NEW TESTAMENT COMMENTARY

VOLUME 2

NEW TESTAMENT COMMENTARY

Geoffrey B. Wilson

VOLUME TWO

PHILIPPIANS – HEBREWS
& REVELATION

THE BANNER OF TRUTH TRUST

THE BANNER OF TRUTH TRUST

Head Office
3 Murrayfield Road
Edinburgh, EH12 6EL
UK

North America Office
PO Box 621
Carlisle, PA 17013
USA

banneroftruth.org

Reprinted 2020

*

ISBN: 978 0 85151 913 5

*

Typeset in 11/14 Adobe Caslon Pro
at The Banner of Truth Trust, Edinburgh

Printed in the USA by
Versa Press Inc.,
East Peoria, IL.

*

Except where noted, Scripture quotations are from
the American Standard Version (1901)

CONTENTS

Philippians

INTRODUCTION

The city of Philippi derived its name from Philip II of Macedon, who refounded it in 356 BC and developed its gold-mining industry. In 167 BC it became part of the Roman Empire, and in 42 BC was the scene of the decisive battle in which Anthony and Octavian defeated Brutus and Cassius. After the war many veterans from the Roman army were settled there and the city was designated a Roman colony. As the citizens of such colonies were very proud of the special privileges conferred by their superior status, they 'were apt to regard themselves as being in but not of the province where they lay' (A. N. Sherwin-White).

However, when Paul and Silas came to Philippi in AD 50, their visit brought the city the greater distinction of being the first in Europe to hear the gospel from Paul's lips. In the first of the 'we' passages of Acts (16:10ff.) Luke gives a vivid eye-witness account of the conversion of three founder-members of the Philippian church: Lydia the seller of purple, the demon-possessed slave-girl whom Paul had cured, and the jailor of the prison. But the church which first met as a small group in Lydia's house was soon to become a flourishing congregation with whom Paul had the happiest relations over many years. On more than one occasion they had shown their love for Paul by sending a gift to supply his material necessities (4:15, 16).

On learning of the apostle's imprisonment, the Christians at Philippi sent Epaphroditus to minister to his needs and bring a further gift (4:18). But this willing service was interrupted by a near-fatal illness and, when Epaphroditus mercifully recovered, Paul deemed it best to send him back to Philippi with this joyous Epistle of thanksgiving (2:25–30). While writing Paul also took the opportunity to deal with several problems which threatened to mar the fellowship of the church. He tactfully seeks to heal a breach caused through a 'personality' clash

(4:2), cuts the ground from under the feet of a 'perfectionist' pressure group (3:12–16), and warns against the danger of listening to the Judaizers (3:2f.). Another purpose served by the letter was to give news of his current circumstances and of his hope of an early release from prison (1:25; 2:24). Where Paul was held captive when he wrote Philippians is a matter of debate, with some scholars favouring Ephesus or even Caesarea, but this commentary follows the traditional view of dating it from near the end of his first Roman imprisonment, about AD 62.

Notwithstanding J. A. Bengel's justly celebrated comment, 'The sum of the epistle is, *I rejoice, rejoice ye*', joy is not the theme of Philippians but is rather its dominant note. The whole letter is suffused with the spirit of joy, and the noun or verb occurs sixteen times in its four chapters. It is remarkable that a prisoner facing a capital charge should write in such a spirit, yet it is the very nature of Christian joy to triumph over adverse circumstances (cf.. *Acts* 16:25). So the Philippians are not exhorted to rejoice because of the happiness of their situation, but because whatever persecution they suffered for the sake of Christ was far outweighed by the joy they had found in him (1:27–30; 4:4–9).

By giving the Epistle the heading, 'The apostle and his friends', the New English Bible draws attention to its leading theme, which is clearly seen in Paul's sustained emphasis upon 'fellowship' or 'communion'. The word basically means 'sharing in something with others', and it may be used to indicate either what is shared ('having a share') or what is given ('giving a share'). The first sense includes sharing in Christ's benefits (1:7), his indwelling power (2:1), and his sufferings (3:10), while the second sense involves making sacrifices to forward his work in the world (1:5). Thus the bond that binds Paul and the Philippians together in Christian fellowship is their common participation in Christ and the work of the 'gospel' (which is another keyword in the Epistle: 1:5, 7, 12, 27; 2:22; 4:3, 15). All this means that there can be no fellowship apart from joint communion with Christ, for it is in him alone that believers are truly made one.

But the outstanding feature of this lovely letter is the majestic 'hymn to Christ' in 2:6–11, which Paul introduces to provide the Christians at Philippi with both the pattern and the dynamic to comply with his exhortations. It is evident that the apostle's purpose is not simply to instruct and edify his readers with profound doctrine; his chief concern is to inspire and motivate them to show the same humility of mind (2:2). This is because Christians cannot work for Christ without also having the mind of Christ. And that involves showing the same spirit of self-denial which made him obedient 'unto death, even the death of the cross' (2:8).

CHAPTER ONE

After greeting the Christians at Philippi, Paul thanks God for their uninterrupted fellowship in the gospel, and confidently expects God to continue his good work in them until its completion in the day of Christ [verses 1–7]. He prays for an increase in their love and knowledge so that they may be made fit for the glory to come [verses 9–11]. The apostle tells how his imprisonment has helped to further the gospel by stimulating others to preach Christ, and though not all do so from the right motives, he still rejoices in the fact that Christ is preached [verses 12–18]. In facing an uncertain future, he is torn between the desire to depart and be with Christ and the need to remain, but he expects to be released for the sake of his assistance to them [verses 19–26]. Paul exhorts them to live worthily of the gospel, and to stand united in its defence, since it is not only given to them to believe on Christ but also to suffer for him [verses 27–30].

1: Paul and Timothy, servants of Christ Jesus, to all the saints in Christ Jesus that are at Philippi, with the bishops and deacons:

Paul associates Timothy with himself in the greeting, not because Timothy played any part in the composition of the letter as Paul's prompt return to the singular demonstrates [verse 3], but because he wishes to prepare the Philippians for Timothy's forthcoming visit [2:19ff.] by showing them that they are colleagues engaged in the same work. This is further emphasized by the joint designation, 'bond servants of Christ Jesus' (F. F. Bruce), which is not an honorific title, but an expression denoting their complete submission to the lordship of Christ. Having been redeemed by Christ from the bondage of sin, they are now totally at the disposal of their new Master. The humility of this address would have special point for readers whose service was in danger of being marred by 'vainglory' [2:3]. 'Many who today love to be called "church workers" should learn what Paul means by "slaves", namely, men who in all their work have no will of their own but only their Owner's will and Word' (R. C. H. Lenski).

To all the saints in Christ Jesus that are at Philippi: Under the Old Covenant Israel was 'holy' in the sense of having been 'set apart' for God's service [*Deut.* 7:6], whereas the gift of holiness is actually conferred upon the beneficiaries of the New Covenant. *All* believers not only have the standing of 'saints' in virtue of their spiritual union with Christ, but are also objectively 'holy' in him because his perfect righteousness is freely put to their account [3:9; *1 Cor.* 1:30; *2 Cor.* 5:21]. 'We do not progress *to* sainthood. We progress *in* sainthood. We progress in sainthood in proportion as we sing alleluias for the initial gift of sainthood' (F. C. Synge). This heavenly union with Christ is here contrasted with the earthly location of the worshipping community. The saints at Philippi are the free-born citizens of heaven [3:20], but their present vocation is to bear witness to Christ amid the pagan darkness of a Roman colony [*1 Pet.* 2:9].

With the bishops and deacons: Presumably Paul singles out these men for special mention because they took the lead in sending assistance to him [4:10-16]. The terms 'elder' and 'bishop' are used interchangeably in the New Testament, the former indicating status, the latter function [cf. *Titus* 1:5–7]. The work entrusted to the 'bishops' (or 'overseers') was the pastoral care of the flock [*Acts* 20:28], while the duties of 'deacons' were chiefly concerned with the administration and finances of the church.

2: Grace to you and peace from God our Father and the Lord Jesus Christ.

In combining the usual Greek and Hebrew forms of greeting, Paul gives them a distinctively Christian content, in which 'grace' points to the undeserved favour of God made known in the Lord Jesus Christ, and 'peace' includes the salvation of the whole man which results from the reception of this grace. These blessings are jointly bestowed by the God whom believers know as their Father, and by their Saviour who is now the ascended Lord of the church [2:9-11].

3: I thank my God upon all my remembrance of you, 4: always in every

supplication of mine on behalf of you all making my supplication with joy, 5: for your fellowship in furtherance of the gospel from the first day until now; 6: being confident of this very thing, that he who began a good work in you will perfect it until the day of Jesus Christ:

There are more frequent references to thanksgiving per page in Paul's letters than can be found in any other Hellenistic author, pagan or Christian (P. T. O'Brien, 'Thanksgiving within the Structure of Pauline Theology', *Pauline Studies*, pp. 54–63). This is because Paul knew that such gratitude was the only appropriate response which could be made to the gift of God's grace. In most of his Epistles Paul begins with a thanksgiving that reflects the situation of his readers and serves to introduce the main theme of the letter. Here, for example, the apostle strikes the keynote of the first two chapters by thanking God for the fellowship of the faithful Philippians in furthering the work of the gospel [verse 5]. He thus has special cause for gratitude as he regularly remembers them in his prayers and makes supplication for them *all* with joy.

Paul's studied repetition of the word 'all' in his opening sentences is remarkable [1:1, 4, 7, 8, 25], and J. B. Lightfoot says that it is 'impossible not to connect this recurrence of the word with the strong and repeated exhortations to unity which the epistle contains [1:27; 2:1–4; 4:2, 3, 5, 7, 1]'. But though Paul was not blind to the failings that needed correction, he could never pray for his friends at Philippi without being filled with joy at the remembrance of their continued participation in the gospel, which was tangibly expressed in their generous giving [cf. *2 Cor.* 8:1–5]. Moreover, they began to share in this work from the first day they received the gospel. 'The communion of the saints was with them a point of practice as well as an article of belief' (John Trapp). Such consistent conduct made Paul confident that the Philippians were the subjects of a genuine work of grace. As their good works were the evidence of God's 'good work' in them, so Paul assures them that God who began that gracious work 'will carry it on to completion until the day of Christ Jesus' (NIV). As well as conveying comfort to believers facing persecution [1:27–30], this assurance also demolishes the pretensions of those who imagined that they had already attained perfection [cf. 3:12,16]. 'It is on the second advent of Christ – and that is the end of the world, and the judgment day – that the Apostle has his eyes set. There is the point of time to which he refers the completeness of our perfecting' (B. B. Warfield). [cf. *1 Thess.* 5:23–24].

7: even as it is right for me to be thus minded on behalf of you all, because I have you in my heart, inasmuch as, both in my bonds and in the defence and confirmation of the gospel, ye are all partakers with me of grace.

It is only right for Paul to think so highly of the Philippians because he regards them in his heart as all being partakers with him of God's grace, both in his bonds and in his defence and confirmation of the gospel. This praise was well deserved. 'For it is much not to hide oneself when a Christian is called to account for the sake of the gospel; it is much when those who are in the same place where he is detained have the courage to remain there, without withdrawing themselves from the danger by flight; it is still more when they dare see and strengthen him, paying him the attentions of love on such an occasion. But it is much more than all this, to seek after him at a distance, to traverse the sea to console him, and not only not to fly away from the place of his prison, but to run thither, and to go many hundreds of leagues to declare themselves on his side. This the Philippians had done, when, having been made acquainted with the detention of St Paul at Rome, they despatched Epaphroditus to visit and to minister to him on their behalf' (Jean Daillé).

Hence the help they sent to the imprisoned apostle together with their willingness to suffer persecution at home for the sake of the gospel showed that they were truly partakers with Paul of God's grace [1:29]. It is probably best to take 'the defence and confirmation of the gospel' in the technical legal sense. Paul sees his witness at his forthcoming trial as a legal validation of the gospel which will receive further confirmation in his acquittal [2:24].

8: For God is my witness, how I long after you all in the tender mercies of Christ Jesus.

As no words can adequately express Paul's yearning for his beloved friends at Philippi, he solemnly appeals to the fact that God who reads every heart, knows the depth and intensity of his feeling for them all. This longing is not mere human affection, but is a love which is the fruit of his spiritual union with Christ, so that 'his pulse beats with the pulse of Christ; his heart throbs with the heart of Christ' (Lightfoot). As a man who is 'in Christ', Paul is gripped by the same love which Christ has for his people, and every true pastor feels something of this affection for the flock committed to his care.

9: And this I pray, that your love may abound yet more and more in knowledge and all discernment; 10: so that ye may approve the things that are excellent; that ye may be sincere and void of offence unto the day of Christ; 11: being filled with the fruits of righteousness, which are through Jesus Christ, unto the glory and praise of God.

Paul's prayers for the churches not only provide the pattern on which their own petitions are to be modelled, but also encourage them to follow the counsel they contain. They are thus a form of indirect exhortation. Hence this particular prayer focuses on those aspects of faith and life which most needed to be stressed at Philippi.

And this I pray, that your love may abound yet more and more in knowledge and all discernment: Paul first prays for an increase in the primary Christian grace of love [*1 Cor.* 13:13], already experienced in love towards God and in their mutual love for one another, so that they may abound more and more. But this request is immediately qualified by the phrase, 'in knowledge and all discernment', for even Christian love may go badly astray unless it is directed aright. 'Misty thought, emotional conduct, and indiscriminate good nature are perilous' (Alfred Plummer). It would seem that the enthusiastic spirit which prevailed in this church was accompanied by a lack of insight. This led to misunderstandings over trifling matters [cf. 4:2], and to giving heed to plausible teachers [cf. 3:1–3, 17–19].

So that ye may approve the things that are excellent: 'Not merely good, rather than bad, but the best among the good, whose excellence none but the more advanced perceive' (J. A. Bengel). Some prefer the rendering, 'so that ye may distinguish the things that differ' (ASV margin), but it does not require much discernment to discriminate between what is good and bad. It is far more difficult to decide what is really excellent and worthy of adoption [cf. 4:8, 9]. Paul is praying that his readers may be enabled to discern and practise those virtues which are vital to the peace and harmony of the church [2:1–3].

That ye may be sincere and void of offence unto the day of Christ: Thus to relate ethics to the End adds an eternal dimension to present conduct. The Philippians must so live in the light of the forthcoming judgment that they will be 'sincere and void of offence' on 'the day of Christ' [*2 Cor.* 5:10]. The word translated as 'sincere' probably means 'tested by the light of the sun' and found 'completely pure' or 'spotless'. This inward purity results in a harmless walk, for 'void of offence' should be understood in the active sense of not causing others to stumble [*1 Cor.* 10:32]. 'The possession of love, and the growth of it in knowledge and discernment, would prevent them from rudely jostling others not of their opinion, or doing anything which, (albeit) with a good intention, might mislead or throw a stumbling-block in the path of those round about them' (John Eadie).

Being filled with the fruits of righteousness, which are through Jesus Christ: This further desire of the apostle for his readers again applies to their present experience. As befits 'the saints' [verse 1], he wishes to see them 'being filled with the fruit of righteousness' (ASV margin). There are two ways of interpreting this difficult phrase. If taken as 'the fruit which consists of righteousness', it means that their lives will be marked by those ethical qualities which are 'the fruit of the Spirit' [*Gal.* 5:22f.]. But when understood as 'the fruit produced by righteousness', it points to the imputed righteousness of Christ as the source of this fruit-bearing [3:9]. Perhaps the Old Testament origin of the phrase [cf. *Amos* 6:12] should incline us to favour the former view instead of restricting 'righteousness' to its forensic meaning. In any case Paul makes it clear that 'the branch cannot bear fruit of itself' by showing that such fruits are the natural and necessary consequence of union with Christ ('which are through Jesus Christ').

Unto the glory and praise of God: Since this spiritual harvest is not a human achievement but the gift of grace, all the glory and praise belong to God [2:11]. As God's 'glory' here refers to the manifestation of his character in redemption, so his 'praise' is the response which that revelation evokes in grateful human hearts [cf. *Eph.* 1:6, 12].

12: Now I would have you know, brethren, that the things which happened unto me have fallen out rather unto the progress of the gospel;

As the Philippians were anxiously awaiting news of their beloved apostle, Paul wants his brethren in the faith to know that the things which have happened to him in Rome have furthered rather than hindered the advance of the gospel. He thus characteristically dwells not on his personal circumstances, about which his readers both then and now would have liked to know more, but concentrates their attention upon the supreme importance of the cause to which he had devoted his life [verse 17].

Apparently at the time Paul wrote this letter, he no longer enjoyed the comparative freedom of his hired lodging [*Acts* 28:30] and was held in stricter custody as he awaited the verdict of his trial, which would either result in his release or his death [verses 19–26; 2:17]. But Paul is far from feeling downcast by this turn of events, for he can perceive that God has made his very imprisonment a means of promoting the faith. It is always God's way to make what threatens to suppress the gospel minister to its advance. The long confinement in Bedford gaol which silenced John Bunyan's preaching only served to make him an evangelist to the whole world through his writing of *The Pilgrim's Progress*. Thus God constantly turns the seeming defeat of his spokesmen into notable victories for the gospel by his providential over-ruling of such opposition [*Gen.* 45:8].

13: so that my bonds became manifest in Christ throughout the whole praetorian guard, and to all the rest;

Paul next explains how the gospel has been advanced. His imprisonment has influenced both those outside the church [verse 13] and those within it [verse 14]. It has become very clear to all that his bonds are not the result of any criminal activity; they are manifestly due to his connection with Christ. 'Waiting under an appeal to the emperor, he had been discovered to be no common prisoner. It had transpired that his official connection with Christ, and his fearless prosecution of the work of Christ, had led to his apprehension and previous trial in Palestine, and not sedition, turbulence, or suspected loyalty – the usual political crimes of his nation. It was widely known that he suffered as a Christian and as an apostle, especially as the preacher of a free and unconditioned gospel to the Gentiles' (Eadie).

Throughout the whole praetorian guard, and to all the rest: The 'praetorium' cannot here refer to a palace or barracks, because 'all the rest' clearly indicates that Paul has a group of people in view, namely, the elite soldiers of the imperial guard who were stationed at Rome. The whole praetorian guard consisted of nine cohorts with a thousand men in each. As the guards who watched over the prisoners were frequently changed, Paul came into close contact with a large number of these men during the years of his captivity, and such was the impression he made upon them that his case was soon 'headline' news in Rome.

14: and that most of the brethren in the Lord, being confident through my bonds, are more abundantly bold to speak the word of God without fear.

And most of the brethren have been made confident in the Lord because of my imprisonment, and are much more bold to speak the word of God without fear (RSV): As the phrase 'in the Lord' lies between 'the brethren' and 'being confident' it can be connected with either, but the latter construction is preferable because it is more in accord with Pauline usage [cf. 2:24; *Rom.* 14:14; *Gal.* 5:10; *2 Thess.* 3:4]. Paul's imprisonment also advanced the gospel by the favourable effect it had upon the majority of believers in Rome. Their confidence in the Lord was renewed through his courageous testimony, and they were thus emboldened to speak the Word of God without fear. They had hitherto preached with some caution, but the brave example set by the apostle now inspired them to speak with far greater daring. Trapp illustrates this verse by quoting from a letter of Bishop Ridley to John Bradford in which he describes his reaction to the death of John Rogers, the first Protestant martyr in Mary's bloody reign: 'I thank our Lord God that since I heard of our dear brother Rogers' departing, and stout confessing of Christ and his truth even unto death, my heart, blessed be God, rejoiced of it; neither ever since that time I have felt any lumpish heaviness, as I grant I have felt sometimes before.'

15: Some indeed preach Christ even of envy and strife; and some also of good will: 16: the one do it of love, knowing that I am set for the defence of the gospel; 17: but the other proclaim Christ of faction, not sincerely, thinking to raise up affliction for me in my bonds.

'We have here a second paradox. It was paradoxical that the

imprisonment of the Apostle should tend to the spread of the Gospel. It was a still greater paradox that the Gospel of love and peace should be preached out of envy and strife' (Plummer). Paul sadly records that among the many thus stimulated to preach Christ with increased boldness, there were some whose zeal sprang from the wrong motives. Since he does not accuse them of false teaching, they are not the Judaizers whom he later so unsparingly condemns [3:2] and elsewhere describes as preaching a different gospel [*Gal.* 1:6-9].

As to a more positive identification of these men, Eadie suggests that they were Jewish believers, who held the essential doctrines of the gospel, but were combative on points of inferior value [cf. *Rom.* 14]. If what united them was their opposition to the apostle of Gentile freedom, 'then such a party might preach Christ, and yet cherish toward Paul all those feelings of envy and ill-will which he ascribes to them'.

Some indeed preach Christ even of envy and strife; and some also of good will: 'The Lord taketh notice, not only of the matter which ministers do preach, whether it be truth or error; but also of the manner how, the ends for which, and the motives from which they preach: even whether they preach Christ "from envy and contention, or from love and good will"; for here Paul taketh notice of it' (James Fergusson).

The one do it of love, knowing that I am set for the defence of the gospel: Those 'of good will' exercise a ministry which stems from a love of real understanding, which recognizes that the imprisoned apostle is set like a soldier at his post for the defence of the gospel, and is as much 'on duty' as the guards who watch over him (R. P. Martin). They knew that he was a willing sufferer for the cause he represented. 'These brethren did not merely "like" Paul; they saw what his office and his imprisonment meant in the plans of God and acted accordingly' (Lenski).

But the other proclaim Christ of faction, not sincerely, thinking to raise up affliction for me in my bonds: But the others, who are envious of Paul's prestige and influence, proclaim Christ in a spirit of rivalry born of selfish ambition, and not from pure motives, thinking that this will add to his distress in prison. 'They attributed their own jealous feelings to the Apostle, and could not conceive a greater worry to him than that he should hear of their success in preaching' (H. A. A. Kennedy).

18: What then? only that in every way, whether in pretence or in truth, Christ is proclaimed; and therein I rejoice, yea, and will rejoice.

But what does it matter? (NIV): Paul's magnanimity is seen in his refusal to allow the personal antagonism towards himself on the part of some preachers to cloud his joy in the only thing that mattered – Christ is proclaimed! 'In pretence' does not mean that these men did not believe what they were preaching, but rather refers to their insincerity in preaching Christ to discomfort Paul [verse 17]. Although the apostle could never rejoice in the preaching of error, he is resolved to rejoice in the preaching of Christ even if it proceeds from impure motives, because he recognized that the power to save lies in the gospel and not the gospeller (Eadie).

As Daillé observes, It is not enough that our actions be good and praiseworthy, if our intentions are not pure and upright. It is to profane the good to do it with a bad end in view, but 'while we detest the abominable profaneness of men who so dreadfully abuse the gospel, let us not cease to rejoice at the good effects which God produces by their hands. Let us hold the thorns of such plants in horror, and gather with thanksgiving the roses which the goodness of God causes to spring from them; and, after the example of the apostle, let us rejoice to see our Christ preached, whatever may be the mind or the hand which presents us His mysteries.'

19: For I know that this shall turn out to my salvation, through your supplication and the supply of the Spirit of Jesus Christ,

Paul is confident that the present situation in which he finds himself shall turn out for his salvation. This citation from Job shows that the apostle sees a parallel to his own experience in the testimony of that much tried Old Testament saint. The whole context deserves to be quoted:

'Hold your peace, let me alone, that I may speak;
And let come on me what will.
Wherefore should I take my flesh in my teeth,
And put my life in my hand?
Though he slay me, yet will I wait for him.
Nevertheless I will argue my ways before him.
This also *shall be my salvation*,

That a godless man shall not come before him.'

Job 13:13–16 (ASV margin)

Although Job and Paul are both on trial, neither has in mind a salvation which guarantees his deliverance from death, for Job says: 'though he slay me', and Paul: 'whether by life, or by death' [verse 20]. They are saved from something far worse than this. Job appeals to God for vindication from the accusations of his false comforters, and Paul desires to be saved from disgracing Christ before the Imperial court. 'Paul says that he knows he will be saved from anything like this. By *this* he refers to his trial: this will turn out safely for him so that he will not disgrace the gospel through cowardice, fear, lack of free utterance, or any inadequacy' (Lenski).

Through your supplication and the supply of the Spirit of Jesus Christ: Paul does not say this in any spirit of self-sufficiency, for he expects his deliverance to come through the prayers of the Philippians and the supply of 'the Spirit of Jesus Christ'. The Spirit is sent by Christ so that Paul can witness to Christ in the hour of trial [*Mark* 13:11; *Luke* 12:11, 12].

20: according to my earnest expectation and hope, that in nothing shall I be put to shame, but that with all boldness, as always, so now also Christ shall be magnified in my body, whether by life, or by death.

The eagerness with which Paul looks for the vindication of the gospel at his trial is vividly expressed by 'earnest expectation'. The word is well defined by Kennedy as 'the concentrated intense hope which ignores other interests, and strains forward as with outstretched head' [cf. *Rom.* 8:19].

The content of this hope is next specified. It is that he may face his ordeal with such courage that he will have no cause to be ashamed, but may be enabled to bear witness to Christ with all the boldness and openness of speech which should characterize one who enjoys the liberty of the Spirit [*2 Cor.* 3:12]. Whatever the result of the trial may mean for Paul, his desire now as always is that 'Christ shall be magnified in my body'. He does not say what he will do, but uses the passive because he is relying upon the supply of the Spirit for the achievement of this great end [verse 19]. So whether the verdict is life or death, the glory of Christ will be promoted and his gospel advanced. 'If he lives, it will be for the service of Christ, which is the highest honour he can pay his Lord. If he has to die, then his readiness to endure death, and his calm courage in enduring, will be the most eloquent testimony to the worth of his Lord' (Kennedy).

21: For me to live is Christ, and to die is gain.

Paul's equanimity in facing these alternatives is explained in a great utterance: 'For *to me* to live is Christ, and to die is gain.' In his experience the only 'life' worthy of the name was that lived in union with Christ and spent in his service, and so for him 'death' was gain because it gave entrance to the immediate presence of Christ. Thus to depart and be 'with Christ' in glory is better by far for Paul [verse 23], but he recognizes that for him to continue living in the flesh may be more needful for his readers [verse 24]. This passage, together with Christ's assurance to the penitent thief, 'Today shalt thou be with me in paradise' [*Luke* 23:43], are both fatal to the view that the intermediate state is one of sleep and unconsciousness. Paul knew that to be at home in the body was to be absent from the Lord, and so he was willing to be absent from the body in order to be 'at home with the Lord' [*2 Cor.* 5:6-8]. 'The souls of believers are at their death made perfect in holiness, and do immediately pass into glory; and their bodies, being still united to Christ, do rest in their graves till the resurrection' (*Shorter Catechism*, Answer to Question 37) [Cf. *Heb.* 12:23: 'The spirits of just men made perfect'].

22: But if to live in the flesh, -if this shall bring fruit from my work, then what I shall choose I know not.

If it is to be life in the flesh, that means fruitful labour for me (RSV): But though death holds no terror for Paul, he does not want the Philippians to suppose that he is simply yearning for death, since a continuance of his earthly life is probably best both for him and them. The significance of Paul's statement lies in the fact that he regards a further lease of life exclusively in terms of bringing forth more fruit. For him 'life in the flesh' was synonymous with 'fruitful labour'. As all his previous missionary service had been blessed with an abundance of fruit, so his one reason for desiring an acquittal was that he might then continue his fruitful labours.

Yet which I shall choose I cannot tell (RSV): If Paul had to choose between promotion to glory and a period of further service, he would not know what to decide. Thus Trapp quaintly says, 'As a loving wife sent for by her husband far from home, and yet loath to leave her children, is in a muse and doubt what to do, so was the apostle.'

23: But I am in a strait betwixt the two, having the desire to depart and be with Christ; for it is very far better: 24: Yet to abide in the flesh is more needful for your sake.

In describing his dilemma, Paul says that he is 'hemmed in on both sides' (Lightfoot). He has the desire 'to depart' (literally, to break camp) and be with Christ, for that is 'very far better' (a triple comparative!). 'The preference of death over life was a personal matter. It was better for him; far better for him to be with Christ, than to be away from Christ; far better to enjoy Christ than to preach Christ; far better to praise Him than to suffer for Him; far better to be in His presence in glory, than to be bound in a prison for Him at Rome' (Eadie). But Paul always put his 'concern for all the churches' [*2 Cor.* 11:28, NIV] before personal considerations, and he knew that it was more necessary for them that he should remain in the body. The contrast between these alternatives is helpfully set forth by William Hendriksen:

Remaining here	*Departing to be with Christ*
Here:	There:
a. A temporary residence, a mere tent-dwelling	A permanent abode
b. Suffering mixed with joy	Joy unmixed with suffering
c. Suffering for a little while	Joy for ever
d. Being absent from the Lord	Being at home with the Lord
e. The fight	The feast
f. The realm of sin	The realm of complete deliverance from sin, positive holiness

25: And having this confidence, I know that I shall abide, yea, and abide with you all, for your progress and joy in the faith;

Although this personal conviction does not amount to prophetic certainty, Paul 'is so confident of the Philippians' need of him that he cannot doubt that this will be God's purpose too' (Kennedy). He will remain alive and stay to serve them, for the sake of their further progress in the faith. His personal longing to depart and be with Christ is thus subordinated to the church's need of his continued ministry. This service would be aimed at forwarding their 'progress and joy in the faith'. The linking together of 'progress' and 'joy' is significant, for it shows that every advance in the faith should be accompanied by a corresponding increase in joy. We know from the Pastoral Epistles that Paul's confidence was justified. He was released and entered upon another term of service before his final imprisonment and martyrdom [*2 Tim.* 4:6–8].

26: that your glorying may abound in Christ Jesus in me through my presence with you again.

So that in me you may have ample cause to glory in Christ Jesus, because of my coming to you again (RSV): When Paul is restored to the Philippians and his ministry among them is renewed, their ground for glorying will be increased by what Christ has done for them through his servant. For the ultimate aim of all ministry is to give further cause for glorying in Christ Jesus. Thus to glory in Christ Jesus means the abandonment of all self-boasting, for unlike the merit-mongers who trust in the flesh, believers are so radically committed to Christ that even the last vestige of trust in themselves is excluded [cf. 3:3: we . . . glory in Christ Jesus, and have no confidence in the flesh']. But the prospect of ministering to them again in the future does not deter Paul from his present duty. So he turns from this happy prospect and sends them the exhortations and instructions which are necessary to deal with the pressing problems they are now facing [1:27ff.].

27: Only let your manner of life be worthy of the gospel of Christ: that, whether I come and see you or be absent, I may hear of your state, that ye stand fast in one spirit, with one soul striving for the faith of the gospel;

Standing emphatically at the beginning of the sentence, 'Only' points to the one essential thing which demands the Philippians' immediate attention, no matter what happens to Paul. The verb which is translated as 'let your manner of life be' literally means 'behave as citizens' (ASV margin). The fact that Paul later alludes to their heavenly citizenship

[3:20] strongly suggests that he has the same idea in mind here. He wants their life as a Christian community to be worthy of the gospel of Christ. 'The exhortation contemplates the Philippians as members of the Christian *commonwealth*. The figure would be naturally suggested to Paul by his residence in Rome, and would appeal to the Philippians as a Roman colony, which was a reproduction of the parent commonwealth on a smaller scale' (Marvin R. Vincent, *Word Studies in the New Testament*, vol. 2, p. 876). In view of the tensions within the church which threatened to mar their witness, Paul's one concern, whether present or absent, is to hear of their united stand for the truth of the gospel against 'the adversaries' [verse 28] who oppose it [cf. *Jude* 3: 'Contend earnestly for the faith which was once for all delivered unto the saints'].

Since the call to stand fast 'in one spirit' is further defined as a striving together 'with one soul', no sharp distinction can be drawn between these terms, which are here virtually used as synonyms in order to underline the need for spiritual unity [cf. *Acts* 4:32]. They must stand fast, like soldiers 'fighting side by side' (Moffatt). This vivid image would remind the Philippians of the phalanx, which consisted of a body of highly trained spearmen who fought together in closed ranks, for this was the tactic which was used by Philip of Macedon and his son Alexander the Great to achieve their great victories. 'The same spirit of unity and valour which had infused the phalanx sent forth for world conquest must now be evidenced by the members of the Church as they contend for the faith of the gospel' (W. L. Lane).

28: and in nothing affrighted by the adversaries: which is for them an evident token of perdition, but of your salvation, and that from God;

And in no way intimidated by your opponents (Arndt-Gingrich): This is the only occurrence in Scripture of a verb which was used for the shying of a frightened horse. The Philippians must not be thrown into a panic by their persecutors, but must face them without fear. As it would appear from Acts 16:13 that there were not enough Jews in Philippi to form a synagogue (a minimum of ten men was required), this opposition must have come mainly from their pagan neighbours, whose devotion to the heathen cults would have been affronted by a faith which condemned all idol-worship. Paul says that such Christian fearlessness under attack provides these persecutors with a token which not only foreshadows their own doom but also points to the salvation of their victims. For in fighting against God's people they are bringing upon themselves that just recompense which consists in 'everlasting destruction from the presence of the Lord' [cf. *2 Thess.* 1:5–9].

And that from God: This shows that God is the author of the Philippians' stability under suffering: 'Their standing firm in contending and being unafraid comes to them "from God" even as Paul adds "graciously granted to you" [verse 29]' (Lenski).

29: because to you it hath been granted in the behalf of Christ, not only to believe on him, but also to suffer in his behalf.

Although Paul's primary concern here is to assure his readers that it is no less a privilege to suffer for Christ than to believe in him [*Acts* 5:41], his words also indicate that the prior grace of faith is just as much a gift of God [*Eph.* 2:8]. 'He says expressly, *"that it is given us to believe in Christ"*, which necessarily implies that this movement itself of our heart, opening to the light of the gospel, and receiving the truth that the preacher presents to it, is a gift of God, and not a work of nature . . . It is He who opened the heart of Lydia to attend to St Paul [*Acts* 16:14]. Paul plants, and Apollos waters; but they are neither of them any thing. It is God which giveth the increase. We are His husbandry, and His work [*1 Cor.* 3:6, 7, 9]. It is He who revealed His secret to Peter; it was not flesh and blood [*Matt.* 16:17]. It is He who revealed His Son to Paul, shining in his heart, that he might enlighten the Gentiles [*Gal.* 1:15]. In fine, it is He who, according to His good pleasure, hides these things from the wise and prudent, and reveals them unto babes [*Matt.* 11:25]' (Daillé).

As to the privilege of suffering, Paul everywhere teaches that this is an essential part of the believer's experience and the badge of authentic discipleship [cf. 3:10; *Acts* 14:22; *Rom.* 5:3; 8:17, 35; *2 Tim.* 1: 8]. This means that 'the persecution of believers is not a fortuitous event, which happens either by chance, or by the malice of men or devils alone. It is God, who guides the whole affair by a special providence. He sees the rage of the enemies of His people. He knows their designs, He perceives all that they are contriving against the gospel, and could (if such were His good pleasure) dissipate both their plans and their efforts in an instant. He lets them alone, and by secret arrangements manages their violence against every one of His servants, as His supreme wisdom sees best. He Himself marks the field where the combat is to be decided. He orders the weapons and the blows, and rules every action. He calls His warrior, and Himself places him in front of the enemy.

'Christian, do not stop at men, and at the appearance of things. Be convinced that it is the Lord who arranges all your trials. You will enter into none but by His permission. But the apostle also shows us, in the second place, that this employment which God gives us, and this calling which He directs us to suffer for Him, is a gift of His grace. I well know that flesh forms quite another judgment, and that of all the favours of God, there is none that it esteems and desires less than this . . . But, if, setting aside the tenderness of the flesh, you will consider the thing itself, what can be esteemed more honourable than suffering for the name of the Lord Jesus? This Jesus is the King of ages, the Prince of angels, the Lord of glory. His gospel is the highest of all truth, it is the salvation of the world, the seed of life and immortality. For what better subject then could we suffer?' (Daillé).

30: having the same conflict which ye saw in me, and now hear to be in me.

The Philippians are engaged in the same conflict which they had seen in Paul when he suffered stripes and imprisonment at Philippi [*Acts* 16:19–24], and now hear about his present imprisonment and trial in Rome [verse 12; 2:25]. They stand together in the great contest of faith to defend the gospel of Christ against their common enemy. For they wrestle not against flesh and blood, but against the powers of darkness whose doom is already sealed by Christ's great victory [*Eph.* 6:12; *Col.* 2:15]. Paul here 'thinks of the conflicts and sufferings of the Christian life itself as a life which in its totality stands under the sign of the cross and in this sign carries the cause of Christ to victory' (E. Stauffer, *TDNT,* vol. 1, p. 139).

CHAPTER TWO

Paul earnestly admonishes the Philippians to maintain the unity of the church by sharing the same mind, which above all consists in humility and selfless concern for their fellow-believers [verses 1–4].

This exhortation is enforced by an appeal to the example of Christ in a lofty passage which celebrates his self-denying love in taking the form of a servant and becoming obedient to the death of the cross, from which God had raised him to the seat of universal sovereignty [verses 5–11]. So they are to work out their own salvation in humble dependence upon God. This involves refraining from disputes and living so blamelessly that Paul would have no cause to be ashamed of them in the day of Christ [verses 12–18]. Paul hopes to send Timothy to Philippi shortly and warmly praises his fidelity. Meanwhile Epaphroditus, now happily recovered from his illness, is returning with this Epistle, and is to be duly honoured for risking his life in Paul's service [verses 19–30].

1: If there is therefore any exhortation in Christ, if any consolation of love, if any fellowship of the Spirit, if any tender mercies and compassions,

Paul begins the most weighty section of the Epistle with an impassioned appeal for unity based on the Christian experience of his readers [verses 1–4]. The repeated 'if' which introduces this fourfold appeal does not express doubt, but rather assumes a condition of reality ('if . . . as is in fact the case'), and thus has the force of an affirmative statement. 'The four clauses seem to be arranged in pairs, one relating to union with Christ and its benefit, the other to communion with the Spirit and its benefit' (Plummer).

If there is therefore any exhortation in Christ: As sharers in Christ's life, the Philippians are under an obligation to heed the exhortation of Christ's apostle to work together in harmony [cf. *1 Cor.* 1:10]. For all who are 'in Christ' are subject to the *rule* of Christ, and must therefore so listen to the *word* of Christ that they may never behave in a way which is contrary to the *mind* of Christ [verse 5].

If there is any solace afforded by love (Arndt-Gingrich): The second appeal is based on the comfort which they have found in Christ's love, for only an experience of his love has the constraining power to silence all disputing and to promote the true spirit of concord between believers [verse 14].

If any fellowship with the Spirit (NIV): Or 'any participation in the Spirit' (RSV). As believers in Christ they are all sharers in the same

Spirit, who has made them fellow-members of the one body [*1 Cor.* 12:13]. This appeal to their spiritual experience is clearly intended to underline the inconsistency of indulging in that spirit of self-assertion which fosters divisions within the church [verses 3, 4]. They must rather seek 'to keep the unity of the Spirit in the bond of peace' [*Eph.* 4:3].

If any tender mercies and compassions: The ground of the final appeal is found in the feelings of affection and sympathy which the Spirit himself inspires. If they now show such tenderness toward one another and forget their differences, they will make Paul's joy complete [verse 2]. 'Chrysostom calls attention to the intense earnestness of these four clauses. The need for unity is so great that exhortation has become entreaty' (Plummer).

2: make full my joy, that ye be of the same mind, having the same love, being of one accord, of one mind;

Although Paul is glad that he can base his appeal to the Philippians on what he knows are the realities of their spiritual experience, his cup of joy will be filled to the brim only if they respond to his urgent call for unity by being 'of the same mind'. The importance of the verb in Paul's argument can be gauged from the fact that no less than 10 of its 23 occurrences in his writings are found in this Epistle.

True spiritual unity, as opposed to mere outward uniformity, depends upon a holy unanimity of thought. Christianity is first and foremost a condition of mind. Hence they cannot work together harmoniously unless they share the same disposition. Paul next shows how this 'thinking the same thing' must work itself out in the life of the church. First, it involves 'having the same love' for one another, as befits those who are loved by the same Saviour and who share the same Spirit [verse 1]. Secondly, it means 'being of one accord, of one mind'. These are to be taken together as providing a '*more precise definition* of the previously mentioned unity of mind: *with harmony of soul cherishing the one sentiment*' (H. A. W. Meyer).

As the inner motivation is the mainspring of all activity, the community of believers must share the same feeling if they are to work together in the same cause. Churches are so often upset by people with 'personality problems' that the very idea of working together may seem like an impossible ideal. Such difficulties can be resolved, but only by the way of lowliness which was exemplified by the Lord himself [verses 3–5; cf. 4:2].

3: doing nothing through faction or through vainglory, but in lowliness of mind each counting other better than himself;

Paul here diagnoses the malaise of the church and points to its remedy. It is clear from 3:12–16 that some were claiming to have already attained spiritual perfection, but to claim a 'glory' belonging to the future state was a form of 'vainglory' that threatened to destroy the fellowship by the party-spirit and jealousy which it introduced (so J.-F. Collange). Such overweening pride is, alas, the most marked feature of those who are convinced of their own perfection. 'Egotism and boastfulness were apparently the perils besetting the Philippian Church . . . It is a strange phenomenon in religious history that intense earnestness so frequently breeds a spirit mingled of censoriousness and conceit' (Kennedy).

Paul offers no palliative for this dire condition, but a radical cure which reaches to the very root of the disease. They must cultivate the lowliness of mind that counts others better than themselves. The Greek moralists despised humility because they regarded it as a form of servile subjection which was at odds with their concept of freedom. But Jesus exploded this false idea of human autonomy by living in perfect obedience to the Father's will [verses 5–8]. For in thus subjecting himself to God, he became the servant of all, and thereby provided the pattern for all authentic service [*Mark* 10:45; *Luke* 22:37]. As Jesus brought this new spirit into the world, so his disciples must be imbued with the same lowliness of mind [verse 5]. In the case of the sinless Jesus, this humility stemmed from his sense of entire dependence upon God as man; whereas in our case, it also springs from the sense of our own sinfulness before God (cf. Trench, *Synonyms,* p. 141).

Perfectionism ministers to pride because it eradicates the sense of sin, but a high regard for self is impossible in those who are convinced of their sinful failings. 'Humility dispels the self-importance which is continually taking and asserting the measure of its own claims, when it comes into contact with others . . . Every man that knows his own heart finds, and must find, much in it to give him a low estimate of himself, and he cannot tell what graces may be cherished in the bosoms of those around him; they may be superior to his own. Nor has he any cause to be vain of any gifts conferred on him – "Who maketh thee to differ?" The original gift, and the impulse to cultivate it, are alike from above . . . But where there is self-assertion or rivalry to secure the "chief seat" and win applause, then the impulses of such vanity necessarily create alienation and disorder' (Eadie).

4: not looking each of you to his own things, but each of you also to the things of others.

This admonition is especially relevant to our day when so many seem to imagine that Christianity consists in 'doing one's own thing', of following one's own spiritual bent, without respect to the welfare of one's fellow-members in the body of Christ. But to exhibit such a concern with 'number one' is to bring the values of the world into the church. Christ has a care for the weakest in his flock as well as for those who believe themselves to be the strongest! What Paul means is well conveyed by Lenski: 'Look to the spiritual interests of others, then also to your own. Do this, all of you, each one.' As Eadie aptly remarks, 'It is not myself alone or in isolation, as if others did not exist, but myself with them and they with me, in earnest brotherhood and love. My object must not be simply to outstrip them in religious attainment, but to bring them and myself to a higher stage of Christian excellence.'

5: Have this mind in you, which was also in Christ Jesus:

Adopt towards one another the same attitude which (was) also (found) in Christ Jesus (C. F. D. Moule): Paul now presses home his call for humility by appealing to Christ as the supreme example of self-sacrificing love. 'It is the spirit which animated our Lord in the act of His incarnation which His apostle would see us imitate. He would have us in all our acts to be like Christ, as He showed Himself to be in the innermost core of His being, when He became poor, He that was rich, that we by His poverty might be made rich . . . If we would follow Christ, we must, every one of us, not in pride but in humility, yet not in lowness but in lowliness, not degrade ourselves but forget ourselves, and seek every man not his own things but those of others . . . Our self-abnegation is thus not for our own sake, but for the sake of others. And thus it is not to mere self-denial that Christ calls us, but specifically to self-sacrifice: not to unselfing ourselves, but to unselfishing ourselves. Self-denial for its own sake is in its very nature ascetic, monkish. It concentrates our whole attention on self-knowledge, self-control – and can therefore eventuate in nothing other than the very apotheosis of selfishness . . . It is not to this that Christ's example calls us. He did not cultivate self, even His divine self. He took no account of self . . . He was led by His love for others into the world, to forget Himself in the needs of others, to sacrifice self once for all upon the altar of sympathy. Self-sacrifice brought Christ into the world. And self-sacrifice will lead us, His followers, not away from but into the midst of men' (B. B. Warfield, 'Imitating the Incarnation', *The Saviour of the World,* pp. 251–69). It should be noted that the appeal here is to the church as a community and not merely to isolated individuals. There is such a thing as the sanctification of the congregation as well as of the individual believer.

6: who, existing in the form of God, counted not the being on an equality with God a thing to be grasped, 7: but emptied himself, taking the form of a servant, being made in the likeness of men; 8: and being found in fashion as a man, he humbled himself, becoming obedient even unto death, yea, the death of the cross. 9: Wherefore also God highly exalted him, and gave unto him the name which is above every name; 10: that in the name of Jesus every knee should bow, of things in heaven and things on earth and things under the earth, 11: and that every tongue should confess that Jesus Christ is Lord, to the glory of God the Father.

As a result of recent study, this majestic passage is now generally regarded as a 'hymn to Christ' of pre-Pauline origin, but the possibility that Paul here incorporates an earlier composition of his own should not be lightly dismissed. In a spirited defence of the apostolic authorship, E. F. Scott points out that Paul's poetic gift is amply demonstrated in many 'splendid outbursts' in his Epistles [cf. *1 Cor.* 13]. According to E. Stauffer, the passage is one of Paul's characteristic incarnation formulas, for he finds the same 'descent-ascent' motif worked into Romans 10:6ff. and concludes that Paul is quoting a 'credal hymn' which he composed at an earlier date. As the hymn is both from the literary and theological point of view 'the work of a master', J.-F. Collange thinks that to deny the authorship to the apostle would be ungracious. More forthright is the judgment of W. G. Kümmel who states that 'nothing compels the conclusion that Paul himself could not have formulated this hymn' (*Introduction to the New Testament,* p. 335). No one today would care to dispute Paul's immense debt to those who were 'in Christ' before him, but in taking over this 'traditional' material he always stamped his personality upon it and made it indisputably his own. It is therefore safer to accept the whole hymn as Paul's rather than to suggest with E. Lohmeyer that those elements which break its metrical symmetry are Pauline additions, for at present we have no means of proving the authenticity of such proposed reconstructions of the hymn. (G. B. Caird provides an interesting critique of Lohmeyer's influential thesis in *Paul's Letters from Prison,* pp. 100–4).

Who, existing in the form of God: Of the many different interpretations of this notoriously difficult passage, the classic view which takes 'form of God' in a metaphysical sense still seems to be the most fruitful, especially since modern Christology proceeds on the highly questionable assumption that the New Testament statements about Christ are a purely 'functional' account of his saving acts. Here the imperfect participle, 'existing', in contrast to the following aorists, refers to Christ's pre-existent state and 'points to indefinite continuance of being' (J. Gwynn).

As the word 'form' was used to denote the essence of a thing, John Murray maintains that 'the form of God' does not mean anything less than Godhood. 'The accent falls upon the fulness of his Godhood, upon his being originally, natively, essentially God in the full possession of all that is distinctive of God in his majesty and glory. This is the dignity of his divine identity, the dignity of unabridged Deity' ('The Mystery of Godliness', *Collected Writings of John Murray*, vol. 3, p. 237). (For a further fine discussion, see B. B. Warfield, 'The Person of Christ according to the New Testament', *Biblical Doctrines*, pp. 176–182, and *The Person and Work of Christ*, pp. 38–44.)

Did not count his existence-in-a-manner-equal-to-God something to cling to (Hendriksen): This focuses upon the humiliation which was involved in Christ's pre-incarnate decision not to cling to his divine 'existential glory, the majesty of his revelation, the greatness and splendour of his manner of being' (S. Greijdanus, cited by J. J. Müller). As Paul reminded the Corinthians of this great act of renunciation to encourage their generosity [*2 Cor.* 8:9], so he administers an implicit rebuke to the quarrelling Philippians by showing them that Christ did not insist upon his rights but in love willingly waived them that he might save the lost [verses 7, 8]. Thus an overriding pastoral purpose ensures that there is no separation of theology and ethics in Paul. He never teaches doctrine for its own sake. His highest theological flights are always related to the down-to-earth problems of Christian living.

But emptied himself, taking the form of a servant: But instead of appearing 'in the form of God', Christ emptied himself by taking 'the form of a servant'. It is not said that Christ 'emptied' (*ekenosen*) himself of his essential equality with God, or of his divine attributes, as is falsely inferred by the proponents of the modern 'kenotic' theory, which has been aptly described by E. Digges La Touche as 'incarnation by divine suicide' (cited by L. Berkhof in *The History of Christian Doctrines*, p. 121). 'Emptied' is here used metaphorically to underline the contrast between the pre-incarnate glory and the incarnate humiliation: 'to show that Christ utterly renounced and laid aside the majesty which he possessed in his original state.

Its most satisfactory definition is found in the succeeding details which describe the incidents of Christ's humanity, and with these exegesis is compelled to stop. The word does not indicate a surrender of deity, nor a paralysis of deity, nor a change of personality, nor a break in the continuity of self-consciousness. Christ's consciousness of deity was not suspended during his earthly life' (Vincent, *ICC*, p. 89). 'Emptied' therefore means that Christ veiled his glory when he 'stripped himself of the insignia of majesty' (Lightfoot). But paradoxically, Christ emptied himself *by taking* (the aorist participle denotes coincident action) the form of a servant, i.e. by an *addition* rather than a subtraction. 'He took the form of a servant while he retained the form of God! It is exactly that which makes our salvation possible and achieves it' (Hendriksen).

Yet though Christ remained essentially one with the Father [*John* 10:30], the stark reality of his servanthood necessarily involved complete subordination to the Father's will, so that he refused every temptation to make independent use of his divine powers during the period of his humiliation [*John* 14:10, 28]. This taking the form of a servant also made Christ subject to the law of God in both its active and passive demands [*Gal.* 4:4, 5]. He came to fulfil all its precepts as our representative, and to exhaust its penalty as our sin-bearing substitute. 'To have taken the form of a servant in reference to any human will or authority would have contradicted his dignity and mission. It was to God the Father that he assumed this relation and it was to the will of the Father that he surrendered himself in the fulness of subjection and obligation' (John Murray) [cf. *John* 6:38; 17:4].

Being made in the likeness of men: As to the manner of Christ's appearing, he was a real man among men, but Paul uses the word 'likeness' to show that in assuming our humanity (sin alone excepted: cf. *Rom.* 8:3) he did not cease to be himself – the eternal Son of God. So though Christ entered upon a genuinely human existence at a definite point in time, his prior existence 'in the form of God' means that the secret of his person cannot be penetrated by those who think of him in merely human terms [*Matt.* 16:16f].

And being found in fashion as a man: This marks an advance on the previous clause. Having become man, Christ was recognized as such by those who saw him 'in the days of his flesh' [*Heb.* 5:7]. The word 'fashion' refers to his external appearance, so that here the contrast 'is between what He *is* in himself, and what He *appeared* in the eyes of men' (Lightfoot). The majority did not see beyond the outward guise, and this failure to perceive his divine dignity meant that his whole earthly walk was one long *via dolorosa* which led inevitably to the cross [cf. *Isa.* 53:2, 3].

He humbled himself, becoming obedient even unto death: First, the pre-incarnate Christ emptied himself *by* taking the form of a servant (verse 7). Then having become man, he humbled himself *by* becoming obedient even up to the point of death. The description covers Christ's entire life upon earth, and shows that his undeviating subjection to the Father's will led him to accept a life of humiliation which culminated in his death. 'This extreme height reached by His obedience was, however, just the extreme *depth* of the humiliation, and thereby at the same time its *end*' (Meyer).

Yea, the death of the cross: The climax is in the word 'cross', and it must have deeply impressed those whose citizenship made them exempt from that hideous form of capital punishment which was reserved for slaves and foreigners. 'Far be the very name of the cross, not only from the body, but even from the thought, the eyes, the ears of Roman citizens' (Cicero). Yet for Christ the greatest anguish of the cross consisted not in the awful physical agony, but in the abyss of spiritual dereliction he experienced as he bore our sin [*Matt.* 27:46; *Gal.* 3:13]. 'He humbled himself to the accursed death of the cross. There were no lower depths possible, for the cross bespeaks the whole curse of God upon sin. It is humiliation inimitable, unrepeated, unrepeatable' (John Murray).

Wherefore also God highly exalted him, and gave unto him the name which is above every name: This is the turning point in the great drama of redemption. In the first part of the 'hymn' attention has been focused on the self-humbling of Christ, but now God takes the initiative by advancing Christ to the place of highest honour. As the reward for Christ's obedience unto death, God highly exalted him, and graciously gave to him the name which is above every name. 'Even Christ receives the recompense as God's *gift of grace*, and hence also He *prays* Him for it, *John* 17:5. The glory of the *exaltation* did not stand to that possessed *before the incarnation* in the relation of a *plus*, but it affected the *entire divine-human* person, that entered on the *regnum gloriae*' (Meyer). 'The name which is above every name' can only be the name 'Lord' (*Kyrios*, verse 11), which is the word used in the Greek version of the Old Testament to render the ineffable name of God, the tetragrammaton YHWH. 'He hath changed the ineffable name into a name utterable by man, and desirable by all the world; the majesty is all arrayed in robes of mercy, the tetragrammaton or adorable mystery of the patriarchs is made fit for pronunciation and expression when it becometh the name of the Lord's Christ' (Jeremy Taylor, cited by Kennedy).

That in the name of Jesus every knee should bow, of things in heaven and things on earth and things under the earth: This expresses the purpose of the exaltation. In adapting the words of Isaiah 45:23 for his purpose [cf. *Rom.* 14:11], Paul here transfers to Christ the universal homage which is there claimed by God. As Eadie says, 'In the name of Jesus' means 'in recognition of it, or of the authority and majesty of Him who bears it . . . If beings bow in recognition of the name of Jesus, it is to Jesus Himself as bearing such a name, that they offer homage.' Paul's threefold classification is comprehensive in its scope, and shows that there is no sphere within the created order which is exempt from Christ's universal lordship. Although the ASV supplies 'things' to make up the sense, the neuter is clearly inappropriate in a passage which speaks of bowing the knee and confessing with the tongue (verse 11). What the apostle has in view is the future submission of all intelligent beings before Christ, whether by choice or by compulsion. 'The first are all the blessed angels and the saints in heaven; the second are all the men on earth; the third are all the demons and the damned in hell. The three groups include all created personal beings. All shall bow in submission and make this acknowledgment or confession with either joy and bliss or dismay' (Lenski).

And that every tongue should confess that Jesus Christ is Lord: In affirming that 'Jesus Christ is Lord', Paul is echoing the earliest creed of the Christian church [cf. *Rom.* 10:9; *1 Cor.* 12:3]. This confession of the present Lordship of Christ which is already made within the context of the church's worship thus anticipates the universal recognition that will follow at the parousia. 'Paul has the exalted Jesus in mind in thus speaking of Him. It was only on His exaltation that Jesus entered upon His dominion. But it by no means follows that he conceived Jesus to have acquired His "Lordship", in the sense of His inherent right to reign, by His exaltation . . . That he recognized that this Jesus had entered upon the actual exercise of His universal dominion only on His resurrection and ascension, and in this sense had received it as a reward for His work on earth [*Phil.* 2:9; *Rom.* 14:9] merely means that, no less than to our Lord Himself, the earthly manifestation of Jesus was to Paul an estate of humiliation upon which glory followed. But the glory which thus followed the humiliation was to Paul, too, a glory which belonged of right to Jesus, to whom His lowly life on earth, not His subsequent exaltation, was a strange experience' (B. B. Warfield, *The Lord of Glory*, pp. 223–225).

To the glory of God the Father: Paul fittingly concludes with a doxology expressing the *ultimate* purpose of Christ's exaltation [verses 9–11]. 'Christ as God has the right to the adoration of the universe, but as God-man He has for His special service received a special investiture. He could not be worshipped at all, if He were not God, and He is now worshipped on this peculiar ground, because He has done and suffered as the apostle tells us. But the prime place is occupied by God the Father, to whom service was rendered by Christ, while the success of such service and its consequent reward by Him are a source of glory to Him. In the honour paid to His exalted Son, His own character is more fully seen and admired' (Eadie).

12: So then, my beloved, even as ye have always obeyed, not as in my presence only, but now much more in my absence, work out your own salvation with fear and trembling;

Having reminded his readers of the exemplary self–sacrifice of Christ, Paul now proceeds to point out its practical bearing upon the life of the church as a whole, thus resuming his appeal to them to show the same lowliness of mind towards one another [verses 1–5]. Hence he is not exhorting them as individuals to work out their personal salvation. He is rather urging them to forsake self-assertive zeal, so that they can all work together for the spiritual health of the whole church as a witnessing community [verse 14ff.]. For a church torn by strife never makes a favourable impact upon the world!

With his own approaching departure in view, Paul seems to have modelled his charge upon Moses' farewell address [*Deut*. 32:1–5]. But whereas Moses rebukes the children of Israel for their past disobedience, Paul believes that he can count upon the Philippians' obedience to the gospel even in his absence, because God is present with them in the power of his enabling grace [verse 13]. At first sight this confidence hardly seems compatible with a feeling of 'fear and trembling', but the other occasions on which Paul used this expression indicate a manward rather than a Godward reference (cf. *1 Cor.* 2:3; *2 Cor.* 7:15; *Eph.* 6:5]. The phrase denotes an attitude of humility in relationship to other men. 'What Paul here demands of the Church is the same humility he called for in verse 3, the same willingness to see something from another's point of view . . . The man who approaches another within the congregation with fear and trembling acknowledges that he has submitted his own life to the power of God and that all vindication proceeds from God alone [1:28]' (W. L. Lane).

13: for it is God who worketh in you both to will and to work, for his good pleasure.

For it is God who works effectively among you: The Philippians do not need to wait for Paul's arrival to reform the flaws in their fellowship, because God himself is effectively at work in their midst (so Collange). As God thus bestows both the power to will and to work, in order to fulfil his good pleasure in restoring the divided community to full spiritual health, it is clear that no room is left for any boasting in human achievement [*Isa.* 26:12]. 'This shows how empty is the presumption of those who divide the glory of our course in the faith between God and ourselves; freely granting that God works in them the beginnings of salvation, but pretending that, after having received the first tokens of His grace, they are afterwards the authors of the rest, which they express by a word full of vanity, saying that they co-operate with God, making themselves, by these means, companions of the Godhead in this work. The apostle here throws down all this project of their pride, pronouncing, gloriously, that *it is God which works in them to will and to do*, the progress and the end, as well as the beginning' (Daillé).

14: Do all things without murmurings and questionings;

'All things' stands at the beginning in the Greek text to emphasize the importance of doing everything in the right spirit. Paul's injunction plainly refers to the internal dissension which was disturbing the peace of the church. Perhaps the two terms are used to indicate cause and effect, for a spirit of grumbling discontent usually leads to ill-natured wrangling. The word 'murmurings' recalls the rebellious complaints of the Israelites against God [*1 Cor.* 10:10], but as the Philippians are clearly not guilty of such presumption, Paul must be alluding to their grumbling amongst themselves. The second term, 'questionings' or disputings, may point to arguments provoked by doctrinal differences.

We know that there were some at Philippi who imagined that they had already attained spiritual perfection [cf. 3:12]. As such people are not noticeably meek in advancing their claims to superior holiness, this attitude of self-assertion would naturally be challenged by the 'ordinary' Christians in the church, and the ensuing arguments would tend to divide the fellowship into opposing camps. This is only a tentative suggestion, because it is obviously impossible for us now to determine the precise situation Paul had in view. But his condemnation of the complaining and arguing that so frequently mars the relationship between believers is certainly not open to question.

15: that ye may become blameless and harmless, children of God without blemish in the midst of a crooked and perverse generation, among whom ye are seen as lights in the world,

The Philippians must avoid all unholy strife [verse 14], in order that they may become the kind of people whose witness will commend itself to outsiders. Paul is here drawing their attention to the vital importance of consistent Christian living, for though God entrusts the treasure of the gospel to frail earthen vessels, the vessels must be clean if their witness is to be effective [*2 Cor.* 4:7]. 'Blameless' not only requires purity of life, but also demands that it may be so evident to all, that no charge can be justly levelled against the witnessing community.

'Harmless' literally means 'unmixed', and indicates that which is free of foreign additions, as of wine unmixed with water or of metal without any alloy in it. The word thus points to a purity which is not contaminated by any foreign element that would alter the character of the church and make void its testimony to the truth. So they must unitedly strive to become 'children of God without blemish', by living up to the privileges which are now theirs by the adoption of grace [*Gal.* 3:26], for it is only when the church is demonstrably different from its pagan environment that any impression is made upon 'a crooked and perverse generation' [cf. *Matt.* 5:13–16]. The latter phrase was part of Moses' accusation against the erring Israelites [*Deut.* 32:5], but Paul applies it to the sinful world of moral darkness in which his readers 'shine like stars in the universe' (NIV). Because they are illuminated by the light of Christ, they are able to reflect that light for the guidance of others, just as the sailor plots his course by the stars.

16: holding forth the word of life; that I may have whereof to glory in the day of Christ, that I did not run in vain neither labour in vain.

This further defines the function of the Philippians as luminaries in a sin-darkened world [verse 15]. It is their missionary rôle to hold forth 'the word of life', i.e. the gospel which alone has the power to bring life to the spiritually dead. 'As they made known its doctrines, and impressed men with a sense of its importance, as their actions, in their purity and harmony, exhibited its life and power, did they hold it forth' (Eadie). Paul urges them to remain faithful to the substance and spirit of the gospel, so that on the day of Christ he may be able to glory in the fact that he did not run or labour in vain. Both metaphors emphasize the energy expended in the fulfilment of his apostolic commission. 'This, then, was a sly goad to stir up the Philippians to constancy and perseverance in the faith; as if he said, Act in such a manner that I may rejoice and glory in your piety, not here only, where every thing is changeable, but also in the great day of Christ; that the good beginnings which I have seen and still see among you may be persevered in and crowned with constancy; that time may cause no change in them, if it be not for the better; so that when the Lord shall appear, after our combats are ended, I may then also have cause to say with joy, to your glory and mine, that I have not laboured in vain' (Daillé).

17: Yea, and if I am offered upon the sacrifice and service of your faith, I joy, and rejoice with you all: 18 and in the same manner do ye also joy, and rejoice with me.

In facing the real possibility of imminent martyrdom, Paul humbly compares his death to a drink-offering that is poured out as the accompanying libation to the sacrificial offering of the Philippians' faith, which is proved genuine by their own willingness to suffer for the gospel [1:29, 30]. It is because Paul knows that his friends are united with him in the great work of advancing the cause of Christ in the world that he can greet even the prospect of death with undaunted joy. So from his grim prison in Rome he rejoices with them all, and bids them also to rejoice with him. Paul here piles up the terms to express his joy under the most adverse circumstances, because he clearly expects his fellow-sufferers at Philippi to meet their trials in the same spirit. And he further puts them on their mettle by using a metaphor which depicts his own suffering as an auxiliary part of the sacrifice made by them. As Lightfoot well says, The apostle's 'language expresses the fundamental idea of the Christian Church, in which an universal priesthood has supplanted the exclusive ministrations of a select tribe or class: see *1 Pet.* 2:5, *a holy priesthood to offer up spiritual sacrifices.* The Philippians are the priests; their faith (or their good works springing from their faith) is the sacrifice: St Paul's life-blood the accompanying libation. Commentators have much confused the image by representing St Paul himself as the sacrificer.'

19: But I hope in the Lord Jesus to send Timothy shortly unto you, that I also may be of good comfort, when I know your state.

Paul now acquaints the Philippians with what he has planned for their benefit [verses 19–30]. He is sending this letter with Epaphroditus without waiting for the result of the trial [verse 25], but as soon as the case is decided Timothy will follow with the news [verse 23]. Although Paul is quite prepared for an unfavourable verdict [verse 17], he still hopes to be acquitted and released for further service [verse 24].

But I hope in the Lord Jesus to send Timothy shortly unto you: Paul often uses the verb 'hope' in formulating his travel plans [*Rom.* 15:24; *1 Cor.* 16:7; *Philem.* 22], and this verse shows that all his plans are made in the full consciousness of his union with the Lord Jesus and in humble dependence upon what is his will for him. 'The Christian is a part of Christ, a member of His body. His every thought and word and deed proceeds from Christ, as the centre of volition. Thus he loves in the Lord, he hopes in the Lord, he boasts in the Lord, he labours in the Lord, etc. He has one guiding principle in acting and in forbearing to act, *only in the Lord* [*1 Cor.* 7:39]' (Lightfoot).

That I also may be of good comfort, when I know your state: R. P. Martin helpfully clarifies the force of this 'also': 'Not only will you be encouraged to have first-hand news of me here, I too shall be heartened when I get news of you at Philippi on Timothy's return.' This means that the main object of Timothy's mission would be to exercise such a ministry in their midst that he would be able to comfort Paul with the report that unity had been restored [1:27].

20: For I have no man likeminded, who will care truly for your state.

I have no one like him, who will be genuinely anxious for your welfare (RSV): Paul is not comparing Timothy with himself (for which he would have written: 'I have no one *else* like myself'), but with others who have no real concern for the welfare of his friends at Philippi [verse 21]. Timothy was unique because only he shared Paul's anxious solicitude for the churches [*2 Cor.* 11:28]. 'There is a right and a wrong anxiety, just as a right and a wrong attention to one's own interests [verse 4]' (Plummer). As Paul's most trusted assistant, Timothy has the best interests of the Philippians at heart, and he is both competent and willing to serve them without regard to the cost to himself.

'Timothy was of a choice and excellent spirit that naturally cared for the Churches' welfare; few such now-a-days' (Trapp).

21: For they all seek their own, not the things of Jesus Christ.

Of the other Christians who might have been entrusted with this important mission to Philippi, Paul sadly records that none was willing to undertake such an onerous task, for they all put their own interests before those of Jesus Christ. Although this reflects no credit on those whom Paul charitably refuses to name, it highlights the self-sacrifice of Timothy, whose single-minded devotion to Christ's cause is demonstrated by his care for the Philippians.

'It may seem at first sight as if it were no great fault to seek one's own; but how insufferable it is in the servants of Christ appears from the fact that it renders those whom it possesses utterly useless. For it is impossible that he who is devoted to self, should spend himself for the Church. Then, you will say, did Paul cultivate men who were worthless and pretenders? I answer that it is not to be understood as if they had been intent only on their own interests, and had no care whatever for the Church, but that, involved in their own private affairs, they were the more negligent to promote the public advantage of the Church. For it must necessarily be, that one or other of two dispositions rules in us: either that, overlooking ourselves, we are devoted to Christ and the things that are Christ's, or that, too intent on our own advantage, we serve Christ perfunctorily' (John Calvin).

22: But ye know the proof of him, that, as a child serveth a father, so he served with me in furtherance of the gospel.

But (Timothy's) proven worth you know: In contrast to such self-seeking, Timothy had given the Philippians first-hand proof of his worth, just as metals are approved by testing [cf. *Acts* 16:3; 19:22; 20:3–6]. 'They were no strangers to his excellence – it had been tested during previous visits' (Eadie).

How as a child (to) a father, he served with me in the furtherance of the gospel: 'The slight want of correspondence between the two parts of the sentence, reflects accurately the twofold relation between the men. To *one another*, they were "as child *to* father"; to *God*, they were alike servants, one "serving *with*" the other' (Gwynn).

23: Him therefore I hope to send forthwith, so soon as I shall see how it will go with me: 24 but I trust in the Lord that I myself also shall come shortly.

This trusted minister of the gospel is therefore the man whom Paul will send to Philippi as soon as the outcome of his trial is known. Then Timothy will bring the news of Paul's condemnation or release. But Paul's trust in the Lord is such that he also expects to visit them shortly [1:25]. We know from the evidence furnished by the Pastoral Epistles that Paul's first trial resulted in his release, and that he enjoyed a further period of useful service before his final imprisonment and death in Rome (c. AD 67).

25: But I counted it necessary to send to you Epaphroditus, my brother and fellow-worker and fellow-soldier, and your messenger and minister to my need;

But I think it is necessary to send back to you Epaphroditus (NIV): Paul next explains his reasons for sending back Epaphroditus with this letter [verses 25–30]. Epaphroditus, whose name means 'charming', is not to be identified with the Epaphras mentioned in *Col.* 1:7; 4:12, and we know nothing more of him than Paul tells us here. In Paul's glowing commendation of this dedicated servant of Christ, the first three terms describe his relation to the apostle, and the final pair his attachment to the Philippians.

My brother and fellow-worker and fellow-soldier: 'My brother in the faith, my fellow-worker in preaching, my fellow-soldier in adversity' (Anselm). Lightfoot points out that the three words are arranged in an ascending scale: 'common sympathy, common work, common danger and toil and suffering'.

And your messenger and minister to my need: As the 'apostle' or appointed delegate of the Philippian church [cf. *2 Cor.* 8:23], Epaphroditus was sent to perform a sacrificial service for Paul by presenting their gift of money [4:18] and ministering to his needs in prison on their behalf [verse 30].

26: since he longed after you all, and was sore troubled, because ye had heard that he was sick:

For he has been longing for you all, and has been distressed because you heard that he was ill (RSV): This states why Paul has decided to send back Epaphroditus at once. It is unlikely that Epaphroditus would have travelled alone to Rome, especially when he was bringing a sum of money to Paul. So if he became ill shortly after their arrival, his companions would take back the unwelcome news on their return to Philippi. This illness naturally intensified his longing to see all his brethren at home, and he was also greatly distressed to realize that news of his condition would have filled them with grief.

27: for indeed he was sick nigh unto death: but God had mercy on him; and not on him only, but on me also, that I might not have sorrow upon sorrow.

Paul here movingly reveals his own reaction to Epaphroditus' illness, which was so serious that he nearly died. But despite his anxiety for the life of his friend, Paul did not heal him by exercising 'the signs of an apostle' [*2 Cor.* 12:12], because 'even in that charismatic era the apostles could not perform miracles whenever they felt so inclined. *Their* will was subject to *God's* will' (Hendriksen). But in graciously restoring Epaphroditus, God showed mercy both to him and to Paul, who was thus spared from being overwhelmed by 'sorrow upon sorrow'. As Eadie says, The sorrow which he already possessed was not the sickness of Epaphroditus, 'for even after his convalescence, he speaks of himself as only lightened in sorrow, but not entirely freed from it. A sorrow would still remain after Epaphroditus had departed, as is intimated in the next verse, the sorrow produced by his present situation – his captivity and all its embarrassments. This statement is in no way inconsistent with what he had written in 1:20, etc, for his condition is there looked at from a very different point of view.'

28: I have sent him therefore the more diligently, that, when ye see him again, ye may rejoice, and that I may be the less sorrowful.

Accordingly, I am sending him (back) the more eagerly in order that when you see him again you may rejoice and I may be less sorrowful (Hendriksen): The Philippians had intended that Epaphroditus should stay with Paul and attend to his needs in prison, but circumstances alter cases [verses 26, 27], and Paul now deems it best to send back their brother so that they may rejoice in his safe return. By sharing in the joy of this reunion

Paul's sorrow will be lessened. 'The original sorrow, which still remains his portion, will be lessened by sympathy with the Philippians' joy at having Epaphroditus home again and in good health' (Plummer).

29: Receive him therefore in the Lord with all joy; and hold such in honour: 30 because for the work of Christ he came nigh unto death, hazarding his life to supply that which was lacking in your service toward me.

Having explained why Epaphroditus is returning earlier than anticipated, Paul now plainly bids the Philippians to give him the welcome he deserves. As he was sent so that they might rejoice [verse 28], they must therefore receive him 'in the Lord' with all joy, for such men are to be honoured and prized.

Because he almost died for the work of Christ, risking his life to make up for the help you could not give me (NIV): Paul here gives the reason for valuing Epaphroditus so highly. The word translated as 'risking' really means that he gambled with his life by staking all in the service of Christ [cf. *Rom.* 16:4]. The noble example of Epaphroditus was followed by others, and certain laymen in the early church who risked their lives in caring for victims of the plague were known as 'the Gamblers'. 'That which was lacking in your service toward me' is an unfortunate rendering which suggests some neglect on the Philippians' part, and Paul's meaning is made much clearer by the NIV. 'The expression is complimentary and affectionate, to the effect that all that was wanting in the matter of their service was their ministration *in person*, which was supplied by Epaphroditus' (Vincent).

CHAPTER THREE

After a further call to rejoice in the Lord, Paul launches into a passionate warning against Judaizers whom he calls 'the mutilators', and shows that he had greater cause than they to trust in the righteousness of the law [verses 1–6]. But the privileges he once prized, he now counts as loss that he may gain Christ and his righteousness, and share in the resurrection from the dead [verses 7–11]. In contrast to the self-deluded who already claimed perfection, Paul still presses on toward the goal, and he enjoins the spiritually mature to strive after the same thing without losing hold of their present attainments [verses

12–16]. In presenting himself as an example to follow, Paul warns against the profligate professors whose god is their belly and who mind earthly things, whereas the true citizens of heaven eagerly await the return of Christ and the glory of the resurrection [verses 17–21].

1: Finally, my brethren, rejoice in the Lord. To write the same things to you, to me indeed is not irksome, but for you it is safe.

For the rest, my brothers, rejoice in the Lord (Hendriksen): 'Finally' is rather misleading because it suggests that Paul is about to conclude the Epistle, whereas the expression is loosely used to introduce a new subject ('for the rest'). As the affectionate address 'my brothers' reminds the Philippians of their glorious position as members of the same spiritual family, it serves to reinforce the renewed exhortation to rejoice [cf. 2:18, 28], but this time Paul defines the sphere of this rejoicing by adding 'in the Lord'. The phrase points to the one ground of rejoicing and also excludes all confidence in the flesh [verse 3]. Believers must indeed rejoice, but they can only do so 'in the Lord': only in union with him and relying solely upon his redemptive achievements on their behalf.

To write the same things to you is no trouble to me, and for you it is a safeguard (Hendriksen): 'The same things' refers to the warning that follows and not to the call to rejoice. Although some suppose this relates to warnings given in previous letters which are lost, it is more likely that the earlier general warning to stand firm against the opponents of the gospel is here applied to the particular threat posed by the Judaizers [1:27– 30]. As a faithful watchman for the souls of men, Paul is so diligent in repeating his warnings that he knows he is pure from the blood of all men [*Ezek.* 33:2–6; *Acts* 20:26].

2: Beware of the dogs, beware of the evil workers, beware of the concision:

The biting sarcasm of Paul's threefold indictment of the Judaizers is intended to ensure that if these emissaries of legalism make their way to Philippi they will be sent packing by the church.

Look out for the dogs (RSV): As a term of reproach, the image suggested by this word was that of the diseased scavenger dogs which roamed about eastern cities, and it thus signified for the Jew all that was impure and unclean [cf. *Rev.* 22:15]. Hence 'dogs' was the Jewish designation for all Gentiles, which Paul here hurls back at the Judaizers: *they* are the dogs, 'for they greedily devour the garbage of carnal ordinances' (Lightfoot).

Look out for the evil-doers (RSV): In their fanatical zeal, these pseudo-missionaries were engaged in the evil work of gaining converts from Gentile churches by corrupting the gospel of God's grace with the leaven of their legalism [cf. *Matt.* 23:15; *2 Cor.* 11:13–15]. 'Instead of *helping* the good cause, they actually *harm* it. They draw the attention away from Christ and his accomplished redemption, and fix it upon an outworn ritual, and upon human worth and attainment in insisting upon its perpetuation and application. Here is Satan's demolition crew. It is working very hard to demolish God's beautiful palace of grace and peace' (Hendriksen).

Look out for those who mutilate the flesh (RSV): Paul denies the honoured title of 'the circumcision' to the apostles of error and scathingly brands them as 'the mutilation'. Their circumcision was of no more value than the gashings of the prophets of Baal, 'because these men were circumcised merely *as regards the body*, and placed their confidence in this fleshly circumcision, but were wanting in the *inner, spiritual* circumcision, which that of the body typified [see verse 3; *Rom.* 2:28f; *Col.* 2:11; *Eph.* 2:11; *Acts* 7:51]. Comp *Gal.* 5:11f. In the absence of this, their characteristic consisted simply in the bodily mutilation' (Meyer).

3: for we are the circumcision, who worship by the Spirit of God, and glory in Christ Jesus, and have no confidence in the flesh:

Paul totally rejects the false claims of the Judaizers and roundly affirms: 'for *we* Christians are the circumcision, for their circumcision is only outward, whereas the *true* circumcision is that of the heart' [*Rom.* 2:25-29; cf. *Deut.* 10:16; 30:6; *Jer.* 4:4; *Ezek.* 44:7]. In the three clauses that follow Paul sets forth the distinguishing characteristics of the true Israel of God [*Gal.* 6:15,16]. 'The notion that God even today recognizes two favoured groups – on the one hand the church and on the other the Jews – is thoroughly unscriptural' (Hendriksen) [cf. *John* 10:16].

Who worship by the Spirit of God: To worship God acceptably requires an inward transformation by the Holy Spirit as the initiator of the

New Covenant [*Jer.* 31:31–34; *Ezek.* 36:26f.], and his enabling promotes that life of *service* which is the true *worship* [cf. *Rom.* 12:1, ASV margin]. 'Christians worship God through the Spirit of God. This is not to be restricted to prayer. It includes all that to which we are impelled by the Spirit. The Christian life fashioned by the Spirit is true *worship*' (H. Strathmann, *TDNT*, vol. 1, pp. 64–5).

And glory in Christ Jesus: This is our only boast! We glory in Christ Jesus 'as Him through whom alone we have attained righteousness, etc, see verse 9; comp. *Gal.* 6:14' (Meyer). The verb used here is one of Paul's favourite and most characteristic words. 'It expresses with great vividness the high level of Christian life at which he is living: "exulting in Christ Jesus". It belongs to the same triumphant mood which finds utterance so often in this Epistle in *rejoice*. This victorious Christian gladness ought to sweep them past all earthly formalism and bondage to "beggarly elements" (Kennedy).

And have no confidence in the flesh: The 'flesh' is another name for external privilege, such as descent, and points to such merit as pride thinks due to formal obedience. It is a ground of confidence opposed to the righteousness of Christ – verse 9' (Eadie).

4: though I myself might have confidence even in the flesh: if any other man thinketh to have confidence in the flesh, I yet more:

Paul here changes from 'we' to the emphatic 'I', as he recounts a vivid snatch of his spiritual autobiography. This is to show that his opposition to the Judaizers was not motivated by envy of their supposed advantages, since he had greater grounds for glorying on that score than they had themselves. So for the sake of argument, he 'places himself on the same standing ground with the Judaizers and, adopting their language, speaks of himself as having that which in fact he had renounced: comp *2 Cor.* 11:18 *since many glory according to the flesh, I will glory also*' (Lightfoot).

Although Paul recognized the 'folly' of such boasting [*2 Cor.* 11:17], it was necessary to list his Jewish credentials before showing that they were unable to provide the perfect righteousness God requires [verses 7–9]. He first lists the advantages which were his by birth [verse 5], and then those which he later acquired by his own efforts [verses 5d, 6].

5: circumcised the eighth day, of the stock of Israel, of the tribe of Benjamin, a Hebrew of Hebrews;

The four advantages by birth are arranged in an ascending scale.

Circumcised the eighth day: The first item in Paul's unimpeachable Jewish pedigree would be all the more impressive if some of the zealous Judaizers were only recently circumcised proselytes. 'Converts to Judaism were circumcised in maturity: Ishmaelites in their thirteenth year. He was thus shown to be neither a heathen nor an Ishmaelite' (Vincent). [*Gen.* 17:9–14; *Lev.* 12:3].

Of the stock of Israel: One who was circumcised on the eighth day could still be the child of proselyte parents, but Paul belonged to the chosen race by direct descent. 'His parents were not grafted into the covenant people, but descended from the original stock' (Lightfoot).

Of the tribe of Benjamin: Moreover, in a day when many Israelites had lost their tribal identity, Paul was proud to be a member of the tribe which gave Israel its first king, after whom he was doubtless named [*Acts* 13:21]. 'This tribe stood high in Jewish estimation, not only as descending from Rachel, Jacob's best-loved wife, but as remaining loyal to the house of David, and, after the exile, forming with Judah the foundation of the future nation' (Kennedy).

A Hebrew of Hebrews: Finally, Paul's racial purity was unspoilt by foreign influences. 'The expression implies characteristics of language and manners. He might be an Israelite and yet a child of Greek-speaking Jews: but his parents had retained their native tongue and customs, and he himself, while understanding and speaking Greek, also spoke in Hebrew on occasion. See *Acts* 21:40; 22:2' (Vincent)

5d: as touching the law, a Pharisee; 6 as touching zeal, persecuting the church; as touching the righteousness which is in the law, found blameless.

Paul's inherited privileges are followed by the three distinctions he had attained by his own choice and training.

As touching the law, a Pharisee: Although the Pharisees (or 'Separated Ones') fought a war on two fronts against the theological 'liberalism' of the Sadducees and the religious 'laxity' of the common people, they were the most influential party in Judaism and were generally respected for their piety (cf. J. Jeremias, *Jerusalem in the Time of Jesus*, pp. 266–

267). To join such a party was the natural choice for an all-or-nothing man like Saul of Tarsus, who studied the law under the famous Gamaliel at Jerusalem [*Acts* 22:3].

As touching zeal, persecuting the church: 'An expression of intense irony, condemning while he seems to exalt his former self' (Lightfoot). Paul thus recalls with shame his fanatical zeal in persecuting the church of Christ [*Gal.* 1:13f], which is assailed when even one member of Christ's body is hurt [*Acts* 9:4f, *1 Tim.* 1: 13]. But on his conversion, the persecutor became one of the persecuted [*Acts* 9:16]. 'He had persecuted, as the Jews are now persecuting him; and in each case the persecution was conscientious' (Plummer) [*Rom.* 10:1–3].

As touching the righteousness which is in the law, found blameless: According to the Pharisaic understanding of what constituted obedience to the law, Paul was blameless in his scrupulous observance of all those minute duties imposed by a tradition intent upon attaining righteousness by works [cf. verse 9]. A close parallel is furnished by the gospel story of the rich young man who claimed to have observed all the law's commands from his youth [*Mark* 10:20]. 'It was at the next step [verse 7] that *he* stopped short. He was unable to "count all things loss for Christ" (Kennedy).

7: Howbeit what things were gain to me, these have I counted loss for Christ.

Yet those things which I formerly reckoned to my credit I have come to count as loss for Christ's sake (F. F. Bruce): Paul's confidence in the Judaistic method of reckoning up his fancied merits was shattered by his encounter with the Risen Christ on the road to Damascus. As his old life and all its cherished values collapsed around him, he realized that the things which he had prized as 'assets' were in fact 'liabilities', and so he bundled them all together and wrote them off as a complete loss. 'In the light of the all-transcending knowledge of Christ the life which trusts in, and appeals to, descent, the Law and achievement, is not just fruitless exertion but harmful in the absolute sense' (H. Schlier, *TDNT,* vol. 3, p. 673).

8: Yea verily, and I count all things to be loss for the excellency of the knowledge of Christ Jesus my Lord: for whom I suffered the loss of all things, and do count them but refuse,

Yes, what is more, I certainly do count all things to be sheer loss because of the all-surpassing excellence of knowing Christ Jesus my Lord (Hendriksen): In addition to the things just mentioned, Paul continues to count *all* things as sheer loss because of the infinitely more valuable gain of knowing 'Christ Jesus my Lord'. As the emphatic fulness of the designation points to the supreme worthiness of the One who is the object of this knowledge, so the warmth with which Paul claims him as '*my* Lord' shows that his knowledge is not based on hearsay but personal communion. Paul at last attained the true 'knowledge of God' when he came to know the Son who had so fully revealed the Father's great love. This knowledge 'is directly connected with the surrender of the soul to Christ, but, as Paul teaches, that always means a close intimacy with Him, from which there springs an ever-growing knowledge of His spirit and will. Such knowledge lays a stable foundation for the Christian character, preventing it from evaporating into a mere unreasoning emotionalism' (Kennedy). [cf. *Eph.* 1:17, 18; 3:19; *Col.* 1:9, 10; 2:2, 3; 3:10].

For whom I suffered the loss of all things: 'These emphatic words suit the mouth of one who had been disowned by his family, and reduced from a position of wealth and influence in his nation to poverty and contempt' (W. M. Ramsay, *St Paul the Traveller and the Roman Citizen*, p. 36).

And do count them but refuse: Paul expresses his utter revulsion at the attempts of the Judaizers to impose the garbage of ceremonial observances upon the Gentile churches [cf. *Gal.* 5:12]. 'All "confidence in the flesh" is contemptuously cast aside and abhorred as dirty muck! [cf. *Isa.* 64:6; *Zech.* 3:3–5] Such is God's estimate of all religious observance and practice which is not rooted in Christ and His atoning merit' (R. P. Martin, *TNTC*).

8b: that I may gain Christ, 9 and be found in him, not having a righteousness of mine own, even that which is of the law, but that which is through faith in Christ, the righteousness which is from God by faith:

Paul's motive in reaching such a radical reassessment is to gain Christ and be found in him. Although many take this to be a reference to the final judgment (cf. Moffatt: 'and be found at death in him'), the context clearly shows that Paul is thinking about his *present* interest in Christ and what is involved in thus finding himself 'incorporate in him' (NEB). Here he explains the meaning of union with Christ, first negatively, and then positively.

Not having a righteousness of mine own, even that which is of the law: In this echo of the apostle's teaching in Romans and Galatians, we have his mature judgment upon the years of fruitless striving to attain righteousness by his own fulfilment of the law's demands [cf. *Rom.* 3:19, 20; *Gal.* 2:16, 21; 3:10]. His encounter with Christ had taught him that his legal righteousness was an external sham that would not pass muster with God, and the whole of his subsequent struggle against placing even a particle of faith in human merit was simply the outworking of that conversion-experience.

But that which is through faith in Christ, the righteousness which is from God by faith: 'But' marks a complete antithesis to such misplaced confidence in the flesh. The only way to attain a right standing with God is through the justifying faith that lays hold of Christ, whose obedience in life and death secured that perfect righteousness which is provided by God and received on the basis of faith [*Rom.* 4:4–6, 23–25]. 'The contrast is between the righteousness which a man can make for himself and the righteousness that God gives him. And the contrast is absolute . . . (Paul) founds salvation solely on an alien righteousness, with the express exclusion of every item of our own righteousness . . . The Gospel, to Paul, consists precisely in this: that we do nothing to earn our salvation or to secure it for ourselves. God in Christ does it all' (B. B. Warfield, 'The Alien Righteousness' in *Faith and Life*, pp. 321–322).

10: that I may know him, and the power of his resurrection, and the fellowship of his sufferings, becoming conformed unto his death; 11 if by any means I may attain unto the resurrection from the dead.

That I may know him (i.e. Christ): Having already spoken of the 'knowledge' of Christ [verse 8], Paul now defines the content of the faith mentioned in the previous verse by explaining what is involved in knowing Christ [verse 10b, c]. In sharp contrast to the perfectionists who claimed to have arrived at the goal [verses 12–16], Paul's great desire is to come to know Christ with ever increasing intimacy, even though that means choosing the way of suffering and death [1:29f].

And the power of his resurrection: This is placed first because it must come first in the order of Christian experience. The reference is not to the power by which Christ was raised from the dead, but to the power which the resurrected Christ exerts over his people in raising them from the sepulchre of their sins to the newness of life in him [*Rom.* 6:4ff., *Eph.* 1:19ff.; 2:5, 6; *Col.* 3:1I]. 'It is the power of the risen Christ as it becomes a subject of practical knowledge and a power in Paul's inner life' (Vincent, *ICC*, p. 104).

And the fellowship of his sufferings, becoming conformed unto his death: Union with Christ also means entering into the fellowship of his sufferings. Paul is not claiming a share in that redemptive travail which was Christ's alone, but is speaking of the afflictions he willingly endures for the sake of Christ and his gospel [cf. *Col.* 1:24]. 'In growing conformity with his death' (NEB) indicates that the process of conformity was advancing – like Him in suffering, like Him in death . . . in all things Paul coveted conformity to His Lord – even in suffering and death' (Eadie). [cf. *2 Cor.* 7–11].

If by any means: The phrase 'expresses not doubt, but rather the eagerness that strives by *all* ways to reach its end' (Gwynn).

I may attain unto the resurrection from the dead: Paul's use of this unique expression – 'the out-resurrection from the dead' – is doubtless dictated by a polemical purpose. It is a telling thrust against those who were claiming to be sinlessly perfect on the basis of their spiritual resurrection with Christ in baptism (so Martin). But complete conformity with Christ will not be attained until the day of his coming, when all believers, whether alive or asleep [*1 Cor.* 15:52], will be glorified together [verse 21]. Paul does not refer to the resurrection of the wicked, because in addressing believers he naturally speaks of their resurrection to glory [cf. *1 Cor.* 15:20–23; *1 Thess.* 4:16, 17].

But that is no reason for supposing that the eternal destiny of the righteous and the wicked will be determined separately rather than at the same general resurrection [cf. *Acts* 17:31f]. The resurrection is here represented as the goal of all Paul's striving, because it is only then that believers will be invested with the body of glory [verse 21]. 'As no one can expect to stand in the last day who has not practised holiness in the fear of God, so no one can hope to attain unto the resurrection of life who has not learned to know Christ and the power of his resurrection and the fellowship of his sufferings, being conformed unto his death. Such a mode of viewing the resurrection need not do away with the other mode of viewing it as a gift of free grace bestowed for the sake of the merit of Christ' (G. Vos, *The Pauline Eschatology*, p. 257).

12: Not that I have already obtained, or am already made perfect: but I press on, if so be that I may lay hold on that for which also I was laid hold on by Christ Jesus.

In countering the false claims of the 'perfectionists', Paul appeals to his own experience to prove that believers are not made perfect in this present life, but he also insists that they must constantly strive for increasing conformity to Christ. The imagery used here is that of the foot-race. Paul runs the Christian race with all the dedication of an athlete who is bent on winning the prize.

This gives us an interesting insight into the psychology of Christian perseverance. The man who is tempted to succumb to the snare of perfectionism will lapse into a state of spiritual complacency. He will consider that he has already arrived at the goal, and regard his fellow-believers as mere 'also rans' in the spiritual race! It is only the consciousness of not yet having arrived which will quicken our endeavours, just as the athlete strains every muscle to finish the course.

Not that I have already obtained, or am already made perfect: The first verb probably points to the time of Paul's conversion, while the second refers to his present state: 'Neither when I became Christ's did I attain, nor, up to this time, have I been perfected' (Vincent). Although 'obtained' has no object, the metaphor suggests that Paul has in view 'the prize' awarded to the victorious athlete [verse 14].

But I press on, if so be that I may lay hold on that for which also I was laid hold on by Christ Jesus: It is in virtue of the grace received in his conversion that Paul still presses on to see if he can grasp the goal for which he was then grasped by Christ. As J. Dupont points out, Christ suddenly seized Paul in an *irresistible way*. 'If Paul is now on the race track, as he describes it in verses 13–14, he has to thank this "start" which came with the Damascus event' ('The Conversion of Paul' in *Apostolic History and the Gospel*, pp. 181, 191).

13: Brethren, I count not myself yet to have laid hold: but one thing I do, forgetting the things which are behind, and stretching forward to the things which are before, 14: I press on toward the goal unto the prize of the high calling of God in Christ Jesus.

Brethren, I count not myself yet to have laid hold: Paul uses the earnest address 'brethren' to introduce an important statement. His emphatic disclaimer is clearly intended to point a contrast with those who thought themselves 'perfect' [verse 15]. The fact that the aged apostle does not even consider himself to be within reach of the prize should give the most convinced perfectionists in Philippi pause for thought, not to speak of their successors today!

But one thing I do: 'There is no need to supply a verb. His Christian conduct is summed up in what follows. Never has there been a more *unified* life than that of Paul as Apostle and Christian' (Kennedy).

Forgetting the things which are behind, and stretching forward to the things which are before: As a *Pharisee* who thought he had arrived at perfection, Saul's present was determined by his past, for perfectionism is based on pride in one's progress in holiness [verses 4–6]. But as a *Christian*, Paul's present efforts are determined by his future goal, and so he forgets past achievements as he presses towards the prize. It is this forgetfulness of the past which frees us to run the Christian race. The competitor who is always looking back over his shoulder will never win that race. Many Christians are so paralysed by past failures or have become so complacent with past successes that they have virtually stopped running the race. But when with Paul we write off our past as a dead loss [verses 7, 8], then we are free to face the future with confidence. The formula for success in the Christian life is simple (but not *easy* like the 'instant' formula of the 'second blessing'!): relegate the past to oblivion, and *strain forward* for the prize which is set before us.

I press on toward the goal to win the prize for which God has called me heavenward in Christ Jesus (NIV): Paul presses on because it is only when the goal is reached that the prize can be grasped. So he strives to attain the prize of 'perfect fellowship with Christ, and his glorification with Christ in the immaculate heritage of heaven hereafter [cf. *2 Tim.* 4:8; *Rev.* 2:10]. This prize is connected with the upward (heavenly, heavenward) call of God which he received at his conversion, when God's saving call to everlasting life came to him "in Christ Jesus", i.e.

by His merit and in communion with Him' (J. J. Müller). The thought of this verse is well expressed in the familiar hymn, 'Fight the good fight':

> *Run the straight race through God's good grace,*
> *Lift up thine eyes, and seek His face;*
> *Life with its path before us lies;*
> *Christ is the way, and Christ the prize.*
>
> J. S. B. Monsell

15: Let us therefore, as many as are perfect, be thus minded: and if in anything ye are otherwise minded, this also shall God reveal unto you:

Let us therefore, as many as are perfect, be thus minded: Paul's gentle irony pinpoints the error of those who consider themselves to be 'perfect' as he picks up their favourite word, and in effect asks them to reconsider its meaning in the light of his personal testimony [verses 12–14]. He is quite prepared to include himself among the 'perfect' so long as they are 'thus minded', for only those who are conscious of their present imperfection will strive to attain the goal which still lies before them. The prospect of being 'perfect' is the Christian's hope; the claim 'to be already "perfect" is always recurring in various forms – all natural but unwarrantable anticipations of heaven on earth. St Paul, by a striking paradox, bids those who hold themselves perfect to prove that they are so by a consciousness of imperfection. If they have it not, he says, they have something yet to learn' (Alfred Barry).

And if in anything ye are otherwise minded, this also shall God reveal unto you: Paul cannot regard the error of the perfectionists with indifference because he knows that to cherish such a delusion as the *truth* will result in misshapen conduct. As one who is sure that he possesses God's truth, the apostle assures those who doubtless boasted of their special 'revelations' that they still stand to profit from a further disclosure of divine truth, for God is sure to show them their mistake.

16: only, whereunto we have attained, by that same rule let us walk.

Only to what you have attained, with the same keep in line! (Lenski) In this exhortation to 'march in line', Paul seeks to safeguard the unity of the church by discouraging the idea that Christians are to be 'spiritual virtuosos' (F. W. Beare), each glorying in his own attainments without regard to the well-being of the body to which he belongs. 'He is anxious for two things - that they should keep on in one course, and that all should keep on together. In both senses he addresses the "perfect"; he will have them understand that they have attained only one thing - to be in the right path, and that it is for them to continue in it; he also bids them refrain from setting themselves up above "the imperfect"; for the very fact of division would mark them as still "carnal", mere "babes in Christ" [*1 Cor.* 3:1–4]' (Barry).

17: Brethren, be ye imitators together of me, and mark them that so walk even as ye have us for an ensample.

By way of application [verses 7–14], Paul exhorts his brothers in the faith to be fellow-imitators of him. As an apostle, he is a man whose unique authority stems from his knowledge of Christ's will for the church, and so there is no egotism in thus presenting himself as an authentic pattern for believers to follow [cf. 4:9]. But here he means something more than: 'Follow my example'. His primary emphasis is: 'Recognize my authority, follow what I say, be obedient' (so W. Michaelis, *TDNT*, vol. 1, p. 668).

And watch closely those who are walking according to the example that we have set you (Hendriksen): In passing from the singular to the plural, Paul has in view the example set by his associates Timothy and Epaphroditus. For their leadership is also in accord with the standard laid down by himself, even though they do not share his special status as a divinely appointed apostle (Martin).

18: For many walk, of whom I told you often, and now tell you even weeping, that they are the enemies of the cross of Christ: 19 whose end is perdition, whose god is the belly, and whose glory is in their shame, who mind earthly things.

For many walk, of whom I told you often: The Philippians must imitate those who exemplify the faith they teach [verse 17], for Paul had often warned them to be on their guard against an evil which was widespread among the Gentile churches, though it had not yet reached them [1:3-8]. The persons described are clearly 'professing Christians who allowed their liberty to degenerate into licence [*Gal.* 5:13]; who, from an altogether superficial view of grace, thought lightly of continuing in sin [*Rom.* 6:1, 12-13, 15, 23]; who, while bearing the name of Christ, were concerned only with their own self-indulgence [*Rom.* 16:18]' (Kennedy).

And now tell you even weeping: The stress of Paul's 'grief would lie in the fact, that they degraded the true doctrine of liberty, so as to minister to their profligate and worldly living. They made use of his name, but did not follow his example' (Lightfoot).

That they are the enemies of the cross of Christ: Such libertines are indeed 'the enemies of the cross of Christ', for though they claim a saving interest in Christ crucified, their sinful lives are a flagrant denial of the faith they confess with their lips. 'The true Christian is the man who is "crucified with Christ", who has "crucified the flesh with its affections and lusts".

The Cross is the central principle in his life. "If any man will come after me, let him deny himself and take up his cross and follow me". Those here described, by their unthinking self-indulgence, run directly in the teeth of this principle' (Kennedy).

Whose end is perdition: Paul states the destiny of these men before specifying the nature of their conduct, so 'that what follows may be read with the greater horror' (Bengel). 'Perdition' points not to the extinction of existence, but to that state of utter ruin and everlasting torment, which is the only appropriate 'end' for the ungodly [*2 Thess.* 1:9; *2 Pet.* 3:7, 16].

Whose god is the belly: Perhaps under the influence of an incipient gnosticism, these 'men of the Spirit' felt that they could indulge their bodily appetites without restraint [*1 Cor.* 6:13], and so surrendered themselves to gluttony and licentiousness.

And whose glory is in their shame: Although they 'gloried' in their freedom to do as they pleased, they did not realize that such slavery to their lusts meant that they were glorying in their 'shame'.

Who mind earthly things: Finally, Paul expresses his amazement at professed believers whose mental horizon was bounded by earthly things! 'In a parallel passage the apostle shows us what these *earthly things* were on which these people set their minds, namely, immorality, indecency, lust, evil desire, greed, evil temper, furious rage, malice, cursing, filthy talk [*Col.* 3:2, 5, 8]' (Hendriksen).

20: For our citizenship is in heaven; whence also we wait for a Saviour, the Lord Jesus Christ:

This advances the reason for rejecting such a misinterpretation of Christian liberty: 'For *our* commonwealth is in heaven' (ASV margin). Since the Philippians lived in a colony whose citizens regarded distant Rome as their native city, they would be quick to grasp Paul's metaphor which shows that heaven is the true homeland of believers (see comment on 1:27). As aliens who have here no continuing city, their life is not rooted in 'earthly things' to which they owe no allegiance, for they belong by the adoption of grace to that heavenly city 'whose architect and builder is God' [*Heb.* 11:10, NIV; cf. *Gal.* 4:26; *Eph.* 2:19; *1 Pet.* 2:11]. It is because the Christian's affections are centred upon 'the things that are above' that his earthly walk will be very different from the walk of those whose minds are still captivated by what is purely temporal [*Col.* 3:1-3].

Whence also we wait for a Saviour, the Lord Jesus Christ: Moreover, it is from heaven that we eagerly await the advent of a *Saviour*, for it is in his capacity as Saviour that the Lord Jesus Christ will complete our final deliverance [verse 21]. Instead of pinning their hopes upon the doubtful divinity of an earthly emperor, believers look for the coming of a Saviour, who has the power both to free them from the bondage of death, and to bestow upon them the glorious liberty of the children of God [*Rom.* 8:21].

21: who shall fashion anew the body of our humiliation, that it may be conformed to the body of his glory, according to the working whereby he is able even to subject all things unto himself.

In contrast to the false claims of the perfectionists, Paul here shows that the tension between the 'already' and the 'not yet' of the Christian's present state can only be resolved when Christ returns to glorify his people. But the fact that the 'prize' of perfection must be bestowed by an act of divine power offers no loophole for the spiritually lazy, for in the meantime all believers must be like the Olympic athlete who spares no effort to attain the goal which still lies before him [verses 11–14].

Who shall fashion anew the body of our humiliation, that it may be conformed to the body of his glory: Far from entertaining the Greek notion of the body as being the tomb of the soul, Paul cannot conceive of any salvation which does not embrace the *whole* man, yet his doctrine of the resurrection is no abstract theory but the living truth of his own experience. In his encounter with the Risen Christ he witnessed the objective reality of 'the body of his glory', while his subjective insight into the significance of this truth was imparted to him by the inward illumination of the Spirit [*Gal.* 1:16]. By way of contrast, he calls our present body 'the body of our humiliation' because it is subject to frailty, sinfulness, mortality, and corruption. As in 2:6–8, the compounds used here mark the difference between what is external and transitory ('fashion') and what is essential and permanent ('form'). Paul thus 'declares a future change of *outward fashion* of body, to result in a full *assimilation of form* (implying the whole *nature*) of the risen Christian to his glorified Lord. He has told us [verse 10] of the gradual process by which the Christian is, in this life, *in course of conforming* to Christ's death. That process, we here learn, is to be consummated by the *change of fashion* of the body, from the natural to the spiritual [*1 Cor.* 15:44], in the Resurrection. Then the entire man, body and soul, shall be *conformable*, – assimilated alike in outward aspect and in inward verity, to the Glory of the Lord' (Gwynn).

According to the working whereby he is able even to subject all things unto himself: The miracle of the resurrection will be accomplished by the same omnipotent power which enables Christ to bring all things under his rule [2:10, 11]. 'His is a sovereign power to which all things are subordinate - all earthly power and authority, enemies and death [cf. *1 Cor.* 15:24-27; *Eph.*1:21, 22]' (Müller).

CHAPTER FOUR

In calling for steadfastness and unity, Paul begs Euodia and Syntyche to resolve their differences, and bids them all to rejoice in the Lord as they show that forbearance towards others which befits those who know that the Lord is at hand [verses 1–5]. They are to be anxious about nothing, for if they commit their needs to God in prayer, the peace of God will guard their hearts and thoughts in Christ Jesus [verses 6, 7]. Finally, he exhorts them to practise every kind of moral goodness, and again urges them to follow his example [verses 8, 9]. Paul thanks them for their ministry to him in prison, although he has learned to be content in all circumstances through the Lord's enabling power [verses

10-13]. Their fellowship in his affliction reminds him of their earlier generosity, and he describes the gift they sent with Epaphroditus as an acceptable sacrifice to God [verses 14–20]. Believers in Caesar's household are specially mentioned in the final greeting, and the letter closes with the usual benediction [verses 21–23]

1: Wherefore, my brethren beloved and longed for, my joy and crown, so stand fast in the Lord, my beloved.

It is unfortunate that this chapter begins with an exhortation which should be regarded as the proper conclusion of the preceding appeal [3:17ff.]. Paul's close attachment to the church at Philippi is shown by his multiplied expressions of love. He not only addresses them as 'my brethren beloved and longed for', but in calling them 'my joy and crown' he lets them know that his joy is bound up with their steadfast perseverance in the faith. 'The Philippian converts are his chaplet of victory, showing that he has not run in vain, ch 2:16' (Vincent). Paul bases his admonition upon the fact of their union with Christ, so that the call to 'stand fast in the Lord' also reveals the secret of such stability [cf. *Eph.* 6:10]. 'So stand' means live in accordance with the pattern just set forth [3:17–21], as you are guided by my precept and my example, as becomes citizens of a heavenly kingdom' (Lightfoot).

2: I exhort Euodia, and I exhort Syntyche, to be of the same mind in the Lord.

Having carefully prepared the ground by stressing the need for unity and humility throughout the letter [1:27; 2:1–5, 14], Paul is at last ready to deal with a sharp personality clash between two prominent women whose quarrel evidently threatened the peace and harmony of the whole church [verse 3]. It is sad to think that our introduction to Euodia and Syntyche is due to the fact that they were at odds with one another. This is the kind of dubious notoriety we would do well to shun! Paul scrupulously avoids taking sides in the dispute and calls upon both women 'to be of the same mind in the Lord', thus making a pointed personal application of his previous admonition to the church [2:2]. To share the Lord's mind involves the adoption of the same attitude of self-sacrificing love [2:5]. As pride is the root cause of such divisions within the church, so humility is the sole remedy for this all too frequent distemper. For the disease can be arrested only when Christians are humble enough to renounce self-interest and take a genuine interest in the concerns of others [2:3, 4]. 'In the Lord' characterizes the specifically *Christian* concord, the moral nature and effort of which are grounded on Christ as their determining vital principle. Paul does not desire a union of minds *apart from* Christ' (Meyer).

3: Yea, I beseech thee also, true yokefellow, help these women, for they laboured with me in the gospel, with Clement also, and the rest of my fellow-workers, whose names are in the book of life.

It is impossible to identify the person whom Paul calls his 'true yokefellow', and the suggestion that this designation be regarded as a proper name (Syzygus, who is asked to live up to his name in uniting these women) is improbable since the word is nowhere else used as a proper name. However, the Philippians would know whom Paul meant, and this partner is urged to help Euodia and Syntyche in resolving their differences, for they shared in Paul's struggles to establish the church at Philippi [*Acts* 16:13], together with Clement (who is otherwise unknown to us) and the rest of the fellow-workers, 'whose names are in the book of life'.

This is intended as an excuse 'for not inserting them here; their names (says he) are written in a much more excellent book than this Epistle of mine. This "Book of Life", of which he speaks, is the register of the kingdom of heaven, wherein are enrolled the names of all the elect . . . For the Scripture, employing frequently things of earth in order to represent to our minds the things of heaven, compares the list of the people of God, whom He has chosen from eternity, and marked as His elect, to a register, in which the names of all the citizens of a town are enrolled. I confess that to us this book is shut up and sealed. God knows them that are His, but will not manifest them fully until that day when the books shall be opened and the sheep separated from the goats. But meanwhile we may judge, although with modesty and charity, by the actions of men, and hold as the elect of God, as citizens of the new Jerusalem, truly enrolled in its registers, those who display in their lives the marks of Divine adoption, such as faith, obedience, love, holiness, perseverance, and other graces. And therefore the apostle scruples not to say, that the "names" of the Philippians in whose conduct and conversation he had observed these holy qualities were written in the "Book of Life"' (Daillé).

4: Rejoice in the Lord always: again I will say, Rejoice.

Paul here returns to the dominant note of the Epistle as he reissues the call to rejoice in the Lord which he repeats for emphasis [3:1]. 'He doubles it to take away the scruple of those that might say, What, shall we rejoice in afflictions?' (G. Herbert cited by Kennedy). They are to rejoice *always*, for 'in the Lord' there is abundant cause for rejoicing even from the depths of a Roman dungeon [cf. *Acts* 16:25; *Rom.* 8:28, 35ff.]. 'No duty almost more pressed in both Testaments than this of rejoicing in the Lord. It is no less a sin not to rejoice than not to repent' (Trapp).

5: Let your forbearance be known unto all men. The Lord is at hand.

The Philippians must not be so preoccupied with their own internal problems as to lose sight of their impact upon the world. Hence Paul urges them to become known for their 'forbearance' to all men. In their relations with others they are to show a gracious and gentle spirit which does not insist upon its rights, since they know that the Lord's coming will vindicate their cause. Because they are assured of heavenly glory, they can afford to be forbearing 'towards all men in spite of every persecution. Faith in their hidden, heavenly plenitude of light and power and life produces a saving gentleness. It is the earthly counterpart of the heavenly glory. Hence it is not weakness or sentimentality. It is the earthly outworking of an eschatological possession [cf. *Phil.* 2:15–6]' (H. Preisker, *TDNT,* vol 2, p. 590). Thus the expectation of the parousia should promote an ethical response of the kind which is a far cry from the unhealthy excitement it so often fosters in those who are more interested in date-fixing than in walking 'worthily of the Lord unto all pleasing' [*Col.* 1:10].

6: In nothing be anxious; but in everything by prayer and supplication with thanksgiving let your requests be made known unto God.

Paul's familiarity with the teaching of his Lord is shown in this warning against being distracted by anxiety [*Matt.* 6:25–34]. Instead of giving way to such carking care, the Philippians are to commit everything to God in prayer. As they lay their specific requests before God, they are to make their supplication with thanksgiving for past mercies and present blessings [*Col.* 4:2]. 'Because many often pray to God amiss, with complaints or murmurings, as though they had just ground for accusing Him, while others cannot brook delay if He does not immediately obey their wishes, Paul joins thanksgiving with prayers. It is as though he had said that those things which are necessary for us ought to be desired from the Lord in such a way that we nevertheless subject our affections to His will, and give thanks while asking. And, unquestionably, gratitude will have the effect upon us that the will of God will be the chief sum of our desires' (Calvin).

7: And the peace of God, which passeth all understanding, shall guard your hearts and your thoughts in Christ Jesus.

And: This has consecutive force: 'and so'. It introduces the blessed result, 'which the compliance with verse 6 will have for the inner man' (Meyer).

The peace of God: This inward peace is bestowed on the basis of Christ's objective achievement, for peace *from* God is founded upon the work of reconciliation which established peace *with* God [*Rom.* 5:1; *Eph.* 2:14ff.]. 'We cannot think of the one, indeed, without thinking of the other; nor can one exist apart from the other. We cannot have peace of heart, until our real and actual separation from God is bridged by the blood of Christ. We cannot have the breach between God and us healed without a sense of the new relation of peace stealing into our hearts' (B. B. Warfield, 'Peace with God' in *Faith and Life*, p. 329).

Which surpasses every (human) *reason* (Vincent): In its power to relieve anxiety the peace of God surpasses all our futile attempts to 'reason' our cares away. 'God's peace produces far better results than human scheming; it is superior to all man's devices for security, and is more efficacious in removing disquietude than any intellectual effort or reasoning power. These often augment disquietude' (Plummer).

Shall guard your hearts and your thoughts: The city of Philippi was guarded by a Roman garrison, so Paul's metaphor would appeal to his readers. 'The peace of God is the garrison of the soul in all the experiences of its life, defending it from the external assaults of temptation or anxiety, and disciplining all lawless desires and imaginations within, that war against its higher purposes' (Kennedy).

In Christ Jesus: God's peace is realized only in union with Christ Jesus, and this relationship requires believers to submit to his gracious rule over their lives [cf. *Col.* 3:15].

8: Finally, brethren, whatsoever things are true, whatsoever things are honourable, whatsoever things are just, whatsoever things are pure, whatsoever things are lovely, whatsoever things are of good report; if there be any virtue, and if there be any praise, think on these things.

In bringing the letter to a close, Paul urges his brothers in the faith to cultivate those good qualities which will command the admiration of their heathen neighbours, though *they* know nothing of the grace that enables believers to manifest such virtues.

Whatsoever things are true: Whatever is 'true' must be understood in the widest sense of all that is true in thought, word, and deed. 'They are to think on "the true" in everything of which it can be predicated – both in reference to God and man, the church and the world, themselves and others – the true in its spiritual and secular relations, in thought, speech, and position' (Eadie).

Whatsoever things are honourable: The word used here comes from the verb 'to worship', and so means 'reverend' (ASV margin), or 'venerable' in the sense of 'worthy of honour'. 'As the Christian is a child of God, an heir of heaven, a brother of the Lord Jesus, a fellow-citizen with the angels, the salt of the earth, and the light of the world, the master and teacher of all men, it is clear that such high qualities must oblige him to maintain a holy and grave deportment; and that he could not fall in with the opposite vices, without betraying his honour and scandalously belying his profession' (Daillé).

Whatsoever things are just: 'Just' should not be restricted to just dealing with men, but must be taken in its broadest meaning: 'whatsoever things are in accordance with eternal and unchanging rectitude' (Eadie).

Whatsoever things are pure: Not merely chaste, but pure in the most comprehensive sense. Whatever things are pure: which are neither tainted nor corrupt – free from all debasing elements, clear in nature, transparent in purpose, leaving no blot on the conscience and no stain on the character' (Eadie).

Whatsoever things are lovely: 'Lovely', which is found only here in the New Testament, refers to whatever others find worthy of admiration and love. 'The apostle speaks only of such things as are not contrary to the will of God, while at the same time they are agreeable and pleasing to men. In this class I would place patience, cheerfulness, sweetness of temper, generosity, and such-like virtues. For although all virtues are beautiful and excellent in themselves, and deserve the approbation and respect of men, being all emanations from God and the fruits of His Spirit, yet nevertheless there are some more pleasing than others' (Daillé).

Whatsoever things are of good report: The alternatives offered in Arndt-Gingrich highlight the difficulty of translating this word which also occurs only here in the New Testament. According to Vincent, the meaning is not 'well spoken of', but 'fair-speaking', and so 'winning' or 'gracious'. Thus 'whatever is of gracious import' would involve expressing what is kind and likely to win people, and avoiding what is likely to give offence' (Plummer).

If there be any virtue, and if there be any praise, think on these things: By switching to conditional clauses, Paul directs the Philippians to exercise their own discernment in approving the things which are morally excellent and worthy of public acclaim. But to 'think on these things' means more than simply meditating upon them [verse 9]. 'He desires us to "think" of them, because the mind is the root of all human actions. It is the mind which influences the ill, stirs up the affections, and conceives and produces every action. He therefore would have the act follow the intention. For it is not merely to indulge the mind in the pleasure of vain speculations that we are to exercise ourselves in this lofty study, but rather that we may put in practice all that we have understood' (Daillé).

9: The things which ye both learned and received and heard and saw in me, these things do: and the God of peace shall be with you.

Paul here presents his own teaching and example as a pattern for the Philippians to follow. 'Learned and received' refer to their instruction in the gospel 'traditions' which he had handed down to them with all the authority of an apostle [cf. *1 Cor.* 11:2, 15:1ff.; *Gal.* 1:9; *1 Thess.* 4:1, 2; *2 Thess.* 2:15]. 'Heard and saw' refer to their experience of his personal conduct both in word and deed. If they do these things, then 'the God of peace' will be with them. 'Not only the peace of God, verse 7, but God himself' (Bengel).

10: But I rejoice in the Lord greatly, that now at length ye have revived your thought for me; wherein ye did indeed take thought, but ye lacked opportunity.

With rare tact and delicacy, Paul expresses his deep appreciation of the gift the Philippians had sent with Epaphroditus, while at the same time maintaining the independence he had found through depending upon Christ for all things [verses 10–18]. 'The passage presents as tactful a treatment of a delicate matter as can well be found in the whole range of high literature' (H. von Soden).

Now I rejoice in the Lord greatly that now at length you caused your concern for my welfare to bloom afresh (Hendriksen): In expressing his great joy in the Lord at the Philippians' revived concern for his welfare, Paul uses a verb which suggests the image of a tree putting forth fresh shoots in the Spring. As this might seem like a reproach for a 'winter of neglect', he at once proceeds to absolve them from any blame by acknowledging that, though their concern for him was constant, they had lacked the opportunity to give it practical expression.

Perhaps this was due to their uncertainty regarding the apostle's movements in recent years, or it may have been because they had no one to send with their gift.

11: Not that I speak in respect of want: for I have learned, in whatsoever state I am, therein to be content.

Although Paul is touched by his friends' practical concern for his welfare, he hastens to dispel any thought of dependence upon their generosity, for he has learned the secret of being content whatever the circumstances. The word 'content' literally means 'self-sufficient', and the Stoics used it of the man who had cultivated an inward detachment from all things and all people, which enabled him to face whatever life brought to him with unshaken resolve. But whereas the Stoic boasted of his self-sufficiency, Paul finds his sufficiency in Christ whose power gives him the victory even in the midst of adversity [verse 13]. 'The contentment which the apostle universally and uniformly possessed, sprang not from indifference, apathy, or desperation . . . It was no egotistic delusion that upheld him, nor did he ever invoke the storm to show that he could brave it. But his mind calmly bowed to the will of God in every condition in which he was placed. For that wondrous equanimity and cheerfulness which far excelled the stolid and stubborn endurance ascribed to heathen stoicism, gave him the mastery over circumstances. He felt the evil, but surmounted it – a purer triumph than with a petrified heart to be unconscious of it' (Eadie).

12: I know how to be abased, and I know also how to abound: in everything and in all things have I learned the secret both to be filled and to be hungry, both to abound and to be in want.

Paul knows from personal experience both how to endure privations and to enjoy an abundance. Since his resources are in Christ, he is neither overwhelmed by poverty nor intoxicated by prosperity. In every situation of life, his serenity is undisturbed because he has learned the secret of true contentment. 'Plenty and hunger, abundance and want - in all these Paul has been initiated. He knows the joys and the cares of life, prosperity and adversity, "good" days and "evil" days, favourable and unfavourable circumstances. And he has learned to be content under all circumstances, be they good or be they evil' (Müller).

13: I can do all things in him that strengtheneth me.

What apparently begins as Paul's comprehensive claim to self-sufficiency ('I can do all things'), paradoxically concludes as an expression of his entire dependence upon Christ ('in him who infuses strength into me'). This great affirmation of faith has been of inestimable comfort to countless Christians down the ages. 'The self-sufficiency of the Christian is relative: an independence of the world through dependence upon God. The Stoic self-sufficiency pretends to be absolute. One is the contentment of faith, the other of pride' (G. G. Findlay).

14: Howbeit ye did well that ye had fellowship with my affliction.

Paul here resumes his thankful recognition of the gift the Philippians had sent to him. For in declaring his independence of human aid, he did not wish to disparage their generosity which gladdened his heart, because he regarded their sacrifice as a noble deed in which they had made common cause with his affliction. By their active support of the imprisoned apostle, they became sharers in the struggle to fulfil his vocation. 'They helped him to carry his burden by means of their material gift, their fellow-feeling and intercession, their interest and their willingness to make sacrifices, and so they had a share in alleviating his hardship in captivity' (Müller) [cf. 1:1].

15: And ye yourselves also know, ye Philippians, that in the beginning of the gospel, when I departed from Macedonia, no church had fellowship with me in the matter of giving and receiving but ye only; 16: for even in Thessalonica ye sent once and again unto my need.

With an upsurge of affection for his beloved friends ('ye Philippians'), Paul gratefully acknowledges that the gift brought by Epaphroditus was not the first he had received from them. For he recalls that not long after their coming to faith in Christ ('in the beginning of the gospel'), when he departed from Macedonia to evangelize Achaia, no other church had shared with him in the cost of that mission [*2 Cor.* 11:9].

'In the matter of giving and receiving' they alone had provided practical support in *giving* what Paul had been glad to *receive*. And even while he was still in Macedonia, they had sent gifts to supply his need on more than one occasion during his stay at Thessalonica.

17: Not that I seek for the gift; but I seek for the fruit that increaseth to your account.

In thus enlarging upon past generosity Paul wishes to make clear that he is not seeking further gifts [verse 18]. 'It is not the gift he covets, but that rich spiritual blessing which the gift secures to its donor' (Eadie). For he sees their gift as a kind of investment in which 'the fruit' or 'interest' is accumulating to their credit. It was Paul's constant aim to enrich his converts by encouraging their growth in grace, and as the Philippians' gift was a tangible evidence of that grace, he is confident that their sacrificial service will be amply rewarded at the last day [cf. 1:11].

18: But I have all things, and abound: I am filled, having received from Epaphroditus the things that came from you, an odour of a sweet smell, a sacrifice acceptable, well-pleasing to God.

However, here I give you my receipt for everything – for more than everything; I am paid in full, now that I have received from Epaphroditus what you sent (NEB): Paul here continues his playful use of commercial metaphors to show that the Philippians have fully discharged their 'debt' to him [2:25–30]. A. Deissmann has shown that the verb 'I have' (meaning 'I have received') frequently occurs in the papyri as a technical expression for the drawing up of a receipt.

An odour of a sweet smell, a sacrifice acceptable, well-pleasing to God: But though Paul is grateful for their gift, his sudden switch to the vocabulary of sacrifice reminds them that its greatest value lay in what it meant to God. It is a fragrant offering that is pleasing to God [*Gen.* 8:21; *Lev.* 1:9]. What was given to meet Paul's needs was in fact an acceptable act of worship [*Rom.* 12:1], and Collange points out that this says something about church 'offerings' which deserves consideration.

19: And my God shall supply every need of yours according to his riches in glory in Christ Jesus.

And my God will meet all your needs according to his glorious riches in Christ Jesus (NIV): As the Philippians have made an offering to God in meeting the needs of his servant, so *his* God will abundantly recompense them by meeting all their needs 'according to', i.e. on a scale that befits his glorious riches in Christ Jesus. God is no man's debtor, and he will not fail to supply the needs of those who gladly make sacrifices to forward his cause in the world.

20: Now unto our God and Father be the glory for ever and ever. Amen.

As worship is the only fitting response to God's bounty, Paul concludes this section of his letter with a doxology, in which he invites his readers to join him in ascribing glory 'to our God and Father' who so wonderfully provides for the needs of his children. This tribute of praise shall endure 'unto the ages of the ages' (ASV margin) – 'an image taken from the cycles or calendars of time, to represent an immeasurable eternity' (Eadie). The truth thus expressed is endorsed by the confessional 'Amen'.

21: Salute every saint in Christ Jesus. The brethren that are with me salute you.

Paul probably wrote the final words of the Epistle in his own hand [*2 Thess.* 3:17]. His closing greeting is unique in that he mentions no one by name, yet he includes everyone by using the singular 'every saint' instead of the usual plural. No doubt this is because he wishes to avoid the appearance of favouring particular individuals when writing to a church which has been suffering from personality clashes between some of its members [4:2]. But there should be no disunity in the church where every saint is 'in Christ Jesus', and Paul's greeting is intended to cement that unity. As the verb 'greet' lacks a subject, it is difficult to decide how this greeting was to be conveyed. Perhaps through the leaders of the church as Vincent suggests, but more probably Paul intends the Philippians to greet one another (so Martin). The brethren with Paul, who also send their greetings, are presumably 'the companions who visited him most frequently in his imprisonment, especially Timothy' (Plummer).

22: All the saints salute you, especially they that are of Caesar's household.

All the Christians in Rome also send their greetings, especially those who belong to Caesar's household, i.e. those engaged in the service of Nero, whether as slaves or freedmen. 'This is worthy of notice; for it is no common evidence of divine mercy that the Gospel had penetrated that sink of all crimes and iniquities. It is also the more wonderful, because it is a rare thing for holiness to reign in courts' (Calvin).

23: The grace of the Lord Jesus Christ be with your spirit.

In the concluding benediction Paul prays for the grace of the Lord Jesus Christ to be with 'your' (plural) 'spirit' (singular). This provides another hint that his paramount concern is to have the whole church united in one spirit. They are all to work together as one person. 'In their whole inner being, in all their thoughts and desires, they must continually share and experience the grace of the Lord' (Greijdanus, cited by Müller).

SOLI DEO GLORIA

BIBLIOGRAPHY

ARNDT, W. F., AND GINGRICH, F. W., *A Greek-English Lexicon of the New Testament* (University of Chicago Press, 1957).

BARRY, ALFRED, *The Epistles to the Ephesians, Philippians, and Colossians (A Bible Commentary for English Readers*, Edited by C. J. Ellicott, vol. 3) (Cassell, n.d.).

BEARE, F. W., *The Epistle to the Philippians* (A. & C. Black, 1973).

BENGEL, J. A., *New Testament Word Studies* (Kregel, 1971).

BERKHOF, L., *The History of Christian Doctrines* (Banner of Truth, 1969).

BRUCE, F. F., *Paul: Apostle of the Free Spirit* (Paternoster Press, 1977).

—— *An Expanded Paraphrase of the Epistles of Paul* (Paternoster Press, 1965).

CAIRD, G. B., *Paul's Letters from Prison* (OUP, 1976).

CALVIN, JOHN, *Galatians–Colossians* (St Andrew Press, 1965).

COLLANGE, JEAN-FRANÇOIS, *The Epistle of Saint Paul to the Philippians* (translated by A. W. Heathcote) (Epworth Press).

DAILLE, JEAN, *An Exposition of Philippians* (Tyndale Bible Society, n.d.).

DOUGLAS, J. D. (ed.), *The New Bible Dictionary* (IVP, 1962).

EADIE, JOHN, *A Commentary on the Greek Text of the Epistle of Paul to the Philippians* (James and Klock, 1977).

FERGUSON, SINCLAIR B., *Let's Study Philippians,* Banner of Truth, 1997.

FERGUSSON, JAMES, *The Epistles of Paul* (Banner of Truth, 1978).

GASQUE, W. WARD, AND MARTIN. RALPH P. (eds.), *Apostolic History and the Gospel* (Paternoster Press, 1970).

GUTHRIE, DONALD, *New Testament Introduction* (Tyndale, 1970)

GWYNN, J., *The Epistle to the Philippians* (John Murray, 1881).

JEREMIAS, JOACHIM, *Jerusalem in the Time of Jesus* (SCM, 1969).

JONES, MAURICE, *The Epistle to the Philippians* (*WC*) (Methuen, 1918).

HAGNER, D. A., AND HARRIS, M. J. (eds.), *Pauline Studies: Essays Presented to F. F. Bruce* (Paternoster Press, 1980).

HENDRIKSEN, WILLIAM, *The Epistle to the Philippians* (Banner of Truth, 1963).

HUNTER, ARCHIBALD M., *Galatians–Colossians* (*LBC*) (John Knox Press, 1959).

—— *Paul and His Predecessors* (Nicholson and Watson, 1940).

KENNEDY, H. A. A., *The Epistle to the Philippians* (*EGT*) (Eerdmans, 1974).

KENT, HOMER A., *Philippians* (*EBC*) (Zondervan, 1978).

KITTEL, G. AND FRIEDRICH, G., *Theological Dictionary of the New Testament,* vols. 1–10 (Eerdmans, 1964–76).

KÜMMEL, W. G., *Introduction to the New Testament* (Revised Edition) (SCM, 1975).

LADD, GEORGE ELDON, *A Theology of the New Testament* (Eerdmans, 1974).

LANE, W. L., *Ephesians–2 Thessalonians* (Scripture Union, 1974).

LENSKI, R. C. H., *The Interpretation of St Paul's Epistles to Galatians, to the Ephesians and to the Philippians* (Augsburg, 1961).

LIGHTFOOT, J. B., *St Paul's Epistle to the Philippians* (Zondervan, 1953).

LOH, I-JIN, AND NIDA, EUGENE A., *A Translators' Handbook on Paul's Letter to the Philippians* (UBS, 1977).

LONGENECKER, RICHARD N., *The Christology of Early Jewish Christianity* (Baker, 1981).

MARSHALL, I. HOWARD, *The Origins of New Testament Christology* (IVP, 1976).

—— 'The Christ-Hymn in Philippians 2:5–11', *Tyndale Bulletin,* 1968, no. 19, pp. 104–27.

MARSHALL, L. H., *The Challenge of New Testament Ethics* (Macmillan, 1946).

MARTIN, RALPH P., *The Epistle of Paul to the Philippians* (Tyndale, 1959.

—— *An Early Christian Confession* (Tyndale, 1960).

—— *Carmen Christi: Philippians 2:5-11 in Recent Interpretation and in the Setting of Early Christian Worship* (CUP, 1967).

—— *Philippians* (*NCB*) (Eerdmans, 1980).

MEYER, H. A. W., *The Epistles to the Philippians and Colossians* (Meyer *NTC*) (T. & T. Clark, 1879).

MICHAEL, J. HUGH, *The Epistle to the Philippians* (*MNTC*) (Hodder & Stoughton, 1943).

MÜLLER, J. J., *The Epistles of Paul to the Philippians and to Philemon* (NICNT) (Eerdmans, 1955).

MURRAY, JOHN, *Collected Writings* vol. 3 (Banner of Truth, 1982).

NEILL, STEPHEN, *Christian Holiness* (Lutterworth, 1960).

PLUMMER, ALFRED, *A Commentary on St Paul's Epistle to the Philippians* (Fleming H. Revell, n.d.).

RAMSAY, W. M., *St Paul the Traveller and the Roman Citizen* (Hodder & Stoughton, 1900).

ROBERTSON, A. T., *Word Pictures in the New Testament,* vol. 1 (Broadman Press, 1931).

SCOTT, ERNEST F., *The Epistle to the Philippians* (*IB*) (Abingdon, 1955).

SHERWIN-WHITE, A. N., *Roman Society and Roman Law in the New Testament* (Baker, 1978).

STAGG, FRANK, *Philippians* (*BBC*) (Broadman Press, 1971).

STANTON, G. N., *Jesus of Nazareth in New Testament Preaching* (CUP, 1974).

STAUFFER, ETHELBERT, *New Testament Theology* (SCM, 1955).

SYNGE, F. C., *Philippians and Colossians* (Torch) (SCM, 1958).

TAYLOR, VINCENT, *The Person of Christ in New Testament Teaching* (Macmillan, 1963).

TRAPP, JOHN, *Commentary on the New Testament* (Sovereign Grace Book Club, 1958).

TRENCH, R. C., *Synonyms of the New Testament* (James Clarke, 1961).

VINCENT, MARVIN R., *The Epistles to the Philippians and to Philemon* (*ICC*) (T. & T. Clark, 1972).

—— *Word Studies in the New Testament* (MacDonald, n.d.).

VOS, GEERHARDUS, *The Pauline Eschatology* (Baker, 1979).

WARFIELD, B. B., *The Person and Work of Christ* (Presbyterian & Reformed, 1950).

—— *Perfectionism* (Presbyterian & Reformed, 1958).

—— *The Saviour of the World* (Banner of Truth, 1991).

—— *The Lord of Glory* (Evangelical Press, 1974).

—— *Faith and Life* (Banner of Truth, 1974).

Colossians

INTRODUCTION

The ancient city of Colossae was situated about 100 miles east of Ephesus in the Roman province of Asia (now Turkey), but in Paul's day its former glory had been eclipsed by the increasing prosperity of nearby Laodicea and Hierapolis. Although the apostle had not visited these cities of the Lycus valley [1:4; 2:1], such was the effect of his ministry at Ephesus that churches were established in each of them [4:13; *Acts* 19:10]. It would appear from 1:7 and 4:12f. that the gospel was brought to this district through the labours of Epaphras (not to be identified with the Epaphroditus of Philippians 2:25, 4:18), who was presumably converted to Christ through Paul's preaching. Epaphras later visited Paul during his Roman captivity, and it was his disturbing account of the situation in Colossae which prompted the apostle to write this Epistle.

As Paul gives no formal statement of the errors he opposes, it is impossible to determine the precise nature of the 'Colossian heresy', but it was evidently a form of syncretism which combined Jewish practices with pagan speculation. The Jewish element in this false teaching called for Gentile observance of the ritual requirements of the law [2:11, 16, 17], while its pagan element encouraged the worship of angelic intermediaries [2:18], and enjoined an asceticism which in its severe treatment of the body went beyond the law's demands [2:20–23]. This curious mixture was produced by the pride that discards divine revelation in favour of human reasoning [12:8], and its inevitable result was the denial of that universal supremacy which belongs to Christ by the double right of creation and redemption [1:14–20]. The appearance of this novel doctrine was hardly a surprising development in a province which was so notorious for the variety and extravagance of its religious beliefs that not even the orthodoxy of the synagogues could be preserved from the prevailing corruption. It therefore seems likely that the Colossian errorists were resident Jews whose acceptance of these pagan notions made them more ready to change the gospel than to be changed by it. It is also apparent that their claim to superior 'knowledge' has certain affinities with later Gnostic teaching, but it is going beyond the evidence to interpret this early deviation from the faith in terms of the developed Gnosticism of the second century as R. McL. Wilson and Edwin Yamauchi have clearly shown.

The relation between Colossians and Ephesians is closer than that which exists between any other of Paul's letters. 'They are *twins*, the offspring of one birth in the writer's mind' (G. G. Findlay). But though these Epistles are so intimately connected that many verses are not only parallel but almost identical in content and style, they show a striking difference in the tone and treatment of their common themes. In Colossians Paul presents his readers with a reasoned defence of the gospel to ward off the threat posed to the church by false teaching, whereas in Ephesians he calmly reflects upon the glorious destiny which belongs to the church in virtue of her union with Christ. The fact that Ephesians lacks a credible 'life-situation' suggests that it was intended as a circular letter, and it is probably to be identified with the letter 'from Laodicea' which is mentioned in 4:16. Thus Paul, as a good physician of souls, sent the right antidote to counteract the poison of error (Colossians), and the right tonic to build up the faith of all believers in Asia Minor (Ephesians).

The brevity of Colossians is no index of its importance, for by unfolding the cosmic implications of Christ's absolute pre-eminence it directs us to trust in the sole sufficiency of his saving work. Although this doctrine is already expressed in germinal form in 1 Corinthians 8:6, it is here stated with greater precision and fulness than is found elsewhere in Paul's writings. As therefore this Epistle forms one of the peaks in the New Testament revelation of Christ, all who desire to reach a correct understanding of his Person must resolve to scale its heights.

The message of Colossians is that believers are complete in Christ, and that faith in him necessarily rules out reliance upon any subsidiary powers, for nothing in the entire universe lies outside the scope of his sovereignty. The contemporary application of this teaching should not escape us in a day when men everywhere are still held in bondage by forces they cannot control. For whether these powers are human or superhuman, none of these things 'shall be able to separate us from the love of God, which is in Christ Jesus our Lord' [*Rom.* 8:39].

CHAPTER ONE

The apostle Paul associates Timothy with him as he salutes the saints at Colossae and invokes the blessing of God upon them [verses 1, 2]. He begins with thanks to God for the good account Epaphras had given him of their growth in grace [verses 3–8]. He prays that they might have the knowledge to walk worthily, and the strength to endure joyfully [verses 9–11]. They are also to give thanks to the Father, who qualified them for the inheritance when he delivered them from the realm of darkness and translated them into the kingdom of his beloved Son, in whom they are redeemed and forgiven [verses 12–14]. In the exalted language of worship Paul next sets forth the pre-eminence of Christ: He is the image of the invisible God, the source and sustainer of creation, the head of the church, and the reconciler of all things to himself [verses 15–20]. And the Colossians, though once estranged from God by evil works, were now reconciled through Christ's death and would be presented without blemish to God, if they continued to believe the gospel of which Paul was a minister [verses 21–23]. The apostle rejoices in his sufferings for the sake of Christ's church, as he fulfils his commission in making known to the Gentiles the once hidden mystery of the indwelling Christ, and strives to present every man perfect in Christ [verses 24–29].

1: Paul, an apostle of Christ Jesus through the will of God, and Timothy our brother,

In introducing himself as an apostle 'through the will of God', Paul shows that his right to address a community of Christians to whom he is personally unknown is founded upon the distinguishing grace which made him the apostle to the Gentiles [2:1; *Eph.* 3:1ff.]. As such he is clothed with the power of the Sender, who entrusted him with the commission to make known to all men 'the mystery of Christ'. And at the outset of an Epistle which stresses the pre-eminence of Christ, the word order of the title, 'an apostle of *Christ* Jesus', is probably intended to fix the attention of its readers upon the unique glory of their exalted

Lord. With himself Paul associates Timothy, his own son in the faith [*1 Tim.* 1:2], and a trusted helper and fellow-worker in the gospel [*1 Thess.* 3:2], but who is here simply designated as 'the brother'. This sets him apart from the apostle as the author of the letter, and also provides a valuable endorsement of its message by a Christian who is well known in the churches.

2: to the saints and faithful brethren in Christ that are at Colossae: Grace to you and peace from God our Father.

Although the Epistle is sent to the Christian community in Colossae, the word 'church' is omitted from the address, perhaps because Paul in his later years preferred to stress the character and calling which made its members Christ's witnesses in the world [cf. *Rom.* 1:7; *Eph.* 1:1; *Phil.* 1:1]. Thus their relation to God is indicated by the term 'saints', while their kinship with other believers is underscored by the word 'brethren'. The noun 'saints' recalls the electing grace which singled out Israel to be God's special possession [*Exod.* 19:6; *Lev.* 11:44], and its application to Christians identifies them as the people of the new covenant [*1 Pet.* 2:9]. Sainthood is at once a gift and a vocation. What is first a *status* conferred, then becomes a *calling* to be followed [*1 Cor.* 1:2]. But this response of faith is only made possible by the determinative act which preceded it. 'Saints are not an eminent sort of Christians, but all Christians are saints, and he who is not a saint is not a Christian' (Alexander Maclaren). In describing the brethren as 'faithful', it is not likely that Paul is hinting at the defection of some in Colossae as J. B. Lightfoot suggests [cf. *Eph.* 1:1], but the adjective more probably refers to the fidelity that is brought forth by the faith which embraces God's objective grace. As the vital phrase 'in Christ' here carries the deeper meaning of incorporation in Christ, it virtually defines the word Christian, and emphasizes the fact that salvation is found only in union with him.

The brief greeting conveys Paul's customary prayer for his readers. It is his wish that they may be blessed with grace and peace 'from God our Father', who is viewed as the ultimate source of this undeserved favour ('grace'), and of the spiritual prosperity ('peace') which results from it. And therein: 'He reproves the folly of this world, in which almost all wish for themselves and their friends, health, riches, and honours; but grace, peace, and other spiritual good things, they neither regard, nor think of. But Christ commands us to *seek first the kingdom of God, Matt.* 6:33' (John Davenant).

3: We give thanks to God the Father of our Lord Jesus Christ, praying always for you,

We always thank God, the Father of our Lord Jesus Christ, when we pray for you (RSV): That there was a church in Colossae was for Paul a cause of profound thanksgiving to God. As he knew that none could be saved without the regenerating grace of God [*Eph.* 2:5], he never congratulates his readers on their faith, but always thanks God for it [cf. verses 12, 13]. If we thus owe our salvation to God, then clearly all the praise must belong to him alone [*1 Cor.* 1:29]. For when all the riches of God's grace are freely lavished upon us, we are under a permanent obligation to pay tribute to that grace in the coinage of our gratitude. The title 'the Father of our Lord Jesus Christ' serves to advertise the fact that God can only be savingly known through the self-giving love by which he has been pleased to reveal himself. For there would have been no good news to preach, if he had not sent his Son into the world to redeem us at measureless cost [verse 14]. So whenever Paul prays for the Colossians, he always begins by thanking God for what he, the Father, has already done for them in Christ before presenting further supplications on their behalf [verse 9]. We should seek to model our own prayers on this apostolic pattern, which teaches us that thanksgiving should always precede intercession.

4: having heard of your faith in Christ Jesus, and of the love which ye have toward all the saints,

This gives the ground of the apostle's thanksgiving. Although he was not personally acquainted with his readers, he had received encouraging news of their faith and love from Epaphras, whose tireless labours had been the means of bringing the gospel to Colossae [verses 7, 8; 4:12]. As we have here two sure marks of a believer – faith in Christ and love to all the saints – those who lack them cannot rightly claim the name of Christian. The construction 'faith in (*en*) Christ Jesus' points not to the object of faith, but to the sphere in which faith lives and acts; for union with Christ is not only the source of life, but also the realm in which it is operative. Hence the expression focuses on the exalted Lord 'as the giver of new life to his people who live under his lordship' (R. P. Martin).

The fruit of this faith was seen in the love which the Colossian believers had 'toward all the saints'. The reference is probably to the entire family of faith [verse 6], for a real love for Christ must also embrace *all* who are his [*1 John* 4:7, 12]. The remarkable repetition of the word 'all' in this Epistle is evidently directed against the exclusiveness and caste-feeling which was fostered by the errorists' claim to superior knowledge [verse 28]. This should teach us that there is no room in the church for any intellectual, spiritual, or social élite, which separates itself from fellow-believers whom Christ has accepted [3:11].

5: because of the hope which is laid up for you in the heavens, whereof ye heard before in the word of the truth of the gospel,

Both spring from the hope stored up for you in heaven (NEB): Hope completes the familiar triad of Christian graces which was probably part of the 'tradition' which Paul received from those who were 'in Christ' before him, but here hope is not co-ordinate with faith and love. It is rather represented as the *source* from which they spring. This hope is not a subjective attitude of expectation, but is the objective *content* of the gospel [verse 23]. It is because the Colossians are assured that the content of the message they received is already stored up for them in heaven that they can remain firm in the faith and show their love to all the saints. Thus the future can be said to determine the present, for what is reserved in heaven for believers now exercises a decisive influence upon their daily conduct.

Whereof ye heard before in the word of the truth of the gospel: There appears to be an implied contrast between the gospel they heard before from Epaphras and the false teaching which had since been presented to them. For they would forfeit their interest in the future, if the 'word of truth' by which this hope came to them was abandoned in favour of the false gospel of 'vain deceit' [2:8]. As the gospel is a word whose whole substance and content is truth, it is necessarily opposed to all the errors invented by men. 'The gospel is not speculation but fact. It is truth, because it is the record of a Person who is the Truth. The history of His life and death is the one source of all certainty and knowledge with regard to man's relations to God, and God's loving purposes to man. To leave it and Him of whom it speaks in order to listen to men who spin theories out of their own brains is to prefer will-o'-the-wisps to the sun' (Maclaren).

6: which is come unto you; even as it is also in all the world bearing fruit and increasing, as it doth in you also, once the day ye heard and knew the grace of God in truth;

Paul gives thanks that the same message of salvation which had reached his readers in Colossae is also in all the world. His object in saying this is to excite their gratitude that the gospel had been sent to them, and to give them a salutary reminder of its universal scope [verse 23]. The apostle's implication is that the universality of gospel truth must not be falsified and narrowed down to a sectarian heresy.

Bearing fruit and increasing: As a tree both bears fruit and grows, so the gospel produces fruit in the conduct of believers [verse 4] and also spreads by winning new converts. That the gospel has the reproductive power to spread throughout the whole world is due to the fact that God himself is at work in it [*1 Cor.* 3:7].

As it doth in you also, since the day ye heard and knew the grace of God in truth: Paul thankfully acknowledges that the Colossians have also lived such fruitful lives from the day they learned what the gospel really is, and were glad to receive it as 'the grace of God' which brings salvation to the undeserving [*Titus* 2:11]. 'He praiseth, both their teachableness, in that this word had fructified in them, from the first day they heard it, and their constancy, for that it continued still fructifying to that time. The earth produceth not fruit, as soon as it hath received the seed: there must be time to mollify the grain; to make it thrust forth, and sprout; to raise it up, and garnish it with fruits. In this spiritual Husbandry, it is not so. The gospel, if rightly received into your heart, will fructify there, from that very moment' (Jean Daillé).

7: even as ye learned of Epaphras our beloved fellow-servant, who is a faithful minister of Christ on our behalf,

In thus commending Epaphras to the Colossians Paul sets the seal of his approval on the teaching which he had delivered to them on the apostle's behalf. It was probably during Paul's stay at Ephesus that Epaphras acted as his representative in taking the gospel to Colossae [*Acts* 19:10]. Paul says two things about Epaphras which are worthy of note. First, he is 'our beloved fellow-servant' or 'fellow-slave'. Something of the warmth of Paul's character is brought out by this reference to the privilege of sharing together in the service of Christ. As the word 'slave' indicates, those who engage in this service have no will of their own, but are entirely under the direction of the Lord who redeemed them from the bondage of sin. Second, he is 'a faithful minister of Christ'. Since such fidelity is the very essence of true service, this commendation implicitly contrasts Epaphras with the false teachers 'in whom an opinion of their own wisdom predominated, when, nevertheless, they were unfaithful towards Christ' (Davenant).

8: who also declared unto us your love in the Spirit.

Epaphras not only took the good news to Colossae, but also brought back to Paul a largely encouraging report of the progress of the new community. That the gospel had taken root in their lives was proved by the presence of the chief fruit of the Spirit [*Gal.* 5:22]. It was through the Holy Spirit that the love of God had been shed abroad in their hearts [*Rom.* 5:5], and it was this supernatural change which enabled them to love all the saints [verse 4]. As love gives man his closest resemblance to God, 'and as it is the great object of the gospel to create and perfect it in the church, it may be safely taken as the index of spiritual advancement' (John Eadie). In view of the very full teaching on the Spirit which is found in Ephesians, it is rather remarkable that this is the only *explicit* reference to the Spirit in Colossians, but this is probably due to the apostle's desire to stress the absolute supremacy of Christ [verse 18]. When Christ is so glorified we have the surest mark of the Spirit's presence, for the whole purpose of his coming is to exalt Christ [*John* 16:14].

9: For this cause we also, since the day we heard it, do not cease to pray and make request for you, that ye may be filled with the knowledge of his will in all spiritual wisdom and understanding,

Paul's prayer for the Colossians is closely connected with the thanksgiving which preceded it [verses 3–8]. He is not only thanking

God for their faith, but is *also* praying that they may continue to grow in grace [verses 9–12]. In thus revealing the content of his fervent intercession, he reinforces his exhortations, stimulates their aspirations, and teaches them how to pray. 'Since the day we heard' echoes 'the similar expression in verse 6. So the apostle's prayer was, as it were, an echo of their faith. An encouragement to them to proceed as they had begun' (T. K. Abbott).

That ye may be filled with the knowledge of his will: As J. Armitage Robinson rightly points out, this is not knowledge in the abstract (*gnosis*), but 'knowledge' (*epignosis*) 'directed towards a particular object', which in this case is the knowledge of God's will as it relates to the conduct of our lives [verse 10]. 'The apostle here made request for something intensely *practical:* not speculations about the divine nature, prying into the divine decrees, nor inquisitive explorations of unfulfilled prophecy, but the knowledge of God's will as it respects the ordering of our daily walk in this world' (Arthur W. Pink). Paul evidently intends to contrast the insubstantial flights of fancy canvassed by the false teachers with the true knowledge which leads to right behaviour.

In all spiritual wisdom and understanding: This knowledge of God's will is conveyed to believers in the form of all wisdom and understanding, and the emphatic position of 'spiritual' at the end of the verse shows that these are not natural virtues but gifts of the Spirit. 'Wisdom' is the practical ability to regulate conduct in the light of God's requirements, while 'understanding' is the capacity to apply this wisdom in every situation which demands a moral decision. For Paul these 'spiritual' gifts stand in direct contrast to the empty pretensions to 'wisdom' [2:23] which proceeded from 'the mind of the flesh' [2:18].

10: to walk worthily of the Lord unto all pleasing, bearing fruit in every good work, and increasing in the knowledge of God;

This spiritual insight is to find concrete expression in the daily round and the common task. 'The end of all knowledge, the Apostle would say, is conduct' (Lightfoot). 'To walk' likens the Christian life to a journey towards heaven, which calls for unwearied advance along the path marked out for such pilgrims [*Isa.* 35:8]. The nature of this progress is specified in the summons to walk 'worthily of the Lord', as befits those who owe their whole salvation *to* him, and who can fulfil this high calling only in virtue of their union *with* him [cf. 2:6]. 'Unto all pleasing' shows that the Christian's great interest in life must be to please his Lord in every respect. Although the word 'pleasing' denotes a cringing and subservient attitude in classical Greek, it has a favourable sense when transferred to the believer's relations to his Lord. 'To do anything to meet, to anticipate, His wishes, is not only the most beneficial but the most absolutely right thing we can do. It is His eternal and sacred due; it is at the same time the surest path to our own highest development and gain' (H. C. G. Moule).

Bearing fruit in every good work, and increasing by the knowledge of God (ASV margin): Paul further explains what is involved in this walk by a return to the image used in verse 6. In thus depicting the calling of believers in terms of the constant fruitfulness and growth effected by the true knowledge of God [*Deut.* 32:2], the apostle implicitly condemns the barren intellectualism of the heretics who gloried in their 'superior' knowledge [2:8].

In the natural realm trees bear only one sort of fruit, but believers are expected to be fruitful 'in every good work' through the power of that divine seed which has been sown in their hearts. 'Unless, therefore, they produce every fruit, they do not answer the nature and efficacy of the seed. For *the fruit of the Spirit* is not one alone, but manifold; viz. *love, joy, peace, patience, longsuffering, goodness, benignity, and the like; Gal* 5:22' (Davenant).

11: strengthened with all power, according to the might of his glory, unto all patience and longsuffering with joy;

Paul concludes his prayer for the Colossians by asking that they may be continually strengthened with all power, 'according to the might of his glory'. Lightfoot points out that 'glory' here stands for the power of God 'as *manifested* to men', and as the parallel passage in Ephesians 1:19, 20 indicates, this divine power was supremely manifested in the resurrection of Christ. Hence the request is that they may be empowered with the same might by which Christ was raised from the dead [cf. *Rom.* 6:4].

Unto all patience and longsuffering with joy: 'Patience' is the brave endurance which triumphs over adverse circumstances, and 'longsuffering' is the capacity to endure the wrongs inflicted by others without being provoked to retaliation. The last words of the verse show that believers are not to meet these trials with Stoic fortitude or gloomy resignation, but are rather to receive them with Christian joy! [cf. verse 24; *Matt.* 5:11; *James* 1:2f.; *1 Pet.* 4:13].

12: giving thanks unto the Father, who made us meet to be partakers of the inheritance of the saints in light;

This is so closely attached to the preceding prayer that at first sight it appears to be a continuation of it. But as Paul never concludes his prayers with thanksgiving, it is more likely that he here glides into a summons (taking 'giving thanks' as an imperative) to his readers to praise God for his saving grace in Christ. [verses 12,14].

Who has qualified you (NIV): By ascribing salvation solely to the action of God, Paul teaches us that it is not within the power of man to make himself fit to receive such a glorious inheritance [*Eph.* 2:1–3]. He first brings down 'the pride of those, that give this glory to free will; boasting, that they have made themselves capable of salvation . . . No, saith the apostle, This wholly appertaineth unto GOD. It is He, that hath made us capable. Of ourselves we cannot so much as think a good thought: so he affirms elsewhere' (Daillé). The aorist tense of the verb points to an instantaneous act which not only confers present grace [verse 13], but also assures future glory [3:24]. The Old Testament colouring of this verse makes 'you' especially significant, for as Gentiles the Colossians might well thank God that they had been admitted to share in what had been the unique privilege of Jews ('the saints', i.e. Jewish believers: cf. *Eph* 2:12, 13).

To share in the inheritance of the saints in the kingdom of light (NIV): As each Israelite was assigned a portion of the promised land by lot, so every believer is given a share in the spiritual inheritance ('the kingdom of light') which that territorial possession prefigured [*Heb.* 3:7–4:11]. 'In other words, the saints, possessed by Christ, themselves possess Christ as their riches and light, and are *qualified* to do so by the grace of the Father who gave the Son for them and to them. The reference is not immediately to the coming glory, but to the present grace' (H. C. G. Moule). [cf. verse 13; *Eph.* 5:8] It should be noted that the Old Testament concept of the inheritance is here spiritualized and applied to the church as the new Israel of God [cf. *1 Pet.* 2:9].

13: who delivered us out of the power of darkness, and translated us into the kingdom of the Son of his love;

Paul now explains that we are qualified to share in this inheritance through what God accomplished in us by converting grace, for it was then that he delivered us from the dominion of darkness and transferred us to the kingdom of his dear Son. Formerly, we were under the devil's authority, not merely as his helpless captives but also as his willing slaves [*Eph.* 2:2]. Thus the misery of our plight by nature is here recalled to enhance our appreciation of the divine power which was put forth to secure our release from this bondage of death [*Isa.* 42:7; *Acts* 26:18]. The absolute nature of the apostle's antithesis shows that there is no middle state between the power of darkness and the kingdom of grace: 'all who breathe are either in the one or the other' (James Fergusson).

And translated us into the kingdom of the Son of love: The same verb is used by Josephus of the Assyrian king Tiglath-Pileser, who transported the conquered inhabitants of Israel to his own kingdom. However, it is not our physical resettlement which Paul has in view, but our spiritual transfer to a present state of grace. 'For God is said to have translated us into the kingdom of his Son, because he hath communicated to us those spiritual gifts, and wrought in us that spiritual condition, which makes us subjects and members of Christ. Therefore, by the kingdom of Christ we must understand all the benefits of grace which are obtained through union with and subjection to Christ our spiritual King' (Davenant). As the phrase 'the Son of his love' points to Christ as the great object of God's love, this love of the Father for the Son thus becomes the pledge of his love for all who are 'in Christ' [*Eph.* 1:6].

14: in whom we have our redemption, the forgiveness of our sins:

Here the liberation of an enslaved people is still in view, but the metaphor has changed from 'the victor who rescues the captive by force of arms [verse 13] to the philanthropist who releases him by the payment of a ransom' (Lightfoot). There can be no doubt that this is the idea conveyed by the word 'redemption', because the parallel verse in Ephesians spells out the price that was paid to secure our release [cf. *Eph.* 1:7: 'through his blood']. If the Colossian errorists had defined 'redemption' in terms of a mystic deliverance through the mere possession of superior knowledge this would explain Paul's insistence upon the *moral* content of the gospel, namely, that the primary blessing of God's great rescue by ransom is 'the forgiveness of sins'. As unforgiven sin presents an insuperable barrier to blessing, so the forgiveness of sins is the priceless boon which opens the door to every other spiritual blessing [*Rom.* 4:6–8]. Although men may fondly claim that forgiveness is God's business, there can be no thought of 'cheap' forgiveness when we remember that our redemption cost God the life of his beloved Son. But we must not overlook the force of the all-important phrase 'in whom', which sets forth the condition of possessing this redemption. For we have the free forgiveness of our sins only as we are found in living union with Christ. 'We cannot get His gifts without Himself' (Maclaren).

15: who is the image of the invisible God, the firstborn of all creation; 16: for in him were all things created, in the heavens and upon the earth, things visible and things invisible, whether thrones or dominions or principalities or powers; all things have been created through him, and unto him; 17: and he is before all things, and in him all things consist. 18: And he is the head of the body, the church: who is the beginning, the firstborn from the dead; that in all things he might have the pre-eminence. 19: For it was the good pleasure of the Father that in him should all the fulness dwell; 20: and through him to reconcile all things unto himself, having made peace through the blood of his cross; through him, I say, whether things upon the earth, or things in the heavens.

The hymnic character of this passage has prompted much critical debate, and attempts have been made to show that a hymn emanating either from Hellenistic Judaism or Gnostic circles has been adapted by the author of Colossians for Christian use. But it is difficult to believe that one of the loftiest statements about Christ in the New Testament could have sprung from such a dubious background, especially when there is evidence to show that the apostle himself is the author of this 'cosmic' Christology. For it represents the logical development of the teaching which is already found in Paul's earlier letters (cf. *1 Cor.* 8:6 for Christ's universal lordship: cf. *Rom.* 12:4f., *1 Cor.* 12:12, 13, 27 for the church as Christ's body). In this great outburst of praise Paul counters the unwarranted speculations of the Colossian heretics by affirming the prominence of Christ in Creation [verses 15–17] and Redemption [verses 18–20].

Who is the image of the invisible God: The word 'image' suggests both Representation and Manifestation (Lightfoot). The important point to note is that in ancient thought an 'image' was not regarded as a mere copy of the object it represented, for it was believed in some way to participate in the substance of that object. 'Image is not to be understood as a magnitude which is alien to the reality and present only in the consciousness. It has a share in the reality. Indeed, it is the reality (H. Kleinknecht, *TDNT*, vol. 2, p. 389). Thus in Christ we see God fully revealed [*John* 14:9], because he alone is the perfect 'image' of 'the invisible God' [verse 19; *2 Cor.* 4:4]. In other words, Christ's revelatory *function* rests upon his essential *relation* as the eternal Son of God [cf. *Phil.* 2:6]. But as the word 'image' also clearly recalls Genesis 1:27, it may be asked how Paul is able to relate this reference to man's creation 'in the image of God' to the pre-existent Son. According to Herman Ridderbos, the answer lies in the fact that Paul's preaching was necessarily determined by the 'redemptive historical outlook' (*Paul – An Outline of His Theology*, p. 77). He nowhere separates Christ's Sonship from his Redeemership, because sinners may never consider what Christ is 'in himself' apart from what he is 'for them'. So it is through the redeeming work of Christ as the Last Adam [*1 Cor.* 15:45] that the original purpose of God in creation is achieved and we see a renewal of the image of God in man [cf. 3:10]. The apostle's thought therefore works back from the historical accomplishment of salvation to the eternal purpose which governed it.

The firstborn of all creation: The contention of the Arians and their successors in the sects today that Christ is here called a creature is refuted by the very wording 'the first-*born*' (rather than 'first-*created*'), and is certainly ruled out by the context [verse 16]. The term 'firstborn' does not refer to temporal priority but to superiority of rank [cf. *Psa.* 89:27]. 'What is meant is the unique supremacy of Christ over all creatures as the Mediator of their creation' (W. Michaelis, *TDNT*, vol. 6, p. 879). As then all things were created through Christ, he stands over against the entire creation as its rightful Lord and Heir [*Heb.*1:1, 2].

Although the designation of Christ as 'the firstborn of all creation' recalls Adam's dominion over the first creation [*Gen.* 1:28ff.], the parallel term 'the firstborn from the dead' [verse 18] shows that Paul is describing Christ's 'primal' sovereignty over creation on the analogy of his significance as the Inaugurator of the new creation. Thus we find that this 'post-redemptive' perspective leads him to explain the meaning of Christ's work in categories which are derived from the first Adam. Accordingly the crucial phrase 'the firstborn from the dead' means that the apostle sees Christ's resurrection as the pivotal event which secured the beginning of the new humanity, so that what was lost under the headship of Adam has now been regained by Christ in a far more glorious way. For the second Adam is the Son of God who has made his people the sharers of his divine life [*1 Cor.* 15:45, 47], whereas the glory that Adam possessed as the 'image of God' and 'the firstborn of all creation' was but the finite reflection of Christ's essential glory as the eternal Son.

For in him were all things created: 'For' introduces the proof of the title given to the Son in the previous clause ('the firstborn of all creation'). Instead of the preposition 'through' which points to the agency of Christ in creation [see below and *John* 1:3; *Heb.* 1:2], 'in' is used here to denote Christ as the 'sphere' in which creation took place. This is because Paul wishes to show 'that the conditioning cause of the act of creation resided in Him. The Eternal Word stood in the same relation to the created Universe as the Incarnate Christ to the Church' (T. K. Abbott). [cf. 2:7, 10; *Rom.* 8:1; *1 Cor.* 1:30; *Eph.* 2:10]. The definite historical act of creation is described by the aorist tense of the verb.

In the heavens and upon the earth, things visible and things invisible: An exhaustive enumeration which brings out the full meaning of 'all things', and thus indicates that the term admits of no exceptions. As therefore every created thing owes its very existence to Christ, it follows that nothing in the entire universe lies outside the scope of his sovereignty [verse 17].

Whether thrones or dominions or principalities or powers: By setting forth Christ as the Creator and Disposer of all spiritual powers, Paul implicitly condemns the false teaching at Colossae, which dethroned Christ from his supremacy by paying homage to angels [2:18]. In comparing this listing of angelic orders with that given in Ephesians 1:21, Lightfoot insists that no stress can be laid on the sequence of names, as though the apostle were formulating a precise doctrine of the celestial hierarchy. He clearly has no patience with this elaborate angelology, and brushes aside these speculations without remarking upon how much or how little truth there may be in them. 'The decisive point for Paul is that in no regard, whether as fate, or nature, or intermediate beings, or servants of God, can these powers either separate the Christian from Christ or lead him to Him' (W. Foerster, *TDNT*, vol. 2, p. 573).

All things have been created through him, and unto him: The final clause presents Christ as the goal of all creation. The phrase 'in him' at the beginning of the verse represented Christ 'as the *conditional* cause of all things. All things came to pass within the sphere of His personality and as dependent upon it. Here He appears as the *mediating* cause; "through him" as in *1 Cor.* 8:6. "Unto him." All things, as they had their beginning in Him, tend *to Him* as their consummation, to depend on and serve Him' (Marvin Vincent). [cf. *Heb.* 2:10; *Rev.* 22:13]

And he is before all things, and in him all things consist: In this summarizing statement Paul reaffirms the absolute 'self-existence' of the eternal Son and declares him to be the Creator and Preserver of all things. The emphatic 'HE IS' recalls Christ's majestic claim, 'Before Abraham was, I AM' [*John* 8:58]. 'He who made all necessarily existed before all. Prior to His creative work, He had filled the unmeasured periods of an unbeginning eternity. Matter is not eternal . . . He pre-existed it, and called it into being. Everything is posterior to Him, and nothing coeval with Him' (John Eadie). But though the Son is independent of all things, all things must depend upon his sustaining power for their continued existence. 'He is the principle of cohesion in the universe. He impresses upon creation that unity and solidarity which makes it a cosmos instead of a chaos' (Lightfoot).

And he is the head of the body, the church: Having demonstrated Christ's sovereignty over creation, Paul next describes his pre-eminence in the church which is his new creation [verses 18–20]. 'And he' is repeated from the preceding verse to emphasize the fact that 'the Creator of the World is also the Head of the Church' (Lightfoot). By placing Christ's redemptive work within the context of his cosmic significance, Paul refutes the false teaching which assigned a reduced rôle to Christ in the economy of salvation and put the Colossians in danger of 'not holding fast the Head' [2:19]. Although the apostle here combines his familiar metaphor of the church as Christ's 'body' with the new concept of Christ as the 'head' of the church, it is important to note that even when they thus appear together both figures retain their independent meaning. 'When Paul writes that man is the head of the woman [*1 Cor.* 11:3], he does not have in view the model of a single body of which the man is the head and the woman is the trunk. Paul goes on to say that Christ is the head of the man and that God is the "head" of Christ. When Paul asserts that the body grows up into the head and is nourished from the head [*Eph.* 4:15, 16], we are not to seek for some physiological model relating the head to the rest of the body. Rather, Christ the head nourishes his body as a man nourishes and cherishes his wife, in a position of authority and primacy' (Edmund P. Clowney, *The Doctrine of the Church*, p. 45). This authority which Christ has over the church as its Head is grounded in the fact that the church owes its origin to him (just as the first woman came from man: cf. *1 Cor.* 11:8), because Paul immediately adds that Christ is 'the beginning, the firstborn from the dead'. In other words, the figure of headship refers to the primacy which belongs to Christ as the source of the church's life, whereas the body metaphor shows that the church belongs to Christ as a wife belongs to her husband [*Eph.* 5:28].

Who is the beginning, the firstborn from the dead: Christ is called 'the beginning' because when he broke the bands of death, his resurrection also ensured that of his people [cf. *1 Cor.* 15:20, 23]. As the One who rose in the power of an endless life, he is then 'the firstborn *from* the dead'. 'Only as he himself is one "from the dead" is Christ "firstborn". Only as he is part of that group which is (to be) raised does he enjoy this exalted status' (Richard B. Gaffin, *The Centrality of the Resurrection*, p. 38). This stands in pointed contrast to verse 16, for while the eternal Son is the Lord of all creation by divine right, he attained the lordship of the church only through the redemptive travail of the cross and the triumph of the resurrection [*Rom.* 1:4].

That in all things he might have the pre-eminence: Or more literally, 'that in all things he alone might become pre-eminent'. 'As He *is* first with respect to the Universe, so it was ordained that He should *become* first with respect to the Church as well . . . The relation between Christ's headship of the Universe by virtue of His Eternal Godhead and His headship of the Church by virtue of His Incarnation and Passion and Resurrection is somewhat similarly represented in

Philippians 2:6 sq. *existing in the form of God . . . taking the form of a servant . . . becoming obedient unto death . . . wherefore also God highly exalted him*' (Lightfoot).

For it was the good pleasure of the Father that in him should all the fulness dwell: This pre-eminence belongs to Christ because it was God's 'good pleasure' [*Luke* 2:14] 'that all the fulness should take up its abode in him' [cf. *John* 1:14, 16]. Many commentators suggest that 'fulness' was a catchword of the Colossian heretics which Paul here takes up in order to refute their teaching, but the non-Gnostic use of the same word in Ephesians makes this unlikely (see further R. P. Martin's article 'Fulness' in *The New Bible Dictionary*, p. 442). As John Murray observes, this verse cannot mean that it was the Father's will that fulness of Deity should dwell in the Son [*John* 1:1, 2]. Hence this fulness must be regarded as the fulness which belongs to Christ as the Word made flesh for our salvation. The fact that Colossians 2:9 refers to Christ's essential Godhood is not incompatible with this conclusion, for the fulness that Christ possesses as the eternal Son does not interfere with 'the fulness he comes to possess for the execution of messianic office'. Moreover, the analogy of Paul's teaching in Ephesians 1:23 'would point to the conclusion that the church is the fulness of Christ, because to the church as the body of Christ is being imparted the fulness that is in Christ. The church is the recipient of that fulness of righteousness, wisdom, knowledge, power, grace, goodness, patience, love, truth, and mercy, which has its permanent abode in Christ, and abides in him in terms of an economy that has no relevance apart from the purpose and realization of this same communication. This fulness believers do not receive as discrete individuals, but in the unity and fellowship of the church as the body of Christ' (*Collected Writings of John Murray*, vol. 2, pp. 301–4).

And through him to reconcile all things unto himself, having made peace through the blood of his cross; through him, I say, whether things upon the earth, or things in the heavens: It was also God's good pleasure to reconcile all things to himself through Christ, whose sacrificial death on the cross was the means by which this peace was secured. Paul clearly underlines the cosmic sweep of Christ's reconciling work by his insistence upon the inclusive scope of 'all things'. As all creation was involved in the consequences of man's sin, so the reconciliation effected by Christ encompasses the whole universe [*Rom.* 8:20ff.; *Eph.* 1:10]. But the final restoration of 'all things' may not be equated with the salvation of 'all beings', for Paul later shows that this 'reconciliation' was only achieved through Christ's conquest of the demonic powers which had introduced the discordant principle of sin into God's world [2:15]. The relevance of the apostle's statement for the Colossians is well explained by William Hendriksen: *Through Christ and his cross the universe is brought back or restored to its proper relationship to God in the sense that as a just reward for his obedience Christ was exalted to the Father's right hand, from which position of authority and power he rules the entire universe in the interest of the church and to the glory of God* [cf. 2:10].

21: And you, being in time past alienated and enemies in your mind in your evil works, 22: yet now hath he reconciled in the body of his flesh through death, to present you holy and without blemish and unreprovable before him:

As those who were once pagan Gentiles, the Colossians are here exhorted to remember with gratitude what Christ's grace has accomplished in delivering them from their former servitude to sin [*Eph.* 2:11, 12]. For when they were thus estranged from God, the hostility of their minds found its outward expression in their evil deeds [*Eph.* 2:2f; 4:18]. 'The apostle charges them not merely with spiritual and latent hostility to God, but with the manifestation of that hostility in open acts of unnatural rebellion' (Eadie).

Yet now hath he reconciled in the body of his flesh through death: That Christ is the subject of the sentence is shown by the unusual expression 'the body of his flesh through (his) death', which is evidently directed against those who taught that angelic intermediaries assisted in the work of reconciliation. In opposing this speculation Paul emphasizes the fact that it was by the putting to death of this body of flesh that reconciliation was achieved, and thereby excludes these spiritual powers from any part in the work of salvation [cf. *Heb.* 2:14ff.].

To present you holy and without blemish and unreprovable before him: Christ's purpose in submitting to the death of the cross was that he might present before himself in glory a people who are so consecrated and cleansed as to be without blemish and above reproach [cf. *Eph.* 5:27; *2 Cor.* 11:2]. Lightfoot (who prefers another construction which makes God the subject of the sentence) gives a *sacrificial* meaning to the verb in his paraphrase: 'He will present you a living sacrifice, an acceptable offering unto Himself.' In rejecting this interpretation, Abbott points out that the meaning of 'to present' is here determined by the *judicial* term 'unreprovable', and rightly observes: 'May we not add that the thought expressed in Lightfoot's paraphrase has no parallel in the N.T.? For Romans 12:1 does not support the idea of God presenting believers to Himself as a sacrifice.'

23: if so be that ye continue in the faith, grounded and steadfast, and not moved away from the hope of the gospel which ye heard, which was preached in all creation under heaven; whereof I Paul was made a minister.

The reality of the Colossians' interest in the reconciliation wrought by Christ will be evidenced by their continuance in the faith. For though Paul assumes that they will so persevere, the presence of false teachers in their midst inevitably puts a question mark against their fidelity, hence his cautionary 'if indeed' (cf. verse 28). Since salvation is through faith in Christ, this is the foundation on which they must build to find true stability, for there is no other way of avoiding the peril of constantly shifting from the sure hope held out by the gospel [*Matt.* 7:24–27].

Which ye heard, which was preached in all creation under heaven; whereof I Paul was made a minister: Here three points are made to stress the importance of continuing in the faith: 1. The gospel they had heard from Epaphras was the means of their conversion [verse 7].

2. As the same gospel had been proclaimed throughout the world, this universality points to its authenticity [verse 6]. Paul's expression probably means that the good news had reached all the important cities of the Empire and was spreading from these centres to the provinces (as the province of Asia was evangelized from Ephesus: cf. *Rom.* 15:19–23).

3. Paul declares that he was made a minister of the gospel. It is not for the purpose of magnifying his office that Paul makes this claim, but to impress on the Colossians that the gospel which they had heard from Epaphras, and which was proclaimed in all the world, was the selfsame gospel that he preached.

24: Now I rejoice in my sufferings for your sake, and fill up on my part that which is lacking of the afflictions of Christ in my flesh for his body's sake, which is the church;

From the remembrance of his call to the ministry Paul returns to the 'now' of his present sufferings as 'the prisoner of Christ Jesus in behalf of you Gentiles' [*Eph.* 3:1]. As Christ's apostle he rejoices in these sufferings, for what he endures in his own person ('in my flesh') is for the benefit of the church ('for his body's sake'), since he is thus filling up what is lacking in 'the afflictions of Christ'. This remarkable expression obviously cannot mean that the atoning sacrifice of Christ on the cross was incomplete and needed to be supplemented by the sufferings of his apostle [cf. 2:13f.]. Moreover, the term 'afflictions' never occurs in the New Testament in connection with the *personal* sufferings of Christ. Paul is speaking rather of his participation in the afflictions of the *corporate* Christ. Such are the afflictions which the glorified Christ reckons as his own because his people bear them for his sake [*Acts* 9:4, 5]. These tribulations are the lot of the believing community on earth [*Acts* 14:22; *1 Thess.* 3:3], for the confession of Christ before men inevitably attracts a share of the same hatred which reached its climax in his crucifixion [*Heb.* 13:13]. And as the tale of 'Messianic woes' must be fulfilled before the end of the age [*Mark* 13:5–27], Paul rejoices in his exceptional vocation of suffering on behalf of the church [*Acts* 9:16], because it serves to bring nearer the new age of glory which Christ will inaugurate at his return [3:4].

25: whereof I was made a minister, according to the dispensation of God which was given me to you-ward, to fulfil the word of God,

In verse 23 Paul spoke of himself as a minister of the gospel, and now he reminds the Colossians of the divine commission which made him a minister of the church at large [verse 24], in case they were tempted to think that their spiritual welfare lay outside the range of his ministry [2:1]. He exercises this ministry towards them in accordance with the 'stewardship' (ASV margin) that has been entrusted to him by God. For though he *serves* men as their minister, he only engages in this service because he has been *appointed* to it by God [cf. *1 Cor.* 4:1, 2; 9:17]. Consequently the steward has no power 'to do any thing of his own head, and after his own phantasy; but only to dispense, what the Master hath given him; and precisely in such manner, as he hath prescribed him' (Daillé). Although some take the phrase 'to fulfil the word of God' to refer to the geographical extension of the gospel (as in verse 23), it is more likely that Paul has in view the universal scope of his commission as the apostle to the Gentiles. His task was 'to fill up the full measure of the Gospel, both in its reception by the Gentiles [verse 27a] and in the moral and spiritual completion of every believer [verse 28]. He toils and contends for nothing less [verse 29]' (A. Lukyn Williams).

26: even the mystery which hath been hid for ages and generations: but now hath it been manifested to his saints,

In this verse the message entrusted to the apostle is more precisely designated by the term 'mystery'. Lightfoot thought that Paul borrowed the word from the heathen mysteries in order to point a contrast between those secret rites and the gospel which is offered to all. But the fact that the singular ('the mystery') is not used in connection with these pagan cults tells against this assumption, as does the appearance of the term in Paul's earlier Epistles [*Rom.* 16:25–27; *1 Cor.* 2:6–10]. The gospel 'mystery' is not an unexplained riddle, but a divine secret which, though proclaimed to all, is understood only by those whom the Spirit of God savingly enlightens [*Mark* 4:11; *1 Cor.* 2:9f.]. Thus God's plan of salvation for Jews *and* Gentiles [cf. *Eph.* 3:3–9], which has been hidden for ages and generations, is *now* revealed to 'his saints', i.e. to *all* believers. 'It came upon the world as a sudden surprise. The moment of its revelation was the moment of its fulfilment' (Lightfoot).

27: to whom God was pleased to make known what is the riches of the glory of this mystery among the Gentiles, which is Christ in you, the hope of glory:

To whom God willed to make known: It was the will of God to make known the mystery to the saints. 'Willed' stands first in the Greek for emphasis. 'The revelation was so momentous in its issue, so signal in its method, and so contrary to human foresight and prejudice, that it proceeded evidently from "the will of God" . . . "Who was I", said Peter, "that I could withstand God?" [*Acts* 11:17]. The Ephesian letter delights to dwell on *God's will* as the cause of the whole counsel and work of salvation' (G. G. Findlay).

What is the riches of the glory of this mystery among the Gentiles: Paul struggles with the limitations of language as he attempts to give adequate expression to the munificence of God's grace. How great are the riches of the divine glory thus outpoured in the revelation of this mystery among the Gentiles! It was in the conversion of the Gentiles that this wealth was fully displayed, 'for it overflowed all barriers of caste or race. Judaism was "beggarly" [*Gal.* 4:9] in comparison, since its treasures sufficed only for a few' (Lightfoot).

Which is Christ in you, the hope of glory: Some prefer 'Christ *among* you', but what is evidently intended to be the climactic statement would be a distinct anti-climax if it referred to nothing more than the beginning of the Gentile mission. 'Christ *in* you Gentiles!' – 'that is the great surprise. None could have foreseen or imagined it. It was God's secret. He has disclosed it to us' (J. Armitage Robinson). The aspect of the mystery revealed in Ephesians concerns the admission of the Gentiles as fellow-heirs with Jewish believers, whereas here Paul stresses their wonderful privilege in knowing the power of the indwelling Christ, whose presence within their hearts constitutes the pledge of future glory [cf. *Rom.* 8:10].

28: whom we proclaim, admonishing every man and teaching every man in all wisdom, that we may present every man perfect in Christ;

Whom we proclaim: In contrast to the false teachers, *we* (i.e. Paul and his fellow evangelists including Epaphras) proclaim Christ! 'Proclaim' belongs to 'the language of mission', but as that involves 'declaring the unique historical reality of Jesus', this word must also be one of 'instruction, admonition and tradition' (J. Schniewind, *TDNT*, vol. 1, pp. 71–2). And since the apostolic proclamation of the gospel presented Christ as the only Saviour [*Acts* 4:12], 'they only preach Christ aright and as they ought to do, who teach that all hope of salvation for mankind is laid up in him alone, and who acknowledge that we receive the riches of divine grace through him alone . . . He who makes Christ a sort of halfway Saviour and Mediator, does not in fact preach him, but the chimera of his own brain' (Davenant).

Admonishing every man and teaching every man in all wisdom: The preaching of Christ is effected through admonition and teaching. Although this dual ministry is seen as the task of the whole community in 3:16, it is primarily the function of the apostle to warn against error and to teach the truth [*Acts* 20:31; *1 Cor.* 4:17]. The phrase 'in all wisdom' probably points to the manner of the teaching rather than its content. The thrice-repeated 'every man' emphasizes the universality of Paul's gospel [3:11], 'in opposition to the doctrine of an intellectual exclusiveness taught by the false teachers' (Abbott).

That we may present every man perfect in Christ: This is the ultimate object of the apostle's preaching. The word 'perfect' can scarcely mean that he intended to make every man an 'initiate' of the gospel mystery; it rather expresses his desire that every man might so grow to full maturity in Christ as to appear before God without confusion in the day of judgment [cf. *Eph.* 4:13]. The universality of Paul's aim is in perfect accord with the *revealed* will of God (as opposed to his secret decree: *Deut.* 29:29), and is therefore an example for all preachers [*1 Tim.* 2:4]. For what 'God himself hath declared to be his will in offering the Gospel, the same also ought to be the will of his Ministers in preaching it' (Davenant).

29: whereunto I labour also, striving according to his working, which worketh in me mightily.

With this great end in view (verse 28), Paul toils to the point of weariness, struggling with intense exertion by means of Christ's supernatural power which works in him mightily. The imprisoned apostle employs this athletic metaphor [*1 Tim.* 4:10] to describe the constant spiritual conflict in which he is engaged on behalf of all the churches [verse 24; 2:1]. But though the striving is Paul's, the effectiveness of his labours is entirely due to Christ's power. As Findlay well says, 'Never do we find this consciousness of the Divine power dwelling in himself expressed by Paul with such joyous confidence as at this period' [cf. *Phil.* 4:13; *Eph.* 3:7, 20].

CHAPTER TWO

Although Paul was personally unknown to the believers at Colossae and Laodicea, he strives that they may be so confirmed in their faith in Christ as to give no heed to the novel doctrines of the false teachers [verses 1–7]. Such specious philosophy is after the rudiments of the world and not after Christ. It is because they are already complete in

Christ, in whom dwells all the fulness of the Godhead, that they must not worship the angelic powers which are subject to his lordship [verses 8–10]. They need no circumcision of the flesh, for in Christ they have received the true circumcision of the spirit. Their baptism had set forth this rising to new life, received from God through Christ's finished work, by which the bond that stood against them was abolished and the defeat of all hostile powers secured [verses 11–15]. It is therefore folly to observe ritual ordinances, which were but a shadow of Christ, when they are now in possession of the reality [verses 16, 17]. The worship of angels, though urged as an exercise in humility, is rather the fruit of carnal pride, because it denies Christ's sole primacy as the Head and Sustainer of his church [verses 18, 19]. If they died with Christ to the mere ideas of men, they must renounce the ascetic practices of human devising which flatter pride, and thus serve only to indulge the flesh instead of mortifying it [verses 20– 23].

1: For I would have you know how greatly I strive for you, and for them at Laodicea, and for as many as have not seen my face in the flesh;

In approaching the purpose of the letter, Paul acquaints his readers with the strife in which he is engaged on their behalf, in order to establish a personal bond with the Christians in the cities of the Lycus valley whom he has never met [4:16]. This conflict is not beyond the bounds of his commission, for as the apostle to the Gentiles, his interest is not limited to the churches of his own founding, but extends to the believers in every community of which he has no first-hand knowledge [cf. *Rom.* 1:13]. 'His prison cell was like the focus of some reverberating gallery in which every whisper spoken all round the circumference was heard and the heart that was held captive there was set vibrating in all its chords by every sound from any of the Churches' (Maclaren).

2: that their hearts may be comforted, they being knit together in love, and unto all riches of the full assurance of understanding, that they may know the mystery of God, even Christ, 3: in whom are all the treasures of wisdom and knowledge hidden.

This expresses the purpose for which Paul strives in prayer: It is that they may be strengthened in heart and welded together in love, and thus attain to the full wealth of that assured understanding which will result in a true knowledge of the mystery of God, namely, Christ. 'Strengthened' is preferable to 'comforted', for the false teaching which threatened the faith of Paul's readers meant that they needed something more than comfort. 'It was not consolation that was required, but confirmation in the right faith' (Abbott).

The importance of the place here assigned to love in the attainment of spiritual understanding should be noted (cf. *Eph.* 3:17f. and 3:14 where the Colossians are urged to put on love, 'the bond of perfection'. 'As against all those who tried to intellectualize the Christian faith, speaking of knowledge (*gnosis*) as if it were an end in itself, Paul emphasizes that the revelation of God cannot be properly known apart from the cultivation of brotherly love within the Christian community' (F. F. Bruce). The experience of being united in love will bring them the spiritual wealth that consists in the complete insight into God's mystery – Christ, who is the very embodiment of the divine wisdom [cf. verse 9 and see comment on 1:2,6].

In whom are all the treasures of wisdom and knowledge hidden: It is probably with a sidelong glance at the rival claims made for angelic intermediaries by the heretics that Paul presents Christ as the sole repository of 'all the treasures of wisdom and knowledge'. The terms 'wisdom' and 'knowledge' also occur together in *Rom.* 11:33 where they describe the character of God as this is revealed in the great drama of redemption, and the fact that here they are virtually fused together by the use of one definite article is perhaps a warning against making subtle distinctions between them. The divine wisdom differs from the derived wisdom of men in that it is original and creative. Paul's attribution of this wisdom to Christ means that he is the personal fulfilment of 'all that the Wisdom of God was, according to the Wisdom Literature, and more still' (C. F. D. Moule). [cf. Prov. 8:22ff.] For Christ is not only the Creator and Preserver of all things [1:16, 17], but he is also the perfect Revealer of God and the one Redeemer of men [1:15, 20].

'Hidden' does not mean kept concealed, but stored up as in a treasure chest. 'The treasures of wisdom are hid, not from us, but for us, in Christ. They who would be wise and knowing, must apply themselves to Christ. We must spend upon the stock which is laid up for us in him, and draw from the treasures which are hid in him. He is the

Wisdom of God, and is *of God made unto us Wisdom*, &c. *1 Cor.* 1:24,30' (Matthew Henry).

4: This I say, that no one may delude you with persuasiveness of speech.

In his first direct reference to the false teachers, Paul warns of the danger of being deluded by their 'plausible (but false) arguments' (Arndt-Gingrich). 'Under this word the Apostle comprehends rhetorical and flattering insinuations, sophistical and intricate subtleties; with which they endeavoured either to insinuate or force an entrance into the minds of men. In short; whatever is so flattering to human reason, by its specious colouring, as to lead a man from Christ, is to be referred to the pernicious *enticing words*. This deceitful sophistry the Apostle condemns in *1 Cor.* 2:4. Not that *persuasiveness of words* is in itself condemnable, for it is a great excellence of speech; but the abuse of it, when it acts by apparent, but false reasons, and is employed to impose upon men' (Davenant).

5: For though I am absent in the flesh, yet am I with you in the spirit, joying and beholding your order, and the steadfastness of your faith in Christ.

For though absent in body, I am with you in spirit, and rejoice to see your orderly array and the firm front which your faith in Christ presents (NEB): Although Paul's imprisonment prevents him from dealing with this menacing situation in person, he assures his readers that he is with them in spirit, and like a general reviewing his troops before the battle, he is confident that their faith in Christ will enable them to maintain 'good order' and 'closed ranks' in the face of the enemy. 'See how by praising them he doth oblige them to regard his advertisements; and by the very consideration of their having so well begun, doth more and more engage them to holy persevering to the end' (Daillé).

6: As therefore ye received Christ Jesus the Lord, so walk in him, 7: rooted and builded up in him, and established in your faith, even as ye were taught, abounding in thanksgiving.

As therefore ye received Christ Jesus as Lord: Paul now exhorts the community to continue in the faith they had 'received' through the ministry of Epaphras [1:7]. This is the technical word for accepting what is handed on by oral tradition [*1 Cor.* 11:23; 15:3], but the tradition here is not merely the doctrine about Christ, for Christ himself is identified with the gospel [cf. Eph. 4:20]. Paul represents Christ, rather than the gospel, as the object of instruction, 'because the central point in the Colossian heresy was the subversion of the true idea of the Christ' (Lightfoot). For in believing the testimony given to Christ Jesus, they had received him *as Lord*, and so were bound to be obedient to him alone [1:10].

Continue to walk in him: As there could be no walking in Christ without a prior reception of him, so this 'ability to walk is the result of communicated animation' (Eadie). In other words, the power to live a new life depends upon daily communion with the living Lord. Thus Christ must be 'the encompassing and guiding and controlling element of every step of life' (J. A. Beet).

Having been rooted, and being built up in him: As usual the richness of Paul's thought leads to the mixing of his metaphors. In the first metaphor Christ is regarded as the soil in which they have been rooted, while in the second he is viewed as the cohesive element in the ensuing process of being built up in the faith. With regard to the first, Daillé points out that those who are rooted in Christ can never be plucked up by any effort, however violent it may be. The winds of false doctrine leave them unmoved, because the sweet sap which they draw from Christ, 'as from a rich soil, doth content them, and purgeth them of that foolish and childish itching humour, which openeth the ears of the weak and unstable to such things. But if you be not thus rooted in CHRIST, it will be no great difficulty to pluck you from the station you are in.'

And being established in the faith, even as ye were taught: To become established in the faith is to continue in the teaching of their faithful pastor Epaphras. Far from interfering with the work of an honoured colleague, Paul places the whole weight of his apostolic authority behind it [1:23].

Abounding in thanksgiving: As thanksgiving is the hallmark of spiritual life, so ingratitude always points to a slight appreciation of gospel grace. This probably accounts for the sustained emphasis upon thanksgiving in Colossians, for only those who fail to realize the fulness of Christ seek some further satisfaction outside of him [verse 10].

A. Lukyn Williams also suggests that there may be an intentional contrast here between the Christian's thanksgiving over everything [3:17] and 'the lack of liberty to be found in the false teaching, verses 16, 21'. [cf. *1 Tim.* 4:3, 4]

8: Take heed lest there shall be any one that maketh spoil of you through his philosophy and vain deceit, after the tradition of men, after the rudiments of the world, and not after Christ:

Paul now warns the Colossians to be on their guard, for they were in danger of being kidnapped by the false teachers! The word 'maketh spoil', meaning to *carry off as booty* or *as a captive*, is here used 'figuratively of carrying someone away from the truth into the slavery of error' (Arndt-Gingrich). If they would avoid this bondage, they must reject that teaching which the preachers of error dignified by the term 'philosophy', and which Paul roundly condemns for its 'vain deceit'. He goes on to expose the true character of this deceptive system in three descriptive phrases: 1. It is 'after the tradition of men'. In contrast to the *divine* origin of the gospel 'tradition' [verse 6], this dogma could not be traced to any higher source than 'the tradition *of men*' [verse 22]. 2. It is 'after the rudiments of the world'. What originates in men clearly cannot transcend the world, and it is therefore futile to seek salvation by the fleshly wisdom that relies upon those rules and regulations which belong to a perishing order. On the much disputed meaning of this phrase see the further comment on verse 20. 3. It is 'not after Christ'. Contrary to the superior claims put forward by the errorists, Paul affirms that their specious reasoning is not in accord with the truth which God has fully revealed in Christ. Every heresy is marked by the failure to conform to this God-given standard.

9: for in him dwelleth all the fulness of the Godhead bodily,

As Eadie observes, Any 'philosophy' not 'after Christ' must be earthly and delusive. It has missed the central truth, 'for in him dwells all the fulness of the Godhead bodily'. Here the term 'the fulness' [see comment on 1:19] is defined by the phrase 'of the Godhead' and the mode of its manifestation is explained by the word 'bodily'. In Romans 1:20 Paul speaks of the 'divinity' of God in reference to the divine qualities which are revealed in the creation; whereas he uses the stronger word, 'Godhead', to show that in Christ there dwells all the fulness of absolute Deity: 'not merely the Divine attributes, but the *Divine nature* itself' (Bengel). Of the many interpretations of 'bodily', the literal is the most natural [cf. *John* 1:14]. 'It is because the fulness took on some visible form in Christ that it became knowable to man. It is worth noting that the verb is in the present tense which points to the continuing effect of the incarnation as an act of revelation' (Donald Guthrie).

10: and in him ye are made full, who is the head of all principality and power:

This great Christological statement leads directly to the practical conclusion which the Colossians are to draw from it. Since they have been made full 'in him', they must not seek by supplementary rites and beliefs the 'completeness' they already possess in Christ alone [verses 1: 17ff.]. 'We are declared to be complete not *from him*, or *by him* only, but *in him* . . . There is no necessity that they who wish to drink of a fountain should enter the fountain itself; because, standing without that, they may draw from thence to quench their thirst: but it is not so with Christ, who is the fountain of grace and righteousness to us, for we cannot receive of his fulness unless we are in him' (Davenant).

Who is the head of all principality and power: This is added to convince them of the futility of invoking angelic powers when these are all subject to the supreme lordship of Christ. But though Christ is described as their 'head', it should be noted that they are not called his 'body', for the special intimacy of that relationship is reserved for Christ's people [1:18].

11: in whom ye were also circumcised with a circumcision not made with hands, in the putting off of the body of the flesh, in the circumcision of Christ; 12: having been buried with him in baptism, wherein ye were also raised with him through faith in the working of God, who raised him from the dead. 13: And you, being dead through your trespasses and the uncircumcision of your flesh, you, I say, did he make alive together with him, having forgiven us all our trespasses; 14: having blotted out the bond written in ordinances that was against us, which was contrary to us: and he hath taken it out of the way, nailing it to the cross; 15: having despoiled the principalities and the powers, he made a show of them openly, triumphing over them in it.

In describing the 'fulness' given by God to the Colossians 'in Christ' [verse 10], Paul lays stress on three things: 1. The spiritual circumcision which was set forth in their baptism; 2. The reality of their participation in Christ's resurrection life; 3. The significance of Christ's triumph over all the powers of evil.

In whom ye were also circumcised with a circumcision not made with hands: This unexpected reference to circumcision suggests that Paul is replying to the claims made for it by the false teachers. But in contrast to the Jewish legalists who made circumcision a condition of salvation [*Acts* 15:1], these 'free thinkers' presumably had their own reasons for recommending it. Possibly they regarded it as a prophylactic against the sins of the flesh [verse 23], as a protection against the power of evil spirits [verse 15], or as the badge of their assumed superiority. But whatever arguments were used to persuade the Colossians to be circumcised, at least it is clear that Paul here cuts the ground from under them, for he assures his Gentile readers that 'in Christ' they were already the recipients of that 'spiritual' circumcision which was 'not made with hands' [cf. *Rom.* 2:29]. The aorist tense points to the time of their conversion and reception into the church by baptism [verse 12].

In the putting off of the body of the flesh, in the circumcision of Christ: Whereas circumcision was a minor physical operation which removed only a portion of the body, in spiritual circumcision 'the whole corrupt, carnal nature is put away like a garment which is taken off and laid aside' (Vincent). [3:9; *Rom.* 6:6]. 'The circumcision of Christ' is the circumcision that belongs to Christ, and is effected through union with him, in contrast to the circumcision of Moses. It is important to note that in this passage the rite of circumcision is not likened to Christian baptism, but contrasted with it.

Having been buried with him in baptism, wherein ye were also raised with him through faith in the working of God, who raised him from the dead: According to the (pre-Pauline) practice of the early church, baptism was not only the funeral of the old life, but also the beginning of an entirely new life [*Rom.* 6:3ff.]. 'They were, in fact, "buried" with Christ when they were plunged in the baptismal water, in token that they had died so far as their old life of sin was concerned; they were raised again with Christ when they emerged from the water, in token that they had received a new life, which was nothing less than participation in Christ's own resurrection life' (F. F. Bruce, *Romans*, p. 136). But this union with Christ, of which the baptismal act was the outward and visible sign, was only experienced through personal faith 'in the working of God' [cf. *Rom.* 4:24; 6:8; 10:9]. 'Faith is the subjective means by which the grace is received; only by a belief in the resurrection can the rising again with Christ be appropriated by the individual. By belief in the resurrection of Christ we believe in the power of God, of which it is an evidence; and this belief, again, is the means by which that power works in the life and produces an effect analogous to that resurrection' (Abbott).

And you, being dead through your trespasses and the uncircumcision of your flesh, you, I say, did he make alive together with him, having forgiven us all our trespasses: 'And you' means 'you as well as Christ', for God who raised Christ from the dead also raised you from the sepulchre of your sins when he quickened you with Christ. As Gentiles, the Colossians had been doubly dead 'through [= by reason of] trespasses' and the 'uncircumcision' of their flesh. They were not only cut off from the life of God by their sins, but their physical condition was then [but not now: cf. *Eph.* 2:11, 12] the true symbol of their unprivileged state as those who lay outside the scope of God's covenant mercy. 'Having forgiven' and 'having blotted out' (in the following clause) are both coincident aorist participles. The first shows that the forgiveness was contemporary with God's quickening grace in conversion, while the second specifies the act by which this comprehensive pardon was secured [verse 14]. As Paul here comes to the heart of Christian experience, he includes himself with all believers ('us'). He is 'eager to claim his share in the transgression, that he may claim it also in the forgiveness' (Lightfoot).

Having blotted out the bond that was against us by its ordinances (ASV margin): Paul now explains how God was able to forgive us all our trespasses. He wiped out the bond which testified against us by means of its unfulfilled demands. Here the figure of a 'bond' is used by the apostle to illustrate the condemning power of the law. The bond was a statement of indebtedness, an IOU signed by the debtor (see *Philem.* 19 for an example of the form). Conscience forces all men to sign this bond, to acknowledge their disobedience to God's revealed will: for the Jew has broken the written law, and the Gentile has not followed the dictates of his heart [*Rom.* 2:15]. But just as writing could be washed off the surface of papyrus because ancient ink contained no acid, so God in his mercy has completely erased the record that stood against us. For on the cross Christ took this bond of sin and condemnation and discharged the debt by exhausting the penalty on our behalf [cf. *Gal.* 3:13; *2 Cor.* 5:21].

And he hath taken it out of the way, nailing it to the cross: Although God is clearly the subject from verse 13, at this point Paul appears to switch his thought to Christ [verses 14b, 15]. This change of subject is suggested by the change in construction, which shows that the bond of indictment against us has been permanently removed by Christ. The phrase that follows explains the way in which Christ rid us of the bond: 'nailing it to the cross'. Paul is probably alluding to the Roman practice of putting a notice over the cross of a crucified man to set forth the crime for which he was condemned. But though the charge under which Christ died was that of claiming to be 'The King of the Jews' [*Mark* 15:26], Paul boldly hails Christ's willing sacrifice as the great victory that forever removed the sentence of death which the law justly pronounced against us [*Gal.* 3:13].

Having despoiled the principalities and the powers, he made a show of them openly, triumphing over them in it: The situation in Colossae leads Paul to depict Christ's death on the cross as the decisive triumph over all the demonic powers of evil, for the false teaching which exalted angels at the expense of Christ clearly owed its inspiration to these defeated powers. 'In it' refers to the cross, where Christ turned apparent defeat into the conquest which disarmed Satan's hosts of their power to retain the spoils [*Luke* 11:22]. 'The paradox of the crucifixion is thus placed in the strongest light – triumph in helplessness and glory in shame. The convict's gibbet is the victor's car' (Lightfoot). As therefore only Christ is Lord, the good angels cannot lead the Colossians to God [*1 Tim.* 2:5], and the bad angels cannot separate them from God [*Rom.* 8:38, 39]. There is but one message of hope that can relieve modern man of his frustration and despair. 'Christ crucified and risen is Lord of all; all the forces of the universe are subject to Him, not only the benign ones but the hostile ones as well. They are all subject to Him as their Creator; the latter are subject to Him also as their Conqueror. And therefore to be united to Him is to be liberated from their thraldom, to enjoy perfect freedom, to overcome all the power of evil because Christ's victory is ours' (F. F. Bruce) [cf. *Eph.* 6:10–18].

16: Let no man therefore judge you in meat, or in drink, or in respect of a feast day or a new moon or a sabbath day: 17: which are a shadow of the things to come; but the body is Christ's.

Since Christ has gained the victory over all hostile powers and is the sovereign Lord of the universe, the Colossians must not capitulate to the false teachers whose rigid demands were presumably designed to please the angelic mediators they worshipped [verse 18]. They must let no one take them to task in the matter of eating and drinking. The error in view is not the adoption of Jewish food laws (which in any case had little to say about drink), but the ascetic abstention which was influenced by pagan thought and practice. For in the ancient world it was believed that fasting made men receptive to ecstatic revelations from the gods.

However, the reference to the observance of annual ('feast day'), monthly ('new moon'), and weekly ('sabbath day') holy days here points to the Judaistic element in this syncretistic 'heresy'. These are dismissed by Paul as 'a shadow of the things to come', because the Mosaic ritual is superseded by the arrival of 'the body' it served for a time to represent [cf. *Heb.* 10:1]. Thus instead of contrasting the *shadow* with the *substance*, Paul again emphasizes the term 'body', which refers to the church as Christ's body. The body belongs to Christ, for spiritual reality is only found in living communion with the Lord, and this discloses the supreme folly of 'not holding fast the Head' [verse 19].

18: Let no man rob you of your prize by a voluntary humility and worshipping of the angels, dwelling in the things which he hath seen, vainly puffed up by his fleshly mind,

Let no one disqualify you by taking pleasure in humility and the worship of angels: Our difficulty in grasping the meaning of what the Colossians must have understood is probably due to Paul's ironical quotation of catchwords used by the false teachers. These men took pleasure in the self-imposed 'humility' of an asceticism [verse 23] which no doubt included the fasting that prepared them to receive their ecstatic visions (see next clause and comment on verse 16). In contrast to such carnal 'humility' which involves scorn for those who do not participate in this mortification of the body, Paul urges them to put on the true humility [3:12] that characterizes the new man in Christ (so W. Grundmann, *TDNT*, vol. 8, p. 22). The heretics further flaunted this spirit of false humility in the worship of angels, for they claimed a superior reverence for God by insisting that he could only be approached through a host of angelic mediators. This was the 'Gnostic' element in the Colossian heresy. It assumed 'that humanity, debased by the contact with matter, must reach after God through successive grades of intermediate beings' (Vincent).

Taking his stand upon the things which he hath seen (ASV margin): The discovery of a second-century inscription in the temple of Apollo at Klaros has thrown light on this puzzling phrase. It refers to someone, who having undergone the rite of initiation, 'entered into' the inner sanctuary, thus '*taking his stand on what he has seen* in the mysteries' (Arndt-Gingrich). This coincidence of language probably points to a form of incipient Gnosticism in Colossae which anticipated later developments. 'If the false teacher were accustomed to say with an imposing air, "I have seen, ah! I have seen!" in referring to his revelations, the apostle's allusion would be obvious and telling' (Findlay).

Vainly puffed up by his fleshly mind: Paul probably chose this phrase to drive home the fact that their asceticism and angel worship, far from securing the destruction of the flesh, proved that they were even controlled by the flesh in the very faculty which stood furthest from it.

19: and not holding fast the Head, from whom all the body, being supplied and knit together through the joints and bands, increaseth with the increase of God.

And not holding fast the Head: Paul here attacks the superior claims of the false teachers by showing that their attachment to Christ was purely nominal. 'They profess to be in "the body" indeed, but to have found a method of growth superior to that available for the *hoi polloi* of Christians' (Lukyn Williams). But none are exempt from the general law that makes the growth of all the members depend upon their vital union with the Head, and this also implies that each individual member sustains an immediate relation to the Head. Hence they 'who feel concern for their salvation ought never to turn their eyes from their Head: for if they are plucked away from him by the wiles of seducers, there is an end of salvation' (Davenant).

From whom the whole body supported and held together by sinews and ligaments (Arndt-Gingrich): In Ephesians 4:16 Paul uses the same 'body' metaphor to illustrate the co-operation of the members in relation to their mutual dependence on the Head; whereas here he sets forth the absolute primacy of the Head in order to show that no member of the body can live, let alone grow, in separation from its Head. 'The difference corresponds to the different aims of the two epistles. In the Colossian letter the vital connexion with the Head is the main theme; in the Ephesian, the unity in diversity among the members' (Lightfoot).

Increaseth with the increase of God: This is the increase that God bestows through Christ, in whom is 'all the fulness of the Godhead' [verse 9]. 'Growth from God, and in conformity with Him, is only to be obtained by holding fast to Christ' (Lukyn Williams).

20: If ye died with Christ from the rudiments of the world, why, as though living in the world, do ye subject yourselves to ordinances,

Since you died with Christ to the basic principles of this world, why, as though you still belonged to it, do you submit to its rules (NIV): The interpretation of this verse depends upon our understanding of the key phrase, 'the rudiments (or elements) of the world'. Many commentators favour the rendering, 'the elemental spirits of the universe' (RSV), because they maintain that such a reference to these astral deities is particularly apt in a passage which refutes angel worship. But A. J. Bandstra asks the pertinent question, 'Does Paul elsewhere say that Christians have died to the angelic, cosmic or demonic powers?' He certainly predicts the final abolition of these powers [*1 Cor.* 15:24], and proclaims their present defeat by Christ [verse 15] 'but nowhere does he speak of believers having died to them. On the other hand, the Apostle does specifically assert that Christians have died to the law [*Gal.* 2:19; *Rom.* 7:4].' Moreover, when Paul here asks the question, 'Why as living in the world are you *dogmatized*?' (cf. verse 14: 'the *dogmata* [i.e. the law of ordinances] which were against us') 'the parallels of *Rom.* 8:12 and 7:6 suggest themselves, where Paul states that Christians are no longer debtors to live according to the flesh, and that they have been discharged from the law, which once held them captive, so that they no longer serve according to the old written code.' Hence Bandstra concludes that Paul chose the term 'not only because it aptly described what for him were the basic forces of the world, namely the law and the flesh, but also because these forces formed the point at which Jewish and Gentile religion met' (*The Law and the Elements of the World,* pp. 68–71). (Compare the usage in *Gal.* 4:3, 9 which is consistent with this interpretation. Herman Ridderbos also rejects the 'cosmic' view, because this verse clearly shows that Paul is thinking 'of the sin-dominated world of men, in which believers are no longer to "live" (which can scarcely be said of the cosmos as universe)', *Paul – An Outline of His Theology*, p. 149.)

Thus Paul is exhorting the Colossians to live out the faith they confessed in their baptism: Since you then died with Christ and put off the body of flesh [verses 11, 12; cf. 3:3], you must no longer behave as though you were still subject to the basic principles of this world – those religious regulations [verses 21, 22] – which are powerless to save and are weak and defenceless before sin.

21: Handle not, nor taste, nor touch 22: (all which things are to perish with the using), after the precepts and doctrines of men?

Paul's scornful reference to the 'No trespassing' signs set up by the false teachers shows that a negative asceticism has nothing in common with the gospel. These prohibitions are arranged in an ascending order of stringency –' Do not take it, do not even taste it, do not so much as touch it!' (Beet) – and are condemned by the apostle on two counts.

1. To abstain from things which are destined to perish with the using cannot possibly promote superior holiness [*1 Cor.* 8:8]. 'The thought is that these things which are merely material, as is shown by their dissolution in the ordinary course of nature, have in themselves no moral or spiritual effect' (Abbott) [*Matt.* 15:17].

2. To submit to the arbitrary rules of men is to exchange gospel liberty for legal bondage [*Isa.* 29:13; *Mark* 7:7]. 'We are free from men not that we may please ourselves, but that we may please Him' (Maclaren) [*1 Cor.* 7:23].

23: Which things have indeed a show of wisdom in will-worship, and humility, and severity to the body; but are not of any value against the indulgence of the flesh.

But they are of no value, serving only to indulge the flesh (RSV margin): The ending of this difficult verse is problematical, but the alternative rendering given here is strongly supported by F. W. Beare and W. Hendriksen, and it has the advantage of bringing the argument to a more forceful conclusion. Paul concedes that such ascetic regulations have indeed an appearance of wisdom, but in reality those who practise the precepts of men pamper 'the flesh' instead of subduing it. For the false wisdom of the 'fleshly' mind finds outward expression in 'self-imposed' worship, spurious 'humility', and unsparing treatment of the body.

This unnatural denial of the needs of the body not only ignores the great gospel command, 'Do thyself no harm' [*Acts* 16:28], but also ministers to the very pride which it was designed to mortify. 'The carnal nature is all the while gratified, even though the body, wan and wasted, is reduced to the point of bare existence. There is more pride in cells and cloisters than in courts and palaces, and oftentimes as gross sensuality. The devotee deifies himself, is more to himself than the object of his homage . . . The entire phenomenon, whatever its special aspect, is a huge self-deception, and a reversal of that moral order which God has established' (Eadie).

CHAPTER THREE

Since the Colossians were raised with Christ and their true life is now hid with Christ in God, they must set their minds on heavenly things, for when the exalted Christ appears they shall also appear with him in glory [verses 1–4]. Therefore they must put to death the sins that belonged to the old life, seeing that they have put off the old man with his doings, and have put on the new man who is being renewed after the image of his Creator; before whom there are no distinctions of race or class since Christ is in all alike [verses 5–11]. As God's elect they must therefore put on all the Christian graces, especially love, peace, and thankfulness. They are to let the word of Christ so dwell in them that they will be enriched in wisdom, edified in worship, and prompted to praise [verses 12–17]. Finally the mutual duties of wives and husbands, parents and children, masters and servants, are each to be regulated by their relation to the Lord [verses 18–4:1].

1: If then ye were raised together with Christ, seek the things that are above, where Christ is, seated on the right hand of God.

As usual in Paul, 'therefore' (here rendered 'then') marks the transition to exhortation [cf. *Rom.* 12:1; *Eph.* 4:1]. 'If' implies no uncertainty, but means 'if, as is the case' or 'since'. Having explained the significance of union with Christ in his death [2:20], Paul now shows that the same bond unites all the members with the resurrection-life of their Head. The reference is not primarily to the subjective experience of his readers, but to the objective benefit which this eschatological event secured for them. The Colossians had entered into conscious possession of this new life by faith and baptism. And since baptism is the visible symbol of union with Christ [*Rom.* 6:3ff.], it becomes for believers 'the demonstrable line of demarcation between the old and the new, and faith in the gospel means a new self-judgment, that of being dead to sin and alive to God' (Ridderbos, Paul, p. 214).

Seek the things that are above, where Christ is: In thus directing the Colossians to 'seek the things that are above', Paul again may be using a slogan of the false teachers in a 'disinfected' sense (H. Chadwick). Instead of heeding such claims to a secret knowledge of heavenly mysteries [2:18], they must realize that they have already been raised to heaven with Christ [*Eph.* 2:6], and that their true life is now 'hid with Christ in God' [verse 3]. Hence they must seek to live in a manner which befits those who belong to this supernal realm with all its transcendent realities [*Phil.* 3:19f.]. 'The exhortation is simply to an actual life consonant with our change of state . . . It is an exhortation to us to be in life real citizens of the heavenly kingdom to which we have been transferred; to do the duties and enter into the responsibilities of our new citizenship' (B. B. Warfield, 'The Hidden Life', *Faith and Life*, pp. 352–3).

Seated on the right hand of God: This clause sets forth the completeness of the Saviour's work and the dignity of his position in language which is clearly derived from Psalm 110:1 [cf. *Heb.* 1:3, 13; 8:1; 10:12; 12:2; *1 Pet.* 3:22; *Rev.* 3:21]. 'Session at the right hand of God means joint-rule. It thus implies divine dignity, as does the very fact of sitting in God's Presence'(W. Foerster, *TDNT*, vol. 3, p. 1089).

2: Set your mind on the things that are above, not on the things that are upon the earth.

This deepens the thought of the previous verse: 'You must not only *seek* heaven; you must also *think* heaven' (Lightfoot). Since earthly thoughts will never sustain a heavenly walk [*Phil.* 3:19], Paul urges them so to set their mind upon things above that the whole of their attitude towards earthly things will be determined by this heavenly orientation [*Matt.* 6:21]. 'The apostle does not urge any transcendental contempt of things below, but simply asks that the heart be not set upon them in the same way, and to the same extent, in which it is set upon things above. The pilgrim is not to despise the comforts which he may meet with by the way, but he is not to tarry among them, or leave them with regret. "Things on earth" are only subordinate and instrumental – "things above" are supreme and final' (Eadie). This antithesis thus condemns the asceticism of the false teachers whose boastful claims to higher knowledge were nullified by their grovelling attachment to 'the basic principles of the world' [2:20f].

3: For ye died, and your life is hid with Christ in God.

For when you renounced the old life in baptism, you then died to all its claims over you, and now that you have put on the new man 'your life is hid with Christ in God'. Here the primary idea is not that of security, but of the present concealment of our essential life. 'The world knows neither Christ nor Christians, and Christians do not even fully know themselves' (Bengel). But though the new life is hidden from the world, and in part from the believer himself, his union with Christ means that he partakes of all the fulness of God [2:9]. If the anatomist cannot even lay bare the principle of physical life, then how much more elusive is the believer's spiritual life both as to its *origin* and *destiny*? 'As to the former, it is hidden with Christ in God; and as to the latter, it shall not be fully revealed till Christ come the second time in glory. But it shall be ultimately disclosed' (Eadie).

4: When Christ, who is our life, shall be manifested, then shall ye also with him be manifested in glory.

The abrupt use of 'when' without a connective brings out the hope more vividly, and fills the reader 'with a sudden light' (Bengel). As

Lightfoot points out, this verse is an advance on the preceding statement ('your life is hid with Christ') in two respects: 1. It is not enough to have said that the life is shared *with* Christ. The Apostle declares that the life *is* Christ [cf. 1 John 5:12]; 2. '*Our*' replaces 'your' as Paul 'hastens to include himself among the recipients of the bounty'.

The Colossians are thus assured that when Christ appears, then they too will appear with him 'in glory'. Although Paul does not stop to define the content of the term, the dominant thought in this context would appear to be the investment of believers with the resurrection body of glory [cf. *Rom.* 8:17; *Phil.* 3:20f, *1 John* 3:2]. 'At present the real dignity of the sons of God is hidden from the eyes of men and indeed from their own eyes, as Christ is hidden from mortal sight. In that day Christ in His essential grandeur will appear and with Him will appear also the grandeur with which He will adorn His servants' (Beet).

5: Put to death therefore your members which are upon the earth: fornication, uncleanness, passion, evil desire, and covetousness, which is idolatry;

In coming to the practical application, it is possible that Paul echoes an early catechism in order to remind the Colossians of the teaching which was delivered to them before their baptism [verses 5–14]. As they had died to the old life of sin when they identified themselves with Christ's death in baptism, so they must put to death the earthly 'members' which are here virtually identified 'with the sins of which they were formerly the instruments' (Bruce). [cf. *Rom.* 6: 19; 7:23] Thus the indicative, 'Ye died' [verse 3], underlies the imperative, 'Put to death', and 'the assurance of the indicative is the urge and the incentive to the fulfilment of the imperative' (John Murray, *Principles of Conduct,* p. 220).

To the sexual sins that were so characteristic of the Graeco-Roman world – immorality, impurity, erotic passion, and evil desire – Paul adds the unrecognized sin of covetousness which he equates with idolatry because the grasping self-seeker makes material gain his god [*1 Tim.* 6:10]. 'Impurity and covetousness may be said to divide between them nearly the whole domain of human selfishness and vice' (Lightfoot).

6: for which things' sake cometh the wrath of God upon the sons of disobedience:

In keeping with his teaching in Romans 1:18ff. Paul declares that these sins call forth the righteous wrath of God who cannot regard this assault upon his holiness with calm indifference. This verse affords no comfort to those modern scholars who wish to personalize 'wrath' in the interests of excusing God from what they deem to be an unworthy emotion. Paul expressly affirms that this is 'the wrath of God', and thus points to the most intense, personal response to sin within the divine being [cf. *John* 3:36; *Eph*. 5:6; *Rev*. 19:15]. But whereas the passage in Romans speaks of the present manifestation of God's wrath, the reference here is probably to its final outpouring on 'the day of wrath' [cf. *Rom*. 2:5]. Although the phrase 'upon the sons of disobedience' is strongly attested, many textual critics regard it as an interpolation from Ephesians 5:6, but it is required to complete the sense and should be retained (so Beet, Abbott, Lenski, and R. E. O. White).

7: wherein ye also once walked, when ye lived in these things;

Or rather, *amongst whom ye also once walked* (ASV margin): Paul's readers once walked with the sons of disobedience and travelled along the same broad way when they used to live in these vile sins. 'They then went along a path trodden by those whose character is derived from, and determined by, the principle of rebellion against God. This justifies the exhortation of verse 5, and prepares a way for that of verse 8' (Beet) [cf. *Eph*. 2:3].

8: but now do ye also put them all away: anger, wrath, malice, railing, shameful speaking out of your mouth: 9: lie not one to another;

'But now' that grace has wrought such a marvellous change in the Colossians, they must discard all the sins of the old life, just as they would cast away a filthy garment. It is difficult to distinguish between 'anger' and 'wrath', though Lightfoot says the former 'denotes a more or less settled feeling of hatred' and the latter 'a tumultuous outburst of passion'. 'Malice' is the malignity that seeks to harm one's neighbour. This ill-will is publicly proclaimed in destructive speech [*Matt*. 12:34]. 'Railing' is the slander by which another's character is defamed.

'Shameful speaking' is the abusive speech which is itself an abuse of the precious gift of language, and is therefore a form of utterance 'quite unfit for *a Christian mouth*' (Findlay) [cf. 4:6]. Paul follows his warning against these vices with a particular injunction against lying. Believers are no longer to lie to one another, because as the parallel passage shows, they are 'members one of another' [*Eph.* 4:25]. As their fellowship is founded upon the truth, lies are bound to injure the body to which they belong, and so they must renounce the corrupt and corrupting deceit which was characteristic of the old man.

9b: seeing that ye have put off the old man with his doings, 10: and have put on the new man, that is being renewed unto knowledge after the image of him that created him:

Paul reminds the Colossians of the significance of the faith confessed in their baptism, for by identifying themselves with the eschatological events of Christ's death and resurrection they had put off the old man and put on the new man. These terms are used by the apostle to express the corporate categories of his thought. The old man is what we once were in Adam, and the new man is what we have become in Christ. The headship of Adam guaranteed solidarity in sin and condemnation, but the coming of Christ introduced a new humanity created after the image of its redeeming Head [1:15]. It is only because believers have put off the old man and his doings that they can be urged to put on those Christian graces which belong to the new man [verses 12ff.]. Thus the order of grace is not 'Do and live' but 'Live and do'.

That is being renewed unto knowledge: But even though believers have already put on the new man, they are not yet perfect and are still under the necessity of being progressively renewed unto that full knowledge of God, which they are destined to attain 'in Christ' [cf. *Eph.* 4:13]. Unlike the speculative knowledge of the false teachers, a true knowledge of God is always intensely practical, since it includes 'the knowledge of His will in all the relations of life' (Lukyn Williams) [cf. 1:9].

After the image of him that created him: The new man, like the first Adam, is created in God's image [*Gen.* 1:27]. But as that image is now made known to us only in the second Adam, he becomes the pattern of the new man [1:15; *Rom.* 8:29; *2 Cor.* 3:18]. 'Renewal after the image of God comes about therefore through the fact that the believer in baptism [*Gal.* 3:27] puts on Christ and thus the new man . . . For this reason to be created after the image of God is the equivalent of bearing, reflecting, being transformed after the image of Christ' (Ridderbos, *Paul*, p. 225).

11: where there cannot be Greek and Jew, circumcision and uncircumcision, barbarian, Scythian, bondman, freeman; but Christ is all, and in all.

In this new humanity the old distinctions that still divide mankind have ceased to count, for differences of race and religion (like Greek and Jew), or of culture (like Greek and barbarian), or of social standing (like slave and free) present no barrier to union with Christ. Such distinctions neither prevent the putting on of the new man, nor do they modify the possession of spiritual privilege and blessing, and this is the glory of Christianity! 'The graces of civilization are not the necessary soil for the graces of the Spirit. Secular enfranchisement is not indispensable to fellow-citizenship with the saints. In the sphere of the new man, those distinctions which obtain in the world exercise no disturbing or preventive influence' (Eadie). The enumeration here suggests that Paul has the special circumstances of his readers very much in mind [cf. *Gal.* 3:28]. The inclusion of the Greeks and the uncircumcised counters the Jewish element in the Colossian heresy, as 'barbarian' serves to dismiss its stress on superior knowledge, while the case of Onesimus would make the reference to slave and freeman especially relevant [4:9; *Philem.* 10].

Greek and Jew, circumcision and uncircumcision: The racial antipathy which existed between Greek (Gentile) and Jew was largely due to their religious differences [*Eph.* 2:11ff.], but the opening of the door of faith to the Gentiles involved the abolition of these inherited privileges and the rite which represented them [*Acts* 10:28; *1 Cor.* 7:19; *Gal.* 5:6, 6:15]. 'If it is no advantage to be born a Jew, it is none to become as a Jew' (Lightfoot).

Barbarian, Scythian: This is not an antithesis, but a climax. The Scythians, 'more barbarous than the barbarians' (Bengel), were 'little better than wild beasts' (Josephus). 'Barbarian' reflects the contempt of the Greek for the language of the 'uncultured', for he regarded their unintelligible utterances as mere sounds without sense ('bar-bar!'). The eminent linguist Max Müller, who traced the beginning of the science of language from the first Day of Pentecost, wrote: 'Not till that word *barbarian* was struck out of the dictionary of mankind and replaced by *brother*, not till the right of all nations of the world to be classed as members of one genus or kind was recognized, can we look even for the beginnings of our science. This change was effected by Christianity.'

Bondman, freeman: Although the *status quo* of slaves is maintained by Paul both in this letter [verse 22–4:1] and that to Philemon, his insistence upon their equal standing in Christ dealt a fatal blow to the idea that a slave was no more than 'a human tool' (Aristotle).

But Christ is all, and in all: 'Christ' stands at the 'end of the sentence, with accumulated emphasis. The Church regards and values each man in his relation to Christ, and bids every other consideration bow to this. He is "all things" – our common centre, our standard of reference, and fount of honour, the sum of all we acknowledge and desire; and he is "in all" – the common life and soul of his people, the substance of all we experience and possess as Christians' (Findlay).

12: Put on therefore, as God's elect, holy and beloved, a heart of compassion, kindness, lowliness, meekness, longsuffering;

Paul follows the demand to renounce the habits of the old life with the positive command to put on the virtues that characterize the new man. The phrase, 'as God's elect', brings the fact of their eternal election to bear upon their present behaviour. It is evident that God's sovereign choice obliges us to put on all the virtues which he recommends to us in the following words. 'For this very thing is the aim and end of his Election, as the Apostle elsewhere informs us, when he saith, That *GOD hath elected us in CHRIST, that we might be holy and blameless before him, Eph.* 1:4' (Daillé). Moreover, as 'holy and beloved' indicates, their election consecrated them to God's service and gave the proof of God's love. These three titles – elect, holy, beloved – are taken from the Old Testament and transferred 'from the Israel after the flesh to the Israel after the Spirit' (Lightfoot). Since the church is a mixed community, the virtues listed by Paul all have to do with personal relationships, and are designed to promote peace and harmony amongst those who by background and temperament were once poles apart.

A heart of compassion: In this, as in everything else, Christ is our supreme example [*Matt.* 9:36; *Mark* 1:41; *Luke* 7:13]. It took Christian compassion to transform the brutal and brutalizing world in which lack of feeling was the Stoic ideal. A heart of compassion is found 'in every regenerate person: he is therefore moved at the very first view of another's misery' (Davenant).

Kindness, lowliness: These are linked because the Christian's attitude towards others is partly determined by his own view of himself (*Phil.* 2:3). 'Kindness', says R. C. Trench, is a beautiful grace 'pervading and penetrating the whole nature, mellowing there all which would have been harsh and austere.' Although Augustine was unmoved by the preaching of Ambrose, he confessed that he was won by the Bishop's kindness: 'And I began to love him, not at first as a teacher of the truth, which I despaired of finding in Thy Church, but as a fellow-creature who was kind to me.' The pagan mind admired self-assertion and despised humility, but Christianity elevated it into a virtue. 'A noble sense was put into the word by the spirit of Christ. Pride has vanished. Others are not beneath our feet. We ourselves are poor sinners. We do not lower ourselves while we are great, as Chrysostom thought; we know that we are *not* great, hence we never even pretend that we are great. So we move among men' (Lenski).

Meekness, longsuffering: These denote the exercise of the Christian temper in its outward bearing towards others. They are best distinguished by their opposites. The first is opposed to 'rudeness, harshness'; the second to 'resentment, revenge, wrath' (so Lightfoot). L. H. Marshall notes that 'meekness' has two elements in it: 1. a consideration for others [see *Gal.* 6:1; *1 Cor.* 11:33; 12:14, 15; *Phil.* 2:4]; 2. a willingness to waive an undoubted right [*1 Cor.* 9: 18]. The real meaning of 'longsuffering' is better conveyed by 'long-temperedness'. It refers 'to the endurance of wrong and exasperating conduct on the part of others without flying into a rage or passionately desiring vengeance. One of the great ethical qualities of God celebrated in Holy Scripture is that He is "slow to anger", and Paul here suggests that the spiritual man shares in this characteristic of God' (Marshall, *The Challenge of New Testament Ethics*, p. 294).

13: forbearing one another, and forgiving each other, if any man have a complaint against any; even as the Lord forgave you, so also do ye:

Paul next enforces the need for mutual forbearance and forgiveness in the Christian community: 'forbearing *one another* and forgiving *yourselves*'. As Vincent remarks, 'The latter pronoun emphasizes the fact that they are *all* members of Christ's body – everyone members one of another – so that, in forgiving *each other* they forgive *themselves*.' This forgiveness is to be as full and free as the divine forgiveness, for in 2:13 Paul uses the same word which literally means 'to grant grace'. The second part of the verse shows that Christ's forgiveness to us is 'the model, and therefore the motive, of our forgiveness of others' (Beet).

14: and above all these things put on love, which is the bond of perfectness.

Above all these, the Colossians are to don the pre-eminent grace of love, which is 'the bond producing perfection' (Moulton-Turner). Others regard love as the bond which binds all the other virtues together, but as the context underlines the unity of the community, it is preferable to see love as the cohesive grace which binds believers together. *'Love, then, is "the bond of perfection" in the sense that it is that which unites believers, causing them to move forward toward the goal of perfection'* (Hendriksen) [*Eph.* 4:13].

15: And let the peace of Christ rule in your hearts, to the which also ye were called in one body; and be ye thankful.

The word represented by 'rule' means literally 'to act as umpire', and from Paul's use of the same word in 2:18 it would seem that he had in mind the umpire who awarded the prize to the winner in athletic contests. The false teachers wished to set themselves up as umpires by awarding the prize for obedience according to their own false standards, but Paul says that the true umpire is within the hearts of believers. This is that peace with God which Christ made through the blood of his cross [1:20]. Instead of heeding the spurious demands of these charlatans, the Colossians must listen to the one authentic umpire, Christ's own peace ruling in their hearts.

To the which also ye were called in one body: Since the goal of their calling is the harmony of the body to which they belong, each member must so acknowledge the headship of Christ [1:18] that no alien spirit is allowed to disturb his reign of peace [cf. *Eph*. 4:3, 4]. 'Strife is the inevitable result when men are out of touch with Him who is the one Source of true peace; but there is no reason why those who have accepted the peace which Christ established by His death on the cross should have any other than peaceful relations among themselves' (Bruce).

And be ye thankful: As the best preservative of this peace, Paul urges them to be always thankful that God has delivered them from the power of darkness and transferred them into the church, which is the domain of Christ's kingly rule [1:13]. 'The command *to give thanks* prevails in this Epistle, as that *to rejoice* in Philippians' (Findlay) [1:3; 2:7; 3:15, 17; 4:2].

16: Let the word of Christ dwell in you richly; in all wisdom teaching and admonishing one another with psalms and hymns and spiritual songs, singing with grace in your hearts unto God.

Let the word of Christ dwell in you richly as you teach and counsel one another with all wisdom (NIV): In comparing this with the closely linked passage in *Eph*. 5:18, 19, we find that the command to be filled with the Spirit is here replaced by 'Let the word of Christ dwell in you richly'. 'In view of the parallelism involved we are bound to conclude that the filling of the Spirit and the richly indwelling Word of Christ are functionally equivalent. That indwelling Word is not some specialized or restricted truth granted only to some in the congregation but "everything I have commanded you" [*Matt*. 28:20], faithfully believed and obeyed . . . The reality of the Spirit's filling work is the reality, in all its breadth and richness, of the ongoing working of Christ, the life-giving Spirit, with his Word. To look for some word other than this word, now inscripturated for the church, is to be seeking some spirit other than the Holy Spirit' (Richard B. Gaffin, *Perspectives on Pentecost*, pp. 33–4). Thus the fellowship of believers is founded upon their mutual submission to 'the word of Christ', the reception of which is marked by the response of praise (as the NIV makes clear). This verse does not therefore mean that believers receive instruction solely by means of song!

And as you sing psalms, hymns and spiritual songs with gratitude in your hearts to God: The importance of singing in the worship of the early church is illustrated in a letter written by Pliny to the Emperor Trajan about AD 112. He reports that the Christians of his province gathered regularly on a fixed day before dawn to sing antiphonally 'a hymn to Christ as God'. It is doubtful whether the terms here used by Paul can be clearly distinguished. 'Psalms' may point to the Christian adoption of the Old Testament Psalter, but in 1 Corinthians 14:26 an ecstatically inspired hymn is evidently in view. 'Hymns' were probably like the samples of Christian praise that seem to be embedded in the New Testament [e.g. *Eph.* 5:14; *1 Tim.* 3:16]. 'Spiritual songs' are so designated to show the source of their inspiration. However, if, as some scholars think, 'spiritual' covers all three terms, then the richness of the early church's worship is expressly attributed to the prompting of the Holy Spirit. Paul insists that such praise should ascend to God from grateful hearts because true worship always demands the response of man's whole being.

17: And whatsoever ye do, in word or in deed, do all in the name of the Lord Jesus, giving thanks to God the Father through him.

The whole field of human conduct is covered by the injunction to 'do all in the name of the Lord Jesus'. There may well be an allusion to the commitment to live under the authority of Christ which was made in baptism [cf. *1 Cor.* 6:11], for the new convert in that act of allegiance placed 'the totality of his life under Christ's lordship' (R. P. Martin). This brief command affords a more comprehensive guide to Christian living than any that could be provided by the heaviest tome of moral casuistry. In every doubtful situation the believer may find sure guidance by asking himself: 'What is the Christian thing to do here? Can I do this without compromising my Christian confession? Can I do it (that is to say) "in the name of the Lord Jesus"?' (F. F. Bruce). The place of thanksgiving in the Christian life is again stressed by Paul when he says that our actions are to be accompanied by the sacrifice of grateful praise which is to be offered through Christ, the only Mediator, in all our approaches to God.

18: Wives, be in subjection to your husbands, as is fitting in the Lord.

Although Paul's brief 'household code' did not threaten the existing social order by offering any incitement to revolutionary change, it brought a new motivation to the old standards of conduct which leavened the lump of paganism and transformed all social relationships. By showing that the 'stronger' and 'weaker' parties in every relationship are equally accountable to Christ, Paul here lays bare their mutual obligations towards one another, for in a one-sided world it would come as a great surprise to some Christians to learn that wives, children, and slaves had rights as well as husbands, parents, and masters. In this verse wives are bidden to be in subjection to their husbands, 'as is fitting in the Lord'.

Some scholars think that the reference to what is fitting points to the adoption of a Stoic maxim, but if so it is Christianized by the addition of the all-important words 'in the Lord'. According to Abbott, the apostle's use of the imperfect tense does not imply 'that the duty has not hitherto been rightly performed, but only that the obligation existed previously'. When even pagans could recognize that wives should be subject to their husbands, it would not be fitting if Christians were more reluctant to acknowledge it! Paul advances the reason for such wifely subjection in Ephesians 5:23. It is found in the headship that makes man the ruling partner in the marriage relation, an arrangement not only established by creation but also endorsed in redemption. Hence Christian wives must understand that equality within the sphere of grace [*Gal.* 3:28; *1 Pet.* 3:7] does not set aside the God-given order for marriage. Nevertheless, the phrase 'in the Lord' clearly sets a limit to this obedience. For wives are only subject to their husbands in what pertains to their legitimate authority *as husbands:* 'everything not contrary to God' (Fausset).

19: Husbands, love your wives, and be not bitter against them.

Turning now to husbands, Paul tells them to love their wives with the self-giving love (*agapao*) that cares for all their needs [cf. *Eph.* 5:25ff.]. 'He saith not, Rule over them, subdue them if they will not submit, but love them, and so win them to your will; make their yoke as easy as may be, for they stand on even ground with you, as yoke-fellows, though they draw on the left side' (John Trapp).

And be not bitter against them: The preposition 'against' probably suggests that what is in view is the bitterness 'vented on the wife though not caused by her' (W. Michaelis, *TDNT*, vol. 6, p. 125). It is a mistake to regard the exhortation as an anti-climax, for many who are polite to all outsiders, 'nevertheless treat their wives and children at home with covert bitterness, because they do not fear them' (Bengel). And, as Lenski observes, this negative is also a litotes which points to the contrary virtue: 'ever be considerate toward them in the way described in Ephesians 5:28, etc.'.

20: Children, obey your parents in all things, for this is well-pleasing in the Lord.

In addressing children Paul makes their natural obligation to obey their parents a summons to religious service: 'for this is well-pleasing in the Lord' [cf. *Eph.* 6:1–3]. 'The love of the child's heart naturally leads it to obedience. Only an unnatural child can be a domestic rebel. Where the parents are Christians, and govern their children in a Christian spirit, obedience should be without exception' (Eadie).

21: Fathers, provoke not your children, that they be not discouraged.

On the other hand, fathers (upon whom the responsibility for the family primarily rests) also have a duty towards their children [*Eph.* 6:4]. They must avoid all that would irritate or exasperate the children – injustice, severity, constant fault-finding, etc. – lest they become discouraged. 'Paul is not commonly regarded as an expert in child psychology, but, where Jesus ben Sira cannot see beyond the menace of the spoilt child, Paul is sensitive to the child's need for encouragement' (G. B. Caird).

22: Servants, obey in all things them that are your masters according to the flesh; not with eye-service, as men-pleasers, but in singleness of heart, fearing the Lord:

In bidding slaves to render uniform obedience to those who are their masters 'according to the flesh', Paul implies that there is another Master who is above the temporal limitations of the existing social order [4:1]. Although many modern versions rightly translate 'slaves', it is perhaps preferable to retain 'servants' because the exhortation 'embodies principles applicable to all posts of subordination' (E. K. Simpson). If Paul had preached 'the social gospel' he doubtless would have encouraged slaves to repudiate their position, with disastrous consequences, yet in sending the converted slave Onesimus back to his master as 'a brother beloved' [*Philem.* 16] he set forth the great principle of religious equality before God which undermined and eventually brought about the abolition of slavery. So here the apostle asks for that heart-obedience which only the redeemed man is able to render to his master.

As the adoption of this ethic led to a transformation of the slave/master relationship, so its widespread absence from the modern industrial scene is diagnosed by John Murray as 'our basic economic ill' (*Principles of Conduct*, p. 103).

Not with eye-service, as men-pleasers: 'The vice was venial in slaves; it is inexcusable, because it darkens into theft, in paid servants – and it spreads far and wide. All scamped work, all productions of man's hand or brain which are got up to look better than they are, all fussy parade of diligence when under inspection and slackness afterwards – and all their like which infect and infest every trade and profession, are transfixed by the sharp point of this precept' (Maclaren).

But in singleness of heart, fearing the Lord: The sincere service which lacks any ulterior motives is prompted by a reverential fear of the Lord. 'Where the all-seeing Master is forgotten, we seek as our highest good the favour of men: and our service sinks down to the external forms which alone lie open to the eye of man. Thus fear of the Supreme Lord saves even the slave from degrading bondage to man' (Beet) [*1 Cor.* 7:23].

23: whatsoever ye do, work heartily, as unto the Lord, and not unto men;

'Here is the secret for all who work for other men, whether they are slaves or free employees: "Throw your soul into the work as if your one employer were the Lord!"' (Lenski). No labour is servile when the Lord's approval is the paramount consideration. Hence the most willing service to men is rendered by those who are bent on pleasing Christ!

24: knowing that from the Lord ye shall receive the recompense of the inheritance: ye serve the Lord Christ.

Paul is not above encouraging such hearty obedience by the prospect of an eternal reward which he describes as 'the inheritance', a significant word since slaves could not inherit any earthly possession. Faithful service is sure to be rewarded, yet this is the reward of grace and not a merited award!

Serve ye the Lord Christ: It is better to take the verb as an imperative. Paul here sums up his charge to slaves in one urgent phrase. 'Since the Lord gives such a reward so rich and blessed, serve ye Him. Look above and beyond human service, and with such a bright prospect in view, serve the Lord Christ. Your masters on earth have no absolute right over you: the shekels they may have paid for you can only give them power over your bodies, your time and your labour, but the Lord has bought you with His blood, and has therefore an indefeasible claim to your homage and service' (Eadie).

25: For he that doeth wrong shall receive again for the wrong that he hath done: and there is no respect of persons.

As masters are reminded in Ephesians 6:9 that 'there is no respect of persons', no acceptance of a man's face, no partiality shown because of his social standing; so here slaves are warned that their low position will not protect them from the same just judgment of their misdeeds. For with the case of Onesimus in mind, Paul would not wish others to think that in pleading for the offender he condoned the offence. 'The low often think that they should be spared on account of their lowness. That is denied' (Bengel).

4:1: Masters, render unto your servants that which is just and equal; knowing that ye also have a Master in heaven.

Finally, Paul calls upon masters to provide their slaves with what is just and fair, because they are also accountable to the same Master in heaven. So since slaves and masters both owe obedience to the one Lord, they need stand in no doubt of how they should behave toward one another. 'The lordship of Christ dominates the whole Epistle. The assertion that the proud master who deemed his fellow-man his chattel is himself a mere *slave* of Christ, sets Christ's authority in a vivid and striking light. This consideration makes the Christian master apprehensive as to his treatment of his dependants. *He* is "in heaven", the seat of Divine authority and glory, whence he shall soon return to judgment' (Findlay).

CHAPTER FOUR

In drawing to a close, the apostle urges his readers to continue in prayer with thanksgiving, and requests them to remember his work in their prayers [verses 2–4]. A concern to present a credible witness must lead them to behave wisely and speak graciously to outsiders [verses 5, 6]. Paul warmly commends the bearers of the Epistle, Tychicus and Onesimus, and conveys the greetings of his companions [verses 7–14]. He gives directions for an exchange of letters between Laodicea and Colossae, and instructs Archippus to fulfil his ministry [verses 15–17]. As usual Paul adds the final greeting in his own hand, and movingly asks them to remember his bonds [verse 18].

2: Continue steadfastly in prayer, watching therein with thanksgiving;

As prayer is the first mark of the Christian life [*Acts* 9:11], so perseverance in prayer is the essential element for continued growth in grace [*Eph.* 6:18]. In calling the Colossians to unceasing prayer, Paul directs them to be watchful in it. It is better to regard this as an independent command. The meaning is not, 'Watch and be attentive during prayer!' but: 'Pray, and at the same time be watchful' (so Lenski) [*Matt.* 26:41].

Such constant watchfulness is necessary to avoid being overtaken by any sudden temptation. 'With thanksgiving' again brings in the characteristic refrain of this Epistle [cf. 1:2; 2:7; 3:15, 17]. Gratitude for Christ's great salvation must be expressed in heart-felt praise! 'Ceaseless prayer combined with ceaseless praise was the atmosphere of Paul's spiritual life' (Beet).

3: withal praying for us also, that God may open unto us a door for the word, to speak the mystery of Christ for which I am also in bonds; 4: that I may make it manifest, as I ought to speak.

Paul also requests prayer for himself and his helpers that God may open unto them a door of opportunity for effective evangelism [*1 Cor.* 16:9; *2 Cor.* 2:12]. 'God opens the door by his providence. Many fail to note this and try to open doors for themselves. When we are spreading the gospel we must follow God's providential indications as to where we ought to work' (Lenski) [cf. *Acts* 16:7,9].

To speak the mystery of Christ, for which I am also in bonds: It was because Paul had proclaimed 'the mystery of Christ' to the Gentiles that he was now a prisoner in chains (see comment on 1:26, 27 and compare *Eph.* 3:1ff.). Paul 'might have been still at large, if he had been content to preach a Judaic Gospel. It was because he contended for Gentile liberty, and thus offended Jewish prejudices, that he found himself a prisoner' (Lightfoot) [*Acts* 21:28; 22:21, 22; 24:5, 6; 25:6, 8].

That I may make it manifest, as I ought to speak: Since the revelation is made in proclamation, Paul desires to be endued with the requisite grace to do justice to the gospel [1:25ff.]. Significantly he makes no request for deliverance from suffering, for he regards what he endures for the sake of the church as a part of his vocation [1:24]. 'If Paul felt his conception of the greatness of the gospel dwarfing into nothing *his* words when he tried to preach it, what must every other true minister of Christ feel?' (Maclaren).

5: Walk in wisdom toward them that are without, redeeming the time.

In regard to those who are outside the church, Paul counsels believers to 'walk in wisdom', 'neither giving offence carelessly, nor taking offence causelessly' (Trapp). They must remember that they are constantly under the critical scrutiny of these 'outsiders' and be conscious of their great responsibility towards them [cf. *1 Cor.* 10:32]. All too often Christians deservedly earn the reputation of being a 'peculiar' people! 'We owe them that are without such a walk as may tend to bring them in. Our life is to a large extent their Bible. They know a great deal more about Christianity, as they see it in us, than as it is revealed in Christ, or recorded in Scripture – and if, as seen in us, it does not strike them as very attractive, small wonder if they still prefer to remain where they are' (Maclaren).

Buying up the opportunity (ASV margin): This means an 'intensive buying' i.e. 'a buying which exhausts the possibilities available' (F. Büchsel, *TDNT*, vol. 1, p. 128). As Christians have a duty to their unbelieving neighbours, they must seize every opportunity for witnessing to the faith, and use it to the full [cf. *Eph.* 5:16].

6: Let your speech be always with grace, seasoned with salt, that ye may know how ye ought to answer each one.

Let your speech always be gracious, seasoned with salt (Hendriksen): Christians are not only to commend the gospel by their lives but also by their lips [*Psa.* 45:3; *Luke* 4:22]. They must always be distinguished by the winsomeness of their speech, which is to be further enhanced by being 'seasoned with salt'. 'Profane men have their saltiness, but he is not speaking of them . . . for he reckons as tasteless everything that does not edify' (John Calvin). Paul probably has in view both the use of salt as a preservative from corruption [*Eph.* 4:29; 5:4], and its function in making food more palatable [*Luke* 14:34].

That ye may know how ye ought to answer each one: 'Not only must your conversation be opportune as regards the time; it must also be appropriate as regards the person' (Lightfoot). No effective witness is given to Christ by rattling off a stereotyped testimony, because this completely ignores the fact that each person has his own special needs. It is worth noting that Paul constantly adapted his speech to his audience [*1 Cor.* 9:22].

7: All my affairs shall Tychicus make known unto you, the beloved brother and faithful minister and fellow-servant in the Lord: 8: whom I have sent unto you for this very purpose, that ye may know our state, and that he may comfort your hearts; 9: together with Onesimus, the faithful and beloved brother, who is one of you. They shall make known unto you all things that are done here.

The bearer of this letter to the Colossians and of all the news from Rome is Tychicus [*Acts* 20:4], Paul's beloved brother and a trusted helper and fellow-servant 'in the Lord', whose ministry is certain to encourage and strengthen their hearts. In our idiom 'I have sent' means 'I am sending' [cf. NIV]. Maclaren draws attention to the indispensable service Tychicus performed in delivering this letter. 'Small things done for Christ are great . . . What is the use of writing letters, if you cannot get them delivered? It takes both Paul and Tychicus to get the letter into the hands of the people at Colossae.'

With Tychicus Paul is returning the runaway slave Onesimus, whose misdeeds are here blotted out by the gracious designation, 'the faithful and beloved brother'. Onesimus could not be placed on a par with Tychicus for the faithfulness of his service, but only for the faithfulness of his belief in the Lord who saved him from his former slavery to sin.

As this faith makes him a member of the redeemed community ('who is one of you'), Paul is confident that he will be welcomed by the Colossian church and pardoned by his wronged master Philemon.

10: Aristarchus my fellow-prisoner saluteth you, and Mark, the cousin of Barnabas (touching whom ye received commandments; if he come unto you, receive him), 11: and Jesus that is called Justus, who are of the circumcision: these only are my fellow-workers unto the kingdom of God, men that have been a comfort unto me.

Paul next sends the greetings of six persons who are with him as he writes [verses 10–14]. The fact that Paul here names Aristarchus [*Acts* 19:29; 20:4; 27:2] as his 'fellow-prisoner' but transfers the title to Epaphras in Philemon 23 may mean that these men took turns in voluntarily sharing the apostle's imprisonment in order to minister to his needs. Paul's commendation of Mark [cf. *2 Tim.* 4:11] is apparently in connection with a projected visit to the churches of Asia, but we are left in the dark as to whether this mission was initiated by Paul or someone else. Although Mark's desertion from the first missionary journey led to a sharp contention between Paul and Barnabas [*Acts* 15:36–41], he had evidently regained Paul's respect by his subsequent service and vindicated his kinsman's confidence in him. It is a strange irony that an otherwise unknown believer, 'Jesus who is called Justus', should have achieved the kind of posthumous fame that many strive for in vain simply because he wanted to send his greetings to the Christians at Colossae!

These three Jewish Christians have proved a comfort to Paul, for they are the only Jews in Rome who are really working with him for 'the kingdom of God' (in contrast to the profitless exertions of the Judaizers!). This pathetic complaint, which confirms what Paul hints at elsewhere [cf. *Phil.* 1:15–17], shows that the rest of the Jews there were hostile to his gospel, though many of them hailed Jesus as their Messiah. 'Even when he was a prisoner, their unrelenting antagonism pursued the Apostle. They preached Christ of "envy and strife". Not one of them lifted a finger to help him, or spoke a word to cheer him. With none of them to say, God bless him! he toiled on. Only these three were large-hearted enough to take their stand by his side, and by this greeting to clasp the hands of their Gentile brethren in Colossae and thereby to endorse the teaching of this letter as to the abrogation of Jewish rites' (Maclaren).

12: Epaphras, who is one of you, a servant of Christ Jesus, saluteth you, always striving for you in his prayers, that ye may stand perfect and fully assured in all the will of God.

Since Aristarchus, Mark, and Jesus named Justus are the only Jews Paul mentions, Epaphras, Luke and Demas must be Gentiles [verses 12–14]. As a native of Colossae and as the founder of the church there [1:7], Epaphras is well described as 'one of you'. In conveying the greeting of this slave of Christ Jesus, Paul informs them that he is always wrestling in prayer on their behalf [verse 2]. 'The effort of Epaphras' prayers was like the intense effort of a Greek athlete contending for a prize. The appropriateness of this phrase is felt by all to whom prayer is a reality' (Beet).

That ye may stand perfect and fully assured in all the will of God: The content of Epaphras' prayers virtually sums up the teaching of the letter. As against the false quest for perfection by legalistic supplements [2:20f.], he asks that they may stand firm in the faith [1:23; cf. *Eph.* 6:11, 13], finding their maturity in the all-sufficient Christ [2:9, 10]. And instead of seeking to complete their faith by some higher revelation, he prays that they may be fully assured 'in all the will of God' [cf. 2:2].

13: For I bear him witness, that he hath much labour for you, and for them in Laodicea, and for them in Hierapolis.

Paul's insistence upon the faithfulness of Epaphras' labours for the Colossian Christians and those in the neighbouring cities of Laodicea and Hierapolis (see Introduction), may be intended to forestall any possible criticism of his having gone to Rome to misrepresent the situation in Colossae or to escape from his responsibilities there. 'This is an example of a good pastor, whom distance cannot induce to forget the Church or prevent him from carrying the care of it with him beyond the sea' (Calvin).

14: Luke, the beloved physician, and Demas salute you.

Luke was one of Paul's closest friends. He was an almost constant companion of the apostle from the time of the second missionary journey (as is shown by the 'we' sections in Acts 16:10–17; 20:5–21:18; 27:1–28:16) until the end of his life [*2 Tim.* 4:11]. Over the years there were doubtless numerous occasions when Paul had reason to be grateful for Luke's professional skill as a doctor, and perhaps not least during his imprisonment in Rome. The fact that both the writers of the Second and Third Gospels were with Paul at this time clearly 'disproves the contention of those who say that Paul knew next to nothing about the historical Jesus' (A. M. Hunter).

Here Demas salutes the Colossians, but in the last crisis he forsook Paul and returned to Thessalonica 'having loved this present world' [*2 Tim.* 4:10]. 'We are not better than the Apostles. If all the light of their wisdom and miracles, could not keep *Demas* from becoming bankrupt of the truth, we ought not to think it strange, if there happen to be among us, some whom belly and vanity do precipitate into the like fault, notwithstanding the clearness and evidence of our holy doctrine' (Daillé).

15: Salute the brethren that are in Laodicea, and Nymphas, and the church that is in their house.

Paul now asks the Colossians to pass on his greetings to the believers in Laodicea, 'and to Nympha and the church in her house' (NIV). Lenski thinks that this house-church was in Hierapolis, because it would be so unlike Paul not to extend a greeting to the Christians there [verse 13]. Be that as it may, Nympha must have been a wealthy woman to have a house large enough to allow the young church to gather for worship in it. No buildings were set apart for public worship until the third century, and so the early Christians were obliged to hold their services in private houses [cf. *Rom.* 16:5; *1 Cor.* 16:9; *Acts* 12:12].

16: And when this epistle hath been read among you, cause that it be read also in the church of the Laodiceans; and that ye also read the epistle from Laodicea.

The letter 'from Laodicea' is probably the one we know as 'Ephesians', for its impersonal nature suggests that it was intended as a circular letter. It is clear from Ephesians 6:21, 22 that Tychicus was also the bearer of this letter, and since he had to pass through Laodicea on his way to Colossae, he would leave a copy there before delivering the Colossian letter. This verse not only shows that Paul's letters were intended to be read to the assembled company of believers when they met for worship [*1 Thess.* 5:27], but also that they were from the first intended for a wider circulation than their initial destination would imply.

17: And say to Archippus, Take heed to the ministry which thou hast received in the Lord, that thou fulfil it.

It seems that Archippus was a member of Philemon's family, possibly his son. In Philemon 2 Paul gives him the honourable title of 'fellow-soldier', and it is reasonable to assume that the church appointed him to be their pastor when Epaphras left for Rome. In thus publicly endorsing the appointment and encouraging him to fulfil his ministry, Paul probably had in mind the urgent need to defend the truth of the gospel by dealing decisively with the errors propagated by the false teachers (so R. P. Martin).

18: The salutation of me Paul with mine own hand. Remember my bonds. Grace be with you.

To mark the letter as genuine Paul now adds the final greeting in his own handwriting [*2 Thess.* 3:17]. 'Remember my bonds' is not an appeal for sympathy, but an exhortation to obey the teaching of this letter. 'His bonds establish an additional claim to hearing. He who is suffering for Christ has a right to speak on behalf of Christ' (Lightfoot) [cf. *Eph.* 3:1; 4:1; 6:20; *Phil.* 9, 13]. Paul's last word to the Colossians is his prayer that the grace of the one authentic gospel which he preaches, may be with them. This very brief benediction is found only here and in 1 Timothy 6:21 and 2 Timothy 4:22.

Soli Deo Gloria

BIBLIOGRAPHY FOR COLOSSIANS AND PHILEMON

Abbott, T. K., *The Epistle to the Ephesians and to the Colossians* (*ICC*) (T. & T. Clark, 1897).

Arndt, W. F., and Gingrich, F. W., *A Greek English Lexicon of the New Testament* (University of Chicago Press, 1957).

Bandstra, Andrew James, *The Law and the Elements of the World* (J. H. Kok, Kampen, 1964)

Beare, Francis W., *The Epistle to the Colossians* (*IB*) (Abingdon, 1955).

Beet, J. Agar, A *Commentary on St Paul's Epistles to the Ephesians, Philippians, Colossians, and to Philemon* (Hodder & Stoughton, 1890).

Bengel, J. A., *New Testament Word Studies* (Kregel, 1971).

Bruce, F. F., *Commentary on Romans* (Tyndale, 1963).

Caird, G. B., *Paul's Letters from Prison* (New Clarendon Bible) (OUP, 1976).

Calvin, John, *Galatians–Colossians* (St Andrew Press, 1965).

—— *Second Corinthians–Philemon* (St Andrew Press, 1964).

Clowney, Edmund P., *The Doctrine of the Church* (Presbyterian & Reformed, 1969).

Daille, Jean, *Sermons on Colossians* (London, 1672).

Davenant, John, *An Exposition of the Epistle of Paul to the Colossians* (Hamilton Adams, 1831/2).

Douglas, J. D. (Editor), *The New Bible Dictionary* (IVP, 1962).

Eadie, John, *Commentary on the Epistle of Paul to the Colossians* (Zondervan, 1957).

Fausset, A. R., *Ephesians* (*JFB*) (Collins, 1874).

Fergusson, James, *A Brief Exposition of the Epistles of Paul* (Banner of Truth, 1978).

Findlay, G. G., *Colossians* (Pulpit Commentary) (Kegan Paul, Trench 1886).

Gaffin, Richard B., *The Centrality of the Resurrection* (Baker Book House, 1978).

—— *Perspectives on Pentecost* (Presbyterian & Reformed, 1979).

Guthrie, Donald, *New Testament Introduction* (Tyndale, 1970).

GUTHRIE, DONALD, *Colossians* (*NBC*) (IVP, 1970).
HENDRIKSEN, WILLIAM, *Colossians and Philemon* (*NTC*) (Banner of Truth, 1971).
HENRY, MATTHEW, *Commentary on the Holy Bible* (various editions).
HUNTER, A. M., *Galatians–Colossians* (*LBC*) (SCM Press, 1966).
KITTEL, G. AND FRIEDRICH, G., *Theological Dictionary of the New Testament,* vols. 1–10 (Eerdmans, 1964–76).
KNOX, JOHN, *The Epistle to Philemon* (*IB*) (Abingdon, 1955).
LENSKI, R. C. H., *The Interpretation of Colossians and Philemon* (Augsburg, 1964).
LIGHTFOOT, J. B., *St Paul's Epistles to the Colossians and to Philemon* (Zondervan, 1961).
LOHSE, EDUARD, *Colossians and Philemon* (Fortress Press, 1971).
MACLAREN, ALEXANDER, *The Epistles of Paul to the Colossians and Philemon* (Hodder & Stoughton, 1888).
MARSHALL, L. H., *The Challenge of New Testament Ethics* (Macmillan, 1946).
MARTIN, RALPH P., *Colossians: The Church's Lord and the Christian's Liberty* (Paternoster Press, 1972).
—— *Colossians and Philemon* (*NCB*) (Oliphants, 1974).
MOULE, C. F. D., *The Epistles to the Colossians and Philemon* (*CGT*) (CUP, 1957).
MOULE, H. C. G., *Colossians and Philemon* (CUP, 1893).
MÜLLER, J. J., *The Epistles of Paul to the Philippians and to Philemon* (*NICNT*) (Eerdmans, 1955).
MURRAY, JOHN, *Collected Writings,* vol. 2 (Banner of Truth, 1977).
—— *Principles of Conduct* (Tyndale, 1957).
PINK, ARTHUR W., *Gleanings from Paul* (Moody Press, 1967).
POOLE, MATTHEW, *Commentary on the Holy Bible* ,vol. 3 (Banner of Truth, 1963).
RADFORD, LEWIS B., *The Epistle to the Colossians and the Epistle to Philemon* (*WC*) (Methuen, 1931).
RIDDERBOS, HERMAN, *Paul – An Outline of His Theology* (Eerdmans, 1975).
ROBBINS, RAY F., *Philemon* (*BBC*) (Broadman Press, 1971).
ROBINSON, J. ARMITAGE, *St Paul's Epistle to the Ephesians* (James Clarke, n.d.).

RUPPRECHT, ARTHUR A., *Philemon* (*EBC*) (Zondervan, 1978).
SCROGGIE, W. GRAHAM, *Know Your Bible,* vol. 2 (Pickering & Inglis, 1956).
SIMPSON, E. K., AND BRUCE, F. F., *Ephesians and Colossians* (*NICNT*) (Eerdmans, 1957).
TRAPP, JOHN, *Commentary on the New Testament* (Sovereign Grace Book Club, 1958).
TRENCH, R. C., *Synonyms of the New Testament* (James Clarke, 1961).
VAUGHAN, CURTIS, *Colossians* (*EBC*) (Zondervan, 1978).
VINCENT, MARVIN R., *The Epistles to the Philippians and Philemon* (*ICC*) (T. & T. Clark, 1972).
—— *Word Studies in the New Testament* (MacDonald, n.d.).
WARFIELD, B. B., *Faith and Life* (Banner of Truth, 1974).
WHITE, R. E. O., *Colossians* (*BBC*) (Broadman Press, 1971).
WILLIAMS, A. LUKYN, *The Epistles of Paul the Apostle to the Colossians and Philemon* (*CGT*) (CUP, 1907).
WILSON, R. MCL., *Gnosis and the New Testament* (Basil Blackwell, 1968).
YAMAUCHI, EDWIN, *Pre-Christian Gnosticism* (Tyndale, 1973).
ZAHN, THEODOR, *Introduction to the New Testament,* vol. 1 (Klock & Klock, 1977).

1 & 2 Thessalonians

INTRODUCTION

After leaving Philippi where they had been so 'shamefully treated' by the magistrates [*1 Thess.* 2:2; cf. *Acts* 16], Paul and Silas took the Egnatian highway through Amphipolis and Apollonia on the hundred-mile journey which brought them to the important city of Thessalonica. Ancient Therme was refounded as Thessalonica in 315 BC by Cassander who named it after his wife, a half-sister of Alexander the Great. Strategically situated at the head of the Thermaic Gulf and endowed with a fine harbour, it was the junction of the great land and sea routes between East and West. These natural advantages had secured its prosperity and attracted a large Jewish colony. Thessalonica was also fortunate in its political privileges, for it was the capital of the Roman province of Macedonia (146 BC), and as a 'free' city (42 BC) its citizens had the right to choose their own rulers or 'politarchs'.

It was probably early in AD 50 when Paul and Silas, accompanied by Timothy, first came with the gospel to Thessalonica. Following his usual practice Paul began the mission in the synagogue. Here for three successive sabbaths he sought to show from the Scriptures that the Messiah had to suffer and rise again, and that the fulfilment of Israel's hope was found in the very Jesus he proclaimed. This revolutionary doctrine was believed by some Jews and many of the 'God-fearing' Gentiles,[1] among whom were quite a number of notable women, with the result that they left the synagogue to meet at Jason's house where Paul and Silas continued to instruct them for a few more weeks. But the loss of their prospective converts to these itinerant teachers so enraged the Jews that they soon contrived a way to bring the visit to

[1] Dissatisfied with what paganism had to offer, such Gentiles were drawn by the teaching of Judaism but repelled by its ritual requirements (cf. Morris, *Tyndale Commentary*, p. 12).

an abrupt end. With the help of some ruffians they caused a riot in the city, and in the hope of laying hands on Paul and his associates they attacked Jason's house. When they failed to find them they brought Jason and some fellow-believers before the politarchs, alleging that these men had received the agitators whose seditious claims for another Emperor called Jesus had turned the world upside down! The civic authorities dared not ignore such a serious charge, but in view of the lack of evidence to support it the accused were bound over to keep the peace and then dismissed. It was therefore to remove the threat of any further action against their Thessalonian friends that the missionaries departed by night for Beroea [cf. *Acts* 17:1–10].

This apparent desertion of the infant church in the face of persecution greatly distressed Paul, especially as he was forced to leave before its members were thoroughly established in their newly-found faith. From Beroea, where the Jews of Thessalonica were again responsible for the interruption of another promising work, the apostle proceeded alone to Athens. Here he was joined by Timothy [*1 Thess.* 3:2], whom he at once sent back to Thessalonica to see how the church was faring in his absence. When Timothy later rejoined Paul in Corinth it was with heartening news of the Thessalonians' firm faith and influential witness. But there were also problems of belief and behaviour which largely stemmed from an inadequate grasp of what Paul had taught them about the return of Christ. As unexpected hindrances had so far prevented a further visit, Paul immediately wrote to express his joy in their progress, to rebut the slanders of his Jewish opponents, and to supply what was lacking in their faith. In regard to Christ's promised appearing, some were discouraged lest loved ones who had died would be at a disadvantage as compared with those who were still alive when it happened, while others were encouraged to idleness by their immediate expectation of this event.

Although Paul's first letter evidently served to correct the sexual laxity which is reflected in 1 Thessalonians 4:3–8, further reports confirmed that the eschatological perplexities in Thessalonica continued unresolved. Accordingly, this was soon followed by a second letter in which he reminded them of the things that must precede the Lord's return, for the imminence of this hope did not imply its immediate fulfilment. Meanwhile he commanded them to lead disciplined and useful lives by earning their own bread and minding their own business. Laziness was no sign of a superior spirituality; the slacker who refused to work should not be supplied with free food! His sharp reproof showed that the apostle would not allow any wedge to be driven between their heavenly interest and the practical concerns of everyday living.

As we read these early documents of the Christian Church today, we are inspired by Paul's intense love for his flock and challenged by the Thessalonians' virile faith. And if we discover that the problems they faced were not peculiar to their day, we also realize that the inspired answers they received are valid for all time.

1 THESSALONIANS

CHAPTER ONE

Paul's associates, Silvanus and Timothy, join with him in sending greetings to the church of the Thessalonians [verse 1]. They thank God for their faith, love, and patience, for these evident tokens of their election show that the gospel came to them not only in word but also in the Spirit's power and in much assurance [verses 2–5]. The Thessalonians became imitators of their teachers and of the Lord, with the result that their witness was an example to the Christians of Macedonia and Achaia, who reported how they had turned from idols to serve the living God and to wait for his Son from heaven [verses 6–10].

1: Paul, and Silvanus, and Timothy, unto the church of the Thessalonians in God the Father and the Lord Jesus Christ: Grace to you and peace.

If this is not Paul's earliest Epistle (probably Galatians was written before it), the greeting is certainly his briefest (only 19 Greek words). This is conventional in form but bears the stamp of its distinctively Christian content. The unusual omission of 'apostle' from the greeting shows that Paul's authority was not in question and that he enjoyed particularly happy relations with the Christians of Macedonia [cf. *Phil.* 1:1].

Paul, and Silvanus, and Timothy: Paul is clearly the real author of the letter [cf. 2:18; 3:5; 5:27], but Silvanus and Timothy are here named as 'the joint asserters and approvers of the truth contained in it' (James

Fergusson). For they both share his concern for the Thessalonians' spiritual progress and also agree on the best means of promoting it. Silas, who was a member of the Jerusalem church and a Roman citizen, replaced Barnabas as Paul's colleague on the second missionary journey [*Acts* 15:40], while Timothy was the young man who joined them at Lystra and was to become the apostle's most trusted lieutenant [*Acts* 16:1].

Unto the church of the Thessalonians in God the Father and the Lord Jesus Christ: Having been called out from idolatry to eternal life by the gospel [verse 9], this company of believers now formed 'the church' whose life was rooted in God and Christ [cf. *Col.* 3:3] – an expression which distinguishes the Persons even as it affirms their absolute equality (see B. B. Warfield, 'God our Father and the Lord Jesus Christ', *Biblical Doctrines*, p. 213). The essence of their faith was in knowing God as their Father and the Lord Jesus Christ as their Redeemer. In the historical Jesus who had died and risen again for their salvation [4:14], they joyfully recognized the Divine Lord and Anointed Deliverer through whom they had been reconciled to God [cf. *Acts* 2:36].

Grace to you and peace: As usual Paul's prayer for his readers is that they may be blessed with the grace that brings peace and prosperity to the whole man. 'Grace is the love of God, spontaneous, beautiful, unearned, at work in Jesus Christ for the salvation of sinful men; peace is the effect and fruit in man of the reception of grace' (James Denney).

2: We give thanks to God always for you all, making mention of you in our prayers;

One old commentator, cited by William Neil, remarks 'There are some prayers in Homer's poems but how few thanksgivings!' But though such ingratitude is characteristic of paganism [*Rom.* 1:21], a constant spirit of thankfulness marks out those who have been made sensible of God's multiplied mercies. Hence Paul, Silas, and Timothy are daily filled with fervent thanksgiving to God as they think of what his grace has wrought in the lives of these Thessalonians. Their prayers for their converts' continuing progress in the faith are pervaded with grateful praise to God because every believer is a standing monument to Divine mercy. This thanksgiving is not therefore a mere rhetorical device intended to win over the readers with fulsome flattery [2:5], but is rather an earnest attempt on the part of the missionaries 'to raise the thoughts of their converts to the God on whom they are wholly dependent, and in consequence to rouse them to fresh efforts' (George Milligan).

3: remembering without ceasing your work of faith and labour of love and patience of hope in our Lord Jesus Christ, before our God and Father;

Continually bearing in mind your work resulting from faith and (your) exertion prompted by love and (your) endurance inspired by hope in our Lord Jesus Christ in the presence of our God and Father (Hendriksen): This verse describes the immediate ground of the thanksgiving, while the following verse discloses its ultimate ground ('knowing . . . your election'). The arrangement of the great triad of Christian graces in the ascending scale of faith, love, and hope is appropriate in a letter which largely deals with the 'hope' of Christ's return; just as it was natural to assign the dominant position to 'love' in the passage devoted to extolling that grace [*1 Cor.* 13:13; cf. 5:8; *Gal.* 5:5, 6; *Col.* 1:4, 5].

Here Paul first thanks God for the work that results from faith. Theirs was no barren assent to a dogma [*James* 2:17], but the dynamic outworking of a life-transforming principle [*Gal.* 5:6]. This work should not be too narrowly defined, though it no doubt included their active propagation of the gospel [verse 8]. He next mentions the laborious toil that is prompted by love. As George Findlay says, work points to *the thing done*, as a matter of achievement: labour indicates the *pains spent* in doing it, as matter of exertion. '*Work* may be easy and delightful; *labour* is toilsome; no selfish man will endure it for another's good. Hence *labour* is the test of *love*.'

This was a new concept of love which was supremely exemplified by Christ, and for which Christians adopted a new word and made it their own (*agape*). It is the self-denying, sacrificial love that gives itself unstintingly in the service of others. Finally Paul refers to the endurance that is inspired by hope in our Lord Jesus Christ. This is not the spirit which suffers with resignation; it is the fortitude which meets trials in the certain hope of the final victory at Christ's coming [cf. verse 6; 3:2–6]. And to speak of this hope naturally brings to mind the day when believers will rejoice in the presence of the God whom they know as their Father [3:13].

4: knowing, brethren beloved of God, your election,

Knowing: 'By the manner of their receiving the gospel, and the evident operation of the graces of God's Spirit, the apostle knew their election of God. We cannot know election as in God's secret decree, but as made manifest in the fruits and effects of it. As there is a knowledge of things *a priori*, when we argue from the cause to the effect, so *a posteriori*, when we argue from the effects to the cause. And thus the apostle came to know their election. Not, we hope it, or conjecture it, but we know it; and not by extraordinary revelation, but by evident outward tokens' (Matthew Poole).

Brethren: So conscious is Paul of the closeness of this bond with his readers that he uses the word twenty-one times in these epistles. As Leon Morris well says, 'There is a sense in which all men may be thought of as brothers. The fraternity of a club or lodge may be very real. But in the sense that matters, brethren are brethren in Christ. The Christian brotherhood is the fellowship of the redeemed'.

Beloved of God: The participle 'beloved' is not in the present tense, 'as though the Thessalonians were simply loved now, in consequence of their newly-acquired Christian worth; it is in the Greek perfect tense, signifying a love existing in the past and realized in the present, the antecedent and foundation of their goodness' (Findlay) [cf. *1 John* 3:1].

Your election: The unexplained reference to 'election' advertises the fact that this truth had formed an essential part of Paul's proclamation of the gospel in Thessalonica. Unlike those who take it upon themselves to conceal what God has been pleased to reveal, the apostle always declared the whole counsel of God [*Acts* 20:27], and not simply that part of it which would not offend the autonomy of the natural man. This is an eternal election of God [*Eph.* 1:4; cf. *2 Thess.* 2:13] to final salvation [*Eph.* 1:11], of a people whom He gave to Christ 'before times eternal' [*2 Tim.* 1:9; *John* 6:38,39; 17:2–12], without respect to their foreseen faith [*Rom.* 9:11], the grand purpose of which is to redound to the glory of his grace [*Eph.* 1:6].

5: how that our gospel came not unto you in word only, but also in power, and in the Holy Spirit, and in much assurance; even as ye know what manner of men we showed ourselves toward you for your sake.

Because our gospel came not unto you in word only (ASV margin): Paul knew the Thessalonians to be elect because 'the Spirit was in us who preached [verse 5], and in you who welcomed the word [verses 6–10]. By saying "our gospel came" instead of "we came with the gospel" [*2 Cor.* 10:4], Paul puts the emphasis more upon the message as the means of realizing God's call than upon the bearers of the message' (James E. Frame). For though preachers must come and speak the message of salvation [*Rom.* 10:14], it needs more than a declaration in 'word only' to bring the dead to life [*Eph.* 2:1] 'Our gospel' means that it was theirs by divine commission and personal experience. They had not run without being sent, nor had they idly spoken of things unknown to themselves – two essential qualifications for effective preaching.

But also in power, and in the Holy Spirit, and in much assurance: Here 'power' (the singular shows that charismatic manifestations are not in view) refers to the clothing of the preachers' words with that vital force which had brought salvation to the Thessalonians [cf. *Rom.* 1:16; *1 Cor.* 2:4]. This benign power [contrast *2 Thess.* 2:9] is always associated with 'the Holy Spirit', whose unique prerogative it is to make the gospel meaningful to men [*1 Cor.* 12:3]. The ambiguity of the final phrase 'in much assurance' is removed in Moffatt's rendering 'with ample conviction on our part'. These preachers were so conscious of the assistance of the Holy Spirit in their ministry that they were fully convinced that God's word would accomplish the work for which He sent it forth [*Isa.* 55:11].

Even as ye know what manner of men we showed ourselves toward you for your sake: Paul now appeals to what the Thessalonians know of the kind of ministry that he and his companions exercised among them as a sufficient reply to the accusations of their opponents [cf. 2:1–12; 17–20]. It seems reasonable to assume that the unbelieving Jews of Thessalonica were responsible for these attacks upon their integrity. Apparently they had said that the missionaries would never return to their deluded converts because they were nothing but wandering teachers who scratched a living by imposing upon the credulous from place to place. Thus they sought to offset the effects of the message they hated by discrediting its messengers.

6: And ye became imitators of us, and of the Lord, having received the

word in much affliction, with joy of the Holy Spirit; 7: So that ye became an ensample to all that believe in Macedonia and in Achaia.

This shows that the subjective confidence of the preachers was verified by the objective change in their hearers. The verb marks the moment when their changed lives gave visible evidence of their election. The example of Christ's witnesses is placed first because 'the Thessalonians came into contact with the model, Christ, through the model copies of Christ, Paul and his companions. If they had not been attracted by the latter they could not have known the former, the chief attraction. So it is the reflection of Christ in us that today induces others to become Christlike' (R. C. H. Lenski).

When amid great tribulation you welcomed the word with joy imparted by the Holy Spirit (Hendriksen): The great change effected by the word they so readily received amid the pressures of persecution was also accompanied by the joy of the Holy Spirit. It was never Paul's practice to portray an easy road to heaven, for he knew that all who become imitators of the Lord are called to share in the rejection which He met from an unbelieving world [3:3, 4; *John* 16:33; *Acts* 14:22; *Phil.* 1:29; *2 Tim.* 1:8]. But the early Christians not only expected persecution as the inevitable accompaniment of genuine discipleship, they also received it as a badge of honour with Spirit inspired joy [*Acts* 5:41].

So that ye became an ensample to all that believe in Macedonia and in Achaia: The result of their imitation of the Lord was that the Thessalonian church became a 'model' or 'pattern' for imitation to all who believed in the provinces of Macedonia and Achaia. News of their faithful witness in the face of heavy trials had radiated from this important centre to encourage believers throughout both provinces to stand firm. Thus an impressive proof of the power of a living faith in Christ was furnished by the fact that the imitators were now the imitated!

8: For from you hath sounded forth the word of the Lord, not only in Macedonia and Achaia, but in every place your faith to God-ward is gone forth; so that we need not to speak anything.

This explains and expands the previous verse. Paul speaks of the gospel, which is the Lord's word to men, as sounding forth from them – the perfect tense indicating not a finished act but a continuing process. Certainly this word did not originate with them, but they had received it so wholeheartedly that its echoes were heard everywhere. Such was the fame of their faith that they had become missionaries to the whole world by way of report!

So that we need not to speak anything, i.e. of your faith in God: 'Where men's deeds speak and commend men, words may be silent. And the apostle might have thought it needful to have divulged these things abroad for the advantage of the gospel, and the examples of others, if he had not been forestalled by the report already spread abroad. The good examples of the people may ease their ministers of some labour in spreading the gospel' (Poole).

9: For they themselves report concerning us what manner of entering in we had unto you; and how ye turned unto God from idols, to serve a living and true God,

For they themselves are reporting about us, what kind of entering in we had among you (Hendriksen): Thus when people keep telling Paul of the success of the Thessalonian mission he can hardly doubt that those it had benefited will know how to deal with the base allegations of his opponents [verse 5; 2:1–12]. What follows gives the substance of these reports in words that are evidently intended to remind them of the preaching through which they had been delivered from the power of darkness [cf. *1 Cor.* 10:19, 20].

And how ye turned unto God: The significance of their conversion was seen in their *turning* from idols to *serve* the living God and in *waiting* for the advent of his Son from heaven [verse 10]. As B. B. Warfield says, 'There are two groups of terms in the New Testament used to express the great change which is experienced by him who enters upon the Christian life. One of these groups includes those terms which describe the change from the manward side, and inform us what part man himself takes in it. The other group includes the terms that 'describe the change from the Godward side, and tell us what part God takes in it. Man repents, makes amendment, and turns unto God; but it is God who renews him, begets him again, quickens or creates him into newness of life. The two groups describe the two sides of the same great occurrence, and must be combined in any complete conception of its nature and implications' (*Selected Shorter Writings*, vol. 1, p. 267).

So though the Thessalonians did turn to God, they were enabled to do so only because the gospel came to them in the power of the Holy Spirit [verse 5].

From idols, to serve: Pagan belief in a multitude of gods meant that the real power in the world was not found in any of them, but in some sort of fate to which even its deities were subject. As man could not enter into a moral relation with this blank necessity, no Greek or Roman could take in the idea of 'serving' a god (Denney). Hence the liberation of the ancient world from the shackles of its superstition required the apostolic witness to the One Supreme God as its Creator and Redeemer, for it is this alone that enables men to regard the whole of life as a moral service which they owe to him [cf. *Rom.* 12:1,2]. 'Only the man who has learned to put himself wholly in subjection to God is truly converted to Him' (John Calvin).

A living: The absence of the article which is reflected in the literal rendering of the ASV draws attention to the *character* of God, who alone has life in himself, 'and is the author and preserver of life unto others, *Acts* 17:28' (Fergusson), in contrast to the lifeless idols of men's hands which cannot move a finger to help their deluded worshippers [cf. *Psa.* 115: 4ff, *Isa.* 40: 18ff.].

And true God: The meaning is not the true as opposed to the false; the contrast is between the true and the unreal. He is '*very* God, as distinguished from idols and all other false gods, the dreams of the diseased fancy of men, with no substantial existence in the world of realities' (R. C. Trench).

10: and to wait for his Son from heaven, whom he raised from the dead, even Jesus, who delivereth us from the wrath to come.

The word 'to await' occurs only here in the New Testament; it 'implies *sustained* expectation' (Findlay). Paul's use of this intensive word in connection with the hope of Christ's appearing is indeed suggestive. As Matthew Poole well says, 'They believed that he was gone to heaven, and would come again, which are two great articles of the Christian faith. And though there was nothing in sense or reason, or any tradition, to persuade them of it, yet they believed it upon the apostle's preaching it. And though the time of his coming was unknown to them, yet their faith immediately put them upon waiting for it. And the certain time of his coming is kept secret, that the saints in every age may wait for it. Though he will not come till the end of the world, yet the saints ought to be influenced with the expectation of it in all generations that do precede it'.

Whom he raised from the dead: 'The theology of Paul is, that the Father raised the Son from the dead, and this resurrection has an evidential connection with the Sonship and the completion of His earthly work [*Rom.* 1:4]' (John Eadie).

Jesus, our Deliverer from the wrath to come (F. F. Bruce): Although the notion seems so strange to modern ears long accustomed to hearing nothing but the love of God, deliverance from the wrath of God was an essential element in the apostolic preaching of the gospel. Here the Jesus who died to become the Deliverer of his people is shown to be one and the same with the glorified Son whose advent they await in the confidence that God has not appointed them to wrath, but to the obtaining of salvation through him [5:9].

'For, though the wrath of God is always being revealed to a greater or less extent in the judgments of God that find expression in the providential ordering of human history, the history both of nations and of individuals, it remains true that in His mercy He endures "with much longsuffering the vessels of wrath fitted to destruction" [*Rom.* 9:22]. In consequence there must be, and the Bible again and again affirms that there will be, a final day of judgment which will prove a day of full salvation for the believer, but will be a day of uttermost wrath for the wicked' (R. V. G. Tasker, *The Biblical Doctrine of the Wrath of God*, p. 37).

CHAPTER TWO

In refuting the charges brought against the missionaries by their opponents, Paul reminds the Thessalonian Christians of the truthfulness and sincerity of their preaching, of the purity of their conduct, and of their strong affection towards them [verses 1–12]. After having toiled so hard among them, Paul and his companions are thankful to God that the Thessalonians not only received the gospel as the word of God but were also prepared to endure the hardships inflicted upon them by their Jewish persecutors [verses 13–16]. The enforced absence from the beloved converts who are his hope and joy is keenly felt by Paul, who had wished twice to return to them, but Satan hindered him [verses 17–20].

1: For yourselves, brethren, know our entering in unto you, that it hath not been found vain:

For you yourselves know, brethren (RSV): This 'you yourselves' is opposed to the 'they themselves' of 1:9 – the Thessalonians know at first-hand what others are merely reporting about them. For 'you are the ones who experienced it. The people in the provinces talk about it far and wide, they have only heard the story, *you* are the ones who *know*' (Lenski). With this brilliant stroke Paul begins his defence against the attacks of the Jews, for clearly no witnesses were better qualified to vouch for the genuineness of the missionaries' motives and methods than their own converts [2:1–12].

Those who have turned from the futile worship of dumb idols are in the best position to know that the 'entering in' of the preachers was not in vain, i.e. it was not empty of reality and power. Our mission to you was not *empty*, or 'hollow, like a vessel that has nothing in it. This is a litotes which states the matter negatively but intends it positively: "not an empty one" = one filled to the brim with most blessed effects. The perfect "has been" = and still remains so to this day' (Lenski).

2: but having suffered before and been shamefully treated, as ye know, at Philippi, we waxed bold in our God to speak unto you the gospel of God in much conflict.

Despite the scarred bodies [*Acts* 16:23] and smarting spirits [*Acts* 16:37] that were the painful badges of their service in Philippi, Paul and Silas entered Thessalonica with the same intense seriousness of purpose with which they had begun their mission in Macedonia. That they were thus undaunted by *injury* and *insult* were credentials sufficient to show the Thessalonians that theirs was not the empty entering in of religious charlatans.

We waxed bold in our God to speak unto you the gospel of God in much conflict: Paul here recalls how they had pursued their commission with the courageous outspokenness born of their confidence in God, for they were supremely conscious of the fact that their message came not from men but from God. This shows us that the gospel is no human expedient to palliate the symptoms of sin; it is God's cure for the fatal condition itself. 'Our age can do with the reminder that the Christian faith is not the accumulated wisdom of pious souls, nor the insight of men of religious genius, but the divine plan for dealing with man's sin' (Morris). The apostle's reference to the fierce strife which their ministry had stirred up in Thessalonica was a telling reminder of the cost of remaining faithful in the face of such violent opposition.

3: For our exhortation is not of error, nor of uncleanness, nor in guile:

This evidently reflects the charges that had been made against Paul and his assistants by their enemies. However, these attacks were so contrary to what their converts knew of them from first-hand experience that they called for nothing more than a flat denial to prove their falsity. Indeed, it is because the appeal of their preaching is that of *God's* gospel [verse 2] – which is the preaching of *God's* Word to men with *his* interests at heart – that it could no more spring from 'error' or 'impurity' than it could be carried out in an atmosphere of 'deceit'. 'Their preaching did not spring from some delusion or mistake. Paul was neither fool nor knave, neither deceived nor deceiver. Nor was his mission a sordid attempt to make a good thing out of preaching, the impure motive being either to secure money [cf. *greed*, verses 5 and 9], or to gain a position of importance [verse 6] and popularity' (James Moffatt). This explanation of the second charge is more consistent with the context than that which restricts it to *sensual* impurity. And though their detractors were certainly not above making the accusation, they were at least astute enough to realize that it could only be greeted with blank incredulity.

4: but even as we have been approved of God to be intrusted with the gospel, so we speak; not as pleasing men, but God who proveth our hearts.

On the contrary (NIV): Paul refutes these accusations by showing that they did not teach error for God had entrusted them with the message; that their motives were not impure for they had been approved by God; and that their methods were not deceitful for their aim was always to please God, not men.

As we have been approved of God to be intrusted with the gospel, so we speak: As they have been 'attested' (Moffatt) by God to preach the gospel, so it is as tried and trusted men that they habitually tell out the good news. That they so stand approved before God is not due to any innate worthiness of their own, but rests solely upon the grace of God by which they were fitted for the exercise of this commission.

Not as pleasing men, but God who proveth our hearts: 'Men be they pleased or displeased, God must not be displeased' (John Trapp). Thus their fidelity to this divine doctrine was the proof of their divine calling, for they preached not to secure the approval of men but to please God [cf. *Gal.* 1:10]. 'The "heart", in the language of the Bible, is not the seat of the feelings alone; it is "the inner man", the real self, the centre and meeting-point of all our thoughts, feelings, and resolves. It is there that God proves us: "The Lord looketh upon the heart". No impure motive or crafty expedient, such as might deceive men, escapes Him. The sense of this continual and omniscient scrutiny makes any kind of dishonesty impossible to the Apostle' (Findlay).

5: For neither at any time were we found using words of flattery, as ye know, not a cloak of covetousness, God is witness;

Paul can also claim that their behaviour in Thessalonica was in complete conformity with these general principles [verses 3, 4]. Their ministry among them had been devoid of flattery, greed [verse 5], and self-importance [verse 6]. Such vices certainly belonged to the verbal tricksters of the day, but they were entirely foreign to the ambassadors of Christ. As to their *words*, the Thessalonians knew that they had not come to them 'with cajoling address' (Frame) in order to gain their own ends. And as to their *motives*, God knew that their preaching was not purely 'a pretext for (satisfying) greed' (Arndt-Gingrich). 'In that which was open to men's observation he appealed to their own testimony; but in regard to what was hidden, to whom could he appeal but to God?' (Augustine).

6: nor seeking glory of men, neither from you nor from others, when we might have claimed authority as apostles of Christ.

The phrase 'we might have claimed authority' is literally 'being able to be in weight' (cf. NEB: 'we might have made our weight felt'). This is the '*weight* of influence which someone enjoys or claims', and it means to 'wield authority, insist on one's importance' (Arndt-Gingrich). Paul's third disclaimer is not that they waived their right to financial support, but that neither in Thessalonica nor elsewhere had they ever come 'seeking' (he does not say 'receiving') honour of men, though as Christ's apostles they had the right to expect it. Since at least Silas and possibly Timothy are included in the term 'apostles', it cannot be used here in its highest meaning of those directly called by Christ, but carries the broader sense of 'missionaries', i.e. those who have been commissioned and sent out by the church [cf. *Acts* 13:4].

7: But we were gentle in the midst of you, as when a nurse cherisheth her own children:

Far from showing themselves to be flatterers given to greed and self-importance, they had manifested a mildness in their midst which was born of pure unselfishness [verses 8, 9, 11]. In spite of the fact that 'babes' (*nepioi*) is the better attested reading, 'gentle' (*epioi*) is to be preferred because it is the only word that makes sense in this context.

As when a nurse cherisheth her own children: 'In this metaphor he expresses two points which he had touched upon, viz. that he has sought neither glory nor gain among the Thessalonians. A mother in nursing her child makes no show of authority and does not stand on any dignity. This, says Paul, was his attitude, since he willingly refrained from claiming the honour that was due to him, and undertook any kind of duty without being ruffled or making any show. In the second place, a mother in rearing her children reveals a wonderful and extraordinary love, because she spares no trouble or effort, avoids no care, is not wearied by their coming and going, and gladly even gives her own life blood to be drained' (Calvin).

8: even so, being affectionately desirous of you, we were well pleased to impart unto you, not the gospel of God only, but also our own souls, because ye were become very dear to us.

This is a clear statement of the truth embodied in the metaphor of the previous verse. It should be noted that Paul speaks of what they gladly did, and not merely of what they were willing to do. Being filled with yearning for the Thessalonians the missionaries had not come to get but to give, and to give not only the gospel of God but also their own 'souls' (or rather *selves*, i.e. their whole being). Truly their entrance was not in vain [verse 1], for theirs had not been the lifeless preaching of loveless hearts. It was an *effective* proclamation because it sprang from this total commitment of themselves in love to those whom they were seeking to reach with the gospel. We must learn that such love is the mainspring of evangelism; without it no souls are won for God.

Because you had become very dear to us (RSV): This deep bond of affection had been forged through the preaching and receiving of God's gospel. For when their conversion had shown the Thessalonians to be beloved of God [1:4], they became still more dear in the eyes of God's servants.

9: For ye remember brethren, our labour and travail: working night and day, that we might not burden any of you, we preached unto you the gospel of God.

This reminder that Paul and his companions had not been a burden on the Thessalonians is a further appeal to their own experience. They well knew what a sacrifice these preachers had made in order to bring them the gospel without charge, toiling to the point of weariness and struggling constantly against hardship.

The expression 'night and day' (i.e. 'a part of the night, a part of the day, and not all night and all day long' – Lenski) indicates the long hours it cost them to maintain their independence while still discharging their God-given commission. Although Paul would accept help from established churches [cf. *Phil.* 4:16; *2 Cor.* 11:8], his policy when planting new churches was to pay his own way by working at his trade as a tentmaker [*Acts* 18:3]. This arduous choice at once freed him from the suspicion of making money out of the gospel and proved the purity of his motives in preaching it.

This is the third time that Paul uses the phrase 'the gospel of God' [verses 2, 8]. In verse 2 it suggests 'the greatness of the charge entrusted to Paul; here, *the greatness of the boon gratuitously bestowed* on the Thessalonians' (Findlay). 'We preached' means that they proclaimed as heralds *God's* gospel, without amendment or alteration of any kind. As Leon Morris crisply comments, 'The gospel preacher is not at liberty to substitute his view of the need of the moment for the God-given message of the cross'.

10: Ye are witnesses, and God also, how holily and righteously and unblameably we behaved ourselves toward you that believe:

Ye are witnesses, and God also, 'Much they could judge of, and on such points he appeals to them; much they could not judge of, and on such points lying beyond their cognizance he appeals to God' (Eadie).

How holily and righteously and unblameably we behaved ourselves toward you that believe: Not as though the conduct of these heralds was otherwise towards unbelievers, but only the believers in Thessalonica were competent to judge the spiritual nature of their devotion towards them. As if to say, 'Whatever unbelievers may think of us, you who believe our message know very well that the way we lived among you was a confirmation and not a contradiction of that testimony'. On the positive side, 'holily' and 'righteously' describe their behaviour before God and men, while 'unblameably' covers the negative aspect of both these relations (so Ellicott).

11: as ye know how we dealt with each one of you, as a father with his own children, exhorting you, and encouraging you, and testifying, 12: to the end that ye should walk worthily of God, who calleth you into his own kingdom and glory.

Paul concludes his apologia with a fresh metaphor which recalls the faithful pastoral care that was given to every convert. 'The Apostle compared himself to a *nurse-mother* [verse 7] in his tender, gentle affection; now he is a *father* in the fidelity and manly strength of his counsels' (Findlay). The dual nature of this 'exhorting' is specified by 'encouraging' and 'testifying' [cf. NEB: 'appealing to you by encouragement, as well as by solemn injunctions']. Thus to encourage and admonish believers is essential for their spiritual progress, which will be in proportion to their grasp of the privileges and the responsibilities of their high calling.

To the end that ye should walk worthily of God: As Findlay points out, a special feature of these Epistles is the continued emphasis which Paul lays on the relation of the Christian believer to God. 'It was *God's* message the apostles of Christ had brought to the Thessalonians [verses 2, 9]; "unto *God*, the living and true", they had "turned from their idols to serve" Him [1:9]. They must, therefore, now live a life "worthy *of God*" – worthy of those who have such a God and are His servants and sons'. Our compliance with this lofty demand becomes a practical possibility only through the enabling power of God's calling [cf. *Phil.* 2:13].

Who calleth you into his own kingdom and glory: The present tense is used because God is calling to that which, in its fullest realization, is still future. For though believers are already by grace the subjects of God's kingly rule, they yet await the final manifestation of the kingdom in glory. 'The *glory* to which He calls us is His own eternal glory, of which all the true members of the Messianic kingdom shall be partakers; comp. *Rom.* 5:2' (Ellicott).

13: And for this cause we also thank God without ceasing, that, when ye received from us the word of the message, even the word of God, ye accepted it not as the word of men, but, as it is in truth, the word of God, which also worketh in you that believe.

And for this reason we on our part thank God without ceasing (Lightfoot): That the labour of Paul and his colleagues had not been in vain affords occasion for the renewed expression of their constant thankfulness to God. 'We on our part' answers to 'you yourselves' in verse 1, and marks the transition from the teachers to the taught. 'Having appealed to the Thessalonians' experience of them as missionaries, they now thank God for their own experience of the Thessalonians as converts' (Alfred Plummer).

That when you received by tradition from us the preached word of God, you accepted it not as the word of men, but as what it really is, the word of God (Ridderbos): This shows us that to change men's hearts requires more than an external hearing of the gospel; they must also welcome it for what it really is, no word of man's devising but the veritable word of God. Now it is because the ascended Lord stands behind the testimony of his apostles that their delivered word is clothed with his authority and can be spoken of as the word of God (so Herman Ridderbos in 'The Canon of the New Testament', *Revelation and the Bible*, p. 194). Hence Paul later urges the Thessalonians to stand fast by holding to the traditions they were taught, 'whether by word, or by epistle of ours' [*2 Thess.* 2:15]. For as the revelation granted to the apostles was unique and unrepeatable it soon became necessary to commit to writing the testimony they first circulated in oral form. 'The apostle cannot, therefore, have any successor who can replace him as bearer of the revelation for future generations, but he must continue *himself* to fulfil his function in the Church today: *in* the Church, not *by* the Church, but *by his word*, "through their word" [*John* 17.20], in other words, by his *writings*' (O. Cullmann, 'The Tradition', *The Early Church*, p. 80).

Which also worketh in you that believe: 'Also' brings forward a further feature of the heard word, which because of its Divine origin 'also' works powerfully in those who 'believe', the present tense showing the condition for the continuing experience of its working.

14: For ye, brethren, became imitators of the churches of God which are in Judea in Christ Jesus: for ye also suffered the same things of your own countrymen, even as they did of the Jews;

The working of this Word within them had been proved by their steadfast endurance of persecution, through which they 'became imitators' [1:6] of the Judean Christians who were similarly afflicted. Such unity in tribulation showed the unity of their faith. For it was their common allegiance to and interest in Christ which had aroused the hatred of the unbelieving. The all-important phrase 'in Christ Jesus' thus distinguishes the Christian from other Judean communities which claimed to be 'of God', but which by their rejection of the Messiah had become synagogues of Satan [cf. *Rev.* 2:9; 3:9].

For ye also suffered the same things of your own countrymen, even as they did of the Jews: The point of the comparison is that both the Jewish Christians of Judea and the Gentile believers at Thessalonica suffered at the hands of their fellow-countrymen. For though the persecution of the Thessalonians was instigated by the Jews, it could not have succeeded without Gentile help [*Acts* 17:5]. Moreover, as the work progressed, the relatives of those converted would not require any encouragement to oppose the teaching which had wrought this unwelcome change in their kith and kin [*Acts* 17:4]. As Denney says, it is the work of God's Word to produce a new character, not only distinct from that of the unconverted but antagonistic to it, so that to the extent that we experience the power of God's Word, we come into collision with the world that rejects it. This suffering is therefore the seal of faith, for it is a sign that believers are being brought by God 'into fellowship with primitive churches, with apostles and prophets, with the Incarnate Son Himself' [cf. *Heb*. 13:12, 13].

15: who both killed the Lord Jesus and the prophets, and drove out us, and please not God, and are contrary to all men; 16: forbidding us to speak to the Gentiles that they may be saved; to fill up their sins always: but the wrath is come upon them to the uttermost.

This implacable opposition to the gospel by the unbelieving Jews, whether at Thessalonica or in Judea, was nothing new since they killed both the Lord and the prophets, and harried the apostles from place to place. 'The crowning sin of the race is put in the forefront; they slew the Lord Jesus; but before the Lord came, they had slain His prophets; and after He had gone, they expelled His apostles . . . What we have here is not a burst of temper, though there is undoubtedly strong feeling in it; it is the vehement condemnation, by a man in thorough sympathy with the mind and spirit of God, of the principles on which the Jews as a nation had acted at every period of their history' (Denney) [*Acts* 7:51f., cf. *Matt*. 21: 38; 23:31].

And please not God, and are contrary to all men; forbidding us to speak to the Gentiles that they may be saved: Not merely 'contrary' in the sense in which Tacitus and others condemned the Jews for their inveterate hatred of the Gentiles, but more specifically for their consistent opposition to the salvation of the Gentiles (*Acts* 22:21f.]. The gravity of Paul's charge lies in the fact that this hostility was directed against the highest interests of mankind, as was shown by their repeated attempts to silence the preachers of the gospel [cf. *Acts* 17:5, 13; 18:12, etc.]

To fill up their sins: Paul does not mean that this 'was their intention; neither does he speak ironically; but speaking as he often does from that Divine standpoint at which all results are intended and purposed results, not outside of, but within, the counsel of God, he signifies that this Divine end was being secured by their wickedness' (Denney). [cf. *Matt*. 23:32].

Always: Eadie explains: At all times in their history, when they killed God's messengers to them, they were filling up their sin, though it was far from reaching its fulness; but 'in Christ's time and ours, by putting Him to death and chasing out His apostles, the measure of their iniquity was at length filled up'.

But wrath is come upon them to the uttermost: Although the exact meaning of 'to the uttermost' is uncertain ('fully' or 'finally' are the most likely alternatives), it can be said that the phrase 'marks the issue to which the *wrath* had arrived: it had reached its extreme bound, and would at once pass into inflictive judgments. As the cup of the *sin* had been gradually filling, so had the measures of the divine *wrath*' (Ellicott). In accordance with the words of Christ [*Luke* 21:20ff.], Paul saw this wrath as sending the woes that would utterly destroy the apostate system of worship (centred in Temple and Priesthood), which had killed the Lord and spurned the overtures of his grace in the gospel. The hope that Scripture holds out to the Jews therefore does not lie in the re-establishment of what was for ever abolished, but consists in looking upon him 'whom they have pierced' [*Zech.* 12:10].

17: But we, brethren, being bereaved of you for a short season, in presence not in heart, endeavoured the more exceedingly to see your face with great desire:

A new section begins here in which Paul replies to the charge of fickle desertion made against them by their Jewish persecutors at Thessalonica [2:17–3:13]. In fact so far were they from being indifferent to the welfare of their converts, that only the briefest period following the enforced separation found them filled with the most intense longing to see them again. Feeling thus suddenly bereft of their loved ones made them all the more anxious to seek a reunion, but these efforts had been frustrated by circumstances beyond their control [verse 18]. In view of all this, how can the Thessalonians believe the slander 'out of sight, out of mind' – that mere physical separation was the sign of spiritual alienation?

18: because we would fain have come unto you, I Paul once and again; and Satan hindered us.

They had made these endeavours, for they *did* wish to return. But as allegations to the contrary depicted Paul as the chief offender, he protests that he had tried 'more than once' (NEB) to re-visit them. The particular circumstances which stood in the way of their return are unknown to us, but behind these checks to their plans Paul could discern the malign opposition of the Evil One himself [cf. *2 Thess.* 2:9;

2 Cor. 12:7]. 'Hindered' is literally 'to *cut a trench*, or *break up a road*, between one's self and an advancing foe, to prevent his progress' (A. R. Fausset), and so the verb vividly conveys Satan's opposition to the progress of the missionaries. For though Satan is always subject to God's overruling, 'within the limits allotted to him he does hinder God's servants' (Morris).

19: For what is our hope, or joy, or crown of glorying? Are not even ye, before our Lord Jesus at his coming? 20: For ye are our glory and our joy.

These incredible insinuations are now effectively dismissed by Paul's rhetorical questions which reveal the intensity of his feeling for the Thessalonians. 'They say you mean nothing to me, but I say you mean everything to me!' Paul 'is not speaking here of the prospect of a reward or of any selfish rejoicing or triumph. The Thessalonians are his hope and joy, and the crown of his glory, as a child of its parent. So Chrysostom: *Who would not rejoice in such a multitude of children, and in the goodness of those children?*' (J. B. Lightfoot). Hence this glorying will be a glorying in what the grace of God has wrought in them through his ministry ('yet not I, but the grace of God which was with me' – *1 Cor.* 15:10).

Or is it not also you in the presence of our Lord Jesus at his coming? (Eadie): According to most authorities (though not most English versions), 'even' does not express the true force of Paul's *kai* which is more accurately represented by 'also'. What this 'also' implies is well noted by Chrysostom: 'Can you imagine that the Jews are right in asserting that we do not care for you as well as for our other converts?' The word 'coming' (*parousia*) was in secular use as a technical expression for a state visit to a city by a sovereign, whose arrival was marked by the presentation of an appropriate gift. Adolf Deissmann cites a papyrus from the third century BC which speaks of contributions for a crown of gold to be presented to the king at his *parousia*. But in contrast to the costly crown expected by earthly monarchs, Paul says that the Thessalonians themselves are 'the crown of rejoicing' which he will present to the Lord at his coming [verse 20]. This is the *parousia* of the King, whose arrival will usher in the new age for all his people. There is therefore nothing provisional about the *parousia*!

'Of a development within the limits of the concept, or a duplication or triplication of the event there is nowhere any trace. It is a point of eventuation, not a series of successive events . . . It designates *the momentous event*, and consequently that which it opens up must needs carry a supreme, absolute weight to the religious consciousness. To conceive of Paul as focussing his mind on any phase of relative consummation . . . inevitably would involve his relegating the eternal things to a rank of secondary importance. It would have meant a repetition, or perhaps a continuation, of the Judaistic scheme of thought' (Geerhardus Vos, *The Pauline Eschatology*, p. 76).

For ye are our glory and our joy. Paul discredits the false accusations of the Jews by showing the strength of his feeling for his beloved converts. Since the Thessalonians are even now his glory and joy, they will remain so at the *parousia*, for they will constitute the crown which he will lay at the Lord's feet.

CHAPTER THREE

Unable to visit Thessalonica himself, Paul recalls how he had sent Timothy to strengthen and encourage them in their trials, and expresses his thankfulness for the good report of their progress received from Timothy on his return [verses 1–10]. He prays that God will guide him to them, and that the Lord will so cause them to abound in love that they may be blameless before God at the Lord's coming [verses 11–13].

1: Wherefore when we could no longer forbear, we thought it good to be left behind at Athens alone;

So, unable to bear it any longer, I made up my mind to be left behind at Athens all alone (Moffatt): As this version makes clear, by 'we' Paul here means 'I'. When Paul came to Athens he sent for Silas and Timothy to join him there [*Acts* 17:14, 15]. Since Silas was apparently unable to leave Beroea at once, Timothy's arrival was all the more welcome. But such was the apostle's anxiety for the Thessalonians that he willingly parted with him for their sake. 'He shows that he had greater consideration for them than for himself by choosing to be left alone rather than that they should be deserted' (Calvin). The pathos of this utterance not only gives us some insight into what Christian fellowship meant to Paul, but also into what it meant to pursue his mission without it in a city that was given over to idolatry [*Acts* 17:16].

2: and sent Timothy, our brother and God's minister in the gospel of Christ, to establish you, and to comfort you concerning your faith;

And sent Timothy, our brother and fellow-worker with God in the gospel of Christ (ASV margin): If this is the right reading (cf. NEB, NIV), Paul warmly commends Timothy as a brother who is not simply a fellow-worker but God's fellow-worker [*1 Cor.* 3:9]. And the sphere in which he works is the gospel of Christ – 'God's great sphere of operation among men. Timothy preached it, and God rendered it efficacious' (Eadie).

In order to strengthen you and to encourage (you) with respect to your faith (Hendriksen): Knowing their faith was under attack [verse 3], Paul sent Timothy to strengthen the Thessalonians and to encourage them to remain steadfast. But it was only because God confirmed Timothy's words in their hearts that these were not empty exhortations, void of any blessed results.

3: that no man be moved by these afflictions; for yourselves know that hereunto we are appointed.

So that no one might be shaken (or disturbed) by these afflictions (Arndt-Gingrich): The purpose of Timothy's mission was therefore to encourage the Thessalonians to 'stand fast' [verse 8] in the midst of persecution.

For yourselves know that hereunto we are appointed: 'We' here means Paul and the Thessalonians, 'representing at the same time all believers. Those afflictions are not accidental on the one hand, and we do not court them or merit them on the other hand, but our position brings them on us, and God by his grace has set us in that position. Why then be shaken by them, for we cannot avoid them, and when with you we forewarned you of them' (Eadie).

4: For verily, when we were with you, we told you beforehand that we are to suffer affliction; even as it came to pass, and ye know.

In fact, when we were with you, we kept telling you that we would be persecuted. And it turned out that way, as you well know (NIV): A comparison with Acts 14:22 shows that it was Paul's policy to teach his converts that these afflictions were an inevitable consequence of their commitment to Christ, for to be forewarned is to be forearmed.

As Findlay says, this is an appeal to the *facts* of the case and the *experience* of the readers. 'The reminder should help to prevent the Thessalonian believers from being "shaken amid these afflictions"; what had happened was natural and expected; it is "no strange thing" [*1 Pet.* 4:12].'

5: For this cause I also, when I could no longer forbear, sent that I might know your faith, lest by any means the tempter had tempted you, and our labour should be in vain.

For this reason, when I could bear it no longer, I sent that I might know your faith (RSV): This rounds off what has gone before [verses 1, 2]. Paul now gives the most emphatic expression to the anxiety which prompted him to send Timothy; he had to know how their faith was faring under these trials. The fact that he could sum up the whole of their Christian experience in this all-inclusive reference to their faith is highly significant. It shows us that the Christian life is pre-eminently the life of faith, for it is by believing the gospel that the Christian lives.

Lest by any means the tempter had tempted you, and our labour should be in vain: At the time Paul sent Timothy he knew that the Thessalonians were faced with the temptation to abandon their faith, though he had no means of knowing whether they had resisted it. Yet by changing from the indicative ('had tempted') to the subjunctive ('our labour should be in vain'), he manages to assure them that even then he was unwilling to believe that his toil had been fruitless – as it would have been if they had succumbed to the temptation. The apostle here attributes the temptation to the activity of the tempter himself [*Matt.* 4:3], whose object in tempting men to sin is to prove them to be reprobate. 'Satan's first work is to keep men from believing, his next is to destroy their faith: young converts are commonly most assaulted' (Poole).

6: But when Timothy came even now unto us from you, and brought us glad tidings of your faith and love, and that ye have good remembrance of us always, longing to see us, even as we also to see you;

But all anxiety was dispelled on Timothy's return to Paul in Corinth (Silas too had arrived from Beroea), and he immediately writes to express his joy in 'the good news' (RSV). There is a fine play on the word, which is nowhere else in the New Testament used of any other but '*the* good news'. 'Timothy's report was, in effect, *gospel* news, as it witnessed to the power of God's message (*the word of God which worketh in you*, 2:13); and it was the best of news to Paul and Silas – a very "gospel" coming to them in return for the Gospel they had brought to the readers [1:5; 2:2 etc.]' (Findlay).

Of your faith and love: i.e. 'faith' in God and 'love' for man, which together comprise 'the sum total of godliness' (Calvin).

And that ye have good remembrance of us always: 'a kindly recollection. In his unselfishness the Apostle had not pressed for an inquiry on this point. But Timothy brings additional information: not only have the Thessalonians not lost faith in God and Christ while under persecution; they have not forgotten the founder of their church, nor turned against him as the cause of this trouble, nor even grown cold toward him, their enthusiasm damped by disappointment' (Walter F. Adeney).

Longing to see us, even as we also to see you: Moreover, Paul was overjoyed to learn that they were as eager to see him as he was to see them, for the bond which united them had made this longing mutual [cf. 2:8, 17; 3:10].

7: for this cause, brethren, we were comforted over you in all our distress and affliction through your faith:

'For this cause' brings together all that was said in the previous verse. Timothy's report had brought much needed comfort to Paul. It had confirmed that his work in Thessalonica was not wasted, and thus enabled him to rise above the hardship and opposition he faced at Corinth, giving him the encouragement to pursue his mission there in the assurance that his labour was not in vain in the Lord [cf. *Acts* 18:5].

Through your faith: 'It was the faith of the Thessalonians about which Paul had directed Timothy to make inquiry. Now it is their faith that cheers the Apostle. The brotherly love and the kindly remembrance were fruits of this faith. If faith had failed, they would have vanished. Although the Apostle does not here develop his doctrine of faith as in the Epistle to the Romans, even this early Epistle reveals his consciousness of the unique importance of the fundamental grace' (Adeney).

8: for now we live, if ye stand fast in the Lord.

Paul seems to have felt that the progress of the gospel in Macedonia and Achaia largely depended upon the success of his work in this key centre [1:8]. And as the failure of that work would have been the death blow to all his hopes, so the report of their faith came to him as a new lease of life that would last for as long as they stood fast in the power of the Lord. The condition upon which Paul's life depended is here expressed by 'if' with the indicative, perhaps to bring out more strongly his confidence that it would certainly be fulfilled (so Milligan). But Paul is thinking of something beyond his own revived energy: the persistence of Thessalonian faith reveals the vitality of the gospel itself, the word at work in believers, ministered by Christ's servants. They 'live' to purpose, in so far as their message lives on in others (Findlay).

9: For what thanksgiving can we render again unto God for you, for all the joy wherewith we joy for your sakes before our God;

These fears for the stability of his beloved brethren in Thessalonica therefore made Paul's joy in the good news of their flourishing faith all the more intense. It is a joy so great that he is unable to return adequate thanks to God for thus granting them the grace of perseverance. 'Paul views everything as coming from God. His first reaction is: "Thank God!": But how can any thanks be commensurate with the gift of joy he and his assistants have received? . . . As though standing in God's presence, Paul and his helpers live and work; from God they receive this as they do every other blessing; their hearts automatically turn to God' (Lenski).

10: night and day praying exceedingly that we may see your face, and may perfect that which is lacking in your faith?

This completes the rhetorical question begun in the previous verse. 'Night and day' (i.e. constantly, as in 2:9) Paul earnestly beseeches God to open the way for his return. For his joy in the Thessalonians has increased his longing to see them again, not only to rejoice in their presence but also to perfect what was lacking in their faith. Thankful though he was for their vigorous and steadfast faith, Paul was too much of a realist not to recognize that it needed to be supplemented by further instruction and by a more perfect obedience to the principles they had already been taught. In the meantime the teaching and admonition he is about to impart will help to make up some of the more important of these shortcomings [cf. 4:1ff. and 4:13ff.]. 'Though his Epistles might avail towards it, yet his personal presence would do more. There is a peculiar blessing attends oral preaching, more than reading. The like prayer he made with respect to the Romans, and upon the same account also, *Rom.* 1:10, 11' (Poole). In the prayer that follows the thought of this verse is repeated; verse 11 echoes verse 10a, while verses 12, 13 echo verse 10b, which by its reference to their present spiritual needs serves to introduce the second part of the letter.

11: Now may our God and Father himself, and our Lord Jesus, direct our way unto you:

In this remarkable petition Paul jointly invoked 'our God and Father' and 'our Lord Jesus' by using the verb 'direct' in the singular; an association which, since it indicates the Lord's oneness 'with the Father in the prerogative of hearing and answering prayer' (Findlay), also points to his deity (cf. *2 Thess.* 2:16 where the names occur in the reverse order). 'Direct' here means to '*make a straight path from us to you*, by the levelling or removal of those obstacles with which Satan has obstructed it' (Lightfoot) [cf. 2:18].

12: and the Lord make you to increase and abound in love one toward another, and toward all men, even as we also do toward you;

'But as for *you*, whether we are again privileged to minister to you in person or not, may "the Lord" (i.e. the Lord Jesus) grant our prayer for your continued growth in grace'. Paul seeks as a gift for his converts from the exalted Lord that outgoing love which abounds and overflows to bless their fellow-believers and their fellow-men, not excluding their persecutors! [5:15; *Matt.* 5:44ff; *Gal.* 6:10] For such love in action is the indispensable evidence of the genuineness of their faith. As Moffatt says, 'No form of *holiness* [verse 13] which sits loose to the endless obligations of this *love* will stand the strain of this life or the scrutiny of God's tribunal at the end' [cf. *Rom.* 13:8–10].

Even as we also do toward you: 'But why make themselves the model, why not Christ and his supreme love, which is the model for us all: "just as the Lord (loves) you"? Because the Lord is here presented as the source of our love, and because the Thessalonians have seen the love of Paul, Silvanus, and Timothy, actual examples of the love produced by the Lord in the hearts of his true followers. If the Lord filled these three with such love, the Thessalonians will see that the Lord can do this also for them' (Lenski).

13: to the end he may establish your hearts unblameable in holiness before our God and Father, at the coming of our Lord Jesus with all his saints.

The purpose of the prayer for love is that Christ may thereby so strengthen their hearts (their inward purposes and desires), that at the judgment-seat of God [*Rom.* 14: 10, NIV] these hearts may be found in a blameless state of holiness. And though this is ultimately the work of the Lord, yet it is a work which demands the active cooperation of the believer [cf. *Phil.* 2:12]. 'The point appears to be that without the strong foundation of love the will might exploit itself in conduct not becoming to the *saint*, that is, specifically, as 4:3–8 suggests, in impurity' (Frame). For selfless *love* is the opposite of the selfish *lust* that satisfies itself at another's expense [4:5].

At the coming of our Lord Jesus with all his saints: 'With all his saints' is explained by 4:13–18. Findlay says: These are not the *angels* of *2 Thess.* 1:7; the term denotes always with Paul *holy men* [*2 Thess.* 1:10]: 'here *the holy dead*, who will "rise first" and whom "God will bring with Him" – with Jesus – when He returns to His people upon earth'. Thus to assure the Thessalonians of the Lord's return with *all* his saints, including their beloved dead whom they feared might miss this great day, would convey much needed comfort to their troubled hearts; whereas a statement about angels would have no relevance to their particular needs. 'The momentous event' (not events!) is therefore a coming *with* the departed saints and a coming *for* the living saints.

CHAPTER FOUR

Paul exhorts the Thessalonians to live according to God's will, for he has not called them to be impure but to be holy [verses 1–8]. He further urges them to increase in brotherly love, and to earn the respect of the unbelieving community by quietly earning an honest living [verses 9–12]. They must not sorrow as men without hope for those who had died before the Lord's coming, because all believers whether living or dead will then be brought together to share eternal fellowship with the Lord [verses 13–18].

1: Finally then, brethren, we beseech and exhort you in the Lord Jesus, that, as ye received of us how ye ought to walk and to please God, even as ye do walk, – that ye abound more and more.

'Finally' is somewhat misleading as Paul is far from finished [cf. *Phil.* 3:1]. The expression rather marks the beginning of the more practical part of the letter and introduces the exhortation and instruction which is based on the report brought back by Timothy. The affectionate term, 'brethren', registers Paul's confidence that as fellow-believers in Christ the Thessalonians will certainly follow the course of conduct he now presses upon them, not in his own name but with all the authority of the Lord who bought them [*1 Cor.* 6:20]. The pattern of living demanded by the gospel is no strange thing, for he has already instructed them in it (see 2:13 for comment on 'received'). And though he gladly acknowledges that they are walking in 'the Way' [*Acts* 9:2], they must make it their constant aim to advance more and more in the path of godliness. For the sole object of the believer's walk must be to please God in all things [*1 Cor.* 10:31]. 'To be pleasing to God appeals to the *gospel* motive for believers, their love for God in the Lord Jesus, and not to the motive of law, the fear of punishment . . . to please ourselves in sin is to turn from God, and this involves a serious calamity; the heathen do not even know God [verse 5], we do' (Lenski).

2: For ye know what charge we gave you through the Lord Jesus.

This is a reminder that their conversion bound them over to a life of obedience. For they had been ransomed from the dominion of sin in order to serve the Lord in perfect freedom [*John* 8:36]. The word 'charges' (ASV margin) has a military flavour and 'is strictly used of commands received from a superior and transmitted to others' (W. E. Vine) [cf. *Acts* 16:24]. What Paul therefore means is that he had delivered these charges to them *on the authority of the Lord Jesus*. An apostle in living union with Christ, Paul's commission is not limited to recalling the words of Jesus; the absolute authority he claims for these commandments is that of the exalted Lord himself. The magnitude of this claim should make those who parade their fresh revelations today pause and ponder whether they really measure up to it!

3: For this is the will of God, even your sanctification, that ye abstain from fornication;

Paul now proceeds to deal with what is lacking in their faith [3:10]. As Frame points out, these exhortations are not haphazard, and it appears from 5:14 that three groups are chiefly in mind: 1. *The weak* who were tempted to indulge in impurity [4:3–8]; 2. *The idlers* who were the most disturbing element in the church [4:9–12; 5:12, 13]; 3. *The faint-hearted* who were anxious both about their dead [4:13–18: the only distinctly new teaching in the Epistle], and about their own salvation [5:1–11].

For this is God's will, your sanctification (Lenski): Paul is not advancing his own ideas; he is enforcing *God's* will. This is not *the* will of God in its entirety, but God's will specifically as it relates to sexual purity [4:3–8]. Sanctification is at once a gift and a demand. It is a *gift* in that believers are objectively holy in Christ [*1 Cor.* 1:30]; it is a *demand* in that it is the will of God that they should become subjectively transformed into Christ's likeness [*2 Cor.* 3:18]. And of necessity such a demand involves 'the separation of the spirit from all that is impure and polluting, and a renunciation of the sins towards which the desires of the flesh and of the mind lead us' (L. Berkhof).

That you abstain from immorality (RSV): Every form of sexual vice was so widespread in Greek society (is our present situation so very different?) that the weak were strongly tempted to relapse into the practices they had been accustomed to regard with indifference. 'What they as Christians needed to remember was that consecration to the true and living God was not only religious but ethical. Whether they had actually tumbled into the abyss or were standing on the precipice is not certain. At all events, Paul's warning with its religious sanction and practical directions sufficed; we hear nothing of "the weak" in the second letter' (Frame).

4: that each one of you know how to possess himself of his own vessel in sanctification and honour, 5: not in the passion of lust, even as the Gentiles who know not God;

That each one of you know how to take a wife for himself (RSV): That 'vessel' here means 'wife' [cf. *1 Pet.* 3:7] is in accord with rabbinical usage, and is supported by the context which forbids fornication [verse 3b] and adultery [verse 6a]. 'It is God's will that every Christian is to know how to act in the matter of sex so as to be pleasing to God [verse 1]. He is to know that God instituted marriage, that each man is to have his own wife, each woman her own husband (monogamy), that every type of fornication is excluded as being contrary to God's will' (Lenski) [*Gen.* 1:28, 2:24; *1 Cor.* 7:2; *Heb.* 13:4].

In sanctification and honour: This is the ethical element in which the acquiring of a wife was to take place: 'The union of man and woman was to be in sanctification and honour, not, as in the case of *fornication*, in sin and shame' (C. J. Ellicott).

Not in the passion of lust like heathen who do not know God (RSV): Since it is through their ignorance of God that the heathen sink into such sins, there could be no greater inconsistency than for those who know God to follow the same shameful course of conduct.

6a: that no man transgress, and wrong his brother in the matter:

That (no one) go beyond what is proper and defraud his brother in this matter (Hendriksen): 'In this matter' shows that the same subject is continued. The euphemism is prompted by Paul's delicacy of feeling, but the flagrant violation of the neighbour's rights which he condemns is clearly adultery [*Exod.* 20:14, 17]. 'He has well said *not to go beyond.* For to each man God has assigned a wife, and has set bounds to nature, that there may be intercourse with one only; therefore, intercourse with another is transgression and robbery, and the taking of more than belongs to one . . . It is more cruel than any robbery, for we grieve not so much when our wealth is carried off, as when marriage is invaded. Dost thou call him thy brother and defraudest him, and that in things which are forbidden?' (Chrysostom).

6b: because the Lord is an avenger in all these things, as also we forewarned you and testified.

Knowing the temptations to licentiousness which surrounded them, Paul had warned the Thessalonians from the beginning, of the fearful consequences of immorality, so that they could not now plead ignorance as an excuse. 'In all these things': in 'everything that concerns the honour of the human person and the sacredness of wedded life; cf. *Heb.* 13:4, *fornicators and adulterers God will judge* . . . There is no reason to suppose that Lord means any other than "the Lord Jesus Christ", through whom God judges the world at the Last Day: cf. *2 Thess.* 1: 7–9; *Acts* 17:31' (Findlay).

7: For God called us not for uncleanness, but in sanctification.

The second reason Paul advances for living a pure life rests in the nature of God's calling. It is inconceivable that a holy God should call them *for* uncleanness. Merely to express the thought exhibits the enormity of the antinomian abuse of grace [*Rom.* 6:1f]. As therefore God is holy [*1 Pet.* 1:14–16], so the Christian must never forget that his vocation is *in* sanctification. 'Holiness is to be the pervading element in which the Christian is to move' (Lightfoot) [*Eph.* 1:4].

8: Therefore he that rejecteth, rejecteth not man, but God, who giveth his Holy Spirit unto you.

The grave consequence of setting aside this instruction provides the third reason for obeying it. For the one who rejects it, rejects not the advice of man but the commandment of God!

Who is ever giving His Spirit, the Spirit whose special characteristic is holiness, to dwell within you (Plummer): A paraphrase which brings out the force of this unusual reference to the Holy Spirit (literally, 'the Spirit of him the holy'). 'Not only did God call the Thessalonians at the first. He is continually breathing His Spirit into them. But the purpose of this is sanctification; the Spirit of God is the Holy Spirit. To live licentiously while receiving this gift is grossly insulting to the Giver. The obligation to purity, growing out of the reception of the Holy Spirit, is similarly urged by the Apostle when writing to the Corinthians: *Know ye not that your body is a temple of the Holy Ghost which is in you, which ye have from God?* [*1 Cor.* 6:19]' (Adeney).

9: But concerning love of the brethren ye have no need that one write unto you: for ye yourselves are taught of God to love one another;

On the subject of love for the brethren, however, Paul is glad to acknowledge that there is no real need to exhort them by *letter* when this grace was so evident in their *lives*. But since he speaks to those not yet made perfect, he urges them to 'abound more and more' [verse 10]. Brotherly love (*philadelphia*) is a word which is elsewhere used in the literal sense of love for blood brothers and sisters. But in the New Testament it is used of the special love Christians bear towards one another as fellow-members of the family of faith, as those who are conscious of having the same Father in heaven. Such brotherly love is of special importance: '1. for it is a testing fruit of regeneration [*1 John* 3:14; 4:8]; 2. its visible existence is a condition of the world's conversion [*John* 17:21]; 3. a token also of true discipleship [*John* 13:35]; 4. while it is obedience to Christ's new commandment, and enforced by his own example [*John* 13:34; 15:17; *Eph*. 5:2]; and is essential to the spiritual growth of the church [*Eph*. 4:16]' (Eadie).

For ye yourselves are taught of God to love one another: The word 'God-taught' (*theodidaktos*) occurs only here in the New Testament. It has no reference to any external instruction but signifies the spiritual teaching of the heart. For though it was by the Word of God that Paul first taught the Thessalonians to love one another, he gratefully recognizes that they were able to learn this lesson only because the Holy Spirit had taught it to their hearts [*Isa*. 54:13; *John* 6:45].

Gracious Spirit, Holy Ghost,
Taught by Thee we covet most
Of Thy gifts at Pentecost,
Holy, heavenly love.
Christopher Wordsworth

10: for indeed ye do it toward all the brethren that are in all Macedonia. But we exhort you, brethren, that ye abound more and more;

As the capital of the province Thessalonica 'was the natural centre of the Macedonian Churches – including Philippi and Beroea, with other communities which had probably sprung up around these principal towns. The Thessalonian Christians were using their position and influence for the good of their brethren around them, and thus giving proof that they had learnt the great lesson of Divine grace' (Findlay). But they must not rest upon this reputation for brotherly love; they must seek to abound in it more and more. Nor is the admonition without special point, for its development shows that what was true of the church as a whole was not true of every member in it [verses 10b–12]. When the passage is compared with 2 Thessalonians 3:6–15 it appears that Paul has in mind those who had stopped work in the imminent expectation of Christ's coming. This idleness was an abuse of brotherly love. For in neglecting the duty of self-support they relied on others to meet their needs, while the time which should have been taken up with work was spent in meddling with matters in which they had no concern.

11: and that ye study to be quiet, and to do your own business, and to work with your hands, even as we charged you;

Make it your ambition to lead a quiet life (NIV): Paul sees that the source of this disturbance is inward, 'the excitement created in the minds of some by the expectation that the day of the Lord was at hand. With Lamentations 3:26 he might have said: "It is good that a man should hope and quietly wait for the salvation of the Lord" . . . Inward tranquillity once restored, outward idleness and meddlesomeness would cease' (Frame).

To mind your own business (NIV): He first mentions that which most disturbed the peace of the church. This was the idlers' interference with the affairs of others, particularly with the church leaders from whom they had doubtless sought support.

And to work with your hands, just as we told you (NIV): During the Thessalonian mission Paul had backed this charge with the force of his own example, which certainly gave no encouragement to the Greek tendency to despise manual labour [*2 Thess.* 3:8; cf. *Mark* 6:3]. 'There can be no better preparation for the coming of Christ than to be faithful in ordinary duties. The man who is doing his work faithfully at the right time is ready to meet Christ. This thought should quiet all feverish apprehension' (E.J. Bicknell).

12: that ye may walk becomingly toward them that are without, and may have need of nothing.

The purpose of this exhortation is now stated, for it is by earning an honest living that they will gain the respect of their pagan neighbours. 'For Christians to be seen neglecting the duty of earning their daily bread while giving themselves up to religious excitement would prejudice their cause in the eyes of the world, which could appreciate the value of sober work, while it could not understand the spiritual pursuits of the new faith' (Adeney).

And be dependent on nobody (RSV): 'The gospel bids us aim not only at brotherly love, but at independence. Remember the poor, it says; but it says also, Work with your hands, that you may preserve a Christian dignity in relation to the world, and have need of no one' (Denney).

13: But we would not have you ignorant, brethren, concerning them that fall asleep; that ye sorrow not, even as the rest, who have no hope.

With his favourite expression for introducing some new instruction [e.g. *Rom.* 11:25; *1 Cor.* 10:1; 12:1], Paul now passes to the topic which was exercising the fainthearted in Thessalonica. As they thought that only those alive at the parousia would be saved, they feared that their brethren who were already dead had forfeited any share in the coming glory. Consequently they mourned for them like pagans who have no hope. The apostle corrects their error in order to comfort them; for there can be no Christian comfort without Christian faith. It is true that sleep is not a distinctively Christian metaphor for death, but in pagan usage the term is not illuminated by any resurrection hope. So Catullus says, 'Suns may set and rise again. When once our brief light has set, one unbroken night of sleep remains.' As Lenski says, 'Behind this word "sleep" and sleeping the pagan sees nothing but his pagan conception of death, to him the word is a mere euphemism. Behind the Christian word lies all the Christian knowledge of the saving facts which actually make death a mere sleep . . . This sleep applies only to the body of the dead believer and not to his soul' [cf. *Luke* 16:19–31; 23:43; *Acts* 7:59; *2 Cor.* 5:8; *Phil.* 1:23; *Rev.* 6:9; 7:9; 20:4].

That ye sorrow not, even as the rest, who have no hope: It is because Paul knows that the Thessalonians have hope through the gospel that he urges them not to sorrow as the unbelieving do. The contrast he draws is not between natural and excessive sorrow, but between Christian hope and pagan sorrow. The finality of death filled the heathen with a feeling of blank despair. It was a sorrow which was unrelieved by any hope of a future reunion with their loved ones. Theocritus makes the representative remark, 'Hopes are among the living, but the dead are without hope'; whereas a Christian inscription in the catacombs begins, 'Alexander is not dead, but he lives above the stars and his body rests in this tomb.'

14: For if we believe that Jesus died and rose again, even so them also that are fallen asleep in Jesus will God bring with him.

Even so them also that are fallen asleep through Jesus will God bring with him (ASV margin): 'If' suggests no uncertainty but points to the logical consequence of believing that Jesus died and rose again. For though the Thessalonians did not doubt that Jesus had risen from the dead, they had not grasped the far-reaching implications of this great event. Accordingly they must realize that not even death can sever the believer's union with Christ whose triumph over the tomb has ensured the resurrection of all who die trusting in him [cf. *Rom.* 8:31–39]. In fact they have double comfort, for Paul not only gives them to understand that the resurrection of the departed saints was secured by the rising of Jesus, but also states that God will bring them with Jesus at the parousia. As believers who have this one gospel hope, they are not therefore to sorrow for their brethren as do those who are altogether without hope. It is only 'through' Jesus, who deprived death of its sting [*1 Cor.* 15:56], that believers can fall asleep in peace. 'It is significant that he does not speak of Christ "sleeping" but uses the word *died*. He died that death which is the wages of sin; and because He endured the full horror implied in that death, He has transformed death for His followers into sleep' (Morris).

15: For this we say unto you by the word of the Lord, that we that are alive, that are left unto the coming of the Lord, shall in no wise precede them that are fallen asleep.

What follows is given on the authority of Christ's own word. It is impossible to determine whether this refers to an otherwise unrecorded saying of Jesus [e.g. *Acts* 20:35], or to a direct revelation made to Paul by the exalted Lord [cf. *2 Cor.* 12:1]. Since 'Paul distinguishes the two classes, the living and the dead, he naturally puts himself among those to whom at the moment he belonged, and who as the living and surviving are contrasted with those who had fallen asleep or died. For there will be a like distinction when the Saviour comes; and to describe the one class the apostle employs the present time and says, "we who are alive and remain". If the Advent were to take place just now, the classification would be literally correct. To the mind of the apostle the second coming was ever present and under this aspect he puts himself and his contemporaries in the one category without actually intending to affirm that they should not taste death till the Redeemer should appear. The clause is thus a vivid way of characterizing all the living as represented by himself and the Thessalonians to whom he writes, while the deceased Thessalonian believers represent all who have died before His appearance and coming' (Eadie).

Shall in no wise precede them that are fallen asleep: 'So little is there a reason to grieve over those who have fallen asleep. Those who are alive at Christ's Parousia shall not even precede those who have died, to say nothing of the fear that there is no hope for them. The living and those who fell asleep shall together be joined in glory to the glorious Lord' (Lenski).

16: For the Lord himself shall descend from heaven, with a shout, with the voice of the archangel, and with the trump of God: and the dead in Christ shall rise first; 17: then we that are alive, that are left, shall together with them be caught up in the clouds, to meet the Lord in the air: and so shall we ever be with the Lord.

For the Lord himself will descend from heaven with a cry of command (RSV): We should not fail to observe that Paul's account of the parousia is strictly confined to a justification of the assurance that when this takes place the living will have no advantage over the departed. For it is the Lord himself who shall descend from heaven to awaken the bodies of those who fell asleep in him with a resistless word of command [cf. *John* 5:28]. As Denney says, 'In that emphatic *Himself* we have the argument of verse 14 practically repeated: the Lord, it signifies, who knows *all* that are His . . . It is not another who comes, but He to whom all Christian souls have been united for ever' [*Acts* 1:11].

With the archangel's call, and with the sound of the trumpet of God (RSV): Possibly the call of the archangel, upon whose identity it is idle to speculate, consists of the sounding forth of God's trumpet, but whatever their precise meaning may be, these expressions can hardly be said to lend support to the notion of a *secret* rapture! Hendriksen reminds us that the trumpet was used to summon the people to meet God [*Exod.* 19:16, 17], and also to signal their deliverance from oppression [*Zech.* 9:14]. 'So also this final trumpet-blast, the signal for the dead to arise, for the living to be changed, and for all the elect to be gathered from the four winds [*Matt.* 24:31] to meet the Lord, may well be interpreted as being also the fulfilment of the trumpet-ordinance in Leviticus 25, and, accordingly, as proclaiming liberty throughout the universe for all the children of God, their everlasting jubilee!'

And the dead in Christ will rise first (RSV): 'This gives us the key to the Apostle's meaning throughout. Being "in Christ", having died as they lived *in Him*, nothing can part them from Him, "neither death nor life" [*Rom.* 8:38]. And when He returns in bodily presence, their bodies must rise to meet Him and do Him homage.' They shall rise *first*, but 'not *before the other dead*, as though theirs were a select and separate resurrection [cf. *John* 5:28, 29]; the antithesis is plainly given in the next verse, – "first", i.e. *before the living saints:* "we shall not take precedence of them, but rather they of us"' (Findlay).

Then we who are alive, who are left, shall be caught up together with them in the clouds to meet the Lord in the air (RSV): This blessed reunion with the departed, now raised to new life on earth, also implies the transformation of the living [*1 Cor.* 15:51] before both are simultaneously snatched up in the clouds – these 'forming the element with which they would be surrounded, and in which they would be borne up' (Ellicott) – to meet their Lord in the air, i.e. the space between heaven and earth. As Paul's purpose here and in *1 Cor.* 15 is to instruct and comfort Christians he says nothing of the destiny of the wicked, but it seems reasonable to assume that this meeting in the air is preparatory to the Lord's return to earth for the final judgment. For in the papyri the word 'meet' was used of the welcome given to a newly arrived magistrate by leading citizens who went out to meet him and escort him back into the city [cf. *Acts* 28:15].

And so shall we ever be with the Lord [cf. 5:10]: Vos points out that 'the word "ever" excludes the conception of a provisional kingdom' ('The Second Coming of Our Lord and the Millennium', *Redemptive History and Biblical Interpretation*, p. 421). This is all that Paul here says about the future life, and for believers it is enough! 'The entire content and worth of heaven, the entire blessedness of life eternal, is for Paul embraced in the one thought of being united with Jesus, his Saviour and Lord' (W. Bornemann).

18: Wherefore comfort one another with these words.

The bereaved Thessalonians would sorrow most of all; the others would want to comfort them. They have genuine comfort to offer which is unlike the empty condolences of the heathen in the face of death: 'Irene to Taonnophris and Philo, good comfort. I was as sorry and wept over the departed one as I wept for Didymas. And all things which were fitting I did, and all mine . . . But, nevertheless, against such things one can do nothing. Therefore comfort one another. Farewell' (*Oxyrhynchus Papyrus* No. 115).

But the apostle's words comfort as nothing else can because they overflow with the real hope that is only given through this authoritative revelation from the Lord who conquered death.

CHAPTER FIVE

Since they know that 'the day of the Lord' would come as a surprise to men at large, the Thessalonians are to be watchful so that they may be found ready for it [verses 1–11]. They are to respect their spiritual guides, to live at peace among themselves, to admonish the idle, to help the weak, and to be patient towards all men. They must renounce the old spirit of revenge and do good to all [verses 12–15]. Refusing to quench the Spirit, they must bring everything to the test, and hold fast to the good while abstaining from every form of evil [verses 16–22]. After praying that God will so sanctify them that they may be blameless at Christ's coming, Paul requests their prayers, commands the public reading of the Epistle to the brethren, and concludes with the benediction [verses 23–28].

1: But concerning the times and the seasons, brethren, ye have no need that aught be written unto you.

Having shown the fainthearted that their fears for the departed were groundless, Paul next allays their anxiety that the day might find them unprepared to meet Christ [verses 1–11]. Probably the mistaken belief that survival until the parousia was necessary for salvation had not unnaturally quickened the Thessalonians' interest in the date and circumstances of Christ's coming. But as Paul has already taught them that spiritual preparedness does not consist in date-setting and sign-watching, nothing further needs to be written on this point [verse 2]; what they do need is the encouragement [verse 11] to live up to the new status [verse 5] that God has given them through Christ [verses 9, 10]. The distinction between the times and the seasons is that the former refers to the duration of the time that must elapse before the advent, while the latter denotes the critical nature of the events that will characterize the end time [cf. *Acts* 1:7].

2: For yourselves know perfectly that the day of the Lord so cometh as a thief in the night.

There is no need to write to them on this matter because they know very well that the time of the parousia has not been revealed by God. For this will be as sudden and unexpected as the coming of a thief who surprises the householder at night [*Matt.* 24:43]. It is evident that Paul has in view the one great event which will wind up the present age and usher in the eternal state [*2 Pet.* 3:10–13]. For he here identifies Christ's coming with 'the day of the Lord' [cf. *2 Thess.* 2:1, 2 where *both* terms are used in the *same* sentence]. 'Some argue that "the day of the Lord" cannot be the hope of the Christian for it is a day of judgment. It is true the term does denote judgment, but not exclusively so, for through this judgment comes the Christian's brightest hope' (Archibald Hughes). It is when the Lord Jesus comes to judge the unbelieving that he also comes to be glorified in his saints [cf. *2 Thess.* 1:7–9 with 'in that day', verse 10].

3: When they are saying, Peace and safety, then sudden destruction cometh upon them, as travail upon a woman with child; and they shall in no wise escape.

This sudden coming of the Lord will take the unbelieving completely by surprise. 'Even though the Lord threatens them with destruction, they have no hesitation in promising themselves peace and every good fortune. And so they fall into this deadly apathy, because they do not see the immediate fulfilment of what the Lord declares will take place. Anything that is not immediately visible to their eyes they consider to be mythical' (Calvin) [*Matt.* 24:37ff; *2 Pet.* 3:3ff.].

Then a sudden (thing) comes upon them, destruction (Hendriksen): The reader is kept in suspense by Paul's vivid word order: sudden – comes – DESTRUCTION! This is not annihilation; it is 'eternal destruction from the face of the Lord' [*2 Thess.* 1:9]. The thought conveyed by the word is therefore that of 'utter and hopeless *ruin*, the loss of all that gives worth to existence' (Milligan) [contrast *Psa.* 16:11].

As travail upon a woman with child; and they shall in no wise escape: As the anguish of a woman's birth-pangs is inevitable [*Isa.* 13:6ff], so the impenitent shall in no wise escape this destruction. 'It still needs emphasis that there are no other alternatives than life with the Lord or eternal loss. One or the other is inevitable' (Morris).

4: But ye, brethren, are not in darkness, that that day should overtake you as a thief.

'But ye, brethren' stands in strong contrast to what is said of the unbelieving in the previous verse. 'Since the Thessalonians are "not in darkness", the coming of day will be no terror or surprise to them. The Day of the Lord will not "Overtake them as a thief", stealing on them suddenly and despoiling them of their treasures unawares, but it will come to them as the welcome daybreak, full of light and joy. To the wicked and careless, by a sad contradiction, the Day of the Lord will be *night*! It is to them "darkness and not light, – yea, very dark, and no brightness in it" [*Amos* 5:20]. But for "the sons of light" [verse 5] it is day indeed, and wears its true character' (Findlay).

5: for ye are all sons of light, and sons of the day: we are not of the night, nor of darkness;

The Thessalonians need not fear that the day of the Lord will catch them unprepared, for since they are all even *now* 'sons of light' – those who belong to the realm of light –Chr ist's coming will also prove them to be 'sons of the day', full sharers in the triumph of that day. 'To the believer the boundary-line between darkness and light is the time of his being brought to the knowledge of Christ. Here, rather than at the moment of his dissolution, or of the Second Advent of Christ, is the great change wrought. From this time forward he is living in the light. And the revelation of a future state presents no such contrast of light and darkness as that which he had already passed' (Lightfoot).

We are not of the night, nor of darkness: The tactful change from 'you' to 'we' (i.e. we believers) is itself an argument for obeying the exhortation [verse 6ff.] that logically follows this reminder of the enlightenment they enjoy in Christ. For having been thus delivered from their former state of darkness it would be the height of folly to fall back into the behaviour-patterns which were characteristic of the old life [cf. *Rom.* 13:12,13; *Eph.* 5:8].

6: so then let us not sleep, as do the rest, but let us watch and be sober.

Paul's conclusion is inescapable. Such a great deliverance obliges Christians to live henceforth in the light; it is not for them to sleep as do the rest. '"Sleep" is natural to those who are "of the night" [comp. *Eph.* 5:11–14]; it is symbolic of the insensibility and helplessness that sin produces' (Findlay). But as befits believers, we must be watchful and sober, remaining *spiritually awake* and *morally alert* throughout the period of waiting for the Lord's coming [cf. *Matt.* 24:42; 25:13; *Mark* 13:35].

7: For they that sleep sleep in the night; and they that are drunken are drunken in the night.

'Sleep and drunkenness belong to the night season, it is the natural time for the one, and it is for many reasons taken advantage of for the other. Believers, on the other hand, are to be wakeful and sober, are not to be like the rest, who are of the night in every sense, it being their element and sphere. What is true of sleepers and drunkards literally is true in a higher and more awful sense of those who lack spiritual illumination' (Eadie) [*Luke* 21:34–36].

8: But let us, since we are of the day, be sober, putting on the breastplate of faith and love; and for a helmet, the hope of salvation.

It is only because the Thessalonians belong to the day that Paul expects them to behave in this way, for he always recognizes the assurance of salvation as the nerve of all ethical endeavour. 'Be sober' here includes the idea of watchfulness (carried over from verse 6) and suggests the simile which 'identifies the Christian's "soberness" with that of the soldier under arms and on guard, in whom drunkenness, or sleep, would be a crime' (Findlay).

Having put on the breastplate of faith and love, and as an helmet, the hope of salvation (Ellicott): The change of tense shows that the sobriety enjoined consists in having donned this spiritual armour and in continuing to wear it. Of the three primary graces which appear here in the same order as before (see comment on 1:3), faith and love are the 'breastplate' that protects the heart, while the certain hope of final salvation is the 'helmet' that covers the head. And though, as Calvin says, Paul mentions only two parts of our equipment, 'he omits nothing that relates to spiritual defence, for those who are furnished with faith, love, and hope, will not be caught unarmed in any respect' [cf. *Rom.* 13: 12; *2 Cor.* 6:7; 10:4; *Eph.* 6: 13ff.].

9: For God appointed us not unto wrath, but unto the obtaining of salvation through our Lord Jesus Christ, 10: who died for us, that, whether we wake or sleep, we should live together with him.

We have this hope because we know by the choice (see comment on 1:4) and calling [2:12] which made us believers that God did not destine us for wrath (see comment on 1:10), though we were 'by nature children of wrath, even as the rest' [*Eph.* 2:3]. The modern refusal to take account of the awful reality of God's anger against sin results in 'a debilitated Christianity, which does not and cannot do what Christ came into the world to do, viz. save men from the wrath to come' (Tasker, op. cit., p 36).

But unto the obtaining of salvation: Our salvation is planned, provided, and bestowed by God; yet we have the duty of 'obtaining' it! This salutary reminder of our responsibility to grasp the proferred grace is in line with the exhortation of verses 6–8 which calls 'the readers to a wakeful, soldierlike activity, such as will be crowned by the "*winning* of salvation", the glorious end for which "God destined" them when He first "called them to His own kingdom and glory" [2:12]' (Findlay) [cf. *1 Tim.* 6:12].

Through our Lord Jesus Christ: 'This is the uniform doctrine of Scripture. Salvation having God for its source, has Christ for its medium (i.e. Mediator). Only through Christ is God known and accessible to us, and only through Him are spiritual blessings conferred upon us by God' (Eadie).

Who died for us, i.e. for our sins: The simplicity of the reference points to the Thessalonians' familiarity with the doctrine of Christ crucified [cf. *1 Cor.* 2:2]. This salvation is mediated to men 'through our' (note the confessional 'our') 'Lord Jesus Christ', and that, through his sin-atoning death 'for us'. The mention of Christ's death for us in such close connection with the wrath of God is too important to overlook. For it clearly implies that Christ averted that wrath from us by taking it upon himself, thus delivering us from our deserved doom [cf. *Rom.* 5:9; *2 Cor.* 5:21; *Gal.* 3:13].

That, whether we wake or sleep, we should live together with him: Resuming the thread of 4:13–17, Paul now assures the Thessalonians that the purpose of Christ's death is that, whether awake or asleep (in the body) at the parousia, 'they shall together live for ever with Him – in His presence, and in communion with Him. Of that life, so blessed and unending, His presence is the primal element and the "chiefest joy"' (Eadie) [*Rom.* 14:8, 9; *2 Cor.* 5:8, 9].

11: Wherefore exhort one another, and build each other up, even as also ye do.

Paul concludes this section with the exhortation to comfort one another [4:18] and build up each other in the faith. 'This is Biblical edification, namely, increase in knowledge, assurance, spiritual strength. It is this upbuilding which will produce the comfort' (Lenski). But he is careful to acknowledge present attainments as he encourages further progress, and so 'guards himself against seeming rebuke, while he intends but to exhort' (Lightfoot).

12: But we beseech you, brethren, to know them that labour among you, and are over you in the Lord, and admonish you;

As it was evidently Paul's practice to ordain elders in every church [*Acts* 14:23], there is no reason to doubt that he refers to those who hold this office. But to persuade the Thessalonians 'to know' (i.e. recognize and respect) them for what they are, he prefers to describe them by the work they do. This is the heavy toil of leading them in the Lord and admonishing them [cf. *Col.* 1:28], 'by the word of encouragement, when this is sufficient, but also by that of remonstrance, of reproof, of blame, where these may be required' (Trench).

13: and to esteem them exceeding highly in love for their work's sake. Be at peace among yourselves.

As Calvin says, This work 'is the edification of the Church, the eternal salvation of souls, the restoration of the world, and in short the kingdom of God and Christ. The excellence and splendour of this work are beyond value. We are, therefore, to think highly of those whom God makes ministers of so great a task'. But he goes on to observe that Paul's description of how this work is to be done [verse 12] shows that 'he certainly does not honour the lazy and the wicked, nor does he point to them as being worthy of it'.

Be at peace among yourselves: This appeal is closely connected with the last. Paul's meaning is that 'the general "peace" is to be kept through affectionate loyalty to the approved leaders; it was disturbed by the *idlers*, whom the Church-officers had to "admonish" [verses 12, 14]' (Findlay) [cf. 4:11; *2 Thess*. 3:6–15].

14: And we exhort you, brethren, admonish the disorderly, encourage the fainthearted, support the weak,

Further we urge you, brothers, warn the idlers, encourage the faint-hearted, cling to the weak (Frame): Some have thought that this is a special charge to the elders of the church, but there is no change of address (cf. 'brethren', verse 12). Ministry is not the monopoly of a special class; the members themselves have a ministry to fulfil to those of their number who are in need of warning, encouragement, and support. The *loafers*, who refuse to work [4:11, 12], are not to be supported in their idleness by the brethren, who are to join their leaders in warning them. On the other hand, they must encourage the *faint-hearted* who were worried about their dead [4:13–18] and also about their own salvation [5: 1–11]. Finally, they must not despise but help (cling to) the *weak*, i.e. those who were tempted to lapse into immorality [4:2–8]. It seems reasonable to accept Frame's classification as substantially correct, even if it is perhaps a little too neat to be exact. For example, it is more than likely that the last group would include some who were spiritually immature rather than morally weak.

14b: be longsuffering toward all. 15: See that none render unto any one evil for evil; but always follow after that which is good, one toward another, and toward all.

'Longsuffering toward all means not only toward all in the three groups mentioned but toward all, including even outsiders, who may be very trying at times because of their hostile actions. The verb means to hold out long before taking action; God himself is longsuffering toward us ' (Lenski).

See that none render unto any one evil for evil, cf. *Rom.* 12:17; *1 Pet.* 3:9: Lightfoot thinks that the repetition of the same phrase 'in all three passages would seem to point to some saying of our Lord as the original'. Be that as it may, the expression certainly reproduces the teaching of Jesus [*Matt.* 5:44], who also fully exemplified it in his life [*1 Pet.* 2:23].

But always keep pursuing the thing that is good (in the sense of beneficial) *in regard to one another and in regard to all* (Lenski): But to avoid retaliation is not enough; all resentment is to be extinguished by the love that eagerly seeks to repay evil with good. For if they would not be overcome of evil, they must 'overcome evil with good' [*Rom.* 12:19–21].

16: Rejoice always; 17: pray without ceasing; 18: in everything give thanks: for this is the will of God in Christ Jesus to you-ward.

Since the duties enjoined in these three pregnant precepts are always binding upon believers Denney aptly refers to them as 'the standing orders of the gospel'. They are concerned with the inner motivation that gives Christian conduct its distinctive stamp.

Rejoice always: 'The joy to which they are exhorted even amidst persecution and suffering is no merely natural joy. It is one of the fruits of the Spirit [*Gal.* 5:22; *Rom.* 14:17; cf. *Acts* 2:46]. It is in no way incompatible with loss and suffering [*Acts* 5:41; *Rom.* 5:3; *2 Cor.* 6:10]. In his letter to the other Macedonian Church Paul not only exhorts them to rejoice, but practises joy himself even in prison, when outward circumstances might well have caused discouragement [*Phil.* 1:4, 18; 4:4, 10, etc]. This joy even in the midst of pain and persecution was one of the great marks of primitive Christianity, which amazed the heathen world, and attracted men to Christ' (Bicknell).

Pray without ceasing: Perpetual prayer in any formal sense is obviously impossible. The meaning is that believers are so to cultivate a spirit of constant prayerfulness that their whole lives will be permeated by the presence of God. 'It is not in the moving of the lips, but in the elevation of the heart to God, that the essence of prayer consists. Thus amidst the commonest duties and recreations of life it is still possible to be engaged in prayer' (Lightfoot). [*Rom.* 12:12; *Eph.* 6:18]

In everything give thanks: Eadie notes that this precept 'is universal in sphere, as the two before it are continuous in time'. As even the most adverse circumstances must work together for the believer's good [*Rom.* 8:28], there is no situation to which he should not respond by giving thanks to God [cf. *Acts* 16:25]. Such gratitude is the fruit of grace and it stands in marked contrast to the thanklessness that characterizes the heathen [*Rom.* 1:21].

For this is the will of God in Christ Jesus to you-ward: They should always rejoice, ceaselessly pray, and in all circumstances give thanks, because '*this* is (the) will of God' – here the absence of the article limits the reference to this particular part of the divine will. 'The will is made known in Christ, and it is in Christ that men are given the dynamic that enables them to carry out that divine will' (Morris).

19: Quench not the Spirit; 20: despise not prophesyings; 21: prove all things; hold fast that which is good; 22: abstain from every form of evil.

Do not quench the Spirit, do not despise prophesying, but test everything (RSV): Since fire is associated with the power of the Spirit [*Matt.* 3:11; *Acts* 2:3; cf. *2 Tim.* 1:6, ASV margin: 'stir into flame the gift of God, which is in thee'], so to smother the Spirit's work is to quench that holy fire. The Thessalonians must not thus suppress the extraordinary operations of the Spirit in their midst. In particular, they are not to despise the gift of prophecy [*1 Cor.* 12:28], which was primarily the forth-telling [*Eph.* 3:5], and occasionally the fore-telling of the divine will [*Acts* 11:28; 21:11], in intelligible speech [*1 Cor.* 14:1–6] under the immediate inspiration of the Spirit. It was by means of these revelations that God was pleased to instruct [*1 Cor.* 14:3] and guide [*Acts* 13:1–3] the early church before the canon of Scripture was complete. But because in such oral communications there was always the danger of receiving pseudo-prophecy as a genuine utterance of the Spirit, they are also to put all prophesying to the test by exercising their powers of spiritual discernment [*1 Cor.* 12: 10; *1 John* 4:1]. It may well be that the abuse of this gift in Thessalonica by enthusiasts who predicted the immediate return of Christ had tempted the more sober-minded to dismiss it as of no value, hence the need for this corrective.

Hold fast what is good, abstain from every form of evil (RSV): What must result from the testing of every manifestation of prophecy is now set forth. Positively, they are to hold fast to the good, the one beautiful and genuine work of the Spirit which makes for the building up of the church [*1 Cor.* 14:12]. Negatively, they are to reject every kind of evil, refusing to be ensnared by any 'revelation' which has been proved counterfeit.

23: And the God of peace himself sanctify you wholly; and may your spirit and soul and body be preserved entire, without blame at the coming of our Lord Jesus Christ.

As the preceding exhortations can only be fulfilled in God's strength [*Phil.* 2:13], Paul now concludes with the prayer that he, who is known as 'the God of peace' through the gospel of redeeming grace [*Acts* 10:36; *Rom.* 5:1; *Col.* 1:20], will himself so sanctify the Thessalonians that no part of their being falls short of entire consecration to him. Clearly this is no piecemeal sanctification effected by human effort, for the radical completeness of the holiness required demands God for its Author [verse 24].

However, 'It is a thing not yet in possession but in petition . . . Paul though promising this perfection as the certain heritage of every Christian man, presents it as a matter of hope, not yet seen; not as a matter of experience, already enjoyed . . . He openly declares, indeed, the term of our imperfection – the point of entrance into our perfection . . . *at the coming of our Lord Jesus Christ*'. Meanwhile 'we are fighting the good fight; we are running the race. The prize is yonder . . . To us it is a weary process. But it is God's way. And He does all things well' (B. B. Warfield, 'Entire Sanctification', *Perfectionism*, pp. 462–4).

And may your spirit and soul and body be preserved entire: Findlay notes that 'wholly', 'implying a totality from which no part is excluded', is now followed by a synonym 'entire' that denotes 'an integrity in which each part has its due place and proportion'. Although some have appealed to this text to justify the view that man is a threefold being, one might as well cite *Mark* 12:30 as the proof of a fourfold doctrine

(F. F. Bruce). Indeed it is quite unwarranted to read a formal definition of the nature of man into Paul's words here when elsewhere he speaks in terms of the duality of man's existence [cf. *Rom.* 8:10; *1 Cor.* 5:5; 7:34; *2 Cor.* 7: 1; *Eph.* 2:3; *Col.* 2:5]. Rather it is the apostle's fervency in prayer that accounts for this fulness of expression. It means that no part of man's life, outward or inward, whether the latter is considered in its 'God-conscious' ('spirit') or its 'self-conscious' ('soul') aspect, is to remain outside the scope of God's sanctifying power (Bruce). 'Be preserved' stands at the end of the sentence for emphasis in the Greek, and like 'entire' is in the singular, as spirit, soul, and body form one whole man.

Without blame at the coming of our Lord Jesus Christ: Since God could not keep otherwise than blamelessly, the thought is that they may be found blamelessly entire at Christ's coming, being thus made fit to stand in the day of judgment and to share in the glory then to be revealed [*Rom.* 8:23; *Phil.* 3:21]. Milligan notes the interesting fact that the word 'without blame', which in the New Testament is confined to this Epistle, has been found inscribed on certain tombs in Thessalonica.

24: Faithful is he that calleth you, who will also do it.

The assurance that the foregoing prayer is no idle wish but a certain hope is firmly grounded in the character of God. It is an invincible confidence because it relies and reckons upon the faithfulness of God as the caller who never fails to complete his covenant engagements [*Num.* 23:19, 20; *Rom.* 8:28–30; *Phil.* 1:6]. Such an assurance must never lead to a presumptuous security in sin, for the true reception of God's grace is always marked by the obedience through which the believer makes his 'calling and election sure' [cf. *2 Pet.* 1:5–11]. On the other hand, it would be cold comfort indeed to take our ever imperfect obedience as the measure of our assurance. For the supreme object of our hope is the faithful God who guarantees our participation in his great salvation. As Leon Morris well says, 'It is profoundly satisfying to the believer that in the last resort what matters is not his feeble hold on God, but God's strong grip on him [cf. *John* 10:28f.].'

25: Brethren, pray for us also (ASV margin).

The addition of 'also' certainly gives an appropriate meaning. As we have just prayed for you [verse 23], so do you 'also' remember us in your prayers. Although an apostle of Christ, it was never above Paul to ask for the prayers of his readers [cf. *Rom.* 15:30; *Eph.* 6:19; *Col.* 4:3; *2 Thess.* 3:1], for he knew that the superhuman demands which were daily made upon him called for nothing less than the impartation of supernatural strength. This is therefore no perfunctory request, but an urgent entreaty to be upheld before the throne of grace by his 'brethren', his fellow-members in the household of faith.

26: Salute all the brethren with a holy kiss.

Since Paul loves all who love the Lord Jesus [*1 Cor.* 16:22, 24], he sends his final greeting to *all* the members of the church, thus ensuring that no one is overlooked. As Chrysostom says, 'Because being absent he could not greet them with the kiss, he greets them through others, as when we say: Kiss him for me.' This is the 'holy' kiss which is exchanged between those who belong to the holy community as the sign of their Christian love for one another. What was then the normal mode of greeting soon proved open to abuse, so that the practice became the subject of numerous regulations in early Councils, and was eventually abandoned in the West during the thirteenth century. Today in our less demonstrative society the same feeling of Christian love may be conveyed, without giving any cause for offence, by a warm handshake (cf. Phillips' paraphrase: 'Give a handshake all round among the brotherhood').

27: I adjure you by the Lord that this epistle be read unto all the brethren.

If Paul at this point took the pen from his amanuensis to add the last words in his own hand [cf. *2 Thess.* 3:17], this would account for the change from the plural to the first person singular. The unexpected solemnity of the charge has provoked much discussion. But when it is remembered that the letter was sent to meet the needs of a situation he could not deal with in person [2:17f], his insistence that it be read to *all* becomes understandable – otherwise the purpose for which it was written would not be achieved [3:10]. Behind this command there is the apostle's conviction that these words would minister grace to the congregation as it met for worship [*Col.* 4: 16], and the practice doubtless marked the first stage in the church's recognition of the canonicity of the New Testament writings [*2 Tim.* 3:16].

28: The grace of our Lord Jesus Christ be with you.

As always with Paul the farewell is a benediction. He prays that 'the grace' – a favourite word and the keynote of his theology – 'of our Lord Jesus Christ' may be with them. He begins and ends all his Epistles on this note of grace, for the grace that is in Christ is their Alpha and their Omega, their first word and their last. 'Whatever God has to say to us – and in all the New Testament letters there are things that search the heart and make it quake – begins and ends with grace . . . All that God has been to man in Jesus Christ is summed up in it: all His gentleness and patience, all the holy passion of His love, is gathered up in grace. What more could one soul wish for another than that the grace of the Lord Jesus Christ should be with it?' (Denney).

2 THESSALONIANS

CHAPTER ONE

After the greeting, Paul thanks God for the Thessalonians' progress in faith and love, and especially for their patience in suffering [verses 1–4]. But the parousia which will bring retribution to their persecutors will also be the day when Christ comes to be glorified in his saints [verses 5–10]. And with that goal in view, Paul prays that God will fulfil his gracious purpose in them [verses 11, 12].

1: Paul, and Silvanus, and Timothy, unto the church of the Thessalonians in God our Father and the Lord Jesus Christ; 2: Grace to you and peace from God the Father and the Lord Jesus Christ.

The address and greeting differ from the form followed in the first Epistle in only two particulars. 1. Here God is called 'our Father', which shows that Paul is thinking of God as the Father of all believers [*Rom.* 8:14–17], rather than as the Father of the Lord Jesus Christ. 2. The added words 'from God the Father and the Lord Jesus Christ' make it plain that the Father and Christ are together the one source of grace and peace. That such a construction could be used without comment not only implies the writer's belief in the deity of Christ, but also takes the readers' acknowledgement of it for granted.

3: We are bound to give thanks to God always for you, brethren, even as it is meet, for that your faith groweth exceedingly, and the love of each one of you all toward one another aboundeth;

We are obliged to give thanks to God always for you, brothers, as is fitting (Hendriksen): Paul, Silas, and Timothy feel impelled as a matter of debt always to thank God for the grace which has made the Thessalonians their brethren in Christ. Moreover, this sense of personal obligation was fittingly in accord with their remarkable spiritual progress [cf. *Phil.* 1:7]. The word 'groweth exceedingly' (*huperauxano*) affords another instance of Paul's fondness for compounds beginning with *huper*, and is suitably applied to faith since it suggest a vigorous organic growth.

No less appropriate is his choice of 'aboundeth' to express the diffusive, or expansive character of their love for one another (Lightfoot). And in their flourishing faith and abounding love Paul saw the encouraging evidence that his prayer for them was already being answered [*1 Thess.* 3:10, 12]. As the apostle often speaks of faith and love without 'hope' [*1 Thess.* 3:6; *Gal.* 5: 6; *Col.* 1:4; *Eph.* 1:15, etc.] there is no need to account for its absence here, though their endurance under persecution implies it [verse 4].

4: so that we ourselves glory in you in the churches of God for your patience and faith in all your persecutions and in the afflictions which ye endure;

From 1 Thessalonians 1:8f. it appears that up to a certain point the missionaries 'refrained from speaking publicly of the success of their mission to Thessalonica, which had advertised itself in the best possible way; but now, out of gratitude to God, and from the sense of what is due to their Thessalonian brethren, they can no longer refrain: "while others have been telling about our work, we ourselves are now constrained to glory in it"' (Findlay). Paul's words here show that the church which had been born in a storm of persecution was still bravely bearing up with unwavering faith under the continuing opposition and attacks of the unbelieving.

5: which is a manifest token of the righteous judgment of God; to the end that ye may be counted worthy of the kingdom of God, for which ye also suffer:

One thought suggests another, so that the sentence is stretched to the end of verse 10. This brave patience and faith in the endurance of these persecutions is seen by Paul as a sure token of the righteousness of God's judgment at the Great Assize when all the injustices of the present life shall be put right [cf. *Phil.* 1:28].

Leon Morris points out that to be counted worthy' is akin to the great Pauline word 'to justify', and does not mean 'to make worthy' but 'to declare worthy'. Although this implies that the attainment of the kingdom is the fruit of grace, the declaration of their worthiness to enter it is no mere legal fiction, but is in complete accord with the facts of the case. In other words, the reality of the Thessalonians' present justification [*Rom.* 3:24, 26] is demonstrated by their willingness to suffer 'for righteousness' sake' [*Matt.* 5: 10]. Such suffering is not only the natural consequence of their commitment to Christ [*Phil.* 1:29], but it also brings them into fellowship with Paul and his colleagues who are enduring the same things on behalf of the kingdom of God. And since Christians are here taught to regard persecution as an anticipation of their vindication by God on the day of judgment, they should never be discouraged by it.

6: if so be that it is a righteous thing with God to recompense affliction to them that afflict you, 7a: and to you that are afflicted rest with us,

'If so be' implies no doubt but confirms the reality, meaning 'as it certainly is'. What Paul is at pains to emphasize is the absolute righteousness of God in the final judgment. Then all present wrongs suffered in the service of God shall be righted in the just punishment of their persecutors. In that day the vast question mark which this conduct has put against the justice of God will receive the answer it deserves [*Matt.* 7:2]. This is what these evil men 'demand of God by their actions, demand again and again, and God would not be righteous if he did not meet this demand upon his righteousness' (Lenski). But for the Thessalonians who are now enduring the pressures of persecution, this judgment will bring the relief of that eternal rest which has been won for them by the justifying righteousness of Christ. 'With us' is a typically Pauline touch and conveys the encouraging assurance that fellowship in suffering must lead to fellowship in glory.

7b: at the revelation of the Lord Jesus from heaven with the angels of his power in flaming fire, 8: rendering vengeance to them that know not God, and to them that obey not the gospel of our Lord Jesus: 9: who shall suffer punishment, even eternal destruction from the face of the Lord and from the glory of his might, 10: when he shall come to be glorified in his saints, and to be marvelled at in all them that believed (because our testimony unto you was believed) in that day.

This section has a rhythmic structure, which some regard as an indication that Paul is quoting a hymn or adapting an apocalypse to Christian use, but it rather suggests that he viewed the Lord's advent with prophetic exultation.

At the revelation of the Lord Jesus from heaven with the angels of his power in flaming fire: The final justification of God [*Rom.* 2:5] will be made manifest to all at 'the revelation' or unveiling of the Lord Jesus. Vos notes that whereas the term *parousia* chiefly concerns believers, the militant effect of the advent upon the disobedient is to the forefront in *apocalypsis* (revelation). In relation to believers 'the appearance of Christ will partake of the character of a "revelation", inasmuch as his glory has not been visibly disclosed to them before' (*The Pauline Eschatology*, p. 79). This is the momentary, miraculous descent of the Lord 'from heaven', attended by 'the angels' who show forth his mighty power, and clothed 'in flaming fire' which is his 'awful robe of glory' (Findlay). In so freely applying to Jesus language that recalls the glorious manifestations of God under the Old Covenant [*Exod.* 3:2; 19:18], Paul shows that the same burning holiness will characterize the revelation of the divine Son from heaven.

Rendering vengeance to them that know not God, and to them that obey not the gospel of our Lord Jesus: 'Vengeance' must not be confused with the vindictiveness of human passion, for the Lord comes to render the retribution which the rebellious deserve. As Findlay says, 'It is the inflicting of *full justice* on the criminal nothing more, nothing less'. Many maintain that 'them that know not God' refers to the Gentiles, while 'them that obey not the gospel' points to the Jews; but it is preferable to regard the expressions as virtually synonymous, with the second merely serving to enhance the meaning of the first. 'So conceived, the two form one extended category including, with the Thessalonian oppressors, all who in their estrangement from God [cf. *Eph.* 4:18] disobey His message conveyed in the Gospel of Christ, their disobedience being the sequence and full expression of a wilful ignorance' (Findlay).

Who shall suffer punishment, even eternal destruction from the face of the Lord and from the glory of his might: 'Shall suffer punishment' means will pay the penalty'. Such persecutors of God's people will pay the just penalty for their misdeeds. As this punishment is 'destruction', the utter loss of blessedness which is entailed in their perpetual banishment from the presence of the Lord, it is the continuation without hope of the most 'unauthentic' existence imaginable – a ruin as 'everlasting' as the bliss of the redeemed [*Matt.* 25:40]. Thus subject to the torment of endless remorse the persecutors will be shut out from the 'glory' of the Lord's might which the salvation of the persecuted so fully reflects [verse 10].

'If the gospel, as conceived in the New Testament, has any character at all, it has the character of finality. It is God's *last word* to men. And the consequences of accepting or rejecting it are final; it opens no prospect beyond the life on the one hand, and the death on the other, which are the results of obedience and disobedience . . . Those who stubbornly refuse to submit to the gospel, and to love and obey Jesus Christ, incur at the Last Advent an infinite and irreparable loss. They pass into a night on which no morning dawns' (Denney).

When he shall come to be glorified in his saints, and to be marvelled at in all them that believed (because our testimony unto you was believed) in that day: These two parallel phrases set forth the significance of the advent for those who by grace have put their trust in Christ. The first means that Christ will be glorified 'in' the persons of his 'saints' whose transformation will perfectly mirror his own glory [*2 Cor.* 3:18; *1 John* 3:2]; the second that Christ will be the object of admiring wonder in 'all' – in every one of those who 'believed'! The aorist tense looks back to the decisive act of faith which has made them sharers in the splendours of 'that day'. Paul's parenthesis assures the much tried Thessalonians that they too will be among this favoured company, because their testimony ('our' includes Silas and Timothy) to the saving truths of the gospel was believed by them. Since the teaching of the apostle here is that the same day which seals the doom of the ungodly also secures the final salvation of all believers, his words clearly rule out the unscriptural notion that the coming of the Lord is in two quite separate stages. 'It is evident that Paul mentions no interval between the time of deliverance and the time of retribution. No period of years elapses. The "rest" and the "destruction" follow in quick succession' (Charles R. Erdman).

11: To which end we also pray always for you, that our God may count you worthy of your calling, and fulfil every desire of goodness and every work of faith, with power;

With this glorious end in view the missionaries not only thank God for the Thessalonians (1:3ff.), but also constantly pray that he may count them worthy of his call to salvation on that day (verse 10).

And that he by (his) power may bring to fulfilment (your) every resolve prompted by goodness and (your every) work resulting from faith (Hendriksen): God having thus begun a good work in them, they ask that he may bring it to completion by the continued exercise of his mighty power [*1 Thess.* 5:24]. And it is because believers are bidden to respond to what the grace of God must first work in them that the petition is also an implied exhortation [*Phil.* 2:13]. Accordingly, they must fulfil every resolve that proceeds from goodness and finish every work begotten by faith. As many have remarked, the best commentary on this prayer is the Easter Collect of the Anglican Church: 'We humbly beseech Thee, that, as by Thy special grace preventing (i.e. preceding) us, Thou dost put into our minds good desires, so by Thy continual help we may bring the same to good effect.'

12: that the name of our Lord Jesus may be glorified in you, and ye in him, according to the grace of our God and the Lord Jesus Christ.

What they ask God to accomplish in the Thessalonians is directed to one end. It is that 'the name of our Lord Jesus' may be glorified 'in' them, and they 'in' him. For as the last day will reveal the full meaning of their union with Christ, so this will bring its revenue of eternal glory to him 'whose name salvation is'. 'This "name" is "glorified", when its full import is recognized, and the worship which it requires is paid to Him who bears it. So in Philippians 2:9, we read how the work and sufferings of Christ will have their consummation when "in t*he name of Jesus* every knee shall bow, and every tongue confess that Jesus Christ is *Lord!*" (Findlay). All who are then found 'in him' shall share in his glory, even as 'servants come in for a share of the honour of the master whose livery they wear' (Adeney).

According to the grace of our God and the Lord Jesus Christ: The acknowledgement of this grace as 'the source, whence all glorification springs', affords another instance of Paul's anxiety to exclude human merit (Lightfoot). That any of the sons of Adam's race are brought to glory is solely due to the undeserved favour of 'our God' and 'the Lord Jesus Christ', who are therefore worthy of all the praise.

CHAPTER TWO

In correcting the mistaken notion that the day of the Lord was at hand, Paul shows that this would be preceded by the great apostasy and the revelation of the man of lawlessness, who will be overthrown by the Lord at his coming, but whose blasphemous pretensions and lying wonders will draw many to perdition because they had no love of the truth [verses 1–12]. But as God had chosen the Thessalonian Christians for salvation, Paul exhorts them to stand fast in his doctrine, and prays that both the Father and the Son may comfort their hearts and establish them in all goodness [verses 13–17].

1: Now we beseech you, brethren, touching the coming of our Lord Jesus Christ, and our gathering together unto him; 2: to the end that ye be not quickly shaken from your mind, nor yet be troubled, either by spirit, or by word, or by epistle as from us, as that the day of the Lord is just at hand;

Now concerning the coming of our Lord Jesus Christ and our gathering together to (meet) him (Hendriksen): Paul now turns to the main purpose of the letter, which is to correct a mistaken belief in the immediacy of Christ's second advent and the assembling to meet him [*1 Thess.* 4:17], and to check the neglect of present duty that this teaching had fostered at Thessalonica [*2 Thess.* 3:6–15]. And since such errors in doctrine can never be expected to promote *right behaviour*, but the contrary, it is not pedantic to insist upon the practical importance of cherishing the *right beliefs!*

We request you, brothers, not to be easily shaken from your (normal state of) mind or disturbed, either by spirit or by word or by letter as from us, to the effect that the day of the Lord has arrived (Hendriksen): Paul is concerned to counter the highly undesirable effects produced by the sensational announcement that 'the day of the Lord' (the period including the events of the end-time) had already arrived, and so the coming of Jesus could be expected at any moment! This had thrown some of the Thessalonians off balance, causing a loss of mental stability which left them in a continuing state of nervous excitement. The faint-hearted felt unfit to meet the Lord, while the idle took it as an excuse to stop work.

They must not thus be swept away from sanity by these 'any moment' adventists who falsely claim his authority for such teaching, whether it purports to be an inspired interpretation or a reported statement of his doctrine, or perhaps even a written communication [cf. 3:17] – a blanket denial which possibly reflects the apostle's own uncertainty of the source of the error. It should be remembered that throughout this notoriously difficult passage Paul is motivated by a purely pastoral purpose. He does not set out to gratify an unlawful curiosity, but deliberately limits his instruction to what is necessary to correct the enthusiasts and to encourage the fearful. Indeed it is only as we realize that prophecy was never intended to provide us with a blueprint of the future that we shall avoid falling into the very error these verses were intended to prevent.

3: let no man beguile you in any wise: for it will not be, except the falling away come first, and the man of sin be revealed, the son of perdition, 4: he that opposeth and exalteth himself against all that is called God or that is worshipped; so that he sitteth in the temple of God, setting himself forth as God.

Let no one deceive you in any way whatever (Frame): Whether this dangerous delusion is propagated in ways already mentioned [verse 2] or in any other way, Paul emphatically warns the Thessalonians not to be deceived by it [cf. *Matt.* 24:4]. 'The doctrine that the day of the Lord had set in was a deception; whatever might be the motives of those who taught it, it was a perilous error and they were to guard against being its dupes' (Eadie).

For (the day of the Lord will not be present) unless first of all there comes the apostasy and there be revealed the man of lawlessness, the son of perdition (Frame): As the clause beginning with 'for' remains unfinished, the bracketed words have to be supplied from verse 2 to make up the sense. There was no factual basis for the agitation at Thessalonica because that day must be preceded by the apostasy and the appearance of the man of lawlessness. *The* apostasy – seemingly a subject in which they had received previous instruction [verse 5] – is the last great religious revolt that is to culminate in the revelation of the one in whom the creature's opposition to God will reach its culmination [cf. *Gen.* 3:5]. Thus the final apostasy of mankind prepares the way for the manifestation of this monstrous figure, the satanically inspired human agent who fully deserves the doom announced by the title 'son of perdition', because in him all wickedness will be summed up [verse 8]. As Vos well says, This should warn us 'not to take for granted an uninterrupted progress of the cause of Christ through all ages on toward the end. As the reign of truth will be gradually extended, so the power of evil will gather force towards the end. The making all things right and new in the world depends not on gradual amelioration but on the final interposition of God'.

He that opposeth and exalteth himself against all that is called God or that is worshipped: Paul's dependence upon Daniel is evident in this description of the activity of the Arch-enemy, whose blasphemous hostility to God was foreshadowed in the desecration of the Jews' Temple in 168 BC by Antiochus Epiphanes in whom the prophecy received its first fulfilment [cf. *Dan.* 7:25; 8:11; 11:31, 36ff.; 12:11]. The phrase, 'that is called God', includes all the so-called gods of the heathen [cf. *1 Cor.* 8:5], while 'or that is worshipped' embraces every object of worship held sacred by men. Carried forward by an impressive display of Satanic power [verse 9], the man who is marked by absolute lawlessness will thus recognize no God but himself.

So that he seats himself in the sanctuary of God, proclaiming himself to be God (Hendriksen): Although Antiochus, who erected an altar to Zeus in the Jewish Temple, and Caligula, who attempted to set up an image of himself there in AD 40, both asserted their divinity, yet the ultimate enormity of an exclusive claim to deity is reserved for the man of sin. Since under the New Covenant no special significance is attached to a particular place of worship [*John* 4:21], it is unnecessary to assume a literal reference to the adversary's entrance into any earthly 'sanctuary' whether Jewish or Christian. 'The "sitting in the temple of God" only sums up in one terse image that unholiest offence offered to the Holiest of Beings' (Vos). What Paul is in fact saying is that this evil person will arrogate to himself the divine status and homage that belongs to God alone. This means that the Lawless One will not be content to masquerade as the Messiah, for such an outright act of self-deification precludes that professed submission to the will of God which this role would demand.

5: Remember ye not, that, when I was yet with you, I told you these things?

We, alas, cannot recall Paul's oral instruction, and therein lies our difficulty! If therefore the interpretation of this passage is beset by many obscurities, it is because we 'have not the key to the cypher with which the Thessalonians had been supplied' (Adeney). If it is legitimate to link *1 John* 2: 18 with this verse, it would seem that the teaching that *Anti-christ*, as opposed to the many antichrists already at work [cf. verse 7], must make his appearance before the end formed part of the general apostolic tradition [cf. verse 15].

The fact that Paul repeatedly told the Thessalonians of events which must *precede* Christ's coming implies reproof that an intelligent grasp of his teaching had not been reflected in their conduct. They should not have been misled by the delusion that the day of the Lord had set in. The apostle's exceptional lapse into the first person singular at this point [cf. 3:16] shows that he is very well aware of what he himself had taught. Probably this jogging of their memory was also intended to avoid 'further explanation in writing on a subject bordering on politics, the more explicit treatment of which might have exposed the missionaries to a renewal in more dangerous form of the charges that led to their expulsion from Thessalonica: see *Acts* 17:6f.' (Findlay).

6: And now ye know that which restraineth, to the end that he may be revealed in his own season. 7: For the mystery of lawlessness doth already work: only there is one that restraineth now, until he be taken out of the way.

And you know what is restraining him now so that he may be revealed in his time. For the mystery of lawlessness is already at work; only he who now restrains it will do so until he is out of the way (RSV): The Thessalonians *knew* what Paul meant; we can only suggest what seems to be the most reasonable interpretation of this cryptic utterance. The mystery of lawlessness is already at work, says Paul, but *something* [verse 6] or *someone* [verse 7] is at present restraining the man of lawlessness until the appointed season for his manifestation (or appearing) has arrived. If it be asked what so restrains the forces of lawlessness, the answer then as now is probably the *rule of law* [verse 6] as this *principle is personified* [verse 7] in well-ordered government [cf. *Rom.* 13:1–6]. Not only would it have been dangerous for Paul to have spoken more plainly of the removal of Roman rule, but the intervening centuries since the disappearance of that Empire have also proved that his vague allusion to the Restrainer was far more appropriate than any specific reference to the contemporary scene.

Nor was this accidental, for like all prophets inspired of God, the apostle spoke better than he knew at the time. What we have here is an example of that foreshortened perspective which is peculiar to the prophet's vision. Paul is able to set forth the events of the end-time, but he does not know or pretend to know *when* these things will take place [cf. *Acts* 1:7]. So with regard to the revelation of the Arch-enemy, he 'did not see whether ten or ten thousand years were involved' (Lenski).

However, the purpose of the prophecy is not to provide believers with a time-table. It is to let them see that not even Satan's final master-stroke is an independent development. Indeed it assures them that nothing is beyond the control of the sovereign God who makes all things work together for the good of his people [*Rom.* 8:28]. Meanwhile the Thessalonians can perceive that 'the mystery of lawlessness' is already secretly at work. 'Already' marks the imminence of the end, for Christians belong to the eschatological period in which the gospel mystery of salvation [*1 Tim.* 3:16] is opposed by this sinister mystery of evil whose content is lawlessness. As therefore the Lawless One will rule only when the restraint of law is removed, so the precursor of his appearing will be the increase of lawlessness.

8: And then shall be revealed the lawless one, whom the Lord Jesus shall slay with the breath of his mouth, and bring to nought by the manifestation of his coming;

After the removal of the restraining power, *then* the Lawless One will be revealed. Without pausing to say whether the period of his ascendancy will be long or short, Paul passes at once to his complete defeat at the very moment of the Lord's appearing. For the apostle's object is not to stimulate interest in the chronology of lawlessness, but to encourage the certain expectation of Christ's ultimate triumph over all the powers of evil.

As Findlay points out, '*Jesus*, the human Name, could not be wanting here, where the overthrow of "the *man* of lawlessness" is in question'. This will be no protracted conflict between evenly matched antagonists, for the returning Lord will instantly slay Satan's mouth-piece and abolish all his power. The two parallel expressions that describe the destruction carry virtually the same meaning. It is fitting that 'the breath of his mouth' should be the terrible weapon with which Christ for ever silences 'this blasphemous assumer of divine prerogative' (Eadie). [cf. *Isa.* 11: 4; *Rev.* 19:15]. In the second the unique combination, 'the manifestation (epiphany) of his coming (parousia)', appears to emphasize the resistless power of the Son of Man, the mere *appearing* of whose *presence* suffices to destroy his adversary.

9: even he, whose coming is according to the working of Satan with all power and signs and lying wonders, 10: and with all deceit of unrighteousness for them that perish; because they received not the love of the truth, that they might be saved.

Paul now reverts to the period preceding this judgment in order to sketch the 'ministry' of Anti-christ and to emphasize its effects upon his dupes. This arch-deceiver also has an advent, he too works signs and wonders, but the infernal parody is after the pattern of Satan's working which is the way of falsehood and death [*John* 8:44]. Hence the appearance of the Lawless One will be accompanied by the supernatural *power* to perform such signs as will authenticate himself and make men *marvel* at him [cf. *Acts* 2:22 where all three terms are used of the miracles of Christ]. The objective reality of these prodigies is not denied, but because they originate in falsehood they are teachers of lies (cf. *Deut.* 13:1–5]. The deceit that is inspired by unrighteousness thus governs the entire manifestation of 'the son of perdition' [verse 3], whose doom will be shared by the deluded [cf. *Matt.* 24:24], even 'those who are on the way to perdition'.

Because they received not the love of the truth, that they might be saved: So 'because' (that is, 'in requital for their refusal': Plummer) they did not welcome the love of the truth which would have brought them salvation, they are justly given over to an infatuation with the lie which leads to their damnation [verses 11, 12]. 'The love of the truth', a remarkable expression which appears only here, shows that their antipathy to the truth was not so much intellectual as moral. Loving darkness rather than light [*John* 3:19], they lacked that commitment to the truth of God which issues in obedience to his will [cf. 1:8]. 'Those of whom the Apostle speaks resist "the truth" with an instinctive, invincible prejudice; for they have no desire to "be saved" from the sins it condemns [*John* 3:20; cf. *2 Cor.* 4:3, 4] . . . It is a just, but mournful result, that rejecters of Christ's miracles become believers in Satan's, and that atheism should be avenged by superstition. So it has been, and will be' (Findlay).

11: And for this cause God sendeth them a working of error, that they should believe a lie:

And so for this reason, it is God that sends them an energy of delusion that they may believe the falsehood (Frame): Not for one moment will Paul leave his readers to imagine that this triumph of Satan is achieved at the expense of God's supremacy over all events. The familiar evasion that God simply 'permits' evil to exist, or that its punishment is merely the outworking of an impersonal law, finds no place in the apostle's thought.[1] Whereas it would seem from verse 9 that Satan alone is responsible for the success of the Lawless One in deceiving his

[1] In a universe created and controlled by God, even the Fall and all its consequences are ordained for the furtherance of his eternal purpose. Although this means that God is the *ultimate* cause of whatever comes to pass, it does not make him the author of sin, because every evil act is the result of a deliberate volition for which its *immediate* agent is responsible. The betrayal of Jesus by Judas is probably the clearest example of this principle of the divine government. In this, Judas remained accountable to God though he could not have done otherwise [*Acts* 4:28], for in yielding to the temptation of Satan he willingly followed his own evil desires [*John* 13:27].

followers, here it is shown that God's ultimate control over the whole process cannot be set aside. The expression 'God sends' indicates a positive, personal act [cf. *Rom.* 1:24, 26, 28]. It is God who sends 'an energy unto delusion' that prepares the way for the final judgment by causing those who rejected the truth to embrace Satan's master-lie and worship Anti-christ (Frame). As one would expect, the apostle faithfully adheres to the prophetic realism of the Old Testament [cf. *1 Kings* 22:29ff.; *2 Chron.* 18:18ff., *Isa.* 19:14; *Ezek.* 14:9]. And indeed this teaching cannot be compromised without exchanging the living God for a finite deity, whose helplessness in the face of rampant evil would deprive men of all comfort.

12: that they all might be judged who believed not the truth, but had pleasure in unrighteousness.

In order that all may be condemned who did not believe the truth but delighted in unrighteousness (Hendriksen): Since these men had no love of the truth, God confirmed their predilection for error by giving them up to the lie, in order that they might receive the unfavourable verdict they deserved in the final judgment. The ground of their condemnation is twofold. So far from trusting in God's truth they did not even give credence to its testimony. They believed neither its promises nor its threatenings. This was because their preferences lay in another direction. For by resolving to take pleasure in wickedness they, like Milton's Satan, had made evil their good (Findlay). Those without 'the love of the truth' will always 'delight in unrighteousness', for between these opposite affections there is no neutral ground.

13: But we are bound to give thanks to God always for you, brethren beloved of the Lord, for that God chose you from the beginning unto salvation in sanctification of the Spirit and belief of the truth: 14: whereunto he called you through our gospel, to the obtaining of the glory of our Lord Jesus Christ.

From the doom that awaits the rebels, Paul turns with relief to the very different destiny which is assured to the Thessalonians by grace. His virtual repetition of the words of 1:3 seems intended to stress the fact that he and his fellow-labourers feel bound to give thanks continually for what God has wrought in them, despite the doubts voiced by the faint-hearted! For the welcome they gave to the truth not only made them their 'brethren', but also showed them to be 'beloved of the Lord' (i.e. Christ; cf. *Deut.* 33:12 which refers to Jehovah). Denney calls this thanksgiving, 'a system of theology in miniature', because it 'covers the whole work of salvation from the eternal choice of God to the obtaining of the glory of our Lord Jesus Christ in the world to come'.

For that God chose you from the beginning unto salvation, i.e. from eternity [cf. *1 Cor.* 2:7; *Eph.* 1:4; *2 Tim.* 1:9]: 'The choice of God is, from its nature, an eternal choice, though His call takes place in time, and through the preaching of the gospel. This divine and ultimate aspect and origin of human salvation the apostle rejoices to contemplate, as, rising above all human instrumentalities, weakness, and failures, it carries all back to His blessed sovereignty and His gracious self-formed purpose, and gives Him all the glory' (Eadie).

Through sanctification by the Spirit and belief in the truth (Hendriksen): When God determines the end, he also ordains the means. Hence this eternal election to salvation was realized in their sanctification *by* the Spirit and belief *in* the truth. Such trust in the truth is the evidence of having been set apart for God by his Spirit. For the human response to the gospel – in conversion [cf. *John* 1:12 and 13] and in the walk that follows it [cf. *Phil.* 1:12 and 13] – is always the result of the divine enabling! 'We have no reason to ask what God decreed before the creation of the world in order to know that we have been elected by Him, but we find in ourselves a satisfactory proof of whether He has sanctified us by His Spirit and enlightened us to faith in His Gospel' (Calvin).

To which (salvation) he also called you through our gospel, with a view to obtaining the glory of our Lord Jesus Christ (Hendriksen): This is at once a reminder of the call of God which came to them through the preaching of the gospel, and an encouragement to persevere to glory. As the remembrance of the awakening call evokes gratitude, so the prospect of the promised consummation inspires hope [verse 16]. The glory of Christ 'is the glory which Christ possesses, and which he shares [cf. *Rom.* 8:17] with "the beloved of the Lord". In other words, *whom he called . . . them he also glorified* [*Rom.* 8:30]' (Frame).

15: So then, brethren, stand fast, and hold the traditions which ye were taught, whether by word, or by epistle of ours.

'So then' points to a logical conclusion. Paul wants the Thessalonians to see what kind of response this understanding of God's gracious purpose should constrain. Instead of being shaken from the faith by wild rumours [verse 2], they are to 'stand fast' in it. The resolve to remain fixed on the rock of revelation is important if one wishes to avoid finishing in the quicksands of speculation.

And hold the traditions which ye were taught: This is not another exhortation; it rather defines the call to stand fast. They would maintain the required stability only by holding fast to 'the traditions' (or teaching) they had been given. As Lightfoot notes, the prominent idea of *paradosis* (*tradition*) 'in the New Testament is that of an authority external to the teacher himself'. So that Paul's use of it amounts to 'a confession that he was not expressing his own ideas, but *delivering* or *handing on* a message that he had received from heaven'. [cf. *Gal.* 1:11, 12 and see the comment on *1 Thess.* 2:13]

Whether by word, or by epistle of ours: 'Ours' qualifies what they are to hold fast, viz. the apostolic tradition, whether spoken or written [*1 Thess.* 2: 13]. It also implies the rejection of every other teaching as lacking the authority to command the consciences of men [cf. *Col.* 2:16ff]. And though we cannot now hear Paul preach in person, this tradition has been faithfully transmitted to us in the pages of the New Testament.

16: Now our Lord Jesus Christ himself, and God our Father who loved us and gave us eternal comfort and good hope through grace, 17: comfort your hearts and establish them in every good work and word.

Now may he, our Lord Jesus Christ and God our Father (Hendriksen): Paul now turns to prayer in order to invoke the divine blessing, without which the preceding exhortation could find no fulfilment in the lives of his converts. The fact that the name of Christ is here placed first serves to emphasize his equality with the Father [cf. *2 Cor.* 13:14]. This is possibly because the immediate context has had Christ's triumph over the Lawless One so much in view.

Who loved us and gave us eternal comfort and good hope through grace: Probably these words ought to be referred to the Father's great act of love in giving his Son to die for us [cf. *John* 3:16], for this 'act is the source of all our consolation and hope' (Lightfoot). Believers enjoy the 'eternal comfort' which will outlast time itself, because they have embraced that 'good hope' whose glorious fulfilment will outmatch their highest expectations. All this is theirs through the supreme gift of God's grace. 'Though the cross of Christ is never mentioned in the two Letters, and His death but twice [*1 Thess.* 4:14; 5:10] in cursory fashion, "the grace of God" therein displayed furnishes the basis and fulcrum of the entire system of doctrine and life in the Epistles' (Findlay).

Comfort your hearts and establish them in every good work and word: Paul's petition on their behalf is short but comprehensive in its scope. He prays that their hearts (or the inner man as seen by God) may be strengthened and settled to do good in all they do or say. For those who cherish a good hope must be seen to live good lives.

CHAPTER THREE

Paul requests the Thessalonians to pray for the spread of the gospel and that he and his companions might be delivered from the persecutors who hindered their work [verses 1, 2]. He assures them of the faithfulness of God, expresses his confidence in their obedience, and prays for their continued progress [verses 3–5]. He next censures the idlers, and requires the rest to withdraw from the company of any brother who refuses to work, so that he may be shamed into mending his ways [verses 6–15]. After a final prayer for his readers, Paul guarantees the authenticity of the letter by adding the closing words in his own handwriting [verses 16–18].

1: Finally, brethren, pray for us, that the word of the Lord may run and be glorified, even as also it is with you; 2: and that we may be delivered from unreasonable and evil men; for all have not faith.

'Finally' (or 'for the rest', cf. *1 Thess.* 4:1) introduces the apostle's treatment of the important practical issues with which the Epistle concludes. But first he asks for a place in their prayers. As ever, he seeks nothing for himself, his sole desire is to see the word of the Lord spread swiftly [*Psa.* 147:15] and be glorified [*Acts* 13:48] in the lives of those who joyfully receive it.

Even as also it is with you: As the original lacks a verb, it is not certain whether Paul refers to the success of their first mission ('as it did among you', RSV), or also intends to include the present progress of the gospel in Thessalonica. Be that as it may, the difficulties that faced him at Corinth doubtless made him long for the Word to run as rapidly through Achaia as it had done in Macedonia.

And that we may be delivered from unreasonable and evil men: With this triumph of the Word in view, they should also pray that its heralds may not be hindered from spreading it by the opposition of certain (= 'the') perverse and wicked men. The apostle clearly has a definite group in mind, which it is not hard to identify. He is thinking of the fanatical attempts of the unbelieving Jews to block the advance of the gospel at Corinth [cf. *Acts* 18:5–17].

For all have not faith: Such implacable hostility to the gospel sadly shows that all men have not faith. Paul is not here stating the obvious; he is in fact explaining what lies behind the activity of these evil men. For as faith puts a man in possession of all the blessings of the world to come, so the lack of it is the mark of belonging to the present evil age. Hence when those without faith exhibit their enmity towards the truth, this antagonism is completely in accord with their nature and their destiny.

3: But the Lord is faithful, who shall establish you, and guard you from the evil one.

Against the persecutors who lack 'faith' stands the 'faithful' Lord (Christ) who will keep his trusting people from being overwhelmed by these assaults, which are really instigated by the Evil One himself. By turning so abruptly from his own trials in Corinth to the dangers which threatened the Thessalonians, Paul shows that he is more concerned about them than he is about himself (Calvin). He therefore assures them of the Lord's strengthening and protecting grace. With regard to the situation in Thessalonica, this guarding will prevent them 'from falling into the snares of the evil one, such as fanaticism, loafing, meddlesomeness, neglect of duty, defeatism (see verses 5–8)' (Hendriksen).

4: And we have confidence in the Lord touching you, that ye both do and will do the things which we command.

Having reminded his friends of the faithfulness of the Lord, Paul tactfully prepares the way for what is to follow [verse 6] by expressing his confidence in their obedience. However, this trust in his converts is not a vote of confidence in human nature! It is a confidence which he has 'in the Lord'. Because he sees in their present obedience the evidence of divine grace at work in their lives, he also expects that they 'will do' (this has some emphasis) what he is about to lay upon them with all the authority of an apostle of Christ.

5: And the Lord direct your hearts into the love of God, and into the patience of Christ.

However, may the Lord incline your hearts to a sense of God's love and to the endurance that Christ alone inspires (Frame): But before Paul begins to admonish the idlers, he commends them all to the Lord (Christ) in this brief but beautiful prayer. For though he has confidence in the Lord that they will do what he commands, 'yet he is certain that the help of the Lord is indispensable to incline their hearts to keep his commandments' (Frame). Therefore he prays that they may be given such a sense of God's love to them that they will want to make his will their own; and that they may manifest the steadfast endurance that Christ alone can inspire.

6: Now we command you, brethren, in the name of our Lord Jesus Christ, that ye withdraw yourselves from every brother that walketh disorderly, and not after the tradition which they received of us.

It is because the Thessalonians are 'brethren' that Paul claims the right to command them 'in the name of', that is, on the authority of 'the Lord Jesus Christ', whose apostle he is. This peremptory address, which was prompted by their failure to heed his milder admonition in the previous letter [*1 Thess.* 4: 11, 12] charges the whole community with the responsibility of disciplining the few who refused to earn their daily bread.

That you hold aloof from every brother walking in disorderly fashion (Findlay): The loyal majority are commanded to hold aloof from every brother who 'breaks the ranks' by stopping work on the excuse that the Lord's advent is near. At least this means that they must not condone his idleness by supplying him with free food, but it may also imply his exclusion from the Lord's Supper. These measures are intended to make him mend his ways [verse 14]; they do not amount to excommunication, for the rest of the congregation is still to regard and admonish him as 'a brother' [verse 15].

And not in accordance with the tradition which you received from us (Findlay): As this disobedient idleness was a serious breach of apostolic discipline, to regard it with complacency would contaminate the whole church. It was contrary to the express instruction given when Paul was with them [verse 10] and reiterated in the first Epistle [*1 Thess.* 4: 11, 12; 5: 14]. On 'tradition' see comment on 2:13. Although 'they' (ASV) is favoured by textual critics, 'you' (RSV, NEB) makes much better sense here.

7: For yourselves know how ye ought to imitate us: for we behaved not ourselves disorderly among you;

The Thessalonians do not need to be told of the obligation to earn their own living, for the teaching they were given had also been conspicuously illustrated in the self-denying lives of their instructors [verse 8]. 'Disorderly', a military term, was applied to soldiers *out of rank*. 'Officers are as much subject to discipline as the rank and file; it was due to their Churches that the Apostles should set an example of a strictly ordered life; with this example before them, which bore exactly upon the point in question, the readers "know" what the nature of their "imitation" should be' (Findlay).

8: neither did we eat bread for nought at any man's hand, but in labour and travail, working night and day, that we might not burden any of you:

'To eat bread' is a Hebraism for gaining a living [cf. *Gen.* 3:19]. It seems likely from *Acts* 17:7 that the missionaries stayed with Jason, but unlike the idle brothers who were begging support from the church *they* worked to pay for their keep. Indeed they chose to accept the most exacting and incessant toil to avoid burdening the Thessalonians with their maintenance. What was said in *1 Thess.* 2:9 to prove that they did not preach for profit, is here repeated as an example to be followed by all, including the work-shy idlers!

9: not because we have not the right, but to make ourselves an ensample unto you, that ye should imitate us.

However, Paul insists that they were entitled to claim the free support of their converts, even though they had waived that right [cf. *1 Cor.* 9:12]. 'Just as Paul wanted to set an example by the work that he did, so that lazy individuals should not eat other people's food like drones, so he was unwilling that this same principle should hurt the ministers of the Word, with the result that the churches would defraud them of their lawful support' (Calvin) [*1 Tim.* 5: 18].

But in order that we might offer ourselves as an example for you to imitate (Hendriksen): 'Ourselves' is thrown forward to emphasize the self-sacrifice which was involved in this waiving of their right to support. These words would make the readers shamefully recall the cost of this mission to the preachers, as they now learned that this unnecessary burden was gladly shouldered to provide them with an example of industry [cf. *1 Thess.* 2:9]. 'The new religion did not teach "the dignity of labour". What it inculcated was just the duty of work' (Adolf Harnack).

10: For even when we were with you, this we commanded you, If any will not work, neither let him eat.

For also, when we were with you, this we used to command you: 'If any one refuses to work, neither let him eat' (Frame): Not content to let their personal example speak for itself, the preachers had often indicated its significance by means of this crisp command. As Frame says, the 'tradition' [verse 6] 'is not a truism: "if any one does not work, he has nothing to eat", but an ethical imperative: "if any one *refuses* to work, he shall not eat"'. It is this *unwillingness* to work which is here stigmatized as a vice. Christians are not called to idleness, but to glorify God in an honourable and useful vocation. For as the following verse mournfully proves, Satan always finds work for idle hands to do! 'The church has therefore seen that this dictum abolishes all false asceticism, all unchristian disinclination to work, all fanatic exaltation above work, all self-inflicted pauperism' (Lenski).

11: For we hear of some that walk among you disorderly, that work not at all, but are busybodies.

For we hear that some among you are conducting themselves in a disorderly manner, not busy workers but busybodies (Hendriksen): These things [verses 6–10] had to be said because Paul and his co-workers have heard that the church is being troubled by a known but unnamed minority, whose disorderly conduct is here condemned in a telling play on words. Such persons are not the *busy workers* they ought to be, but have become the *busybodies* they ought not to be! Unmindful of their own duty [cf. *1 Tim.* 5:8], these idlers were meddling in the affairs of others, and then looking to the church to supply their needs. Believing that the Lord's return was at hand [2:2], they tried to persuade others to join them in waiting for it. In the meantime they expected to live on the charity of their less spiritual brethren who were still working!

12: Now them that are such we command and exhort in the Lord Jesus Christ, that with quietness they work, and eat their own bread.

Paul now turns to command and exhort the idlers. This time he refers to them as those who are 'in the Lord Jesus Christ', which points to the privileges and obligations that belong to the believers. Hence it is both an acknowledgment of their standing and an appeal to live up to it. Further evidence of the apostle's tact in dealing with these offenders is seen in his choice of the indirect and impersonal address 'them that are such' (meaning 'people of this kind') in preference to 'you idlers' or even 'those idlers'. Instead of depending upon others for their keep, these persons are here commanded to live on the fruits of their own labours. 'With quietness' is not the opposite of the meddlesomeness mentioned in the previous verse, 'but of the feverish excitement of mind stimulated by the belief that the *Parousia* was at hand' (Frame) [cf. *1 Thess.* 4: 11; *1 Tim.* 2:2].

13: But ye, brethren, be not weary in well-doing.

As for the rest who have obeyed the tradition, Paul urges them not to become weary 'in well-doing', i.e. 'in your honourable course' (Lightfoot) [cf. *Gal.* 6:9]. The reference is quite general and should not be restricted to the duty of almsgiving. The meaning within the context is well expressed by Hendriksen: 'Do not be misled. Do not let a few people who neglect *their* duty keep *you* from doing *yours*. Never grow tired of doing what is right, honourable, excellent.'

14: And if any man obeyeth not our word by this epistle, note that man, that ye have no company with him, to the end that he may be ashamed.

If anyone does not obey our instructions in this letter, take note of that man and do not associate with him, so that he may be ashamed of himself (Bruce): This tells the faithful majority what to do should any one of the idlers disregard Paul's letter and persist in his disobedience. 1. They are to 'take note of that man', not by naming him publicly but by inwardly resolving to avoid him in future. 2. They are to withdraw [verse 6] from all close association with him, 'so that he may be ashamed of himself', i.e. 'made to turn and look into himself, and so be put to shame' (Fausset). The realization of his shame would thus lead to the reformation of his conduct and his restoration to the full fellowship of the church.

15: And yet count him not as an enemy, but admonish him as a brother.

This shows the spirit in which this discipline was to be carried out. He was not to be regarded as an enemy, but admonished as a 'brother'. The false idea that Christ's return was imminent had led him to neglect his immediate duty, 'but he was still to be counted a brother, as he had not forsaken the faith, or cut himself off from communion by notorious immorality, or by a relapse into heathen creed and profligacy'. Hence he was to be dealt with kindly; 'undue severity was to be avoided, the purpose being not to frown him away, but to win him back' (Eadie).

16: Now the Lord of peace himself give you peace at all times in all ways. The Lord be with you all.

With the recognition that these prescriptions to promote the peace of the church will avail nothing without the divine blessing, Paul concludes with the prayer that Christ, the Lord of peace [*Col.* 1:20] may give them 'peace at all times in all ways'. Clearly this includes far more than outward concord. He is praying that in every circumstance of life they may have an abiding sense of that peace which alone ensures the spiritual prosperity of the whole man (Morris).

The Lord be with you all: As in verse 18, Paul includes the 'disorderly brethren', 'who even more than others need the control of "the Lord" and the calming effect of his "peace". In the Benedictions of *1 Cor.* 16:24, *2 Cor.* 13:13, *all* has the like pointed significance' (Findlay).

17: The salutation of me Paul with mine own hand which is the token in every epistle: so I write.

The greeting by the hand of me Paul; this fact is a token of genuineness in every letter; this is the way I write (Frame): Like his contemporaries, it was Paul's habit to dictate his letters to an amanuensis and then add the concluding greeting in his own handwriting.[1] As is the case here, he sometimes calls attention to this personal touch in order to attest the genuineness of the Epistle [cf. *1 Cor.* 16:21; *Gal.* 6:11; *Col.* 4:18; and *Philem.* 19, though he probably wrote the whole of this himself]. In this instance it was added because of the uncertainty that is hinted at in 2:2, and to show the Thessalonians that no letter which purported to come from him was to be received as authentic without his characteristic autograph [*Gal.* 6:11]. This proof of authenticity would also prevent any erring member from disputing the apostolic origin of the preceding injunctions. Although 'every letter' suggests that Paul wrote many more letters than have come down to us [cf. *1 Cor.* 5:9], this should cause us no concern, as we possess as many as God intended us to have. Enough indeed to show us the way of salvation and lead us to heaven!

18: The grace of our Lord Jesus Christ be with you all.

As always Paul commends his readers to the grace that is theirs in the Lord Jesus Christ. Those who but a short time before had been heathens and whose Christian course since then had been far from easy, are here reminded once more of the all-sufficient grace of their Saviour. 'Although he has left them, they are not really alone. The free love of God, which visited them at first uncalled, will be with them still, to perfect the work it has begun. It will beset them behind and before; it will be a sun and a shield to them, a light and a defence. In all their temptations, in all their sufferings, in all their moral perplexities, in all their despondencies, it will be sufficient for them. There is not any kind of succour which a Christian needs which is not to be found in the grace of the Lord Jesus Christ' (Denney).

SOLI DEO GLORIA

[1] Frame refers to Deissmann's reproduction of a letter dated September 13, 50 AD, from one Mystarion to a priest, in which the *farewell* and the date are written in another hand, a circumstance that 'proves that somebody at that date (about the time of our letter) closed a letter in his own hand without expressly saying so'.)

BIBLIOGRAPHY

Adeney, Walter F., *Thessalonians and Galatians* (*Century Bible*) (T. C. & E. C. Jack, 1902).

Arndt, W. F.–Gingrich, F. W., *A Greek English Lexicon of the New Testament* (University of Chicago Press, 1957).

Berkhof, L., *Systematic Theology* (Banner of Truth, 1959).

Best, Ernest, *The First and Second Epistles to the Thessalonians* (*BNTC*) (A. & C. Black, 1972).

Bicknell, E. J., *1 & 2 Thessalonians* (*WC*) (Methuen, 1932).

Bruce, F. F., *1 & 2 Thessalonians* (*NBC* revised) (IVP, 1970).

—— *An Expanded Paraphrase of the Epistles of Paul* (Paternoster Press, 1965)

Calvin, John, *1 & 2 Thessalonians* (St Andrew Press, 1961).

Cullmann, Oscar, *The Early Church* (SCM, 1976).

Denney, James, *The Epistles to the Thessalonians* (*EB*) (Hodder & Stoughton, 1892).

Eadie, John, *The Epistles to the Thessalonians* (James and Klock, 1977).

Ellicott, C. J., *The Epistles to the Thessalonians* (Zondervan, 1957).

Erdman, Charles R., *The Epistles of Paul to the Thessalonians* (Westminster Press, 1966).

Fausset, A. R., *1 & 2 Thessalonians* (*JFB*) (Collins, 1874).

Fergusson, James, *The Epistles of Paul* (Banner of Truth, 1978).

Findlay, G. G., *The Epistles to the Thessalonians* (*CBSC*) (CUP, 1891).

—— *The Epistles to the Thessalonians* (*CGT*) (CUP, 1904).

Frame, James E., *The Epistles to the Thessalonians* (*ICC*) (T. & T. Clark, 1912).

Grier, W. J., *The Momentous Event* (Banner of Truth, 1970).

Guthrie, Donald, *New Testament Introduction* (Tyndale, 1970).

Hendriksen, William, *1 & 2 Thessalonians* (*NTC*) (Banner of Truth, 1972).

Hughes, Archibald, *A New Heaven and a New Earth* (Marshall, Morgan & Scott, 1958).

Lenski, R. C. H., *1 & 2 Thessalonians* (Augsburg, 1961).

Lightfoot, J. B., *Notes on the Epistles of St Paul* (Zondervan, 1957).

MEETER, JOHN E. (ed.), *The Shorter Writings of B. B. Warfield* vol. 1 (Presbyterian & Reformed, 1970).

MOFFATT, JAMES, *1 & 2 Thessalonians* (*EGT*) (Eerdmans, 1974).

MILLIGAN, GEORGE, *St Paul's Epistles to the Thessalonians* (Macmillan, 1908).

MORRIS, LEON, *1 & 2 Thessalonians* (*TNTC*) (Tyndale, 1956).

—— *1 & 2 Thessalonians* (*NIC*) (Eerdmans, 1959).

NEIL, WILLIAM, *The Epistles of Paul to the Thessalonians* (*MNTC*) (Hodder & Stoughton, 1950).

PLUMMER, ALFRED, *A Commentary on St Paul's First Epistle to the Thessalonians* (Robert Scott, 1918).

—— *A Commentary on St Paul's Second Epistle to the Thessalonians* (Robert Scott, 1918).

POOLE, MATTHEW, *A Commentary on the Holy Bible,* vol. 3 (Banner of Truth, 1963).

RIDDERBOS, HERMAN, in *Revelation and the Bible* (Tyndale, 1965).

TASKER, R. V. G., *The Biblical Doctrine of the Wrath of God* (Tyndale, 1970).

TRAPP, JOHN, *Commentary on the New Testament* (Sovereign Grace Book Club, 1958).

TRENCH, R. C., *Synonyms of the New Testament* (James Clarke, 1961).

VINCENT, MARVIN R., *Word Studies in the New Testament* (Macdonald, n.d.).

VINE, W. E., *Expository Dictionary of New Testament Words* (Oliphants, 1958).

VOS, GEERHARDUS, *The Pauline Eschatology* (Baker Book House, 1979).

—— *Redemptive History and Biblical Interpretation* (Presbyterian & Reformed, 1980).

WARFIELD, B. B., *Biblical Doctrines* (Banner of Truth, 1988).

—— *Perfectionism* (Presbyterian & Reformed, 1958).

YOUNG, ANDREW W., *Let's Study 1 & 2 Thessalonians* (Banner of Truth, 1999).

The Pastoral Epistles

INTRODUCTION

Since the eighteenth century, the letters to Timothy and Titus have been known as the 'Pastoral' Epistles, because they are largely concerned with the duties of those who are called to lead the flock of God. Unlike the anonymous Epistle to the Hebrews, these letters not only bear Paul's name, but are addressed to two of his most trusted assistants. As the apostolic authorship is amply supported by both the external and internal evidence, the authenticity of the Pastorals did not become a 'problem' until the rise of modern scepticism. The five arguments advanced against their genuineness have centred upon (1) the *historical setting*, (2) the *ecclesiastical situation*, (3) the *doctrinal viewpoint,* (4) the *heresy condemned*, and (5) the *linguistic differences*.

It is arbitrary to dismiss the *historical data* contained in these Epistles on the assumption that the execution of Paul took place at the end of his two-year imprisonment in Rome, for the triumphant conclusion of Acts suggests vindication rather than martyrdom [*Acts* 28:30, 31], and this view is confirmed by Paul's own expectations of an early release from captivity [*Phil.* 1:25; 2:24; *Philem.* 22]. Although the sequence of Paul's movements after he was set free is problematical, it would appear that he travelled east before making his long awaited trip to Spain [*Rom.* 15:23, 24]. If we assume that he was released in AD 63, Paul may have visited Crete on the way to Ephesus and Colossae, and then returned through Macedonia for a stay at Philippi before proceeding to Nicopolis, where he spent the winter. A mission to Spain of at least a year probably followed in the Spring of AD 64, but when we next hear of Paul he is again in Asia Minor. It is possible that Paul was re-arrested after further ministry in Ephesus, for the journey back to Rome seems to have been via Miletus, Troas, and Corinth [*2 Tim.* 4:13, 20]. Amid all these uncertainties, we can at least be sure that Paul wrote 1 Timothy and Titus while he was still at liberty, and 2

Timothy during his final imprisonment in Rome [c. AD 67]. Hence the commentary follows this order.

There is no ground for supposing that the *ecclesiastical situation* reflected in the Pastorals requires a date later than the lifetime of Paul. By the time of Ignatius [c. AD 115] a resident bishop exercised authority over the elders and deacons of the local church, but here there are only two orders of ministry, for the terms 'bishop' and 'elder' are still used interchangeably as they are in Acts [20:17, 28; cf. *Titus* 1:5, 7]. Moreover, Timothy and Titus clearly have a roving commission to act as the apostle's personal representatives to the churches, and are not monarchical bishops after the second-century pattern. Directions are given for the enrolling of widows worthy of the church's support, but the existence of an official 'order' of widows cannot be proved from the passage [*1 Tim.* 5:3–16].

A further difficulty concerns the difference in the *doctrinal viewpoint* of these letters. Critics adversely compare the continued stress upon the need to maintain orthodoxy ('*the* faith' as a deposit rather than 'faith' in Christ) and piety ('godliness') with the striking originality of Paul's thought. But as A. Sabatier observed, 'Paul was an apostle before he was a theologian. To him the need of conservation was more urgent than that of innovation. His gospel was, above everything else, a message that he had received, and that he had to deliver and defend' [cf. *1 Cor.* 15:1–11; *Gal.* 1:6–9; *2 Thess.* 2:15]. It should therefore occasion no surprise to find that Paul's parting counsels emphasize the importance of preserving the apostolic gospel in both purity of doctrine and of life.

There is now little support for identifying the *heresy condemned* with the fully developed Gnostic systems of the second century. The error seems to reflect a Jewish form of incipient gnosticism, not unlike but not more advanced than the false teaching which is refuted in the Colossian Epistle. The Judaistic origin of this deviation from the faith is proved by the references to the law, circumcision, genealogies, and 'Jewish fables' [*1 Tim.* 1:7; *Titus* 1:10, 14; 3:9], while pagan influences apparently led to a dualistic understanding of the world which would account for the ascetic prohibition of marriage and certain foods [*1 Tim.* 4:3–5; *Titus* 1:14, 15]. Presumably the belief that the 'resurrection is already past' [*2 Tim.* 2:18] was due to the same proto-gnostic tendency to spiritualise what was a fundamental article of Christian belief [*1 Cor. 15*: 20].

But the major objection to the Pauline authorship centres upon the *linguistic differences* between the Pastorals and other Pauline Epistles. Although much has been made of the occurrence of 306 words which are not found elsewhere in Paul's writings, it is quite unreasonable to deny Paul their use when critics admit that the 2,177 words of the other ten Epistles do not represent the apostle's entire vocabulary (Donald Guthrie). Moreover, it is surely self-evident that different subjects call for different modes of expression. As we do not demand that Shakespeare's Sonnets should exhibit a certain percentage of Hamlet words, 'we should not expect that an author's favourite expressions would be distributed over the pages of his book like the spots on a wall-paper pattern' (Newport J. D. White). It should also be recognized that the probable quotation of much traditional material (including confessions of faith, and doxologies or hymns) accounts for many of the stylistic peculiarities of these Epistles.

Those who suppose the Pastorals to be the spurious productions of a post-apostolic imitator are encased in the problems of their own making. 'If there are difficulties in vindicating the Pauline authorship, it is still more difficult to prove in whole or in part how a forger could manufacture three such Epistles as these are, in form and contents, and foist them on the Apostle Paul' (J. E. Huther). The gravest ethical questions are raised by the refusal to receive the Epistles as Paul's authentic utterances. For the denial of their apostolic origin demands the invention of so many personal allusions and circumstantial details as to make their fabricator's professed concern for the truth nothing less than a piece of consummate hypocrisy. Although the term 'pseudonymous' may lend a certain dignity to the deception, it does not remove the moral difficulty, and it is far more realistic 'to assume that an author's own claims are valid unless they are psychologically improbable' (Guthrie). We have briefly tried to show that there are very good grounds for maintaining that Paul was in fact the author of these farewell letters to Timothy and Titus, but perhaps the most impressive proof of their apostolicity may be seen in the immense gulf which separates them from the pathetically pedestrian literature of the second century.

1 Timothy

CHAPTER ONE

Paul greets Timothy as his true child in the faith, and exhorts him to refute the irrelevant myths and genealogies spread by those who want to be teachers of the law, for they are as ignorant of the meaning of the law as they are of the glorious gospel which was committed to the apostle [verses 1–11]. As a former persecutor Paul is a conspicuous example of the divine mercy, and he praises God for calling him to preach Christ, who came into the world to save sinners [verses 12–17]. Accordingly Timothy is urged to remain faithful to his commission, and is warned of such men as Hymenaeus and Alexander, who have made shipwreck of their faith [verses 18–20].

1: Paul, an apostle of Christ Jesus according to the commandment of God our Saviour, and Christ Jesus our hope;

This is not merely a private letter to a faithful helper, for the official character of the address shows that Paul intended it to be read to the church at Ephesus, where he had left Timothy to act as his representative in dealing with the threat posed to the faith by false teachers [verse 3]. In introducing himself as 'an apostle' ('one sent forth') of Christ Jesus, Paul is clearly using the word in its highest sense, since he is one of that select company who received the gospel from the Lord himself [*Gal.* 1:12]. 'The distinguishing features of an apostle were, a commission directly from Christ: being a witness of the resurrection: special inspiration: supreme authority: accrediting by miracles: unlimited commission to preach and to found churches' (Marvin Vincent).

The order 'Christ Jesus' is more frequent in Paul, particularly in the Pastorals (25 times), perhaps because his experience began with the revelation of Christ's heavenly glory; whereas 'Jesus Christ' is the form favoured by writers like Peter and John, who had come to faith in the Messiah through a knowledge of his earthly life.

According to the commandment of God our Saviour, and Christ Jesus our hope: The linking together of God and Christ as the co-ordinate sources of Paul's apostleship is highly significant, for it gives clear evidence of his belief in the deity of Christ. At the outset of a letter which combats false teaching, Paul is careful to emphasize that he is not a self-appointed teacher of his own ideas, but is sent forth to preach the gospel by the command of God 'our Saviour' and Christ Jesus 'our hope'. The confessional 'our' is itself an appeal to the Ephesian church not to exchange the verities of the gospel for the vain myths of men. The title 'Saviour' is applied to God six times in the Pastorals, and this shows that God's free offer of salvation must be extended to all men, in contrast to the exclusive claims of the false teachers who limited salvation to those who had the superior discernment to join their clique. As God is the author of our salvation, so Christ is the embodiment of our hope. Our risen and glorified Lord is himself our hope, because his triumph over sin and death provides the objective pledge of our final redemption [*Phil.* 3:20,21; *Col.* 1:27, *1 John* 3:2].

2: unto Timothy, my true child in faith: Grace, mercy, peace, from God the Father and Christ Jesus our Lord.

Paul warmly addresses Timothy as his true spiritual child whom he has begotten in the sphere of faith. Timothy was converted through Paul's ministry at Lystra, and later became a constant companion of the apostle [*Acts* 16:1–3]. According to tradition, Timothy was martyred by a mob at Ephesus in AD 97 for opposing the licentious idolatry of the cult of Diana. In greeting Timothy [cf. *2 Tim.* 1:2], Paul appropriately adds 'mercy' to his usual 'grace' and 'peace' since the experience of the divine mercy 'produces fitness for the Gospel ministry, verses 13, 16; *2 Cor.* 4:1; *1 Cor.* 7:25' (J. A. Bengel). As ministers commend the mercy of God to others, they must never forget that they need to be partakers of it themselves. 'If they know aright what they are, and what they should be, they will be ever throwing themselves on God's mercy' (Patrick Fairbairn). 'Grace' is God's undeserved favour in forgiving sinners, as 'mercy' is his spontaneous compassion in freeing them from the misery entailed by their disobedience, while 'peace' is that aspect of salvation which results from an experience of this grace and mercy. Thus God extends his 'grace' to men as they are *guilty*, and his 'mercy' to them as they are *miserable* (R. C. Trench). In the final clause Paul again emphasizes the divine dignity of Christ by showing that this triple blessing is conjointly bestowed by 'God the Father and Christ Jesus our Lord'.

3: As I exhorted thee to tarry at Ephesus, when I was going into Macedonia, that thou mightest charge certain men not to teach a different doctrine, 4: neither to give heed to fables and endless genealogies, which minister questionings, rather than a dispensation of God which is in faith; so do I now.

I write to thee now, as I exhorted thee to tarry at Ephesus, when I was going into Macedonia: It is probably better to supply what Paul leaves unexpressed at the beginning of verse 3 rather than at the end of verse 4 as in the ASV (*'so do I now'*). Upon his release from Rome, Paul sent Timothy to Philippi to find out how the church there was faring [*Phil.* 2:19], and evidently arranged to meet Timothy at Ephesus after returning from Colossae. As Paul was anxious to fulfil his promise to visit Philippi [*Phil.* 2:24], he delegated the task of dealing with the false teachers at Ephesus to Timothy, and he now writes to confirm this commission so that none can question the authority of his representative.

That thou mightest charge certain men not to teach a different doctrine, neither to give heed to fables and endless genealogies: No doubt Paul knew the identity of those responsible for introducing these alien novelties, but his refusal to name them was probably intended to avoid giving such would-be 'teachers of the law' [verse 7] any standing in the community of faith. In this Jewish teaching the gospel of God's free grace was displaced by fanciful myths and interminable genealogies, not unlike the unwholesome allegorical inventions found in Philo or the apocalyptic Book of Jubilees [cf. 4–7, Titus 1:14; 3:9].

They promote useless speculations rather than divine training that is in faith (Arndt-Gingrich): Here it would seem that the word *oikonomia* ('dispensation') should be taken in the subjective sense of training in the way of salvation. Paul judges this teaching by its results. He brands such empty arguments as 'useless speculations,' because they cannot promote the godly discipline which accompanies faith.

5: But the end of the charge is love out of a pure heart and a good conscience and faith unfeigned:

In contrast to the false teaching which results in strife and sterile questionings, the goal of the charge given by Timothy to the church at Ephesus is the love which can only spring from a real experience of the grace of God. Instead of pointing to the divine origin of this love [*Rom.* 5:5], Paul here gives a threefold description of its proximate source, because he wishes to stress the inner sincerity which always distinguishes a genuine profession from its plausible counterfeits. 1. *A pure heart.* In Scripture 'the heart' stands for the totality of man's innermost self [*Prov.* 4:23], and so 'a pure heart' points to the radical inward renewal which enables a man to love and serve God with single-minded devotion [*Matt.* 5:8; *2 Tim.* 2:22]. 2. *A good conscience.* The word 'conscience', literally means 'a knowing with', and is the term frequently used by Paul to designate that innate faculty of self-judgment by which a man tries his own thoughts and actions [*Rom.* 2:15]. To experience freedom from the guilt of sin and be led by the Spirit is to enjoy the blessing of a 'good' conscience, but no testimony is given by the 'branded' or 'seared' conscience of those who have rejected the truth in favour of Satan's lies [4:2]. 3. *Faith unfeigned.* With a sidelong glance at the false teachers, Paul speaks of the 'unhypocritical' faith which needs no actor's mask to conceal its insincerity [*2 Tim.* 1:5]. For instead of the true faith which works by love and thus fulfils the law [*Rom.* 13:10; *Gal.* 5:6], theirs was a faith which drew men into profitless speculations and vain talking [verses 4,6].

6: from which things some having swerved have turned aside unto vain talking;

It was from this triad of graces that the false teachers had wandered away, having missed the goal by turning off into meaningless chatter. The secret of much unsatisfactory and unprofitable preaching is disclosed by the folly of these men. Since they had not the root of the matter in them, 'they naturally fell to discoursing about vain questions, the debatable and speculative points about which they *could* find themselves at home . . . If the heart is not *in* the great things of the gospel, if it is out of accord with their deep spiritual tone, it cannot delight to speak of them, and will be only too glad to turn aside to inferior topics' (Fairbairn).

7: desiring to be teachers of the law, though they understand neither what they say, nor whereof they confidently affirm.

The errorists wanted to be teachers of the law, but as they had no insight into the meaning of the law and its relationship to the gospel [verse 8], they did not know what they were saying and could not grasp the things about which they spoke with such superficial confidence. The same feature may be observed in all those who deviate from the truth of the gospel. They announce their errors with the stubborn assurance that is born of ignorance!

8: But we know that the law is good, if a man use it lawfully,

In case his disparaging reference to 'teachers of the law' should appear to reflect upon the law itself, Paul immediately adds that the law is good [*Rom.* 7:12, 16], provided it is used lawfully. This deliberate play on words is very much to the point. 'The law itself, because it is law, dictates its lawful use and condemns every abuse as being unlawful. All pretending law teachers stand condemned by the very law they pretend to teach' (R. C. H. Lenski). The would-be law teachers in Ephesus swerved from the path of truth when they made the law the spring-board for their fanciful interpretations. Confusing the law with the gospel, they could not see that the law was given primarily to bring sin to light and condemn evil-doers. Paul's standpoint here is in complete accord with the teaching of the great evangelical Epistles [cf. *Rom.* 7:7–25; *Gal.* 3:19–25]. Since the law was added 'for the sake of transgressions', it is designed not for a righteous man, but 'for the lawless and unruly' [verse 9]. And because Timothy knows this, he will know how to 'use the law', 'not in Jewish fashion as a yoke for the saint, but as a whip for the sinner' (George G. Findlay).

9: as knowing this, that law is not made for a righteous man, but for the lawless and unruly, for the ungodly and sinners, for the unholy and profane, for murderers of fathers and murderers of mothers, for manslayers, 10: for fornicators, for abusers of themselves with men, for men-stealers, for liars, for false swearers, and if there be any other thing contrary to the sound doctrine; 11: according to the gospel of the glory of the blessed God, which was committed to my trust.

Against the mixture of law-teaching and licence championed by the errorists, Paul lays down the general principle that the law was not made for a 'righteous' man. Although this word is used in its widest sense, the believer is evidently in view. Unlike the wicked, the Christian is no longer under the condemning power of the law, because he now desires to act in conformity with its requirements [cf. *Rom.* 8:1–4; *Gal.* 5:23]. In a characteristic enumeration Paul sets forth the positive function of the law. The list follows the order of the Ten Commandments. The first three pairs cover offences against God, while the vices mentioned are all violations of the second table of the law. 'In each case extreme forms of the sin are chosen to emphasize the strength of evil in the heathen world and the real need of law for those who have not heard of the gospel: cf. *Rom.* 1:21–32' (Walter Lock).

But for the lawless and unruly: The active enmity of sinners towards God is demonstrated in their refusal to acknowledge the Creator's lordship over them. When dependent creatures thus assert their own autonomy, they choose that self-determination which inevitably leads to self-destruction, since the disobedient cannot escape the awful punishment threatened by the law they have despised. The distinction between the two terms is well noted by Marvin Vincent: 'In the one case no legal obligation is recognized; in the other, subjection to law is refused.'

For the ungodly and sinners: These are very properly linked together, because the man who is without inward reverence for God always reveals his defiance in many outward acts of rebellion, and so deliberately falls short of the true goal of his existence (cf. the *Shorter Catechism*, Answer to Question 1: 'Man's chief end is to glorify God, and to enjoy him for ever') [*1 Pet.*4:18; *Jude* 15].

For the unholy and profane: Here the negative is again correctly combined with the positive, for the man to whom nothing is sacred has the same secular spirit as Esau, who sold his birthright for one miserable meal [*Heb.* 12:16]. 'Profane' comes from the word 'threshold', and strictly means what may be trodden, hence unhallowed. The profane are therefore those 'who walk over everything and make it as common as dirt' (Lenski).

For smiters of fathers and smiters of mothers (ASV margin): Probably the sin condemned is not parricide, but that of dishonouring parents. 'For this extreme and outrageous violation of the Fifth commandment the punishment of death was provided in the Mosaic law' (J. H. Bernard) [*Exod.* 21:15].

For manslayers: Or murderers. Violators of the Sixth Commandment show a total disregard for the sanctity of life. As murder is the supreme manifestation of human hate and a direct assault upon the image of God in man, it is a crime for which the only appropriate punishment is death [*Num.* 35:16]. 'It is the sanctity of life that validates the death penalty for the crime of murder' (John Murray, *Principles of Conduct*, p. 122).

For immoral persons, sodomites: Persons guilty of two of the most repulsive breaches of the Seventh Commandment. Sexual laxity, especially as this is manifested in the perverted practice of sodomy, always heralds the decline of a civilization and is a certain mark of the wrath of God [*Rom.* 1:18, 27]. Notwithstanding the modern churchmen who condone and even advocate homosexuality, Paul categorically states that none who indulge in such a vile sin shall inherit the kingdom of God [*1 Cor.* 6: 9].

For kidnappers: 'A man's most precious possession is *himself*, and the worst form of thieving (condemned in the Eighth Commandment) is that practised by slave-dealers, whose booty is not *things*, but *persons*' (Bernard) [*Exod.* 21:16; *Deut.* 24:7].

For liars, for false swearers: Those who break the Ninth Commandment usually contradict, distort, or suppress the truth to gain some dishonourable end, but the worst form of lying is that which is solemnly confirmed by an oath.

And if there be any other thing contrary to the sound doctrine: Paul rounds off the catalogue with an inclusive clause covering whatever else is contrary 'to the sound (or healthy) doctrine'. By his repeated use of this phrase, the apostle implicitly contrasts the cancerous teaching of the ignorant legalists with the wholesome influence of the gospel [*2 Tim.* 4:3; *Titus* 1:9, 2:1].

According to the gospel of the glory of the blessed God: This is loosely attached to the whole of the preceding statement concerning the place of the law in Christian instruction [verses 8–10]. The law subserves the interests of the gospel by restraining evil-doers and convicting them of their sin, but it must never be regarded as an essential supplement to the gospel, because justification does not come by our striving to render obedience to the law [*Acts* 13:39; *Rom.* 3:20]. 'The gospel of God's glory is the gospel which peculiarly displays His glory – unfolds this to the view of men by showing the moral character and perfections of God exhibited as they are nowhere else in the person and work of Christ' (Fairbairn) [cf. *2 Cor.* 4:4]. On the expression 'the blessed God' (cf. 6:15), Bengel succinctly remarks, 'The Blessed blesses.' As God contains all blessedness in himself, so he is the source of all blessing for men. 'The epithet seems added from the rush of personal feeling as the sense of the present love and mercy of Christ (never long absent) comes to him strongly in penning the words' (A. E. Humphreys).

Which was committed to my trust: Or 'with which I was entrusted'. This is an essential reminder of Paul's authority, for it emphatically affirms his divine commission against the 'teachers of law' [verse 7], and thus prepares the way for what follows [verses 12–14].

12: I thank him that enabled me, even Christ Jesus our Lord, for that he counted me faithful, appointing me to his service;

Although at first sight this may only seem to be a personal aside, it is no mere digression, but is in fact an integral part of Paul's argument. For his own history not only provides a signal example of the divine mercy, but also illustrates the disastrous effects of legalistic zeal [verse 13; *Phil.* 3:6]. 'In a word, the law was for the *condemnation* of sinners, the gospel was for the *saving* of sinners and the ministration of forgiveness' (C. J. Ellicott). Hence Timothy must at once stop the pretended law-teachers, if the Ephesians are not to exchange the blessings of the gospel for the ministration of death. In this passage Paul speaks with such an intensity of feeling that his readers cannot fail to take the lesson to heart (see comment on verse 1). 'Here speaks the very soul of Paul. Here is doctrine turned into life. Past experience burns undimmed, confession of sin, confession of faith, gratefulness, burst into praise and doxology' (Lenski).

I thank him: As Paul can never forget the encounter on the way to Damascus which turned him into a preacher of the faith he once persecuted, so he never ceases to be grateful to Christ who then enabled him, counted him trustworthy, and appointed him to his service. The proof of Christ's enabling was seen in the trust thus committed to Paul. 'He saith, *Christ enabled me*, that is, endowed him with fidelity, zeal, courage, and all other qualifications requisite for that honourable and difficult ministry, *2 Cor.* 3:5,6 . . . His faithfulness was not the cause or motive, but the fruit and effect, of the grace of God in calling him to the ministry. This he expressly declares, *1 Cor.* 7:25, *hath obtained mercy to be faithful.* If our Saviour had only discovered his fidelity, without bestowing that grace upon him, there had not been a reason of such affectionate thanksgiving; for that always supposes some favour and benefit received' (Matthew Poole).

Service: It is the mark of Paul's humility that he chooses to describe his vocation by the lowly word *diakonia.* Its use here clearly attests the apostolic authorship of the Pastorals, since no second-century writer would have applied to an apostle a term which was then associated with the service of deacons.

13: though I was before a blasphemer, and a persecutor, and injurious: howbeit I obtained mercy, because I did it ignorantly in unbelief,

Paul's purpose in recalling his sinful past is to magnify the super abounding grace he was shown [verse 14]. This self-indictment is arranged on an ascending scale: he was before 'a blasphemer' who denied Christ and forced others to do the same [*Acts* 26: 11]; 'a persecutor' who by his relentless pursuit of the Lord's people persecuted the Lord himself [*Acts* 22:4,7]; and 'injurious', being a man of violence with an outrageous disregard of other men's rights. Yet such a sinner still came within the scope of God's mercy, because he 'did it ignorantly in unbelief'. Guilty though he was, his unbelief was not a clear-eyed rejection of the truth [*Mark* 3:28–30], for he acted with the zeal which was not according to knowledge [*Acts* 26:9; *Rom.* 10:2]. This ignorance was deeply culpable, but it was not unpardonable. For Jesus responded to the ignorance of his murderers with a prayer for mercy, and that was the mercy which overtook the persecutor on the road to Damascus [*Luke* 23:34].

14: and the grace of our Lord abounded exceedingly with faith and love which is in Christ Jesus.

It was the conviction of the enormity of his transgressions that gave Paul this deep and abiding consciousness of the superabundance of the Lord's forgiving grace [verse 15]. While a fanatical adherence to the law had made him the helpless prisoner of sin, grace alone brought the captive the new life of love and liberty which is found in union with Christ Jesus. This was something that those in Ephesus over whom the law was exerting the same fatal fascination would do well to bear in mind! 'He mentions *faith and love*, the two principal graces, in opposition to the reigning sins in his unconverted state: faith in the doctrine of the gospel, in opposition to his former ignorance and infidelity; and love to Christ and believers, in opposition to his former rage and cruelty against them' (Poole). It is worth noting that this verse, together with verse 15, was the origin of the title of John Bunyan's spiritual autobiography, *Grace Abounding to the Chief of Sinners.*

15: Faithful is the saying, and worthy of all acceptation, that Christ Jesus came into the world to save sinners; of whom I am chief.

Faithful is the saying: This is the first of the five 'Faithful sayings' which are found in the Pastoral Epistles [1:15; 3:1; 4:9; *Titus* 3:8; *2 Tim.* 2: 11]. It is significant that scarcely thirty years after the crucifixion Paul is thus able to remind his assistants of the gospel message by means 'of a body of utterances in which the essence of the gospel has been crystallized by those who have tasted and seen its preciousness. Obviously the days when this gospel was brought as a novelty to their attention are past . . . The gospel has been embraced and lived; it has been trusted and not found wanting; and the souls that have found its blessedness have had time to frame its precious truths into formulas . . . They are dug from the mine of the Christian heart indeed, but they come to us stamped in the mintage of apostolic authority' (B. B. Warfield, 'The Saving Christ', reprinted in *The Person and Work of Christ,* pp. 549–60).

And worthy of all acceptation: The primary thought here is not that the gospel is worthy to be accepted by all, but that it is deserving of 'complete acceptance in every way, without reservation, without hesitation, without the least doubt' (Lenski).

That Christ Jesus came into the world sinners to save: 'That' introduces the brief but marvellously full 'saying' which sums up the whole gospel in only eight Greek words. It is a joyful declaration of the purpose of Christ's coming into the world of sin and death. He descended into the sphere of evil for no other reason than to save poor lost sinners ('sinners' is placed before the verb for emphasis in the Greek). He who eternally existed in the form of God willingly took the form of a servant in order to die the death our sins deserved [cf. *Phil.* 2:5–11]. 'Jesus did all that is included in the great word *'save'*. He did not come to induce us to save ourselves, or to help us to save ourselves, or to enable us to save ourselves. He came to save us. And it is therefore that His name was called Jesus –bec ause He should save His people from their sins. The glory of our Lord, surpassing all His other glories to usward, is just that He is our actual and complete Saviour; our Saviour to the uttermost' (Warfield, op. cit., p. 557).

Of whom I am chief: By at once applying the saying to himself, Paul responds to it in the same way he would have others respond to it (verse 16). He says 'I am' and not 'I was', for though his sinful past has been blotted out by the mercy of God, he is acutely conscious of the fact that he is not yet made perfect [*Phil.* 3: 12]. 'In the experiences of personal religion each individual man is alone with God. He sees nought but the Holy One and his own sinful self [cf. *Luke* 18:13, *to me the sinner*]. And the more familiar a man becomes with the meeting of God face to face the less likely is he to be deceived as to the gulf which parts him, limited, finite, defective, from the Infinite and Perfect' (White).

16: howbeit for this cause I obtained mercy, that in me as chief might Jesus Christ show forth all his longsuffering, for an ensample of them that should thereafter believe on him unto eternal life.

But I was mercifully dealt with for this very purpose, that Jesus Christ might find in me the first occasion for displaying all his patience (NEB): In the previous verse the word 'chief' (*protos*) signifies 'foremost in rank', but here it takes on the temporal meaning of 'first in time'. Such was the former persecutor's pre-eminence in sin that it served to demonstrate the full extent of Christ's patience. 'Greater longsuffering He could not show in any case than in mine, nor find a sinner that so required *all* His longsuffering; not a part only' (John Chrysostom).

For a pattern to them which should hereafter believe on him to life everlasting (AV): Paul sees himself as a 'pattern', the 'prototype' or 'outline sketch' of the kind of sinners Jesus came to save. 'His meaning is that right from the very beginning God showed this example of His grace that could be seen clearly and widely, so that no one should doubt that if only he comes to Christ in faith, he may obtain pardon. All our distrust is removed when we see in Paul a visible type of that grace which we seek' (John Calvin). All who are saved by Christ 'believe *on* him *unto* eternal life' (ASV). This means that they continue to rest their faith on Christ until they attain eternal life, whereas temporary believers always reveal the falsity and inadequacy of their profession by falling short of the promised goal.

17: Now unto the King eternal, immortal, invisible, the only God, be honour and glory for ever and ever. Amen.

The remembrance of the abounding grace he was shown prompts Paul to break forth into a fervent doxology [6:15; *Rom.* 11: 36]. 'The King eternal' literally means 'the King of the ages', and the title evidently springs from the Jewish view of the two ages, the present age and the age to come. 'God was King in both spheres, and indeed of the "ages of the ages" as the phrase *for ever and ever* suggests' (Donald Guthrie). The three adjectives – immortal, invisible, only – provide a striking description of the nature of God. Unlike mortal man, God is incorruptible and so immortal [cf. *Rom.* 1:23]. As God is also invisible, he is beyond human examination [6:16], and can be known only by those to whom he chooses to reveal himself [*Heb.* 11:27]. And he is the *only* God as opposed to all the finite deities of man's invention [*1 Cor.* 8:4, 5]. 'To Him alone belong honour and glory, and to Him they belong to all eternity' (Fairbairn). The liturgical 'Amen' ('So be it!') is an emphatic invitation to every believer to set his own seal to the truth thus affirmed.

18: This charge I commit unto thee, my child Timothy, according to the prophecies which led the way to thee, that by them thou mayest war the good warfare;

In returning to the original charge given to Timothy [verses 3, 5], Paul now affectionately reminds his spiritual child [verse 2] of the prophetic revelation of God's will which had brought him into the ministry. For as Timothy faced the difficult task of preserving the purity of the faith in the church at Ephesus, he was to remember the divine initiative in his calling so that he would be encouraged to rely upon the divine power in fulfilling it. Clearly the reference is to the ministry of Christian prophets, who exercised an important function in the early church, but the gift of inspired prophecy was no longer required after the canon of Scripture was complete. 'Since we no longer have prophets, since we do not have our Lord with us as he was with the disciples, and since we do not have new organs of revelation as in apostolic times, Scripture in its total extent, according to the conception entertained by our Lord and his apostles, is the only revelation of the mind and will of God available to us. This is what the finality of Scripture means for us; it is the only extant revelatory Word of God' (John Murray, 'The Finality and Sufficiency of Scripture', *Collected Writings*, vol. 1, p. 19).

In speaking of 'the *prophecies* which led the way to thee', Paul apparently has more than one occasion in view. The commissioning of Paul and Barnabas suggests that there was also a prophecy which led Paul to choose Timothy as his assistant during the course of the second missionary journey [cf. *Acts* 13:1–3; 16:1–3] and this was followed by a further revelation of the divine will at Timothy's ordination [4:4]. And it is by reliance upon the Word of God thus given that he is to 'war the good warfare' by defending the faith against the attacks of the false teachers [verses 3–12].

19: holding faith and a good conscience; which some having thrust from them made shipwreck concerning the faith:

As the need for a moral response to the gospel is here clearly underlined, it is perhaps preferable to take both references to 'faith' in the subjective sense, though the first of these would undoubtedly include 'right belief'. Paul's point is that Timothy must be careful to maintain 'a good conscience' if he wishes to retain his 'faith' [cf. 1:5]. This is precisely where the false teachers went wrong, for when they violently thrust aside the claims of conscience they inevitably made shipwreck of their faith. According to the apostle, the problems of unbelief are not due to certain intellectual difficulties but to moral failure. And this is because a bad conscience always brings forth the corrupt teaching that is congenial to it [*Matt.* 7:15–20]. 'The metaphor of a shipwreck is very apt, for it suggests that if we wish to reach port with our faith intact, we should make a good conscience the pilot of our course, or otherwise there is danger of shipwreck; faith may be sunk by a bad conscience as by a whirlpool in a stormy sea' (Calvin).

20: of whom is Hymenaeus and Alexander; whom I delivered unto Satan, that they might be taught not to blaspheme.

Two of the false teachers at Ephesus are cited as examples to be avoided. Another reference to Hymenaeus is found in *2 Tim.* 2:17, 18 (see note there), but nothing further is known of Alexander, who is not to be identified with the two other men of the same name mentioned in *Acts* 19:33 and *2 Tim.* 4:14. By instructing the church to excommunicate these opposers of the truth, Paul delivered them over to the power of Satan [cf. *Job* 2:6; *1 Cor.* 5:5]. It is almost certain that this would also involve the supernatural infliction of some form of bodily punishment, but the final clause suggests that its purpose was remedial [*Acts* 13:8–11]. It was hoped that this stern discipline would make them stop reviling God's word and bring them to repentance.

CHAPTER TWO

In keeping with the universal scope of the gospel, Paul urges that prayer is to be made for all men, especially those in authority, so that believers may lead a peaceful and godly life [verses 1, 2]. Such prayer is well-pleasing to God who desires the salvation of all men. For there is but one God and one Mediator, Christ Jesus, who gave himself as a ransom for all, and it was to testify to this that Paul was appointed an apostle to the Gentiles [verses 3–7]. With regard to the conduct of worship, he directs that in praying for others men must not be at variance among themselves, while women are to be modest in dress and demeanour [verses 8–10]. Remembering man's priority in creation and her part in the world's sin, a woman ought rather to learn than to teach. But she shall be saved by accepting the rôle of motherhood assigned to her, and by living in faith, love, holiness, and chastity [verses 11–15].

1: I exhort therefore, first of all, that supplications, prayers, intercessions, thanksgivings, be made for all men; 2: for kings and all that are in high place; that we may lead a tranquil and quiet life in all godliness and gravity.

In this section the stress which Paul lays on the word 'all' suggests that he is contrasting the universal scope of the gospel with the spirit of Jewish exclusiveness fostered by the false teachers [verses 1–7]. For he 'would naturally be anxious that the Christian Church should not fail, as the Jews had done, in recognizing the universality of its mission' (Lock). Hence his first concern is to underline the primary importance of praying for all men, especially for kings and all those in authority, so that peace may be preserved and piety may flourish unhindered by persecution or strife. A godly life is always the best advertisement for Christianity, but we are to pray that our witness can be given in that climate of peace which is most conducive to the spread of the gospel in the world. 'The supplication of faithful intercessors for the common weal lays invisible restraint on the powers of darkness and their tools and brings reinforcement to honest rulers from the Governor among the nations (*Psa.* 22:28). Lack of prayer menaces national as well as individual welfare. Civil government may be grievously perverted, but divine sanction ratifies its right to exist' (E. K. Simpson). [cf. *Rom.* 13:1–7, *1 Pet.* 2: 13–17].

The apostle enforces the urgency of the duty by the use of four synonyms: 'supplications' are the requests which spring from a keenly felt sense of need; 'prayers' is a general term covering every form of reverent address to God; 'intercessions' is a word that primarily refers to 'free familiar prayer, such as boldly draws near to God' (R. C. Trench), though here it clearly takes on the added meaning of prayer on behalf of others [cf. *Rom.* 8:27, 34; *Heb.* 7:25]; 'thanksgivings' for past mercies must always accompany our requests for further blessings. Trench points out that thanksgiving is the one aspect of prayer which will continue in heaven, where it will be larger, deeper, fuller than here. For only there will the redeemed know how much they owe to their Lord, 'while all other forms of prayer, in the very nature of things, will have ceased in the entire possession and present fruition of the things prayed for' [*Rev.* 7:12].

3: This is good and acceptable in the sight of God our Saviour: 4: who would have all men to be saved, and come to the knowledge of the truth.

Such prayer is 'good and acceptable in the sight of God', who is again called 'our Saviour' (see comment on 1:1). This is the criterion by which all worship must be tested, for as Calvin remarks, 'The only genuine rule for right and proper action is to look to God's good pleasure and to undertake only what He approves.'

Who would have all men to be saved: That God would have all men to be saved is shown by his provision of a ransom sufficient for all [verse 6]. Hence the church may never hug the gospel to itself, but must always seek to fulfil its commission to preach the good news to every creature [*Mark* 16:15]. As God is full of compassion, 'he desires not the death and destruction of any [*Ezek.* 33:11], but the welfare and salvation of all. Not that he has decreed the salvation of all, for then all men would be saved; but he has a good will to the salvation of all, and none perish but it is their own fault, *Matt.* 23:37' (Matthew Henry).

And come to the knowledge of the truth: The ultimate aim of salvation is to come to the full knowledge of the truth as this is embodied in Christ [*John* 14:6; *Eph.* 4:21]. Consequently the rescue from sin and ignorance must be followed by 'an advance from this first knowledge of one's true self as a sinner to the complete and perfect knowledge of the truth . . . The word for full knowledge, *epignosis*, is repeated four times in these Epistles, *2 Tim.* 2:25; 3:7, *Titus* 1:1, and is contrasted with the knowledge, falsely so called, of the heretical teachers, cf. 6:20; *Titus* 1:16' (Humphreys).

5: For there is one God, one mediator also between God and men, himself man, Christ Jesus, 6: who gave himself a ransom for all; the testimony to be borne in its own times;

As a further confirmation of the universality of the gospel, Paul cites what seems to be an extract from an early creed, which was probably already current in Ephesus. It crisply sets forth the unity of God, the mediatorial work of Christ, and the universal scope of his vicarious atonement.

For there is one God: This affirms the basic belief of Judaism, which pious Jews recited daily in the Shema: 'Hear, O Israel: The LORD our God is one LORD' [*Deut.* 6:4]. But what the Jews failed to grasp was that this one God whom they worshipped must also be the God of the Gentiles, and in Romans 3:29, 30 Paul refutes Jewish exclusivism by appealing to the unity of God to justify the universal scope of his mission [cf. *1 Cor.* 8:6].

One mediator also between God and men, himself man, Christ Jesus: With the advent of Christ, Job's pathetic cry for an umpire was answered [*Job* 9:32, 33], because he is the one mediator who could bridge the infinite gulf which separated the holy God from sinful men [*John* 14:6].

This unique function belongs to Christ in virtue of the fact that he alone is both God and man. But while his deity is here assumed, his humanity is emphatically asserted in order to show 'that he belongs to all men without distinction' (A. Oepke, *TDNT*, vol. 4, p. 619).

Who gave himself a ransom for all: This is clearly based on the words of the Lord [*Mark* 10:45], but here the indefinite 'for many' is replaced by the universal 'for all', and instead of the simple noun, we have a rare compound which 'emphasizes the thought of substitution; it is a substitute-ransom that is signified' (Leon Morris). God not only desires the salvation of all men [verse 4], but Christ's finished work is of sufficient value to expiate the sin of all men. 'There are no claims of justice not yet satisfied; there is no sin of man for which an infinite atonement has not been provided. "All things are now ready". Therefore the call to "come" is universal . . . The extent to which a medicine is offered is not limited by the number of persons favourably disposed to buy it and use it. Its adaptation to disease is the sole consideration in selling it, and consequently it is offered to everybody' (W. G. T. Shedd, *Dogmatic Theology*, vol. 2, p. 482).

The testimony to be borne in its own times: The phrase is too brief for its precise meaning to be clear. It appears to be Paul's own comment on the preceding citation. 'The testimony' probably refers to the witness which the apostle and all future teachers have to give (verse 7). 'The crowning message of revelation, redemption by the blood of the Lamb, must be published abroad as the supreme panacea for all the ills that flesh is heir to' (Simpson).

7: whereunto I was appointed a preacher and an apostle (I speak the truth, I lie not), a teacher of the Gentiles in faith and truth.

As a final proof that the church must pray for all men [verses 1, 2], Paul appeals to his own appointment by God [1:1] to be a 'herald' (NIV) and an apostle whose distinctive commission made him a teacher of the Gentiles [*Acts* 22:21; *Eph.* 3:1ff.]. 'His Epistles therefore should be highly prized by us Gentiles, and diligently studied' (John Trapp). The parenthesis, in which Paul gives the Ephesians a characteristic assurance of his truthfulness (see comment on 1:1), should be connected with what follows, as in Romans 9:1. For the purpose of this vehement statement is to underline the universality of

Paul's mission against the exclusivist ideas of the errorists. The apostle exercised his ministry 'in (the sphere of) faith and truth', which means that he was used by God to bring the Gentiles to 'living faith in the truth of the gospel' (William Hendriksen).

8: I desire therefore that the men pray in every place, lifting up holy hands, without wrath and disputing.

In resuming the subject of prayer, Paul next gives directions on how the men are to pray 'in every place', i.e. wherever there is a community of believers [*1 Cor.* 1:2; *1 Thess.* 1:8]. The apostle thus makes it plain that in public worship men have the responsibility of leading the congregation in prayer [*1 Cor.* 14:34f].

Lifting up holy hands: It was the Jewish habit to pray with uplifted hands [*1 Kings* 8:22], and 'the custom passed over into the primitive church, as may be seen from the mural paintings in the catacombs' (Marvin R. Vincent). The adjective 'holy' shows that the outward gesture must be a true expression of the pure intention and devotion of the heart [*Psa.* 66:18].

Without wrath and disputing: 'Either would mar the charity which prays for all men' (Bernard). With regard to the first, Jeremy Taylor remarked, 'Anger is a perfect alienation of the mind from prayer'; and concerning the second, Bernard notes that 'in our prayers we leave our differences behind us'.

9: In like manner, that women adorn themselves in modest apparel, with shamefastness and sobriety; not with braided hair, and gold or pearls or costly raiment; 10: but (which becometh women professing godliness) through good works.

'In like manner' indicates that Paul is still speaking about the conduct of public worship, but the relevance of his remarks on the dress and deportment of women also extends to the effect of their behaviour upon society, since 'good works' are the 'fitting ornament' of women who make a profession of 'godliness' [5:10; cf. *1 Pet.* 3:1–6]. As ostentation and extravagance in dress hardly point to a mind set on heavenly things [*Col.* 3:2], Christian women are to dress modestly, 'with decency and propriety' (NIV). 'The outward modesty which makes itself known in the dress, is to be accompanied by inward purity and chastity, since the former would otherwise be of no account' (Huther). Obviously, the practical application of the principle here set forth will always be expressed in a manner that is considered appropriate to the cultural and social climate of the time. What is important is to remember the unchanging principle: 'Let all things be done decently and in order' [*1 Cor.* 14:40].

11: Let a woman learn in quietness with all subjection. 12: But I permit not a woman to teach, nor to have dominion over a man, but to be in quietness.

Although Paul elsewhere shows that women have equal standing with men in Christ [*Gal.* 3:28], he also insists that fellowship in Christ does not remove the natural distinction between the sexes, which was established by the priority given to man in creation [verse 13]. Paul will not permit a woman to assume the place of leadership in the church as an authoritative teacher of doctrine, because that would set aside the order of nature and put her in the position of exercising authority over the men in the congregation.

'Paul refers to teaching *Scripture* and not to imparting intellectual secular information to the mind. The public teacher of God's people does not only tell others what they need to know, but in the capacity of such a teacher he stands before his audience to rule and govern it with the Word . . . No woman may step into the place of the man without violating the very Word she would try to teach to both women and men. Her effort to do so would be self-contradictory in God's eyes despite what the world may say' (Lenski). Since the prohibition only applies to the conduct of public worship, a woman can teach other women [*Titus* 2:3, 4], take a Sunday school class, and instruct her own children [*Titus* 1: 5; 3:14, 15]. But when in church, she is to learn in silence, and must not try to usurp the teaching function which is denied to her by the Word of God.

13: For Adam was first formed, then Eve; 14: and Adam was not beguiled, but the woman being beguiled hath fallen into transgression:

Paul gives two reasons for this ban. First, he appeals to the fact that Adam was created before Eve [*Gen.* 2:21ff.], and in the light of *1 Cor.* 11: 8f. ('the man is not of the woman, but the woman of the man: for neither was the man created for the woman; but the woman for the man'), this means that 'the origin and *raison d'être* of woman are to be found in man' (H. Schlier, *TDNT*, vol. 3, p. 679). As therefore God's purpose in creating Eve was to provide a 'help meet' for Adam [*Gen.* 2:20], it is unlawful for a woman to take to herself the headship which belongs to man.

Secondly, Paul shows that Eve's part in the Fall was due to her being deceived [*2 Cor.* 11:3]. 'The Serpent deceived the woman; the woman did not deceive the man, but persuaded him: *Gen.* 3:17, *thou hast hearkened to the voice of thy wife* . . . In the preceding verse [verse 13], we are taught why the woman should not *exercise authority,* now, why she should not *teach*; more easily deceived, she more easily deceives' (J. A. Bengel). Paul puts all the emphasis on the word 'deceive' (mentioned twice), in order to drive home this particular lesson. He is not blaming Eve to excuse Adam, for he shows in Romans 5:12ff. that the whole race was ruined by the transgression of the *one man* who was its Head.

15: but she shall be saved through her childbearing, if they continue in faith and love and sanctification with sobriety.

Instead of hankering after the teaching office which does not belong to her (verse 11), let the woman gratefully receive the divinely ordained role of motherhood [5:14; *Titus* 2: 5], notwithstanding the unnatural prohibition of marriage advocated by the false teachers [4:3]. Of course Paul is not saying that she will win salvation 'through' or by means of childbirth. The preposition used here is the *dia* of accompanying circumstances, and the assurance thus conveyed is that she shall be saved 'in' her child-bearing. It is by accepting her proper sphere that she fulfils her true destiny. This is the plain meaning of the words. To take 'the childbearing' as a veiled reference to the Incarnation, is fanciful, to say the least!

If they continue in faith and love and sanctification with sobriety: Paul has been either speaking of women, in the plural or of woman in a generic sense from verse 9 and so the sudden transition to the plural 'they' should occasion no surprise. To bear and rear children is indeed a 'good work' [verse 10], but women are not saved in a manner that is different from men. As they are saved the moment they believe, so they must continue in faith and the state of grace ('love and sanctification with sobriety' or chastity) if they are to attain the promised consummation [cf. *Col.*1: 23].

CHAPTER THREE

Paul here specifies the qualifications required of those who aspire to leadership in the church. A bishop or overseer must be above reproach, not a recent convert, but a man who is able to teach, and whose well-ordered family life provides an example to the church and commands the respect of the community at large [verses 1–7]. The same high moral standards must also be evident in those who are chosen to serve as deacons and deaconesses [verses 8–13]. He hopes to visit Timothy soon, but meanwhile stresses the importance of observing these directions, since they outline the conduct that is proper to the church. Anyone who is tempted to belittle the church by a careless walk is reminded that it is nothing less than God's household, the very pillar and bulwark of the truth. Paul now cites part of a hymn to show that the secret of godliness was revealed through the One whom all believers worship as their Incarnate and Glorified Lord [verses 14–16].

1: Faithful is the saying, If a man seeketh the office of a bishop, he desireth a good work.

Faithful is the saying: The second of the 'faithful sayings' omits the words 'and worthy of all acceptation' [1:15; 4:9], because its application is limited to a particular group. Its purpose is not to proclaim the message of the gospel, but to commend the ministry of the gospel [*2 Tim.* 2:2]. 'The particular response which is in view is the encouragement of those who should seek the good work of serving as a bishop' (George W. Knight, *The Faithful Sayings in the Pastoral Epistles*, p. 144).

If a man seeketh the office of a bishop: In the apostolic church the two terms 'elder' and 'bishop' were used interchangeably to designate the same person [*Titus* 1:5–7]. 'The term "elder" indicates the mature spiritual experience and understanding of those so described; the term "bishop", or "overseer", indicates the character of the work undertaken' (W. E. Vine). [*Acts* 20:28; *1 Pet.* 5:2,3]. It is evident that the kind of seeking here intended is 'not the prompting of a carnal ambition, but the aspiration of a heart which has itself experienced the grace of God, and which longs to see others coming to participate in the heavenly gift' (Fairbairn).

He desireth a good work: 'It is a work, a business, not ease; *Acts* 15:38; *Phil.* 2:30' (Bengel). In the following verses it is made clear that such a work can only be accomplished by men of good character [verses 2–7].

2: The bishop therefore must be without reproach, the husband of one wife, temperate, sober-minded, orderly, given to hospitality, apt to teach;

In the fifteen qualifications which follow, Paul stresses that the man who aspires to the ministry must be an example to the flock. The first seven describe the virtues with which he must be endowed [verse 2], the next seven indicate the vices from which he must be exempt and outline his conduct in regard to his family and the church [verses 3–6], while the last relates to his reputation in the world outside [verse 7].

Without reproach: The list begins with the general qualification of blamelessness. The word used literally means 'not to be laid hold of', and so not open to just censure. 'Every faithful pastor must be such as against whom no just exception can be laid, no gross fault objected. Involuntary failings and unavoidable infirmities have a pardon, of course, both with God and all good men' (Trapp)

The husband of but one wife (NIV): The same high moral standard is required of deacons [verse 12]. It does not mean that a single man cannot serve or that an overseer cannot marry again following the death of his first wife [*Rom.* 7:1–3]. 'The emphasis is on one wife's husband, and the sense is that he have nothing to do with any other woman. He must be a man who cannot be taken hold of on the score of sexual promiscuity or laxity' (Lenski).

Temperate, self-controlled, respectable (NIV): As to his personal qualities, he must be a man who is not given to any kind of excess, whose well-disciplined mind finds its natural expression in a well-ordered respectable life.

Given to hospitality: This word literally means 'loving strangers'. In a day when inns were dens of extortion and vice, there was a great need to provide safe lodging for Christian travellers and for those made fugitives by persecution [*Rom.* 12:13; *Heb.* 13:2; *1 Pet.* 4:9].

Apt to teach: It is only here and in verse 5 that Paul touches on the actual work of an overseer. As well as possessing a sound knowledge of the faith, he must have the ability to teach it to others [*2 Tim.* 2:2; *Titus* 1:9]. 'What is required here is not merely a voluble tongue, for we see many whose easy fluency contains nothing that can edify. Paul is rather commanding wisdom in knowing how to apply God's Word to the profit of His people' (Calvin).

3: no brawler, no striker; but gentle, not contentious, no lover of money;

Of the next five on the list, the one positive virtue required is sandwiched between four negatives. 'No brawler' is no improvement on the AV's 'not given to wine' (cf. NIV). The word signifies 'a common tippler, whether he drinks to the loss of his reason or no; a winebibber, that makes bibbing at a tavern his trade: no sitter at wine' (Poole). In his conduct toward others, the overseer must be 'no striker' either with tongue or hand [*2 Cor.* 11:20], but is to be of a 'gentle' and forbearing spirit. As befits a minister of the new covenant, he will not be a man who is always insisting upon his '*legal* rights, lest they should be pushed into *moral* wrongs' (R. C. Trench). 'Not contentious' shows that the herald of God's peace must not stir up strife with quarrelsome words. The usefulness of many a ministry has been destroyed by a failure to radiate the peace which was only proclaimed from the pulpit and not shown in the life. Finally, the one who directs others to heaven must not be 'a lover of money' [6:9–11; *Matt.* 6:19–21]. This is a needful word of warning, for the earth-bound desires of a covetous spirit always clip the wings of faith and love.

4: one that ruleth well his own house, having his children in subjection with all gravity; 5: (but if a man knoweth not how to rule his own house, how shall he take care of the church of God?)

In contrast to the unscriptural demand of the Roman Catholic Church for a celibate priesthood [4:3], Paul takes it for granted that the overseer will be a married man with a family, because 'those who know ordinary life and are well practised in the duties that human relationships impose, are far better trained and fitted to rule in the Church' (Calvin). Thus the good pastor will be a man whose 'gravity' or calm dignity will secure the respect and ready obedience of his children. Paul's rhetorical question argues from the lesser to the greater. For if a man is unable to govern his own family, he is clearly not fitted for the more difficult task of caring for the church of God, 'which is a larger society, with all the members of which he is not so constantly present, and over whom he hath not such a coercive power, and as to whom a far greater care must be taken' (Poole).

6: not a novice, lest being puffed up he fall into the condemnation of the devil.

In his directions to Timothy, Paul insists that the overseer must not be a 'novice', a 'newly planted' convert, or he may become blinded by 'a smoke-screen of pride' (A. T. Robertson) and 'fall under the same judgment as the devil' (NIV). As pride was the cause of the devil's downfall, those in high places of spiritual responsibility must take care to keep low before God [*Isa.* 14:12–15; *Luke* 10:17,18; *2 Pet.* 2:4; *Jude* 6]. The absence of this directive from the parallel passage in Titus is an indication that church organization in Crete was in a very much less advanced state than in Ephesus. In the case of newly formed churches, the apostles had to appoint converts to this office, 'because no others were available; and men appointed in such circumstances would have no temptation to be puffed up any more than would the leaders of a forlorn hope' (White). But the situation was quite different in a well-established church where the elevation of a novice to a position of prestige might fill him with pride and cause him to fall.

7: Moreover he must have good testimony from them that are without; lest he fall into reproach and the snare of the devil.

The final qualification laid down by Paul for the overseer of the local church is that he must have 'a good reputation with outsiders' (NIV). It is true that unbelievers have no right to interfere with the affairs of the church, but because they have the law of God written in their hearts [*Rom.* 2:15], their moral judgments are regarded by Paul as being worthy of respect. 'There is something blameworthy in a man's character if the consensus of outside opinion be unfavourable to him; no matter how much he may be admired and respected by his own party' (White). To appoint a man of doubtful reputation to a place of leadership in the Christian community would expose him to the reproach of men and 'the snare of the devil', who is here represented as the great hunter of souls [cf. 6:9; *2 Tim.* 2:26]. The idea is that 'the disgrace incurred by the one who has not a good testimony from the non-Christians, is used by the devil as a snare, not only to tempt him, but also to seduce him into apostasy from the gospel' (Huther).

8: Deacons in like manner must be grave, not double-tongued, not given to much wine, not greedy of filthy lucre; 9: holding the mystery of the faith in a pure conscience.

Although the Seven appointed to serve in Acts 6 are not actually called 'deacons', it seems reasonable to assume from the practical duties assigned to them that they were the forerunners of those who were later given this title [*Phil.* 1:1]. 'The qualifications looked for in deacons stress sound character and a firm hold on the true faith. There is no mention of capacity for teaching or the like. It may perhaps be inferred that the primary tasks of the deacons were administrative and financial. The scriptural references seem to make it clear that the diaconate formed one of the two recognized orders constituting the local ministry of the Christian Church' (Leon Morris, *Ministers of God*, p. 90). Deacons must also be men of serious character and dignified bearing; not saying one thing to one man and something different to the next, as did Bunyan's parson Mr Two-tongues; not addicted to wine; and not out for dishonest gain. With regard to the last, Charles R. Erdman remarks, 'Judas was not the last treasurer who betrayed his Lord for a few pieces of silver.'

Holding the mystery of the faith in a pure conscience: 'The mystery of the faith' is the revelation given in Christ of the once hidden purpose of God [verse 16; *Rom.* 16:25, 26]. But the accent here falls on the ethical demand for a pure conscience [1:5, 1:19]. 'It is as if the pure conscience were the vessel in which the mystery of the faith is preserved' (B. Weiss).

10: And let these also first be proved; then let them serve as deacons, if they be blameless.

'Also' indicates that deacons no less than overseers must be men of blameless (or 'unaccused') character [verses 2–7]. Let them 'first be proved' does not refer to a formal examination or a period of probation, but clearly has in view the general verdict of the local church concerning their life and conversation [*Acts* 6:3].

11: Women in like manner must be grave, not slanderers, temperate, faithful in all things.

It would be strange if Paul singled out deacons' wives for special mention when the wife of the overseer held a much more influential position in the church, and it is preferable to understand the repetition of 'in like manner' [verse 8] as making another group and thus introducing the qualifications required of women who serve as deacons. They too must be dignified, not retailers of 'devilish' gossip ('slanderers' is literally 'devils'), but temperate and reliable in everything. Their duties included assisting at the baptism of women, pastoral work among the sick and poor, and carrying official messages [*Rom.* 16:1, 2]. 'Thus while the New Testament prohibits women from assuming the rôle of leadership in the church [2:11–12; *1 Cor.* 14:34], they do appear as having a significant ministry in the church along with men in the subordinate auxiliary rôle of the diaconate' (Robert L. Saucy).

12: Let deacons be husbands of one wife, ruling their children and their own houses well. 13: For they that have served well as deacons gain to themselves a good standing, and great boldness in the faith which is in Christ Jesus.

In reverting to the male diaconate, Paul requires them to maintain the same high standard of family life as that laid down for the overseer (see comment on verses 2, 4–5). Those who serve faithfully in this subordinate office 'gain to themselves a good standing' among their fellow-believers and in the community at large, and this consciousness of their personal integrity also gives them 'great boldness in the faith which is in Christ Jesus'. But, such boldness 'is only truly safe and humble if it moves in an atmosphere of faith in the protecting and strengthening presence of Christ Jesus. Here the dominant quality and requisite of all Christian service, personal faith in Christ Jesus, is recalled' (Parry).

14: These things write I unto thee, hoping to come unto thee shortly; 15: but if I tarry long, that thou mayest know how men ought to behave themselves in the house of God, which is the church of the living God, the pillar and ground of the truth.

In disclosing his purpose in writing to Timothy, Paul enables us to grasp the inner meaning of the Pastoral Epistles, for the passage forms the bridge between the preceding regulations about the ministry and the onslaught against false teaching which follows. The abiding significance of the lesson thus taught by the apostle is that unless the church is careful to maintain a faithful ministry it will be impossible to preserve the purity of its faith in Christ [verse 16].

Paul here sets forth the dignity of the church in a threefold description that is designed to underline the kind of conduct which reverence for God demands. First, we must realize that the church is not simply a voluntary association of men, but the very dwelling-place of God. 'There are good reasons why God should call the Church His House, for not only has He received us as His sons by the grace of adoption, but He Himself dwells in the midst of us' (Calvin). Secondly, in contrast to the folly of worshipping dumb idols, the life of the believing community is derived from, and determined by, the inspiring and directing presence of 'the living God' [*2 Cor.* 3:3; *1 Thess.* 1:9; *Heb.* 12:22]. Finally, the church is the very 'pillar and bulwark of the truth' (RSV). As the recipient of God's truth, the church is committed to uphold and defend it against the attacks of those whose teaching emanates from the father of lies [4:1f.].

As Fairbairn well says, 'The truth is not of the church's making, but of God's revealing: she has it, not as of her own, but from above; and has it not to alter or modify at her own will, but to keep as a sacred treasure for the glory of God and the good of men . . . Rightly understood, therefore, this passage determines nothing for Rome, or for any church which rests its claim to apostolicity on historical descent. The grand test is, does she hold by the truth of God? Is she in her belief and practice a witness for this? Or does she gainsay and pervert it?' [*2 Tim.* 3:16f.].

16: And without controversy great is the mystery of godliness;

He who was manifested in the flesh, justified in the spirit,
Seen of angels, Preached among the nations,
Believed on in the world, Received up in glory.

It is generally agreed that Paul here quotes a fragment of an early Christian hymn. The lines fall naturally into three contrasting pairs: (1) flesh-spirit, (2) angels-nations, (3) world-glory. 'The movement of thought is spatial rather than chronological because the important point is that the Saviour has reunited heaven and earth' (Robert H. Gundry, 'The Form, Meaning and Background of the Hymn Quoted in 1 Timothy 3:16' in *Apostolic History and the Gospel*, p. 207).

And confessedly great is the mystery of piety: All believers unite in confessing the supreme importance of the mystery which God has revealed in the gospel, for they know that the secret of true piety is nothing less than Christ himself [cf. *Col.* 1:27]. 'And a "mystery of godliness" the gospel is called, because, being believed, it transformeth men into the same image, and stirs up in them admirable affections of piety' (Trapp).

He who was manifested in the flesh / Justified in the spirit: Although the quotation is abruptly introduced with the pronoun 'who', none of Paul's readers 'would hesitate to supply the subject, Jesus Christ' (B. B. Warfield). In this couplet the contrast is not between the humanity and divinity of Christ, but between two successive stages of his life. The incarnate Son 'was manifested in the flesh' during the period of his humiliation, but he was justified in the realm of the Spirit when by his resurrection he entered into the state of exaltation. As Christ died under the cloud of our guilt [*2 Cor.* 5:21], we could not be justified until the resurrection of our Surety removed this verdict of condemnation and effectively affirmed the representative character of his perfect righteousness [*Rom.* 4:25].

'Christ's resurrection was the *de facto* declaration of God in regard to his being just. His quickening bears in itself the testimony of his justification. God, through suspending the forces of death operating on Him, declared that the ultimate, the supreme consequence of sin had reached its termination. In other words, resurrection had annulled the sentence of condemnation (G. Vos as cited by Richard B. Gaffin, to whom I am indebted for the substance of this comment).

Seen of angels / Preached among the nations: Since the hymn celebrates the triumph of Christ incarnate, 'seen of angels' probably refers to the worship accorded by the angelic host to Christ at his ascension [*Phil.* 2:9f.], and this would fit in with the final line, 'received up in glory'. 'Preached among the nations' shows that the early church was eager to fulfil its missionary mandate to preach the gospel to every creature, and the hymn's stress on the universal scope of the gospel leads Robert

Gundry to make the interesting suggestion that it may have originated in Syrian Antioch, the church which sent forth Paul and Barnabas to evangelize the Gentiles [*Acts* 11:19–26; 13:1ff.]. As Bernard notes, The revelation to Gentiles is *mediate*, by preaching, while 'the revelation to the higher orders or created intelligences is *immediate*, by vision'.

Believed on in the world / Received up in glory: The final couplet sets forth the consummation of Christ's saving work on earth and in heaven. 'Believed on in the world' points to the amazing result of the universal preaching of the good news [*Col.* 1:23]; 'received up in glory' means that Christ was taken up to the realm of glory and there enthroned in the seat of all authority and power.

CHAPTER FOUR

Through the Spirit the apostle warns Timothy of the rise of deceitful teachers, who will enforce ascetic practices in violation of the declared will of God [verses 1–5]. Timothy can best combat such errors by teaching the true faith, avoiding unprofitable speculations, and providing an example of godly living. He must be diligent in fulfilling his ministry and developing his gift, so that his progress may be seen by all. For in thus taking heed to himself and his doctrine, he will save both himself and his hearers [verses 6–16].

1: But the Spirit saith expressly, that in later times some shall fall away from the faith, giving heed to seducing spirits and doctrines of demons,

Since Paul places all the emphasis on the Spirit as the divine author of the prediction, we cannot be certain that the apostle was the recipient of this revelation, but it is not improbable in view of his previous warning to the same church [*Acts* 20:29, 30]. 'In later times' does not refer to the remote future (as in 'the last days' of *2 Tim.* 3:1), but to an impending crisis of which the first signs are already present [verses 3–5]. The apostasy of 'some' from their profession of 'the faith' will be due to their paying attention to deceiving spirits and the doctrines taught by demons. Engaged as he was in a spiritual conflict, Paul knew very well that his wrestling was not against flesh and blood, but against the malevolent powers of darkness [*Eph.* 6:12]. 'They are the *ultimate*, the false teachers of the next verse being the *proximate*, cause of the errors about to appear in the Church' (Bernard).

2: through the hypocrisy of men that speak lies, branded in their own conscience as with a hot iron;

Through the specious falsehoods of men whose own conscience is branded with the devil's sign (NEB): Since the false teachers are engaged in the devil's work, their conscience is branded with the sign which indicates his ownership. The metaphor is taken from the practice of branding slaves and criminals. 'The meaning is that they are in bondage to secret sin. Proclaiming a doctrine which makes strong ascetic demands, they are themselves controlled by self-seeking and covetousness. They are secretly the slaves of satanic and demonic powers which make them their instruments' (J. Schneider, *TDNT*, vol. 3, p. 644).

3: forbidding to marry, and commanding to abstain from meats, which God created to be received with thanksgiving by them that believe and know the truth.

Paul here shows that the spurious spirituality which pretends to attain a higher perfection by abstaining from outward things is an impeachment of the wisdom of God in creation [*Gen.* 1:31]. Having already endorsed the divine ordinance of marriage [2:15; 3:2, 12], the apostle condemns the devilish demand for celibacy by implication rather than by argument, but elsewhere he clearly teaches that the unlawful requirements of asceticism can never be the means of promoting a superior state of sanctity [cf. *Col.* 2:20–23]. With regard to the prohibition of certain foods, Paul insists that such a ban is contrary to the will of God, who created these gifts 'to be received with thanksgiving by them that believe and know the truth'. Ignorance, far from being the mother of devotion, keeps its votaries in bondage to the superstition which prevents them from receiving God's blessings with gratitude. In contrast to the unbelieving Jews or to the half-instructed 'weak brethren' [*Rom.* 14:21], believers who fully know the truth have no scruples in freely partaking of that bounty which they thankfully acknowledge to be the fruit of God's covenant love.

4: For every creature of God is good, and nothing is to be rejected, if it be received with thanksgiving: 5: for it is sanctified through the word of God and prayer,

'For' introduces the reason for the whole of the preceding statement [verse 3]. Because the goodness of God is manifested in creation, every creature he made is good, and therefore nothing is to be rejected or thrown away, provided it is received with thanksgiving [*Gen.* 1:31; *Mark* 7:15; *Acts* 10:15]. As if to anticipate the objection that some foods were expressly forbidden by the Mosaic Law, Paul repeats the condition of blessing to show that '*thanksgiving* disannuls the Law in each particular case. Nothing over which thanksgiving can be pronounced is any longer included in the category of things tabooed' (White). For the food is thus 'sanctified through the word of God and prayer'. 'It becomes holy to the eater; not that it was unclean in itself, but that his scruples or thanklessness might make it so to him' (Lock). In this clear reference to grace before meals [*Mark* 6:41; 14:22; *Acts* 27:35], the Word of God and prayer are joined together, because we speak to God on the basis of his Word and use expressions which are taken from it. The early examples of such prayers which have come down to us are 'packed with Scriptural phrases' (Bernard).

6: If thou put the brethren in mind of these things, thou shalt be a good minister of Christ Jesus, nourished in the words of the faith, and of the good doctrine which thou hast followed until now:

By submitting these truths to the brethren [verses 4, 5], Timothy will fortify them against error [verses 1–3], and prove himself a good minister of Christ Jesus. Although some prefer the praise of men, a godly pastor would rather choose 'to be accounted a good servant of Christ, so that during the whole of his ministry this should be his only aim' (Calvin). Timothy will attain this goal by continuing to be nourished by 'the words of the faith and of the good doctrine' – for it is loyal adherence to the objective truth of the gospel that makes a good minister – and this is the course he has followed until now. 'Many who have purely learned Christ from their boyhood afterwards fall away with the passing of time, but Paul says that Timothy was not one of them' (Calvin) [*2 Tim.* 3:14, 15].

7: but refuse profane and old wives' fables. And exercise thyself unto godliness:

In sharp contrast to 'the good doctrine', Timothy must have nothing to do with those unholy myths which resemble the tall stories told by credulous old women [1:4; *Titus* 1:14]! 'The *myths* with which the heretics offer supposed religious truths are profane. They have nothing to do with God and lead astray from Him. It can hardly be said more plainly that the *myths* and NT religion are mutually exclusive' (G. Stählin, *TDNT*, vol. 4, p. 787). Instead of giving heed to such folly, Timothy is to train himself for a life of godliness. As true godliness is rooted in Christ's saving work, it is fundamentally the *gift* of God's grace [*Titus* 2:11, 12]. But it is also a *demand* in that our growth in grace calls for an obedience to God's will which requires strenuous self-discipline [verses 8,10; 6:11, 12].

8: for bodily exercise is profitable for a little; but godliness is profitable for all things, having promise of the life which now is, and of that which is to come. 9: Faithful is the saying, and worthy of all acceptation.

Most commentators are agreed that the formula of verse 9 refers back to verse 8, because this is more like a proverbial saying than verse 10, which rather appeals to Christian experience to confirm its truth ('for'). The third of the 'faithful sayings' contrasts the limited value of gymnastic exercise ('profitable for *a little*') with the absolute value of godliness ('profitable for *all things*'). The far greater superiority of godliness consists in its 'having promise of the life which now is, and of that which is to come'. Godliness is profitable, not because it offers a guarantee of worldly prosperity [6:5ff.], but because it carries with it a promise of that everlasting life 'in which we already participate in the period of Christ, and to which we look forward in fulness then' (G. Stählin, *TDNT*, vol. 4, p. 1120). As God is the giver of this new life in Christ [*2 Tim.* 1:1], he remains the object of hope [*Titus* 1:2], so that even present struggles can be regarded as a preparation for future glory [verse 10]. Thus 'the distinction is not between two kinds of life, but the two conditions under which the one life is lived' (Parry).

10: For to this end we labour and strive, because we have our hope set on the living God, who is the Saviour of all men, specially of them that believe.

The experience of Paul and his fellow-labourers is a standing testimony to the truth of the saying [verse 8]: For with this end in view they toil and struggle [*Col.* 1:29], because they have fixed their hope on God (the) *living*, who is 'therefore able to give life now and hereafter' (Lock). The further description of God as 'the Saviour of *all* men' is evidently directed against the rigorous demands of the false teachers, and is intended to show that God is not merely the Saviour of a handful of ascetics [verses 3, 4]. For God's offer of salvation applies to all men without distinction [2:4], and this calls for the universal proclamation of his word of grace in order to bring the lost to faith [*Titus* 1:3].

But to reassure any Christians who were disturbed by the exclusive claims of the heretics, Paul adds that God is *especially* the Saviour of believers because the expectations of those whose hope is placed in the living God can never be disappointed. It is a mistake to detach this verse from its 'life-situation' and make it either a prop for universalism or the enemy of predestination. We shall be able to avoid such errors only as we seek to interpret every text within its particular context.

11: These things command and teach.

In case Timothy had any misgivings about his task in Ephesus, Paul encourages him to leave his hearers in no doubt of his authority. Although teaching precedes commanding in point of time, 'command' is here placed before 'teach' because the church had to be recalled to certain fundamental truths which were in danger of being forgotten ('these things' = verses 6–10). 'Teach the tractable, command the obstinate, lay God's charge upon all' (Trapp).

12: Let no man despise thy youth; but be thou an ensample to them that believe, in word, in manner of life, in love, in faith, in purity.

Timothy was relatively youthful for the heavy responsibility of acting as the apostle's representative in Ephesus, even though he was probably between 35 and 40 years of age. Hence his character and conduct must be such as to give none any occasion to despise his lack of years. No doubt the exhortation was also intended to have a salutary effect on the Ephesian congregation, 'for no Greek maxim was more familiar than the subordination of youth to age' (E. K. Simpson). So if he is to command respect, Timothy must be an 'ensample' to believers, i.e. 'not merely an example *to* them but a model *for* them' (Bernard). [cf. *Titus* 2:7f.] Paul indicates five spheres in which this pattern is to be made distinct. As to outward conduct, both speech and conduct must be above reproach, and with respect to inward disposition, it should be clear that this has been shaped by the three essential graces of love, faith, and purity.

13: Till I come, give heed to reading, to exhortation, to teaching.

Paul has already indicated that he hopes soon to visit Ephesus [3:14], and meanwhile Timothy is to devote himself to the work of the ministry. Three aspects of this work are singled out for special mention. First, there is the public reading of the Scripture, a practice taken over from the synagogue [*Luke* 4:16, 17; *Acts* 15:21; *2 Cor.* 3:14]. Apostolic letters were also read to the congregation, and we see in this tacit recognition of their inspiration and authority the origin of the New Testament canon [*Col.* 4:16; *1 Thess.* 5:27; *2 Pet.* 3:15, 16; *Rev.* 1:3]. Next came the exhortation or sermon that followed the reading and was based upon it. This was also an adoption of what was the custom in the synagogue [*Acts* 13:15]. Finally, there is the teaching or catechetical instruction, which served to explain the doctrines of the faith to new converts and provided them with the guidelines for Christian living [cf. *Rom.* 12:7; *Titus* 2:1–14].

14: Neglect not the gift that is in thee, which was given thee by prophecy, with the laying on of the hands of the presbytery.

In urging Timothy not to neglect the gift that is in him, Paul is not implying that he is failing in his duty, since the negative simply expresses what is positively required: 'Always be giving this your diligent attention!' But the exhortation is necessary because 'the gift' is not a magical endowment which works without the co-operation of its recipient; 'it may be neglected and needs to be kindled into a flame (see *2 Tim.* 1:6). To neglect God's gifts, whether of nature or of grace, is a sin' (Bernard). The gift which is in view is that which fitted Timothy for the work of the ministry. Paul's choice of Timothy at Lystra was confirmed by prophetic utterances [1:18; *Acts* 16:1–3], and the impartation of the gift was recognized in connection with the symbolic laying on of hands by the elders in which Paul also joined [*2 Tim.* 1:6; cf. *Acts* 13:1–3]. 'The essence of the matter does not lie in the particular official hands that ministered in Timothy's ordination;

but the grace was God's immediate and inward bestowment, attested by the voice of His Spirit in the Church, then sealed and acknowledged on the Church's part in the appropriate form' (Findlay).

15: Be diligent in these things; give thyself wholly to them; that thy progress may be manifest unto all.

After reminding Timothy of the gift which qualified him for the task, Paul now bids him to be diligent in the exercise of his ministry [verses 12–14]. He must be so absorbed in these duties that his 'progress' (a word often used of progress in philosophy by Stoic writers) may be evident to all. Two points are significant here: 1. that the true spiritual progress of the Christian is visible to others as well as himself, and 2. that although in the pastoral exhortation of this section *progress* seems to be a matter of human effort, 'in the last resort, as the development of a grace, it is like all genuine NT *progress* a gift of God' (G. Stählin, *TDNT*, vol. 6, p. 714).

16: Take heed to thyself, and to thy teaching. Continue in these things; for in doing this thou shalt save both thyself and them that hear thee.

Paul concludes with a double charge: 1. Timothy must take heed to himself, for the minister must be the first to profit from the truth which he presses upon his hearers [*2 Tim.* 2:6], lest having preached to others he should find himself rejected [*1 Cor.* 9:27]; 2. He must take heed to his own presentation of the truth, for those under his care must not only be instructed in 'the doctrine', but also have their particular needs met with the right word at the right time [*Prov.* 15:23]. This is followed by the assurance that if Timothy perseveres in 'these things' (i.e. all the preceding injunctions which were summed up in verse 15) he shall save both himself and those who hear him. 'Save' here means full and final salvation.

'Nor should it seem strange that Paul ascribes to Timothy the work of saving the Church, for all that are won for God are saved and it is by the preaching of the Gospel that we are gathered to Christ. And just as the unfaithfulness or negligence of a pastor is fatal to the Church, so it is right for its salvation to be ascribed to his faithfulness and diligence. It is indeed true that it is God alone who saves and not even the smallest part of His glory can rightly be transferred to men. But

God's glory is in no way diminished by His using the labour of men in bestowing salvation' (Calvin) [*Eph.* 4:11].

CHAPTER FIVE

With regard to church discipline, Paul first shows that Timothy's admonitions must be suited to the age and sex of the persons addressed [verses 1, 2]. In dealing with widows, it is necessary to distinguish between those in need of the church's support and those with relatives who are well able to take care of them [verses 3–8]. No widow under the age of sixty may be enrolled unless she is known to be of good character, and younger widows should be encouraged to marry again and bring up a family [verses 11–16]. Elders are to be honoured and rewarded for their work; no accusation should be received against an elder without proof, but those found guilty of an offence must be openly reproved that the rest may fear to imitate them [verses 17–21]. Timothy is charged to act without prejudice, cautioned against ordaining any man in haste, and bidden to shun all that is evil [verses 21, 22]. After advising Timothy to take a little wine for the sake of his health, Paul reverts to the need for discernment in judging character because outward appearances can be very deceptive [verses 23–25].

1: Rebuke not an elder, but exhort him as a father; the younger men as brethren: 2: the elder women as mothers; the younger as sisters, in all purity.

In fulfilling the pastoral office Timothy must show church members the same respect he would give to his own family. An older man (the word here does not refer to an 'elder' of the church, cf. verse 17) should not be harshly rebuked, but entreated as a father. Although the others named are also governed by the verb 'exhort', it is possible that Paul passes from the idea of admonition to Timothy's general relations with the various groups in his flock (J. N. D. Kelly). He must treat younger men as brothers, the elder women as mothers, and the younger women as sisters. In the latter case he adds the cautionary clause, 'in all purity', since nothing 'will so easily make or mar the young preacher as his conduct with young women' (A. T. Robertson).

3: Honour widows that are widows indeed.

As the duty of supporting widows was recognized by the church from the beginning [*Acts* 6:1], it is not surprising to find Paul endorsing this practice. But at the outset of his discussion he lays down the important qualification: 'Honour widows that are widows *indeed*', i.e. those who are truly bereft, having neither husband nor kinsfolk to support them [verse 4]. In contrast to the common disparagement of widows, the word 'honour' recalls the fifth commandment [*Exod.* 20:12], and thus shows that they are not only entitled to respect but to material provision as well [*Matt.* 15:4ff].

4: But if any widow hath children or grandchildren, let them learn first to show piety towards their own family, and to requite their parents: for this is acceptable in the sight of God.

But if a widow has a family, the responsibility for her support rests with them and not the church. Let her relatives learn that their first duty is to practise piety towards their own family, and 'make a return to those who brought them up' (Arndt-Gingrich). A ready fulfilment of this natural obligation is not only reasonable, but is also approved of God because it is in accordance with his revealed will [*Exod.* 20: 12].

5: Now she that is a widow indeed, and desolate, hath her hope set on God, and continueth in supplications and prayers night and day.

This gives the characteristics of the true widow who is eligible to receive the support of the church. Having been left entirely alone, she has fixed her hope on God, the Guardian of widows, and like Anna is given to constant prayer [*Luke* 2.37]. The expression 'night and day' is 'indicative of the *when* rather than the *how long*; not *throughout* night and day, but *by* night as well as *by* day a steady and regular habit of devotion' (Fairbairn) [cf. *1 Thess.* 3:10].

6: But she that giveth herself to pleasure is dead while she liveth.

By contrast the widow who only lives for pleasure is spiritually dead even while she lives, and has no claim on the church's charity [cf. *Rev.* 3:1]. 'Life in worldly pleasure is only life in appearance' (H. J. Holtzmann).

7: These things also command, that they may be without reproach.

Timothy must take care that Paul's instructions concerning widows are obeyed, for to maintain a credible witness it is necessary to ensure that those supported by the church, whether bishops [3:2] or widows, are seen to lead lives which are above reproach.

8: But if any provideth not for his own, and specially his own household, he hath denied the faith, and is worse than an unbeliever.

Paul's strong language appears to indicate that some in Ephesus were trying to evade the duty of supporting their own relatives by making the church responsible for them [verse 4]. Such a man stands condemned on two counts: 1. he has denied 'the faith' in the practical sense of failing to fulfil the duties it inculcates [*Exod.* 20:12]; 2. he is worse than an unbeliever not only because many pagans perform the duty [*Rom.* 2:14], but also because he has the law of Christ to guide him [*Gal.* 6:2, 10]. 'Faith does not set aside natural duties, but perfects and strengthens them' (Bengel) [*James* 2:14–17].

9: Let none be enrolled as a widow under threescore years old, having been the wife of one man, 10: well reported of for good works; if she hath brought up children, if she hath used hospitality to strangers, if she hath washed the saints' feet, if she hath relieved the afflicted, if she hath diligently followed every good work.

To ensure that the generosity of the church is not abused, Paul next specifies the qualifications of 'true' widows [verse 3]. No widow under the age of sixty is to be put on the list of those entitled to receive regular support. (Naturally this ruling would not prevent a younger widow from receiving whatever help was necessary in time of need.) As to her character, she must have been a faithful wife and be well known for her good works. 'The wife of one man' clearly cannot mean 'only once married', since the apostle advises younger widows to marry again [verse 14; cf. 3:2, 12].

What is meant by 'good works' is explained by the five examples which are introduced by the word 'if'. A widow who is worthy of the church's support will have brought up her children well (assuming she had a family), been given to hospitality and the attendant courtesy of washing her guests' feet, and in short, will have devoted herself to 'all kinds of good deeds' (NIV). Some have claimed that the passage already points to the enrolment of an 'official' order of widows, and that the list given in verse 10 even hints at their duties, despite the fact that the verbs used all refer to their past conduct! 'But there is no proper evidence whatever to show that such widows as those here mentioned by the apostle were invested with any sort of office, or were called to do anything but such pious and free-will service as their own hearts might prompt, and their limited opportunities might enable them to perform' (Fairbairn).

11: But younger widows refuse: for when they have waxed wanton against Christ, they desire to marry; 12: having condemnation, because they have rejected their first pledge.

With regard to younger widows, Paul directs Timothy to refuse to put them on the roll for permanent support, for when they are swayed by sensual desires that alienate them from Christ, they wish to marry. In view of the advice given in verse 14, the condemnation thus incurred could hardly be due to the rejection of a 'pledge' not to remarry. 'This is not an apostolic beginning of monastic orders. Paul is not in one breath keeping widows from remarriage and in the next breath urging this very thing' (Lenski). 'First pledge' literally means 'first faith' (ASV margin), and the particular danger envisaged is that a younger widow, in whom the sexual impulse is still strong, might allow her natural affection to override her first loyalty to Christ and marry a pagan. By entering into such a union, she would bring judgment upon herself, and disgrace upon the faithful community whose fellowship she had publicly renounced.

13: And withal they learn also to be idle, going about from house to house; and not only idle, but tattlers also and busybodies, speaking things which they ought not.

Moreover, if younger widows were placed on the list for full support, this would encourage idleness and leave them free to gossip and meddle with affairs which were no concern of theirs. To warn Timothy of the undesirable consequences of such unwise charity, Paul draws a vivid picture of these young women gadding about from house to house, 'speaking of things better left unspoken' (NEB). 'As vagrants, or as pedlars opening their packs, and dropping here a tale and there a tale.

A practice flatly forbidden by God, *Lev.* 19:16, "Thou shalt not go up and down as a talebearer among thy people"' (Trapp).

14: I desire therefore that the younger widows marry, bear children, rule the household, give no occasion to the adversary for reviling: 15: for already some are turned aside after Satan.

In view of these dangers, Paul counsels younger widows to marry, if, as the context makes clear [verses 11, 12], they can marry 'in the Lord' [*1 Cor.* 7:39]. Then bringing up a family and managing the home will keep them so busy that 'the adversary' (i.e. the devil or his agents, cf. 4:1) will be given no opportunity for slander. Paul's explanatory remark shows that he was not merely theorizing in verses 11–13, but speaking from sad experience. Some of the younger widows had already thrown off their allegiance to Christ and turned aside after Satan. 'Therefore the apostle would have them regarded as beacons, warning the church not to continue the over-indulgent treatment it had begun to exhibit toward such' (Fairbairn).

16: If any woman that believeth hath widows, let her relieve them, and let not the church be burdened; that it may relieve them that are widows indeed.

In rounding off his discussion of widows, Paul shows that the Christian woman with dependent widows in her family should support them and not let the church be burdened with them, so that the church can help those widows who are really destitute. This instruction would apply both to the woman whose husband was not a believer, and to the woman of means who managed her own household (like Lydia, *Acts* 16:14f.). The longer reading of the AV – 'believer (masc.) or believer (fem.)' was probably due to copyists who 'felt that a restriction of the principle of this verse to Christian women was unfair' (Bruce M. Metzger, *A Textual Commentary on the Greek New Testament*, p. 642).

17: Let the elders that rule well be counted worthy of double honour, especially those who labour in the word and in teaching.

After showing how widows are to be honoured [verses 3–16], the apostle next enforces the duty of honouring the spiritual leaders of the church, who are here called 'elders' rather than 'overseers' to draw attention to the dignity of their position (cf. comment on 3:1). The elders who rule well [3:4, 5] should be counted worthy of double honour, i.e. they should be honoured not only for the sake of their office, but also for the excellence of their work. This double honour applies especially to elders who are giving all their energies to preaching and teaching [3:2]. But if the primary meaning of 'honour' is to the fore, the next verse suggests that the idea of remuneration was also present in Paul's mind [verse 18], for he 'was thinking particularly of the honour which the church was bound to show to their elders by presenting them with the means necessary for their support' (Huther).

18: For the scripture saith, Thou shalt not muzzle the ox when he treadeth out the corn. And, The labourer is worthy of his hire.

As in *1 Cor.* 9:9, Paul's quotation of *Deut.* 25:4 is an argument from the lesser to the greater: 'If God commands men to care for the oxen which tread out the corn, how much more does this principle hold good for ministers who labour to provide men with the Bread of Life?' Although the second quotation is evidently introduced as a well-known saying of the Lord [*Luke* 10:7], we can not be sure that Paul intended to include it in the category of Scripture. But even if the opening formula applies only to the first quotation, the close connection ('and') shows that the words of Jesus had the same normative authority for the church as the written word of God, i.e. the Old Testament (cf. comment on 4:13). On the other hand, Paul may have seen the original text of Luke's Gospel, in which case this 'would be the earliest instance of the Lord's words being quoted as "Scripture"' (Lock).

19: Against an elder receive not an accusation, except at the mouth of two or three witnesses. 20: Them that sin reprove in the sight of all, that the rest also may be in fear.

Since the ministry is a prime target for Satan's malice, no accusation against an elder is to be entertained without evidence from two or three witnesses [*Deut.* 19:15; *Matt.* 18:16; *2 Cor.* 13:1]. 'If to be accused were sufficient to make a man guilty, no good minister should be innocent . . . Truth hath always a scratcht face. Men hate him that reproveth in the gate. Every fool hath a bolt to shoot at a faithful preacher' (Trapp). But elders who are found guilty of sin must be publicly rebuked so that other believers ('the rest') may fear to follow their bad example. Paul is here speaking of sins that give rise to public scandal, for if any elder 'commits a fault not in that category, it is clearly preferable that he should be admonished privately rather than openly accused' (Calvin).

21: I charge thee in the sight of God, and Christ Jesus, and the elect angels, that thou observe these things without prejudice, doing nothing by partiality.

Paul solemnly charges Timothy to carry out the preceding disciplinary instructions with perfect fairness, neither prejudging the case nor showing any favouritism. As the apostle's every act is governed by his awareness of the divine presence, he fittingly reminds Timothy that his administration of the church comes under heavenly scrutiny. For every church leader needs to be reminded that his conduct is witnessed by 'God *and* Christ Jesus, *and* the elect angels'. The first 'and' joins God with Christ as divine, while the second marks off 'the elect angels' as creatures who owe their existence to God. The angels of heaven are here described as 'elect' in contrast to the fallen angels, 'who did not keep their position of authority but abandoned their own home' [*Jude* 6, NIV].

22: Lay hands hastily on no man, neither be partaker of other men's sins: keep thyself pure.

Do not be over-hasty in laying on hands in ordination, or you may find yourself responsible for other people's misdeeds; keep your own hands clean (NEB): Paul here impresses upon Timothy the importance of ensuring that only men of unquestioned integrity are appointed to the ministry. For if he neglects to guard this holy office against profane intruders, he may find himself sharing the blame for their sins. It is as he thus seeks to preserve the purity of the church that he will keep himself pure. This seems to be the primary meaning of the final clause, though a more general reference cannot be ruled out. Some interpreters maintain that this laying on of hands refers to the formal restoration of penitents to membership, 'but there is no trace in the New Testament of the existence of this custom in apostolic times' (Huther) [cf. 4:14; *2 Tim.* 1: 6].

23: Be no longer a drinker of water, but use a little wine for thy stomach's sake and thine often infirmities.

Perhaps a desire to clarify the preceding exhortation ('keep thyself pure') prompted the apostle to warn Timothy against practising self-discipline at the expense of his health. Apparently Timothy drank only water in case others should think he was addicted to wine [3:2]. But in view of Timothy's frequent ailments, Paul urges him to take a little wine as a remedy for these infirmities. 'How few there are today who need to be forbidden water, how many rather that need to be restricted to drinking wine soberly!' (Calvin).

24: Some men's sins are evident, going before unto judgment; and some men also they follow after. 25: In like manner also there are good works that are evident; and such as are otherwise cannot be hid.

These general statements resume the thought of verse 22. Although the wise choosing of elders is undoubtedly difficult, the task will be made much easier if Timothy remembers that conduct always affords the best guide to character. Paul first describes those who are unfit for office. The sins of some men are so obvious that they rush before them to judgment, proclaiming their guilt in advance; whereas 'there are others whose offences have not yet overtaken them' (NEB), but careful enquiry will usually succeed in bringing them to light. Similarly, fitness for office is made evident by good works, which cannot remain hidden, even if they are not immediately apparent. If Timothy bears these guidelines in mind, he will ensure that unworthy men are not ordained and that good men are not overlooked.

CHAPTER SIX

The apostle directs Christian slaves to honour their masters so that the gospel is not dishonoured, while those with believing masters must not presume upon the bond of Christian love but should serve them even better [verses 1, 2]. The proud corrupters of the true faith are next denounced, for they not only engage in sterile controversies, but also make their religion a pretext for gain. The real gain of godliness with contentment is contrasted with the illusory pursuit of riches, which has proved to be the root of all kinds of evil for many [verses 3–10]. Paul charges Timothy to fight the good fight of faith, and to witness a good confession without reproach as he keeps in view the approaching advent of Christ, whose appearing shall reveal the full glory of the world's only Ruler [verses 11–16]. Wealthy believers must not trust in uncertain riches, but are exhorted to be rich in those good works by which they can lay up for themselves true treasure in heaven [verses 17–19]. Paul's final appeal urges Timothy to guard the deposit, and to shun the profane sophistries which have ensnared some, while his closing benediction embraces the whole church [verses 20–21].

1: Let as many as are servants under the yoke count their own masters worthy of all honour, that the name of God and the doctrine be not blasphemed. 2: And they that have believing masters, let them not despise them, because they are brethren; but let them serve them the rather, because they that partake of the benefit are believing and beloved. These things teach and exhort.

In dealing with the delicate question of the attitude to be adopted by converted slaves towards their masters, Paul neither preaches revolutionary change nor even a resigned acceptance of the *status quo*, but reminds them of the importance of their position as ambassadors of the gospel [cf. *Titus* 2: 10]. Hence all who are under the yoke as slaves should not only bow to the authority of their unbelieving masters, but also regard them as worthy of all respect. For while such ungrudging service will commend the gospel they profess, 'the name of God' would be blasphemed if pagans 'could point to Christians doing their ordinary duties badly as the effect of their religion' (Parry).

In those cases where Christian slaves are blessed in having believing masters, they must not behave as though their equality before God had erased the civil distinction between them. Instead of despising or looking down on their masters, they should serve them all the better, 'because those who benefit from their service are believers, and dear to them' (NIV). Timothy must continue to teach and exhort 'these things' concerning the duty of slaves, so that the church might not be charged with undermining the foundations of society by encouraging a rebellious spirit in slaves.

3: If any man teacheth a different doctrine, and consenteth not to sound words, even the words of our Lord Jesus Christ, and to the doctrine which

is according to godliness; 4: he is puffed up, knowing nothing, but doting about questionings and disputes of words, whereof cometh envy, strife, railings, evil surmisings, 5: wranglings of men corrupted in mind and bereft of the truth, supposing that godliness is a way of gain.

The warmth of Paul's words here shows how far removed he is from the Laodicean indifference of the modern church towards those who teach a 'different' doctrine which is quite alien to the apostolic faith [cf. *Gal.* 1:6–9]. According to the apostle, the church must reject any one whose teaching does not agree with the healthy words 'of our Lord Jesus Christ', for that is the only doctrine which is in conformity with and conducive to godliness [*Titus* 1:1]. The reference is not to the words spoken directly by the Lord, but to the fact that the exalted Christ is both the ultimate *source* of the apostles' doctrine and the great *subject* of all their preaching.

He is puffed up with conceit, he knows nothing; he has a morbid craving for controversy and for disputes about words (RSV): Paul next provides Timothy with a penetrating analysis of the 'psychology of error' (Lenski). The false teacher is inflated with the pride that blinds him to the truth, but though he knows nothing as it really is, he does not hesitate to confine the entire cosmos within the strait-jacket of his preconceived ideas. Instead of delighting in the healthy words of the gospel, he is morbidly absorbed with useless speculations and hair-splitting 'disputes about words' (our 'logomachies'). 'The wit of heretics and schismatics will better serve them to devise a thousand shifts to elude the truth than their pride will suffer them once to yield and acknowledge it' (Trapp).

That result in envy, quarrelling, malicious talk, evil suspicions and constant friction between men of corrupt mind, who have been robbed of the truth and who think that godliness is a means to financial gain (NIV): Paul lists five social consequences which stem from the mind that is diseased by pride: 1. 'envy', provoked by more brilliant speculations; 2. 'quarrelling' with the proponents of these theories; 3. 'malicious talk', the slandering of such rivals; 4. 'evil suspicions', doubting the honesty of those who beg to differ from them; 5. 'constant friction', the mutual irritation which exists between those who propagate contrary errors. Although these false teachers were once acquainted with the truth, they were never possessed by it, and have now been defrauded of any interest in it through the innate depravity of their minds. The essential secularity of their thought is demonstrated by their mercenary motives. They care neither for God nor man, but simply don the mask of religion in order to enrich themselves [*Titus* 1:11].

6: But godliness with contentment is great gain: 7: for we brought nothing into the world, for neither can we carry anything out; 8: but having food and covering we shall be therewith content.

But if godliness is not a gainful trade, there is great gain in the godliness which is coupled with 'contentment' [cf. 4:8]. The word literally means 'self-sufficiency', and it was used by the Cynics and Stoics to describe the wise man whose inner resources make him independent of all outside help. What the word means to Paul is made plain in *Phil.* 4:11–13. 'Godliness is ever accompanied with contentment in a greater or lesser degree; all truly godly people have learned with St Paul, in whatever state they are, to be therewith content' (Matthew Henry). It is evident that such a lack of dependence upon worldly possessions is the only reasonable attitude for believers to adopt (note the three 'we' verbs). For we brought nothing into the world, and we can take nothing out of it [*Job* 1:21; *Eccles.* 5:15]. 'Whatever a man amasses by the way is in the nature of luggage, no part of his truest personality, but something he leaves behind at the toll-bar of death' (E. K. Simpson). So if we have food and shelter, we shall be content with these necessaries and not hanker after luxuries. 'For nature is content with a little and all that goes beyond natural usage is superfluous. Not that a more liberal use of possessions should be condemned as bad in itself, but a desire for it is always sinful' (Calvin).

9: But they that are minded to be rich fall into a temptation and a snare and many foolish and hurtful lusts, such as drown men in destruction and perdition.

Those who have fixed their desires upon wealth as their highest good soon find they are following a downward path, which brings them sorrow in this world and eternal perdition in the next. In falling a prey to this temptation, they are caught like an animal in a trap, and are held fast by 'many foolish and hurtful lusts'. 'The desires in question are foolish, because they cannot be logically defended; they are hurtful, because they hinder true happiness' (White). Such lusts plunge men into 'destruction and perdition'. 'The combination (found only here) is emphatic, "loss for time and eternity"' (Lock).

10: For the love of money is a root of all kinds of evil: which some reaching after have been led astray from the faith, and have pierced themselves through with many sorrows.

Although money is not in itself evil, the *love* of money is a root of all kinds of evil. 'The sentiment is, that there is no kind of evil to which the love of money may not lead men, when it once fairly takes hold of them' (Fairbairn). In thus reaching after money 'some have wandered away from the faith and pierced their hearts with many pangs' (RSV). A departure from the faith is inevitable when gold displaces God in man's affections, and Paul clearly knows some in Ephesus who have exchanged spiritual treasure for material wealth with tragic consequences to themselves [*Matt.* 6:24]. For instead of gaining joy and satisfaction from their riches, they suffer the pangs of conscience and the anguish of disillusionment. 'Many a millionaire, after choking his soul with gold-dust, has died from melancholia!' (Simpson).

11: But thou, O man of God, flee these things; and follow after righteousness, godliness, faith, love, patience, meekness.

Paul bases this personal appeal to Timothy upon an emphatic reminder of what he is by the grace of God: 'But *thou*, O man of God'. The title was given to Old Testament prophets and is especially appropriate to one who is called to serve God in the ministry of the gospel, though obviously this does not mean that other Christians are to be something less than this [cf. *2 Tim.* 3:17]. As befits a man of God, Timothy is ever to flee 'these things', i.e. the love of money and its attendant evils. On the positive side, he must be constant in his pursuit of the Christian virtues. The six named here fall into three pairs. 1. 'Righteousness' and 'godliness' cover the whole of the Christian's duty: upright conduct towards man, and reverent devotion towards God. 2. 'Faith' and 'love' are linked together as the animating principles of the Christian life. 3. 'Patient endurance' and 'meekness' denote the conduct proper to a Christian amid the enmity and opposition of the world to Christ's gospel, 'the former being opposed to submission, the latter to exasperation' (Huther) [cf. *2 Tim.* 2:25].

12: Fight the good fight of the faith, lay hold on the life eternal, whereunto thou wast called, and didst confess the good confession in the sight of many witnesses.

Fight the good fight of faith (AV): Having hinted at the need for perseverance and strenuous effort, Paul now exhorts Timothy to fight the good fight 'which faith in a man wages against all that hinders and opposes; not a fight for "the faith" as against false teachers, but faith's fight for the prize of the high calling' (Parry) [*1 Cor.* 9:24f.; *Phil.* 3:12f.].

Lay hold on the life eternal: This cannot be the reward bestowed at the end of the contest, since Timothy is urged to grasp eternal life even while he continues to fight the good fight. But in realizing by faith what he possesses in Christ, he can live a life which is *qualitatively* different from his former walk, and this is because the future has already invaded his present experience [cf. 4:8].

To which you were called when you made the good confession in the presence of many witnesses (RSV): As the context shows that the calling in view is that to salvation and not service, these words must refer to Timothy's baptism rather than his ordination (see the further comment on the next verse).

13: I charge thee in the sight of God, who giveth life to all things, and of Christ Jesus, who before Pontius Pilate witnessed the good confession; 14: that thou keep the commandment, without spot, without reproach, until the appearing of our Lord Jesus Christ:

The credal content of this solemn charge to Timothy has led scholars to suggest that Paul is here citing part of a baptismal confession (note the reference to God as Creator, and to Christ's witness before Pilate and his second coming in judgment). In the primitive church baptism was preceded by careful instruction in the faith, and was administered in the presence of the congregation when the candidates were required to make a public profession of their faith in Christ [verse 12; *Rom.* 10:9; *1 Cor.* 12:3; *Phil.* 2:11]. Now just as Timothy had confessed at his baptism, 'Jesus is Lord', so Jesus had made the same 'good confession' by witnessing to his own kingship before Pilate [*Mark* 15:2]. The commandment which must be kept 'without spot, without reproach' is therefore 'the charge laid on Timothy in his baptism, for the once-for-all confession of obedience to the divine Lord made in baptism can fittingly be appealed to at any subsequent time' (G. R. Beasley-Murray, *Baptism in the New Testament*, pp. 205–6). Although the 'appearing' of Christ in glory was always at the forefront of Paul's thought, he never pretended to know the date of the Lord's return, but is content to affirm that it will occur at the appropriate time determined by God (verse 15, 'which God will bring about in his own time', NIV).

15: which in its own times he shall show, who is the blessed and only Potentate, the King of kings, and Lord of lords; 16: who only hath immortality, dwelling in light unapproachable; whom no man hath seen, nor can see: to whom be honour and power eternal. Amen.

If the time of Christ's appearing is fixed by God, then every intervening event must also be under his sovereign control, and this leads Paul into a magnificent outburst of praise which expands the thought of his opening doxology [cf. 1:17].

Who is the blessed and only Potentate: The first epithet describes the absolute bliss which God possesses in himself; the second, the absolute sovereignty of his power over all things.

The King of kings, and Lord of lords, i.e. 'the King of those reigning and the Lord of those ruling': 'He means that the powers of this world are subject to His supreme dominion, depend upon Him, and stand or fall at His will' (Calvin).

Who only hath immortality: 'He only has immortality; he only is immortal in himself, and has immortality as he is the Fountain of it, for the immortality of angels and spirits is derived from him' (Matthew Henry).

Dwelling in light unapproachable: God dwells in a realm of light of such dazzling radiance that mortal man can neither approach nor apprehend him [cf. *Psa.* 104:2].

Whom no man hath seen, nor can see: 'Even a beatific vision of heaven will not consist of a sight of God as God, but rather as He shines forth in a manifestative and communicative way in the person of Christ, as suited to finite capacities' (Arthur Pink) [*Exod.* 33:20; *John* 1:18].

To whom be honour and power eternal. Amen: Paul concludes this sublime doxology by ascribing honour and power to God, as the One who is supremely worthy of all worship and praise, and he seals it with the solemn word of confirmation ('Amen' = 'so be it').

17: Charge them that are rich in this present world, that they be not highminded, nor have their hope set on the uncertainty of riches, but on God, who giveth us richly all things to enjoy; 18: that they do good, that they be rich in good works, that they be ready to distribute, willing to communicate; 19: laying up in store for themselves a good foundation against the time to come, that they may lay hold on the life which is life indeed.

Paul now returns to the subject of riches [verses 9, 10], and outlines the instruction Timothy must give to believers who are rich, as wealth is reckoned 'in this present world'. 1. Regarding the dangers to be avoided: he is to charge them not to be high-minded, to prevent them from becoming 'purse-proud' and looking down on their poorer brethren; he is to warn them not to have their hope set on 'uncertain' riches [*Prov.* 23:5], but on God 'who endows us richly with all things to enjoy' (NEB). Clearly this is a shaft directed against the ascetic demands of the heretics [4:1–5]. 'No good purpose is served by pretending that God did not intend us to enjoy the pleasurable sensations of physical life' (White). 2. Regarding the duties to be enjoined: he is to charge them to do good and be rich in good works, which means they must be ready to share their wealth and be quick to recognize the claims of Christian fellowship. In this way they will lay up treasure for themselves as a firm foundation for the future, so that they may grasp that which is life indeed [cf. *Matt.* 6:19,20]. Paul's teaching here 'is in exact accord with Christ's in *Matt.* 25:34–40, 46b. Salvation, to be sure, is entirely *by grace through faith* [*Eph.* 2:8; *Titus* 3:5], but the reward is *according to works* [*Dan.* 12:3; *2 Cor.* 5:10; *Rev.* 20:12]' (William Hendriksen).

20: O Timothy, guard that which is committed unto thee, turning away from the profane babblings and oppositions of the knowledge which is falsely so called; 21: which some professing have erred concerning the faith. Grace be with you.

Paul virtually sums up the message of the Epistle in his final appeal to Timothy, which was probably written in his own hand [*2 Thess.* 3:17].

O Timothy, guard the deposit which is committed unto thee (ASV margin): Paul earnestly exhorts Timothy to guard that 'deposit' (i.e. the 'sound doctrine' of the gospel), which has been entrusted to his safe-keeping. 'What is a deposit? It is something that is accredited to thee, not invented by thee; something that thou hast received, not that thou hast thought out; a result not of genius but of instruction; not of personal ownership but of public tradition; a matter brought to thee, not produced by thee, with respect to which thou art bound to be not an author but a custodian, not an originator but a bearer, not a leader but a follower' (Vincent of Lérins [5th century]).

Turning away from the profane babblings and oppositions of the knowledge which is falsely so called: On the negative side Timothy is to spurn the empty chatter which opposes the true gospel in the name of 'knowledge' [cf. 1: 3, 4]. 'Any speculation, any philosophising, any form of learning, any scientific theorizing which sought to intrude itself, in the way of modifying it in the least respect, upon the Gospel of Christ, – which is a sacred deposit committed to its ministers not to dilute or to alter or to modify, but to learn, hold, guard and preach, – would be characterized by Paul without hesitation as among the profane inanities and contradictions of knowledge falsely so called' (B. B. Warfield, 'The Inviolate Deposit', *Faith and Life*, p. 388).

Which some professing have missed the mark concerning the faith (ASV margin): This is another veiled reference to the false teachers [cf. 1:19]. 'In their profession of a knowledge which was secular in its method and shallow in its character, they failed in maintaining their own faith in God revealed in Christ, the only sure qualification for true knowledge' (Parry).

Grace be with you: Paul uses the plural 'you' in this brief benediction, because he knew that his letter to Timothy would also be read to the church at Ephesus.

2 Timothy

CHAPTER ONE

Paul affectionately greets Timothy, for whom he constantly prays, and longs to see, having received a reminder of his sincere faith which dwelt first in his grandmother and mother [verses 1–5]. He urges him to stir up the gift of God which is in him, and not to be ashamed of the testimony of the gospel, but to be ready to suffer for it by the power of God, who saved and called them both into his service (verses 6–10). It is due to his fidelity to the gospel that Paul is now a prisoner, but he is not ashamed, for he has entrusted himself to the Lord's safe-keeping [verses 11, 12]. Timothy must hold fast the sound teaching and guard the good deposit with the help of the Holy Spirit [verses 13, 14]. This appeal is enforced by the sad reminder of the general desertion of Paul's converts in Asia, and on the other hand by the bright example of the faithfulness shown by Onesiphorus [verses 15–18].

1: Paul, an apostle of Christ Jesus through the will of God, according to the promise of the life which is in Christ Jesus, 2: to Timothy, my beloved child: Grace, mercy, peace, from God the Father and Christ Jesus our Lord.

The opening salutation is very similar to that of the First Epistle to Timothy, but as Paul here calmly faces the last great crisis of his life, he reaffirms that he is an apostle of Christ Jesus 'through the will of God in accordance with the promise of life which is in Christ Jesus'. His apostleship was the result of that promise, for 'had there been no such *promise* there could have been no *divinely willed apostle* to proclaim the promise' (Hendriksen). This is the promise of everlasting life – beginning in grace and perfected in glory – which is found in union with Christ Jesus [verse 10; *1 Tim.* 4:8]. In addressing Timothy as 'my beloved child', Paul expresses the fatherly affection he feels for his own son in the faith, and thus sets the tone for this heartfelt and deeply moving letter of farewell. The greeting is identical with that given in *1 Tim.* 1:2 (see comment there).

3: I thank God, whom I serve from my forefathers in a pure conscience, how unceasing is my remembrance of thee in my supplications, night and day 4: longing to see thee, remembering thy tears, that I may be filled with joy; 5: having been reminded of the unfeigned faith that is in thee; which dwelt first in thy grandmother Lois, and thy mother Eunice; and, I am persuaded, in thee also.

Instead of reflecting upon his own sad plight, Paul begins in a spirit of gratitude to God. This is prompted by the treasured memories he has of his beloved child and by some recent reminder of Timothy's faith from without, conveyed perhaps by letter or messenger. The apostle affirms that he serves God with the same purity of conscience which characterized the worship of his forefathers, because the faith he proclaimed was the true fulfilment of Israel's ancestral hope [*Acts* 24:14–16]. 'Paul always maintained that the Gospel was the divinely ordained sequel of Judaism; not a new religion, but the fulfilment of "the promise made of God unto our fathers" [*Acts* 26:6]' (White). He assures Timothy that he constantly remembers him in his prayers 'night and day' [cf. AV and *1 Tim.* 5:5], and as he recalls Timothy's tears at their last parting, he longs to see him again that he may be filled with joy.

Whatever reminded Paul of Timothy's sincere faith in Christ naturally led him to think of the prior conversion of Timothy's grandmother Lois and his mother Eunice. This probably took place during Paul's first visit to Lystra [*Acts* 14:6], for when he returned Timothy's mother was already a believer [*Acts* 16:1]. Finally, by expressing his confidence in the genuineness of Timothy's faith, Paul provides the basis for the ensuing appeal, viz. that Timothy should bear a courageous testimony to the truth in the face of affliction.

6: For which cause I put thee in remembrance that thou stir up the gift of God, which is in thee through the laying on of my hands.

It is because Paul knows the reality of Timothy's commitment that he urges him to keep stirring into flame the gift of God which is in him. The bestowal of this ministerial gift was symbolized through the laying on of the apostle's hands at his ordination. Although this was an act in which the elders also joined, Paul only mentions his own part in that service here, since he is stressing the significance of the spiritual bond in his personal relationship with Timothy (see comment on *1 Tim.* 4: 14). The exhortation shows that the gift for service does not operate automatically, but requires the active co-operation of its recipient to keep it ablaze [cf. *1 Thess.* 5:19]. Paul does not imply that Timothy had been failing in his duty, for his use of the present infinitive rather means that his 'child' is to continue to fan the flame as he had been doing. This clarion call for untiring zeal in God's service demands the constant attention of every Christian worker, for frail flesh is prone to the lassitude which allows spiritual ardour to burn very low.

7: For God gave us not a spirit of fearfulness: but of power and love and discipline.

What God gave to Paul and Timothy for the work of ministry was not a spirit of craven fear, 'but a spirit of power and love and sound judgment' (Bruce). These are the three graces which are especially needed as the storm clouds of persecution begin to loom large on Timothy's horizon [verse 8]. 1. 'Power' is the divine dynamic which imparts the strength to work on, to endure adversity, and to die if need be; 2. 'Love' is the self-denying grace which banishes fear [*1 John* 4:18] and is ready to risk all to save the flock; 3. 'Sound judgment' ensures that power and love are exercised with wisdom, and thus provides an essential safeguard against the dangers of fanaticism.

8: Be not ashamed therefore of the testimony of our Lord, nor of me his prisoner: but suffer hardship with the gospel according to the power of God;

In view of this divine enduement [verse 7], Timothy must never be ashamed to testify about our Lord, even though the witness to a crucified Messiah inevitably excited the enmity and scorn of the world. White points out that the construction used here forbids the supposition that Timothy had actually done what Paul warns him against doing. It is a call to continued fidelity which urges Timothy not to become ashamed rather than to stop being ashamed. Paul also adds the touching appeal, 'nor of me his prisoner', for though he insists that he is the Lord's prisoner and not Caesar's [cf. *Eph.* 3:1], when an acknowledged leader is treated like a criminal his assistants are automatically involved in the same disgrace. Instead of yielding to such a feeling of shame, let Timothy join with Paul in suffering for the gospel [cf. NIV], according to the power that God gives [verse 7]. For the power given is always commensurate to the sufferings to be endured [*2 Cor.* 12:9, 10].

9: who saved us, and called us with a holy calling, not according to our works, but according to his own purpose and grace, which was given us in Christ Jesus before times eternal, 10: but hath now been manifested by the appearing of our Saviour Christ Jesus, who abolished death, and brought life and immortality to light through the gospel,

Theodore of Mopsuestia (c. 350–428) gives well the connecting thought which carries Paul here 'from his appeal for boldness into another of his exulting Gospel anthems. "Take," he says in effect, "take great pains, bear long pains – for a gift so great, so age-long"' (cited by Humphreys).

Who saved us, and called us with a holy calling: Since our salvation is wholly of God, which he accomplished without our aid, his almighty power is sufficient to sustain us throughout every crisis of life [4:18]. And as we are called with a holy calling, we must draw on that power to live as befits the free-born citizens of heaven [*1 Cor.* 1: 2; *Phil.* 2:12, 13; 3:20].

Not according to our works, but according to his own purpose and grace: As in Titus 3:5ff, Paul inserts a characteristic disclaimer of man's merit, and emphasizes that our salvation is due solely to God's own sovereign purpose and grace. If we had merited the gospel, 'it had been hard to suffer for it; but our salvation by it is of free grace, and not according to our works, and therefore we must not think much to suffer for it' (Matthew Henry).

Which was given us in Christ Jesus before times eternal: 'Before we existed, it was given to us, the Mediator even then receiving it' (Bengel). Thus our temporal trials, however severe they may be, are put into their proper perspective by the certainty of God's electing grace in Christ Jesus [cf. *Eph.* 1:4].

But hath now been manifested by the appearing of our Saviour Christ Jesus: Although the term 'appearing' is elsewhere used of Christ's return in glory, it here refers to the glorious dawning of God's eternal purpose of grace, which was embodied and made effective through the coming in the flesh of our Saviour.

Who abolished death, and brought life and immortality to light through the gospel: Through his redemptive travail Christ has broken the power of death [Heb. 2:14], and brought 'life' and 'immortality' to light. The believer's present experience of new 'life' in Christ will be consummated in the 'immortality' or incorruptibility of the resurrection body [1 Cor. 15:53–57-, Phil. 3:21]. It is by means of the gospel that this revelation is made effective, 'for it is the power of God unto salvation' [Rom 1:16].

11: whereunto I was appointed a preacher, and an apostle, and a teacher.

The mention of the word 'gospel' leads Paul to state his own relation to it. It is for this gospel that he was appointed a herald, and an apostle, and a teacher (see note on *1 Tim.* 2:7). So conscious was he of the great honour thus bestowed upon him that he could feel no shame in suffering for the gospel [verse 12].

12: For which cause I suffer also these things: yet I am not ashamed; for I know him whom I have believed, and I am persuaded that he is able to guard that which I have committed unto him against that day.

The phrase 'also these things' marks the climax in Paul's long career of suffering, since he was now facing the prospect of being executed as a criminal. Yet he is not ashamed to be found in such straits, 'for I know him whom I have believed', i.e. the Saviour who triumphed over death and brought to light 'life and immortality' [verse 10]. Hence Paul is convinced that Christ is able to guard that which he has deposited with Him until that day [4:8]. In other words, he is assured of Christ's ability to save and keep him to the very end. The alternative view takes 'the deposit' to be the gospel entrusted to Paul [cf. RSV, NEB], on the ground that it harmonizes with Paul's charge to Timothy in verse 14. Although this neatly deals with a difficulty, the intensely personal nature of Paul's affirmation of faith may be said to favour the traditional interpretation adopted above.

13: Hold the pattern of sound words which thou hast heard from me, in faith and love which is in Christ Jesus.

In resuming his advice to Timothy [verses 6–8], Paul next urges him to remain true to the 'pattern' or 'model' (rather in the sense of *standard*. Arndt-Gingrich) set by his own teaching. In contrast to the diseased words peddled by false teachers, Timothy's ministry must be firmly based upon the 'healthy' words of the apostle's doctrine (see comment on *1 Tim.* 1:10). But this must be done in that spirit of faith and love, which is the fruit of living in union with Christ Jesus. For without the enlivening presence of faith and love even the purest teaching is bound to degenerate into a dead orthodoxy.

14: That good thing which was committed unto thee guard through the Holy Spirit which dwelleth in us.

'That good deposit' (ASV margin) is the gospel message committed to Timothy, which he is to guard by the power of the Holy Spirit. This means he must rely upon the help of the Holy Spirit, who indwells all believers, and more particularly assisteth the ministers of the gospel. We can neither keep our minds sound in the faith, as to the doctrine of it, nor our souls steady in the exercises of faith or love, without the assistance of the Holy Spirit' (Poole).

15: This thou knowest, that all that are in Asia turned away from me; of whom are Phygelus and Hermogenes.

As an incentive to fidelity, Paul reminds Timothy of some notable examples of disloyalty and loyalty [verses 15–18]. Clearly 'turned away from *me*' cannot refer to apostasy, but presumably points to the moment of the apostle's re-arrest when he was deserted by the Christians of Asia, who seem to have been influenced by Phygelus and Hermogenes. 'These two are named because they were the most conspicuous in their unfaithfulness to the apostle' (Huther).

16: The Lord grant mercy unto the house of Onesiphorus: for he oft refreshed me, and was not ashamed of my chain; 17: but, when he was in Rome, he sought me diligently, and found me 18: (the Lord grant unto him to find mercy of the Lord in that day); and in how many things he ministered at Ephesus, thou knowest very well.

In contrast to the desertion of the majority, Onesiphorus (which means 'profit-bringer') had lived up to his name by ministering to Paul's needs in prison. He was not ashamed to be associated with a chained apostle, and diligently searched the prisons of Rome until he found him. As the grateful recipient of this mercy, Paul prays that the Lord may show mercy to the household of Onesiphorus [*Matt.* 5:7], and that the Lord (Christ) will grant him to find mercy from the Lord (God) on judgment day.

Moreover, this man's ministry to the imprisoned apostle was but the climax of his service, for Timothy knows very well how much valuable assistance he had rendered to the Christians at Ephesus. Those who wish to find a scriptural warrant for prayers for the dead assume that Paul's prayer for the household of Onesiphorus [cf. 4:19] must mean that he was now dead. But it is more likely that Onesiphorus was separated from his family by distance rather than by death, and such a prayer would be entirely natural if he were still with Paul in Rome or on his way home.

CHAPTER TWO

Paul bids Timothy to be strong, and to ensure that the apostolic tradition is preserved through a succession of faithful teachers [verses 1–2]. He is to suffer hardship as a good soldier of Christ, because the facts of the gospel and the experience of the apostle prove that the endurance of such suffering is the necessary prelude to reigning with Christ in glory [verses 3–13]. In training others Timothy must warn them against engaging in useless word-battles which greatly hinder those who listen. As to himself, he must strive after God's approval as a workman who correctly interprets the word of truth [verses 14, 15]. He is to avoid the vain disputing that promotes ungodliness, and may even overthrow the faith of some, and must remember that the foundation of God stands secure, for the Lord knows those who are his [verses 16–19]. As a purified vessel is made fit for honourable use, so Timothy should see that his profession is matched by his practice. He must shun foolish controversies, and as the Lord's servant must show gentleness when dealing with his opponents in the hope of leading them to a change of heart and freeing them from the devil's clutches [verses 20–26].

1: Thou therefore, my child, be strengthened in the grace that is in Christ Jesus.

This emphatic appeal is based on Timothy's filial relation to Paul. As a son bears the likeness of his father, so Timothy is to exhibit his spiritual kinship with the apostle by his continued fidelity to the gospel. He cannot do this in his own strength, but only as he is inwardly strengthened by means of the grace that is in Christ Jesus [*Eph.* 6:10]. 'Weak grace may evidence pardon of sin; but it is strong grace that can overcome the temptations of Satan, *1 John* 2:12, 14, and bear up the heart in strong consolation. The blessing upon man in the first creation was, "Increase and multiply"; in the second, "Grow in grace, be strong", &c.' (Trapp).

2: And the things which thou hast heard from me among many witnesses, the same commit thou to faithful men, who shall be able to teach others also.

Those same gospel truths which Timothy had heard Paul proclaim among many witnesses over the years, he must now entrust to faithful men who will be competent to teach others also. The apostle does not speak of secret doctrines privately imparted to Timothy, but clearly refers to the truths which he preached throughout his public ministry. 'This is the true apostolic succession of the ministry: not an uninterrupted line of hands laid on which extends back to the apostles themselves so that all ordinations which are not in that line are null and void; but a succession of true apostolic doctrine, the deposit of what we still hear from Paul in his writings, this held by us in faithful hearts with competency to teach others these same things. The apostle did not evidently expect the future teachers of the church to produce new or different teaching. The gospel is changeless in all ages' (Lenski).

3: Suffer hardship with me, as a good soldier of Christ Jesus. 4: No soldier on service entangleth himself in the affairs of this life; that he may please him who enrolled him as a soldier.

Endure hardship with us (NIV): Since the ministerial calling places Timothy in the front line of the battle, he must be willing to endure hardship along with his comrades, as a good soldier of Christ Jesus. As Calvin notes, this warfare does not consist in inflicting evil upon others, and so the stress lies not on the offensive capacities of the soldier, but on his iron discipline in facing the onslaught of the enemy. Such discipline is the result of his total commitment, for no soldier on active service allows himself to become entangled in the affairs of civilian life, because his one aim is to satisfy the officer who enlisted him. The issue here is not that of pay (as in *1 Cor*. 9:7), 'but of a radical turning aside from all the cheerful or sad demands of life and a turning to full readiness in relation to Christ' (C. Maurer, *TDNT*, vol. 6, p. 641).

5: And if also a man contend in the games, he is not crowned, except he have contended lawfully.

Paul's second image is drawn from the Greek games, and his point is that a professional athlete is not rewarded with 'the victor's crown unless he competes according to the rules' (NIV). This would include both the preliminary training and the regulations governing the race itself. 'As applied to the Christian minister the training is that of *1 Tim.* 4:7, the regulations those of the law of Christ, especially those laid down here in verses 10–12' (Lock).

6: The husbandman that laboureth must be the first to partake of the fruits.

The truth set forth in this third illustration is that the farmer's hard work entitles him to the first share of the crop. Hence ministers who toil long and hard in God's service will be the first to rejoice in seeing the fruits of their labours safely harvested. 'It is the man who has bathed himself in sweat to secure a harvest who has the premier title to its produce. Labour expended on an object renders it our own' (Simpson). Thus, when taken together, these three metaphors show that the ministry of the gospel demands: 1. the wholehearted devotion of the soldier; 2. the self-discipline of the athlete; 3. the wearisome toil of the farmer.

7: Consider what I say; for the Lord shall give thee understanding in all things.

If Timothy will reflect on the meaning of what Paul has just said, he will see that he must suffer his share of hardship before he can enjoy the reward which is implied in each of the preceding figures (the victory after battle; the prize after the race; the harvest after much labour). Let Timothy duly ponder the apostle's teaching, and the Lord will give him the enlightenment he needs. So we cannot expect to grasp the meaning of Scripture unless we give our minds to it, but true spiritual understanding is always the Lord's gift to us.

8: Remember Jesus Christ, risen from the dead, of the seed of David, according to my gospel:

If it be asked why Paul here introduces this pregnant statement of the central facts of the gospel entrusted to him, the answer cannot lie in the need to remind Timothy of the truth of the doctrine, but rather in its application to the hardships he must endure as the preacher of a faith outlawed by men. Hence it should be seen as a call to follow the path marked out by the Saviour who suffered the agonies of the cross before he was crowned with glory and honour. 'Remember it for thine encouragement; that Christ, for a reward of his sufferings, was both raised and exalted, *Phil.* 2:9' (Trapp). Timothy will be strengthened for the conflict as he keeps in mind the raised and reigning heir of David's line, Jesus Christ, with whom we shall also live and reign in glory [verses 11, 12].

9: wherein I suffer hardship unto bonds, as a malefactor; but the word of God is not bound.

It is for this gospel that Paul is suffering 'even to the point of being chained like a criminal' (NIV). The strength of his language indicates how deeply he felt the shame and degradation of his imprisonment, but he rejoices in the fact that the word of God is not chained! 'Persecuting powers may silence ministers and restrain them, but they cannot hinder the operation of the Word of God upon men's hearts and consciences; that cannot be bound by any human force' (Matthew Henry).

10: Therefore I endure all things for the elect's sake, that they also may obtain the salvation which is in Christ Jesus with eternal glory.

Because Paul knows that his sufferings promote the advance of the gospel, he willingly endures all things for the sake of 'the elect', i.e. those whom God has predestined and chosen for salvation [*Rom.* 8:33; *Col.* 3:12; *Titus* 1:1]. His sufferings thus have an evangelistic purpose: it is that the elect 'also' (they as well as he) may obtain the salvation which is 'in Christ Jesus'. He here views his apostolic vocation in the light of God's electing grace, because his sufferings could never help to save those who were not so chosen [cf. *Col.* 1:24: 'for his body's sake, which is the church'].

On the other hand, the investment of the elect 'with eternal glory' requires the use of the means ordained by God to achieve that end [cf. *2 Thess.* 2:13, 14]. As an instrument of God's saving purpose, the apostle Paul knew that his testimony in preaching, writing, and suffering 'was for all countries and for all time; and the elect of this present age are in many ways reaping the benefit of his self-denying and devoted labours' (Fairbairn).

11: Faithful is the saying: For if we died with him, we shall also live with him: 12: if we endure, we shall also reign with him: if we shall deny him, he also will deny us: 13: if we are faithless, he abideth faithful; for he cannot deny himself.

The last of the five faithful sayings in the Pastorals is another fragment of an early Christian hymn, which some scholars have seen as a 'Hymn to Martyrdom', but the language used suggests that it rather belongs to a baptismal setting.

For if we died with him, we shall also live with him: These words clearly recall *Rom.* 6:8, and point to baptism as the decisive past-event which marked the end of the old life and the beginning of the new [*Rom.* 6:3, 4]. If we died with Christ in his once-for-all death to sin [*Rom.* 6: 10], then we shall also certainly live with him [*Rom.* 6:4–6].

If we endure, we shall also reign with him: Between our past death and future hope, there lies our present responsibility, and this accounts for the omission of the preposition 'with him' from the verb 'endure' [cf. *Rom.* 8:17]. If we continue to endure to the end of our earthly course, then we shall also reign with him in glory. Thus reigning *with* Christ is the reward promised to those who now suffer *for* him.

If we shall deny him, he also will deny us: But another dreadful possibility has to be faced. If we shall perchance disown Christ, then he too will disown us [*Matt.* 10:33]. In contrast to the comfort of the first two lines, we have here a warning against the dire consequences of apostasy. It is by heeding such warnings that the elect are brought safely to heaven [*Heb.* 6:9].

If we are faithless, he abideth faithful; for he cannot deny himself: But as not every act of unfaithfulness amounts to outright apostasy, the fourth line brings a final word of comfort to believers who are troubled by their frequent failure to live up to their profession. 'What if we do not always remain steadfast? Does our every "denial" cause Christ to deny us for ever? No, if we are faithless, he abides faithful, for he cannot deny himself . . . The Christ with whom we have died remains faithful to us, not in the final analysis because of our faithfulness, but because he cannot deny himself' (George W. Knight, *The Faithful Sayings in the Pastoral Letters*, p.136) [cf. *Rom.* 3:3].

14: Of these things put them in remembrance, charging them in the sight

of the Lord, that they strive not about words, to no profit, to the subverting of them that hear.

This verse sets forth Timothy's duty as a trainer of other teachers, the 'faithful men' mentioned in verse 2. The charge which Paul had laid on him must also be passed on to them. For they need to be reminded that the whole object of their ministry is to benefit their hearers, and not to upset their faith! Hence Timothy must warn them before God not to engage in useless word-battles, as this only 'subverts' (literally: turns upside down) those they should be building up.

15: Give diligence to present thyself approved unto God, a workman that needeth not to be ashamed, handling aright the word of truth.

Turning back to Timothy, Paul urges him to make every effort to present himself to God as one approved. He is to be like a workman who has no need to be ashamed of the quality of his work. And for Timothy this entails 'handling aright the word of truth'. According to Arndt Gingrich, the idea conveyed by the use of the word in *Prov.* 3:6 and 11:5 is that of cutting a straight road through a forest or difficult country so that the traveller may go directly to his destination. This suggests that it here means: '*guide the word of truth along a straight path* (like a road that goes straight to its goal), without being turned aside by wordy debates or impious talk'.

16: But shun profane babblings: for they will proceed further in ungodliness, 17: and their word will eat as doth a gangrene: of whom is Hymenaeus and Philetus; 18: men who concerning the truth have erred, saying that the resurrection is past already, and overthrow the faith of some.

Timothy must avoid the godless chatter of the false teachers whose only 'progress' is towards even more ungodliness! For the effect of their teaching upon the church is like the spreading of a gangrenous growth which eats into the flesh. Of these errorists, Paul specially mentions Hymenaeus [*1 Tim.* 1:20] and Philetus, who had gone astray from the truth by teaching that the resurrection had already taken place, and this was upsetting the faith of some. Like the sceptics in Corinth, they rejected the future resurrection of the body, presumably on the ground that they had already experienced the resurrection of the soul in baptism

[*Rom.* 6:4; *Col.* 2:12]. 'It was altogether a spiritual thing in their account, a quickening merely of the soul's activities to newness of life; and thus, by their excess in spiritualising, they loosened the very foundations of the Christian system; for the position they assumed involved by necessary inference the denial of Christ's resurrection, and the saving efficacy of His death [*1 Cor.* 15:12–19]' (Fairbairn).

19: Howbeit the firm foundation of God standeth, having this seal, The Lord knoweth them that are his: and, Let every one that nameth the name of the Lord depart from unrighteousness.

But despite the false teachers and their deluded followers, Paul assures Timothy that God's firm foundation still stands secure – i.e. the true church remains unmoved by such errors [cf. *1 Tim.* 3:15] – because its inviolability is guaranteed by the divine seal. This seal bears two inscriptions which recall the abortive rebellion of Korah, Dathan, and Abiram against Moses, the true servant of the Lord. After expressing confidence in the Lord's vindication of his leadership, Moses exhorts the people to depart from the tents of these wicked men [*Num.* 16:5, 26]. As applied to the present crisis, the first inscription underlines the eternal security of the church, while the second stresses the purity which is required to provide public proof of its secret election. These are but two sides of the same coin, for God's election is always to holiness [*Eph.* 1:4]. Hence the Lord's true servants will show that they are really known of God by forsaking wickedness which in this context refers to the false teaching that is both dishonouring to God and ruinous to men.

20: Now in a great house there are not only vessels of gold and of silver, but also of wood and of earth; and some unto honour, and some unto dishonour. 21: If a man therefore purge himself from these, he shall be a vessel unto honour, sanctified, meet for the master's use, prepared unto every good work.

Paul explains the mixed state of the church in the gospel age by another metaphor. In a great house there are many vessels with functions which vary according to their worth. Those of gold and silver are set aside for honourable use, but those of wood and earthenware are used for menial purposes and are discarded after having served their purpose. So the presence of false teachers in the church is only a temporary phenomenon, which serves to warn the faithful of the perils of apostasy. Paul therefore advises Timothy to cleanse himself 'from these', i.e. he is to separate himself from men like Hymenaeus and Philetus [verse 17]. In this way he will prove himself to be a vessel 'unto honour', for in having been thus set apart for holy service, he is now useful to Christ his Master, and is permanently prepared for every good work.

22: But flee youthful lusts, and follow after righteousness, faith, love, peace, with them that call on the Lord out of a pure heart.

As Timothy was still a young man [see *1 Tim.* 4:12], Paul bids him flee from all youthful desires (e.g. impatience, conceit, dogmatism, contentiousness, as well as sexual lust) which are inconsistent with the positive virtues he must pursue, namely, righteousness, faith, love, and peace. For in so doing he will keep company with those who 'call on the Lord out of a pure heart', which clearly implies that the pastor must not be less holy than his flock! The exhortation thus shows that character is more important than charisma. As Fairbairn well says, 'A sound moral condition is above all things essential to fitness for effective ministerial service in the divine kingdom. Other things may more or less be helpful, but this is indispensable.'

23: But foolish and ignorant questionings refuse, knowing that they gender strifes.

Paul again warns Timothy not to have anything to do with the foolish and uninstructed speculations of the false teachers [cf. *1 Tim.* 1:4; 4:7]. Parry points out that the second adjective is a very shrewd hit, for it denies the exact quality on which such teachers would pride themselves. 'These speculations show a half-educated mind, untrained to see the real points at issue and the true importance of things.' If Timothy appeared to endorse these futile questionings, believers would be distracted from the verities of the faith and become engaged in strifes which would divide and destroy the church.

24: And the Lord's servant must not strive, but be gentle towards all, apt to teach, forbearing, 25: in meekness correcting them that oppose themselves; if peradventure God may give them repentance unto the

knowledge of the truth, 26: and they may recover themselves out of the snare of the devil, having been taken captive by him unto his will.

Timothy is here further advised that the Lord's servant, like his supreme Exemplar [*Matt.* 12:19], must not strive. He must not delight in controversy, but is to be kind to all, showing skill in teaching, and bearing evil without resentment' (Arndt-Gingrich). '*Gentle* unto all men, so he will be *apt to teach*; *forbearing* towards opponents, so he will be able to *correct*' (Bengel). For there is always the possibility that God may give them the grace of the possibility that God may give repentance, thus enabling them to turn from their errors and leading them into the full knowledge of the truth, which they now falsely claimed to possess. Only such a divinely given change of heart can arouse them from the stupefaction of their sinful state, so that they can escape from the snare of the devil, in which they were held captive to do his will. This means that sinners are so drugged by the devil's potions that they mistake bondage for freedom, and remain his willing slaves until they are brought to their senses by the power of God's grace.

CHAPTER THREE

Paul predicts that the last days will be marked by unparalleled moral decadence when a form of godliness will be professed but its power denied. Those who already exhibit such characteristics must be avoided by Timothy, for their deception of weak-minded women and their opposition to the truth shows them to be men of counterfeit faith, whose folly will become evident to all [verses 1–9]. After a reminder of his own teaching and the sufferings he endured for the gospel, Paul urges Timothy to show the same faithfulness in the face of persecution [verses 10–12]. As deceivers wax worse, Timothy is to abide in the truths he had learned, being assured that the sacred writings which he had known from childhood were able to make him wise unto salvation through faith in Christ. All Scripture is inspired by God, and is therefore able to equip the man of God for all his work [verses 13–17].

1: But know this, that in the last days grievous times shall come.

Since such opposition to the truth is characteristic of this present evil age, Timothy must neither be surprised nor dismayed by it, but is to recognize that the church will face terrible times 'in the last days' before

Christ's return [*2 Pet.* 3: 3; *Jude* 18]. For as the end approaches there will be a fearful increase in wickedness, when evil men will abound in the same vices which have already appeared in those whom Timothy is now to avoid [verses 2:5, 13; 4:3, 4]. 'The revelations Paul has received are God's advance warnings to fortify his ministers and their churches. Paul, approaching his end, is passing these warnings on' (Lenski).

2: For men shall be lovers of self, lovers of money, boastful, haughty, railers, disobedient to parents, unthankful, unholy, 3: without natural affection, implacable, slanderers, without self-control, fierce, no lovers of good, 4: traitors, headstrong, puffed up, lovers of pleasure rather than lovers of God;

'Lovers of self, lovers of money' provides the key to this list of vices, for moral corruption is the inevitable consequence of the misdirected love which seeks self-gratification through the things that money can buy [*1 Tim.* 6:10], and thus makes men 'lovers of pleasure rather than lovers of God'. This self-centredness naturally leads to the self-assertiveness that is boastful, proud, abusive' (NIV). The megalomania which enthrones self is also devoid of any sense of natural decency, for it is unfilial, unthankful, unholy, unloving, and unforgiving! In the remaining seven terms the aggressive character of such egoism comes strongly to the fore. It is given to false accusation, and will go to any lengths to satisfy its lusts. Its brutality is not tempered by any love of the good, while its treacherous and reckless conduct is inspired by an overweening conceit.

5: holding a form of godliness, but having denied the power thereof: from these also turn away.

In his final charge Paul clearly has the Ephesian Judaists in mind. He accuses them of hypocrisy in holding to the outward semblance of godliness, when their actions prove that they are strangers to the regenerating power of the gospel, which they have in effect totally denied. And from these false teachers Timothy is to turn away.

6: For of these are they that creep into houses, and take captive silly women laden with sins, led away by divers lusts, 7: ever learning, and never able to come to the knowledge of the truth.

Men of this kind propagate their errors by worming their way into houses and misleading weak-minded women, burdened with sins and led on by various desires, who are always learning but never able to reach a knowledge of the truth [see comment on *1 Tim.* 2:4]. As Satan's strategy was first to deceive Eve, so heretical teachers have often chosen to spread their falsehoods by the same method. Impressionable women, oppressed by feelings of guilt, are eager to try any quack remedy which does not require them to abandon their sins. Hence their morbid curiosity in religious novelties prevents them from coming to a realization of the truth.

8: And even as Jannes and Jambres withstood Moses, so do these also withstand the truth; men corrupted in mind, reprobate concerning the faith.

Just as Jannes and Jambres opposed God's spokesman before Pharaoh, so do these men oppose the truth of the gospel. This is a shrewd shaft against the sectaries. Since they are so fond of Jewish myths and genealogies, let them recall how the Egyptian magicians who opposed Moses were confounded [*Exod.* 7:11; 9:11]. Although their names are not given in the Old Testament record, they were preserved by Jewish tradition, with which Paul was familiar through his rabbinical training under Gamaliel [*Acts* 22:3].

The apostle here brands these errorists as men whose minds have been hopelessly corrupted, and who are therefore utterly rejected so far as the faith is concerned. As the organ by which the truth is received is corrupt, they are disqualified, for they cannot even accept the doctrines of the gospel let alone teach them to others.

9: But they shall proceed no further: for their folly shall be evident unto all men, as theirs also came to be.

But Timothy need not fear that these men will be any more successful than Jannes and Jambres were in opposing the truth. For despite the threat posed by the heretics, their progress is more apparent than real, and the hollowness of their pretensions will soon be revealed. 'Truth must prevail in the end, and imposture cannot permanently deceive' (Bernard).

10: But thou didst follow my teaching, conduct, purpose, faith, longsuffering, love, patience, 11: persecutions, sufferings; what things befell me at Antioch, at Iconium, at Lystra; what persecutions I endured: and out of them all the Lord delivered me.

But in contrast to the teachers of error, Timothy is fully qualified to teach the true faith, having closely followed the steps of his master and observed the example thus set both in doctrine and life. Paul describes the content of this course of instruction in a list of nine items. 'My teaching' is naturally placed first and covers what the apostle taught and the way he taught it, while 'conduct' shows that his manner of life was perfectly consistent with the truth he confessed. Paul was sustained in his 'purpose', his steadfast resolve to devote his life to the furtherance of the gospel, by his own 'faith' in God's word. His 'longsuffering' enabled him to persevere in his labours until the fruit appeared, and this was made possible by his outgoing 'love' for the lost. 'Patience, persecutions, sufferings' refer to what Paul willingly suffered for the sake of the gospel, and he instances what befell him at Pisidian Antioch, Iconium, and Lystra because these events must have made a profound impression upon the young Timothy [cf. *Acts* 16:1f with 13:50; 14:2, 5, 19].

As Paul looks back at the persecutions he endured, he adds 'yet out of them all the Lord rescued me' in order to teach Timothy to rely upon the same help in similar straits. 'The Lord ever rescues his people, frequently *from* death, sometimes *by means of* death. Either way, nothing ever separates them from his love' [*Rom.* 8:38, 39] (Hendriksen).

12: Yea, and all that would live godly in Christ Jesus shall suffer persecution.

Moreover, Paul's experience was not exceptional, for persecution is the lot of all who intend to live a godly life in union with Christ Jesus [cf. *Acts* 14:22]. The world's hostility to the gospel will not always be of the same intensity, but in so far as it 'retains its native character, those who are bent on leading in it lives of piety shall have to meet persecution' (Fairbairn) [*John* 16:33; *1 John* 3: 13]

13: But evil men and imposters shall wax worse and worse, deceiving and being deceived.

But though untouched by such distress, evil men and imposters of the kind already mentioned [verses 2–9] will progress from bad to worse, deceiving and being deceived. As teachers their success will be limited [verse 9], but they will increase in wickedness through becoming the dupes of their self-chosen errors. For those who set out to deceive others are themselves brought under the enslaving power of the same delusion.

14: But abide thou in the things which thou hast learned and hast been assured of, knowing of whom thou hast learned them;

Paul again makes an emphatic contrast between Timothy's sure grounding in the truth and the deceptive delusions of the false teachers [cf. verse 10]: 'But as for you, continue in what you have learned, and have become convinced of, because you know those from whom you learned it' (NIV). Timothy was certain of the truth of what he had learned, because the content of that teaching was closely reflected in the character of his teachers. As Paul's son in the faith, Timothy obviously owed most to the apostle himself, but the next verse shows that the primary reference is to the formative influence exercised upon Timothy by his mother and grandmother [1:5].

15: and that from a babe thou hast known the sacred writings which are able to make thee wise unto salvation through faith which is in Christ Jesus.

It is due to the fidelity of these teachers that Timothy's knowledge of the Old Testament Scriptures stretches back to his earliest years. Paul affirms that the 'sacred' writings, in contrast to all those of purely human origin, are uniquely able to give the wisdom that leads to salvation. As a guide to salvation, the Old Testament is not a revelation that is complete in itself, for it points forward to Christ as the fulfiller of all its promises. Hence Paul's qualifying phrase is directed against the 'vain jangling' to which the Scriptures were being subjected by those who had rejected the key to their correct interpretation [*Luke* 24:44ff.]. The endless genealogies and Jewish myths 'on which these letters pour contempt, were the stock-in-trade of men versed in the allegorical method, and who practised a puerile and speculative treatment of inspired Scripture. So the occasion has come to formulate the doctrine of inspiration implicit throughout St. Paul's teaching [see specially *Rom.* 15:4 and *1 Cor.* 10:11]. That doctrine exhibits in the words "through faith that is in Christ Jesus" its specially Pauline stamp and character' (Findlay).

16: Every scripture inspired of God is also profitable for instruction, for teaching, for reproof, for correction which is in righteousness:

This translation is open to serious objection in that it suggests there may be other scriptures which are not inspired by God. Since the sentence lacks a main verb, 'is' has to be supplied by the translators, but it is more natural to insert this immediately after the subject, 'scripture'. The same construction is found in *1 Tim.* 4:4, which, Simpson drily notes, no one translates: 'every good creature of God is also not one of them to be rejected'! Moreover, the absence of the article does not invariably require the rendering 'every', for it would be equally foolish to translate *Acts* 2:36 as 'every house of Israel' instead of 'all (the) house of Israel' [cf. *Eph.* 2:21; 3:15].

Paul's thought here is accurately conveyed by the AV, but the NIV gives the literal meaning of his words: All Scripture is God-breathed. As Warfield was at pains to point out, the Greek term does not mean that God inspired ('breathed into') the Scripture or its human authors, but that Scripture is the product of divine spiration ('breathed out by God'). 'What it affirms is that the Scriptures owe their origin to an activity of God the Holy Ghost and are in the highest and truest sense His creation. It is on this foundation of Divine origin that all the high attributes of Scripture are built' (*The Inspiration and Authority of the Bible*, p. 296).

And profitable for teaching, for reproof, for correction, and for training in righteousness (RSV): It is precisely because all Scripture is God-breathed that it is so universally profitable. The Word of God provides a complete guide to doctrine and practice. As to doctrine, it is profitable for teaching the truth and for refuting all falsehood. As to practice, it is profitable for restoring the fallen and for training in all righteous living.

17: that the man of God may be complete, furnished completely unto every good work.

God's purpose in thus providing the Scripture is that the man of God may be completely equipped for every good work. Although in this context 'the man of God' appears to refer to the Christian leader, the title may also be fitly applied to every believer [see comment on *1 Tim.* 6:11]. The Scripture 'is so full a direction, that Christians need not go down to the Philistines to whet their tools, nor be beholden to unwritten traditions, or to the writings of pagan philosophers, for directions what to do, how to worship God, or manage any part of their conversation either as to their general calling, or as to their particular relations' (Poole).

CHAPTER FOUR

In his final charge to Timothy, Paul presses him to preach the Word and to fulfil his ministry, even though some may prefer the myths of men to the truth of God [verses 1–5]. As for Paul, the contest is over, and he now awaits the crown which the Lord will also give to all who have set their hearts on his appearing [verses 6–8]. Timothy is to come as soon as he can, bringing Mark with him, and also Paul's cloak, books, and parchments [verses 9–13]. He is also to be on his guard against Alexander the coppersmith who did Paul much harm [verses 14, 15]. All deserted Paul at his first defence, but the Lord enabled him to proclaim the message and delivered him from the lion's mouth [verses 16, 17]. And he is confident that the Lord will deliver him from every evil work and bring him safely to his heavenly kingdom [verse 18]. After various greetings, and a last word of entreaty, the letter ends with a prayer and the benediction [verses 19–22].

1: I charge thee in the sight of God, and of Christ Jesus, who shall judge the living and the dead, and by his appearing and his kingdom: 2: preach the word; be urgent in season, out of season; reprove, rebuke, exhort, with all longsuffering and teaching.

In this paragraph the Epistle reaches its climax as Paul solemnly adjures Timothy to remain faithful to his charge now that the time of his own departure is at hand [verses 1–8]. Since Timothy must one day give an account of his stewardship, Paul lays this mandate upon him in the presence of God and of Christ Jesus, who shall judge the living and the dead [*Acts* 10:42; 17:31; *2 Cor.* 5:10]. By immediately adding, 'and by his appearing and his kingdom', Paul shows that he expected the day of universal judgment to coincide with Christ's glorious appearing and the consummation of his kingdom. It is clear from verse 18 that the goal which Paul has in view is the heavenly kingdom, and not an earthly millennium! The appearing 'is for all men alike, the kingdom is for the blessed alone' (Lenski). The five imperatives which follow summon Timothy to the urgent fulfilment of his duty.

Preach the word: Timothy's primary task is to preach the gospel, and this is the first duty of every minister [*1 Cor.* 9:16, 17]. The Word is the objective deposit of truth which is entrusted to the man of God [1:14]. He is not to give the people stones instead of bread, by publishing his own opinions or delivering lectures in philosophy – not even 'Christian' philosophy! His task as a herald of God's grace means that he must preach the Word, the whole Word, and nothing but the Word [*Acts* 20:27]. The remaining imperatives show how this great work is to be done.

Be urgent in season, out of season: 'that is, at all times; for what may seem to the careless or lukewarm unseasonable occasions for making mention of the truth, will often by the zealous and faithful pastor be found opportunities of usefulness' (Fairbairn).

Reprove, rebuke, exhort, with all longsuffering and teaching: As there can be no healing without hurting, the preacher must make it his aim to convict the conscience and rebuke the sin of his hearers before encouraging them with the comforts of the gospel [*Jer.* 8:11]. In each aspect of this ministry, he must show himself to be a sound teacher of the Word, by bringing the truth to bear upon the particular circumstances of his people. And he is also to do it 'with all longsuffering', neither losing patience with them nor despairing of their salvation.

3: For the time will come when they will not endure the sound doctrine; but, having itching ears, will heap to themselves teachers after their own lusts; 4: and will turn away their ears from the truth, and turn aside unto fables.

Paul urges Timothy to be diligent in proclaiming the truth, because he foresees that the time will come when men will not put up with 'the sound doctrine' [see comment on *1 Tim.* 1:10]. But they will be driven by their own desires to accumulate for themselves teachers who will tickle their 'itching ears', i.e. ears 'which were always pricking with an uneasy desire for what would gratify the taste of a carnal, self-willed heart' (Fairbairn). This explains why the truth so seldom gets a hearing. Such people refuse to listen to it, and prefer to turn aside to empty myths. They delight to hear 'fables, any idle stories, or impertinent discourses, provided they touch not their lusts' (Poole).

5: But be thou sober in all things, suffer hardship, do the work of an evangelist, fulfil thy ministry.

In contrast to those who are intoxicated by error, Timothy must retain that clarity of mind and sound judgment which will enable him to persevere in his God-given calling without faltering. This will mean accepting the hardship which is involved in doing the work of an evangelist, i.e. preaching the gospel. With Paul's example before him [verses 6–8], he must not allow the prospect of suffering to deter him from fulfilling his ministry. 'Timothy is exhorted to make actual the potentialities of his ministry with the utmost wholeheartedness' (Simpson).

6: For I am already being offered, and the time of my departure is come.

In drawing attention to the beauty of Paul's 'swan-song' [verses 6–8], Findlay says that no passage in his Epistles is more finely touched with the apostle's genius. 'These verses have an ideal fitness as the apostle's final record and pronouncement upon his own career . . . Nor has Christian faith since found any higher expression of its sense of victory in the presence of death'. 'As for me' (NEB) does more justice to Paul's emphatic 'for I', since the phrase tacitly reminds Timothy of the urgent need to redouble his efforts now that Paul has reached the end of his ministry. What was contemplated as a possibility in *Phil.* 2:17 is now a certainty, and Paul's life is already being poured out like a drink offering upon God's altar [cf. *Num.* 15:1–10].

It would appear from *Rom.* 15:16 that Paul regarded his mission to the Gentiles in terms of an offering to God, and now that sacrificial service will be completed by his approaching death. The metaphorical use of such cultic imagery must not be pressed; it clearly does not mean that Paul is offering some kind of secondary atonement. The word 'departure' was used of loosing a ship from its moorings, or of a soldier striking his tent, but probably neither image is in view here as the word was a common euphemism for death. What this departure meant for Paul is vividly conveyed in *Phil.* 1:23, where he speaks of his 'desire to depart and be with Christ; for it is very far better'.

7: I have fought the good fight, I have finished the course, I have kept the faith:

The imminence of Paul's departure enables him to look back on the long contest in which he has been engaged from the vantage point of victory. 'I have fought the good fight' recalls *1 Tim.* 6:12 (see comment there), and refers to his success in contending for 'the prize of the high calling of God in Christ Jesus' [*Phil* 3:14]. This is placed first because Paul is a Christian before he is an apostle [verse 8]. 'I have finished the course' continues the athletic metaphor, though the figure is changed from the wrestling-match to the race [cf. *1 Cor.* 9:26]. Paul's life-long ambition is at last fulfilled now that he has completed his course of Christian service [*Acts* 20:24}. With the final member of this triad Paul drops the metaphor and states the literal fact: 'I have kept the faith'. He has guarded and transmitted intact the sacred deposit of the gospel [1:14]. 'Through all trial, and mockery, and persecution, and suffering, he had held fast by the saving truths which he received by special revelation from above, and which as a chosen vessel he was sent forth to declare to a perishing world' [*Gal.* 1:12; *Acts* 9:15] (Fairbairn).

8: henceforth there is laid up for me the crown of righteousness, which the Lord, the righteous judge, shall give to me at that day; and not to me only, but also to all them that have loved his appearing.

Having now finished his course, Paul only has to await the due reward of his labours, which the Lord the righteous judge will give to him 'at that day', i.e. the day of Christ's appearing. The crown is the recompense for a righteous life; 'it is that kind and measure of bliss which the wrestler in righteousness alone is either entitled or prepared to enjoy' (Fairbairn). A comparison of this verse with *1 Cor.* 9:25 would suggest that 'the crown of righteousness' is to be identified with the 'incorruptible' crown of eternal life. But the promised 'reward' nevertheless remains a divine donation, and must be received as a gift, because all Paul's work is the fruit of God's grace [*1 Cor*. 15: 10]. Moreover, this gift of eternal life is not for Paul alone, but for all who 'have loved his appearing'. Such a love for Christ's return affords the only adequate motivation for living righteously in this present evil age [*1 John* 3:2, 3]. 'The perfect tense is used because their love will have continued up to the moment of their receiving the crown' (White).

9: Give diligence to come shortly unto me: 10: for Demas forsook me, having loved this present world, and went to Thessalonica; Crescens to Galatia, Titus to Dalmatia.

In these closing sentences Paul outlines his present circumstances without a trace of self-pity, but there is deep pathos in the last picture they give us of the great apostle [verses 9–18]. As he awaits the final crisis in his cold, cheerless dungeon, he longs to see his 'beloved child' once more. Timothy must do his best to come quickly, because Paul is almost alone, following the desertion of Demas to Thessalonica, and the departure of Crescens to Galatia and Titus to Dalmatia (now Croatia). Evidently Crescens and Titus were despatched to do the Lord's work, but Demas deserted Paul because he gave up the love of Christ's appearing for the love of this present world [verse 8].

11: Only Luke is with me. Take Mark, and bring him with thee; for he is useful to me for ministering. 12: But Tychicus I sent to Ephesus.

Luke very likely acted as Paul's secretary in taking down this Epistle. 'The faithful Luke bides still with the age-worn apostle, to whom he could best minister in his painful weakness and suspense. His comradeship must have been the bright spot in the encircling gloom of his close captivity. There is a tremulous note in the *only*' (Simpson). Timothy is also to pick up Mark and bring him to Rome, for Paul had long since changed his opinion of Mark and now finds him useful in the ministry [*Acts* 13:13; 15:38; *Col*. 4:10, *Philem*. 24]. 'I sent' is probably the epistolary aorist, 'I am sending'. If so, it identifies Tychicus as the bearer of the letter and suggests that Paul was sending him to Ephesus to supervise the work there during Timothy's absence.

13: The cloak that I left at Troas with Carpus, bring when thou comest, and the books, especially the parchments.

With winter approaching [verse 21], Paul feels the need for the heavy cloak which he left at Troas with Carpus, and he asks Timothy when he comes to bring this together with his books and precious parchments. Perhaps these writings included parts of the Greek Old Testament, and collections of the Lord's sayings which Paul may have wished to hand on to Luke [*Luke* 1:1–4]. Be that as it may, it is clear that Paul desired to make good use of whatever time was left to him by continuing his reading and study. Paul's request may be aptly compared with that made by William Tyndale from his damp cell to the governor of Vilvorde Castle. He begged for a warmer cap and cloak, a woollen shirt, but 'most of all my Hebrew Bible, Grammar and Vocabulary, that I may spend my time in that pursuit'.

14: Alexander the coppersmith did me much evil: the Lord will render to him according to his works: 15: of whom do thou also beware; for he greatly withstood our words.

Paul here recalls a specific occasion when he suffered a great deal of harm through this man's implacable opposition to the gospel in order to warn Timothy to be on his guard against him. Since we know nothing further about 'Alexander the coppersmith', the nature of his offence remains a matter of conjecture. Perhaps he had been instrumental in securing Paul's re-arrest (Simpson), or he may have been the leading witness for the prosecution at Paul's first hearing in Rome (Lenski). But Paul is content to leave the issue in higher hands, for 'the Lord will render to him according to his works' [*Deut*. 32:35; *Rom*. 12:19]. Although this is a prediction and not an imprecation, the certainty of the Lord's judgment upon such an adversary of the truth caused Paul no distress. 'If God is a moral governor; if sin is a reality; those who know themselves to be on God's side cannot help a feeling of joy in knowing that evil will not always triumph over good' (White).

16: At my first defence no one took my part, but all forsook me: may it not be laid to their account.

Paul sadly records that at the preliminary investigation (*prima actio*), which preceded the trial proper in Roman law (*secunda actio*), no one had the courage to speak up for him in court. All the Christians in

Rome deserted him in his hour of need, but he forgives their failure and prays that it may not be held against them [*Luke* 23:34; *Acts* 7:60]. 'He would have it to be reckoned as a proof of weakness, not of false-heartedness' (Fairbairn).

17: But the Lord stood by me, and strengthened me; that through me the message might be fully proclaimed, and that all the Gentiles might hear: and I was delivered out of the mouth of the lion.

In contrast to the failure of his friends, Paul triumphantly affirms the faithfulness of the Lord, who stood by him and imparted the strength which enabled him to bring his ministry to its completion in the capital of the pagan world. Paul did this by preaching the gospel to the vast throng of Gentiles who had come to hear the trial, which was probably held in one of the large basilicas in Rome.

'We annex a territory by the mere act of planting our country's flag on a small portion of its soil; so in St Paul's thought a single proclamation of the gospel might have a spiritual, almost a prophetical, significance, immeasurably greater than could be imagined by one who heard it' (White). Paul's inspired 'apologia' made such a deep impression upon the court that he was rescued from the lion's mouth. Presumably the expression is an oblique reference to his temporary reprieve from Nero's malice. 'After his first examination Paul could still write to Asia bidding Timothy and Mark come to him, which shows that he looked forward to a considerable interval before the next stage of his trial' (W. M. Ramsay, *St Paul the Traveller and the Roman Citizen*, p. 361).

18: The Lord will deliver me from every evil work, and will save me unto his heavenly kingdom to whom be the glory for ever and ever. Amen.

Paul knows that he has reached the end of his earthly course [verse 7], and does not expect to be acquitted at his next appearance in court. But past deliverances assure him that the Lord will rescue him from every evil work and bring him safely to his heavenly kingdom. The machinations of the Evil one and his human agents can inflict no abiding harm upon one who enjoys Christ's protection. 'Christ's kingdom here on earth is where he rules with his grace and his gospel; Christ's heavenly kingdom is where he rules with heavenly glory'

(Lenski). As Paul joyfully anticipates his transfer to that state of bliss [*Phil.* 1:23], he ascribes all the glory to Christ in a fervent doxology which he seals with an emphatic 'Amen'. 'The very hope produces a doxology: how much more the realization!' (Bengel).

19: Salute Prisca and Aquila, and the house of Onesiphorus.

Paul sends greetings to his staunch friends and fellow workers, Prisca and Aquila, the much travelled Jewish couple [*Acts* 18:2], who are evidently back in Ephesus again [cf. *Rom.* 16:3]. Prisca is usually named first, and this may indicate her great ability. Paul also greets the household of Onesiphorus, because he knew that Onesiphorus was not with his family when this letter was written [see comment on 1:16–18].

20: Erastus remained at Corinth: but Trophimus I left at Miletus sick.

This Erastus is probably the companion of Timothy mentioned in *Acts* 19:22. Trophimus was the innocent cause of the Temple riot in Jerusalem which led to Paul's first arrest [*Acts* 21:29]. It is not without contemporary significance that an apostle with the gift of healing left unhealed an associate who was sick! As Simpson notes, 'Miracles of healing were not at the command of their performers. There may be a reason in the divine counsels for a believer's sickness as well as for his health.'

21: Give diligence to come before winter. Eubulus saluteth thee, and Pudens, and Linus, and Claudia, and all the brethren.

Paul makes a last appeal for Timothy to do his best to come before the winter, and sends the greetings of four Roman Christians who are otherwise unknown to us, unless Linus is the man who was to become bishop of Rome. Probably none of them had sufficient standing in the city to support Paul in court [verse 16]. As for the rest, his heart is large enough to account them 'brethren' still.

22: The Lord be with thy spirit. Grace be with you.

These are the last words of the great apostle. He first prays that the Lord may be with Timothy's spirit, and then embraces all believers in the final benediction, 'Grace be with you all!' (NEB). Paul thus ends his ministry on the same note with which it began [*Acts* 13:43], for what was his 'signature' in every Epistle is also his final prayer for the church [*2 Thess.* 3:17,18].

TITUS

CHAPTER ONE

In greeting Titus as his true son in the faith, Paul also describes the content of the message entrusted to him [verses 1–4]. Titus was left in Crete to set things in order and appoint elders, who must be good men and able teachers of sound doctrine [verses 5–9]. The character given to the Cretans by one of their own poets is exemplified by the deceivers who spread the leaven of legalism for base gain. Titus must rebuke them sharply that they may be sound in the faith, for though their Jewish mentors professed to know God, their evil deeds proved that they were strangers to the truth [verses 10–16].

1: Paul, a servant of God, and an apostle of Jesus Christ, according to the faith of God's elect, and the knowledge of the truth which is according to godliness,

Instead of a brief personal greeting to a trusted associate, we have here a lengthy salutation whose official tone suggests that it was intended by Paul to provide Titus with the necessary authorization for his mission in Crete [verses 1–4]. In calling himself 'a servant of God', Paul indicates his complete submission to the divine will, and in claiming the title 'an apostle of Jesus Christ', he points to the commission he received from Christ, who sent him forth as his messenger to the Gentiles [*Acts* 22:21]. Paul's service and apostleship are in perfect accord with the elect's faith and knowledge of the truth. So if the Cretans are indeed God's elect, their faith and knowledge will be in harmony with the testimony of Christ's own apostle, for that is the only doctrine 'which is according to godliness'. By thus insisting upon the essential connection between faith and godliness, Paul at once strikes the keynote of the Epistle and tacitly condemns the ungodly myths peddled by the false teachers. As God chose us to be holy [*Eph.*1:4], the only convincing evidence of our election is found in that life of godliness which is the fruit of faith [*2 Pet.* 1:5–10].

2: in hope of eternal life, which God, who cannot lie, promised before times eternal; 3: but in his own seasons manifested his word in the

message, wherewith I was intrusted according to the commandment of God our Saviour;

As an apostle of Jesus Christ, Paul takes his stand on 'the hope of eternal life', which inspires all his labours and enables him to endure present afflictions cheerfully [cf. *2 Tim.* 1:1; *1 Cor.* 15:19]. In contrast to the untruthful Cretans [verse 12], God who cannot lie [*1 Sam.* 15:29], promised this eternal life from all eternity [cf. *2 Tim.* 1:9]. The reference is to the pre-temporal purpose of God. As the covenant of redemption was ratified before the creation of the world [*John* 17:24], so the time of its manifestation is appointed by the divine decree [*Gal.* 4:4; *Eph.* 1:10]. This revelation of God's Word is made in the message of the gospel, which Paul emphatically claims was entrusted to him, 'according to the commandment of God our Saviour' [*Eph.* 3:8; *1 Tim.* 1:11–13].

The Cretan errorists can claim no such authority for their perverse deviations from the truth. The designation of God as '*our* Saviour' is strongly confessional, and it challenges the church in Crete to remain true to the apostolic faith. The clear teaching of this passage is that no man should take upon himself any office in the church without *God's* call. 'Whoever would find comfort in themselves, or clear and justify their callings to others, or do good in the place of the body where they are set, they must be able to prove that they are not intruders but called by this calling and commandment of God. As Paul performed every duty in the church by virtue of his extraordinary calling, so they must by virtue of their ordinary' (Thomas Taylor).

4: to Titus, my true child after a common faith: Grace and peace from God the Father and Christ Jesus our Saviour.

The intimate address 'my true child after a common faith' implies that Titus had been converted through Paul's ministry. The faith they shared was the faith common to all the elect, as opposed to the disruptive Jewish myths spread abroad by the heretics. A Gentile by birth, Titus probably became a Christian during the mission to Antioch [*Acts* 11:25, 26; *Gal.* 2:1–3]. The otherwise unaccountable omission of his name from Acts lends plausibility to the suggestion that he was a relative of Luke (cf. W. M. Ramsay *St Paul the Traveller and the Roman Citizen*, p. 390). Be that as it may, it is clear from his success at troubled

Corinth that Titus was endowed with the right qualities to deal with the difficult situation in Crete [*2 Cor.* 2:13; 7:6–15; 8:6, 16–18; 12:18]. As usual in Paul, the greeting 'Grace and peace' denotes the undeserved favour of God and the spiritual well-being that flows from it. These divine blessings are conjointly bestowed by God the Father and Christ Jesus 'our Saviour'. The title applied to the Father in the previous verse is here transferred to Christ, since our salvation is equally the gift of the Father's electing love and Christ's redeeming work.

5: For this cause left I thee in Crete, that thou shouldest set in order the things that were wanting, and appoint elders in every city, as I gave thee charge;

'As I gave thee charge' shows that Paul is not giving Titus a new directive, but providing him with the written authorization for the task already laid upon him. First, he is to 'straighten out what was left unfinished' (NIV). This would include checking the false teachers, and instructing believers in the doctrine that promotes godliness [1:10, 11; 2:1–10]. Secondly, he is to appoint elders in every city. The method of selection is not specified, but probably Titus would encourage each congregation to choose suitable men whose appointment he would then formally confirm [cf. *Acts* 14:23]. As in *1 Tim.* 3:2ff., Paul emphasizes the moral qualities which are required in those who are to lead the flock.

'The danger was lest talent and cleverness should carry the day, and the leadership of the Church fall into the hands of men deficient in the elements of a worthy Christian character . . . Self-seeking teachers had insinuated themselves into the Christian societies, who knew how to impose on the credulous or unstable by their show of learning and asceticism . . . Entrance into the ministry must be barred to such candidates as these; and officers must be chosen whose character commanded the respect of the community, and who would be likely to exert a wholesome and steadying influence on the Church's life, at a time of transition and feverish unrest' (Findlay).

6: if any man is blameless, the husband of one wife, having children that believe, who are not accused of riot or unruly.

The qualifications for elders are very similar to those given in *1 Tim.*

3: 1–7, but the fact that deacons are not mentioned here suggests that the organization of the church in Crete was less advanced than at Ephesus. Although God has committed the treasure of the gospel to earthen vessels, they must be *clean* vessels if their testimony is to be effective. The message proclaimed with the lips lacks all credibility unless it is first embodied in the life. Thus the character must be in accord with the calling: a man who is blameless, a faithful husband (see comment on *1 Tim.* 3:2), and a wise father (see comment on *1 Tim.* 3:4, 5). Since older men were chosen as elders, their suitability could best be gauged by the way in which they had brought up their children [*Prov.* 22:6]. Paul only wants men with believing children, and not men whose children have a reputation for profligacy or disobedience.

7. For the bishop must be blameless, as God's steward; not self-willed, not soon angry, no brawler, no striker, not greedy of filthy lucre,

The sudden switch from 'elder' to 'bishop' proves that they are interchangeable terms, the first denoting the office, and the second describing the function (see comment on *1 Tim.* 3:1). The 'bishop' or overseer must be blameless because he is the steward of God's household, the church [cf. *1 Tim.* 3:15]. Paul defines what it means to be 'blameless' in a series of five negatives [verse 7] and seven positives [verses 8, 9]. On the negative side, a representative list is given of the vices which the worker in *God's* household must not have: 1. he will not arrogantly insist on having his own way without any regard to the opinions of others; 2. he will not be quick-tempered since pastoral work requires great patience; 3. he will not be given to much wine (see comment on *1 Tim.* 3:3); 4. he will not strike his opponents with blows or with words; 5. he will not be motivated by a desire for base gain, either by making his teaching the means of enriching himself (as the heretics did, verse 11), or by misappropriating church funds (as Judas did, *John* 12:6).

8: but given to hospitality, a lover of good, sober-minded, just, holy, self-controlled;

On the positive side the bishop will be: 1. hospitable (see comment on *1 Tim.* 3:2); 2. a lover of what is good, whether good men, good deeds, or good things; 3. well-disciplined in thought and behaviour; 4. just in all his dealings with others; 5. devout in his dedication to God; 6. self-controlled because Spirit-filled [cf. *Gal.* 5:23].

9: holding to the faithful word which is according to the teaching, that he may be able both to exhort in the sound doctrine, and to convict the gainsayers.

Lastly, the Christian minister must hold fast to the trustworthy word which is in accordance with the apostolic teaching [cf. *Rom.* 6:17: 'the pattern of teaching'], 'so that he can encourage others by sound doctrine and refute those who oppose it' (NIV). Only 'the truth, the whole truth, and nothing but the truth' is equal to the twofold task of building up the faithful and exposing the errors of its adversaries. Calvin warns against the dangerous fickleness 'whereby a pastor does not steadfastly maintain the doctrine of which he should be the unshaken protagonist. In short, there is required in a pastor not only learning but such zeal for pure doctrine that he will never depart from it'.

10: For there are many unruly men, vain talkers and deceivers, specially they of the circumcision, 11: whose mouths must be stopped; men who overthrow whole houses, teaching things which they ought not, for filthy lucre's sake.

It appears that there were many self-appointed teachers within the church, especially Jewish Christians, whose erroneous doctrines were undermining the faith of whole families [cf. *2 Tim.* 3:6]. Paul wisely refrains from repeating their false teaching, but roundly denounces them as rebels who flout the authority of the church by the voluble but empty rhetoric which deceives the unwary.

'Note the difference between these and godly pastors, who are according to God's heart. They feed God's people with wisdom and understanding, while the other feed with vanity and wind; these have their gifts and calling from God, and speak every word from Him and for Him; the other, like the Devil's cooks, are ever blending impurities with the truth, that it may be never purely tasted. Like untrusty solicitors, they speak one word for God and two for themselves' (Taylor). The mouths of these men must be muzzled, so that no further damage is done to the church [cf. *1 Tim.* 1:3, 4]. Finally, the duplicity of such falsehood is revealed by its motivation. For whereas the true shepherds preach the truth for its own sake, the emissaries of error do their deadly work 'for filthy lucre's sake'. 'If Balaam's eye is upon Balak's gold, it must needs be blinded; and when covetousness has become the conscience of men, no wonder if they speak, write, or attempt anything, if it will help them forward to their expected wages' (Taylor).

12: One of themselves, a prophet of their own, said, Cretans are always liars, evil beasts, idle gluttons.

In quoting the testimony of Epimenides, whom the Cretans revered as a prophet, Paul has his readers on the horns of a dilemma. They must either agree with this verdict on their character, or repudiate the charge and make their own seer a liar. In fact the Cretan reputation for lying was so notorious in the ancient world that the verb 'to Cretize' meant 'to lie and cheat'. As to the ferocity of the Cretans, Epimenides also said that the absence of wild beasts from Crete was supplied by its human inhabitants! The further stigma 'idle gluttons' accuses them of the laziness that desires satisfaction without the exertion of earning an honest living. The character given to the Cretans by this heathen poet is exemplified by the errorists who spread Jewish myths for base gain [verses 13, 14].

13: This testimony is true. For which cause reprove them sharply, that they may be sound in the faith,

Paul endorses the truth of this saying, and therefore instructs Titus to administer a sharp reproof to 'the gainsayers' [verse 9]. Because their false teaching threatened the whole church, the severity of the rebuke must be equal to the gravity of the danger, both to those they deceived and to themselves as the self-deceived [cf. *2 Tim.* 3:13]. But though the disease calls for drastic treatment, the true surgeon of souls only cuts to achieve a cure. There is a remedial purpose in view. It is 'that they may be sound in the faith'. 'Much vituperation would have been saved had Christians always had this saving purpose in mind when dealing with those erring from the faith' (Guthrie).

14: not giving heed to Jewish fables, and commandments of men who turn away from the truth.

Paul next diagnoses the source of this disease. It arises from professed Christians giving heed to a form of teaching which is quite alien to the gospel. To insist on preserving the purity of the faith may seem unadventurous to some, but it is impossible to improve what is fixed and final by the addition of a medley of Jewish myths and human regulations [cf. 3:9 and see comment on *1 Tim.* 1:3, 6]. 'God's truth must not thus be bartered for the fallacies and fables of men. Fallible sanctions cannot usurp the place of infallible' (Simpson). The Cretan deceivers had learned their aberrations from men who persisted in rejecting the truth, i.e. from Jews whose ascetic demands were probably not unlike those reflected in the Colossian 'heresy' [*Col.* 2:22 and see Introduction].

15: To the pure all things are pure: but to them that are defiled and unbelieving nothing is pure; but both their mind and their conscience are defiled.

The apostle here affirms the principle, 'To the pure all things are pure', in order to repudiate the prohibitions insisted upon by these outside teachers, whose defiled conscience led them to regard as unclean things which were in themselves capable of pure use [*1 Tim.* 4:4; cf. *Luke* 11:41; *Rom.* 14:20; *1 Cor.* 6:12; 10:23] Purity is not promoted by the ritualistic scruples of the Jewish legalists, who contaminate everything they touch because both their mind and conscience are polluted by unbelief. 'Since in God's sight there is no purity apart from faith, it follows that unbelievers are all unclean. Thus they will not obtain the cleanness they desire by any laws or regulations, for being themselves impure, nothing in the world can be pure to them' (Calvin).

16: They profess that they know God; but by their works they deny him, being abominable, and disobedient, and unto every good work reprobate.

Paul has already branded the Jewish controversialists as 'men who turn away from the truth' [verse 14], but because they professed to know God, they were able to palm off their errors on the self-appointed teachers within the church [verse 13].

Whereas Paul hopes that a sharp reproof may restore the latter to soundness in the faith, he unsparingly condemns the unconverted outsiders whose fair words are belied by their evil deeds. Such men are 'abominable' or detestable in the sight of God, because they are 'disobedient' in their resolve to cling to the traditions of men rather than yield to the truth of the gospel, and are therefore disqualified from doing anything good. 'This last is like a final judgment. Like coins or metals that are tested as to genuineness these confessors of God are found spurious, utterly to be rejected' (Lenski).

CHAPTER TWO

In contrast to such errors, Titus must insist upon conduct that is consistent with the sound teaching. Paul outlines the behaviour expected of each group within the community, and urges Titus to exercise a model ministry [verses 1–10]. For the grace of God which brings salvation teaches men to renounce sin and to lead godly lives as they look for the return of Christ, who died to make his people zealous of good works. Titus is to teach these things with all authority so that none may despise him [verses 11–15].

1: But speak thou the things which befit the sound doctrine:

In contrast to the disease of heresy, Titus must continue to speak what befits sound doctrine, for wholesome teaching promotes the spiritual health which is manifested in an obedient walk [cf. *1 Tim.* 1:10].

'Christianity is primarily, indeed, a doctrine, but only that it may be in the true sense a life; and the two can never be kept apart from each other in the public teaching of the church without imminent peril to both' (Fairbairn).

2: that aged men be temperate, grave, sober-minded, sound in faith, in love, in patience:

The older men of the church are to set an example of spiritual maturity which is in keeping with their age. Titus should exhort them to be: 1. 'temperate', not given to excess of any kind; 2. 'grave', possessing the dignity that is worthy of respect; 3. 'sober-minded' or self-controlled [cf. 1:8]; 4. 'sound in faith, in love, in patient endurance', personal qualities which would have a stabilizing influence in a community disturbed by false teaching.

3: that aged women likewise be reverent in demeanour, not slanderers nor enslaved to much wine, teachers of that which is good;

Similarly, the older women are to conduct themselves in a manner which is proper to their holy calling, so that their very walk and motion, their countenance, speech, silence, may present a certain dignity of holy propriety' (Jerome). The two negatives, 'not slanderers nor enslaved to much wine', point to the attendant dangers of indulging the Cretan penchant for idleness [1:12]. They should rather fill their time by being 'teachers of that which is good'. This does not refer to public instruction, but to the informal advice and help they can give to the younger women, by word and example [verses 4, 5].

4: that they may train the young women to love their husbands, to love their children, 5: to be sober-minded, chaste, workers at home, kind, being in subjection to their own husbands, that the word of God be not blasphemed:

Paul shows a fine regard for what is proper in delegating to older women the duty of training young women in their domestic duties. In view of the crucial effect of her influence upon society, Paul lists seven characteristics which are essential to the key rôle of the Christian wife and mother. The first pair are also first in importance: she is to be devoted to her husband and children, for such love will inspire and make light of every other duty. The second pair – 'sober-minded, chaste' – designate the self-control and purity which is to inform all her conduct. The third pair specify that she is to fulfil her household duties with kindness, for where this is lacking even the most efficient housekeeping is a doubtful boon. Finally, Paul requires wives to be subject to their own husbands, because it had to be shown that the natural relation between husband and wife was perfected rather than annulled by grace [*Eph.* 5:22, 23; *Col.* 3:18]. The final clause probably qualifies all seven items: 'that the word of God be not blasphemed' [cf. *Isa.* 52:5; *1 Tim.* 6:1]. 'If the observed effect of the Gospel were to make women worse wives it would not commend it to the heathen' (White).

6: the younger men likewise exhort to be sober-minded:

As a young man himself, Titus is instructed to urge the younger men to be self-controlled, and to show them what this means by his own example [verses 7, 8]. The admonition is brief, but comprehensive in its scope. For the greatest need of young men is to have their natural impetuosity firmly curbed by a prudent self-restraint.

7: in all things showing thyself an ensample of good works; in thy doctrine showing uncorruptness, gravity, 8: sound speech, that cannot be condemned; that he that is of the contrary part may be ashamed, having no evil thing to say of us.

As a minister of the gospel, Titus must be concerned about his public image. In all things he must strive to show himself as an example of good works, for his witness will not be effective unless his teaching is visibly embodied in his life. His teaching is to be marked by two important personal qualities. 'Uncorruptness' or 'soundness' expresses 'the single-mindedness and sincerity which a teacher of sacred things should exhibit. It signifies his wholeheartedness, while *gravity* rather has reference to his outward demeanour' (Bernard).

The content of his teaching must be in conformity with the apostolic 'deposit' [*2 Tim.* 1:14]: 'sound' or healthy speech which cannot be condemned, so that any opponent will be shamed into silence. By adding 'having no evil thing to say of us', Paul reminds Titus that any failure on his part would also reflect on the apostle whom he represented in Crete.

9: Exhort servants to be in subjection to their own masters, and to be well-pleasing to them in all things; not gainsaying; 10: not purloining, but showing all good fidelity; that they may adorn the doctrine of God our Saviour in all things.

Christian slaves must be taught to give their masters satisfactory service by obeying them in all things. This will involve the avoidance of two vices to which slaves were especially prone: 1. 'not gainsaying', not answering back; 2. 'not purloining, not taking their masters' property for themselves. With reference to the latter, Humphreys remarks, 'Almost all trades, arts, and professions were at this time in the hands of slaves; and so all tricks of trade, all mercantile or professional embezzlement and dishonesty, are covered by the word'. But believers must show themselves to be so trustworthy that they may in all respects adorn the doctrine of God our Saviour. As the word 'adorn' is used of the setting of a jewel, to 'adorn the doctrine' means that it will be 'set off', and exhibited in a favourable light by the faithful conduct of those who profess it (so Bernard).

11: For the grace of God hath appeared, bringing salvation to all men, 12: instructing us, to the intent that, denying ungodliness and worldly lusts, we should live soberly and righteously and godly in this present world; 13: looking for the blessed hope and appearing of the glory of the great God and our Saviour Jesus Christ; 14: who gave himself for us, that he might redeem us from all iniquity, and purify unto himself a people for his own possession, zealous of good works.

As the opening 'for' indicates, Paul now points to the grace of God as the motivating power which enables believers to fulfil the ethical demands of the gospel [verses 1–10]. This is 'the first of the two Evangelical outbursts of that "spring of living water" in St. Paul's own heart which kept his life and teaching always green and fresh' (Humphreys) [cf. 3:4–7].

For the grace of God hath appeared, bringing salvation to all men: Paul once again stresses the universal scope of the gospel by affirming that the grace of God has been revealed in the visible earthly appearance of Christ, the Sun of Righteousness, whose coming dispelled the darkness of our nature's night. The gospel is good news for all men, 'because, when God calls upon men universally to believe, he does not call upon them to believe that they are elected, or that Christ died for them in particular. He calls upon them to believe that Christ died for sin, for sinners, for the world . . . The atonement is not offered to an individual either as an elect man, or as a non-elect man; but as a man, and a sinner, simply' (Shedd). (See also comment on *1 Tim.* 1:1; 2:4, 6; 4:10.)

Instructing us, to the intent that, denying ungodliness and worldly lusts, we should live soberly and righteously and godly in this present world: The point of the whole paragraph is to underline the educative function of grace in transforming our present life, for the triumph of God's grace must be shown in the fruit of godly living [*Matt.* 6:20; *Gal.* 5:22, 23]. This 'categorical imperative' involves the once-for-all denial of the ungodliness and worldly lusts which characterized the old life, and the aorist participle may point to the baptismal vow as marking this decisive break with the past (see comment on *1 Tim.* 6: 12, 13). The renunciation of the past makes way for the positive aim expressed by the three adverbs which follow. 'Sobriety keeps the house, and moderates the mind at home; righteousness looks forth and gives every man his due abroad; piety looks up to God and gives Him His right' (Taylor).

Looking for the blessed hope and appearing of the glory of the great God and our Saviour Jesus Christ: The vivid expectation of Christ's return provides the grand incentive to such godly living. According to Paul, 'the blessed hope' of believers is not a secret event, for he immediately defines it as the visible appearance of the glory of Christ on the last day [*1 Tim.* 6:14; cf. *Matt.* 16:27]. 'We can only conclude that the distinction between the Rapture of the Church and the Revelation of Christ is an inference which is nowhere asserted by the Word of God and not required by the terminology relating to the return of Christ . . . The parousia, the apokalypse, and the epiphany appear to be a single event. Any division of Christ's coming into two parts is an unproven inference' (G. E. Ladd, *The Blessed Hope,* p. 69). Since Christ's deity will then be manifested, Paul here fittingly adds 'great God' [cf. *Rom.* 9:5] to the title 'our Saviour' [1:4]. The passage provides us with a clear testimony to the proper deity of Christ, and it should occasion no surprise that Paul, 'who everywhere thinks and speaks of Christ as very God, should occasionally call him by the appropriate designation' (B. B. Warfield, *The Lord of Glory*, p. 255).

Who gave himself for us, that he might redeem us from all iniquity, and purify unto himself a people for his own possession, zealous of good works: Paul next explains the twofold purpose of Christ's substitutionary sacrifice [*Mark* 10:45; *Gal.* 1:4; *1 Tim.* 2:6]. 1. He gave himself to redeem us from all iniquity (or lawlessness), i.e., he 'paid the price to buy us free and take us away from all lawless living (ungodliness and worldly lusts, verse 12)' (Lenski). 2. He gave himself to purify for himself 'a people for his own possession'. This last phrase recalls *Exod.* 19:5 and its application to Christians identifies the Church as the New Israel [cf. *Gal.* 6:16, *Phil.* 3:3; *1 Pet.* 2:9f.].

As our cleansing from the defilement of sin has qualified us for God's service, it is fitting that we should be 'zealous of good works'. 'Give God thine affections, else thine actions are still-born, and have no life in them. Now zeal is the extreme heat of all the affections, when they are seething or hissing hot, as the apostle's word is, *Rom*. 12:11, when we love God and his people out of a pure heart fervently . . . Let God's love in the work of our redemption be duly pondered (as here), and it will fire us up to a holy contention in godliness' (Trapp).

15: These things speak and exhort and reprove with all authority. Let no man despise thee.

Paul's closing words look back to 2:1. Titus must continue to give practical instruction in Christian living within the proper doctrinal setting. He is not only to speak these things, but is to exhort the people and reprove them as necessary, with all the authority of his divine commission. The final admonition appears to be addressed as much to the Cretans who will hear it read out as to Titus himself. He must not permit any man to 'despise' him. The original word literally means, 'to think round a thing; hence, to have thoughts beyond, to disregard'. He is so to conduct himself that no man will be able to evade the force of his words.

CHAPTER THREE

The Cretans must be taught to obey the civil authorities and to live at peace with all men [verses 1, 2]. These duties are enforced by the reminder of their former sinful state, and the unmerited kindness of God in the bestowal of that free salvation which made them the heirs of eternal life [verses 3–7]. The evidence of this great change is to be seen in the good works of believers, but useless speculations which engender strife are to be shunned [verses 8, 9]. After two warnings the obstinate heretics are to be avoided as being self-condemned [verse 11]. When Artemas or Tychicus arrives, Paul requests Titus to join him at Nicopolis, and to give whatever help Zenas and Apollos may need on their journey. Such assistance befits believers, who are to show the fruits of their profession by serving others. After the customary salutations, Paul concludes with a benediction which embraces all the Christians in Crete [verses 12–15].

1: Put them in mind to be in subjection to rulers, to authorities, to be obedient, to be ready unto every good work, 2: to speak evil of no man, not to be contentious, to be gentle, showing all meekness toward all men.

Titus must remind the unruly Cretans of their obligation to obey the civil authorities, and to be ready for any good work which will be of benefit to the community [*Rom.* 13:1ff.; *1 Tim.* 2:2]. In contrast to their former mode of life [verse 3], they are now to reflect the kindness of God in their conduct towards all men.

On the negative side, they are not to revile any man, nor be contentious (this word literally means, 'non-fighters'). Positively, they are to be gentle or forbearing, willing to yield their rights to others, 'showing *all* meekness to *all* men'. Such meekness 'is an inwrought grace of the soul; and the exercises of it are first and chiefly towards God, when we accept his dealings with us without disputing . . . He that is meek indeed will know himself a sinner among sinners; or if there was One who could not know Himself such, yet He too bore a sinner's doom and endured therefore the contradiction of sinners [cf *Matt.* 11:29: "I am meek and lowly of heart"]; and this knowledge of his own sin will teach him to endure meekly the provocations with which they may provoke him, and not to withdraw himself from the burdens which their sin may impose upon him [*Gal.* 6: 1; *2 Tim.* 2:25]' (R. C. Trench).

3: For we also once were foolish, disobedient, deceived, serving divers lusts and pleasures, living in malice and envy, hateful, hating one another.

Paul's use of the plural 'we' shows that his statement is true of all believers including himself and Titus: We have good reason to manifest such meekness toward the unsaved when we remember that we were once like them ourselves [cf *Eph.* 2:1–3]. A mournful proof of the depravity of human nature is provided by this sevenfold description of our former sinful state. At that time we also were: 1. '*foolish*', without understanding through the blinding effect of sin upon the mind [*Eph.* 4:18]; 2. '*disobedient*', to both God and man, rebelling against the dictates of conscience and the constraints of the law; 3. '*deceived*', made to wander from the true way through following the reasonings of unbelief, 4. '*serving divers lusts and pleasures*', being dominated by the desire for self-gratification; 5. '*living in malice and envy*', showing ill-will towards others and coveting what is theirs; 6. '*hateful*', made detestable to others through the self-centredness of sin; 7. '*hating one another*', for mutual hatred is the inevitable result of such sinful egocentricity.

4: But when the kindness of God our Saviour, and his love toward man, appeared, 5: not by works done in righteousness, which we did ourselves, but according to his mercy he saved us, through the washing of regeneration and renewing of the Holy Spirit, 6: which he poured out upon us richly, through Jesus Christ our Saviour; 7: that, being justified by his grace, we might be made heirs according to the hope of eternal life.

The fourth of the Faithful sayings [verse 8] ascribes the work of salvation entirely to God, and so focuses on the way in which that salvation is applied to sinners that many scholars think Paul is here quoting part of a baptismal creed or hymn, which faithfully echoes his own teaching. As Warfield well says, These sayings 'represent the form which his doctrinal expositions had taken as current coin in the churches, no longer merely Paul's teaching, though all of that, but the precious possessions of the people themselves, in which they were able to give back to him a response from their listening hearts' (The Way of Life' in *Faith and Life*, p. 394).

But when the kindness of God our Saviour, and his love toward man, appeared: 'But' marks the great change wrought in us by the action of God [*Eph.* 2:4ff.]. It was when 'the kindness' of God and his 'love-toward-man' (our 'philanthropy') appeared in the first coming of Christ [2:11; *2 Tim.* 1:10], that he saved us through the renewing power of the Holy Spirit, and consequently we now gladly confess him to be God *'our Saviour'!*

Not by works done in righteousness, which we did ourselves: The emphatic denial that man can contribute anything to his salvation is an essential element in Paul's gospel and in all authentic preaching [*Rom.* 3:27, 28; 4:2–6; 9:11; *Gal.* 2:16; *Eph.* 2:9; *2 Tim.* 1:9]. For as Trapp pithily remarks, 'We that are bankrupts in Adam, would yet fain be doing, and think to be saved for a company of poor beggarly duties; as bankrupts will be trading again, though but for pins, etc.'.

But according to his mercy he saved us, through the washing of regeneration and renewing of the Holy Spirit: Having ruled out any thought of obtaining salvation by co-operating with God, this positive statement attributes our salvation solely to the mercy of God, which found expression in the sovereign bestowal of his regenerating grace [cf. *Eph.* 2:4, 5]. The actual application of the redemption wrought by Christ is the work of the Holy Spirit, who imparts new life to man in 'regeneration', and this 'renewal' (RSV) is the radical once-for-all change that makes him a new creature [*2 Cor.* 5:17]. Since both these terms are used to explain how God saved us, there is no reference here to the progressive work of sanctification which does call for the active co-operation of believers [*Rom.* 12:1, 2]. 'Washing' clearly has some reference to baptism, and this word was chosen because it could point to both the outward ordinance and the inner spiritual reality which that rite symbolized. Hence in the baptismal setting of this saying, believers 'confess that God has already saved them through the radical inner washing wrought by the Holy Spirit, a washing that may be spoken of as regeneration and renewal. And they do so at the time when they receive that which signifies that washing, even baptism' (George W. Knight, *The Faithful Sayings in the Pastoral Letters*, p. 111).

Which he poured out upon us richly, through Jesus Christ our Saviour: Although 'he poured out' recalls the prophecy which received its primary fulfilment on the day of Pentecost [*Joel* 2:28ff.], the reference here is to the work of the Spirit in regeneration and conversion [*Rom.* 5: 5; *1 Cor.* 2:12; *Gal.* 4:6, *Eph.* 1:13]. This rich bestowal 'is expressly connected with the mediation of Christ, who as Saviour has opened the way for it, and Himself sends forth the Spirit as the fruit of His work on earth, and the token of its acceptance with the Father. So that the whole Trinity appears here as concurring in the blessed work of our salvation' (Fairbairn) [cf *Luke* 24:29; *Acts* 2:33].

That, being justified by his grace, we might be made heirs according to the hope of eternal life. This expresses the final purpose of God in the bestowal of the Spirit. It is that, having been justified by his grace (i.e. declared righteous 'through the redemption that is in Christ Jesus', *Rom.* 3:24; cf. 2:14), we might at once become 'heirs' in accord with the sure hope of eternal life. 'The apostle is speaking not of the future, but of the present condition of believers. They are heirs of eternal life; but they are so in hope, not yet in actual possession; for *eternal life* in its full meaning is something future, *Rom.* 6:22, 23' (Huther).

8: Faithful is the saying, and concerning these things I desire that thou affirm confidently, to the end that they who have believed God may be

careful to maintain good works. These things are good and profitable unto men:

In contrast to the dogmatism of ignorance [*1 Tim.* 1:7], Titus knows the reality of the evangelical truths set forth in the preceding 'faithful saying' [verses 4–7]. Hence he is to affirm 'these things' with confidence, being convinced of their practical bearing on the conduct of believers. For a genuine experience of God's grace must be reflected in a life of gratitude [*Rom.* 12:1ff.]. 'It is most significant and suggestive that the apostle held that good works were most certainly assured by a theology which gives special prominence to the free unmerited grace of God' (White).

9: but shun foolish questionings, and genealogies, and strifes, and fightings about the law; for they are unprofitable and vain.

Titus must shun the foolish speculations and genealogies, which lead to disputes and quarrels about the law, for they are unprofitable and vain [see comment on 1:14 and *1 Tim.* 1:4]. He must teach the sound doctrine that promotes godliness [1:1], and not emulate the folly of those who had turned aside to matters which did not relate to the truth of salvation. 'In teaching we are always to have regard to usefulness so that all that is not conducive to godliness may be excluded. There is no doubt that the sophists in their ranting about things of no worth boasted of them as highly worthy and useful to know, but Paul does not admit any usefulness except in building up faith and a holy life' (Calvin).

10: A factious man after a first and second admonition refuse; 11: knowing that such a one is perverted, and sinneth, being self-condemned.

A 'factious' man here refers to an 'opinionative propagandist who promotes dissension by his pertinacity' (Simpson). If he still persists in his self-chosen opinions after having been twice warned of his error, Titus must have nothing more to do with him, 'recognizing that a man of that sort has a distorted mind and stands self-condemned in his sin' (NEB). For though he may not be condemned by his own conscience, he is at least condemned by his own action. 'He is self-condemned because his separation from the Church is due to his own acknowledged act. He cannot deny that his views are antagonistic to those which he once accepted as true; he is condemned by his former, and, as St Paul would say, his more enlightened self' (White).

12: When I shall send Artemas unto thee, or Tychicus, give diligence to come unto me to Nicopolis: for there I have determined to winter.

In closing Paul informs Titus that he will send either Artemas (who is mentioned only here) or Tychicus [*Acts* 20:4; *Eph.* 6:21; *Col.* 4:7; *2 Tim.* 4:12] to replace him in Crete, and when thus released instructs him to proceed to Nicopolis in Epirus (on the west coast of Achaia), where the apostle had decided to spend the winter.

13: Set forward Zenas the lawyer and Apollos on their journey diligently, that nothing be wanting unto them. 14: And let our people also learn to maintain good works for necessary uses, that they be not unfruitful.

Paul next requests Titus to give Zenas and Apollos, who are evidently the bearers of this letter, whatever assistance they may need to continue on their journey. 'Those that labour in the Lord's work must have all necessary accommodations and encouragements. They must be set forth and brought forward on their journey and in their negotiations worthy of God, *3 John* 6' (Trapp).

This will also provide the Christians of Crete with an opportunity to learn how to help others in urgent need, so that they do not prove to be unfruitful professors. Nothing further is known of Zenas who was probably a Roman jurist, but Apollos is almost certainly the eloquent Alexandrian who preached at Corinth [*Acts* 18:24; *1 Cor.* 1:12; 16:12].

15: All that are with me salute thee. Salute them that love us in faith. Grace be with you all.

As the workers with Paul join in sending their greetings to Titus, so Titus is to pass on these greetings to those who 'love us in faith', i.e. 'in the sphere of faith'. The brief benediction embraces all the Cretan believers, and this shows that Paul intended the whole church to hear his letter.

SOLI DEO GLORIA

BIBLIOGRAPHY

ARNDT, W. F., AND GINGRICH, F. W., *A Greek English Lexicon of the New Testament* (University of Chicago Press, 1957).

BARRETT, C. K., *The Pastoral Epistles* (OUP, 1963).

BEASLEY-MURRAY, G. R., *Baptism in the New Testament* (Paternoster Press, 1972).

BENGEL, J. A., *New Testament Word Studies* (Kregel, 1971).

BERNARD, J. H., *The Pastoral Epistles* (*CGT*) (CUP, 1899).

BRUCE, F. F., *Paul: Apostle of the Free Spirit* (Paternoster Press, 1977).

—— *Expanded Paraphrase of the Epistles of Paul* (Paternoster Press, 1965).

CALVIN, JOHN, *The Epistles to Timothy and Titus* (St. Andrew Press, 1964).

EARLE, RALPH, *1 & 2 Timothy* (*EBC*) (Zondervan, 1978).

ELLIS, E. EARLE, *Paul and His Recent Interpreters* (Eerdmans, 1961).

ERDMAN, CHARLES R., *The Pastoral Epistles* (Westminster Press, 1966).

FAIRBAIRN, PATRICK, *The Pastoral Epistles* (James and Klock, 1976); reprinted as *1 & 2 Timothy and Titus* (Banner of Truth, 2002).

GAFFIN, RICHARD B., *The Centrality of the Resurrection* (Baker Book House, 1978).

GASQUE, W. WARD, AND MARTIN, RALPH P. (eds.), *Apostolic History and the Gospel* (Paternoster Press, 1970).

GEISLER, NORMAN L. (ed.), *Inerrancy* (Zondervan, 1979).

GUTHRIE, DONALD, *The Pastoral Epistles and the Mind of Paul* (Tyndale, 1956).

—— *The Pastoral Epistles* (*TNTC*) (Tyndale, 1957).

—— *New Testament Introduction* (Tyndale, 1970).

HENDRIKSEN, WILLIAM, *1 & 2 Timothy and Titus* (Banner of Truth, 1957).

HENRY, MATTHEW, *Commentary on the Holy Bible* (various editions).

HIEBERT, D. EDMUND, *First Timothy* (Moody Press, 1957).

—— *Second Timothy* (Moody Press, 1958).

—— *Titus & Philemon* (Moody Press, 1957).

—— *Titus* (*EBC*) (Zondervan, 1978).

HINSON, E. GLENN, *1–2 Timothy and Titus* (*BBC*) (Broadman Press, 1971).
HUMPHREYS, A. E., *The Epistles to Timothy and Titus* (CUP, 1895).
HUTHER, J. E., *The Pastoral Epistles* (*Meyer NTC*) (T. & T. Clark, 1881).
KELLY, J. N. D., *The Pastoral Epistles* (A. & C. Black, 1963).
KENT, HOMER A., *The Pastoral Epistles* (Moody Press, 1958).
KITTEL, G. AND FRIEDRICH, G., *Theological Dictionary of the New Testament,* vols. 1–10 (Eerdmans, 1964–76).
KNIGHT, GEORGE W., *The Faithful Sayings in the Pastoral Epistles* (Presbyterian & Reformed, n.d.).
LADD, GEORGE E., *The Blessed Hope* (Eerdmans, 1956).
LENSKI, R. C. H., *The Interpretation of Paul's Epistles to Timothy and Titus* (Augsburg, 1961).
LOCK, WALTER, *The Pastoral Epistles* (*ICC*) (T. & T. Clark, 1966).
METZGER, BRUCE M., *A Textual Commentary on the Greek New Testament* (United Bible Societies, 1971).
MORRIS, LEON, *Ministers of God* (IVP, 1968).
—— *The Apostolic Preaching of the Cross* (Tyndale, 1965).
MURRAY, JOHN, *Collected Writings,* vol. 1 (Banner of Truth, 1976).
—— *Principles of Conduct* (Tyndale, 1957).
PARRY, R. ST. JOHN, *The Pastoral Epistles* (CUP, 1920).
PINK, ARTHUR W., *Gleanings from Paul* (Moody Press, 1967).
POOLE, MATTHEW, *Commentary on the Holy Bible,* vol. 3 (Banner of Truth, 1963).
RAMSAY, W. M., *St Paul the Traveller and the Roman Citizen* (Hodder & Stoughton, 1900).
ROBERTSON, A. T., *Word Pictures in the New Testament,* vol. 4 (Broadman Press, 1931).
SABATIER, A., *The Apostle Paul – Appendix on the Epistles to Timothy and Titus* by G. G. Findlay (Hodder & Stoughton, 1903).
SAUCY, ROBERT L., *The Church in God's Program* (Moody Press, 1972).
SHEDD, W. G. T., *Dogmatic Theology* (Klock & Klock, 1979).
SIMPSON, E. K., *The Pastoral Epistles* (Tyndale Press, 1954).
STOTT, JOHN R. W., *Guard the Gospel* (IVP, 1973).
TAYLOR, THOMAS, *An Exposition of Titus* (Christian Classics, n.d.).

TRAPP, JOHN, *Commentary on the New Testament* (Sovereign Grace Book Club, 1958).

TRENCH, R. C., *Synonyms of the New Testament* (James Clarke, 1961).

VINCENT, MARVIN R., *Word Studies in the New Testament* (MacDonald, n. d.).

VINE, W. E., *Expository Dictionary of New Testament Words* (Oliphants, 1958).

WARFIELD, B. B., *The Person and Work of Christ* (Presbyterian & Reformed, 1950).

—— *The Inspiration and Authority of the Bible* (Marshall Morgan & Scott, 1959).

—— *Faith and Life* (Banner of Truth, 1974).

—— *The Lord of Glory* (Evangelical Press, 1974).

WHITE, NEWPORT J. D., *The Epistles to Timothy & Titus* (*EGT*) (Eerdmans, 1974).

YAMAUCHI, EDWIN, *Pre-Christian Gnosticism* (Tyndale, 1973).

Philemon

INTRODUCTION

Lightfoot maintains that this Epistle holds a unique place in Paul's writings because 'it is the only strictly private letter which has been preserved'. But the greetings at the beginning and end of the letter suggest that it was intended for a public hearing. Hence this brief epistle is to be seen not simply as a private letter from one personal friend to another, but rather 'as an apostolic letter about a personal matter' (R. P. Martin). For though the letter is the very model of tact and courtesy, it is also the authoritative utterance of Christ's apostle, and Paul makes it clear to Philemon that he expects him to do even more than he asks [verse 21].

Paul writes to Philemon to intercede for his runaway slave Onesimus [verse 10]. Apparently he robbed his master and headed straight for Rome, but instead of finding refuge in the crowded city, he somehow came into contact with Paul and was converted. The once worthless slave now began to live up to his name, and proved so 'profitable' [verse 11] to Paul that he would have liked to keep him as his friend and helper, if he had not felt obliged to return him to his wronged master in Colossae. But because the slave who ran away as a pagan is returning as a Christian, Philemon is asked to grant far more than a mere pardon to the repentant Onesimus, for he is to receive him as 'a brother beloved' [verse 16]. It can be safely assumed that Philemon did respond to Paul's appeal, since he would not have kept a letter which he refused to obey.

Onesimus was converted at about the same time that Paul received news from Epaphras of the threat to the faith which had arisen in Colossae. Paul therefore entrusted Tychicus with the responsible task of protecting Onesimus from arrest by slave catchers on the return journey [*Col.* 4:9], and of delivering the letters to the Laodiceans (probably our 'Ephesians', see comment on Colossians 4:16) and the

Colossians, together with this covering letter to Philemon. Although it is often remarked that Paul stops short of asking Philemon to give Onesimus his freedom, it may be questioned whether the thought ever crossed Paul's mind, for in the social conditions of the time emancipation could be a doubtful boon amounting only to the freedom to starve. But if this letter presented no revolutionary challenge to the social structures of the day, the implications of its teaching were bound to prove fatal to slavery in the end.

The outstanding value of this short Epistle is helpfully summarized by W. Graham Scroggie under seven heads. 'Its *Personal* value consists in the light which it throws upon the character of Paul. Its *Ethical* value consists in its balanced sensitiveness to what is right. Its *Providential* value consists in its underlying suggestion that God is behind and above all events. Its *Practical* value consists in its application of the highest principles to the commonest affairs. Its *Evangelical* value consists in the encouragement it supplies to seek and to save the lowest. Its *Social* value consists in its presentation of the relation of Christianity to slavery and all unchristian institutions. And its *Spiritual* value consists in the analogy between it and the Gospel Story' (*Know Your Bible*, vol. 2, p. 201).

Paul links Timothy with himself in greeting Philemon, his family and the church in his house [verses 1–3]. He thanks God for the news of Philemon's faith in Christ and love for the saints which has given him much joy [verses 4–7]. As Christ's prisoner, Paul appeals to Philemon on behalf of Onesimus, who has become his own son in the faith. The once unprofitable slave is now so profitable that Paul would have preferred to keep him, if he had not been under the obligation of returning him to his master [verses 8-14]. Paul suggests that the desertion of Onesimus was overruled so that Philemon might receive back a brother beloved instead of a slave [verses 15, 16]. He pleads with Philemon to refresh his heart by receiving Onesimus, and offers to repay any debts incurred by the fugitive slave, though he reminds Philemon of his even greater debt to himself [verses 17–20]. He is confident that Philemon will do more than he asks, and expresses the hope that he will soon be a guest at Philemon's home [verses 21, 22]. As usual Paul conveys the greetings of his companions, and concludes the Letter with the benediction [verses 23–25].

1: Paul, a prisoner of Christ Jesus, and Timothy our brother, to Philemon our beloved and fellow-worker, 2: and to Apphia our sister, and to Archippus our fellow-soldier, and to the church in thy house:

By introducing himself as 'a prisoner of Christ Jesus' [verses 9, 10, 13, 23], Paul enlists the sympathy of Philemon and implicitly contrasts his own suffering with the trifling sacrifice he is asking him to make. 'How could Philemon resist an appeal which was penned within prison walls and by a manacled hand?' (Lightfoot). Since Paul had never been to Colossae, Philemon was presumably converted during Paul's ministry in Ephesus [verse 19], where he must have also met Timothy [*Acts* 19:22]. The greetings sent by Timothy thus serve to remind Philemon that fellow-believers are bound together in the bonds of brotherhood. But it is clear that Timothy played no part in the composition of the letter because Paul speaks in the singular from verse 4. Moreover, there is special significance in addressing Philemon as 'our beloved', for it is a reminder that he belongs to a community of mutual love [verse 9; *Rom.* 1:7], which is patterned upon the self-giving love of the One who gave himself for its salvation [*Eph.* 5:25]. Hence Philemon must extend that same love to the slave whom Paul calls 'a brother beloved' [verse 16]. Philemon is also Paul's 'fellow-worker', and as such he shares in the common task of witnessing to the gospel by word and deed [verses 5, 7], and by consecrating his house to Christ's service [verse 2].

Apphia, a 'sister' in the Lord, is evidently Philemon's wife. As the lady of the house she had to supervise the duties of the slaves, and so her own response to Paul's appeal for Onesimus would be a crucial factor in influencing the decision of her husband. In a letter addressed to a Christian 'household', it is fair to assume that Archippus is Philemon's son. If Colossians 4:17 means that he was given pastoral responsibility in the absence of Epaphras, this would explain why the younger man is described by the stronger term – 'fellow-soldier' – which 'seems to indicate an activity requiring more pains and self-denial' (Theodor Zahn). J. Knox's idea that Archippus was the master of Onesimus and the real recipient of the letter is an exegetical flight of fancy which is unworthy of the serious attention it has received. The return of Onesimus would also concern the 'church' [*Col.* 4:15] which gathered in Philemon's house, 'because it was in that congregation that

Onesimus would have to be recognized as a Christian. Further, some at least of the worshippers there would be his fellow-servants, with whom he must be properly reinstated' (Lukyn Williams).

3: Grace to you and peace from God our Father and the Lord Jesus Christ.

Paul greets all the believers at Philemon's house and prays that they may enjoy grace and peace 'from God our Father and the Lord Jesus Christ' – a formula that shows the source of these blessings. Grace is the unmerited favour of God which brings sinners to salvation in Christ, and peace is that state of spiritual well-being that flows from the reception of this grace. 'There is no grace unless God bestows it, and there is no real peace unless it flows forth from God's reconciliation with sinful man' (J. J. Müller).

4: I thank my God always, making mention of thee in my prayers,

Paul's thanksgivings fulfil a function similar to that of the overture in an opera, for they introduce the themes to be elaborated in the body of the letter (J. Knox). So in verses 4–7 no fewer than seven of the terms used by Paul are later taken up and woven into his argument: 'love' [verses 5, 7, 9, 16]; 'prayers' [verse 22]; 'sharing', 'partner' [verse 17]; 'the good', 'goodness' [verse 14]; 'heart' [verses 12, 20]; 'refreshed' [verse 20].

I thank my God always: Since God alone is the author of salvation, Paul does not congratulate Philemon on having conducted himself as a Christian, but gives God all the praise which is his due. Moreover, Paul not only thanks God for what he has already accomplished in Philemon's life, he also prays that God will complete the good work which he has begun in his heart [*Phil.* 1:6].

5: hearing of thy love, and of the faith which thou hast toward the Lord Jesus, and toward all the saints;

Presumably Paul heard of Philemon's faith and love from Epaphras [*Col.* 1:7, 8; 4:12]. 'Love is first mentioned, as more noticed. But faith is the mother-grace, the womb wherein love and all the rest of that heavenly offspring are conceived' (Trapp). Paul is glad that Philemon is so forward in showing love for all the saints because he is about to ask for a further demonstration of it [verses 9, 16]. This emphasis upon love results in a criss-cross arrangement of the clauses in the sentence (*chiasmus*):

love	faith
toward (*pros*) the Lord Jesus	for (*eis*) all the saints

6: that the fellowship of thy faith may become effectual, in the knowledge of every good thing which is in you, unto Christ.

(Praying) that the sharing to which your faith gives rise may effectively impart the knowledge of every good thing that is in us and that leads us closer to Christ: The meaning of almost every word in this difficult verse is disputed. But if 'fellowship' is here taken as 'sharing', then Paul is praying that the generosity which was prompted by Philemon's faith might promote 'the knowledge of every good thing which is in us'. This is not some form of theoretical enlightenment; it is that concrete knowledge of 'the good' which God desires believers to perform [*Rom.* 12:2; *Gal.* 6:10; *1 Thess.* 5:15]. Paul is thus preparing Philemon for the request that follows, so that his 'goodness should not be as of necessity, but of free will' [verse 14]. And by acting out what God's grace has first worked in, Philemon will be drawn closer to Christ. Alternatively, 'unto Christ' may mean that this deed will advance Christ's cause and so serve to glorify him.

7: For I had much joy and comfort in thy love, because the hearts of the saints have been refreshed through thee, brother.

Paul speaks of the great joy and comfort he had in the news of Philemon's love. This love appears to have found active expression in a particular deed by which 'the hearts of the saints have been refreshed'. No doubt Philemon had used his wealth to minister to the needs of his fellow-believers in some time of crisis, and this may have been in connection with the great earthquake of AD 60. By placing 'brother' last in the sentence, Paul turns this one word into a highly effective appeal. As Philemon had shown himself to be a true Christian brother in the past, he is again called to live up to this description by the way in which he received Onesimus.

8: Wherefore, though I have all boldness in Christ to enjoin thee that which is befitting, 9: yet for love's sake I rather beseech, being such a one as Paul the aged, and now a prisoner also of Christ Jesus:

Since Paul has been given impressive proof of Philemon's love, he will not invoke his authority as an apostle to command what ought to be done. He prefers to entreat 'for love's sake'. This phrase does not refer to the love of Philemon or Paul, but to 'love absolutely, love regarded as a principle which demands a deferential respect' (Lightfoot). Paul reinforces his appeal by reminding Philemon that it is made by an old man who is also a prisoner for the sake of Christ. 'Such is the man who now forbears to use his indisputable authority and merely makes a request' (Beet). Although some versions prefer 'ambassador' (RSV, NEB), it is virtually certain that Paul means 'old man', since he would not use an official title in making what is essentially a personal appeal. There is no ground for doubting the accuracy of the description, for at this time Paul would be nearly sixty, and prematurely aged by his sufferings.

10: I beseech thee for my child, whom I have begotten in my bonds, Onesimus,

'After having so carefully prepared the way, Paul at last comes to the purpose of the letter. He again uses the verb 'I beseech', but this time mentions the object of his request. He is appealing to Philemon on behalf of his child, whom he has begotten in his bonds [*1 Cor.* 4:15]. Paul's use of this expression does not mean that 'it was done by his own power, but only through his instrumentality; for it is not the work of any man to reshape and renew a human soul in the image of God, and it is with this act of spiritual regeneration that he is now dealing' (Calvin).

This tactful preamble is designed to enlist Philemon's sympathy before Paul dramatically reveals the name of his child: 'It is Onesimus!' (Moffatt). Paul's plea for Onesimus is often compared with the letter written by Pliny the Younger in which he asks Sabinianus to forgive his freedman for having run away. But though both letters deal with a similar situation, the contrasts are more striking than the resemblances. Pliny is uncertain of the future good conduct of the freedman, but Paul has no doubt about the slave's. In assuming that Sabinianus will be justly angry, Pliny begs him not to resort to torture; whereas Paul not only counts on Philemon's forgiveness but also expects him to receive his slave as a brother beloved [verse 16]. Pliny sternly threatened the freedman, but there is no hint that Paul spoke severely to the slave (so Scroggie). Pliny's letter appeals to Stoic virtue, but Paul's reckons on the response of Christian love.

11: who once was unprofitable to thee, but now is profitable to thee and to me:

Onesimus, whose name means 'profitable', must have rendered very grudging service to his master before his flight. But Paul here assures Philemon with a playful touch of humour that the slave who had once been *unprofitable* to him is now *profitable* to them both [Col. 3:22ff.; verse 13]. 'Christianity knows nothing of hopeless cases. It professes its ability to take the most crooked stick and bring it straight, to flash a new power into the blackest carbon, which will turn it into a diamond' (Maclaren).

12: whom I have sent back to thee in his own person, that is, my very heart:

This verse shows the strength of Paul's affection for his new son in the faith [verse 10]. 'In Onesimus, Paul sends his own heart, a part of himself, all his own tender emotions as they are centred in Onesimus. Can there be a question as to how Philemon will treat what Paul sends him?' (Lenski).

13: whom I would fain have kept with me, that in thy behalf he might minister unto me in the bonds of the gospel: 14: but without thy mind I would do nothing; that thy goodness should not be as of necessity, but of free will.

Onesimus gave evidence of the great change in his life by serving Paul so faithfully that he would have liked to keep him. And though the imprisoned apostle might well have claimed such service from Philemon in the person of his slave, he resolved to do nothing without Philemon's consent so that his goodness would not appear constrained but freely willed. It is because love cannot be compelled that Paul refuses to intrude on a decision that must be Philemon's own (so

Lohse). Some have thought that Paul is here asking Philemon for the return of Onesimus. But in the light of what follows [verses 15, 16], his deliberately vague reference to 'thy goodness' evidently means that 'Philemon's kindly reception of Onesimus must not even seem to be constrained' (Vincent).

15: For perhaps he was therefore parted from thee for a season, that thou shouldest have him for ever;

Instead of fixing Philemon's attention upon the desertion of Onesimus, Paul uses a euphemistic expression which suggests that God had overruled this evil for good. 'He does not say *he parted himself*, but *he was parted:* since the design was not Onesimus' own to depart for this or that reason: just as Joseph also, when excusing his brethren, says [*Gen.* 45:5] *God did send me hither*' (Chrysostom as cited by Lightfoot). Hence it seems that God's purpose in this brief parting was that Philemon might enter into a new relationship with Onesimus which not even death could dissolve [verse 16].

16: no longer as a servant, but more than a servant, a brother beloved, specially to me, but how much rather to thee, both in the flesh and in the Lord.

Although Onesimus was still a slave, he could no longer be treated merely as a slave, for he was far more than that. The relationship between master and slave is now on an entirely different plane, because both are in Christ [*1 Cor.* 7:21–24; *Col.* 3:11].

The grace of God has made the slave 'a brother beloved'. Onesimus is especially loved by Paul, but how much more should this be true of Philemon, since Onesimus belonged to him in the double sense of being both his slave and his brother. 'In the flesh Philemon had the brother for a slave; in the Lord he had the slave for a brother' (H. A. W. Meyer).

17: If then thou countest me a partner, receive him as myself.

If then Philemon considers Paul as his 'partner' [v 6], a sharer in the same faith, he is to receive Onesimus as he would the apostle himself! For to do otherwise would be to deny the reality of that bond which makes all believers fellow-members of the body of Christ.

18: But if he hath wronged thee at all, or oweth thee aught, put that to mine account;

What Paul only expresses hypothetically is in fact the case, for Onesimus must have robbed Philemon of a considerable sum to have paid for the long journey to Rome. To remove this obstacle to their reconciliation, Paul himself undertakes the responsibility for the debt and asks Philemon to charge it to his account. But though the offer is made in all seriousness, the next verse shows that Paul did not really expect it to be taken up.

19: I Paul write it with mine own hand, I will repay it: that I say not unto thee that thou owest to me even thine own self besides.

Here Paul takes up the pen from his amanuensis, and presents Philemon with his signed IOU. This promise to pay would be legally binding, but the creditor is at once reminded that he owes much more than a sum of money, even his own self! Philemon's obligation to Paul thus far exceeds the loss he had sustained through Onesimus, for he owed his salvation to Paul's ministry. And as this is a claim which can never be repaid, Paul is confident that Philemon will not press him for the payment of the lesser debt. 'By putting it this way, Paul wishes to remind Philemon of the pardon he himself received, to make him understand how grace freely received calls to remission of debt, when a fellow sinner also comes to conversion' (C. Bouma, cited by Müller).

20: Yea, brother, let me have joy of thee in the Lord: refresh my heart in Christ.

The confirmatory particle 'yea' gathers up all that Paul has said on behalf of Onesimus, and introduces a final personal plea to Philemon: 'Let me have some benefit from you in the Lord' (Arndt-Gingrich). He who owes the right to be called 'brother' to Paul's ministry is now able to bring some benefit to his benefactor by receiving back the slave as his 'brother' in the same family of faith [verse 16]. Since Philemon had refreshed the hearts of the saints with his deeds of love [verse 7], he must not neglect this opportunity of refreshing Paul's heart. The phrases 'in the Lord' and 'in Christ' are perhaps meant to remind Philemon that only the Lord could enable him to show such grace to the one who had wronged him.

21: Having confidence in thine obedience I write unto thee, knowing that thou wilt do even beyond what I say.

Paul is writing with every confidence in Philemon's obedience, but as the apostle has chosen to entreat rather than command [verse 8], the obedience in view here must be that of the disciple to his Lord. With the earthly master's obedience to his Master in heaven thus assured, Paul knows that Philemon will do even more than he says. To understand this as a veiled request to give Onesimus his freedom is certainly rash. As it is enough for Paul to have shown that Onesimus is a brother to be loved, he refuses to specify how that love is to be expressed, and this is left entirely to the Christian judgment of his friend.

22: But withal prepare me also a lodging: for I hope that through your prayers I shall be granted unto you.

Since Paul evidently anticipates an early release from prison, he asks Philemon to prepare a guest room for him. 'There is a gentle compulsion in this mention of a personal visit to Colossae. The Apostle would thus be able to see for himself that Philemon had not disappointed his expectations' (Lightfoot). Paul expresses the hope that God will answer the prayers of the church ('your' is plural) on his behalf, so that he may be soon restored to them.

According to Philippians 2:24, Paul was planning to visit Macedonia after being set free, and perhaps he intended to come to Colossae via Macedonia. Although he makes no mention of travelling west to Spain [*Rom.* 15:23, 24], the testimony of Clement (AD 95) suggests that he fulfilled this long cherished ambition before he was again arrested and brought back to Rome to suffer death at the hands of Nero (c. AD 67).

23: Epaphras, my fellow-prisoner in Christ Jesus, saluteth thee; 24: and so do Mark, Aristarchus, Demas, Luke, my fellow-workers.

Five of Paul's companions send their greetings (see comments on Colossians 4:10–14), but here he calls Mark, Aristarchus, Demas, and Luke his fellow-workers. Calvin says of the later desertion of Demas: 'And if one of Paul's assistants became weary and discouraged and was afterwards drawn away by the vanity of the world, let none of us rely too much on our own zeal lasting even one year, but remembering how much of the journey still lies ahead, let us ask God for steadfastness.'

25: The grace of our Lord Jesus Christ be with your spirit. Amen.

After addressing Philemon in the singular from verse 4, Paul reverts to the plural 'your' as he prays that Christ's grace may rest on the entire community who will hear the letter read out as they meet for worship [verse 2]. Paul's loveliest letter is thus brought to a fitting conclusion with the same word of 'grace' which is his mint-mark in every Epistle.

[The bibliography for Colossians and Philemon is at the close of the commentary on Colossians.]

SOLI DEO GLORIA

Hebrews

INTRODUCTION

It is certain that the first readers of this Epistle knew its author [13:18, 22], but this knowledge has been lost to posterity because he did not put his name to it. Consequently the identity of the writer remains one of the unsolved mysteries of New Testament introduction. Its attribution to the Apostle Paul is more convenient than convincing, and the many modern attempts to establish the author's identity have failed to pierce this veil of anonymity (though Luther's choice of Apollos – *Acts* 18:24–28 – still seems the likeliest guess!). However, the providential suppression of the name of its human author is evidently intended to focus attention upon the divine origin of the message itself. When God is acknowledged as the real speaker it is of no consequence if a particular voice he chooses to use cannot be recognized [1:1].

It is almost as great a problem to determine the identity of those addressed by the writer. Some scholars have suggested that it was intended for Gentile readers, but the argument of the letter strongly supports the traditional belief that it was sent to Hebrew Christians. It is reasonable to suppose that they were living in Rome [13:24], where the threat of further persecution tempted them to renounce their faith in Christ and return to the safety of a religion which was acknowledged by the State [10:32–34, 12:4]. The author's treatment of his theme suggests a date shortly before the fall of Jerusalem in AD 70, when the sacrificial system was abruptly terminated by the destruction of the Temple.

Hence this 'word of exhortation' was called forth by the failure of these Jewish believers to grasp the absolute finality of that revelation which God has given to men in Christ. They must understand that those rites and ceremonies under which the gospel was typically set forth in former days have been superseded by the advent of the one in whom they have found their perfect fulfilment. That priesthood in which men 'were not suffered to continue by reason of death' has been abolished by the once-for-all redemptive achievement of Christ who is 'a priest for ever after the order of Melchizedek'. For when the true glory of Christ's heavenly Priesthood is discerned all earthly pretensions to the sacerdotal office must be abandoned.

CHAPTER ONE

The keynote of the whole Epistle is struck in its grand opening statement which introduces Christ both as the revealer and fulfiller of God's last word to men. For though God formerly spoke to the fathers in the prophets, it is only in the Person and work of his Son that he has fully revealed himself. Thus Christ, in his teaching office (Prophet), redeeming work (Priest), and heavenly session (King), is the one Mediator through whom we must now make all our approaches to God [verses 1–3]. Since the Jews believed that the law was ministered by angels, it was necessary for the author to prove the Son's superiority over these exalted creatures [verse 4]. Hence he appeals to the testimony of Scripture in a series of seven quotations. The first three which are cited set forth the essential dignity of the Son [verses 5, 6,]; the fourth and fifth contrast the obedience of the angels with the sovereignty of the Son [verses 7–9]; the sixth shows that the angels are related to Christ as creatures to their Creator [verses 10–12]; and the seventh points to the Son's present enthronement at God's right hand, whereas the angels pursue their ministries in order to fulfil the Son's commands [verses 13, 14].

1: God, having of old time spoken unto the fathers in the prophets by divers portions and in divers manners, 2: hath at the end of these days spoken unto us in his Son, whom he appointed heir of all things, through whom also he made the worlds; 3: who being the effulgence of his glory, and the very image of his substance, and upholding all things by the word of his power, when he had made purification of sins, sat down on the right hand of the Majesty on high;

In this sublime announcement of the Epistle's theme its author is not merely reminding those who had been privileged to receive the divine oracles of the undisputed fact that God had spoken to the fathers, but he rather seeks to underline the preparatory and progressive character of that revelation. In former days God spoke to Israel 'in the prophets' at various times and in a great variety of ways. These men were not free to interpret the message they had received from God in words of their own choosing, for the divine impulse under which they spoke extended to the very words they uttered [*2 Pet.* 1:21].

Geerhardus Vos makes the following comment on the significance of the preposition which is used here: 'To say that God was speaking in the prophets need not detract at all from their intelligence, but it does serve to emphasize the absolute character of the resultant prophecies. We need not be concerned so much about the processes of revelation, provided we maintain a firm conviction that the product of revelation is truly the infallible Word of God. This we find in Hebrews, which lays strong stress on the fact that the revelation was *in* the prophets.'

Among men in general there is unbelief in the Word of God because it is commonly mistaken for a purely human word which may be rejected without fear of punishment. Micaiah, it was held, could not have spoken God's Word, for his testimony was not acceptable to Ahab, and Jehoiakim at a later date burnt the scroll which, in his view, was no more than the pessimistic utterance of a very troublesome prophet. But God vindicated his Word, and incidentally his servants, in the judgment which overtook those who opposed it [*1 Kings* 22; *Jer.* 36]. Yet that which sinners use as an excuse for their repudiation of Scripture is in fact the mark of its gracious character. It is for our safety that God veils his glory and sends his Word to us through his servants the prophets who speak as we are able to hear it. For when God did speak directly to the children of Israel they had no doubt that it was God who spoke to them, but they were so terrified by it that 'they said unto Moses, Speak thou with us, and we will hear; but let not God speak with us, lest we die' [*Exod.* 20:19]. Those who now stubbornly refuse to hear Moses and the prophets will believe their testimony one day, for there are no agnostics in hell [*Luke* 16:19–31].

It is therefore spiritual suicide to neglect that Word which was written by human hands, but which is nevertheless the veritable speech of the living God addressed to our hearts. 'No matter whether written by Moses, the Prophets, or the Apostles of our Lord and Saviour, the one subject of the Bible is the Man Christ Jesus, 'who is over all, God blessed for ever' [*Rom.* 9:5]. The testimony of Jesus is the spirit of prophecy, therefore thus saith the Lord himself, 'Search the Scriptures', for Moses wrote of Me, David wrote of Me, the Prophets wrote of Me, and they are they which testify of ME' (Brownlow North, *The Rich Man and Lazarus*, pp. 108–9).

Hath at the end of these days spoken unto us in a Son (ASV margin): It was at the end of these days of Messianic expectation that God spoke his last word 'unto us' in his Son. Christ's fulfilment of Israel's ancestral hope not only brought to an end the period of promise, but also marked the beginning of 'the age to come'. These Hebrew believers could only contemplate a return to the tangible ceremonies of the Levitical system because they had completely failed to grasp the distinctive character of the dispensation in which they were now living. Such a lack of spiritual discernment always leads to the same result, for where ignorance concerning the purpose of Christ's coming prevails, a relapse into some form of ritualism becomes inevitable.

In former times God spoke to the fathers 'in *the* prophets', but now he has spoken 'unto us in *a* Son'. Or rather 'One who is Son', for the absence of the definite article here underlines the essential deity of him who is *by nature* a Son. 'God spake to us in one who has this character that He is Son' (Westcott). It is the transcendent dignity of the One through whom this final revelation is made which emphasizes the great responsibility of those who are the recipients of it. 'But last of all he sent unto them his son' [Matt. 21:37]. After sending his own Son, God had no one greater to send. Thus Christ is God's last word to man.

'In opposition to this *gradual revelation* of the mind of God under the Old Testament, the apostle intimates that now by Jesus, the Messiah, the Lord hath at once begun and finished the whole revelation of his will, according to their own hopes and expectation. So, Jude 3, the faith was 'once delivered unto the saints;' not in *one day*, not in *one sermon*, or by *one person*, but at *one season*, or under one dispensation, comprising all the time from the entrance of the Lord Christ upon his ministry to the closing of the canon of Scripture; which period was now at hand. This season being once past and finished, no new revelation is to be expected, to the end of the world. Nothing shall be added unto nor altered in the worship of God any more. God will not do it; men that attempt it, do it on the price of their souls' (John Owen).

Since those addressed were faltering in their profession of faith because they entertained an inadequate view of Christ, their instructor immediately corrects this basic error by setting forth his unique glory in seven majestic assertions. The pre-eminence of the Son guarantees the superiority of that revelation which is mediated to mankind solely through him. In these days when the propagandists from the cults aggressively hawk their spurious wares from door to door, it is vital for us to realize that a truncated Christology forms the foundation of all false teaching, and that it never fails to produce a deformed Christianity [*2 John* 7–11].

Whom he appointed heir of all things: 1. This was the Father's eternal appointment of the Son to be the mediatorial heir of the universe. For though he possessed a natural authority over all things as the eternal Son, he became incarnate so that through his obedience unto death he might acquire the lordship with which he is even now invested. Moreover, the future universal recognition of Christ's sovereignty over the whole of the created order cannot fail to be realized because it is the subject of this divine decree [*Phil.* 2:9–11]. But since grace promises all believers a share in this dominion, John Trapp quaintly exhorts, 'Be married to this heir, and have all!' [*Rom.* 8:17].

Through whom also he made the worlds: 2. Next, it is explicitly affirmed that the universe was given its existence by the Son's fulfilment of the Father's creative fiat. In his comment on Colossians 1:16, J. B. Lightfoot draws attention to the fact that the Alexandrian Jew, Philo, commonly used the same preposition, 'through' (*dia*), to describe the purely passive and instrumental role which he assigned to the Logos (the Word) in the work of creation. However, if the writers of the New Testament adopted Philo's language, both here and in John 1:3, they certainly discarded his thought, for in Scripture the Eternal Word is represented as the 'co-operating agent' in the creation of the universe (*Commentary on Colossians*, p. 155). The word which is translated in this verse as 'worlds,' usually means 'ages' (ASV margin), and this suggests the further thought that Christ continues to uphold and direct 'the universe, including all space and ages, and all material and spiritual existences' (A. R. Fausset). None but the Lord of the ages could comfort his followers with the assurance, 'Lo, I am with you always, even unto the consummation of the age' [*Matt.* 28:20, ASV margin].

Who being the effulgence of his glory: 3. Whereas the previous statements described the splendour of the Son in terms of the Father's decree, in this verse there is a portrayal of what the Son is in his own nature. Here we are told that all the brightness of God shines forth from him who is the very 'radiance of his glory' (Arndt-Gingrich). The divine glory which once rested upon the 'tent of meeting' has been fully manifested in the Incarnate Word who 'tabernacled among us,' 'full of grace and truth' [*John* 1:14, ASV margin].

'Among the many causes of the extreme attachment of the Jews to the Mosaic economy, this was no doubt one, that such splendid displays of the Divine majesty had been made in connection with it; but the Apostle points them to *the glory that excelleth,* and intimates to them, that humble as was the external appearance of Jesus of Nazareth, He was the true Shekinah, in whom dwelt the Godhead bodily – the real, substantial, adequate representation of the King eternal, immortal, and invisible, whom no eye hath seen, or can see' (John Brown).

And the impress of his substance (ASV margin): 4. This phrase shows that the Son 'is both personally distinct from, and yet literally equal to, Him of whose essence He is the adequate imprint' (H. P. Liddon) [*2 Cor.* 4:4; *Col.* 1:15]

As Calvin observes, the term 'reminds us that God is known truly and firmly only in Christ. His likeness is not just veiled and concealed, but is an express image which represents God Himself, just as a coin bears the image of the die-stamp from which it is struck'. Although we cannot 'by searching find out God' [*Job* 11:7], yet he is perfectly made known to us through him who said, 'he that hath seen me hath seen the Father' [*John* 14:9]. Thus these two words, 'effulgence' and 'impress', which occur only here in the New Testament, suggest complementary images corresponding to the terms 'co-essential' and 'only-begotten': for it is in Christ that the *revelation* of God's glory is seen ('effulgence'), and it is in him that the divine *essence* is made intelligibly distinct for man ('impress') –(so Westcott).

And upholding all things by the word of his power: 5. This impressive declaration attributes to the Son the guiding of all things in the universe to their appointed goal. 'Christ is therefore represented as the *Author of providence* in the broadest sense. To say that He does this *by the word of his power* amounts to an attestation of His *divine* power' (Vos) [Col 1:16–17].

'This abundantly discovers the vanity and folly of them who make use of the creation in an opposition unto the Lord Christ and his peculiar interest in this world. His own power is the very ground that they stand upon in their opposition unto him, and all things which they use against him consist in him. They hold their lives absolutely at the pleasure of him whom they oppose; and they act against him without whose continual supportment and influence they could neither live nor act one moment: which is the greatest madness and most contemptible folly imaginable' (John Owen)

When he had made purification of sins: 6. The setting of this statement shows that it is impossible to grasp the meaning of the atonement unless it is seen within the context of eternity. The scandal of the cross is only removed when we understand that Christ suffered 'by the determinate counsel and foreknowledge of God,' and that he did this to make purification of sins. Thus our apprehension of the essential glory of the Mediator will be the measure of our glorying in the cross [*2 Cor.* 8:9; *Phil.* 2:6–81. The sacrificial language used here suggests that what was foreshadowed in the purifications prescribed by the Levitical law has been finally fulfilled in Christ's one perfect sacrifice [9:26]. 'By himself' [AV] is omitted by the ASV, but the Greek usage expresses the same thought. As Westcott puts it: 'Christ Himself, in His own Person made the purification: He did not make it as something distinct from Himself, simply provided by His power'. In other words, Christ 'was at once priest and victim – priest to offer the sacrifice, and victim to bear the sin, here considered as a defilement that must be purged away' (George Smeaton).

Sat down on the right hand of the Majesty on high: 7. Upon the completion of his atoning work Christ sat down in the place of supreme dignity and power as the enthroned Priest-King of his people [*Psa.* 110:1]. In contrast to the Levitical priests who stood during their ministrations because their work was never finished [10:11], our High Priest [8:1] assumed this position of universal authority 'when he had offered one sacrifice for sins for ever' [10:12]. 'Angels and men stand before the throne, the Son sits, not in idleness, but in active power and rule' (R. C. H. Lenski).

4: having become by so much better than the angels, as he hath inherited a more excellent name than they.

The author now begins a series of comparisons in order to prove that the superiority of the New Covenant resides in the excellence of the Mediator through whom it is inaugurated Although this verse refers to Christ's Sonship as the Messiah his fitness to fulfil this function rests upon that essential dignity which he always possessed as the Son of God [verse 2]. Christ's eternal ascendancy over the angelic hosts was apparently eclipsed during the baffling interlude of his passion, but his absolute supremacy over them was openly demonstrated when he entered into the Messianic inheritance, and 'sat down on the right hand of the Majesty on high' as the triumphant Son of Man [1:3, 2:7, 9].

Throughout this chapter 'the angels are not compared with Christ merely as exalted creatures, but also as revealers and administrators, in which respects also Christ is superior to them' (Vos). In the giving of the law to Israel God was separated from man by a double mediation – by angelic intermediaries and by Moses – but in hailing Jesus as our 'Emmanuel' we gratefully recognize that in the gospel God himself has stepped alongside us in the glorious person of his only begotten Son [*Deut.* 33:2; *Psa.* 68:17; *Matt.* 1:23; *Acts* 7:53; *Gal.* 3:19]. The favourite adjective of the writer appears here for the first time, though it is not difficult 'to see behind the apologetic *better* the dogmatic *best*" (A. B. Bruce) [1:4, 6:9, 7:7, 19, 22; 8:6 (twice); 9:23; 10:34; 11:16, 35, 40; 12:24].

5: For unto which of the angels said he at any time, Thou art my Son, This day have I begotten thee? and again, I will be to him a Father, and he shall be to me a Son?

This is the first of seven citations from the Old Testament which are introduced to substantiate the foregoing assertion. Here the interrogative form demands a negative reply, for what is predicated of the Son in Psalm 2:7 is never attributed to the angels in Scripture. On this John Owen makes the significant observation, 'An argument, then, taken negatively from the authority of the Scripture in matters of faith, or what relates to the worship of God, is valid and effectual, and here consecrated for ever to the use of the church by the apostle.' Thus the silence of Scripture affords no licence for the practice of those rites and ceremonies which owe their origin to the sinful imaginations of men rather than to the positive commandment of God [*Isa.* 8:20]. Angels are collectively referred to as the 'sons of God' in the Old Testament [*Job* 38:7], 'but *Son* is singular to Christ, and incommunicable to any other' (Matthew Poole).

'This day' has no reference to the eternal generation of the Son, an interpretation which Calvin quite rightly dismissed as a 'Subtlety', but rather points to the particular time when Christ's claim to divine Sonship was decisively vindicated. Since the resurrection marked the beginning of Christ's exaltation, it makes no material difference whether the fulfilment of this prophecy is referred to that event, as it is in Acts 13:33, or whether it is applied to the pre-eminence of the Ascended Christ, as it is in verses 4, 5 and in chapter 5:5. For as John Murray has well said on Romans 1:4, 'Everything antecedent in the incarnate life of our Lord moves toward the resurrection and everything subsequent rests upon it and is conditioned by it' (*The Epistle to the Romans,* p. 12).

The second testimony which could never be ascribed to angels is taken from 2 Samuel 7:14 and respects the promise which God made to David concerning the establishment of the kingdom under his son Solomon, but it is evident that the primary fulfilment of this oracle did not exhaust its meaning. It also spoke prophetically of the Father's relation to the Messianic Son who 'was born of the seed of David according to the flesh' [*Rom.* 1:4], for it was under Him alone that the Davidic throne could be established 'for ever' [*2 Sam.* 7:13]. As 'the eternal and natural relation that is between the Father and Son' cannot be the subject of a promise, John Owen therefore explains the verse in the following way. 'If it be asked on what account God would thus be a father unto Jesus Christ in this peculiar manner, it must be answered that the radical, fundamental cause of it lay in the relation that was between them from his eternal generation; but he *manifested* himself to be his father, and engaged to deal with him in the love and care of a father, as he had accomplished his work of mediation on the earth and was exalted unto his throne and rule in heaven.'

6: And when he again bringeth in the firstborn into the world he saith, And let all the angels of God worship him.

And again, when he bringeth in (AV): The third quotation is apparently taken from *Deut.* 32:43, LXX, though the same thought is also found in *Psa.* 97:7, LXX. The supporters of the translation favoured by the ASV refer the verse to the second advent, but as the evidence for this is not conclusive it is better to adhere to the AV where 'again' simply signifies the bringing forth of a further proof.

It is the constant aim of the writer to make his readers realize that 'the age to come' began with the heavenly investiture of Christ, and it is the present subjection of the inhabited earth to the sovereignty of the exalted Mediator which made necessary a change in worship. Hence the worship which the angels were commanded to pay to Jehovah under the old economy is now transferred to Christ as the 'firstborn' of God's new creation, a term which indicates his 'supreme rank and Lordship' over all things [*Col.* 1:15].

It should be particularly noted that it was God the Father who instituted this change in worship, for he does not promise 'to accept any thing but what is of his own appointment; so that it is the greatest folly imaginable to undertake any thing in his worship and service but what his appointment gives warrant for' (John Owen). The verse reveals the foolishness of those who would withdraw their allegiance from the One whom even angels worship, for 'Whatever diversity of opinion there may be among men as to worshipping Christ Jesus, there is obviously but one mind and one heart in heaven' (John Brown).

7: And of the angels he saith, Who maketh his angels winds, and his ministers a flame of fire:

In the fourth quotation, this time from *Psa.* 104:41 the word 'maketh' underlines the inferiority of the angels to the Son. 'He is the Son; they are the creatures of God. *Only begotten* is the description of His mode of existence; *made* is the description of theirs. *All* their powers are communicated powers; and however high they may stand in the scale of creation, it is in that scale they stand, which places them infinitely below Him, who is so the Son of God as to be "God over all, blessed for ever"' (John Brown). This graphic description of the angels' service does not imply any transformation of their essence, but rather suggests that 'they are clothed with God's powers to accomplish His will in the realm of nature' (Thomas Hewitt) [12:18; *Exod.* 19:16, 18].

8: but of the Son he saith, Thy throne, O God, is for ever and ever; And the sceptre of uprightness is the sceptre of thy kingdom. 9: Thou hast loved righteousness, and hated iniquity; Therefore God, thy God, hath anointed thee with the oil of gladness above thy fellows.

The creaturely obedience of the angels is now contrasted with the divine sovereignty of the Son in this fifth quotation, which is from *Psa.* 45:6, 7. As H. C. Leupold says, the vocative 'O God' is the simple and obvious translation, and modern critical attempts to evade it appear to be based on the prior assumption that such a confession of the deity of the Messiah is impossible (despite *Isa.* 9:6). Yet the king who is addressed as 'God' in verse 8, is at the same time distinguished from God in verse 9, which speaks of 'God, thy God'. 'This paradox is consistent with the incarnation, but mystifying in any other context. It is an example of Old Testament language bursting its banks, to demand a more than human fulfilment (as did *Psa.* 110:1, according to our Lord)' (Derek Kidner).

But of the Son he saith, Thy throne, O God, is for ever and ever: As God's messengers the angels are endowed with marvellous powers, but they remain creatures who are always subject to the Creator's sovereign will. Incomparably exalted above them is the Son to whom alone this throne belongs. Earthly emperors might indeed blasphemously arrogate divine honours to themselves, but because this King is truly hailed by God as 'God' his kingdom must endure for ever. 'His it was by natural inheritance, as God the Son; and as man united to the Godhead, he inheriteth the privileges of that person. This natural dominion over all things remaineth for ever' (Poole) [*Col.* 1:16]

And the sceptre of uprightness is the sceptre of thy kingdom: Unlike the kings of this world whose decisions are often influenced by partiality or prejudice, the Son exercises his royal rule in perfect righteousness [*Isa.* 11:5]. Our own history shows that those monarchs who insisted upon their divine right to rule were conspicuously lacking in this divine attribute! But Christ's kingdom is an everlasting kingdom, because none but he could bring in everlasting righteousness [*Dan.* 9:24].

Thou hast loved righteousness, and hated iniquity: During the period of his humiliation Christ proved his undeviating attachment to righteousness and his inflexible hatred of iniquity, wherefore 'also God highly exalted him, and gave unto him the name which is above every name' [*Phil.* 2:9].

Therefore God, thy God, hath anointed thee with the oil of gladness: This is a description of the heavenly coronation which followed the victorious completion of Christ's earthly ministry. It is to this event that Peter alludes when he told the Jews on the day of Pentecost 'that God hath made that same Jesus, whom ye have crucified, both Lord and Christ' [*Acts* 2:36]. The unalloyed joy of this occasion distinguishes it from that unction of the Spirit which Christ received when 'he was a man of sorrows, acquainted with grief and exposed to innumerable evils and troubles' (John Owen).

Above thy fellows: 'The angels cannot be intended; their inferiority to the Son is so insisted on here that they could scarcely be described as His "fellows". It is most likely that the reference is to the "many sons" of chapter 2: 10, whom the first born Son is not ashamed to call His 'brethren' [2:11] . . . Their joy is great, because of their companionship with Him, but His is greater still' (F. F. Bruce).

10: And, Thou, Lord, in the beginning didst lay the foundation of the earth, and the heavens are the works of thy hands: 11: They shall perish; but thou continuest and they all shall wax old as doth a garment; 12: And as a mantle shalt thou roll them up, as a garment, and they shall be changed but thou art the same, and thy years shall not fail.

The sixth quotation is again from the Psalms. *Psa.* 102:25–27, LXX is cited to show that the angels owe even their very existence to Christ. This work of creation obviously cannot be ascribed to Christ as man, yet it is here properly assigned to him as the eternal Son who became incarnate for our salvation [*John* 1:3; *Col.* 1:16]. In verse 12 the Son is further identified as the author of that cataclysmic judgment which finally shall usher in 'new heavens and a new earth, wherein dwelleth righteousness' [*2 Pet.* 3:13].

Despite the apparent fixity of the created order, the Word of God declares that the cosmos must suffer change, but Christ continues for ever in the glorious unity of his Divine-human person [13:8]. This should teach us that 'such is the frailty of the nature of man, and such the perishing condition of all created things, that none can ever obtain the least stable consolation but what ariseth from an interest in the omnipotency, sovereignty, and eternity of the Lord Christ' (John Owen).

Swift to its close ebbs out life's little day;
Earth's joys grow dim, its glories pass away;
Change and decay in all around I see;
O Thou who changest not, abide with me.
Henry F. Lyte

13: But of which of the angels hath he said at any time, Sit thou on my right hand, till I make thine enemies the footstool of thy feet?

The seventh quotation – *Psa.* 110:1 – is introduced by a rhetorical question that demands a negative reply. God never addressed any angel in such terms, but the author plainly infers that he did so speak to the Son. This Psalm is cited more frequently in the New Testament than any other, and it is also the foundation upon which the whole superstructure of the Epistle is built. It is the repeated application of the fourth verse of the psalm to Christ which gives the letter its distinctive character, for it shows that he exercises this universal dominion as the enthroned Priest-King, thus combining in his own person two offices which were always kept separate in Israel. In verse one, David hails the Messiah as his Lord because only One who was himself divine could be advanced by Jehovah to the place of supreme power.

'As he was God, he was David's Lord, but not his son; as he was man, he was David's son, and so absolutely could not be his Lord; in his person, as he was God and man, he was his Lord and his son, – which is the intention of our Saviour's question, *Matt.* 22:45' (John Owen).

Till I make thine enemies the footstool of thy feet? The image is taken from conquerors who emphasized their triumph by placing their feet upon the necks of the conquered [*Josh.* 10:24; *Heb.* 10:13]. Although the word 'till' does not indicate a time when Christ shall cease to reign, *1 Cor.* 15:24 does refer to the end of Christ's mediatorial rule. This passage is explained by Charles Hodge, 'When that is done, i.e., when he has subdued all his enemies, then he will no longer reign over the universe as Mediator, but only as God; while his headship over his people is to continue for ever.' As the church is still constantly attacked by the enemies of Christ it is worth recalling Calvin's timely comment on this verse: 'Certainly if we are to believe what our eyes see, then the kingdom of Christ seems to be on the verge of ruin. But this promise that Christ will never be dragged from His throne but that rather He will lay low all His enemies, banishes from us all fear.'

14: Are they not all ministering spirits, sent forth to do service for the sake of them that shall inherit salvation?

This question, which requires an affirmative response, places the subordination of the angels in strong contrast with the previous declaration of the Son's sovereignty. As their name implies, they are God's messengers 'sent forth to do service for the sake of them that shall inherit salvation'. This refers to the future possession of the heavenly inheritance. Salvation is a present reality of Christian experience, but its full realization awaits the forthcoming consummation. Those who receive salvation as an inheritance clearly have contributed nothing towards it, and this divine patrimony is bestowed upon none but sons [*John* 1:12, 13]. 'The angels serve in reference to that salvation which the Son, thus exalted above them, has procured for man. *They* stand before God as ministers awaiting His commands, but *the Son* sits at God's right hand: *they* minister to God and man, but *the Son* rules; and everything, even against its will, must bow to His dominion' (Franz Delitzsch).

CHAPTER TWO

It is the distinctive style of the author to interlace his exposition with exhortation, and in the first of these he warns of the danger of drifting from God's great salvation in Christ [verses 1–4]. He next explains that Christ's seeming inferiority to the angels during the period of his humiliation was the essential prelude to his exaltation, which fulfilled the prophecy that promised universal sovereignty to man [verses 5–9]. As the intrusion of sin meant that man's destiny could only be achieved through suffering, it was both necessary and fitting that the Son should become like his brethren, for it is through his vicarious endurance of sin's penalty that he has brought many sons to glory [verses 10–13]. Christ's purpose therefore in becoming man was to deprive the devil of the power of death, and to liberate those held captive by its dreadful bondage [verses 14, 15]. Hence the incarnation was the indispensable qualification for Christ's priesthood. For since his gracious design was not to help the angels but the seed of Abraham, he had to be made like his brethren in order to represent them before God and to make propitiation for their sins. Thus, having suffered being tempted, he is able to succour them that are tempted [verses 16–18].

1: Therefore we ought to give the more earnest heed to the things that were heard, lest haply we drift away from them.

Our author here interjects the first of the warnings with which his argument is punctuated. 'Therefore,' as Christ is so infinitely exalted above the angels, both in his person and his station, how urgent was the need for these Hebrews to give diligent attention to the message of salvation they had heard through the preaching of the gospel [4:2; *Rom.* 10:17]. This appeal to the glory of Christ lays the axe to the root of the tree of indifference, for a careless hearing of God's Word always stems from a failure to apprehend the unique majesty of the Mediator [*Matt.* 17:5]. It was this spiritual lassitude which had exposed them to the very real danger of drifting away from their desired haven. 'Lapse from truth and goodness is more often the result of inattention than of design. Drifting is a mark of death: giving heed, of life. The log drifts with the tide: the ship breasts the adverse waves, because someone is giving earnest heed' (Marvin R. Vincent).

2: For if the word spoken through angels proved steadfast, and every transgression and disobedience received a just recompense of reward;

Since there was a strict enforcement of the sanctions denounced against the transgressors of that revelation which was given through the mediation of angels [*Acts* 7:53; *Gal.* 3:19], then clearly those who neglect the salvation which was first spoken through the Lord will be punished with far greater severity [verse 3]. This argument expressly contradicts the illogical notion that despisers of the gospel will be treated with greater leniency than those who disobeyed the law of Moses [*Matt.* 11:20–24]. For if then 'every transgression' (each stepping aside from the law) and 'disobedience' (which results from an unwillingness to hear) received its *exact requital* or *just penalty,* those who now disregard the gospel must expect a judgment commensurate with the gravity of their guilt in refusing to heed God's own Son.

3: how shall we escape, if we neglect so great a salvation? which having at the first been spoken through the Lord, was confirmed unto us by them that heard;

How shall we escape: By expressing the warning in the form of a question, the writer appeals to the readers' own judgment, and thus makes his dissuasive from their contemplated apostasy far more effective than if he had positively declared, 'We shall not escape.'

If we neglect: To slight the gospel by neglect amounts to a rejection of its proffered pardon, and will be judged as such. 'Can any man perish more justly than they who refuse to be saved?' (John Owen).

So great a salvation? To believe the gospel is actually to receive that salvation, the greatness of which is beyond our computation and comprehension [*John* 3:16]. Thus the proper end in the publishing of the gospel is the salvation of those to whom it is sent; the incidental result is the damnation of those who spurn it [*John* 12:48; *2 Cor.* 2:15, 16].

Which having at the first been spoken through the Lord: The greatness of this salvation is attested by three indisputable facts [verses 3, 4]. 1. It was directly introduced by the Lord Himself. As the promised prophet [*Deut.* 18:18, 19], he 'came preaching the gospel of God' [*Mark* 1:14], and his own witness to himself gave the apostolic preaching not only its basis and content, but also its authority and power [*Luke* 4:21, 24:44].

Was confirmed unto us by them that heard: 2. It was faithfully transmitted to us by Christ's appointed witnesses. 'We heard it [verse 1] from those who heard, the immediate followers of the Lord. The writer thus puts himself in the second generation of Christians. They are not said to have heard the gospel directly from the Lord. Paul, on the other hand, claims that he received the gospel directly from Christ [*Gal.* 1:11]' (Vincent).

4: God also bearing witness with them, both by signs and wonders, and by manifold powers, and by gifts of the Holy Spirit, according to his own will.

God also bearing witness with them: 3. It was evidenced by signs and wonders, manifold deeds of power, and the supernatural endowments of the Spirit. This confident appeal to the miraculous display of divine power which accompanied the apostolic proclamation of the gospel obviously could never have been made if the wonders here described were completely unknown to the recipients of this Epistle. But it is equally unreasonable to expect the continuous manifestation of similar signs when there is now no new gospel to confirm and the canon of Scripture is complete. These gifts 'were part of the credentials of the Apostles as the authoritative agents of God in founding the church. Their function thus confined them to distinctively the Apostolic Church, and they necessarily passed away with it' (B. B. Warfield).

So also A. W. Pink: 'As there were *offices* extraordinary (apostles and prophets) at the beginning of our dispensation, so there were *gifts* extraordinary; and as successors were *not* appointed for the former, so a continuance was never intended for the latter . . . We no longer have the apostles with us and therefore the supernatural gifts (the communication of which was an essential part of "the *signs* of an apostle" – *2 Cor.* 12:12) are absent.'

5: For not unto angels did he subject the world to come, whereof we speak.

These Hebrews had become discouraged partly because they did not as yet possess those external blessings which they associated with the world to come. Their preoccupation with the future had made them blind to their present spiritual privileges, a disease which the author seeks to cure by insisting upon the reality of Christ's present rule. The old world was placed in subjection to the angels when sin broke man's dominion over it, but the new world began with the heavenly enthronement of Christ as the victorious Son of Man. Christianity 'thus marks the beginning of the future world. The author speaks of the great salvation of Christianity, which is so great because God has subjected the inhabited world to the rule of His people. This was the original goal of creation, but it was effected only in Christ. With Christ, therefore, we have a new creation' (Vos).

6: But one hath somewhere testified saying, What is man, that thou art

mindful of him? or the Son of man, that thou visitest him? 7: Thou madest him a little lower than the angels; Thou crownedst him with glory and honour and didst set him over the works of thy hands: 8a: Thou didst put all things in subjection under his feet.

In confirmation of his contention the author reminds his readers of a passage of Scripture which is well known to them, even if he has yet to teach them its prophetic meaning – *Psa.* 8:4–6. The Psalmist is filled with awe as he surveys the vastness of the heavens, and he marvels at the Creator's goodness in appointing frail and feeble man to the high dignity of being his vice-regent on earth. With man's *exaltation* over the created order in mind, it was natural for David to say that man was made only 'a little lower than the angels'.

But like every prophet he spoke better than he knew at the time [*1 Pet.* 1:10,11], and the inspiration of the same Spirit here leads this 'minister of the new covenant' to apply the same phrase to the *humiliation* of Christ [verse 9]. For as Westcott says, 'Words which were used of man in himself became first true of One Who being more than man took man's nature upon Him. In such a case the description of dignity was of necessity converted initially into a description of condescension.' Thus the destiny which Adam forfeited through sin was regained and realized through the obedience of the Son of Man who endured the shame of the cross for the sake of the joy that was set before him [12:2].

8b: For in that he subjected all things unto him, he left nothing that is not subject to him. But now we see not yet all things subjected to him.

Although the author's repetition of 'all things' shows that God has excepted nothing from the dominion of man, present experience sadly proves that the full accomplishment of this divine decree is still awaited.

9: But we behold him who hath been made a little lower than the angels, even Jesus, because of the suffering of death crowned with glory and honour, that by the grace of God he should taste of death for every man.

However, the application of the prophecy to Jesus exhibits the certainty of its realization, for faith perceives that the final glorification of the members is guaranteed by the present exaltation of the Head. And the fact that Jesus is now 'crowned with glory and honour' is here represented as the abiding consequence of the matchless stoop which had made him 'a little lower than the angels'. 'In becoming man Christ took upon Him a nature that was *capable* of dying. This the angels were not; and in *this* respect He was, for a season, made lower than they' (A. W. Pink). Yet his death was no peaceful quietus, for he willingly came to drain to its bitterest dregs the cup which our sins had mingled (James Denney).

That: The word expresses purpose and introduces the clause which explains the reason for Christ's death.

By the grace of God: 'This intimates that unmerited grace prompted God to give His Son, and to transfer guilt to Him. In short, whatever was vicarious was of grace in a special sense. A penal death was the effect of justice; but to admit a Surety-substitution was of grace' (George Smeaton).

He should taste of death: 'So that Christ by tasting of death had experience, knew what was in death, as threatened unto sinners. He found out and understood what bitterness was in that cup wherein it was given him' (John Owen).

For every man: The scope of this declaration is determined by the context, which shows that Christ died for 'them that shall inherit salvation' [1:14], the 'many sons' [2:10], those who are 'sanctified' [2:11], his 'brethren' [2:11, 12], and the 'children' whom God had given him [2:13]. 'Christ did taste death for every son to be brought to glory and for all the children whom God had given to him. But there is not the slightest warrant in this text to extend the reference of the vicarious death of Christ beyond those who are most expressly referred to in the context. This text shows how plausible off-hand quotation may be and yet how baseless is such an appeal in support of a doctrine of universal atonement' (John Murray, *Redemption – Accomplished and Applied*, p. 61).

10: For it became him, for whom are all things, and through whom are all things, in bringing many sons unto glory, to make the author of their salvation perfect through sufferings.

Although man idly dreams of salvation without atonement, this is a forcible reminder that it can never be safe to dispense with what is deemed to be necessary by him who is the Creator of all things and the sovereign Disposer of all events. The readers of the Epistle must resist the temptation to renounce their faith in a crucified Messiah, because the glorification of the 'many sons' could only be secured through the humiliation of their redeeming Head, who thus became the 'author' of their salvation.

As Geerhardus Vos points out, the word 'perfect' does not mean that 'Christ stood in need of moral improvement'. It rather indicates that his endurance of these sufferings perfectly fitted him to exercise this office for his people: 'Christ draws us after Himself to salvation. He led the way to glory' (Vos) [*Acts* 3:15]. 'Such is the desert of sin, and such is the immutability of the justice of God, that there was no way possible to bring sinners unto glory but by the death and sufferings of the Son of God, who undertook to be the captain of their salvation' (John Owen).

11: For both he that sanctifieth and they that are sanctified are all of one: for which cause he is not ashamed to call them brethren,

The character of this salvation is further defined by this description of the work which Christ performs for his people. He is the author of their sanctification. This does not here refer to a continuous process; it means that Christ has cleansed his people from their sin in order to make them fit to serve God. As Vos observes, 'Purifying, sanctifying, perfecting, lie with Paul in the moral subjective sphere, as is especially clear in the case of 'sanctification'. But in Hebrews the last named [i.e. sanctification] has as a rule nothing to do with the subjective moral transformation of the believer. It describes, on the contrary, what has been done through the sacrifice of Jesus outside of the believer, to render the way to God open for him. In Pauline language we should call this "justification," although that would not exactly reproduce the point of view' (*The Self-Disclosure of Jesus*, p. 301).

Now it is because the sanctifier and the sanctified are partakers of the same nature that 'he is not ashamed to call them brethren'. Pink points out that if 'all of one' alluded to God as their common Father this denial of shame would have been entirely out of place, for 'he could not then do otherwise than call them brethren'. But in fact the whole passage is intended to bring out 'the oneness of Christ with His people in their humiliation. In other words, the apostle is not here speaking of our being lifted up to Christ's level, but of His coming down to ours'.

12: saying, I will declare thy name unto my brethren, in the midst of the congregation will I sing thy praise.

Three testimonies are next introduced to prove that Christ is the Head of a new order of humanity, the first of which is from *Psa.* 22:22. This is from that part of the psalm which predicts the triumphant sequel to the Messiah's sufferings [*John* 20:17]. 'The constitution of the congregation or "church" (Greek: *ekklesia*), with Christ in the midst revealing God to His brethren, is possible only because of His sacrifice' (A. M. Stibbs).

13: And again, I will put my trust in him. And again, Behold, I and the children whom God hath given me.

It is because the national rejection of the Messiah was foreshadowed by Isaiah's own experience that his words are here fitly applied to Christ [*Isa.* 8:17–18]. Although his faithfulness to the divine commission had separated him from the nation at large the prophet continued to trust in God. However this isolation was not complete, for his ministry also resulted in the emergence of an elect remnant, even 'the children whom God hath given me' [*Isa.* 6:13].

'This identification extended not only to his disciples, of whom we read, but also to his children. These children were given him precisely for the express purpose of being identified with him in his trust in God. They were children of prophetic significance. Centuries later this was repeated, on a higher plane, in Christ. Again there was an unparalleled necessity for Christ to put his trust in God, and also there arose a close identification between Christ and the believers' (Vos). This passage, which is unique in describing believers as the children of Christ, strongly emphasizes his humanity. For Christ could not save the children whom God had given him in the eternal covenant of grace without first becoming their Kinsman-Redeemer, and he could not put his trust in God except as he was made man [*John* 17:2].

14: Since then the children are sharers in flesh and blood he also himself in like manner partook of the same; that through death he might bring to nought him that had the power of death, that is, the devil;

'Flesh and blood' were foreign to his existence as the eternal Son of God, but Christ willingly 'partook of the same' in, order to secure the salvation of his children. In thus stating the purpose of the incarnation, the author also removes its stigma, for as John Owen rightly insists, 'the first and principal end of the Lord Christ's assuming human nature, was not to reign in it, but to suffer and die in it'.

That through death he might bring to nought him that had the power of death, that is, the devil: The vital truth, which is so memorably expressed in this striking paradox, is that Christ's death was indispensably necessary to free his people from death's fearful bondage [verse 15]. For the children of Christ could only be delivered from the devil's dominion by his dying the death which was properly theirs. It was his vicarious endurance of the penalty of sin which annulled death's condemning power over them and made it but the portal to eternal life [*1 Cor.* 15:55–57]. 'Jesus suffered and overcame death; the devil, wielding death in his hand, succumbed' (J. A. Bengel).

15: and might deliver all them who through fear of death were all their lifetime subject to bondage.

'The judgment of God always shows itself in consciousness of sin. It is from this fear that Christ has released us, by undergoing our curse, and thus taking away what was fearful in death. Although we must still meet death, let us nevertheless be calm and serene in living and dying, when we have Christ going before us. If anyone cannot set his mind at rest by disregarding death, that man should know that he has not yet gone far enough in the faith of Christ' (Calvin) [9:27].

Scripture proclaims freedom from the fear of death through the finished work of Christ, but the best that atheistic philosophy can recommend to modern man is the free acceptance of death as the natural termination of his existence. Those who choose to experience such an authentic 'existence' thereby deprive themselves of that 'life' more abundant which is found only in the living Lord himself [*Rev.* 1:18].

As Robert Reymond puts it, 'Existentialism is fatalistic in its view that death can never be overcome and nihilistic in its view that death is the most proper possibility of human existence . . . Existentialism leaves men precisely where it finds them – lost, and without a Saviour' (*Introductory Studies in Contemporary Theology*, pp.166–7).

16: For verily not to angels doth he give help, but he giveth help to the seed of Abraham.

Although it is true that the verb used here does not directly describe Christ's assumption of our humanity, he could not have helped men without first becoming man himself. The idea of 'help' or 'succour' is by a metaphor drawn from the literal meaning 'of laying hold of another to rescue him from peril' (Thayer). It has this sense in 8:9 where God is said to have 'taken his people by the hand to deliver them from the land of bondage. Thus it is not of angels but of men that the Son of God takes hold. There is justice but no salvation for the angels who lost their first estate. 'Here sovereign grace interposeth, – the love of God to mankind, *Titus* 3:4. As to the angels, he "spared them not," *2 Pet*. 2:4. He spared not them, and "spared not his Son" for us, *Rom*. 8:32' (John Owen).

'The seed of Abraham' not only properly refers to the immediate readers of this Epistle, but also fitly includes the whole family of faith [*Gal*. 3:7].

17: Wherefore it behooved him in all things to be made like unto his brethren, that he might become a merciful and faithful high priest in things pertaining to God, to make propitiation for the sins of the people.

Here we are given the first *distinct* [1:3] intimation of what is to be the Epistle's leading theme by the word 'high priest', which 'is a shadow cast before from the great section of chapters 5–10' (C. J. Vaughan). As it was God's good pleasure to help men, it was incumbent upon Christ to be conformed to his brethren in 'all things', sin only excepted [4:15]. Hence our Mediator was taken from among men [5:1], in order that 'he might become a *merciful* and *faithful* high priest'. It is preferable with Westcott to relate both adjectives to Christ's work for men, rather than to refer 'faithful' to God. 'Our High-priest is "merciful" in considering the needs of each sinful man, and "faithful" ("one in whom the believer can trust") in applying the means which He administers.'

The expression 'to make propitiation for' appears here with sins as the object, and as it is obviously impossible to propitiate sin, it has been urged with some cogency that the word 'expiation' should be adopted instead (cf. H. Bushnell's definition: 'We propitiate only a person, and expiate only a fact or act or thing' – cited by L. Morris). But as F. F. Bruce remarks, 'if sins require to be expiated, it is because they are sins committed against someone who ought to be propitiated'. Christ therefore made propitiation *in respect of* the sins of his people, and it is by this satisfaction of divine justice that he gained access to God on their behalf.[1] As the Jews did not expect a suffering Messiah, the cross was the great stumbling block to their faith in him, but this explanation of the purpose of Christ's humiliation is sufficient to demonstrate its necessity.

18: For in that he himself hath suffered being tempted, he is able to succour them that are tempted.

Christ's triumph over the temptations which arose out of his sufferings, gave him the perpetual ability to 'succour them that are tempted'. As Westcott well says 'The power of sympathy lies not in the mere capacity for feeling, but in the lessons of experience. And again, sympathy with the sinner in his trial does not depend on the experience of sin but on the experience of the strength of the temptation to sin which only the sinless can know in its full intensity. He who falls yields before the last strain.'

CHAPTER THREE

Having shown that Christ is superior to the angels who were the spiritual agents in the giving of the law, the author now proceeds to prove that he is superior to Moses, the human agent through whom God gave the law to Israel. If only they will consider Christ, they will see that though Moses was a faithful servant in God's house, a far greater glory belongs to the faithful Son who rules over it. But to remain in that house, they must maintain their faith in Christ to the end [verses 1–6]. This point is enforced in a second warning, which reminds them of the judgment that overtook their forefathers, who were prevented from taking possession of the promised inheritance by their wilful

[1] John Owen makes the following important points on the word 'propitiate'. 'In the use of this word, then, there is always understood, (1st) An *offence*, crime, guilt, or debt, to be taken away; (2dly) A *person offended*, to be pacified, atoned, reconciled; (3rdly.) A *person offending*, to be pardoned, accepted; (4thly.) A *sacrifice* or other means of making the atonement. Sometimes one is expressed, sometimes another, but the use of the word hath respect unto them all.'

unbelief. So if they would avoid their fate, they must obey the truth by responding to the 'today' of God's grace in the gospel [verses 7–19].

1: Wherefore, holy brethren, partakers of a heavenly calling, consider the Apostle and High Priest of our confession, even Jesus;

In this chapter the author approaches the problem of proving Christ's superiority to Moses with great finesse, as any criticism of their renowned Leader and Lawgiver would only antagonize his readers and prevent all further discussion. In fact this point was conceded in principle when he established the Son's ascendancy over the angels, for even the Jews did not regard Moses as being equal to them. However, it will be seen that in exalting Christ he does not find it necessary to belittle Moses.

Wherefore: Seeing then that we have such a sympathetic High Priest [2:17,18], we must look to him alone for help in our time of need [4:14–16].

Holy brethren: An address which would remind these Hebrews that the faith they professed at once made them members of a holy brotherhood and separated them from their unbelieving kinsmen [2:11].

Partakers of a heavenly calling: The earthly rest of Canaan only faintly reflected the reality of the heavenly inheritance which Christ calls his people to share. 'In the word "heavenly" there is struck for the first time, in words at least, an antithesis of great importance in the Epistle, that of this world and heaven, in other words that of the merely material and transient and the ideal and abiding. The things of this world are material, unreal, transient; those of heaven are ideal, true, and eternal' (A. B. Davidson).

Consider: The word means 'notice in a spiritual sense, fix the eyes of the spirit upon someone' (Arndt-Gingrich). If the author 'could but get the Hebrew Christians to "*consider* the Apostle and High Priest of their profession," his object of keeping them steady in their attachment to Him was gained. It is because men do not know Christ that they do not love Him; it is because they know Him so imperfectly that they love Him so imperfectly. The truth about Him as the Great Prophet and the Great High Priest well deserves consideration – it is "the manifold wisdom of God". It requires it; it cannot be understood by a careless, occasional glance' (John Brown).

The Apostle and High Priest: The prophetic and priestly functions of Christ are here closely conjoined by the single definite article. The writer avoids giving the title 'apostle' to the first preachers of the gospel in 2:4 because he chooses to reserve it for the One whom God has sent into the world and through whom God is supremely revealed to man [1:1, 2] 'As Prophet, Christ is God's representative to His people; as Priest, He is their representative before God. As the Apostle He speaks *to* us from God, as our High Priest He speaks *for* us to God' (Pink).

Of our confession, even Jesus: 'Confession' here refers to the faith or religion we profess (cf. NEB), and 'our' is emphatic. 'In "*our* religion" it is Jesus who is *apostle and high priest,* not Moses' (James Moffatt). Christianity superseded Judaism, because it saw that the Son was greater than his faithful servant [verses 5, 6].

2: who was faithful to him that appointed him, as also was Moses in all his house.

The verse disarms prejudice by according Moses the highest praise. In the household of God, Moses resembles Jesus in his faithfulness, for though he was not without personal failings, his ministerial fidelity was beyond question. 'He withheld nothing of what God revealed or commanded, nor did he add any thing thereunto; and herein did his faithfulness consist' (John Owen) [*Num.* 12:7]. But the faithfulness of Moses could be exercised only during the limited period of his earthly service; whereas Jesus, in faithfulness to God who appointed him, ever lives to exercise the offices of Apostle and High Priest ('*being* faithful'). [*Acts* 2:36]

3: For he hath been counted worthy of more glory than Moses, by so much as he that built the house hath more honour than the house. 4: For every house is builded by some one; but he that built all things is God.

As Christ is the builder of this household, his glory far excels that of Moses who was but a servant in it and a member of it. Christ is worthy of their worship for the supernatural work of salvation which has been entrusted to him by God demands nothing less than divinity for its accomplishment. It is because Christ is the Saviour of the whole people of God who form this house that he is here said to be its builder. As a member of the redeemed community Moses was no more than a part of the house, though he was the revered leader of the Old Testament heirs of Christ's great salvation. And since Christ built the house of salvation in accordance with the plan furnished by the Father's decree, there is no incongruity in the further affirmation that God is the builder of all things.

5: And Moses indeed was faithful in all his house as a servant, for a testimony of those things which were afterward to be spoken;

Instead of calling Moses a bondservant, the writer uses another word which suggests that his service was freely rendered, and thus underlines the dignity of his position in all 'God's house' (ASV margin) [cf. *Num.* 12:7]. Yet there was no finality in the institutions and testimonies he delivered to Israel, for these all pointed forward to the promised Messiah [*Luke* 24:27; *John* 5:46; *Heb.* 10:1]. Moreover, he plainly acknowledged the preparatory character of the revelation which was mediated through him when he predicted the advent of another Prophet whom God would raise up from among them [*Deut.* 18:15]. 'And here the apostle takes his leave of Moses, he treats not about him any more; and therefore he gives him as it were an honourable burial. He puts this glorious epitaph on his grave, "Moses, a faithful servant of the Lord in his whole house"' (John Owen).

6: but Christ as a son, over his house; whose house are we, if we hold fast our boldness and the glorying of our hope firm unto the end.

Moses and Christ are both said to be faithful, but similarity falls short of identity, for faithfulness is to be gauged by the sphere in which it is exercised. The faithfulness of Moses was finite and temporal, but that of Christ is infinite and eternal. Moses was *within* the house as a faithful *servant*; Christ faithfully presides over the same house as the Messianic *Son*. In Christ there is therefore a radical spiritual continuity between the period of promise and the age of fulfilment [*1 Cor.* 10:4; *Heb.* 11:26].

Whose house are we, if we hold fast our boldness and the glorying of our hope firm unto the end: Their profession of faith in Christ had marked them out as members of this household, but they must be careful to maintain their personal trust in the Christian hope [*Rom.* 5:2]. And believers may rest assured that this is no delusory hope, for Christ himself is the substance of it. Those who fail to continue 'firm unto the end' do not overthrow the doctrine of the final perseverance of the saints; they simply prove that they were never really a part of Christ's house. 'The Hebrews were ever in danger of subordinating the future to the present, and of forsaking the invisible (Christ in heaven) for the visible (Judaism on earth), of giving up a profession which involved them in fierce persecution. Hence their need of being reminded that the proof of *their* belonging to the house of Christ was that they remained steadfast to Him to the end of their pilgrimage' (Pink).

7: Wherefore, even as the Holy Spirit saith, Today if ye shall hear his voice,

As the AV correctly indicates, the parenthetical quotation of *Psa.* 95:7–11 is introduced to enforce the exhortation 'Wherefore . . . take heed' [verse 12]. The relevance of this testimony to the crisis of decision which now faced them is strikingly conveyed in the words 'as the Holy Spirit saith'.

In describing this psalm as the authoritative utterance of the Holy Spirit the writer not only points to its inspiration, but also emphasizes the peril of regarding Scripture as a dead letter, for its divine Author continues to speak directly to mankind in it [4:12]. 'Today' refers to that period of grace which God grants to men. Those who fall short of the promised inheritance do so by their failure to respond to the last of these daily invitations. Thus their disbelief of the Word of God is an act of disobedience which effectively excludes them from entering into 'his rest' [verses 18,19]. God's Word is always 'Today,' but it is never safe to presume that he will say it again 'Tomorrow!' [*2 Cor.* 6:2] The author is fearful lest his readers should have reached just such a point of no return, for he compares their situation with that which faced their fathers in the wilderness.

8: Harden not your hearts, as in the provocation, Like as in the day of the trial in the wilderness,

Harden not your hearts: 'It is to the *heart* God's word is addressed, that moral centre of our beings out of which are the issues of life [*Prov.* 4:23]. There may be conviction of the conscience, the assent of the intellect, the admiration of the understanding, but unless the heart is moved there is no response' (Pink).

As in the provocation, in the day of temptation in the wilderness (AV): 'Temptation' and 'provocation' probably allude to separate incidents, though the names 'Massah' (temptation) and 'Meribah' (strife) are linked together in *Exod.* 17:7. If the reference is to Rephidim *and* Kadesh, then these examples of Israel's unbelief which occurred at the beginning and the end of their wanderings in the wilderness suggest that the whole of their course was characterized by a progressive hardening of heart [*Exod.* 17:1–7; *Num.* 20:1–13].

9: Where your fathers tried me by proving me, And saw my works forty years.

In the desert they put God to the test to see if he were worthy of their trust, and these experiments with the divine government were extended over no less than forty years! This period of time would be of special significance for the descendants of these doubters, if this letter was written shortly before AD 70, and it was now nearly forty years since Jesus had accomplished the new 'exodus' [*Luke* 9:31] at Jerusalem.

10: Wherefore I was displeased with this generation, And said, They do always err in their heart: But they did not know my ways;

'Displeased' is far too mild a word, for the Psalmist expressed God's vehement anger and loathing with that generation. The word should warn us that there is nothing impersonal in God's righteous reaction to man's obduracy. This wrath was called forth by their deliberate rejection of God's gracious leading. 'Always' points to the permanent and prevailing bent of their character. As this condition was habitual their case was hopeless. For though they were so highly favoured with the knowledge of God's will, they went astray in their heart 'and' (AV) preferred to walk in their own ways ('cared not to take my road' – Moffatt), thus proving their complete unfitness to enter into the rest of God.

11: As I sware in my wrath, They shall not enter into my rest.

As 4:8–11 makes clear, the disobedience which excluded them from the earthly rest of Canaan also debarred them from sharing in the eternal rest of heaven, 'for God took their faith or unbelief in this proximate sense as having an eternal and final effect' (Vos).

'Old Testament examples are New Testament instructions' (John Owen) [*1 Cor.* 10:11].

12: Take heed brethren, lest haply there shall be in any one of you an evil heart of unbelief, in falling away from the living God:

All are affectionately addressed as 'brethren', but each is warned of the peril he faced, for none could abandon Christ without also 'falling away from the living God' [2:3]. It is perfectly safe to depart from the dead gods of the heathen, but it is otherwise with him who lives to make his threatened punishments an awful reality [10:31]. The faithless heart is here described as 'evil' because the root of all apostasy is the primal sin of unbelief [*Gen* 3:1]. It might be thought that 'turning back to Judaism would not be apostasy from the living God; that is the opinion of modernists and their Unitarianism. But the writer calls that unbelief' (Lenski) [cf. 6:4–6; *John* 5:23, 17:3]

13: but exhort one another day by day, so long as it is called To-day; lest any one of you be hardened by the deceitfulness of sin:

They are urged to improve each day of grace by mutual exhortation in order to escape being hardened by the deceitfulness of sin, which in this particular case 'would be the illusion of faithfulness to the past' (Vincent). Sin first gained its power over mankind by assuming an attractive disguise, but its hideous character is revealed by the Word of God which strips it of this fair façade. It is only when the mask is so pierced that sin loses its power to charm [*Gen.* 3:13; *2 Cor.* 11 1:3; *Gal.* 6:7].

'All the devices of sin are as fair baits whereby dangerous hooks are covered over to entice silly fish to snap at them, so as they are taken and made a prey to the fisher' (William Gouge).

14: for we are become partakers of Christ, if we hold fast the beginning of our confidence firm unto the end:

'We have become partners with Christ' (A. T. Robertson) is a charitable acknowledgment of their profession which must be proved genuine by their patient perseverance to the end. As Kenneth Wuest well says: 'Again as in verse 6, the question is not one of the *retention* of salvation based upon a *persistence* of faith, but of the *possession* of salvation as evidenced by a *continuation* of faith'. This expression should not be understood in the Pauline sense of mystical union with Christ; it rather points to their participation in Christ's heavenly kingdom [12:28].

15: while it is said, To-day if ye shall hear his voice, harden not your hearts, as in the provocation.

It is probably best to regard this repetition of the quotation as beginning a new section (as in NEB), which enforces the lesson to be learned from the example of their forefathers [verses 15–19]. The warning note that is sounded in 'while it is said' is well brought out by J. B. Phillips' paraphrase, 'These words are still being said for our ears to hear.'

To-day: The urgency of the appeal arises from the fact that there will not always be this opportunity to hear God's voice. For the doors of God's rest are closed to all who fail to heed this warning and refuse to respond to the voice of grace in the blessed day of salvation.

16: For who, when they heard, did provoke? Nay, did not all they that came out of Egypt by Moses?

The author chooses to set forth the consequences of Israel's unbelief in a series of questions, because this 'favourite device of the diatribe style' (Moffatt) was better fitted to touch the consciences of his readers than a simple statement of the facts [verses 16–18].

For who . . . did provoke? 'The writer would say, "My warning against apostasy is not superfluous or irrelevant: *for*, consider; *who* were they that provoked God? They were those who had fairly begun their journey to Canaan, as you have begun your Christian course. *They* provoked God, so may *you*"' (Vincent).

Did not all . . . ? 'They were so numerous that they practically constituted the whole generation of the exodus. So far from its being true that a good ending necessarily follows a good beginning, a whole generation of God's chosen people failed to reach the Land of Promise because they provoked God' (Vincent) [cf. *Num.* 26: 63–65].

17: And with whom was he displeased forty years? was it not with them that sinned, whose bodies fell in the wilderness?

As the questions of the previous verse identified those who rebelled against God, so this double question graphically drives home the exemplary judgment which overtook them [*1 Cor.* 10:5–11]. 'What a long, long line of graves – the saddest in the world! They came out of the bondage of Egypt under faithful Moses [verse 5], but they fell as corpses in the wilderness!'(Lenski).

18: And to whom swore he that they should not enter into his rest, but to them that were disobedient?

As the word implies ('to refuse belief and obedience'– Thayer), they *disobeyed* because they *disbelieved*. 'Unbelief passed into action' (Westcott). That 'disobedient' thus virtually anticipates the 'unbelief' of verse 19, shows that the author here virtually treats them as convertible terms. And this usage is in harmony with the Christian conviction that unbelief in the gospel is the supreme act of disobedience [*John* 16:9].

19: And we see that they were not able to enter in because of unbelief.

And so we see . . . (Lenski): This introduces the irrefutable conclusion of the argument. The exclusion of unbelievers from the promised rest of God is not only an undeniable fact, but also a moral necessity. These people *justly* perished in the wilderness, because they divested themselves of all their interest in the promised inheritance through their unbelief. 'And let not others entertain better hopes of their condition hereafter, whilst here they follow their example; for, – No unbeliever shall ever enter into the rest of God' (John Owen).

CHAPTER FOUR

In this chapter the author draws a parallel between the typical rest of Canaan and the real rest that is offered to believers in Christ. He warns his discouraged Hebrew readers not to follow the example of their ancestors who did not believe the good news they had heard, for God has sworn that the unbelieving shall not enter into his rest. It is true that Joshua did lead the next generation into the promised land, but the fact that years later God repeated his offer of rest through David shows that the true rest cannot be identified with the earthly inheritance. Thus there remains a sabbath rest for the people of God. For it is through Christ, whose work far excels that of Joshua, that the believer is able to enter into that rest in which he has ceased from his own works, and this means that the pattern set by God's creation-rest is now fulfilled [verses 1–10]. Therefore we must strive to enter this rest lest anyone should fall through the same disobedience to God's living Word, which is quick to discern and punish the first stirrings of unbelief in the heart. For all things are revealed to the gaze of God with whom we have to do [verses 11–13]. So the Son of God for our High Priest, we must hold fast our confession and come boldly to the throne of grace to receive the succour and strength we need [verses 14–16].

1: Let us fear therefore, lest haply, a promise being left of entering into his rest, any one of you should seem to have come short of it.

Therefore, while the promise of entering his rest remains, let us fear lest any of you be judged to have failed to reach it [RSV]: As the promised 'rest' of Canaan only typified the eternal inheritance [3:14], the promise of entering into God's rest remained open. But they had reason to fear lest any one of them should *be judged* to have missed it after the evil example of their faithless forbears [3:19]. This translation of *dokeo* gives a better sense than 'seem' (ASV), 'for the knowledge of certain judgment is a greater reason to fear than any appearance of failure' (Thomas Hewitt).

Such warnings against apostasy are misunderstood when they are thought to teach that true believers may fall away and be lost. For just as accidents are avoided by obeying the road signs which are put up for our safety, so we are preserved from the dangers of our pilgrimage by paying heed to those warnings which are annexed to the promise of salvation. This truth is further illustrated by Paul's experience on the voyage to Rome. He had been divinely assured that *all would be saved* despite the loss of the ship [*Acts* 27:22–25], but that did not prevent him from warning the centurion that *none could be saved* if the sailors were allowed to desert the ship [*Acts* 27:31]. So those ordained to salvation only obtain it by using the appointed means to that end. Therefore all who know the plague of their own hearts will never deem it safe to dispense with what God considers to be necessary for their spiritual safety [6:9, 10:35; *1 Cor.* 10:12].

2: For indeed we have had good tidings preached unto us, even as also they: but the word of hearing did not profit them, because it was not united by faith with them that heard.

The lesson to be learned from the past must not be lost upon the readers, for their fathers in the wilderness also heard the glad tidings of salvation, but 'the word which they heard did not benefit them, because it was not united by faith with the hearers' (Arndt-Gingrich). As in the parable of the Sower, the fault lies not with the message but with the unresponsive hearts of the hearers. To listen to the gospel while remaining destitute of faith is to come short of God's promised rest. The author wants every wavering Hebrew to understand that faith must be mixed with the preached word if it is to profit those who hear it. 'Faith and the promise meeting make a happy mixture, a precious confection' (John Trapp).

3: For we who have believed do enter into that rest; Even as he hath said,
As I sware in my wrath, they shall not enter into my rest:
although the works were finished from the foundation of the world.
4: For he hath said somewhere of the seventh day on this wise, And God
rested on the seventh day from all his works; 5: and in this place again,
They shall not enter into my rest.

For we are entering into the rest, (we) who have come to believe (Lenski): Unlike the unbelieving who failed to profit from the preached word [verse 2], *we* are entering into God's rest because we have believed the promise. For it was through our commitment to the gospel that life became a pilgrimage to the heavenly inheritance [11:13–16], which we shall soon enjoy 'if we hold fast the beginning of our confidence firm unto the end' [3:14].

As he hath said . . . : For of the faithless Israelites God sware that they should not enter into his rest, although his rest was ready for man since the completion of the work of creation. This further citation of *Psa.* 95:11 [3:11] therefore implies that believers may still enter this rest. 'Wherever there is a promise, there a threatening in reference unto the same matter is tacitly understood. And wherever there is a threatening, that is no more than so, be it never so severe, there is a gracious promise included in it; yea, sometimes God gives out an express threatening for no other end but that men may lay hold on the promise tacitly included. The threatening that Nineveh should perish was given out that it might not perish. And John Baptist's preaching that the axe was laid to the root of the trees was a call to repentance, that none might be cut down and cast into the fire' (John Owen).

And God rested on the seventh day: This means that God established the pattern upon which man's life was to be built by following the cycle of his creative activity with this day of rest [*Gen.* 2:2]. In Hebrew thought the word 'rest' has a positive meaning and 'stands for consummation of a work accomplished and the joy and satisfaction attendant upon this. Such was its prototype in God . . . For mankind, too, a great task awaits to be accomplished, and at its close beckons a rest of joy and satisfaction that shall copy the rest of God. Before all other important things, therefore, the Sabbath is an expression of the eschatological principle on which the life of humanity has been constructed . . . It teaches its lesson through the rhythmical succession of six days of labour and one ensuing day of rest in each successive week. Man is reminded in this way that life is not an aimless existence, that a goal lies beyond' (Geerhardus Vos, *Biblical Theology,* p.140).

They shall not enter into my rest: It is significant that the divine sentence pronounced on rebellious Israel is again repeated *after* the testimony which confirmed that God's rest had been available to man from the beginning. For it is an emphatic reminder of the solemn truth that this rest will never be attained by the disobedient [cf. 3:18].

6: Seeing therefore it remaineth that some should enter thereinto, and they to whom the good tidings were before preached failed to enter in because of disobedience,

In summing up the preceding verses [3–5], the author concludes that it is God's desire that men should enter into his rest, and that this gracious design cannot be frustrated by the disobedience of those to whom this good news was first preached. The refusals of unbelief can never nullify the promise of an entrance into God's rest, for others will be bidden to take their place [*Matt.* 22:8–10; *Acts* 13:46].

7: he again defineth a certain day, To-day, saying in David so long a time afterward (even as hath been said before), To-day if ye shall hear his voice, harden not your hearts.

It makes no material difference whether the author regarded the 95th Psalm as a composition of David's (as in the Septuagint) or whether 'saying in David' simply means 'in the book of David'. What matters is that God is still speaking this word of warning and invitation to these faltering Hebrews through the testimony of 'David'. And if they should choose to ignore these repeated admonitions they have no reason to expect that they will fare any better than those who perished in the wilderness for exactly the same fault.

8: For if Joshua had given them rest, he would not have spoken afterward of another day.

Moreover, if this rest had been enjoyed by those who eventually possessed Canaan under the leadership of Joshua, then God would not have fixed another day for entering into it so long a time afterward' [verse 7]. For the temporal settlement of the promised land was but a faint shadow of the true rest into which the people of God are conducted by their 'Joshua' who is, as Trapp says, 'Jehovah our Righteousness' [*Matt.* 11:28–30].

9: There remaineth therefore a sabbath rest for the people of God.

The word *sabbatismos* occurs only here in the New Testament and it means the 'keeping of a Sabbath'. As those addressed might feel that their faith in Christ had deprived them of a Sabbath rest, the author seeks to allay these fears by showing that Christ's work invested it with a new significance.

The Sabbath was a creation ordinance which placed the day of rest at the end of the six days of labour, but when Adam sinned it became impossible for man to attain the rest of God by his own efforts. This now required nothing less than a second creation, and by keeping the Sabbath on the first day of the week, 'the people of God' gladly acknowledge that their entrance into this rest depends entirely upon the redemptive achievement of Christ. 'Believers knew themselves in a measure partakers of the Sabbath-fulfilment. If the one creation required one sequence, then the other required another. It has been strikingly observed, that our Lord died on the eve of that Jewish Sabbath, at the end of one of these typical weeks of labour by which His work and its consummation were prefigured. And Christ entered upon His rest, the rest of His new, eternal life on the first day of the week, so that the Jewish Sabbath comes to lie between – was, as it were, disposed of, buried in His grave' (Vos, *Biblical Theology*, p. 142).

10: For he that is entered into his rest hath himself also rested from his works, as God did from his.

In verse 9 we have the collective 'people of God', but here the author uses the singular because he is stating a principle which holds good in every case. 'When one, who as a believer belongs to God's people, dies, he enters God's rest and, like God, rests from his works. It is true of all God's people who have already died and will be true of all his people who shall die at some future time' (Lenski).

11: Let us therefore give diligence to enter into that rest, that no man fall after the same example of disobedience.

The urgency of this exhortation stems from the very real danger of falling short of God's rest. Once again the allusion is to those whose carcasses 'fell' in the wilderness, and here the verb points to the complete ruin of any one who follows 'the same example of disobedience' [3:17]. For as Trapp remarks, 'God hangs up some malefactors, as it were in gibbets, for a warning to others.' In order to avoid this unhappy fate it is vital that they spare no pains and make every effort to enter into that rest which is offered to them in the gospel.

12: For the word of God is living and active, and sharper than any two-edged sword, and piercing even to the dividing of soul and spirit, of both joints and marrow, and quick to discern the thoughts and intents of the heart.

In case anyone might be tempted to treat God's Word as a 'dead' letter which could be ignored with impunity, the admonition is reinforced by the stern reminder that it is 'living, and active', and so is quick to detect and punish the first secret stirrings of unbelief in the heart. The context makes it certain that the phrase 'sharper than any two-edged sword' has no reference to the activity of the divine Word in regeneration, but rather describes its terrible power to execute the sentence which it passes upon rebels who resist its testimony. The qualities attributed to the Word of God show that it is regarded in its *judicial* power (Fausset). As it excluded the disobedient Israelites from the rest which was represented to them by Canaan, so it shall exclude 'Christian' apostates from the heavenly inheritance. On the expression 'piercing even to the dividing of soul and spirit, of both joints and marrow', F. F. Bruce remarks: 'It would indeed be precarious to draw any conclusions from these words about our author's psychology, nor is it necessary to understand them in the sense of the Pauline distinction between soul and spirit.'[1]

13: And there is no creature that is not manifest in his sight: but all things are naked and laid open before the eyes of him with whom we have to do.

Since 'everything is open and laid bare to the eyes' (Arndt Gingrich) of the One to whom we must give account, how important it is for us to strive earnestly to enter his rest. The general sense of 'laid open' is clear enough, but there is uncertainty regarding the metaphor from which it is derived. E. K. Simpson associates it with the wrestler's grip on the throat of his opponent, but it is probably preferable to think of the victim's neck being bent back to expose it for the thrust of the knife. Whatever the truth of the matter, we may certainly agree with Simpson when he says that the figure represents 'either the denuded or helpless plight of all created persons or forces when brought face to face with their Creator and Lord' (cited by F. F. Bruce). Hence Calvin wisely concludes, 'Whenever His Word is set before us, we must tremble, because nothing is hid from Him.'

[1] J.G. Machen regards the threefold division of man's nature into body, soul, and spirit as a serious error because it encourages what he calls 'an "empty-room" view of the presence of God in the redeemed man.' It suggests that only the 'spiritual' part of man requires renovation, whereas Scripture teaches 'that the whole man, corrupt before because of sin, is transformed by the regenerating power of the Spirit of God.' *The Christian View of Man*, pp. 139–44. See also *Collected Writings of John Murray*, vol. 2, pp. 23–33, and the full discussion in Louis Berkhof's *Systematic Theology*, pp. 191–4.)

14: Having then a great high priest, who hath passed through the heavens, Jesus the Son of God, let us hold fast our confession.

Having then a great high priest: 'Then' does not denote a logical deduction, but simply serves to introduce the Epistle's main theme, which is to show the superiority of Christ's heavenly priesthood over that earthly succession which it has completely superseded [4:14–10:18]. The assertion is at once a word of encouragement and an emphatic reply to the taunts of their unbelieving kinsmen, who would assail the validity and efficacy of this 'new' religion on the ground that it had no high priest to intercede for its misguided adherents. 'The author not only claims that such a High Priest does in fact exist, but by his use of *great* asserts that He is a person of high distinction and power and, therefore, greater than Aaron' (Hewitt).

Who hath passed through the heavens, Jesus the Son of God: The appearing of Jesus in glory affords convincing proof that his sacrifice was acceptable to God and assures his people of the prevailing power of his intercession on their behalf. However, this same Jesus is none other than the Son of God for our author does not speak of the conferment of divine honours upon a mere man, but plainly refers to the exaltation of him who is natively and essentially the eternal Son [1:1–3]. As the Aaronic High Priest passed through the veil into the Holiest place, 'so this great High Priest had passed through the heavens and appeared among eternal realities. So that the very absence of the High Priest which depressed them, was itself fitted to strengthen faith. He was absent because dealing with the living God in their behalf' (Marcus Dods).

Let us hold fast our confession: It is a characteristic of the author's style to include himself in his exhortations [4:1, 11, 16; 6:1; 10:22, 23, 24; 12:1 [twice], 28; 13:13, 15]. They must at all costs maintain their subjective confidence in Jesus the Son of God or else they will never participate in the objective benefits of his great salvation [2:1, 6:6].

15: For we have not a high priest that cannot be touched with the feeling of our infirmities; but one that hath been in all points tempted like as we are, yet without sin.

The double negative is equal to a strong affirmation. In case the contemplation of the Son's glory should lead them to suppose that he had no capacity for sympathy, they are given the immediate assurance that in Jesus they have a compassionate High Priest who has fully shared their 'infirmities' [5:2]. Bengel turns the ambiguity of this word to good account by saying that in respect of us it includes the idea of sin, but in respect of Christ it is excluded [7:26].

'The Son of God, had He never become incarnate, might have pitied, but He could not have sympathized with His people . . . The truth is, He not only can be touched, but cannot but be touched. The assertion is not, It is possible that He may sympathize; but, It is impossible that He should not' (John Brown).

Without sin: The meaning is not that Jesus triumphed over temptation, though that is of course true, but that there 'was no latent sin in Jesus to be stirred by temptation and no habits of sin to be overcome' (A. T. Robertson). Yet the fact that Jesus *could not sin* [*John* 14:30] in no way diminishes the terrible reality of his conflict with the powers of evil [5:7]. The sinner who capitulates to the first solicitation to evil cannot claim to have felt the full power of temptation. It was otherwise with Jesus who experienced the anguish of temptation to an unimaginable degree, for his immaculate person was subjected to the continuous assaults of the Tempter.

As G. C. Berkouwer puts it, 'Christ's sinlessness does not nullify the temptation but rather demonstrates its superiority in the teeth of temptation' (*The Person of Christ,* p. 263). Thus, having suffered 'being tempted, he is able to succour them that are tempted' [2:18].

16: Let us therefore draw near with boldness unto the throne of grace, that we may receive mercy, and may find grace to help us in time of need.

Let us therefore draw near: This gospel exhortation reflects the assurance which casts out the spirit of bondage and fear, and enables all believers to draw near to God in worship [*Rom.* 8:15]. We have here specifically ritual language. Note, for example, 4:16; 7:25; 10:1, 22. This language is used not only of the believers, but also of the officers in the sanctuary, that is, of the priests. 'Back of this stands the idea that the priest *brings near* his sacrifice, as well as *bringing near* those who follow him. So we are brought near by Jesus as our High Priest and Forerunner' (Vos).

With boldness unto the throne of grace: We are to be thus always drawing near to God with holy boldness, because we know that through the finished work and present mediation of our great High Priest, we are approaching not a throne of judgment but a throne of grace.

That we may receive mercy, and may find grace to help us: 'The twofold aim corresponds with the twofold necessity of life. Man needs mercy for past failure, and grace for present and future work. There is also a difference as to the mode of attainment in each case. Mercy is to be "taken" as it is extended to man in his weakness; grace is to be "sought" by man according to his necessity' (Westcott).

In time of need: Or 'for timely help': 'before we are overwhelmed by temptations, when we most need it; such as is suitable to the time, persons, and end designed [*Psa.* 104:27]. A supply of grace is in store for believers against all exigencies; but they are only supplied with it, according as the need arises' (Fausset).

CHAPTER FIVE

The author next shows that the priesthood of Christ is superior to that of Aaron, because the compassion and divine appointment of Christ fulfil the essential requirements of this office. For every high priest is taken from among men, as he could not sympathize with his clients unless he shared their infirmity, and he must also be called by God to undertake this ministry [verses 1–4]. As to his authority, Christ did not glorify himself, but God appointed him to be a priest for ever after the order of Melchizedek [verses 5, 6]. As to his sympathy, Christ's full humanity was attested by his agony in the garden, for it was through his sufferings that he became the author of eternal salvation, being named of God a high priest after the order of Melchizedek [verses 7–10]. Of this Melchizedek the author has many things to say, which he fears his spiritually retarded readers will find difficult to understand. For though by now they ought to be teachers, they still need the milk that belongs to inexperienced babes, rather than the solid food of the discerning adult [verses 11–14].

1: For every high priest, being taken from among men, is appointed for men in things pertaining to God, that he may offer both gifts and sacrifices for sins:

In verses 1–4 it is shown that the Jewish High Priest was required to have a compassionate concern for those he represented before God, and that the effectiveness of his ministrations rested upon the reality of a divine call to undertake this office. These requirements were perfectly met in Christ who became the High Priest of his people by divine appointment, and who is qualified to sympathize with them by his unique experience of suffering on their behalf [verses 5–10].

For every high priest, being taken from among men, is appointed for men in things pertaining to God: The mediation of Christ depended upon his kinship with those he came to redeem, for in order to manage the religious interests *of* men, every High Priest was to be 'taken *from among* men' [2:9–18].

That he may offer both gifts and sacrifices for sins: John Owen says that 'the proper and principal work of a priest' is the offering of those 'gifts and sacrifices' which sin made necessary, and therefore 'where there is no proper propitiatory sacrifice there is no proper priest'. Hence the Christian ministry is not an order of sacrificing priests! For Christ's priesthood 'leaves no room for any sacrifice or any sacrificial offering for sin in heaven or on earth. What ministers of the Gospel have to offer of propitiation for acceptance is for acceptance not in heaven, but on earth; is offered not to the Holy God, but to rebel hearts of sinful men. It is to be offered not to Him against whom we have sinned, but from Him, and in behalf of Him, to those who have rebelled against Him. And what they have to offer to sinners for acceptance by sinners is the fruit of the completed work of offering for sins. As regards the great matter of expiation and satisfaction, they must bear faithful testimony to the truth, "It is finished"' (Nathaniel Dimock, *The Sacerdotium of Christ,* p. 80).

2: who can bear gently with the ignorant and erring, for that he himself also is compassed with infirmity; 3: and by reason thereof is bound, as for the people, so also for himself, to offer for sins.

These verses indirectly assert the superiority of Christ's priesthood. For the Jewish High Priest had first to offer for his own sins before he acted on behalf of the people, and it was this knowledge of his own infirmity which enabled him to 'bear gently with the ignorant and erring' (as opposed to the presumptuous sinner, cf. 10:26 with *Num.*

15:30). He was bound to have a fellow-feeling for those he represented because he was himself a sinner, yet this measured mildness cannot be compared with the boundless sympathy which the sinless Son of God feels for those who have wandered from the way [4:15].

4: And no man taketh the honour unto himself, but when he is called of God, even as was Aaron.

The author here pointedly reminds his readers that in contrast to the corruption of the priestly office in contemporary Judaism, Israel's first High Priest exercised a valid ministry because he was commissioned by God for this service; whereas all worship which is offered without a divine command is performed without divine approval and incurs divine judgment [*2 Chron.* 26:16–21].

'As it is the promise of God to govern the Church, so He reserves to Himself alone the right to lay down the order and manner of its administration. On this I base the principle that the papal priesthood is a spurious one, because it was fabricated in a human workshop. God nowhere commands that a sacrifice should now be offered to Him for the forgiveness of sins. He nowhere ordains that priests should be appointed for this purpose. Therefore when the Pope installs his priests to make sacrifices, the apostle says that they are not to be considered lawful unless perchance by some new and special law they exalted themselves above Christ, who Himself did not dare to take this honour on Himself, but waited for the word of the Father' (Calvin).

5: So Christ also glorified not himself to be made a high priest, but he that spake unto him, Thou art my Son, This day have I begotten thee:

Christ was like Aaron in that he also did not advance himself to the position of High Priest, but was appointed to this office by the Father [*John* 8:54]. When Christ took his rightful place in heaven, God proclaimed him to be his Son, and it is his essential Sonship which qualifies him to exercise such a perpetual priesthood. Yet Christ's triumphant enthronement did not mark the beginning of his priesthood, for this divine testimony was but the public announcement of that eternal decree by which he was ordained the Mediator of his people. And it was in Christ's priestly offering of himself upon the cross that this decree passed into the realm of historical accomplishment

[9:13, 14]. This is the second time that *Psa.* 2:7 is quoted; see also the comment on 1:5.

6: as he saith also in another place, Thou art a priest for ever after the order of Melchizedek.

That God declared Christ to be a priest is confirmed by an appeal to *Psa.* 110:4, which also indicates that he belongs to a different order of priesthood from that of Aaron. As the promised deliverer is shown to be a prince of David's line in the first verse of the same psalm [1:13], it is evident that he can lay no claim to the priestly functions which pertained exclusively to the house of Levi. However, Christ's priesthood infinitely transcends the Levitical order for it is patterned upon the unique precedent afforded by Melchizedek, the Priest-King of Salem, and the Messiah therefore permanently unites in his own person the two offices which were always distinct in Israel [*Gen.* 14:18].

7: Who in the days of his flesh, having offered up prayers and supplications with strong crying and tears unto him that was able to save him from death, and having been heard for his godly fear,

The author turns next to the experience of suffering which fitted Christ to be a sympathetic High Priest [verses 7–9]. While the phrase 'who in the days of his flesh', would seem to refer to the whole period of his humiliation, the rest of the verse appears to point to his agony in Gethsemane.

'These prayers, accompanied with strong crying and tears, to Him who was able to save Him from death, imply the endurance of penal death. Did he fear the mere corporeal suffering which many a martyr has met with fortitude? Sinless nature no doubt shrinks from death, but it was something of a far other quality which gave rise to the agony and amazement which weighed so heavily on the Son of God, – viz., the second death, the full infliction of wrath at the hand of God, for the sins, not of one man, but of the whole company of the elect. The curse of the law under which He spontaneously placed Himself struck the soul as well as the body [*Gal.* 3:13]. More was comprehended than bodily pain, as might be argued from the horror and recoil of the Redeemer from the cup which was to be drunk. Besides, corporeal sufferings would not have sufficed for men's redemption, for He redeemed the soul as well as the body [*1 Cor.* 6:20]: He assumed both soul and body; and He offered both in our room, as was necessary to expiate guilt incurred in both and by both. . . Hence, while the Lord Jesus continued amid all His agony the object of divine love as the only-begotten of the Father, He endured all the curse, wrath and infliction justly to be awarded to the sin He bore on His own body... Though the Surety was in Himself the beloved Son, He was, as the sin-bearer, under the hiding of His Father's face when He poured out these prayers with strong crying and tears' (George Smeaton).

Now it is said that these supplications were answered because of 'his godly fear'. Yet how can this statement be reconciled with the fact that he died? The solution of this difficulty is found in the conditional nature of the prayers which Christ offered. For though he could not but *wish* that the cup might pass from him, he nevertheless submitted himself entirely to the Father's will, and it was this *definite petition* which was fully granted [*Matt.* 26:39; *Mark* 14:36; *Luke* 22:42,]. 'The ultimate obedience was learned in Gethsemane, after Gethsemane and on the cross the obedience was only carried out' (Lenski).

8: though he was a Son, yet learned obedience by the things which he suffered;

Son though he was (Moffatt): In 12:5f. the author teaches that painful discipline is the lot of all true sons of the Father, and that every son, because he is a son, has to suffer. Jesus, however, had to suffer not because *but although* he was 'Son', which shows that he is Son in a unique sense. As the divine Son [1:1f.], 'it might have been expected that he would have been exempt from such a discipline' (Moffatt). But as the appointed Mediator of a sinful people, Jesus had to learn that obedience which found its perfection in atoning suffering, even the death of the cross'. Here '*learning obedience* signifies *bringing out into the present conscious experience of action* that which was already present in principle. There is a great difference, of course, between the mere principle and even the desire to obey, and the actual carrying out of the desire' (Vos) [10:7].

9: and having been made perfect, he became unto all them that obey him the author of eternal salvation;

And having been made perfect: 'As to the term *perfection* (*teleiosis*), we must adhere strictly to the meaning *fitting for the office*. The experience of learning was a moral experience, to be sure; but the perfection attained was not moral perfection, but a perfect fitness for His office' (Vos).

He became unto all them that obey him: Although this qualification clearly limits salvation to the obedient, it does not ascribe that salvation to their obedience. Christ is the author of salvation, but the reality of our interest in it must be attested by an obedient walk [*John* 14:15]. The words would have particular force for those who were beginning to waver in their profession. 'There is, there can be, no salvation through Christ to men living and dying in unbelief, impenitence, and disobedience' (John Brown).

The author of eternal salvation: In 2:10 'the thought was of Christ going before the "many sons" with whom He unites Himself. Here the thought is of that which He alone does for them. In the former passage He is the great Leader who identifies Himself with His people: in this He is the High priest who offers Himself as an effectual sacrifice on their behalf' (Westcott).

10: named of God a high priest after the order of Melchizedek.

'Having been made perfect' Christ entered the heavenly sanctuary and was greeted by God as the High Priest of a more excellent order than that of Aaron. The significance of this designation is explained in the seventh chapter of the Epistle. 'God nameth or calleth things as they are, and as he hath made them; and this was done openly, and with the most illustrious solemnity, at his ascension into heaven, when God set him down on his right hand in the presence of all the surrounding angels, who did all submit to him as their Head and King, and acknowledge him as the great royal High Priest of God, as was foretold' (Matthew Poole) [*Psa.* 110:1, 4].

11: Of whom we have many things to say, and hard of interpretation, seeing ye are become dull of hearing.

The closing word of the previous verse marks a skilful transition from instruction to an extended exhortation [5:11–6:20]. He has much to say to them concerning Melchizedek as a type of Christ, but he fears that the sluggishness of their hearing offers an insuperable impediment to the doctrine he wishes to deliver to them [6:12]. The obscurity does not reside in the teaching, but in that spiritual insensitivity which is the invariable result of coldness of heart. This crushing rebuke is therefore intended to arouse them from their torpor so that his words may not fall upon deaf ears.

12: For when by reason of the time ye ought to be teachers, ye have need again that some one teach you the rudiments of the first principles of the oracles of God; and are become such as have need of milk and not of solid food.

The charge is substantiated by the reminder that their progress in the faith bears no relation to what might have been justly expected of them. They ought now to be teachers, whereas they still needed to be taught the first rudiments of the faith, and to be fed with milk because they were unable to digest solid food [*1 Cor.* 3: 1ff.].

Of the oracles of God: 'Viz., of the Old Testament. Instead of seeing Christ as the end of the Old Testament, they were relapsing towards Judaism, so as not only not to understand the typical reference to Christ of such an Old Testament personage as Melchizedek, but even more elementary references' (Fausset).

13: For every one that partaketh of milk is without experience of the word of righteousness; for he is a babe. 14: But solid food is for fullgrown men, even those who by reason of use have their senses exercised to discern good and evil.

Their spiritual immaturity was evidenced by the fact that they were restricted to a diet of milk, and so they were 'without experience of the word of righteousness'. The context would seem to rule out any reference to justification, and the expression is probably to be understood as a synonym for the Christian faith. Arndt-Gingrich points out that as righteousness 'constitutes the specific virtue of Christians, the word becomes almost equivalent to Christianity'. On the other hand, 'solid food is for fullgrown men' whose experience enables them to discriminate between what is good and what is harmful. The lesson is plain to see: as indolence accounted for their lamentable ignorance of Christian truth, so every faculty must be kept in vigorous exercise to ensure healthy spiritual growth [*Prov.* 13:4].

CHAPTER SIX

If these faltering pilgrims are to press on to perfection, they must leave behind the ABC of the gospel, and advance to a more mature understanding of Christ's person and work [verses 1–3]. Since a refusal to advance would expose them to the dreadful danger of apostasy, the author issues a solemn warning against this sin from which no recovery is possible [verses 4–8]. But despite his stern words, he is persuaded of the reality of their faith by their many deeds of love, and he encourages them to go on to inherit the promises [verses 9–12]. For we like Abraham must patiently wait for God to make good his immutable promise, which has been doubly confirmed to us by his oath. Hence our hope has a sure anchorage within the veil, because Jesus has entered heaven on our behalf, having become a High Priest after the order of Melchizedek [verses 13–20].

1: Wherefore leaving the doctrine of the first principles of Christ, let us press on unto perfection; not laying again a foundation of repentance from dead works, and of faith toward God, 2: of the teaching of baptisms, and of laying on of hands, and of resurrection of the dead, and of eternal judgment.

Although the author reproaches his readers for their failure to assimilate the rudiments of the faith [5:12], it is not his purpose to lay again this elementary foundation, for by now they ought to be able to grasp that solid teaching which will enable them to press on to maturity. It is significant that these 'first principles' of the gospel were also features of Jewish faith and practice, because it would be more difficult for people who were already familiar with these doctrines 'to appreciate their new Christian content than for pagans who met them for the first time' (William Neil). The six fundamentals mentioned are arranged in three pairs, and may have formed part of a primitive catechism.

Repentance from dead works, and of faith toward God: The first word of the gospel is the call to repent [*Mark* 1:15], and this involves the radical redirection of the whole life. For no man can be saved without renouncing his sins, recognizing that they are 'dead works' which separated him from the living God and kept him in the sphere of death

[9:14]. The sequel to repentance is here simply described as 'faith toward God', because the author is addressing Jews who are convinced of the unity of God, and he wishes to show them that 'faith in God, the God of salvation, is not distinct from, but inclusive of, faith in our Lord Jesus Christ (as in *John* 14:1)' (Delitzsch).

Of the teaching of baptisms, and of laying on of hands: When the readers were brought to faith in Christ they had been taught the vital difference between Christian baptism and all the religious washings it displaced, including ritual cleansings [9:10] and every other kind of baptism for initiates [*Acts* 19:1ff]. In the early church baptism was followed by the 'laying on of hands', an act which was associated with the gift of the Holy Spirit, though the case of Cornelius clearly shows that the coming of the Spirit was not dependent upon it [*Acts* 10:44–48]. 'The main point in Acts is that baptism and the reception of the Spirit necessarily belong together' (E. Lohse, *TDNT*, vol. 9, p. 432).

And of resurrection of the dead, and of eternal judgment: Except for the Sadducees [*Acts* 23:8], the Jews also believed these doctrines, but did not connect them 'with Jesus, who is the Resurrection and the Life and the judge at the last day. The foundational doctrine of Christianity gave Jews what they could not attain in their work-righteousness and empty Judaism: the sure hope of a blessed resurrection in Jesus and the certainty that they would be justified in the eternal judgment' (Lenski). [9:27, 10:37; *Acts* 17:31; *Rom.* 10:1–4]

3: And this will we do, if God permit.

If God permit: It is the author's earnest desire to teach his readers that doctrine which should lead them to spiritual maturity [verse 1], but he fears that perhaps their unbelief had so provoked God that he would not grant them further light [*Luke* 8:18]. For even the sun's meridian splendour brings no illumination to sightless eyes! Hence this reverent proviso: 'If God permit'; that is, 'If God give me life and ability, and you capacity and stability; for many fall away, whose damnation sleepeth not' (Trapp).

4: For as touching those who were once enlightened and tasted of the heavenly gift, and were made partakers of the Holy Spirit, 5: and tasted the good word of God, and the powers of the age to come, 6: and then

fell away, it is impossible to renew them again unto repentance; seeing they crucify to themselves the Son of God afresh, and put him to an open shame.

This very severe warning is intended to arouse the readers to a lively sense of the awful danger which faced them, for what they calmly considered to be a return to the faith of their fathers is shown as an act of apostasy from which no recovery is possible. The author hopes to recall them from the brink of disaster by an alarming description of those who totally fall away from the profession of the Christian faith [verse 9]. This class of persons once appeared to be truly regenerate but their subsequent course sadly proved that they had neither part nor lot in this matter' [*Acts* 8:21].

Many have appealed to this passage as proving that it is possible for the truly converted to fall away and be lost. But this presupposes that what is here predicated of such apostates must point to the possession of saving faith, rather than the temporary enjoyment of great spiritual privileges. For though the 'fruits of the atonement enjoyed by some non-elect persons are defined in very lofty terms' [10:29; *2 Pet.* 2:20, 21], it must 'be marked with equal emphasis that these fruits or benefits all fall short of salvation, even though in some cases the terms used to characterize them are such as could properly be used to describe a true state of salvation' (John Murray, *Collected Writings,* vol. 1, p. 68).

For as touching those who were once enlightened: This refers to their acceptance of the doctrine of the gospel, for unless they had first professed its truth they could not have fallen away from it [*1 John* 2:19]. 'The sin against the Holy Ghost, though similar, is not identical with this; for *that* may be committed by those outside the church (as in *Matt.* 12:24, 31, 32); *this,* only by those *inside'* (Fausset).

And tasted of the heavenly gift: 'There is a goodness and excellency in this heavenly gift which may be tasted or experienced in some measure by such as never receive them in their life, power, and efficacy. They may taste, – 1. Of the *word* in its truth, not its power; 2. Of the *worship* of the church in its outward order, not in its inward beauty; 3. Of the *gifts* of the church, not its graces' (*Works of John Owen,* 'On the Nature and Causes of Apostasy', vol. 7, p. 25) [*Matt.* 7:22, 23; *Mark* 6:20; *Luke* 10:17–20; *John* 6:70; *1 Cor.* 13:1f.].

And were made partakers of the Holy Spirit: 'Not by an inhabitation of his person in them, but by his operations in them, whereby he is trying how far a natural man may be raised, and not have his nature changed . . . He is proving by his gifts to them how much supernatural good, and workings towards salvation, they are capable of, without the putting forth of the exceeding greatness of his power to make them new creatures'(Poole).

And tasted the good word of God, and the powers of the age to come: The powers of the world to come are projected into the present age through the ministry of the Spirit in the proclamation of the Word of God. The preaching of the good news is therefore a foretaste of the heavenly state. This emphasis upon 'the presence of the future' would have a salutary effect upon the readers, who appear to have been disillusioned because they did not yet possess the external blessings which they associated with the Messianic Kingdom. To cure them of this religious externalism, the author insists that believers are already in vital connection with the heavenly world. For he shows them in chapter 12:2f. that what belongs to the end 'is present for the most part, only certain features of it being reserved for the future. The internal, spiritual part is the important part, and this we have now' (Vos).

And then fell away: This fall is final and without remedy. The faith of God's elect endures to the end; temporary faith withers and dies [*Matt.* 13:20–22].

It is impossible to renew them again unto repentance: Here is the first of the four impossible things which are mentioned in this Epistle [6:18, 10:4, 11:6]. It is worth noting that in the impressive word order of the original language, 'impossible' emphatically stands at the head of the sentence [cf. verse 4 in the AV]. The impossibility resides in the apostates themselves, for the complete repudiation of the doctrine which formerly they embraced means that a further preaching of the gospel would be entirely lost upon them [*Matt.* 7:6].

Seeing they crucify to themselves the Son of God afresh, and put him to an open shame: 'The apostate crucifies Christ on his own account by virtually confirming the judgment of the actual crucifiers, declaring that he too has made trial of Jesus and found Him no true Messiah but a deceiver, and therefore worthy of death. The greatness of the guilt in so doing is aggravated by the fact that apostates thus treat *the*

Son of God, 10:29' (Marcus Dods). Hence the heinous nature of their sin makes repentance impossible.

7: For the land which hath drunk the rain that cometh oft upon it, and bringeth forth herbs meet for them for whose sake it is also tilled, receiveth blessing from God: 8: but if it beareth thorns and thistles, it is rejected and nigh unto a curse; whose end is to be burned.

A telling illustration from the realm of nature sets forth the solemn truth that the hearing of the gospel is fraught with eternal consequences for either weal or woe. The land which is blessed by God with frequent showers of rain is expected to bear useful fruits for those by whom it is tended, but that which produces only thorns and thistles is 'rejected' (the word here has personal overtones, cf. *2 Cor.* 13:5ff.), 'nigh unto a curse' [*Gen.* 3:17f], and destined to utter destruction.

Whose end is to be burned: 'The end of briers and thorns is the fire, they are to be burnt up by it; and this will be the final issue with apostates, to be destroyed by a Christ whom they have rejected, with eternal fire, chapter 10:27, 12:29; *Matt.* 3:12, 25:41; *2 Thess.* 1:7–9' (Poole).

9: But, beloved, we are persuaded better things of you, and things that accompany salvation, though we thus speak.

By means of this affectionate address ('beloved' is used only here in the Epistle), the author seeks to assure his readers that his stern admonition was prompted by a sincere concern for their spiritual welfare, and though 'he had spoken it *unto them*, he did not speak it *of them*' (John Owen). For he had every reason to hope that the past evidences they had given of their faith indicated something more than an empty profession [verse 10]. The assurance is in no sense a retraction of the warning, but is rather intended to dispel any prejudice which might prevent it from having the desired effect upon them. As 'things that belong to salvation' (ASV margin) had been manifested in their lives, so now they are shown 'the one road they must travel without turning back' (G. C. Berkouwer, *Faith and Perseverance*, p. 119).

10: for God is not unrighteous to forget your work and the love which ye showed toward his name, in that ye ministered unto the saints, and still do minister.

Since God is not unrighteous he cannot fail to reward the service which a reverence for his name inspired, yet this is an award of grace, and not a merited reward [*Luke* 17:10]. 'The butler may forget Joseph, and Joseph forget his father's house; but forgetfulness befalls not God, to whom all things are present, and before whom there is written a book of remembrance for them that fear the Lord, and think upon his name, *Mal.* 3:17' (Trapp). In thus ministering to their fellow believers in distress they showed their interest in the gospel [10:32–34], for 'those brethren who, being loved in and for God, do evidence to these Hebrews that they are passed from death to life, *1 John* 3:14' (Poole).

11: And we desire that each one of you may show the same diligence unto the fulness of hope even to the end: 12: that ye be not sluggish, but imitators of them who through faith and patience inherit the promises.

The author hopes that a consideration of the end of those who renounce their profession will prove so salutary that each of them may be encouraged to display that zeal which leads to the 'full realization' of the Christian hope. He does not wish them to become '*sluggish*, but imitators of them who through faith and patience inherit the promises'. The use of the same word (*nothros*) in chapter 5: 11 shows that it was their 'dullness' in hearing which made it necessary to warn them against becoming 'sluggish' in their hope. For a careless hearing of the Word of God at first diminishes and eventually extinguishes the hope of salvation. But the promised inheritance can only be possessed by those who entertain a living hope; hence they are urged to imitate the patient perseverance of their forefathers, whose faith is so eloquently commended in the eleventh chapter of the Epistle.

13: For when God made promise to Abraham, since he could swear by none greater, he swore by himself, 14: saying, Surely blessing I will bless thee, and multiplying I will multiply thee. 15: And thus, having patiently endured, he obtained the promise.

God condescended to confirm with an oath the promise he made to Abraham, for though this could add nothing to the trustworthiness of his word, it comforted Abraham to have it so emphatically endorsed. But as none is greater than God, the only way in which he could take such an oath was to swear by himself, a precedent which incidentally attests the legitimate use of oaths in human relations [verse 16].

Although Abraham knew that the earlier promise of a numerous posterity depended for its fulfilment upon the child of his old age, yet he did not withhold that child from God, and this unquestioning obedience was rewarded by the solemn ratification of the promise, the substance of which is reproduced in verse 14 [11:19; *Gen.* 12:2f, 2,2:16f.]. Abraham received a partial fulfilment of the promise in this life, and at death entered more fully into its blessings [*Matt.* 8:11; *John* 8:56]. Thus the Hebrews are reminded of the illustrious example of their revered progenitor in order to encourage them in the exercise of that patient endurance which results at last in the possession of the promised salvation.

16: For men swear by the greater: and in every dispute of theirs the oath is final for confirmation.

The use to which the oath is put in human affairs serves to illustrate the divine oath [verse 17f.]. For when men swear by the greater name of God this has two results, negative and positive: 1. it ends all contradiction; 2. it establishes that which it attests. 'An oath is a decisive appeal to the highest power to close all controversy. Therefore in condescension God interposed an oath to give to His promise this additional pledge of immutability for our encouragement' (Westcott).

17: Wherein God, being minded to show more abundantly unto the heirs of the promise the immutability of his counsel, interposed with an oath;

So God 'interposed with an oath' – he acted as his own Guarantor in pledging the fulfilment of the promise – in order that Abraham's spiritual heirs might be assured of his unchangeable resolve to secure their salvation [1:14; *Rom.* 8:17; *Gal.* 3:26–29, 4:26–28].

'His word is sufficient, yet tendering our infirmity he hath bound it with an oath, and set to his seal. His word cannot be made more true, but yet more credible. Now two things make a thing more credible: 1. The quality of the person speaking; 2. The manner of the speech. If God do not simply speak, but solemnly swear, and seal to us remission of sins, and adoption of sons by the broad seal of the sacraments, and by the privy seal of his Spirit, should we not rest assured?' (Trapp).

18: that by two immutable things, in which it is impossible for God to lie, we may have a strong encouragement, who have fled for refuge to lay hold of the hope set before us:

The complete veracity of God's Word is at once a grand incentive to the Hebrew Christians to persevere in the hope which they had embraced and a tacit rebuke for their tendency to waver in that hope. The bare *promise* of God should be sufficient to command their belief, but when it is reinforced by his *oath*, the complete impropriety of continuing to doubt the One for whom 'it is impossible to lie' is apparent. Hence these 'two immutable' assurances afford the strongest possible encouragement to believers to remain steadfast in their profession

Who have fled for refuge to lay hold of the hope set before us: Whatever may be the precise meaning of this metaphor it is plain that it refers to the protection which the Christian hope provides against an impending catastrophe. A burning conviction of the fearful reality of the final judgment saved the first preachers of the gospel from any sense of embarrassment as they solemnly warned their hearers to 'flee from the wrath to come'. Although there may be an allusion here to the cities of refuge mentioned in *Num.* 35, the context appears to favour a nautical reference. Thus F. F. Bruce comments: 'We are refugees from the sinking ship of this present world-order, so soon to disappear; our hope is fixed in the eternal order, where the promises of God are made good to His people in perpetuity.'

19: which we have as an anchor of the soul, a hope both sure and steadfast and entering into that which is within the veil;

Here the Christian hope is likened to the 'anchor of the soul'. The figure is not to be pressed, but simply means 'that we are moored to an immoveable object' (A. B. Davidson). It is a hope that is fixed in the unseen but real sanctuary of heaven. Therefore the stability of this hope 'is undisturbed by outward influences (*sure*), and it is firm in its inherent character (*steadfast*)' (Westcott).

20: whither as a forerunner Jesus entered for us, having become a high priest for ever after the order of Melchizedek.

Where as a forerunner there entered in in our behalf Jesus (Lenski): The human name of Jesus, placed emphatically at the end of the sentence, points to the necessity of his sacrificial death [2:9–18]. For it was only because he made our doom his own that he has entered heaven as a forerunner 'for us'. The word 'forerunner' is not used elsewhere in the New Testament. 'It expresses an entirely new idea, lying completely outside of the Levitical system. The Levitical high priest did not enter the sanctuary as a forerunner, but only as the people's representative. He entered a place into which none might follow him; in the people's stead, and not as their pioneer. The peculiarity of the new economy is that Christ as high priest goes nowhere where his people cannot follow him. He introduces man into full fellowship with God' (Vincent).

Having become a high priest for ever after the order of Melchizedek: This must not be taken as meaning that Jesus did not 'become' our eternal high priest 'until he entered heaven. That is the same as saying that the Jewish high priest became high priest only the moment he entered behind the veil' (Lenski). The clear teaching of this Epistle is that Jesus entered heaven, there to make intercession for us *in virtue of the once-for-all priestly offering of himself upon the cross* [9:11–14, 24–28, 10:10–14]. The repetition of the word 'Melchizedek' marks an adroit return to the point at which this digression began [5:10], and introduces the instruction which was promised on this theme [5:11, 7:1ff].

CHAPTER SEVEN

The author has already adduced the testimony of Psalm 110:4 to show that Christ is a priest after the order of Melchizedek [5:6], and now he appeals to Gen. 14:18ff. to explain why this priesthood is superior to that of the Levitical order. Firstly, the names of Melchizedek, the Priest-King of Salem, who blessed Abraham after the slaughter of the kings, are suggestive of the righteousness and peace of Christ's priestly reign. Secondly, it is significant that nothing is said of his birth and death, for it means that Melchizedek always appears in the narrative as a ministering priest, and this fittingly illustrates the eternal priesthood of the Son of God [verses 1–3]. Moreover, Abraham confessed the superiority of Melchizedek when he gave him the best of the spoils, so that it could even be said that Levi paid tithes to

Melchizedek in the person of his father Abraham [verses 4–10]. Now if perfection could have been attained through the Levitical priesthood, then the Psalmist would not have spoken of the rise of a priesthood pertaining to another tribe, for it is evident that our Lord was not of Levi but of Judah [verses 11–14]. And as the permanence of this priesthood is guaranteed by Christ's endless life and God's immutable oath, it has replaced that imperfect order which required many priests, because they were removed from their office by death [verses 15–24]. Wherefore Christ is able to save all who draw near to God through him, seeing he ever lives to intercede for them [verse 25]. For it was fitting that we should have such a spotless High Priest, who had no need to offer daily sacrifices, first for his own sins, and then for the sins of the people: for he made the one perfect sacrifice for sin when he offered up himself. For the law appoints weak men as high priests, but the oath which came after the law, appoints a Son who has been made perfect for ever [verses 26–28].

1: For this Melchizedek, king of Salem, priest of God Most High, who met Abraham returning from the slaughter of the kings and blessed him, 2: to whom also Abraham divided a tenth part of all (being first, by interpretation, King of righteousness, and then also King of Salem, which is, King of peace; 3: without father, without mother, without genealogy, having neither beginning of days nor end of life, but made like unto the Son of God), abideth a priest continually.

The author now explains how the high-priesthood of Jesus is typically set forth in the brief appearance of the mysterious figure who blessed Abraham after his victory over the four kings, and to whom he paid tithes [*Gen.* 14:18–20]. As in Paul where the gospel-promise given to Abraham is seen to precede the law, so this original interpretation demonstrates that the law 'has no eternal validity as a way of salvation' by showing that Christ's priesthood was already foreshadowed in the same book of Genesis (so G. Schrenk, *TDNT*, vol. 5, p. 1021).

For this Melchizedek . . . abideth a priest continually: Although the intervening description fills in the details of Abraham's encounter with the Priest-King of Salem, the words 'abideth a priest continually' express the real point of the Melchizedek priesthood. This priesthood resembles that of Christ because the snapshot we are given of

Melchizedek in Scripture leaves him in the permanent possession of his office. So as we see him in that picture 'which is a prophetic copy of another, he is a priest continually' (Davidson).

John Owen rightly insists upon the fundamental importance of this surprising disclosure for a true understanding of the person and work of Christ. 'The first personal instituted type of Christ was a priest; this was Melchizedek. – There were before *real* instituted types of his work, as sacrifices; and there were *moral* types of his person, as Adam, Abel, and Noah, which represented him in sundry things; but the first person who was solemnly designed to teach and represent him, by what he was and did, was a priest. And that which God taught herein was, that the foundation of all that the Lord Christ had to do in and for the church was laid in his priestly office, whereby he made atonement and reconciliation for sin. Every thing else that he doth is built on the supposition hereof. And we must begin in the application where God begins in the exhibition. An interest in the effects of the priestly office of Christ is that which in the first place we ought to look after. This being attained, we shall be willing to be taught and ruled by him, and not else.'

Verses 1, 2a: In spite of the degenerate polytheism of his neighbours, the sacred narrative describes Melchizedek as a 'priest of God Most High,' a designation which distinguishes him as a servant of the only true God. He also ruled over the city of Salem, which is almost certainly to be identified with Jerusalem. Moreover, even the patriarch Abraham freely acknowledged the greatness of this man by whom he was blessed [verse 7], and to whom he gave 'a tenth out of the chief spoils' [verse 4].

Verse 2b: The author finds a typical significance in the words 'Melchizedek' and 'Salem', for the first means 'King of righteousness' while the second refers to the blessings of 'peace' which flow from his righteous rule. *This is ever the order with God.* The peace which is enjoyed by those who dwell in Salem is based upon the justifying righteousness of their great Priest-King. For as Luther says, 'It is impossible for one to have this peace without faith, that is, the righteousness of God' [*Psa.* 85:10; *Isa.* 32:17; *Rom.* 5:1, 14:17].

Verse 3: In this verse the reasoning proceeds on the premise that even the silence of Scripture is pregnant with meaning. 'Melchizedek was an historical person and not eternal, still as a Scriptural figure he was regarded as eternal, being without recorded father or mother or genealogy, and having no recorded beginning of days nor end of life. In these respects he is like unto the Son of God, that is, stripped of all earthly attachments. As such, then, he is also a type of Christ. Thus *as he appears in Scripture* he may be regarded as enveloped in an atmosphere of eternity' (Vos). This refusal to see anything in Melchizedek save that which is taught in Scripture leads Calvin to conclude that, 'In dealing with everything that has to do with Christ we must scrupulously observe that we do not accept anything that is not from the Word of God.'

Melchizedek's priesthood was unlike the Levitical order in that it was not limited to a prescribed period, nor did it depend for its exercise upon a carefully preserved genealogy; for his office was derived from his personal dignity, and in this he resembled the Son of God. For the immeasurable superiority of Christ's priesthood over the earthly order which it replaced rests upon the divine dignity of his eternal Sonship. Hence John Owen pertinently observes, 'that Christ, abiding a priest for ever, hath no more a vicar, or successor, or substitute in his office, or any deriving a real priesthood from him, than had Melchizedek'.

4: Now consider how great this man was, unto whom Abraham, the patriarch, gave a tenth out of the chief spoils.

These Hebrew Christians are now earnestly urged to consider an amazing spectacle: here is the respected founder of their race paying the very best of the booty to a Gentile priest! 'Abraham's doing homage to Melchizedek is a plain proof that, in his sacred character, Melchizedek was superior to any of the religious officers under the legal economy' (John Brown).

5: And they indeed of the sons of Levi that receive the priest's office have commandment to take tithes of the people according to the law, that is, of their brethren, though these have come out of the loins of Abraham: 6: but he whose genealogy is not counted from them hath taken tithes of Abraham, and hath blessed him that hath the promises. 7: But without any dispute the less is blessed of the better.

Even though they were brethren in virtue of their descent from a common ancestor, the people were obliged by the law of God to pay tithes to the sons of Levi because the priesthood belonged to them. As Melchizedek obviously had no place in the Levitical line, Abraham did not present tithes to him as a matter of legal obligation, but in voluntary recognition of his superiority as 'priest of God Most High'. In verse 6 the author draws attention to Abraham's dignity as the possessor of the divine promises in order to enhance the greatness of the One by whom he was blessed, for it is beyond dispute that 'the less is blessed of the better'. Lenski further notes that 'hath taken tithes' and 'hath blessed' are perfect tenses, which are used to convey 'the lasting significance and effect of these priestly acts'.

8: And here men that die receive tithes; but there one, of whom it is witnessed that he liveth.

This verse points a further contrast between the sons of Levi and Melchizedek, for while the former are dying men even as they receive tithes, the silence of Scripture concerning the latter's death is a positive witness to the fact that he lives. 'The actual historical Melchizedek no doubt died, but the Melchizedek of the sacred narrative does nothing but LIVE – fixed, as it were, in unchangeable existence by the pencil of inspiration, and so made the type of the Eternal Priest, the Son of God' (Delitzsch).

9: And, so to say, through Abraham even Levi, who receiveth tithes, hath paid tithes; 10: for he was yet in the loins of his father, when Melchizedek met him.

In fact, 'to use just the right word' (Arndt-Gingrich), Levi 'hath paid tithes' (perfect tense again) to Melchizedek in the person of the patriarch Abraham, whose acknowledgment of this priest was a representative act which involved all his descendants. Lenski enters a vigorous protest against the suggestion that this forms an apologetic conclusion to what even the author regards as an artificial argument. Such objections have no force when countless acts of ancestors are regarded in the same way today! 'Did Adam's act not put death upon all of us [*Rom.* 5:12]? When a king abdicates, does that not count also for his sons and for their sons? When I squander my property, do my heirs still retain it? Why speak of Levi as not personally giving assent to what was done by Abraham before Levi was born? Although he was at that time unborn and gave no personal assent, did Levi not share in Abraham's blessing, both that which was bestowed by God and that which was pronounced by Melchizedek?'

11: Now if there was perfection through the Levitical priesthood (for under it hath the people received the law), what further need was there that another priest should arise after the order of Melchizedek, and not be reckoned after the order of Aaron?

If the Levitical order had achieved the end for which the priestly office had been instituted by God, then clearly the Psalmist would not have spoken of the rise of a different kind of priest [*Psa.* 110:4]. This failure is heightened by the words in parenthesis, for in stating that the people received the law 'on the basis' of this priesthood, the author certainly implies the inadequacy of its mediation in dealing with the problem of sin. For though Israel rendered an outward obedience to the laws which regulated the service of the earthly sanctuary, yet its priests remained powerless to effect that inward cleansing of the conscience which alone could 'make perfect them that draw nigh' [10:1]. Hence the need of another order of priesthood was proved by the defectiveness of their ministrations.

12: For the priesthood being changed, there is made of necessity a change also of the law.

Since the priesthood was the very basis of the law [verse 11], a change in the priesthood necessarily involved a change in the law. In fact Psalm 110 heralded the abolition of the entire legal system with all its ceremonial ordinances. The Jews were mistaken if they believed that the Levitical priesthood was established as a permanent institution by an unalterable law. For the law rested on the priesthood, so when God set aside that priesthood, he also dispensed with the law by which it was regulated. 'These means and these laws served their temporary purpose; and when the time came, they had to be changed for something that would be permanent, complete, eternal' (Lenski).

13: For he of whom these things are said belongeth to another tribe, from which no man hath given attendance at the altar.

This change in the law concerning the priesthood was demanded by the Psalmist's prediction, for the One of whom he spoke was excluded from offering the sacrifices prescribed under that law because he did not belong to the tribe of Levi [*Psa.* 110:1, 4]. 'Seeing Christ himself had no right to minister at the material altar, the re-introduction of such altars is inconsistent with the perpetual continuance of his priesthood' (John Owen).

14: For it is evident that our Lord hath sprung out of Judah; as to which tribe Moses spake nothing concerning priests.

'For as we very well know, *our* Lord is of the tribe of Judah!' David expressed his personal interest in the Messiah when he addressed him as 'my Lord' [*Psa.* 110:1], and Lenski suggests that the author's use of the pronoun 'our' is intended gently to recall his readers to their confession of faith in Christ. Many scriptures plainly foretold that the Messiah was to belong to the tribe of Judah [e.g. *Gen.* 49:8–10; *Isa.* 11:1–5; *Mic.* 5:2], while the words 'hath sprung' refer to the historical appearance of this promised 'Branch' [*Jer.* 23:5; *Zech.* 3:8, 6:12].

The lack of a positive appointment to the priesthood in the law of Moses excluded the men of Judah from exercising this office as effectively as if it had been expressly forbidden to them [*Jer.* 7:31; *Col.* 2:20–23]. 'That a ceremony is not expressly forbidden by Scripture does not warrant its practice, because the Scriptural rule excludes all religious ceremonies which are not of Divine appointment. Their not being commanded is therefore a sufficient reason for refusing them' (Samuel Palmer, *The Nonconformist's Catechism*, 1773, reprinted in *Sermons of the Great Ejection*, p. 212, Q. 34).

15: And what we say is yet more abundantly evident, if after the likeness of Melchizedek there ariseth another priest, 16: who hath been made, not after the law of a carnal commandment, but after the power of an endless life:

Although the fact that Jesus sprang from the tribe of Judah makes it clear that the law has been changed [verse 14], this is 'yet more abundantly evident' from the character of his priesthood, which is first described *negatively* and then *positively*.

Not after the law of a carnal commandment (or lit. *fleshen* commandment): 'The Law of the Aaronic priesthood had reference to descent from a particular tribe, to bodily conditions, to marriage, in a word to "flesh", a word which expresses all that which is mortal and perishable. A priesthood created and exercised under such a fleshen commandment can have no effects outside of the principle which regulates it; it can never extend its influence into the region of spirit and life' (Davidson).

But after the power of an indissoluble life (ASV margin): It was otherwise with Christ whose 'physical death as Man was no dissolution of His eternal life as God' (A. M. Stibbs). And it is because this perpetual life is the inalienable possession of the Risen Christ that he is able freely to bestow it upon his people [7:25].

17: for it is witnessed of him, Thou art a priest for ever after the order of Melchizedek.

In proof of the perpetuity of Christ's priesthood the author here appeals to the Scripture upon whose testimony his teaching has been based [verse 11f.]. As Vaughan observes: 'The typical Melchizedek had this indestructible life only from the studied mysteriousness of the Scripture record of him. Christ the antitype of Melchizedek has it in right of His resurrection to die no more (*Rom.* 6:9f. *Christ being raised from the dead dieth no more . . . but in that he liveth, he liveth unto God*)'.

18: For there is a disannulling of a foregoing commandment because of its weakness and unprofitableness 19: (for the law made nothing perfect), and a bringing in thereupon of a better hope, through which we draw nigh unto God.

The introduction of a 'better hope,' through which we draw near to God [10:19–22], meant the abrogation of the 'foregoing commandment' which brought nothing to completion. 'For, indeed, that law made nothing perfect. It did not make a perfect priest; it did not make perfect expiation; it did not afford perfect peace of conscience; it did not give real, far less perfect, sanctification. If it had, it would have been permanent' (John Brown).

However, in spite of its preliminary character, the ceremonial law possessed a spiritual value because it foreshadowed the grace which was to be revealed in Christ. The rites which were practised under its provisions derived their efficacy from his forthcoming sacrifice, after which the divine authority for their continuance was withdrawn [cf.

Matt. 27:51 with 10:19, 20]. Therefore those who still continued to cling to the shadow actually forfeited the substance it had once represented.

'The "better" hope is that which springs from belief in the indestructible life of Christ and the assurance that that life is still active in the priestly function of intercession. It is the hope that is anchored within the veil fixed in Christ's Person and therefore bringing us into God's presence and fellowship' (Marcus Dods).

20: And inasmuch as it is not without the taking of an oath 21: (for they indeed have been made priests without an oath; but he with an oath by him that saith of him, The Lord sware and will not repent himself, Thou art a priest for ever);

Moreover, the selfsame scripture provides a further proof of the superiority of the Melchizedek priesthood by showing that God confirmed it with a solemn oath [*Psa.* 110]. The fact that no such oath was made in connection with the Levitical order showed the provisional nature of their service, for the legal dispensation was but a preparation for the advent of the Promised Seed [*Gal.* 3:17–27]. Westcott points out that the stress laid on the oath suggests the contrast which Paul draws between 'the promise' and 'the Law' in the Galatian Epistle. 'The Law is an expression of the sovereign power of God who requires specific obedience: the oath implies a purpose of love not to be disturbed by man's unworthiness.'

22: by so much also hath Jesus become the surety of a better covenant.

The sentence which was broken by the parenthesis of the previous verse is now completed. It is the divine oath which distinguishes Jesus (his name being placed last in the sentence for emphasis) as the surety of a better covenant (*diatheke*). The importance of this word to the author's argument may be gauged from the fact that this is the first of seventeen times he uses it in this Epistle, whereas it only occurs another sixteen times in the rest of the New Testament. R. V. G. Tasker has noted that 'The Biblical covenants between God and man, though they call for obedience and faith on man's part, are essentially divine dispositions, manifestations of His saving grace. In these covenants, though there are two parties, there is one disposer' (*The Gospel in the*

Epistle to the Hebrews, p. 16).[1] But though the Mosaic covenant was good, this is *better*, because the fulfilment of its promises is not suspended upon the obedience and faith of its beneficiaries, for even these were purchased for them by their Surety [*Psa.* 110:3; 8:6–13]. This word 'surety' (*enguos*) appears only here in the New Testament. It means that Jesus 'is the Personal guarantee of the terms of the new and better covenant, secured on the ground of His perfect sacrifice [verse 27]' (W. E. Vine).

23: And they indeed have been made priests many in number, because that by death they are hindered from continuing: 24: but he, because he abideth for ever, hath priesthood unchangeable.

A further and final proof of the inferiority of the Levitical priesthood is now brought forward. It is an incontrovertible fact that there were many Jewish high priests because death always made the appointment of a successor necessary. One by one they were stopped by death. But the priesthood of Christ is never-ending, for *he* ever lives to intercede on behalf of his people [verse 25].

Unchangeable: Or 'indefectible'. Our author here affirms that Christ's priesthood 'is in its very nature unsupersedable, that finality inheres in it . . . In the one flawless Mediator we descry priesthood at its summit-level. His unique endowments exhaust the requisites of the office and invest it with ineffaceable validity' (E. K. Simpson in *The Evangelical Quarterly*, July 1946, p. 188).

25: Wherefore also he is able to save to the uttermost them that draw near unto God through him, seeing he ever liveth to make intercession for them.

Wherefore also he is able to save to the uttermost: It follows from the foregoing that Christ is able perfectly to secure the complete salvation of all those for whom he acts as priest. 'Those who endeavour to come unto God any other way but by Christ, as by saints and angels, may do well to consider whether they have any such office in heaven as by virtue whereof they are able to save them to the uttermost . . . All false religion is but a choice of other things for men to place their trust in,

[1] For a fuller explanation of the word COVENANT, see the magisterial discussion by John Murray in *The New Bible Dictionary*, pp.264–8.

with a neglect of Christ. And all superstition grows on the same root, in all effects or instances of it, be they great or small' (John Owen). [*John* 14:6]

Them that draw near unto God through him: Thus the Hebrews must realize that, 1. They can no longer rely on the mediation of a superseded order of priests; 2. They are *required* to come unto God through that 'new and living way' which has been opened up by Christ [cf. 10:19–22 with 10:25]. 'Attendance unto the service, the worship of God in the gospel, is required to interest us in the saving care and power of our high priest. – Men deceive themselves, who look to be saved by him, but take no care to come to God in holy worship by him' (John Owen).

Seeing he ever liveth to make intercession: The unambiguous teaching of this Epistle is that the ministry of Christ in heaven is one of intercession and not sacrifice [verse 27; 9:12, 25, 26; 10:10, 12; 13:12]. 'He is a priest now, not to offer sacrifice but as the permanent personal embodiment of all the efficacy and virtue that accrued from the sacrifice once offered. And it is as such he ever continues to make intercession for his people' (John Murray, *Redemption –Accomplished and Applied*, p. 28).

H. B. Swete warns us against entertaining a purely carnal conception of this intercession: 'The New Testament does not represent Him as an *orante*, standing ever before the Father, and with outstretched arms, like the figures in the mosaics of the catacombs, and with strong crying and tears pleading our cause in the presence of a reluctant God; but as a throned Priest-King, asking what He will from a Father who always hears and grants His request. Our Lord's life in heaven is His prayer. But in the days of His flesh He prayed as we pray, and one of His prayers of intercession [John 17] remains to help the Church to realize in some measure the ends which He sets before Him in His intercessory life' (*The Ascended Christ*, pp. 95–6).

For them: Cf. *John* 17:9. 'Christ intercedes for *all* those for whom He has made atonement, and for those *only*. This may be inferred from the limited character of the atonement, and also from such passages as *Rom.* 8:34; *Heb.* 7:25, 9:24, in every one of which the word "us" refers to believers' (Louis Berkhof, *Systematic Theology*, p. 404).

26: For such a high priest became us, holy, guileless, undefiled, separated from sinners, and made higher than the heavens;

We are here bidden to reflect upon the perfection of this new Priesthood which is exactly adapted to our case and need. For 'Unholy sinners do stand in need of *a holy priest* and a *holy sacrifice*' (John Owen). *HOLY* describes what Christ is in himself. As befits 'the Holy One' (i.e. the Messiah, *Acts* 2:27), his character is absolutely holy, and his will is in complete accord with that of the Father [10:7]. *GUILELESS* sets forth what Christ is in relation to men. His complete lack of evil feeling towards men is positively expressed in that loving service which is the fruit of having triumphed over the full power of temptation [4:14–16]. *UNDEFILED* underlines the inherent nature of Christ's priesthood. As Moffatt notes, the word suggests a contrast between the *real* purity of Jesus and the *ritual* purity of the Levitical high priest [Lev. 21:10–15]. *SEPARATED FROM SINNERS* indicates the abiding result of Christ's victory over sin and death [9:28]. This local separateness 'implies no spiritual barrier: rather it is essential to the exercise of the mediatorial intercession, and even to the universal and impartial accessibility (compare *Eph.* 4:10, *that he might fill all things*)' (Vaughan). *MADE HIGHER THAN THE HEAVENS* explains the previous phrase by enlarging upon the present heavenly glory of our great High Priest [4:14]. Calvin shows the necessity for this exaltation by his remark, 'No one can unite us with God except someone who reaches to God.'

27: who needeth not daily, like those high priests, to offer up sacrifices, first for his own sins, and then for the sins of the people: for this he did once for all, when he offered up himself.

The supreme eminence of Christ's Person therefore explains the superior efficacy of his Priesthood over that of Aaron and his successors: for, 1. their sacrifices were frequent, his was final; 2. they were sinners, he is sinless; 3. they offered animals, he offered himself! Thus the verse introduces the idea of Christ's self-offering which is to be fully expounded in chapters 9 and 10.

For this he did once for all: 'The passages which make mention of Christ's ONE oblation, or of His offering Himself ONCE, are conclusive as to the fact of His being a priest on earth; for that word ONCE cannot be understood of what is done in heaven. It must refer to His death as a historic fact, completed and finished here below. It is against all reason to affirm that the sacrifice was offered once, if it still continues; for the expression ONCE, or ONE OFFERING, plainly contrasts the completed sacrifice with the continuous intercession which evermore proceeds upon it. Nor does the Epistle stop there: the analogy instituted between the fact that it was appointed to all men once to die, and the one atoning death of Christ [9:27], leaves us in no doubt that we must view that sacrifice as completed on the cross' (George Smeaton).

28: For the law appointeth men high priests, having infirmity; but the word of the oath, which was after the law, appointeth a Son, perfected for evermore.

The disparity is even more starkly displayed in the concluding contrast which crowns the whole argument. The law appointed men with sinful infirmities, but the word of the oath appointed a Son who has been 'perfected for evermore'. This means that 'all sacrifices had been consummated in the one Sacrifice, all priesthoods absorbed in the one Priest. The offering had been made once for all: and, as there were no more victims, there could be no more priests' J. B. Lightfoot, 'The Christian Ministry,' appended to *The Epistle to the Philippians,* p. 265).

Therefore, 'Plurality of priests under the gospel overthrows the whole argument of the apostle in this place; and if we have yet priests that have infirmities, they are made by the law, and not by the gospel' (John Owen).

CHAPTER EIGHT

Since our High Priest is now enthroned in the true tabernacle of heaven, he clearly has a superior priesthood to those whose ministrations are of necessity confined to the earthly copy of these heavenly realities. He is thus the Mediator of a better covenant, which is founded upon better promises, than that which was given through Moses [verses 1–6]. For if the first covenant had been faultless, there would have been no point in the prophetic promise of a new covenant, whose very announcement by Jeremiah implied that the existing covenant was already old and obsolete [verses 7–13].

1: Now in the things which we are saying the chief point is this: We have such a high priest, who sat down on the right hand of the throne of the Majesty in the heavens, 2: a minister of the sanctuary, and of the true tabernacle, which the Lord pitched, not man.

In this section of the Epistle the author enters upon an extended comparison of Christ's priestly ministry with that which was exercised by mortal men [8:1–10:18]. The discussion naturally rests upon what has gone before, but the main point to remember is that Christ ministers in the heavenly sanctuary and not in an earthly tabernacle made with hands [9:24]. For unlike those priests who performed their service in the tabernacle erected by man (Moses), Christ is a minister of the true tabernacle which was pitched by God himself. This 'does not imply that the tabernacle in the wilderness was not also most truly pitched at God's bidding, and according to the pattern which He had shown [*Exod.* 25:40]; but only that it, and all things in it, were weak earthly copies of heavenly realities' (R. C. Trench, *Synonyms of the New Testament*, pp. 26–27).

The greatness of Christ's priesthood is further revealed by the place which he occupies in the real sanctuary above [1:3]. For whereas the Levitical high priest entered the earthly 'holy place' but once a year, and then only to stand briefly before the symbol of God's throne, Christ our Priest-King sat down on the throne of the divine Majesty in heaven itself! And the essential point which the unsettled readers must grasp is that their unseen Mediator so reigns in glory in order to minister all the riches of his grace to them [11:1].

John Owen makes a characteristically vigorous application of this truth: 'The church hath lost nothing by the removal of the old tabernacle and temple, all being supplied by this sanctuary, true tabernacle, and minister thereof. – The glory and worship of the temple was that which the Jews would by no means part withal . . . And in later ages men ceased not, until they had brought into Christianity itself a worship vying for external order, ceremony, pomp, and painting, with whatever was in the tabernacle or temple of old; coming short of it principally in this, that *that* was of God's institution for a time, *this* of the invention of weak, superstitious, and foolish men. Thus is it in the church of Rome. And a hard thing it is to raise the minds of men unto a satisfaction in things merely spiritual and heavenly . . . But "unto them that believe Christ is precious." And this "true tabernacle," with his ministration, is more unto them than all the old pompous ceremonies and services of divine institution, much more the superstitious observances of human invention.'

3: For every high priest is appointed to offer both gifts and sacrifices: wherefore it is necessary that this high priest also have somewhat to offer.

A priest without a sacrifice is like a childless mother, for he is expressly appointed in order to make such offerings. Therefore if Christ is a priest he too must 'have had something to offer' (NEB margin). The tense of the verb used here definitely excludes all thought of a continuous offering, and as F. F. Bruce observes, 'is consistent with our author's repeated emphasis on the singularity of the sacrifice which Christ offered [7:27, 10:12]'. But 'because Christ's crowning act of priesthood, His offering of Himself, was done in relation to the actual presence of God, and not in relation to the earthly figure sanctuary in Jerusalem, it was, as the writer to the Hebrews saw it, done in the true heavenly tabernacle and not in the shadowy earthly one. In other words, though Jesus died outside the city of Jerusalem, His deed as a priestly act was done in heaven, or in the heavenlies, as Paul himself might have said, and not just on earth' (A. M. Stibbs, *The Finished Work of Christ,* p. 25). 'If any one else can offer the body of Christ, he also is the minister of the true tabernacle. – For the Lord Christ did no more, He did but offer himself; and they that can offer him, do put themselves in his place' (John Owen).

4: Now if he were on earth, he would not be a priest at all, seeing there are those who offer the gifts according to the law;

Indeed the mere fact that Christ did not belong to the tribe of Levi prevented him from presenting the offerings prescribed by the law. His descent from Judah meant that he could never officiate as a priest in the earthly sanctuary [7:13, 14], though of course he acted as a priest on earth when he 'suffered without [outside] the gate' in order to sanctify the people [13:12].

5: who serve that which is a copy and shadow of the heavenly things, even as Moses is warned of God when he is about to make the tabernacle: for,

See, saith he, that thou make all things according to the pattern that was showed thee in the mount.

These priests ministered in the tabernacle which was but a copy of the reality it represented. It provided only 'a pale reflexion' (Souter) of the heavenly things. Nevertheless it was a copy which God had commanded Moses to make, and it was this alone which invested it with spiritual meaning. But this meaning could not be conveyed to men if Moses were permitted to introduce any innovation into the worship of God, and therefore he was strictly admonished to make everything precisely according to the pattern which had been shown to him on the mount.

Hence Calvin concludes, 'By thus emphasizing the rule that He has laid down, He forbids us to depart from it in the very slightest. For this reason all the forms of worship produced by men fail, and also those things which are called sacraments and yet have not come from God . . . We must beware that in wishing to fit our own inventions to Christ we do not so change Him (as the papists do) that He becomes unlike Himself. It is not permissible for us to invent anything we like, but it belongs to God alone to show us *according to the pattern that was showed thee.*'

6: But now hath he obtained a ministry the more excellent, by so much as he is also the mediator of a better covenant, which hath been enacted upon better promises.

But as the case now stands, Christ has obtained a more excellent ministry for he is the mediator of a better covenant 'which has been (legally) enacted on the basis of better promises' (Arndt-Gingrich). With this emphatic repetition of the word 'better' the keynote of the Epistle is again struck. 'At every point Christianity is better than Judaism' (A. T. Robertson). The superiority of this covenant lies in the fact that its promises are guaranteed by the perfect satisfaction which has been rendered to God by its Mediator on behalf of those he represented [7:22, 27]. A covenant requires a mediator or 'middleman' to bring together the contracting parties, and Christ effected this union between God and his people by means of that reconciling work which secured the interests of both parties, because it met the claims of justice and mercy. In the verses that follow the author shows that the Scripture speaks of the 'better promises' on which this covenant rests: they consist in, 1. the renewal of the heart [verse 10]; 2. the universal knowledge of God [verse 11]; 3. the complete forgiveness of sins [verse 12].

7: For if that first covenant had been faultless, then would no place have been sought for a second.

If the Sinaitic covenant had not manifestly failed to produce the obedience it demanded, there would have been no occasion to search for a new covenant to replace it. That such a search for something better was going on even while that dispensation remained in full force is proved by the testimony of Jeremiah [verses 8–12]. The author thus shows that 'the Levitical system answered to a covenant which was recognized as imperfect and transitory by an Old Testament prophet, since he spoke of a divine purpose to establish a new covenant' (Vincent).

8a: For finding fault with them, he saith,

This appeal to Scripture substantiates the bold assertion of the previous verse [*Jer.* 31:31–34]. 'There is a subtle delicacy of language in this insensible shifting of the blame from the covenant to the people. The covenant itself could hardly be said to be faultless, seeing that it failed to bind Israel to their God; but the true cause of failure lay in the character of the people, not in the law, which was holy, righteous, and good' (F. Rendall, *The Epistle to the Hebrews*, p. 65). 'The old covenant was faulty because it did not provide for enabling the people to live up to the terms or conditions of it. *It* was faulty inasmuch as it did not sufficiently provide against their faultiness' (Marcus Dods).

He saith (legei): The significance of this 'subjectless' phrase is well brought out in a comment by B. B. Warfield: 'Like Philo, the author of the Epistle to the Hebrews looks upon Scripture as an oracular book, and all that it says, God says to him: and accordingly, like Philo, he adduces its words with a simple "it says", with the full implication that this "it says" is a "God says" also' (*The Inspiration and Authority of the Bible*, p. 346).

8b: Behold, the days come, saith the Lord, that I will make a new covenant with the house of Israel and with the house of Judah; 9: not

according to the covenant that I made with their fathers in the day that I took them by the hand to lead them forth out of the land of Egypt; For they continued not in my covenant, and I regarded them not, saith the Lord. 10: For this is the covenant that I will make with the house of Israel after those days, saith the Lord; I will put my laws into their mind, and on their heart also will I write them: and I will be to them a God, and they shall be to me a people: 11: And they shall not teach every man his fellow-citizen, and every man his brother, saying, Know the Lord: For all shall know me, from the least to the greatest of them. 12: For I will be merciful to their iniquities, and their sins will I remember no more.

In this important prophecy the covenant which God made with Israel at Sinai is unfavourably compared with the new covenant which would eventually supersede it. The author has no other purpose in quoting it than to prove that its promises have been fulfilled by Christ and that his church now constitutes the New Israel of God.[1] As the terms of the Mosaic covenant were rendered null and void by the disobedience of the people, God therefore speaks of a new covenant which cannot be broken because it will ensure the spiritual response of those with whom it is made by providing for the internal renovation of their character. Under the gracious provisions of this covenant, God promises to inscribe his law upon the hearts of his people, who shall all know him 'from the least to the greatest', *for* 'their sins will I remember no more'.

1. *I will put my laws into their mind, and on their heart also will I write them* [verse 10]: At Sinai the proclamation of the law was accompanied by the most terrible portents, yet even this awesome disclosure did not succeed in securing Israel's obedience to its demands [12:18–21]. Indeed the perverse obduracy of the human heart is such that until God is pleased to renew it by his Spirit it cannot render any obedience to his law [*Ezek.* 36:26–27]. 'It is clear from this how much force free will has, and what rightness there is in our nature before God renews us. We will and we choose, and we do so of our own accord, but our will is carried away by an almost raging impulse to resist God and cannot in any way submit to His justice. So it comes about that the

[1] O. T. Allis subjects the teaching of those who claim 'that the Christian Church is a mystery parenthesis which interrupts the fulfilment to Israel of the Kingdom prophecies of the Old Testament' to a devastating examination in his book *Prophecy and the Church*.

Law is fatal and deadly for us as long as it remains written on tablets of stone, as Paul says in *2 Cor.* 3:3. In short, we accept God's command obediently when He changes and corrects the native wickedness of our hearts by His Spirit; otherwise He will find nothing in us but evil passions and a heart wholly given to wickedness. It is clearly laid down that a new covenant is to be made by which God will write His laws on our hearts, because otherwise it will be of no effect' (Calvin).

2. *All shall know me* [verse 11]: It is clear from the preceding promise that far more is signified by this than mere notional knowledge *about* God. It rather speaks of that personal knowledge of God which is ever expressed in a practical conformity to the divine will. This knowledge is neither sacramentally conveyed through a hierarchy of self-styled priests, nor is it individually communicated in any mystical fashion apart from the Word of God. 'No new prophets appear with new messages. We have all God's Word; and each has it in his own hand. We can by it even test those who stand up to preach and to teach it. "From their small up to their great" is correct: from our children and our catechumens up to our great theologians; God's saving revelation, complete at last, is accessible to all alike. It is the fulfilment of the prophecy of Jeremiah and of *Isa.* 54:13; 11:9; *Hab.* 2:14; *Joel* 2:28; *John* 6:45; *1 John* 2:20,27' (Lenski).

3. *Their sins will I remember no more* [verse 12]: The word 'for' which introduces the final promise indicates that the former blessings are based upon a full satisfaction for sin. As the old covenant was not ratified without the sprinkling of the blood of sacrifice, so the new covenant could not be inaugurated without the shedding of Christ's blood [9:19–22; *Exod.* 24:6–8].

And this is the meaning which Christ himself attached to his death when he took the cup and told the amazed disciples, 'This cup is the new covenant in my blood, even that which is poured out for you' [*Luke* 22:20]. His willing submission to the death of the cross was a divine necessity because the mercy of God is never exercised at the expense of his righteousness [*Rom.* 3:24–26]. God could only forgive the sins of his people in a manner which was consistent with his holiness [*Psa.* 85:10]. Thus it took nothing less than the blood of One who was divine to make good this promise of a free pardon for guilty sinners [*Acts* 20:28]. Moreover, the non-remembrance of their sin also implies the imputation of Christ's righteousness to their account, for when God 'forgets their sins, he will have their persons in everlasting remembrance, *Psa.* 112:6' (Poole) [*Rom.* 5:18–21].

13: In that he saith, A new covenant, he hath made the first old. But that which is becoming old and waxeth aged is nigh unto vanishing away.

By saying 'a new covenant,' he antiquates the first (Moffatt): In fixing upon this one word 'new' (*kainos*) the author here stresses the superiority of that covenant which has made the former one obsolete; whereas in 12:24 he describes it as 'fresh' (*neos*) in point of time as compared with the ancient one it has replaced.

And whatever is antiquated and aged is on the verge of vanishing (Moffatt): If Jeremiah spoke of a 'new' covenant so long ago, how much nearer is the old order now to vanishing away! It is in a state of senile decrepitude, 'like an old, old man who is sinking into his grave. To such a thing the readers would go back if they again became Jews' (Lenski). The sacrificial system did indeed vanish away with the destruction of the temple in AD 70. 'Thus the Sinaitic superstructure became antiquated. But its foundation, the Abrahamic covenant, was never abrogated, and still stands today, as the abiding basis of the new superstructure, the new covenant' (Martin J. Wyngaarden, *The Future of the Kingdom in Prophecy and Fulfilment,* p. 124) [*Gal.* 3:15–17].

CHAPTER NINE

The author's description of the furniture and service of the tabernacle shows that the old covenant was a dispensation of distance. For though the priests daily ministered in the Holy place, entrance to the Holy of holies was barred to all, except the High Priest on the annual Day of Atonement. And this ban proved the inadequacy of these carnal ordinances to effect that inward purification which would bring the worshipper near to God [verses 1–10]. But in contrast to the High Priest's yearly entrance into the Holy of holies Christ once for all entered the real sanctuary of heaven in virtue of his perfect sacrifice for sin, having obtained eternal redemption [verses11, 12]. If then the blood of animals removed outward defilement and gave ritual purity, how much more shall the blood of Christ, who through his own eternal Spirit offered himself without blemish to God, cleanse their conscience from dead works to serve the living God? [verses 13, 14]. It is by his sacrificial death that Christ is the Mediator of a new covenant, for the blessings of this testament could not have been received without the death of its testator [verses 15–17]. Thus even the provisions of the first covenant had to be ratified by the shedding of blood, apart from which there is no remission [verses 18–22]. But though the copies of heavenly things required cleansing by blood, the heavenly things themselves called for better sacrifices than these. For Christ has not entered a holy place made with hands, but heaven itself, there to appear before God for us. Unlike the Levitical high priest he does not have to make repeated sacrifices for sin, for he has now once suffered to put away sin by the sacrifice of himself. And as it is appointed unto men once to die, and after this the judgment; so Christ, having been once offered to bear the sin of many, shall appear the second time in glory to consummate the salvation of his people [verses 23–28].

1: Now even the first covenant had ordinances of divine service, and its sanctuary, a sanctuary of this world.

Now the first covenant had indeed a divinely appointed pattern of ministry and a holy place in which this service was performed. The tabernacle which God instructed Moses to make was a worldly sanctuary with a heavenly meaning, but precisely because it was so firmly fixed upon the earth it could not afford access to the heavenly reality it dimly represented [8:5].

2: For there was a tabernacle prepared, the first, wherein were the candlestick, and the table, and the showbread; which is called the Holy place.

This tabernacle was 'made' in contrast to that which was 'not made with hands' [verse 11]. No more is said of the tabernacle than is necessary to advance the author's argument. He makes no mention of the outer court but simply gives a brief description of the tent itself, the first compartment of which was the sanctuary, or 'the Holy place,' and this contained the lampstand and the table of showbread [*Exod.* 25:23–29,37:10–24].

The candlestick (*luchnia*): Better, light-stand or lamp-stand. W.E. Vine points out that 'candlestick' is a serious mistranslation: 'There is no mention of a candle in the original either in the Old Testament or in the New Testament. The figure of that which feeds upon its own substance to provide its light would be utterly inappropriate. A lamp is supplied by oil, which in its symbolism is figurative of the Holy Spirit.'

3: And after the second veil, the tabernacle which is called the Holy of holies; 4: having a golden altar of incense, and the ark of the covenant overlaid round about with gold, wherein was a golden pot holding the manna, and Aaron's rod that budded, and the tables of the covenant; 5: and above it cherubim of glory overshadowing the mercy-seat; of which things we cannot now speak severally.

As there was a curtain at the entrance of the sanctuary, the veil which divided this first compartment from 'the Holy of holies' is here called 'the second veil'. The 'golden altar of incense' *belonged* (cf. '*having*' with 'in which,' verse 2) to the Holy of holies, though it was *placed* 'within the outer sanctuary in order to be daily served by the ordinary priests' (Delitzsch) [*Exod.* 30:1–6,40:5]. Beyond the veil lay the ark of the covenant in which were deposited the tables of testimony, Aaron's rod that budded, and the pot with manna in it, while the mercy-seat, which formed the lid of this sacred chest, was overshadowed by the cherubim of glory [*Exod.* 16:33–34, 25:16–22; *Num.* 17:10]. It is not the author's intention to speak of the individual significance of these things, though doubtless he could have done so had it been within the scope of his present purpose. He chooses instead to describe what took place within this earthly tabernacle on the annual day of Atonement.

6: Now these things having been thus prepared, the priests go in continually into the first tabernacle, accomplishing the services; 7: but into the second the high priest alone, once in the year, not without blood, which he offereth for himself, and for the errors of the people:

Although the ordinary priests served God continually in the holy place to which they enjoyed unhindered access without blood, entrance to the inner sanctuary was forbidden to all except the high priest, but even he could enter it only once a year, and then not without the blood of sacrifice. Furthermore, 'this sacrificial blood was not finally efficacious, for fresh blood had to be shed and a fresh entry made into the holy of holies year by year' (F. F. Bruce).

As verse 8 makes clear, the author is here contrasting the unsatisfactory service of the Levitical high priests with the complete finality of Christ's sacrifice. 'Offereth' is in the present tense to mark the fact that their work was never finished. For though the chief end of their ministry was to offer sacrifices for sins, they failed to reach the end of their task. And this was because they always brought an offering which only served to recall the sins it could not really remove [10:3, 4], whereas Christ began his priesthood by making an end of sin, and then in virtue of that sacrificial death he entered in once for all into the holy place, having obtained eternal redemption' [verse 12].

Secondly, it should be noted that 'offereth' only loosely describes the high priest's function, for it is not said where or when the offering was made. But it is plain from Lev. 16:15 that the *offering* of the sacrifice preceded the *sprinkling* of the blood upon the mercy-seat. What this indicates is that the blood secured the high priest's safe access into the holiest place; it did not provide him with the means of continuing the work of offering after entrance had thus been gained. The passage therefore provides no grounds for supposing that Christ continues 'to offer' his blood in heaven. In this Epistle his sacrificial offering is firmly located on earth [13:12], and it is repeatedly shown that this one perfect offering for sins admits of no repetition or continuation.

8: the Holy Spirit this signifying, that the way into the holy place hath not yet been made manifest, while the first tabernacle is yet standing;

By means of this restriction the Holy Spirit virtually declared that the way into the heavenly sanctuary was not open while the worship carried on in the earthly tabernacle continued in accordance with God's appointment. This period came to an end with the death of Christ, when the rending of the temple veil was the supernatural sign that at last this barrier had been removed [*Matt.* 27:51]. The author does not mean that there was no experience of gospel grace under the Old Testament, but 'that unimpeded access to the presence of God was not granted until Christ came to accomplish His sacrificial ministry' (F. F. Bruce).

9: which is a figure for the time present; according to which are offered both gifts and sacrifices that cannot, as touching the conscience, make the worshipper perfect,

That the way into the holiest was thus barred is 'a parable bearing on the present crisis' (W. Manson). It should convince the readers of the futility of returning to a system that brought nothing to perfection, for the gifts and sacrifices which were offered in connection with the earthly tabernacle could never make the worshipper complete, because in themselves they possessed no power to cleanse his conscience [verse 14]. Although they sufficed to secure his ceremonial purity, they were a means of grace only insofar as they pointed forward to the final sacrifice of Christ. 'Nothing can give perfect peace of conscience with God but what can make atonement for sin. And whoever attempt it any other way but by virtue of that atonement, will never attain it, in this world nor hereafter' (John Owen).

10: being only (with meats and drinks and divers washings) carnal ordinances, imposed until a time of reformation.

Moreover, the carnal service of the worldly sanctuary gave evidence of its provisional character, for these rites were only imposed until 'the time of the new order' (Arndt Gingrich). [*Acts* 15:10] The arrival of the promised Seed meant that those who still rashly continued to observe these ordinances did so without a divine warrant and in consequence were left with nothing but the empty husks of a superseded ritual.

11: But Christ having come a high priest of the good things to come, through the greater and more perfect tabernacle, not made with hands, that is to say, not of this creation,

But when Christ appeared as a high priest of the good things that have come (RSV): This better reading is in line with the 'realized eschatology' of the author. For though believers are still pilgrims on their way to Zion [11:16], spiritually speaking they have already arrived [12:22–24]! The present possession of these heavenly blessings was secured 'through' the triumphant entrance of our great high priest into that sanctuary which is not of this world because it is 'not made with hands' [*Acts* 7:48, 17:24]. The official designation 'Christ' not only draws attention to the Messianic fulfilment of what was typified in the material copy, but also indicates the representative nature of his entry into heaven by which the salvation of his people is assured. For God's acceptance of the person of the Mediator is the indisputable proof of the efficacy of the sacrifice he had offered on their behalf [8:3]. As P. E. Hughes explains, the reason that 'tabernacle' and 'the holy place' [verse 12] are treated as synonymous terms is because the veil which divided the earthly tent into two chambers has been abolished by Christ's death [verse 8]. *Thus Christ entered the true tabernacle (of heaven) which is the true sanctuary (of God's presence).*

12: nor yet through the blood of goats and calves, but through his own blood, entered in once for all into the holy place, having obtained eternal redemption.

As the opening disclaimer shows, Christ not only ministers in a better place [verse 11], he also offered a better sacrifice. The blood of goats and calves brought the Levitical high priest only once a year into the holy place of the earthly tabernacle, but it was 'through his own blood' that Christ entered 'once for all' into heaven itself. H. C. G. Moule correctly states, 'Blood *shed* is not a vehicle of power, but an evidence of death, especially by sacrifice or execution'. So what these high priests had in common was that they both entered a sanctuary in virtue of a sacrificial death. To give evidence of that death the earthly high priest took *with him* the blood of another victim, but as Christ was both priest and sacrifice he presented only *himself!* 'His "entering in" as the Crucified One Risen *is* the presentation' (Moule, *Outlines of Christian Doctrine,* pp. 85, 105).

Christ thus 'entered in not with, but "through his own blood," that is, by means of or because of, His death as Man, when His human blood was shed. So, in the heavenly glory, He does not sprinkle, and never has actually sprinkled, blood upon some heavenly mercy-seat' (A. M. Stibbs, *The Meaning of the Word 'Blood' in Scripture*, p. 18). The remarks of John Owen on the verse are to the same effect: 'It is a vain speculation, contrary to the analogy of faith, and destructive of the true nature of the oblation of Christ, and inconsistent with the dignity of his person, that he should carry with him into heaven a part of that material blood which was shed for us on the earth. This some have invented, to maintain a comparison in that wherein is none intended. The design of the apostle is only to declare by virtue of what he entered as a priest into the holy place. And this was by virtue of his own blood when it was shed, when he offered himself unto God'. Yet it is this unscriptural idea which is given support by the RSV, 'taking his own blood', an inexcusable inaccuracy which is justly criticized by both F. F. Bruce and T. Hewitt.

Having obtained eternal redemption: What Christ obtained by his death was *eternal* redemption in contrast with the *temporary* deliverance effected by the Levitical sacrifices. As these sacrifices sufficed for all who were represented by the earthly high priest, so the sacrifice of Christ actually saves all who are included within the scope of his work. He did not die to secure a mere possible redemption of all men, but purposely 'to give his life a ransom *for many*' [*Mark* 10:45]. 'It is to beggar the concept of redemption as an elective securement of release by price and by power to construe it as anything less than the effectual accomplishment which secures the salvation of those who are its objects. Christ did not come to put men in a redeemable position but to redeem to himself a people' (John Murray, *Redemption – Accomplished and Applied*, p. 63).

13: For if the blood of goats and bulls, and the ashes of a heifer sprinkling them that have been defiled, sanctify unto the cleanness of the flesh:

This justifies the preceding affirmation [verse 12]: 'For if the blood sacrifices of the tabernacle served to purify the *flesh* from ceremonial uncleanness, then how much more shall the blood of Christ cleanse the *conscience* from dead works to serve the living God?' The defilement produced by physical contact with a dead body excluded the person affected from the congregation of Israel, but the sprinkling of the ashes of an heifer provide a ritual cleansing which again fitted him to join in the worship of God [*Num*. 19]. 'The spiritual Israelite derived, in these legal rites, spiritual blessings not flowing from them, but from the Antitype. Ceremonial sacrifices released from *temporal penalties* and *ceremonial disqualifications*: Christ's sacrifice releases from *everlasting penalties* [verse 12] and *moral impurities of conscience* disqualifying from access to God [verse 14]' (Fausset).

14: how much more shall the blood of Christ, who through the eternal Spirit offered himself without blemish unto God, cleanse your conscience from dead works to serve the living God?

If therefore even the blood of animals sufficed to secure such an external purification, how much more shall the blood of Christ effect the moral cleansing of the conscience?

Not all the blood of beasts,
On Jewish altars slain,
Could give the guilty conscience peace,
Or wash away the stain.

But Christ, the heavenly Lamb,
Takes all our sins away;
A sacrifice of nobler Name,
And richer blood than they.
Isaac Watts

Who through his eternal spirit offered himself (ASV margin): This means that 'in virtue of his inseparable and unchangeable Divine Nature Christ was Priest while he was victim also' (Westcott). In other words, that which gave Christ's sacrifice its atoning value was the *voluntary* character of that act, for he was at once 'the sacrificing Priest' and 'the sacrificed Lamb' (Lenski). And because he made the offering through his *eternal* spirit, which could not be extinguished by death (7:16: 'the power of a life that cannot be destroyed'- NEB), he entered heaven once-for-all 'having obtained *eternal* redemption' [verse 12]. Thus the reference is not to the Holy Spirit, 'but to the Spirit which was His own, that is, to *Christ's divine nature.* Also, the word *eternal* here means *heavenly*. Therefore the meaning is that *through the heavenly aspect of His deity* Christ makes the offering. This is also borne out by the opening words of the Epistle: ". . . the Son, after he had made propitiation of sins in himself". The verb here is in the middle voice, which is significant, indicating something taking place *within Christ's Person'* (Vos).

Without blemish unto God: The efficacy of the Levitical offerings depended upon the outward perfection of the sacrifice, but what Christ offered to God was *Himself*, an offering without inward blemish or moral impurity of any kind [*1 Pet.* 1:19].

Cleanse your conscience from dead works to serve the living God? 'We must note the aim of atonement, which is *to serve the living God.* We are not cleansed by Christ so that we can immerse ourselves continually in fresh dirt, but in order that our purity may serve the glory of God. He [the author of Hebrews] goes on to say that nothing can proceed from us which is pleasing to God until we are cleansed by the blood of Christ. Since we are all enemies of God before our reconciliation, all that we do is likewise hateful to Him. The beginning of true worship is therefore reconciliation. Because no work is so pure or free from sin as to be pleasing to God by itself, cleansing by the blood of Christ which destroys all stains must necessarily intervene. This is the true contrast between the living God and dead works' (Calvin).

15: And for this cause he is the mediator of a new covenant, that a death having taken place for the redemption of the transgressions that were under the first covenant, they that have been called may receive the promise of the eternal inheritance.

It is on account of the infinite superiority of his sacrifice that Christ is the Mediator of the new 'covenant' (the same word, *diatheke*, is used in verses 16, 17 in the sense of a 'testament'). The old covenant extended a promise of eternal life, but it was unable to confer it, for the blood of animals could never provide a real atonement for sin. As therefore nothing less than the death of Christ could cancel the guilt of those 'called' in the former dispensation, Christians of New Testament days had no reason to be offended by it; for *all* who receive the 'eternal' inheritance do so in virtue of that 'eternal' redemption [verse 12] which was obtained by means of Christ's 'eternal' spirit [verse 14]. Thus the real value in the typical sacrifices of the old covenant is found in the one perfect sacrifice to which they pointed. 'It is Christ's death that gives worth to the types that pointed to him. So then the atoning sacrifice of Christ is the basis of the salvation of all who are saved before the Cross and since' (Robertson).

16: For where a testament is, there must of necessity be the death of him that made it. 17: For a testament is of force where there hath been death: for it doth never avail while he that made it liveth.

Having mentioned a 'death' and an 'inheritance' in the previous verse, the author here slides easily into the second meaning of *diatheke* as a 'last will and testament'. It has been pointed out that this change of meaning appeared so natural to the Greek commentators on this

Epistle that they make no remark on it. 'There is no more possibility or feasibility of interference with the effective application of the blessings of the covenant than there is of interfering with a testamentary disponement (or disposition) once the testator has died. This use of the testamentary provision of Roman law to illustrate the inviolable security accruing from the sacrificial death of Christ serves to underline the unilateral character of the new covenant. One thing is apparent, that a testament is a unilateral disposition of possession. How totally foreign to the notion of compact, contract, or agreement is the disposition or dispensation which can be illustrated in respect of its effective operation by a last will!'(John Murray, *The Covenant of Grace*, p. 30).

18: Wherefore even the first covenant hath not been dedicated without blood.

In this verse the reference to the blood of sacrifice shows that the author reverts to the concept of a 'covenant.' Those who were tempted to look askance at the blood of Christ are here reminded that the Sinaitic covenant was not inaugurated without the shedding of blood [*Exod.* 24:3–81]

19: For when every commandment had been spoken by Moses unto all the people according to the law, he took the blood of the calves and the goats, with water and scarlet wool and hyssop, and sprinkled both the book itself and all the people, 20: saying, This is the blood of the covenant which God commanded to you-ward.

Several details in this description are not found in the Exodus narrative but though the sources used by the author are no longer available for our scrutiny we are not thereby obliged to doubt the accuracy of his inspired account of the matter [*2 Tim.* 3:16]. What he wishes to emphasize is that all the provisions of that covenant were solemnly ratified by Moses when he sprinkled both the book and the people with the blood which he then identified as 'the blood of the covenant'.

21: Moreover the tabernacle and all the vessels of the ministry he sprinkled in like manner with the blood.

Subsequently even the tabernacle itself and all its sacred vessels required to be cleansed by blood so that they might be used by sinners without receiving defilement from them [*Lev.* 16:14–20].

22: And according to the law, I may almost say, all things are cleansed with blood, and apart from shedding of blood there is no remission.

In fact under the law 'I may almost say, all things are cleansed with blood,' without which 'there is no remission'. Although those who could only afford a bloodless offering still obtained remission, such exceptions nevertheless derived their efficacy from the universal rule on which they were based [*Lev.* 5:11–13]. The author's insistence upon this principle makes it hard to see how there can be any remission of sins granted through the 'unbloody' offering of the mass. 'There is in the mass no real Christ, no suffering, and no bleeding. And a bloodless sacrifice is ineffectual. The writer of the book of Hebrews says that "apart from shedding of blood there is no remission" of sin [9:22]; and John says, "The blood of Jesus his Son cleanseth us from all sin" [*1 John* 1:7]. Since admittedly there is no blood in the mass, it simply cannot be a sacrifice for sin' (L. Boettner, *Roman Catholicism*, p. 227). This is therefore an unscriptural practice which 'dishonours and degrades the one perfect and all-sufficient sacrifice of Christ, by representing it as repeated, or rather caricatured, daily and hourly by the juggling mummery of a priest' (William Cunningham, *Historical Theology*, vol. 2, p. 143).

23: It was necessary therefore that the copies of the things in the heavens should be cleansed with these; but the heavenly things themselves with better sacrifices than these.

But while such animal sacrifices sufficed to cleanse the earthly sanctuary, 'better sacrifices' than these were needed to purify heaven for man's entrance. This plural is used because the verse states only the general principle, though presently it will be shown that this access into God's presence was effected by 'one sacrifice' [10:12]. 'The earthly tabernacle, as God's dwelling, might have been supposed to be hallowed by his presence and to need no cleansing, but being also his meeting-place with men it required to be cleansed. And so our heavenly relations with God, and all wherewith we seek to approach him, need cleansing.

In themselves things heavenly need no cleansing, but as entered upon by sinful men they need it. Our eternal relations with God require purification' (Marcus Dods).

24: For Christ entered not into a holy place made with hands, like in pattern to the true; but into heaven itself, now to appear before the face of God for us:

Christ therefore has not entered a holy place made with hands which was but a copy of the celestial reality, but has appeared in heaven itself as the representative of a people who now enjoy through him continuous and unrestricted access into the very presence of God. 'It is enough that Jesus should *show himself for us* to the Father: the sight of Jesus satisfied God in our behalf. He brings before the face of God no offering which has exhausted itself, and, as only sufficing for a time, needs renewal; but he himself is in person, by virtue of the eternal Spirit, i.e., the imperishable life of his person, now and for ever freed from death, our eternally present offering before God' (Delitzsch).

25: nor yet that he should offer himself often, as the high priest entereth into the holy place year by year with blood not his own;

Unlike the Levitical high priest who entered the holy place each year 'with blood not his own', Christ made the unrepeatable offering of his own blood through which he entered into the heavenly sanctuary once-for-all. 'Whatever had the greatest glory in the old legal institutions, carried along with it the evidence of its own imperfection, compared with the thing signified in Christ and his office. – The entrance of the high priest into the holy place was the most glorious solemnity of the law; howbeit the annual repetition of it was a sufficient evidence of its imperfection' (John Owen).

26: else must he often have suffered since the foundation of the world: but now once at the end of the ages hath he been manifested to put away sin by the sacrifice of himself.

The sufficiency of this offering is proved by its finality; for if its benefits did not extend to former generations [verse 15] then Christ must have suffered repeatedly from the time that man first became a sinner. But since he did not so suffer, it is evident that he made a complete offering for the sins of his people. For *He* did not painlessly present the blood of others but offered *Himself*, and this entailed mortal suffering which clearly cannot be repeated. Hence those who presume to present this offering anew have fallen back to the level of a superseded priesthood! For true Christian worship leaves the sacrifice where 'God the Lord of time placed it – at that exact historical moment in the third decade of our chronology. It is the saving consequences of that atoning act, not the act itself, which become a present event in our worship' (Oscar Cullmann, *The Christology of the New Testament*, p. 99).

But now once at the end of the ages hath he been manifested to put away sin by the sacrifice of himself: But now that Christ has been historically manifested he has annulled sin's power by exhausting its penalty in his priestly self oblation upon the cross. 'At the end of the ages' marks the end of the period of preparation. Since God had determined that there was to be one sacrifice for all generations, the occurrence of that sacrifice marked the beginning of the age to come, and closed the period of symbolism and expectation.

27: And inasmuch as it is appointed unto men once to die, and after this cometh judgment; 28: so Christ also, having been once offered to bear the sins of many, shall appear a second time, apart from sin, to them that wait for him, unto salvation.

The author appeals to the universal fact of death to confirm his statement that Christ's death was 'once for all'. 'Man dies once, and the next thing before him is judgment. So Christ died once and the next thing before him is the Advent' (Vaughan). Death became a divine appointment for man through his one primal act of disobedience, and the judgment which must follow it registers the unfavourable verdict of God upon a sinful life. Such a verdict could only be reversed through a vicarious satisfaction for sin, and this Christ accomplished in accordance with the prophecy of Isaiah (cf. 53:12: 'he bare the sin of many'). The dreadful anguish with which Cardinal Newman's Gerontius faced the Great Assize is in startling contrast to the New Testament which speaks of the believer's 'boldness in the day of judgment' [*1 John* 4:17]. Plainly this is not a presumptuous confidence, for the assurance of his complete absolution from all guilt is based upon the full satisfaction which Christ made for his sin. It is to be further noted that the extent of the atonement is determined by the number who are finally saved by it. The passage represents the second advent of Christ, this time without even the imputation of sin, as the climactic event which will consummate the salvation of 'the many' for whom he once suffered.

'It is the great exercise of faith, to live on the invisible actings of Christ on the behalf of the church. So also the foundation of it doth consist in our infallible expectation of his second appearance, of our seeing him again, Acts 1:11 . . . The present long-continued absence of Christ in heaven is the great trial of the world. God doth give the world *a trial by faith in Christ*, as he gave it *a trial by obedience in Adam*. Faith is tried by difficulties. When Christ did appear, it was under such circumstances as turned all unbelievers from him. His state was then a state of infirmity, reproach, and suffering. He appeared in the flesh. Now he is in glory, he appeareth not. As many refused him when he appeared, because it was in outward weakness; so many refuse him now he is in glory, because he appeareth not. Faith alone can conflict with and conquer these difficulties' (John Owen) [*Rev.* 22:20].

CHAPTER TEN

In summing up his argument, the author points out that the repeated sacrifices prescribed by the law only served to remind the people of their sinfulness, for it is impossible that the blood of animals should take away sins [verses 1–4]. As foretold by the Psalmist, this great lack was supplied when Christ came into the world to sanctify his people through the once-for-all offering of his own body on their behalf [verses 5–10]. For whereas the Levitical priests daily stand to offer those sacrifices which can never take away sins, Christ sat down on the right hand of God after he had offered the one perfect sacrifice for sins, having thus secured the complete reinstatement of his people in accordance with Jeremiah's prophecy of the new covenant [verses 11–18]. Therefore as Christ has opened up a new and living way to God, let us boldly enter the holy place through the redeeming merit of our great Priest [verses 19–22]. Let us hold fast our confession, and encourage one another, not forsaking the assembling together for worship as the day of the Lord's return draws near [verses 23–25]. Waverers are again solemnly warned that if they wilfully renounce their interest in Christ, they will incur a judgment far more severe than that which overtook the despisers of the law, as befits those who have trampled under foot the Son of God himself [verses 26–31]. Let them recall the former days of faith, when they joyfully endured much persecution, so that they do not now cast away the prospect of their reward. Let us then remember our identity: we are not of those who shrink back to perdition, but of those who have faith to the saving of the soul [verses 32–39].

1: For the law having a shadow of the good things to come, not the very image of the things, can never with the same sacrifices year by year, which they offer continually, make perfect them that draw nigh.

Having proved the finality of Christ's sacrifice, the author next insists upon its perfection. He begins by conceding that the law had indeed a shadow of the good things to come, but a shadow could never fulfil the expectations to which it gave rise. But at last this unsubstantial promise had given place to the very image itself, for the new age which was inaugurated by the finished work of Christ 'is not merely a reproduction of the Heavenly Reality, but its actual substance, the Reality itself come down from heaven' (Vos). Thus the law could never make perfect those who sought to draw near to God through the continuous succession of sacrifices which it prescribed, and this was because 'no repetition of the shadow can amount to the substance' (A. B. Davidson).

2: Else would they not have ceased to be offered? because the worshippers, having been once cleansed, would have had no more consciousness of sins.

The question summons the readers to reflect on the significance of these repeated offerings, for if any one of them had been adequate to pacify the consciences of the worshippers by effecting a real purification of sins then this would have brought the series to an end. The impotence of these offerings is therefore self-confessed. The argument used here suggests that the Epistle was written before AD 70 when the destruction of the temple ensured the cessation of all sacrifices. 'All peace with God is resolved into a purging atonement made for sin: "Being once purged"' (John Owen).

3: But in those sacrifices there is a remembrance made of sins year by year.

'It would not have occurred to an observant Jew under the Mosaic covenant to say that the Day of Atonement involved an annual "remembrance" of sins; he would have said, rather, that there was an annual *removal* of sins. Our author might have replied, truly enough, that the ritual designed to effect the removal of sins necessarily involves their remembrance; but he is influenced chiefly by the promise that under the new covenant God will remember His people's sins no more. Since the new covenant is contrasted with the old, the implication is that there was no such absolute wiping out of sins from the divine record under the sacrificial law' (F. F. Bruce).

4: For it is impossible that the blood of bulls and goats should take away sins.

He does not deal here with the positive value of what had been a divine appointment, but only shows what these sacrifices could not do when considered in themselves. This trenchant judgment was timely, for to forsake Christ in order to return to a system of worship that had outlived its usefulness, would amount to an accounting of 'the precious blood of Christ' as inferior in value to the blood of beasts which could never take away sin. 'This obvious truth needs no proof. There is no relation between the physical blood of animals and man's moral offence' (Marcus Dods).

5: Wherefore when he cometh into the world, he saith, Sacrifice and offering thou wouldest not, but a body didst thou prepare for me; 6: In whole burnt offerings and sacrifices for sin thou hadst no pleasure: 7: Then said I, Lo, I am come (in the roll of the book it is written of me) to do thy will, O God.

The author sees a prophetic anticipation of the whole earthly course of Christ in the words uttered by David in Psalm 40:6–8. 'It is not as if Christ, and *not* David, were the speaker: David speaks; but Christ, whose Spirit already dwells and works in David, and who will hereafter receive from David His human nature, now already speaks *in* him' (Delitzsch).

Sacrifice and offering thou wouldest not: This is not a rejection of sacrifices as such; it rather affirms the common prophetic doctrine that ritual offerings are worthless without corresponding obedience of heart and life [*Mic.* 6:6–8; *1 Sam.* 15:22; *Psa.* 50:8–14, 51:16f., *Isa.* 1:11f., *Jer.* 7:21f, *Hos.* 6:6; *Amos* 5:21f.]. What is new here is David's inspired recognition of the fact that sacrifices cannot adequately express his devotion to God, and so he speaks 'as if his self-offering will be the sacrifice to end all sacrifices' (Derek Kidner). The sacred rhetoric of David thus prophetically points forward to the only One who could bring it to fulfilment.

But a body didst thou prepare for me: The quotation follows the Greek version of the Psalm, and Lenski suggests that its substitution of 'a body didst thou prepare for me' for the Hebrew 'mine ears hast thou digged' (AV margin) was due to the desire of the translators to make it more intelligible to Greek readers. In either case, there is no material difference in meaning, for attentive hearing prepares for obedient service [*Isa.* 50:4–7]. And it was Christ's voluntary submission to the will of God which distinguished the offering of his body from the forced and non-rational offering of the bodies of beasts in sacrifice. As E. Schweizer points out, This emphasis on the fact that Jesus consciously offered up his body in sacrifice is a new use [verses 5, 10], for elsewhere 'body' is practically never used in the vocabulary of sacrifice (*TDNT*, vol. 7, p. 1058).

Then said I, Lo, I am come . . . to do thy will, O God: The language vividly expresses the eager promptitude of Christ's complete dedication to the will of God. 'There is nothing of irresponsibility or adventure in Christ's life and death. It is all obedience, and therefore it is all revelation. We see God in it because it is not His own will but the will of the Father which it accomplished. Even when we come to consider its relation to sin, this must be borne in mind. Atonement is not something contrived, as it were, behind the Father's back; it is the Father's way of making it possible for the sinful to have fellowship with Him (James Denney, *The Death of Christ*, p. 122).

8: Saying above, Sacrifices and offerings and whole burnt offerings and sacrifices for sin thou wouldest not, neither hadst pleasure therein (the which are offered according to the law), 9: then hath he said, Lo, I am come to do thy will. He taketh away the first, that he may establish the second.

These words of the Messiah therefore show that God's dissatisfaction with the sacrifices which were offered according to the law pointed forward to their replacement by his own perfect obedience to the divine will. Hence the abrogation of the first must mean the establishment of the second: so that those who continue to offer such sacrifices, whether animal or material (as opposed to the spiritual 'sacrifices' of 13:16; *Rom.* 12:1, 2), after Christ's definitive sacrifice are guilty of the sin of flagrant opposition to the will of God!

10: By which will we have been sanctified through the offering of the body of Jesus Christ once for all.

'The will of God, with which we are here concerned, is not satisfied by an obedience which comes short of death. For it is not merely the preceptive will of God, His will that men should do right and live according to His holy law, which Christ came to fulfil; it is His gracious will, a will which has as its aim that sinful men should be constituted into a people for Himself, a will which has resolved that their sin should be so dealt with as no longer to keep them at a distance from Him; a will, in short, that sinners should find a standing in His sight. And in that will we are sanctified, not merely by Christ's fulfilment of the law of God as it is binding on man in general, but by His fulfilment of the law as it is binding on sinful men, by His obedient suffering of death as that in which God's mind in relation to sin finds its final expression' (James Denney).

Once for all: That which has been completed *for* the believer obviously cannot refer to a gradual process *within* the believer. Accordingly, this 'sanctification' is the objective achievement of Christ which has secured the purification of his people and for ever set them apart for the service of God. It has a forensic import which is analogous to the Pauline concept of 'justification'.

11: And every priest indeed standeth day by day ministering and offering oftentimes the same sacrifices, the which can never take away sins: 12: but he, when he had offered one sacrifice for sins for ever, sat down on the right hand of God; 13: henceforth expecting till his enemies be made the footstool of his feet.

The Levitical priests must *stand* as they daily offer the very same sacrifices which can never take away sins. But this Priest after he had offered one sacrifice for sins for ever, *sat down* on the right hand of God [1:3]. Christ's heavenly enthronement bears witness to the eternal validity of that one historic sacrifice by which he made reconciliation for iniquity and brought in everlasting righteousness [*Dan.* 9:24]. The author's intention in echoing the word of *Psa.* 110:1 in verse 13 is probably to warn the readers 'not to let themselves be numbered among the enemies of the exalted Christ, but rather to be reckoned as His friends and companions by preserving their fidelity to the end' (F.F. Bruce) [3:14, 10:26–31].

14: For by one offering he hath perfected for ever them that are sanctified.

This verse rules out the possibility of any further offering for sins either on earth or in heaven, for it affirms that Christ has perfected for ever those who are consecrated to God by his one offering on their behalf. According to John Flavel this means, 'that the oblation made unto God by Jesus Christ, is of unspeakable value, and everlasting efficacy, to perfect all them that are, or shall be sanctified, to the end of the world' (*Works*, vol. 1, p. 155).

15: And the Holy Spirit also beareth witness to us; for after he hath said, 16: This is the covenant that I will make with them after those days, saith the Lord: I will put my laws on their heart, and upon their mind also will I write them; then saith he, 17: And their sins and their iniquities will I remember no more. 18: Now where remission of these is, there is no more offering for sin.

Earlier in the Epistle [8:8f.] the author had drawn the attention of his readers to the newness of that covenant which had made the first old, but here he appeals once more to this testimony of the Holy Spirit in order to underline its finality [*Jer.* 31:31f.]. God's promise that he will no more remember the sins of his people is the outstanding feature of the new covenant, for the continual remembrance of sins under the old economy showed the insufficiency of its constant sacrifices to atone for sin [verse 3]. But Christ blotted out the sins of his people beyond recall when he offered himself to God on their behalf. His death ratified the new covenant and abolished the old order. Thus where there is the full remission of sins, no possibility of any further offering for sin remains. The author's emphatic reiteration of this truth was necessary for those who were thinking of going back to Judaism and all its sacrifices, but it must be noted that the general character of his final word includes every kind of supposed offering for sin. For since Christ's sacrifice all other sacrifices for sin are utterly futile and meaningless.

19: Having therefore, brethren, boldness to enter into the holy place by the blood of Jesus,

Exposition now gives place to exhortation, and the remainder of the Epistle is devoted to a detailed application of the eloquent appeal which begins in this verse and extends to verse 25. He addresses his readers as 'brethren' to remind them of the privileges which are inseparable from their profession of faith in Christ, for it is as those who realize that their acceptance by God rests entirely upon the sacrificial death of their great High Priest that he bids them boldly to enter the heavenly sanctuary. 'Christians do not enter the holiest *with* the blood of Jesus, for then they would be priests, anew opening up the way, whenever they approached, by a new offering; the view of the passage is that the way is opened up once for all by the offering of the Son [9:12, 28; 10:12], and lies for ever open because He abides before the face of God for us [9:24]; and it is on this fact, called here the blood of Jesus, that the glad confidence of believers in regard to entrance is based' (A. B. Davidson).

20: by the way which he dedicated for us, a new and living way, through the veil, that is to say, his flesh;

This entering into the presence of God is by that fresh and living way which Jesus has *inaugurated* by his sacrifice, for the veil barred man's access to 'the holy place' until *he* opened up the way. The Old Testament way into the sanctuary was simply a lifeless pavement trodden by the high priest, and by him alone' (Delitzsch); whereas the 'living way' is of vital and perpetual efficacy because the *living* and *life-giving* Saviour is that way [7:251.

Through the veil, that is to say, his flesh: As there was no way into the inner sanctuary of the tabernacle except through the veil, so the flesh of Jesus affords the only means of access to the heavenly sanctuary [*Mark* 15:38]. 'The crucified Christ is the entrance, the entrance veil.

"No man cometh to the Father but *by me*", (John 14:6), by my blood, by my flesh, by this veil. This veil shuts out and forever hides the Father from all those who spurn it as the means of entry' (Lenski).

21: and having a great priest over the house of God;

This further reminder of the greatness of the Priest who now presides over the house of God is designed to encourage their confident approach to the throne of grace, and also to warn them against any return to the ministrations of a discarded priesthood. 'Christ could not be a high priest unless the former priests were divested of their office, since theirs was a different order. He means therefore that all those things which Christ changed at His coming are to be let go. He sets Him over the whole house of God so that whoever wishes to have a place in the Church must submit to Christ and choose Him and no other as his leader and ruler' (Calvin) [3:1–6, 4:14–16].

22: let us draw near with a true heart in fulness of faith, having our hearts sprinkled from an evil conscience: and having our body washed with pure water,

It is in virtue of Christ's one offering for sin and the perfection of his priesthood that they are exhorted to draw near [comment on 4:16] to God 'with a true heart in full assurance of faith' (AV). These are the prime requisites in every approach to God: *sincerity of heart,* because he desires 'truth in the inward parts' and hates all hypocrisy, falsehood, and deceit [*Psa.* 51:6; *John* 4:24]; *full assurance of faith*, because 'he that cometh to God must believe that he is, and that he is a rewarder of them that seek after him' [11:6].

Having had our hearts sprinkled from an evil conscience and having had our bodies washed with pure water (Wuest): As these perfect participles point to unrepeatable acts with abiding effects, they 'express not conditions of approach to God which are yet to be achieved, but conditions already possessed' (Marcus Dods). This cultic language recalls the purification which the Levitical priests had to undergo before they were fit to approach God [*Exod.* 29:4, 21], but the author evidently pours a Christian content into these terms. In effect he is saying, 'We believers have experienced through the death of Christ that once-for-all *inward cleansing* from sin which was given its *outward expression* in our baptism.' Thus the Christian's subjective confidence [verse 22a] must always be based upon his personal interest in Christ's objective work [verse 22b].

23: let us hold fast the confession of our hope that it waver not; for he is faithful that promised:

Since the author knows that the Christian's confidence in the promise is best sustained by a firm conviction of the reliability of the Promiser, he reinforces this call to continue in the faith by reminding his readers that the attainment of the hope they had confessed is based on the unchanging faithfulness of God [11:11; *1 Cor.* 1:9; *1 Thess.* 5:24]. Perseverance is the hallmark of a genuine interest in Christ, but inconstancy imperils the eternal inheritance, for the hope of salvation is liable to wither when the frank confession of it wavers.

24: and let us consider one another to provoke unto love and good works;

In place of the selfish individualism which only fosters strife, they must constantly seek to encourage and edify one another by those deeds of love which will express the reality of their fellowship in Christ. The professing church today sorely stands in need of a renewal of such 'provocations'! [*Phil.* 2:1–5] It is worth noting that 'love' here completes the familiar triad of Christian virtues ('faith', verse 22; 'hope', verse 23; 'love'. verse 24; cf. *1 Cor.* 13:13 and *1 Thess.* 1:3).

25: not forsaking our own assembling together, as the custom of some is, but exhorting one another; and so much the more, as ye see the day drawing nigh.

It is because the New Testament knows nothing of a solitary Christianity that the author presses upon his readers the duty of assembling together for worship, instruction, and mutual encouragement. Even if it is not welcome, this warning is nevertheless necessary for their spiritual welfare, as the partial neglect of the means of grace is the first step towards a total decline from grace. Indeed the sluggishness of some should rather serve to quicken them to greater diligence in the encouragement of one another, and all the more so as they see 'the day drawing nigh'. The early church did not consider the second advent of Christ to be an interesting topic for cold chronological calculation, for it lived in the earnest expectation of that momentous event [*Rev.* 22:20]. The actual situation which this verse reflects is beyond our ken, but it seems likely that the letter was sent in the first place to Jewish Christians in Rome, some of whom were leaving the meetings of the church and contemplating a return to the Jewish synagogues to avoid further persecution [verses 32–34].

26: For if we sin wilfully after that we have received the knowledge of the truth, there remaineth no more a sacrifice for sins,

As under the law there was no forgiveness of deliberate sin, sin committed 'with a high hand' [*Num.* 15:30, AV margin] so under the gospel there is no provision for the reinstatement of those who wilfully fall away from their profession of faith in Christ. Both classes of sinners are worthy of the same sentence of death, for both are guilty of rejecting God's 'covenant' outside of which there is no salvation [verse 29]. Hence the sternness of the author's warning matches the wickedness of the sin. He shows his readers the awful doom that awaits apostates on the day of judgment [verse 27f.], in order that they might realize the consequences of severing their connection with Christ by a permanent withdrawal from the Christian assembly [verse 25; cf. *1 John* 2:19].

What we have here is a dreadful disclosure of the fate which must inevitably overtake anyone who, after having professed an interest in Christ's salvation, then deliberately and defiantly repudiates it. This settled *state* of rebellion against the gospel, is not to be confused with isolated *acts* of sin which may be committed through weakness or ignorance. The warning of 6:4–8 has the same sin in view, but there the psychological aspect is stressed: the fact that repentance and renewal is impossible. Here the emphasis is linked with God's terms of salvation: there is no sacrifice to wipe out this sin.

There remaineth no more a sacrifice for sins: It is because Christ's sacrifice is the only sacrifice for sin, that the man who wilfully rejects that sacrifice in order to return to the dead works and lifeless service of Judaism, finds that there is no other sacrifice for sin to which he can have recourse.

27: but a certain fearful expectation of judgment, and a fierceness of fire which shall devour the adversaries.

Having spurned the sacrifice of Christ, there remains for the apostate only a fearful expectation of the furious fire of divine judgment which is to devour the adversaries [12:29; *Rev.* 21:8]. The word 'certain' indicates a punishment of 'undefined, undefinable magnitude – something that is inexpressible, inconceivable . . . The most dreadful conception comes infinitely short of the more dreadful reality. We can only say of it, "It is a certain fearful punishment which the apostate has to expect"' (John Brown).

28: A man that hath set at nought Moses' law dieth without compassion on the word of two or three witnesses: 29: of how much sorer punishment, think ye, shall he be judged worthy, who hath trodden under foot the Son of God, and hath counted the blood of the covenant wherewith he was sanctified an unholy thing, and hath done despite unto the Spirit of grace?

The equity of the judgment is vindicated by the enormity of the offence, for if the person who set at nought the law of Moses was punished without mercy, then it is evident that the sin of one who is guilty of despising the Son must be visited with far greater severity [*Deut.* 17:2–7]. This sin is unpardonable because a contemptuous rejection of the gospel is nothing less than a trampling under foot of the Son of God, a profanation of the blood of the new covenant, and a scorning of the Spirit of grace.

The blood . . . wherewith he was sanctified: Although the apostate never was regenerate he was once externally dedicated to God by a profession of faith in Christ's atoning blood, and it was from this alone that he fell away. John Murray states that there is a certain sense in which it can be said that Christ died for the non-elect, but the benefits which they derive from the atonement are only temporary. 'The difference can be stated bluntly to be that the non-elect do not participate in the benefits *of* the atonement and the elect do. The non-elect enjoy many benefits that accrue *from* the atonement but they do not partake of the *atonement*' (*Collected Writings*, vol. 1, pp. 69).

30: For we know him that said, Vengeance belongeth unto me, I will recompense. And again, The Lord shall judge his people.

The author now appeals to the Hebrew Christians' own knowledge of the absolute rectitude of the Judge as he introduces two quotations which confirm the righteousness of the sentence which is to be executed upon all such despisers of the gospel. 'It is a most profitable exercise for the soul to be often engaged in contemplating the Divine attributes, pondering God's almighty power, ineffable holiness, unimpeachable veracity, exact justice, absolute faithfulness and terrible severity. Christ Himself has bidden us "fear Him which is able to destroy both soul and body in hell" [*Matt.* 10:28]. The better God's character be known, the more we heed that exhortation of Christ's, the clearer shall we perceive that there is nothing unsuited to the holiness of God in what Scripture affirms concerning His dealings with the wicked. It is because the true nature of sin is so little viewed in the light of God's awful holiness, that so many fail to recognize its *infinite* demerits' (A. W. Pink).

Vengeance belongeth unto me, I will recompense: Both quotations are from the Song of Moses. The first, *Deut.* 32:35, appears in the version followed by Paul in *Rom.* 12:19. Although in their original setting these words refer to the vengeance which will overtake the enemies of Israel, they state a principle of universal application, for as John Trapp tersely remarks, 'If God will avenge his elect, *Luke* 18:7, how much more his Son and his Spirit!'

And again, The Lord shall judge his people: This is taken from the next verse, *Deut.* 32:36, where the words mean that the Lord will do judgment *for* his people, i.e. in the sense of vindicating them. Here they are quoted to show that those who forsake his covenant cannot expect to escape his righteous judgment, for when greater privileges are lightly esteemed heavier judgment is incurred [cf. *Amos* 3:2].

31: It is a fearful thing to fall into the hands of the living God.

The dumb idols of the heathen could neither help nor punish their self-deceived devotees, but because Israel's God lives he has the power to fulfil every promise and to make his threatened judgments a frightful reality. Thus 'it is a fearful thing to fall into the hands of the living God', for 'mortal man, however inimical he may be, cannot carry his enmity beyond death, but the power of God is not confined to such narrow limits. We often escape from men, we cannot escape the judgment of God' (Calvin).

32: But call to remembrance the former days, in which, after ye were enlightened, ye endured a great conflict of sufferings;

As with the earlier warning, so this is followed by words of encouragement [6:9f.]. Here the author bids them recall a particular occasion, soon after their 'enlightenment', when their faith had emerged unscathed from a great contest of sufferings. Although this persecution was severe it appears from 12:4 that no Christian lives were lost, and this would rule out Jerusalem as the scene of their trial. W. Manson suggests that the Epistle was written to Jewish Christians in Rome shortly before Nero's bloodbath (AD 64), and that these verses (verses 32–34) refer to their experiences during AD 49 when the Emperor Claudius ordered all Jews to leave the city because, according to Suetonius, 'they were constantly indulging in riots at the instigation of Chrestus' [cf. *Acts* 18:2]. 'If we assume that the name "Chrestus" here is a garbled form of Christus, the meaning will be that Messianic agitations breaking out among the Jews at Rome had drawn down upon them the unfavourable notice of the public authorities, the guardians of the peace, and Claudius acted accordingly . . . The most plausible explanation of the whole episode is that Christian propaganda had been introduced into the synagogues at Rome and had created considerable ferment' (W. Manson, *The Epistle to the Hebrews*, p. 41).

33: partly, being made a gazing-stock both by reproaches and afflictions; and partly, becoming partakers with them that were so used.

This specifies the two ways in which the faith of the Hebrews had been severely tested soon after their conversion. Their own confession of Christ had brought them public reproaches and sufferings, and these afflictions were intensified by their voluntary association with fellow believers who were enduring the same persecution.

34: For ye both had compassion on them that were in bonds, and took joyfully the spoiling of your possessions, knowing that ye have for yourselves a better possession and an abiding one.

Despite the personal risk involved, they did not shrink from visiting those of their brethren who were imprisoned for the sake of the gospel, and willingly ministered to their needs [*Matt.* 25:36]. Moreover, they were enabled to meet the loss of their worldly goods with joyful fortitude because they knew that they had a better eternal inheritance. 'This will make a rich amends for all they can lose and suffer here. In heaven they shall have a better life, a better estate, better liberty, better society, better hearts, better work, every thing better' (Matthew Henry) [*Matt.* 6:19–21; *1 Pet.* 1:4].

35: Cast not away therefore your boldness, which hath great recompense of reward.

Since you showed such courage in those days, do not now cast away your confident confession which has 'great recompense of reward'. This is 'of a kind which no mercenary self-seeker would seek: holiness will be its own reward; self-devotion to Christ will be its own rich recompense' (Fausset) [*Gen.* 15:1; *Matt.* 5:12, 10:32].

36: For ye have need of patience, that, having done the will of God, ye may receive the promise.

If they are to receive the promised salvation they have need of patience both to do and to bear the will of God. For it is only the recognition that the will of God includes the afflictions that accompany a profession of faith in Christ which enables the believer to sustain them [*1 Pet.* 4:19]. 'The consideration of eternal life as the free effect of the grace of God and Christ, and as proposed in a gracious promise, is a thousand times more full of spiritual refreshment unto a believer, than if he should conceive of it or look upon it merely as a reward proposed unto our own doings or merits' (John Owen).

37: For yet a very little while, he that cometh shall come, and shall not tarry. 38: But my righteous one shall live by faith: and if he shrink back, my soul hath no pleasure in him.

The exhortation to patient endurance is now confirmed by a free quotation of *Hab.* 2:3, 4 according to the Septuagint. In the original Hebrew the prophet Habakkuk is bidden to wait for the promised vision ('*it* will surely come'), whereas in the Greek version the advent of a person is awaited ('*he* will surely come'). This messianic interpretation is endorsed by the author, who also inverts the two parts of *Hab.* 2:4 [verse 38], so that '"my righteous one" becomes the subject of both parts of the verse' (F. F. Bruce).

For yet a very little while: The phrase may be a reminiscence of Isaiah 26:20, LXX, but since the author's mind is so steeped in Scripture it is not necessary to assume that this is a conscious quotation. After having suffered so much they must not think the time has come to abandon their faith. Let them hold fast to their original confidence, and in a very little while they will receive the promise.

He that cometh shall come, and shall not tarry: For Christ shall soon appear and bestow the promised glory. 'He will most certainly come; his very name is still "the coming One". He has received that name because of his first coming but also because of his second coming' (Lenski) [*Matt.* 11:3].

But my righteous one shall live by faith: Since the believer can only be described as God's 'righteous one' because he is justified by faith [*Rom.* 1:17; *Gal.* 3:11], he clearly cannot retain that standing before God unless he continues to believe.

'The apostle's purpose is to show that those who are reckoned just before God can only live by faith. The future tense of the word "live" shows the continuity of life' (Calvin).

And if he shrink back, my soul hath no pleasure in him: Yet *if* this same 'righteous' man were to shrink back, then God would take no pleasure in him, for only 'he that endureth to the end shall be saved' [*Matt.* 10:22]. 'Christ hath no delights in dastards, turn-coats, run-a-ways, he will not employ them so far as to break a pitcher, or bear a torch, (*Judg.* 7:7)' (Trapp).

39: But we are not of them that shrink back unto perdition; but of them that have faith unto the saving of the soul.

Thus believers cannot escape from the necessity of choosing between these alternatives. They must realize that to renounce their interest in Christ is to 'shrink back unto perdition'. In that event their loss would be total and final.

However, their past history convinces the writer that they will not prove to be reprobates, but that they are of that number who believe 'unto the saving of the soul'. And it is to inspire such perseverance that the illustrious faith of their ancestors is so splendidly recalled in the verses which now follow [11:1ff.].

CHAPTER ELEVEN

To enforce the need of patient endurance, the author first explains the nature of faith, and then illustrates its achievements during the period of promise. His inspiring list of the great heroes of faith, who continued to trust in God through many trials, is roughly chronological and stretches from Abel to the Maccabean martyrs [verses 1–38]. This roll-call of faith serves to remind the readers of their greater privileges under the gospel. For though these noble men and women endured so much, they did not live to see their hope fulfilled in Christ: God having determined that the Old Testament saints should be perfected together with all New Testament believers [verses 39, 40].

1: Now faith is assurance of things hoped for, a conviction of things not seen.

Now faith is confident assurance of the things we hope for (Arndt-Gingrich): Faith does not *give* 'substance' (AV) to the things hoped for, but is rather the subjective assurance of their reality. It is solely because the objects of hope have an existence quite apart from faith that faith in them is not misplaced. It is this which distinguishes saving faith from the faith of the imagination, for only those who put their trust in the promises of God are delivered from embracing a miserable delusion. 'By *faith* we are sure of eternal things that they ARE; by *hope* we are confident that WE SHALL HAVE them. Hope presupposes faith [*Rom.* 8:25]' (Fausset).

A conviction of things not seen: Such faith is more than a bare assent to a set of theological propositions; it is a regulative principle of life [*Gal.* 2:20]. Thus it was 'by faith' in what was unseen that the elders overcame all the obstacles which were presented to them by the eye of sense. As Moffatt observes, the writer is not giving an abstract definition of faith, but is describing it 'as an active conviction which moves and moulds human conduct. The happiest description of it is, "seeing Him who is invisible" [verse 27]'.

2: For therein the elders had witness borne to them.

Moreover it was 'in' (and not outside) the sphere and exercise of this faith that the fathers were approved of God, for without faith it is impossible to please him [verse 6]. The statement thus prepares the readers for the great roll-call of faith which follows [verses 4–38]. They must realize that the achievements of the heroes they so much admire were all wrought 'by faith'. So if they now renounce their faith in Christ in order to return to Judaism, 'they do not desert *to* but *from* these men and these women and thereby place their names on that horrible list marked "Perdition" [10:39]'(Lenski).

3: By faith we understand that the worlds have been framed by the word of God so that what is seen hath not been made out of things which appear.

Indeed it is faith alone which enables us to perceive that the universe was not made out of pre-existing materials but that it owes its existence to the creative word of God [*Gen.* 1:3; *Psa.* 33:6, 9]. 'Creation is here represented as a fact which we apprehend only by faith. By faith we understand (perceive, not comprehend) that the world was framed or fashioned by the word of God, that is, the word of God's power, the divine fiat, so that the things which are seen, the visible things of this world, were not made out of things which do appear, which are visible, and which are at least occasionally seen. According to this passage the world certainly was not made out of anything that is palpable to the senses' (Berkhof, *Systematic Theology*, pp. 133–4).

This verse therefore serves two important purposes: 1. It completes the author's description of faith by confirming that it is 'a conviction of things not seen' [verse 1]; 2. It lays the essential foundation for the life of faith in all its manifestations. For without faith in God as the sovereign Creator of the world it is impossible to trust in his power to preserve and govern all things for the final good of his people [*Rom.* 8:28; *Rev.* 4:11].

4: By faith Abel offered unto God a more excellent sacrifice than Cain, through which he had witness borne to him that he was righteous, God bearing witness in respect of his gifts: and through it he being dead yet speaketh.

The faith of Abel must not be artificially restricted to the spirit in which he offered his sacrifice, for it also includes his obedience to what must have been a divine appointment [*Rom.* 10:17]. It was not by fancy, but by faith that he 'brought of the firstlings of his flock and of the fat thereof'. If Scripture does not provide us with an account of the institution of expiatory sacrifice, yet it can hardly be without significance that 'the very first recorded instance of acceptable worship in the family of Adam brings before us bleeding sacrifices, and seals them with the divine approbation. They appear in the first act of worship, *Gen.* 4:3, 4. They are emphatically approved by God as soon as they appear' (A. A. Hodge, *The Atonement*, p. 124). The worship of Cain was not accepted, because he wilfully ignored the consequences of the fall. His gift of 'the fruit of the ground' merely acknowledged God as the creator and sustainer of life, whereas saving faith is pre-eminently faith in the promised redemption [*Gen.* 3:15].

God must have visibly signified his acceptance of Abel's offering for Cain was displeased by it. It is likely that he sent fire from heaven to consume the sacrifice [*Gen.* 15:7; *Lev.* 9:24; *Judg.* 6:21; *1 Kings* 18:38; *2 Chron.* 7:1]. 'Whomsoever God accepts or respects, he testifieth him to be righteous; that is, to be justified, and freely accepted with him. This Abel was by faith antecedently unto his offering. He was not made righteous, he was not justified by his sacrifice; but therein he showed his faith by his works: and God by acceptance of his works of obedience justified him, as Abraham was justified by works; namely, declaratively; he declared him so to be' (John Owen).

In adducing the example of Abel the author evidently has in mind its particular bearing upon those who were being persecuted for their faith [12:4], for as he later shows, the blood of faith's *first* martyr still cries to God for vindication [12:24; cf. *Gen.* 4:10; *Rev.* 6:9–11]. 'Thus, Abel is not only a type of the persecution and suffering of the godly, but gives a pledge of the certain vengeance which God will take in due time upon their oppressors' (A. W. Pink) [*Luke* 18:7, 8].

5: By faith Enoch was translated that he should not see death; and he was not found, because God translated him: for he hath had witness borne to him that before his translation he had been well-pleasing unto God:

Enoch, like Elijah after him [*2 Kings* 2:11], did not taste death, for God took him directly to heaven. This immediate glorification of the body is also to be shared by those who are alive at Christ's coming

[*1 Cor.* 15:51, 52; *1 Thess.* 4:16, 17]. 'This verse does not teach that Enoch had faith to be translated. God translated him because he lived a life in which He was pleased. It was by faith that he lived that life. The Mosaic commentary on his life is in the words "Enoch walked with God" [*Gen.* 5:22]' (K. Wuest).

Since Enoch was spiritually 'translated' [*Col.* 1:13] long before his physical removal from the earth, it follows that those who wish to join God in heaven must first give evidence on earth of a similar transformation of heart and life [*Rom.* 12:2]. 'He changed his place, but not his company, for he still walked with God, as in earth, so in heaven' (Trapp). The second part of the verse means: Enoch pleased God *prior* to his translation and this fact is permanently recorded in the witness borne to him by the Scripture *after* his translation.

6: and without faith it is impossible to be well-pleasing unto him; for he that cometh to God must believe that he is, and that he is a rewarder of them that seek after him.

Before he goes on to speak of Noah, the author here pauses to apply the lesson that the Hebrews must learn from the example of Enoch. Since *Gen.* 5:22–24 affirms that Enoch was well-pleasing to God, he must have been a man of faith, for without faith it is impossible to please him at all. 'Where God hath put an impossibility upon any thing, it is in vain for men to attempt it. From the days of Cain multitudes have been designing to please God without faith, – all in vain; like them that would have built a tower whose top should reach to heaven' (John Owen).

And this means that the man who draws near to God must believe that he is, and that he is a rewarder of them that seek after him. The first point involves far more than a notional assent to the existence of a 'First Cause' or 'Supreme Being'; it is to believe in the self-existent living God as he has been pleased to reveal himself in his works, in his Word, and in his Son [1:2]. Secondly, the man of faith will approach God with the conviction that he will graciously receive and reward him [*Gen.* 15:1; *Jer.* 29:13]. 'So that Enoch's faith, and the faith of every one who approaches God, verifies the description of verse 1: the unseen must be treated as sufficiently demonstrated, and the hoped-for reward must be considered substantial' (Marcus Dods).

7: By faith Noah, being warned of God concerning things not seen as yet, moved with godly fear, prepared an ark to the saving of his house; through which he condemned the world, and became heir of the righteousness which is according to faith.

Noah received the warning of the impending deluge with implicit faith despite every appearance to the contrary, and, filled with reverential awe, he built an ark for the saving of his family. During the 120 years of God's longsuffering the faithful witness of Noah as 'a preacher of righteousness' amounted to a divine condemnation of the universal unbelief which greeted his unwelcome message. Thus Noah's righteous conduct attested the reality of his justification, for his interest in 'the righteousness which is according to faith' (i.e. *by the rule of, on a principle of faith*, cf Rom. 4:13, 9:30, 10:6) was proved by his unswerving fidelity to this exacting commission [*Gen.* 6:9f.; *2 Pet.* 2:5].

'The example is the more instructive, as it naturally, and almost necessarily, brings before the mind the fearfully destructive efficiency of unbelief. The world that perished had materially the same message delivered to them as that which Noah received. Had they repented, there is no reason to doubt that the fearful infliction would not have taken place. Noah believed, and feared, and obeyed, and was saved. They disbelieved, and mocked, and were disobedient, and perished' (John Brown).

8: By faith Abraham, when he was called, obeyed to go out unto a place which he was to receive for an inheritance; and he went out, not knowing whither he went.

This verse begins the section in which the faith of the patriarchs is reviewed [verses 8–22]. Abraham was by nature no different from any other child of Adam, for until he was called by the Lord he lived with his family in the heathen city of Ur where they 'served other gods' [*Josh.* 24:2].

God had no plans for the conversion of that city, but it was his will to call one man out of it. Abraham at once obeyed the divine demand to renounce the past, leaving home for an unspecified destination, thus acknowledging that he had been effectually called by the grace of God [*Gen.* 12:1f.]. This call is distinguished from all other plausible pretences by the unquestioning obedience which it secures. 'Obedience is faith's daughter. Faith hath not only to do with the grace of God, but with the duty of the creature' (Thomas Manton).

To go out unto a place which he was to receive for an inheritance: It is clear from verse 10 that Abraham looked for a better inheritance than the land of promise in which he lived as a stranger. Indeed the author is at pains to point out that the pilgrim life of the patriarchs proved that they hoped for far more than the possession of an earthly inheritance, and this was because their faith had grasped the spiritual nature of the promise [verses 13–16].

And he went out, not knowing whither he went: If Abraham knew not whither he went, yet he knew who had called him, and that was enough. 'Abraham winked, as it were, and put his hand into God's, to be led whithersoever he pleased' (Trapp). In the same way the readers are to abandon the visible shadows of Judaism in favour of the invisible substance of Christianity [*2 Cor.* 4:18].

'Nothing but the faith of the gospel can induce a man to abandon the world and commence a pilgrimage towards heaven. And wherever there is the faith of the gospel, there will be the commencement and prosecution of such a pilgrimage. If Abraham had continued in Mesopotamia, or stopped short of Canaan, it would have been a proof that he did not believe the divine testimony; and whatever men may profess, if they continue to love the world, and become "weary in well-doing", it is clear evidence that they have not believed the gospel' (John Brown) [2 Tim. 4:10].

9: By faith he became a sojourner in the land of promise, as in a land not his own, dwelling in tents, with Isaac and Jacob, the heirs with him of the same promise:

Moreover faith enabled Abraham, as it did Isaac and Jacob after him, to live as self-confessed aliens in the land of promise, dwelling in tents, without so much as a square foot to call their own, except for the purchase of a burial place for Sarah [*Gen.* 23; *Acts* 7:5]. 'The tent-life of the patriarchs demonstrated their pilgrim character: it made manifest their contentment to live upon the *surface* of the earth, for a tent has no foundation, and can be pitched or struck at short notice. They were sojourners here and just passing through this wilderness-scene without striking their roots into it' (A. W. Pink). He whose heart is fixed upon things above holds loosely to the things of earth [*Col.* 3: 1, 2]. 'A little in the world will content a Christian for his passage, but all the world, and ten thousand times more, will not content a Christian for his portion' (Jeremiah Burroughs, *The Rare Jewel of Christian Contentment*, p. 43) [13:5; *Phil.* 4:11; *1 Tim.* 6:6, 8].

10: for he looked for the city which hath the foundations, whose builder and maker is God.

Abraham was content with his earthly lot because he looked for that city with unshakeable foundations [12:28] 'whose architect and maker is God' (ASV margin). 'There is *an instinct of immortality* in saintship. He who lives to God *knows* that he must live for ever (*Matt.* 22:32)' (Vaughan). The word 'city' not only suggests the idea of permanence, but also brings to mind an ordered society under the divine government. 'The object of his desire was social and not personal only' (Westcott).

11: By faith even Sarah herself received power to conceive seed when she was past age, since she counted him faithful who had promised:

This takes note of Sarah's faith, though Abraham remains the subject of the sentence as in verse 9: *By faith he also, together with Sarah, received power to beget a child* (H. H. Esser, *NIDNTT*, vol. 1, p. 378). 'At first she laughed, through unbelief, at the unlikelihood; but afterward she bethought herself, and believed. This latter is recorded, the former pardoned. So *Gen.* 18:12, 'Sarah laughed within herself, saying, After I have waxen old shall I have pleasure, my lord being old also?' Here was never a good word but one, viz. that she called her husband lord, and this is recorded to her eternal commendation, *1 Pet.* 3:6. Isaac then was not a child of nature, but of the mere promise; so are all our graces. We bring forth good things, as Sarah's dead womb brought forth a child' (Trapp).

12: wherefore also there sprang of one, and him as good as dead, so many as the stars of heaven in multitude, and as the sand, which is by the sea-shore, innumerable.

As was shown in the previous verse, Sarah shared her husband's faith in the divine promise, and in fact her belief in the revelation that she would bear a son was a condition for the fruitfulness of Abraham's faith. 'If the Jews are now proud of their origin, they must look to its cause. Whatever they are is to be attributed to the faith of Abraham and Sarah. It follows from this that they cannot hold or defend the position which they have attained except on the basis of faith' (Calvin). [*Gen.* 15:5, 17:15–22, 22:17; *Isa.* 51:1, 2; *Rom.* 4:16–21]

13: These all died in faith, not having received the promises, but having seen them and greeted them from afar, and having confessed that they were strangers and pilgrims on the earth.

These all died in faith: The verses which follow [verses 13–16] cannot apply to the antediluvians mentioned by the author for they were not pilgrims in a strange land, and of course Enoch did not die! They rather point the lesson to be learned from the eminent example set by the founders of Israel [verses 8–12]. This verse conveys something more than an objective account of their obedience; it 'gives an internal picture of their mind and how they felt themselves to be, a consciousness which they preserved even up to death' (A. B. Davidson).

Not having received the promises: Since God was pleased on numerous occasions to confirm and expand the original promise made to Abraham, the plural is used here. Thus the patriarchs believed the promises, which were centred in the Messiah through whom all the nations of the earth were to be blessed, yet they all died without having seen their fulfilment [verses 39,40]. If then they lived and died triumphantly on bare promises, how dare those who have seen their fulfilment falter in their allegiance to Christ?

But having seen them and greeted them from afar: 'They were like pilgrims to the Holy City who see its towers and spires on the horizon, ecstatically point to the vision, and shout their acclaim. This is all they had during their earthly lives' (Lenski) [*John* 8:56].

And having confessed that they were strangers and pilgrims on the earth: As the reality of their heavenly calling made evident their renunciation of the world, they inevitably attracted the *hostility* which was accorded to 'strangers' in the ancient world, while as 'pilgrims' or 'sojourners' they willingly bore the *stigma* of having no rights of residence in an alien land [cf. *Eph.* 2:12ff.; *Phil.* 3:20].

14: For they that say such things make it manifest that they are seeking after a country of their own.

In confessing themselves to be pilgrims on earth they declared that their true homeland was in heaven. 'Whosoever professes he has a Father in heaven, confesses himself a stranger on earth; hence there is in the heart an ardent longing, like that of a child among strangers, in want and grief, far from his *fatherland'* (Luther).

15: And if indeed they had been mindful of that country from which they went out, they would have had opportunity to return.

Indeed if their thoughts had been fixed upon the country they had left then there was nothing to stop their return to it. Hence their exile was entirely voluntary. In the same way the readers had ample opportunity to end their pilgrimage of faith and return to the attractions of Judaism. But those who are truly called of God do not revert to the old life, not for lack of opportunity, but because they no longer desire it; whereas Demas returned to this present world for no other reason than that he still loved it! [*2 Tim.* 4:10]

16: But now they desire a better country, that is, a heavenly: wherefore God is not ashamed of them, to be called their God; for he hath prepared for them a city.

The patriarchs had this sense of exile because their hearts were set on a better country and firmer settlement than could be found anywhere, but in heaven. By this expectation they gave God the credit for meaning more by his promises than the *letter* indicated, for they had respect to their *spirit* rather than the thing promised. Hence God is not ashamed to be called their God, and this is proved by the fact that he has prepared for them a city to justify the expectations which they had based upon his power and goodness. The patriarchs showed that they understood that God, in giving these promises, became their God; therefore God was not ashamed of them, and this showed itself especially in his naming himself 'the God of Abraham, Isaac and Jacob' [*Exod.* 3:15] (so Marcus Dods).

17: By faith Abraham, being tried, offered up Isaac: yea, he that had gladly received the promises was offering up his only begotten son; 18: even he to whom it was said, In Isaac shall thy seed be called: 19: accounting that God is able to raise up, even from the dead; from whence he did also in a figure receive him back.

As there could be no fulfilment of the divine promise without Isaac, the command to sacrifice his only son was the supreme test of Abraham's faith in God [*Gen.* 21:12, 22:1–18]. God normally tries the faith of his people by requiring their continued trust in his word despite the occasional apparent contradictions of his providential dealings with them. But Abraham was subjected to a far more severe test, because the command to slay Isaac was in *direct* contradiction to the promise that 'In Isaac shall thy seed be called'.

But Abraham refused to let his obedience to the command cancel his trust in the promise, for he reckoned that God was well able to raise up his son even from the dead [*Gen.* 22:5]. And it was because Abraham was actually in the process of offering up Isaac when he was stopped, that the receiving back of his son was virtually a resurrection from the dead. For though 'Isaac did not in fact rise from the dead, yet it seemed to be a kind of resurrection when he was snatched back suddenly and miraculously by the unexpected grace of God' (Calvin).

20: By faith Isaac blessed Jacob and Esau, even concerning things to come.

By faith Isaac believed the revelation which God made to him concerning the respective destinies of Jacob and Esau. And it was because he was fully conscious of the inspiration under which he had spoken that he made no attempt to revoke the blessing after the discovery of Jacob's deceit [*Gen.* 27:33]. Instead he bowed to the divine decree even though it set aside the law of primogeniture and overruled his own inclinations [*Rom.* 9:10–13].

The Hebrew Christians also had received a revelation of things to come to which they must either give their unhesitating assent or else resign themselves to sharing Esau's bitter lot [12:16, 17].

21: By faith Jacob, when he was dying, blessed each of the sons of Joseph; and worshipped, leaning upon the top of his staff.

It was faith which enabled Jacob, when he lay dying in Egypt, to predict the future inheritance of Ephraim and Manasseh in Canaan [*Gen.* 48: 1f.]. The inference here is that those who do not lay hold of the promised blessings in faith cannot be the true descendants of the one who did.

And worshipped, leaning upon the top of his staff: This incident took place before the patriarchal benediction mentioned in the first part of the verse [*Gen.* 47:31]. The difference between the Septuagint, 'upon the top of his staff', and the Hebrew, 'upon the bed's head', is only a matter of punctuation. The Septuagint reads the unpointed Hebrew word M–TT–H as MATTEH, *staff*, whereas it is pointed in the Massoretic text as MITTAH, *bed*. In this instance it seems likely that the former is the more accurate reading, and it certainly makes better sense. As death drew near, Jacob made Joseph swear that he would not leave his body in Egypt but that it would be taken to Canaan for burial there, and then he worshipped God, supporting his now feeble frame upon his staff, which was the symbol of his pilgrim state [*Gen.* 32:10]. Thus the fact that Jacob arranged to take possession of Canaan, 'as it were, by his dead body, was a very strong expression of his full persuasion that in due time his posterity should, according to the divine promise, possess it as an inheritance' (John Brown).

22: By faith Joseph, when his end was nigh, made mention of the departure of the children of Israel; and gave commandment concerning his bones.

At the end of his long life Joseph predicted the exodus of the children of Israel from Egypt, saying, 'God will surely visit you' [*Gen.* 50:24, 25]. As one who was second only to Pharaoh himself, his body might well have been laid to rest in some grand Egyptian tomb, but he entertained a far higher hope than this. For he publicly expressed his faith in the promised salvation by commanding that his bones should join in the exodus from Egypt and be buried in Canaan. 'To take an example from hence of digging men's bones out of their graves, of enshrining and placing them on altars, of carrying them up and down in procession, of adoring them with all signs of religious veneration, applying them unto miraculous operations, in curing diseases, casting out of devils, and the like, is fond [foolish] and ridiculous' (John Owen).

23: By faith Moses, when he was born, was hid three months by his parents, because they saw he was a goodly child; and they were not afraid of the king's commandment.

Five examples of faith from the life of Israel's greatest leader, Moses, are next instanced, the first of which recalls the faith of his parents [verses 23–29]. When Amram and Jochebed saw the beauty of Moses they resolved to defy the barbarous mandate which ordered the death of every son born of Hebrew parents, and they hid him in the house for three months, not fearing Pharaoh's impious decree [*Exod.* 2:2; *Acts* 7:19]. They evidently believed the beauty of their child to be a special token of the divine favour which marked him out for a high destiny [cf. *Acts* 7:20, ASV margin, 'Moses . . . was fair unto God']. We are not told whether they received a more specific revelation of God's will concerning the child, but in any case some appreciation of the divine purpose to be fulfilled through Moses is implied in the author's ascription of faith to Amram and Jochebed' (F. F. Bruce).

24: By faith Moses, when he was grown up, refused to be called the son of Pharaoh's daughter; 25: choosing rather to share ill treatment with the people of God, than to enjoy the pleasures of sin for a season;

When Moses was forty years old he renounced the position he enjoyed in Egypt as the adopted son of Pharaoh's daughter in order to share the reproach of the people of God [*Exod.* 2:11, 12; *Acts* 7:23, 24]. This was not the act of a pioneer revolutionary made in the interests of any earthly Utopia. It was not because he was of the same race that Moses chose to share the lot of a persecuted people, but because he knew them to be 'the people of God'. 'The faith of Moses enabled him to estimate aright the objects before him, and to forecast the future of the People of God, and oppose it to the temporary glory of sin. "Sin" in his case would have been apostasy, and there lies a delicate appeal to the Hebrews in his example' (A. B. Davidson).

The pleasures of sin: 'It is a common thing for a scripture to speak of a certain thing as if it were, and to say that it is, when it is only supposed to be so by others. For example, "There be gods many, and lords many" [*1 Cor.* 8:5]; not that there really were any such gods, but that by others they were reckoned so to be. Similarly in this text, he speaks according to the manner of men concerning the pleasures of sin, as they are reputed . . . It is false pleasure, and what truer misery is there than false joy? It is like the pleasure of the man who receives much money, but it is all counterfeit, or the pleasure of the man who dreams of a feast and awakes so hungry and vexed that he could eat his dream. For this reason sin should be doubly hated, because it is ugly and false, because it defiles and mocks us' (Ralph Venning, *The Plague of Plagues*, pp. 208–10).

26: accounting the reproach of Christ greater riches than the treasures of Egypt: for he looked unto the recompense of reward.

Geerhardus Vos points out that the phrase 'the reproach of Christ' is explained by the exhortation, 'Let us therefore go forth unto him without the camp, bearing his reproach' [13:13]. 'This reproach is thus seen to be a reproach which Christ Himself first bore and which we now bear together with Him. So we must similarly interpret the reproach of Christ borne by Moses. This does not imply that Moses had a prophetic knowledge of the sufferings of the future Messiah, but rather that the reproach which Moses bore was objectively identical with the reproach suffered by Christ and His people throughout the ages. This implies, therefore, that back of all the reproaches and sufferings which God's people have endured, stood Christ. How this appeared to Moses' own subjective consciousness is told us in 11:25, "choosing rather to share ill treatment with the people of God . . ."'

For he looked unto the recompense of reward: The fleeting treasures of Egypt could not capture Moses' affections for he looked forward to an eternal inheritance [verse 6]. 'Let the things of this world be increased and multiplied into the greatest measures and degrees imaginable, it alters not their kind. – They are temporary, fading, and perishing still; such as will stand men in no stead on their greatest occasions, nor with respect unto eternity' (John Owen).

27: By faith he forsook Egypt, not fearing the wrath of the king: for he endured, as seeing him who is invisible.

The strange attempt to reconcile this verse with Moses' fearful flight to Midian should be abandoned [*Exod.* 2:14, 5]. It must refer to the events associated with the exodus, which is here ascribed to the faith of Moses because it was accomplished under his inspired leadership. 'Not fearing the wrath of the king' describes his fearless demeanour before Pharaoh as he repeatedly demanded the release of God's people [*Exod.* 10:28, 29]. By 'seeing him who is invisible' Moses withstood the wrath of this earthly potentate, and was able to lead the children of Israel out of Egypt without fear of what might be done to prevent their escape.

28: By faith he kept the Passover, and the sprinkling of the blood, that the destroyer of the firstborn should not touch them.

Moses 'instituted the passover' (ASV margin) for no other reason than that God had commanded it. He instructed the people to offer the appointed sacrifice and to sprinkle their door posts with the blood, for he was fully persuaded that this unusual measure would protect them from the destroyer as he passed through the land in terrible judgment [*Exod.* 12].

'That which God would for ever instruct the church in by this ordinance is, that unless we are sprinkled with the blood of Christ, our paschal Lamb, no other privilege can secure us from eternal destruction. – Though a man had been really an Israelite and had with others made himself ready that night for a departure, which was a high profession of faith, yet if the lintel and posts of his door had not been sprinkled with blood, he would have been destroyed. And on the other hand, where there is this sprinkling of blood, be the danger never so great or so near, there shall be certain deliverance. "The blood of sprinkling speaks better than the blood of Abel"' (John Owen) [*John* 1:29; *1 Cor.* 5:7].

29: By faith they passed through the Red sea as by dry land: which the Egyptians assaying to do were swallowed up.

As John Owen notes, 'the whole is denominated from the better part', for the vast majority of those who passed safely through the Red Sea later perished miserably in the wilderness because of their unbelief [3:7–19; *Exod.* 14:11; *1 Cor.* 10:5]. But on this occasion the temporal deliverance of the many was effected by the saving faith of the few: e.g. Moses, Aaron, Caleb, and Joshua [*Rom.* 9:6].

Which the Egyptians assaying to do were swallowed up: '*Rash presumption* [is] mistaken by many for *faith*: with similar presumption many rush into eternity. The same thing done by the believer and by the unbeliever is not the same thing. What was *faith* in Israel was *presumption* in the Egyptians' (Fausset).

30: By faith the walls of Jericho fell down, after they had been compassed about for seven days.

The next example of faith which is celebrated by the author is separated from the exodus by an interval of forty years. This period is passed over in silence because he regards the wanderings in the wilderness as the years of unbelief. A signal instance of the power of united faith is provided by the fall of Jericho, for after Joshua and the children of Israel had marched silently round this apparently impregnable citadel for seven days its walls at last collapsed before their triumphant shout of faith. The Hebrews are called to a similar exercise of faith in the power of God to conquer all the bastions of unbelief [*Josh.* 6; *Zech.* 4:6–7; *2 Cor.* 10:3–5].

31: By faith Rahab the harlot perished not with them that were disobedient, having received the spies with peace.

No doubt the surprising inclusion of Rahab in the roll of those whose faith is specially praised is an implied rebuke to the readers [*Josh.* 2]. For if an Amorite harlot believed the reports she had heard of the God of Israel so that she perished not with them that were disobedient', then how can the children of the covenant renounce their interest in the promised Messiah? Calvin says that she is only described as 'the harlot' in order to magnify the grace of God in reclaiming her from such a disgraceful past, for it is certain that 'her faith is the evidence of her repentance' [*Josh.* 6:25; *James* 2:25]. Indeed she later married a prince of Judah, and shares with 'Ruth the Moabitess' an honoured place in the genealogy of the Saviour himself [*Matt.* 1:5].

32: And what shall I more say? for the time will fail me if I tell of Gideon, Barak, Samson, Jephthah; of David and Samuel and the prophets:

Although the list is far from exhausted, lack of time forces the author rapidly to sum up the achievements [verses 32–34] and the sufferings of faith [verses 35–38] in a brilliant final paragraph. The order remains roughly chronological, for apart from David, all those named here belong to the period of the Judges, while some of the later descriptions clearly refer to the courageous endurance of the Maccabean martyrs. By this rhetorical device the readers are faced with a long line of witnesses who remained faithful to their calling. Will they now waver in theirs?

33: who through faith subdued kingdoms, wrought righteousness, obtained promises, stopped the mouths of lions, 34: quenched the power of fire, escaped the edge of the sword, from weakness were made strong, waxed mighty in war, turned to flight armies of aliens.

A powerful impression is produced by the cumulative effect of this swift inventory of faith's exploits. With all the skill of an orator, the writer, in nine terse clauses delivered in 'sledgehammer style' (Robertson), invites them to 'See what faith has wrought!' Some of the items are readily identified; others have a more general reference.

Who through faith subdued kingdoms: Gideon conquered the Midianites [*Judg*. 7]; Barak the Canaanites [*Judg*. 4]; Samson the Philistines [*Judg*. 14f.]; Jephthah the Ammonites [*Judg*. 11]; and David the Philistines [*2 Sam*. 5:17], the Moabites [*2 Sam*. 8:2], and the Ammonites [*2 Sam*. 10:12]. That all those victories were achieved with weaker forces than those of their enemies demonstrates that faith is a mighty weapon! [cf. *1 Sam*. 14:6].

Wrought righteousness: This probably refers to the righteous rule exercised by those mentioned in the previous verse [cf. *2 Sam*. 8: 15]. 'Conquerors used their success for the furtherance of right. Righteousness was shown to be the solid foundation of enduring power: *Isa*. 9:7, 54:14; *1 Kings* 10:9' (Westcott).

Obtained promises: The Old Testament saints lived long enough to see many promises fulfilled, though they died without having seen the fulfilment of the Messianic promises [cf verses 13, 39].

Stopped the mouths of lions: In the next three clauses personal deliverance is in view. The first may be referred to the youthful exploits of Samson and David [*Judg*. 14:5, 6; *1 Sam*. 17:35], and to Daniel's courage in his old age [*Dan*. 6:22].

Quenched the power of fire: Here Shadrach, Meshach, and Abed-nego at once spring to mind [*Dan*. 3:12ff]. 'It was not only the flame, but the very nature of the fire, which in the power of faith they quenched and overcame, when they walked in "the midst of the furnace"' (Delitzsch).

Escaped the edge of the sword: Either in battle, or when pursued by enemies, as David escaped from Saul [*1 Sam*. 18:11], and Elijah from Jezebel [*1 Kings* 19:3].

From weakness were made strong: The last three clauses show how God's strength was received through faith. Although the main reference here is probably to Samson [*Judg.* 16:28], Hezekiah's recovery from sickness may not be ruled out [*2 Kings* 20:1–7].

Waxed mighty in war: A possible reminiscence of Barak's annihilation of Sisera's host [*Judg.* 4:16], though all Israel's notable victories were the fruit of faith in the divine promise [cf. *2 Chron.* 14:9–12; 20: 14–25].

Turned to flight armies of aliens: In 'aliens' we have 'a comprehensive word for the enemies of Israel all along the sacred history, but it certainly includes the Maccabean struggle, and so prepares for the distinct reference to that later period in the verses which follow' (Vaughan).

35: women received their dead by a resurrection: and others were tortured, not accepting their deliverance; that they might obtain a better resurrection:

The author now begins a harrowing account of what faith can suffer. 'There was never any greater instance of the degeneracy of human nature unto the image of the devil than this, that so many of them have been found, and that in high places of power, emperors, kings, judges, and priests, who were not satisfied to take away the lives of the true worshippers of God by the sword, or by such other ways as they slew the worst of malefactors, but invented all kinds of hellish tortures whereby to destroy them' (John Owen). In this verse an extreme contrast is drawn between the women who were delivered from the suffering of bereavement by a resurrection which restored their children to an earthly life [*1 Kings* 17:17–24; *2 Kings* 4:18–37], and the refusal of the Maccabean martyrs to recant under the most fiendish tortures because they looked for 'a better resurrection' than a mere respite from earthly suffering [*2 Macc.* 7:9, 11, 14; *2 Cor.* 4:17, 18].

36: and others had trial of mockings and scourgings, yea, moreover of bonds and imprisonment: 37: they were stoned, they were sawn asunder, they were tempted, they were slain with the sword: they went about in sheepskins, in goatskins; being destitute, afflicted, ill-treated

Others whose sufferings fell short of martyrdom, nevertheless endured cruel mockery, scourging, bonds, and imprisonment [e.g.

1 Kings 22:24–27; *Jer.* 20:2, 37:15], while some were stoned, sawn asunder, or slain with the sword. In view of the context many regard the words 'were tempted' as an incongruous insertion, but A. B. Davidson points out that the manuscript authority favours this reading and that 'the reference must be to cruel tortures practised on men to procure apostasy'. According to tradition Jeremiah was stoned to death in Egypt, and Isaiah was sawn asunder during Manasseh's evil reign (for biblical examples, see *2 Chron.* 24:20–22; *Jer.* 26:23). The same fidelity to God forced others to wander about like wild animals, destitute of even the common necessities of life.

38: (of whom the world was not worthy), wandering in deserts and mountains and caves, and the holes of the earth.

The author's parenthetic judgment is well expounded by Trapp: 'They were fitter to be set as stars in heaven, and be before the Lord in his glory. The world was not worthy of their presence, and yet they were not thought worthy to live in the world.'

On 'caves' Fausset remarks, 'Palestine, from its hilly character, abounds in fissures and caves, affording shelter to the persecuted, as the fifty hid by Obadiah and Elijah [*1 Kings* 18:4, 13, 19:8, 13]; Mattathias and his sons [*1 Macc.* 2:28, 29]; Judas Maccabeus [*2 Macc.* 5:27].'

39: And these all, having had witness borne to them through their faith, received not the promise, 40: God having provided some better things concerning us, that apart from us they should not be made perfect.

Even though all these heroes obtained a good report through faith, they did not receive the fulfilment of the promise during their life on earth. For 'God had something better in view for us, (and so purposed) that they should not attain the Perfection apart from us' (W. Manson's translation). Or as Moffatt explains it: 'God in his good providence reserved the messianic *perfection* of Jesus Christ until we could share it.' Thus the Old Testament saints could not reach 'perfection' without us because the fulfilment of that promise awaited our day! For though they have already attained the bliss that belongs to 'the spirits of just men made perfect' [12:23], the final consummation of their hope still awaits the end of the age [9:28], when all the people of God shall be glorified together. 'If those on whom the great light of grace had not yet shone showed such patience in bearing their ills, what effect ought the full light of the gospel to have on us? A tiny spark of light led them to heaven, but now that the sun of righteousness shines on us what excuse shall we offer if we still hold to the earth?' (Calvin).

CHAPTER TWELVE

Since such a noble succession of witnesses have gone before them, the Hebrews are urged to discard every weight and to run with patience the race that is set before them, looking unto Jesus the pioneer and perfecter of faith, who endured the cross for the sake of the joy that was set before him and is now seated at the right hand of God [verses 1, 2]. When they consider what he suffered for them, they have no cause to become fainthearted, especially if they remember that God's fatherly chastisements prove their sonship and also serve to make them partakers of his holiness [verses 3–10]. Although no chastening is enjoyable at the time, it afterwards yields the fruit of righteousness in those who are exercised by it. Therefore they must brace themselves for the conflict, and pursue peace with all men and the sanctification without which no man shall see the Lord; looking carefully lest any man should despise his spiritual birthright after the evil example of Esau who found no place of repentance, though he sought it diligently with tears [verses 11–17]. In Christ they are not confronted with the terrible portents of a vanished legal order, for they have not come to Mount Sinai but to the heavenly realm of Mount Zion, in which the redeemed rejoice before God through the merits of the Mediator whose blood speaks better than that of Abel [verses 18–24]. If they refuse to hear God who now speaks to them from heaven in the Person of his Son, they will incur a far more dreadful judgment than that which befell the despisers of the law. As therefore we receive through Christ a kingdom which cannot be shaken, let us serve God with godly fear, remembering that he is a consuming fire[verses 25–29].

1: Therefore let us also, seeing we are compassed about with so great a cloud of witnesses, lay aside every weight, and the sin which doth so easily beset us, and let us run with patience the race that is set before us,

Therefore let us also: The author again graciously identifies himself with his disheartened readers [10:39], in order to encourage them to exercise the same faith by which their distinguished 'forerunners' were approved of God [11:4–40].

Seeing we are compassed about with so great a cloud of witnesses: This does not mean that this host of 'witnesses' are the heavenly spectators of what takes place in the earthly arena, for as used here the word almost has the sense of 'martyr' [cf. *Acts* 22:.20; *Rev.* 2:13, 17:6]. As Lenski points out, it is unbiblical to suggest that the spirits of the departed are still hovering about us to watch our progress. 'These saints are not "witnesses" that see our faith and testify about us; God does not ask them to testify about us. They are witnesses whose life, works, sufferings, death attest their own faith, and testify to us through the pages of Holy Writ and in other history that they were true men of faith indeed.'

Lay aside every weight: As the athlete disciplines himself to discard everything that would impede his progress in the contest for which he has entered, so also every weight must be laid aside in the Christian race. An immoderate use of that which is not in itself sinful can become a great hindrance to the Christian. 'The Christian runner must rid himself even of innocent things which might retard him. And all that does not help, hinders. It is by running he learns what these things are. So long as he stands he does not feel that they are burdensome and hampering' (Marcus Dods) [cf. *Phil.* 3:8–14].

And the sin which doth closely cling to us (ASV margin): The figure compares sin to a loose garment entangling the limbs of the runner, which thus reduces his speed and retards him in his course. The reference is not to some sin in particular, but to sin itself. As Vaughan remarks, The AV rendering 'the sin which doth so easily beset us' catches 'the point of the expression admirably until it is perverted into *the besetting sin* as something different from *the whole body of sin*'. Those who would be reckoned as serious competitors in this race must therefore strip off the clinging garment of sin!

And let us run with patience the race that is set before us: After the negative preparation comes the positive demand for persistent progress. 'Patience' is not passive forbearance, but 'patient endurance'. It is the lack of stamina that distinguishes the would-be contestant from the successful athlete. In the Christian race, which is not a short sprint but a long distance contest, there are no prizes for those who do not persevere to the end of the course [contrast *Acts* 20:24; *2 Tim.* 4:7, 8].

2: looking unto Jesus the author and perfecter of our faith, who for the joy that was set before him endured the cross, despising shame, and hath sat down at the right hand of the throne of God.

Looking unto Jesus: The author now reveals the great secret of Christian perseverance. The strength to run this race is only imparted when our gaze is constantly fixed upon the great object of faith. 'Nor shall we endure any longer than whilst the eye of our faith is fixed on him. From him alone do we derive our refreshments in all our trials' (John Owen).

The pioneer and perfecter of faith: This glory belongs uniquely to Jesus because: 1. As the *founder* of faith he alone blazed the trail of salvation [2:10]; 2. As the *example* of faith he alone brought faith to its perfection. 'Christ in the days of his flesh trod undeviatingly the path of faith, and as the Perfecter has brought it to a perfect end in his own person. Thus he is the leader of all others who tread that path' (W. E. Vine).

Who for the joy that was set before him endured the cross, despising shame: This indicates the nature of Christ's example. As in verse 16, the preposition *anti* means 'in exchange for': just as Esau sold his birthright for the price of a single meal, so in order to gain the joy that was set before him Jesus paid the price of the 'cross' (the word occurs only here in the Epistle), despising its shame. The joy envisaged was not a selfish joy; it was the joy to be achieved through that redemption which would accomplish the salvation of all his people [*Isa.* 53:11].

And hath sat down at the right hand of the throne of God: In drawing attention to the contrast between he 'endured' and 'hath sat down', Westcott comments: 'The fact of suffering is wholly past but the issue of it abides for evermore.' Thus faith recognizes 'this Jesus' as the one whom God has made 'both Lord and Christ' [*Acts* 2:36]. He who once suffered on earth now rules from heaven [*Matt.* 28:18]. The Hebrews must believe this however much present circumstances may appear to contradict it [12:3f.]. And so must we!

3: For consider him that hath endured such gainsaying of sinners against himself, that ye wax not weary, fainting in your souls.

'For' introduces the reason for fixing their gaze upon Jesus; to consider what he had to endure will show how light their sufferings are by comparison. Let them reflect upon what it meant for the *sinless One* patiently to bear the implacable hatred of *sinners* against himself [*Isa.* 53:7]. 'The constant consideration of Christ in his sufferings is the best means to keep up faith unto its due exercise in all times of trial' (John Owen) [*1 Pet.* 2:21–24].

4: Ye have not yet resisted unto blood, striving against sin:

Unlike 'the captain of their salvation' the Hebrews have not as yet suffered death in striving against sin, though they have 'endured a great conflict of sufferings' because of their confession of faith in him [10:32–34]. The particular sin of unbelief to which these unexpected hardships had exposed them is here personified as a formidable foe who must be resisted even at the cost of life itself. 'This sin would win if in fear of blood the readers would relinquish their faith; it would be vanquished if the readers, unafraid of a bloody death, held fast to their faith' (Lenski).

5: and ye have forgotten the exhortation which reasoneth with you as with sons, My son, regard not lightly the chastening of the Lord, nor faint when thou art reproved of him; 6: For whom the Lord loveth he chasteneth, And scourgeth every son whom he receiveth.

The readers were repining under the opposition they encountered because they had forgotten the Scripture that addresses them as children who must receive with meekness the chastening of their heavenly Father [*Prov.* 3:11, 12; cf. *Job* 5:17; *Psa.* 94:12; *Rev.* 3:19]. Although the hardhearted man steels himself against feeling the stroke, and the fainthearted man reels under it, the child of God is neither to despise correction nor to despair when he is reproved; otherwise he will fail to profit from the experience.

For whom the Lord loveth he chasteneth: God punishes his enemies; he chastens his children. The one is the judicial infliction of his wrath; the other is the proof of his parental love. 'The same hand – but not the same character – gives the stroke, to the godly and the ungodly. The scourge of the judge is widely different from the rod of the Father' (Charles Bridges, *Commentary on Proverbs*, p. 31 n). Moreover, this fatherly discipline pertains only to the present life. 'There is no chastisement in heaven, nor in hell. Not in heaven, because there is no sin; not in hell, because there is no amendment. Chastisement is a companion of them that *are in the way*, and of them only' (John Owen).

7: It is for chastening that ye endure; God dealeth with you as with sons; for what son is there whom his father chasteneth not?

If they would endure rightly, they must endure intelligently (Moffatt). They must recognize that the reason for such chastening is found in God's fatherly relation to them, for what son is there whom his father does not correct? 'Corrections are pledges of our adoption and badges of our sonship. One Son God hath without sin, but none without sorrow. As God corrects none but his own, so all that are his shall be sure to have it; and they shall take it for a favour too, *1 Cor*. 11:32' (Trapp).

8: But if ye are without chastening, whereof all have been made partakers, then are ye bastards, and not sons.

These weary Hebrews might well think that they would not suffer if they were really God's sons, but in fact the reverse is the case. For if they did not so suffer, they would not be God's sons! 'Saints, saith God, think not that I hate you, because I thus chide you. He that escapes reprehension may suspect his adoption. God had one Son without corruption, but no son without correction. A gracious soul may look through the darkest cloud, and see a God smiling on him' (Thomas Brooks, *Precious Remedies against Satan's Devices*, pp. 85–6).

9: Furthermore, we had the fathers of our flesh to chasten us, and we gave them reverence: shall we not much rather be in subjection unto the Father of spirits, and live?

'This comparison is made in several parts. The first is that if we give so much reverence to the fathers of whom we are born after the flesh that we submit to their discipline, much more honour is due to God who is our spiritual Father. The second is that the discipline by which fathers bring up their children is only useful for this present life, but God looks further to sanctify us for eternal life. Thirdly, mortal men chastise their children as they think good, but God applies His discipline with the wisest purpose and the highest wisdom so that there is nothing in it that is out of control' (Calvin).

And live? 'We are reminded by this that nothing is more fatal to us than to refuse to give ourselves in obedience to God' (Calvin).

10: For they indeed for a few days chastened us as seemed good to them; but he for our profit, that we may be partakers of his holiness.

'The fathers of our flesh' chastened us according to what 'seemed good to them', but God with unerring wisdom designs it for our spiritual good. 'What the Author means to bring out by saying that the chastisement of earthly parents is for a few days, is the brevity and comparative unimportance of our connection with our natural parents; their chastisement is for a short time as the duration of our relation to them is short, and indeed their chastisement, if wise, has in view to make us able to be independent of them; God's chastening has another view, to make us partakers of His holiness, to unite us to Him in character and likeness more and more. It is not the duration of the chastisement that is the point of the passage; it is the duration of our relation in each case to him who chastens' (A. B. Davidson).

11: All chastening seemeth for the present to be not joyous but grievous; yet afterward it yieldeth peaceable fruit unto them that have been exercised thereby, even the fruit of righteousness.

Certainly no chastening is regarded as an enjoyable experience at the time, but rather grievous. But it later yields peaceable fruit to those who have been exercised by it, even (the fruit of) 'righteousness,' the word being placed last in the sentence for emphasis. The stoical endurance of that which was intended to be *felt* can never produce such fruit! [*Isa*. 9:8–12] For it is only when we are 'exercised' by this discipline that a harvest of righteousness is reaped in our lives. And it is indeed 'peaceable fruit' because the victory of faith brings peace in God and peace of conscience.

12: Wherefore lift up the hands that hang down, and the palsied knees;
13: and make straight paths for your feet, that that which is lame be not turned out of the way, but rather be healed.

The practical application of this teaching is couched in language which is evidently taken from *Isa*. 35:3 and *Prov*. 4:26. In verse 12 the bracing of the body stands for the spiritual resolution with which

Christians are to meet adversity. Instead of wilting under chastisement, they are to lift up the listless hands and strengthen the paralysed knees.

And make straight paths for your feet, that that which is lame be not put out of joint but rather be healed (ASV margin): No advance in the Christian way is possible while the community halts between two opinions, for they cannot follow the straight path of grace until they make a final break with Judaism [*1 Kings* 18:21]. 'Inconsistency and vacillation in the general body of the church would create a way so difficult for the lame, that their lameness would become dislocation, and they would perish from the way; on the other hand, the habit of going in a plain path would restore them to soundness' (A. B. Davidson).

14: Follow after peace with all men, and the sanctification without which no man shall see the Lord:

The following verses [verses 14–17] set forth the indispensable conditions for receiving the promised blessings of the gospel.

Peace continue to pursue with all (Lenski): If this were one of a series of general admonitions, the reference would be to 'all men' [cf. *Rom.* 12:18], but in the present context the thought centres on 'the crippled souls' in their company and so the parallel is *Rom.* 14:19: 'peace with all the members of the church so that no dissension may afford anyone cause for turning from Christ' (Lenski).

And the sanctification without which no man shall see the Lord: 'Sanctification' is well described by Westcott as 'the preparation for the presence of God'. It is 'the bringing of the consecrated person into harmony of life and character with the consecration' (Vaughan). As the Hebrew believers had been separated unto God by their confession of faith in Christ, so they are to live the life that befits those who are so separated [cf. *Rom.* 6:19, 22].

15: looking carefully lest there be any man that falleth short of the grace of God; lest any root of bitterness springing up trouble you, and thereby the many be defiled;

Looking carefully whether there be any man that falleth back from the grace of God (ASV margin): It would be foolish to infer from this that the saints of God can fall from grace and be lost, because the author has in view only the '*phenomenal* aspect of religion' (Vos). He is making the simple point that anyone who abandons his profession of Christ in favour of a return to Judaism is left behind in the wilderness of unbelief, and it is to guard against this danger that he exhorts them all to be overseers of one another [3:12f.].

Lest any root of bitterness springing up trouble you, and thereby the many be defiled: If anyone among them thus falls back from gospel grace, it is not merely a loss for himself, it is also a danger for many others. Such a man would be like the springing up of a bitter root which spreads its defilement to the whole congregation, so making it unfit to worship God [*Deut.* 29: 18; *Josh.* 7:25]. 'Himself bitter against Christ, he embitters others against Christ, poisons them, if you will' (Lenski) [cf. *Gal.* 5:9].

16: lest there be any fornicator, or profane person, as Esau, who for one mess of meat sold his own birthright.

By recalling Esau's irrevocable act of folly, the author now warns the waverers that spiritual blessings when once renounced cannot be regained [verses 16, 17]. The reference is not to sexual immorality, which is dealt with later in the Epistle [13:4], but to the peril of religious infidelity. The 'fornication that he has in mind is illustrated by the profane choice of Esau, who forfeited the blessing of God in favour of a paltry secular benefit. Thus the word 'fornicator' is 'used here in the Biblical sense of idolater' (R. V. G. Tasker).

Who for one mess of meat sold his own birthright: As the first-born, Esau possessed spiritual privileges which were distinctively his own, until he rashly bartered them away for a miserable morsel of meat – such a 'cheap meal', says Calvin, as that 'by which Satan habitually lures the reprobate' [*Gen.* 25:29–34].

17: For ye know that even when he afterward desired to inherit the blessing, he was rejected; for he found no place for a change of mind in his father, though he sought it diligently with tears.

Now the warning is driven home. For the Hebrews know that though Esau afterward desired to have the blessing he had despised, he found it impossible to reverse the consequences of his sinful choice. In fact his profane irreverence was further manifested in the desire to occupy the place he had so light-heartedly abandoned. Having sold his birthright as something of no value, he nevertheless desired *to inherit* the blessing which belonged to it! 'He asserted the prerogative of birth, a gift of God, when he had himself recklessly surrendered it' (Westcott).

For he found no place of repentance (ASV margin): It is going against the natural construction of the words to refer this repentance to a change of mind on the part of Isaac (as in the ASV text). It was Esau who sought but could not find a place of 'repentance'. The word as used here means more than a mere change of mind; it refers to 'a change of mind undoing the effects of a former state of mind' (A. B. Davidson). The message for the readers is loud and clear: It is 'impossible again to renew to repentance' those who wilfully renounce their spiritual birthright, for after the gospel has been rejected there is no place for a change of mind which will secure them the final blessing [6:6, 10:26].

Though he sought it diligently with tears: 'It' being the blessing he now so belatedly desired. 'He might have had it formerly without tears; afterwards, though weeping, he was rejected' (Bengel) [*Gen.* 27:34f.].

18: For ye are not come unto a mount that might be touched, and that burned with fire, and unto blackness, and darkness, and tempest, 19: and the sound of a trumpet, and the voice of words; which voice they that heard entreated that no word more should be spoken unto them;

The issue facing the Hebrews is now crystallized in one magnificent sentence [verses 18–24]. As the superiority of the new covenant infinitely transcends that of the old economy which it has superseded, so those who despise the grace so fully exhibited in it will be visited by sanctions even more severe than those which attended the giving of the law [2:2–4].

The welcome absence of the awesome sensible phenomena which characterized the Sinaitic revelation must not lead them to doubt the ultimate reality of that supersensible world to which they have been brought by the gospel. For the very same voice which spoke to the people from a material mountain now addresses them from heaven itself! Well might the author earnestly urge them to 'See that ye refuse not him that speaketh' [verse 25] [cf. *Exod.* 19:16–19; 20:18–21; *Deut.* 4:11f.].

Which voice they that heard entreated that no word more should be spoken unto them: As the people heard the direct speech of God from out of the fire and darkness which surrounded the mount they were stricken with terror, for 'the speaking of the law doth immediately discover the invincible necessity of a mediator between God and sinners' (John Owen) [*Exod.* 20:19; *Deut.* 5:25].

20: for they could not endure that which was enjoined, If even a beast touch the mountain, it shall be stoned; 21: and so fearful was the appearance, that Moses said, I exceedingly fear and quake:

Moreover, the fact that the people could not bear the rigour of the command to slay by stoning any trespassing beast clearly showed that this approach to God was at the same time a fearful shrinking back. Although the words attributed to Moses are not an exact quotation from the Old Testament, there is no need to doubt that they accurately represent his state of mind on that occasion. For if only the *remembrance* of the sight led him to express himself in similar terms [*Deut.* 9:19], he must have been even more terrified by the reality itself [cf. *Exod.* 19:10ff.].

'The effect of this terror extended itself unto the meanest of beasts, and unto the best of men,' and, argues John Owen, if the 'mediator himself of the old covenant was not able to sustain the dread and terror of the law: how desperate then are their hopes who would yet be saved by Moses!' (i.e. by their obedience to the law, cf. *Rom.* 10:1–5).

22: but ye are come unto mount Zion, and unto the city of the living God, the heavenly Jerusalem, and to innumerable hosts of angels, 23: to the general assembly and church of the firstborn who are enrolled in heaven, and to God the judge of all, and to the spirits of just men made perfect, 24: and to Jesus the mediator of a new covenant, and to the blood of sprinkling that speaketh better than that of Abel.

But ye are come unto mount Zion, and unto the city of the living God, the heavenly Jerusalem: Mount Zion is here spiritualized to suggest an image of that heavenly realm to which the Hebrews have already been brought by grace. Thus in leaving Mount Sinai for Mount Zion they have exchanged the sensuous for the spiritual; the place of temporal manifestation for the eternal abode of the righteous; and the dread sense of separation from God for the gracious privilege of unbroken communion with God through Jesus Christ. 'As Jerusalem was distinguished into two cities, the superior and the inferior; so is the Church into triumphant and militant; yet both make up but one city of the living God' (Trapp).

And to innumerable angels in festal gathering (RSV): 'Sinai, too, had its angels, but they did not appear in festal assembly, see *Acts* 7:53 and *Gal.* 3:19. The word "myriads" or ten thousands is repeatedly used with reference to angels [*Dan.* 7:10; *Jude* 14; *Rev.* 5:11]. Since Christ has entered heaven after his work of redemption, the whole angel world rings with festal panegyrics [*Rev.* 5:1–12]' (Lenski).

And to the assembly of the first-born who are enrolled in heaven (RSV): Those who still tread the pilgrim path on earth may rejoice in the knowledge that their names are already written in heaven, and that before long they will join that vast company which forms the church triumphant [*Luke* 10:20; *Rev.* 21:27]. 'All the people of Christ are the "first-born" children of God, through their union with Him who is The First-born *par excellence;* their birthright is not to be bartered away, as was Esau's' (F. F. Bruce).

And to a judge who is God of all (RSV): This reminder that they have already come before a judge who is the God of all creation serves a dual purpose. For God is both the *discerner* of the true among the professing (a note of warning), and 'the *avenger* of the true Church, now under persecution and temptation (a note of comfort)' (Vaughan) [10:27,30,31; *Luke* 18:7, 8].

And to the spirits of just men made perfect: 'The souls of the just when separated from their bodies, do not wander up and down in this world, nor hover about the sepulchres where their bodies lie; nor are they detained in any purgatory, in order to their more perfect purification; nor do they fall asleep in a benumbed stupid state: but do forthwith pass into glory, and are immediately with the Lord' (John Flavel, *Works*, vol. 3, p. 38) [*Luke* 23:43].

And to Jesus the mediator of a new covenant: In contrast to the antiquated covenant which it replaced, this 'new' (*neos*) covenant is both recently established and ever fresh and young. Its Mediator is here simply called 'Jesus' – 'the *human* name so full of the *saving* character [*Matt.* 1:21], so attractive therefore to the struggling and militant church' (Vaughan). 'Believers have not now access unto, or dependence on, a Moses, a mere man, and a servant, declaring God's will, only a sinner himself, trembling in his office, and weary of his clients, and whose ministry is vanishing, as his person dying; but unto God the Son himself incarnate, a Son-mediator, making sons, and bringing them nearer to God, satisfying the law for them and writing it on their hearts; above all sin himself, though a sacrifice for it, who is able to save to the uttermost, for that he ever liveth to intercede for them, chapter 1:1–3, 3:6, 7:26; Rev. 1:13' (Poole).

And to the blood of sprinkling that speaketh better than that of Abel: Abel and Jesus were both slain by wicked hands, but whereas Abel's blood cried for vengeance on him by whom it was shed, that of Jesus pleads for the pardon of guilty sinners, and so speaks 'better' than a martyr's blood [*Gen.* 4:10; *Luke* 23:34]. It is here called 'the blood of sprinkling' since it cleanses only those to whom it is applied in faith [*1 John* 1:7].

25: See that ye refuse not him that speaketh. For if they escaped not when they refused him that warned them on earth, much more shall not we escape who turn away from him that warneth from heaven:

The preceding comparison is enforced by a final appeal not to capitulate to the prompting of unbelief which could stifle the voice which still speaks to them in grace from heaven [2:2f., 10:29]. In the *innocent* request that God should not speak directly to them at Sinai, the author 'sees *prefigured* the *sinful* refusals of the voice of God in the onward history of Israel, and draws a note of warning from them for Christian days' (Vaughan) [cf. 3:7ff.]

26: whose voice then shook the earth: but now he hath promised, saying, Yet once more will I make to tremble not the earth only, but also the heaven. 27: And this word, Yet once more, signifieth the removing of those things that are shaken, as of things that have been made, that those things which are not shaken may remain.

At Sinai God's voice shook the earth, but according to Haggai 2:6 there is a day coming when he will shake both heaven and earth. By underlining the words, 'yet once more', he shows us that the second shaking will be final. It will sweep away all things temporal so that the unshakeable eternal realities may remain. The forthcoming consummation thus has a positive purpose: it is the establishment of a new heaven and a new earth which shall become the heritage of the redeemed [2:5; *Rom.* 8:19; *2 Pet.* 3:13; *Rev.* 21:1–5]. If therefore the Hebrews would not fall short of this eternal inheritance, they must not refuse to hear what God in these last days is speaking to them in his Son.

28: Wherefore, receiving a kingdom that cannot be shaken, let us have grace, whereby we may offer service well-pleasing to God with reverence and awe: 29: for our God is a consuming fire.

'Let us have grace' is more accurately rendered 'let us be thankful' (Arndt-Gingrich). The grace which has invested them with all the privileges of citizenship in an immovable kingdom must constrain an overwhelming sense of gratitude to God. This will find its natural expression in service that is well-pleasing to him because it proceeds from those whose lives are permeated by 'godly fear and awe' (ASV margin). This reverential fear of God accompanies every genuine experience of his redeeming love, for the nearer we are brought to God by grace, the greater will be our sense of the infinite gulf which separates the creature from the Creator [cf. *Isa.* 6:1f.].

For our God is a consuming fire: These words are taken from *Deut.* 4:24 which warns Israel that their covenant relationship with God ('*our* God') would not protect them from the devouring fire of divine judgment if they incurred his jealousy by lapsing into the sin of idolatry. An abiding consciousness of the ineffable holiness of God offers the best deterrent against the commission of sin, and therefore every child of grace prays, 'Unite my heart to fear thy name', for he knows that it is impossible to combine a love of sin with a love for God [*Psa.* 86: 11]. 'Even those who stand highest in the love and favour of God, and have the fullest assurance thereof, and of their interest in Him as their God, ought, not withstanding, to fear Him as a sin-revenging God and a consuming fire' (Ezekiel Hopkins: *Sermon on Hebrews 12:28–29*).

CHAPTER THIRTEEN

After various exhortations concerning social and religious duties, there is a final appeal to renounce the vain ritual of a superseded order and to share Christ's reproach by joining him outside the camp of Judaism [verses 1–17]. The author requests the prayers of his readers that he might soon be restored to them, and formally concludes the letter with a majestic benediction and doxology [verses 18–21]. He urges them to heed his word of exhortation, gives news of Timothy's release, sends greetings, and ends with a brief benediction [verses 22–25].

The author's 'word of exhortation' [verse 22] is more like a homily than a letter, but in his concluding words he reverts to Paul's familiar pattern of reminding the readers of their obligation to live out what they believe. He begins his 'ethical' appendix with a brief paragraph of crisp precepts which set forth the Christian's social duties [verses 1–6].

1: Let love of the brethren continue.

Whenever this command is 'more honoured in the breach than the observance', Christianity ceases to exist, for God refuses to accept the professed service of those who are without love for the brethren. Hence the need to insist upon the *continuance* of this love! The primary importance of this injunction makes it unnecessary to imagine that it was called forth by any particular situation. It is everywhere insisted upon throughout the New Testament [e.g. *John* 13:34; *Rom.* 13:8; *1 Cor.* 13; *1 Thess.* 4:9; *1 Pet.* 1:22; *1 John* 2:10; 3:11, 23; 4:7, 11, 12, 21]. As Westcott observes: 'The love of the Jew for his fellow Jew, his "brother", was national: the Christian's love for his fellow-Christian is catholic. The tie of the common faith is universal, and in proportion as the ill-will of those without increased, it became necessary to deepen the feeling of affection within.'

2: Forget not to show love unto strangers: for thereby some have entertained angels unawares.

A readiness to welcome travellers and a compassionate concern for those under affliction are two ways in which this brotherly love is to be manifested [verses 2, 3]. They must not neglect to offer hospitality to strangers for in so doing 'some have entertained angels unawares', not as though they will receive such supernatural visitors as Abraham once did, but they may well find that some of their guests resemble *angels* (i.e. *messengers*) in proving to be true messengers of God to them [*Gen.* 18]. Moffatt points out that there were pressing reasons for the exercise of this kindly virtue in the primitive church, because inns were notorious not only for their extortionate charges but also for their low moral standards. Such accommodation was obviously unsuitable for travelling Christians on both these counts.

3: Remember them that are in bonds, as bound with them; them that are ill-treated, as being yourselves also in the body.

But while strangers seek hospitality [verse 2], prisoners must be sought out in order to be helped. From the foundation of the church, Christians, in obedience to the Lord's teaching [*Matt.* 25:36], and often at great risk to themselves, ministered to the needs of such as suffered imprisonment for the gospel's sake. This help was given in several ways: either by personally visiting them to alleviate their suffering through gifts and sympathy [*2 Tim.* 1:16], or by subscribing money to purchase their release, or by praying for them [*Col.* 4:3, 18]. The author next bids his readers remember that they also are in the body; for when one member of the Christian community suffers, all the members suffer with it [*1 Cor.* 12:26]. 'This is the ideal which each believer must strive to realize' (Westcott).

4: Let marriage be had in honour among all, and let the bed be undefiled: for fornicators and adulterers God will judge.

After mention of the body, the sanctity of the marriage bond is next enforced. This is not a statement defending marriage against a false asceticism as the AV wrongly suggests, but a serious warning not to indulge in any sexual relationship outside that honourable estate. Since sin entered the world human society always has been permissive, but Christians have been rescued from this degradation by the amazing grace of God [*1 Cor.* 6:9–11]. Fornicators and adulterers generally escape human condemnation, but *God* (placed last in the sentence for emphasis) will judge those whom man does not punish [10:30]. And then the immoralities which now are so flippantly regarded will be viewed in a very different light!

5: Be ye free from the love of money; content with such things as ye have: for himself hath said, I will in no wise fail thee, neither will I in any wise forsake thee. 6: So that with good courage we say, The Lord is my helper; I will not fear: What shall man do unto me?

Finally, Christians must be free of the *love* of money, which Paul says is the root of all evil [*1 Tim.* 6:10]; and be content with what they have, knowing that with God as their satisfying portion they will lack for nothing [*Matt.* 6:31–33]. This exhortation is supported by two quotations which confirm that the assurance of God's presence with them should remove all anxious care. As the first of these recalls the words of encouragement given to Joshua when their forefathers were on the verge of entering Canaan [*Josh* 1:5], there is a peculiar fitness in applying it to the crisis which these Jewish Christians were now facing. The second is taken from *Psa.* 118:6, and it expresses the response they ought to be able to make to the promise of God's perpetual presence. 'If He has said, I will never leave, WE may well say, What shall MAN do?' (John Brown) [cf. *Rom.* 8:31f.].

7: Remember them that had the rule over you, men that spake unto you the word of God; and considering the issue of their life, imitate their faith.

The closing appeal makes it clear that fidelity to Christ demands a final break with Judaism and involves the bearing of his reproach outside the camp [verses 7–17]. 'There would be no meaning in exhorting the Hebrews to remember their former teachers unless the exhortation were an indirect way of exhorting them not to swerve from the faith in the form in which those departed teachers had delivered it to them' (A. B. Davidson). A consideration of the end of their pilgrimage provides the grand incentive to imitate their faith. The Hebrews cannot expect to finish their earthly course in the same way unless they abide in the same faith. Although these leaders died in the faith they had so long confessed, there is no need to assume that they also died as martyrs for it, as some have suggested.

8: Jesus Christ is the same yesterday and to-day, yea and for ever,

The verse affirms that Jesus Christ is still the same to-day as he was yesterday declared to be by their former teachers [verse 7], and he will remain the same throughout eternity. This declaration of an unchanging Christ is therefore a summons to an unchangeable faith in him. Hence Trapp remarks, 'This was the sum of their sermons, and is the substance of their and your faith; which therefore you must stick to, standing fast in the street which is called Straight, *Acts* 9:11, and not whirred about with divers and strange doctrines'.

9: Be not carried away by divers and strange teachings: for it is good that the heart be established by grace; not by meats, wherein they that occupied themselves were not profited.

Be not carried away by divers and strange teachings: 'He calls the teachings which lead us away from Christ *diverse*, since there is no other simple and pure truth than the knowledge of Christ. He calls them *strange*, since God does not regard as His anything that is outside Christ. By this we are warned how we should proceed if we want to attain due proficiency in Scripture, for anyone who does not take a straight course to Christ is a wanderer' (Calvin).

For it is good that the heart be established by grace: Their hearts cannot be made firm without their determined adherence to the doctrine they had already received, because the gospel is the sole channel through which the saving grace of God is mediated to mankind.

Not by meats, wherein they that walked were not profited (ASV margin): Since the meticulous observance of such distinctions did not profit those who practised them, it would be sheer folly to exchange the principle of grace for the empty ritual of a vanished order. As the writer goes on to say 'we have an altar', the word 'meats' almost certainly refers to the priestly privilege of partaking in those sacred meals which were provided by meat which had been first offered in sacrifice. The main point to be grasped is that the difference between 'grace' and 'meats' – between the Christian faith and Judaism – is one of complete antithesis. For the grace of the gospel cannot co-exist with the lifeless performance of an external religious code, which is here summed up in the pregnant term 'meats' [cf 9:10]. 'The Apostle refers to "teachings", not to practices; it is not implied that the Hebrews were in a locality where the practices were carried on, they were being carried aside by the doctrines' (A. B. Davidson).

10: We have an altar, whereof they have no right to eat that serve the tabernacle.

Although Christians do not have a visible altar on which many kinds of sacrifices are offered, this does not mean that they are without an altar of their own. This 'altar' is Christ's once-for-all sacrifice which fulfilled what was foreshadowed on the Day of Atonement. On that occasion no part of the offering was reserved for the priests, for after the high priest had presented the blood within the sanctuary, the bodies of the beasts were burned outside the camp [*Lev.* 16:27]. Accordingly those who continue to 'serve the tabernacle' thereby debar themselves from any part in the offering of Christ. The benefits which Christ purchased for his people by his death cannot be enjoyed by those who remain inside the camp which crucified the Lord of glory! The observations of John Owen on this verse have lost none of their force over the years, and they are as pertinent today as when they were first written.

'*Obs. I.* That the Lord Christ, in the one sacrifice of himself, is the only altar of the church of the New Testament.

Obs. II. That this altar is every way sufficient in itself for the end of an altar, namely, the sanctification of the people; as verse 12.

Obs. III. The erection of any other altar in the church or, the introduction of any other sacrifice requiring a material altar, is derogatory to the sacrifice of Christ, and exclusive of him from being our altar.'

11: For the bodies of those beasts whose blood is brought into the holy place by the high priest as an offering for sin, are burned without the camp. 12: Wherefore Jesus also, that he might sanctify the people through his own blood, suffered without the gate.

It was because all the sins of the congregation were laid upon the bodies of these beasts that they were devoted to destruction outside the camp. In the same way Christ the sinless One became an outcast when the sins of his people were laid to his account, and he suffered outside the gate in order to exhaust the curse he bore for them [*Gal.* 3:13]. It was this vicarious bearing of the curse of sin which effected the sanctification of those he represented. Moreover, this suffering not only served to separate a people unto himself, it also finally severed his connection with an apostate nation. 'When the Lord Jesus carried all the sins of his own people in his own body unto the tree, he left the city, as a type of all unbelievers, under the wrath and curse of God' (John Owen).

13: Let us therefore go forth unto him without the camp, bearing his reproach. 14: For we have not here an abiding city, but we seek after the city which is to come.

The climax of the Epistle is reached in this moving appeal. No place remains for the Hebrews within the city which had rejected and crucified their Lord (a statement which would have little point if Jerusalem had already been destroyed). They must abandon the rites and ceremonies of Judaism from which the glory had departed, in order to join Christ outside the camp, for it is impossible to evade bearing his reproach without also losing his presence [11:26; *Luke* 9:23; *Phil.* 3:4–10]. Furthermore, any reluctance to renounce the protection of those religious privileges which were centred upon an earthly city would be dispelled by remembering that their real security lay in remaining faithful to their heavenly calling. 'The main business of believers in this world is diligently to seek after the city of God, or the attainment of eternal rest with him; and this is the character whereby they may be known' (John Owen) [11:10, 13–16; *Phil.* 3:20].

15: Through him then let us offer up a sacrifice of praise to God continually, that is, the fruit of lips which make confession to his name.

John Owen notes that the next three verses give a summary of Christian duty under three heads: *Spiritual*, with respect to God, verse 15; *Moral*, with respect to men, verse 16; and *Ecclesiastical*, with respect to Christian leaders, verse 17.

Through him then: 'Through him' is the same as through him alone. 'There is a profane opinion and practice in the papal church about offering our sacrifices of prayer and praise to God by others; as by saints and angels, especially the blessed Virgin. But are they our altar? Did they sanctify us by their blood? Did they suffer for us without the gate? Are they the high priests of the church? Have they made us priests unto God; or prepared a new and living way for our entrance unto the throne of grace? It is on account of these things that we are said to offer our sacrifice by Christ; and it is the highest blasphemy to assign them unto any other'. It therefore follows that, 'Whatever we tender unto God, and not by Christ, it hath no other acceptance with him than the sacrifice of Cain' (John Owen).

Let us offer up a sacrifice of praise to God continually: The sacrifices which believers now offer are not carnal but spiritual. They are the sacrifices of praise and thanksgiving, of beneficence and almsgiving [verse 16]. Clearly, as defined here and elsewhere in the New Testament, true worship is essentially inward and ethical [cf. *Rom.* 12: 1, 2; *James* 1:27].

That is, the fruit of lips which make confession to his name: In the passage here quoted the prophet makes a figurative use of sacrificial language in order vividly to express the reality of Israel's repentance [cf. *Psa.* 50:12–15, 51:15–17]. 'Covering God's altar with the calves of our lips, *Hos.* 14.3. This shall please the Lord better than an ox or bullock that hath horns and hoofs; *Psa.* 69:31' (Trapp).

16: But to do good and to communicate forget not: for with such sacrifices God is well pleased.

The sincerity of their love for God will be shown by a practical concern for the needs of others [*1 John* 3:17]. As they have been careful to do this very thing in the past, so they are to maintain the same ministry in the future [6:10]. This fellowship is sacrificial because it involves the Christian in sharing his temporal blessings with those in need, and with such service God is well pleased. Moreover, he who has freely received, will freely give, for an experience of grace is always reflected in a life of gratitude [*Matt.* 25:35–40; *Rom.* 12:13; *Gal.* 6:6; *Phil.* 4:18].

17: Obey them that have the rule over you, and submit to them: for they watch in behalf of your souls, as they that shall give account; that they may do this with joy, and not with grief: for this were unprofitable for you.

The author previously referred to the fidelity of their former leaders in the faith; now he urges them to obey their present guides [verses 7, 17]. 'It is their duty so to *obey* whilst they (the rulers) teach the things which the Lord Christ hath appointed them to teach; for unto them is their commission limited, *Matt.* 28:20: and to *submit unto their rule* whilst it is exercised in the name of Christ, according to his institution, and by the rule of the word, and not otherwise. When they depart from these, there is neither obedience nor submission due unto them' (John Owen).

For they watch in behalf of your souls, as they that shall give account; that they may do this with joy, and not with grief: Like faithful shepherds, they watch in the interest of your souls, and they do this under the constant pressure of knowing that one day they must render to the Chief Shepherd an account of the care they have taken of his sheep.

For if you are unwilling to obey their teaching, they will not be able to render a joyful account of their oversight on the great day of reckoning [verse 20; *Ezek.* 33:7–9; *Phil.* 2:16].

For this were unprofitable for you: An impressive understatement! 'While *they* groan, *you* would do worse than groan. All the advantage of having faithful leaders and watchmen would not only be lost but would turn into the opposite. It is bad when no one rings the alarm and warns, it is a thousand times worse for you and for me when we are deaf to a true warning' (Lenski) [*2 Thess.* 1:7–9].

18: Pray for us: for we are persuaded that we have a good conscience, desiring to live honourably in all things. 19: And I exhort you the more exceedingly to do this, that I may be restored to you the sooner.

In referring to himself for the first time, the author requests the prayers of his readers. 'The allusion to his purity of conduct, and strong assertion of his consciousness of it, in regard to them and all things, when he is petitioning for their prayers, implies that some suspicions may have attached to him in the minds of some of them. These suspicions would naturally refer to his great freedom in regard to Jewish practices' (A. B. Davidson). Although he is not detained in prison [verse 23], it seems that he is engaged on some mission which hinders his return, but he hopes that he may be soon 'restored' to them. Events would prove whether it was in fact God's will that he should return to them, yet as John Owen wisely observes, prayer is not to be ruled by the secret purposes of God. 'According unto our present apprehensions of duty, we may lawfully have earnest desires after, and pray for such things as shall not come to pass'.

20: Now the God of peace, who brought again from the dead the great shepherd of the sheep with the blood of an eternal covenant, even our Lord Jesus, 21: make you perfect in every good thing to do his will, working in us that which is well-pleasing in his sight, through Jesus Christ; to whom be the glory for ever and ever. Amen.

Having requested prayer for himself, the author concludes with a marvellously comprehensive prayer for his readers which recapitulates the message of the entire Epistle.

Now the God of peace, who brought again from the dead the great shepherd of the sheep: It is in the raising up from the dead of 'our Lord Jesus' that

God is known as the 'God of peace', because the resurrection is the proof of our reconciliation.

'Christ, as the great shepherd of the sheep, was brought into the state of death by the sentence of the law; and was thence led, recovered, and restored, by the God of peace . . . Had not the will of God been satisfied, atonement made for sin, the church sanctified, the law accomplished, and the threatenings satisfied, Christ could not have been brought again from the dead . . . The death of Christ, if he had not risen, would not have completed our redemption, we should have been "yet in our sins"; for evidence would have been given that atonement was not made. The bare resurrection of Christ, or the bringing him from the dead, would not have saved us; for so any other man may be raised by the power of God. But the bringing again of Christ from the dead, "through the blood of the everlasting covenant", is that which gives assurance of the complete redemption and salvation of the church' (John Owen).

So though Israel had been led by other shepherds in former days, the Hebrews must recognize that it is only by heeding the voice of this 'great shepherd' that they can enjoy God's peace, for he alone ever lives to guide, guard, and rule over the *one* flock of God [*John* 10:1–28; *1 Pet.* 2:25, 5:4].

In the blood of an eternal covenant (ASV margin): 'In the blood' means that Christ was raised in virtue of his own sacrificial blood-shedding which had abolished the old covenant and established an eternal covenant, so that now 'there is no more offering for sin' [10:18]. If then the resurrection 'is the *result* of the Saviour's sacrifice offered in blood, it is impossible that the Ascension of the Saviour can be *in order* to the offering of that blood of sacrifice in heaven' (N. Dimock, *The Sacerdotium of Christ*, p. 113).

Even our Lord Jesus: Since this is the Epistle's only reference to Christ's resurrection, it is significant that the author who has dwelt so lovingly upon the human name 'Jesus' should here add the title 'Lord', thus pointing to the universal dominion with which he was then invested. The appeal of the confessional 'our' should not be overlooked.

Make you perfect in every good work to do his will (AV): Although by nature we are completely unfit to perform any good work, for we have neither the inclination nor the capacity to do God's will, the grace that bestows an interest in 'the blood of the everlasting covenant' imparts the capacity to do works which God accounts 'good' because they are the fruit of our union with Christ ('*through* Jesus Christ') [*Eph.* 2:10].

Working in us that which is well-pleasing in his sight: Nothing but an experience of grace will supply us with the key which enables us to understand the Pauline paradox: 'Whatever good we *do*, God *does* in us [*Phil.* 2:13]' (Fausset).

Through Jesus Christ, to whom be the glory for ever and ever. Amen: 'The doxology may be to the God of peace to whom the prayer is addressed, more probably it is to Jesus Christ, last-named and the great figure who has been before the mind throughout the Epistle' (Marcus Dods).

22: But I exhort you, brethren, bear with the word of exhortation: for I have written unto you in few words.

What follows his prayer is in the nature of a postscript. First he urges them as 'brethren' to 'bear with the word of exhortation' even though it should cut across their most cherished prejudices. 'Sharp though it be, and to the flesh tiresome, yet suffer it. Better it is that the vine should bleed than die. But many are like the nettle, touch it never so gently, it will sting you' (Trapp). In view of the critical decision facing them [verse 13], he says that he has written briefly. For though the letter is long by New Testament standards, it could be read aloud to the congregation in less than an hour.

23: Know ye that our brother Timothy hath been set at liberty; with whom, if he come shortly, I will see you.

Next he informs them of the release of Timothy with whom he hopes to visit them, provided Timothy arrives before he is obliged to start his journey. 'All that we can infer from this reference to an imprisonment of Timothy of which we have no other information is that probably the readers and certainly "the writer stood in some relationship to the Pauline world-mission circle"' (F. F. Bruce).

24: Salute all them that have the rule over you, and all the saints. They of Italy salute you. 25: Grace be with you all. Amen.

The usual Christian greetings and the benediction bring the Epistle to a close. If 'they of Italy' refers to those resident in Italy, then the writer is in Italy himself. But it is more likely that this refers to a group living outside Italy, and in that case, the writer, who is also abroad, is addressing a community whose most probable location is Rome. The benediction is identical to that found in Titus. And it is this word 'grace' which sums up all the blessings of that new and better covenant of which Jesus Christ is the sole Mediator.

SOLI DEO GLORIA

BIBLIOGRAPHY AND ACKNOWLEDGMENTS

The author expresses his grateful thanks to the following authors and publishers who kindly gave permission to reproduce quotations from their copyright works.

ALLIS, O. T., *Prophecy and the Church* (Presbyterian & Reformed, 1954).

BERKOUWER, G. C., *Faith and Perseverance* (Eerdmans, 1958).

—— *The Person of Christ* (Eerdmans, 1954).

BROWN, COLIN (ed.), *The New International Dictionary of New Testament Theology*, vol. 1 (Paternoster Press, 1975).

BRUCE, F. F., *The Epistle to the Hebrews* (*NLC*) (Marshall, Morgan & Scott, 1964).

CALVIN, JOHN, *The Epistle to the Hebrews* (Oliver & Boyd, 1963).

CULLMANN, OSCAR, *The Christology of the New Testament* (SCM, 1963).

DENNEY, JAMES, *The Death of Christ* (Tyndale, 1964).

HEWITT, THOMAS, *Hebrews – Introduction and Commentary* (*TNTC*) (Tyndale, 1960).

KIDNER, DEREK, *Psalms 1–72 – Introduction and Commentary* (*TOTC*) (Tyndale, 1973).

KITTEL, G. AND FRIEDRICH, G., *Theological Dictionary of the New Testament* (vols. 1–10) (Eerdmans, 1964–76).

LENSKI, R. C. H., *The Interpretation of the Epistle to the Hebrews* (Augsburg, 1961).

MCKELVEY, R. J., *The New Temple* (OUP, 1969).

MORRIS, LEON, *The Apostolic Preaching of the Cross* (Tyndale Press, 1965).

MURRAY, JOHN, *Collected Writings*, vols. 1 & 2 (Banner of Truth, 1976, 1977).

—— *The Covenant of Grace* (Tyndale, 1956).

—— *Redemption – Accomplished and Applied* (Banner of Truth, 1961).

NEIL, WILLIAM, *The Epistle to the Hebrews* (Torch) (SCM, 1955).

ROBERTSON, A. T., *Word Pictures of the New Testament,* vol. 5 (Broadman, 1932).

STIBBS, A. M., *The Finished Work of Christ* (Tyndale, 1955).

—— *The Meaning of the Word 'Blood' in Scripture* (Tyndale, 1958).

—— *Commentary on Hebrews* (IVP, 1970).

TASKER, R. V. G., *The Gospel in the Epistle to the Hebrews* (Tyndale, 1956).

VINE, W. E., *Expository Dictionary of New Testament Words* (Oliphants, 1958).

VOS, GEERHARDUS, *Biblical Theology* (Banner of Truth, 1975).

—— *The Self-Disclosure of Jesus* (Eerdmans, 1954).

—— *The Teaching of the Epistle to the Hebrews* (Eerdmans, 1956).

WYNGAARDEN, MARTIN J., *The Future of the Kingdom in Prophecy and Fulfilment* (Baker, 1955).

The following books were also consulted:

ARNDT, W. F. AND GINGRICH, F. W., *A Greek English Lexicon of the New Testament* (University of Chicago Press, 1957).

BENGEL, J. A., *New Testament Word Studies* (Kregel, 1971).

BERKHOF, L., *Systematic Theology* (Banner of Truth, 1959).

BOETTNER, LORAINE, *Roman Catholicism* (Banner of Truth, 1966).

BRIDGES, CHARLES, *Commentary on Proverbs* (Banner of Truth, 1968).

BROWN, JOHN, *The Epistle to the Hebrews* (Banner of Truth, 1972).

BURROUGHS, JEREMIAH, *The Rare Jewel of Christian Contentment* (Banner of Truth, 1964).

CUNNINGHAM, WILLIAM, *Historical Theology* (Banner of Truth, 1960).

DAVIDSON, A. B., *Hebrews* (*HBC*) (T. & T. Clark, 1959).

DELITZSCH, FRANZ, *Commentary on the Epistle to the Hebrews* (T. & T. Clark, 1880).

DIMOCK, NATHANIEL, *Our One Priest on High* (Longmans, Green, 1910).

—— *The Sacerdotium of Christ* (Longmans, Green, 1910).

DODS, MARCUS, *The Epistle to the Hebrews* (*EGT*) (Eerdmans, 1974).
FAUSSET, A. R., *Hebrews* (*JFB*) (Collins, 1874).
FLAVEL, JOHN, *Works*, vols. 1 & 3 (Banner of Truth, 1968).
GUTHRIE, DONALD, *New Testament Introduction* (Tyndale Press, 1970).
HENRY, MATTHEW, *Commentary on the Holy Bible* (various editions).
HODGE, A. A., *The Atonement* (Evangelical Press, 1974).
HODGE, CHARLES, *1 Corinthians* (Banner of Truth, 1958).
HUGHES, PHILIP E., *Commentary on the Epistle to the Hebrews* (Eerdmans, 1977).
LEUPOLD, H. C., *Exposition of the Psalms* (Baker, 1961).
LIGHTFOOT, J. B., *Commentary on Philippians* (Zondervan, 1968).
—— *Commentary on Colossians and Philemon* (Zondervan, 1961).
LUTHER, MARTIN, *Lectures on Hebrews* (*Works*, vol. 29) (Concordia, 1968).
MACHEN, J. G., *The Christian View of Man* (Banner of Truth, 1965).
MANSON, WILLIAM, *The Epistle to the Hebrews* (Hodder & Stoughton, 1966).
MOFFATT, JAMES, *The Epistle to the Hebrews* (*ICC*) (T. & T. Clark, 1924).
MOULE, H. C. G., *Outlines of Christian Doctrine* (Hodder & Stoughton, 1894).
MURRAY, JOHN, *The Epistle to the Romans* (*NIC*) (Eerdmans, 1960).
NAIRNE, A., *The Epistle to the Hebrews* (*CGT*) CUP, 1922).
NORTH, BROWNLOW, *The Rich Man and Lazarus* (Banner of Truth, 1960; reprinted as *A Great Gulf Fixed*, 1999).
OWEN, JOHN, *An Exposition of Hebrews* (Banner of Truth, 1991)
—— *Works*, vol. 7 (Banner of Truth, 1965).
PALMER, SAMUEL, 'The Nonconformist's Catechism' (*Sermons of the Great Ejection*) (Banner of Truth, 1962).
PINK, ARTHUR W., *An Exposition of Hebrews* (Baker, 1954).
—— *The Holy Spirit* (Baker, 1970).
POOLE, MATTHEW, *Commentary on the Holy Bible*, vol. 3 (Banner of Truth, 1963.)
RENDALL, FREDERIC, *The Epistle to the Hebrews* (Macmillan, 1888).
REYMOND, ROBERT L., *Introductory Studies in Contemporary Theology* (Presbyterian & Reformed, 1968).

SKILTON, JOHN (ed.), *The New Testament Student at Work*, vol. 2 (Presbyterian & Reformed, 1975).

SMEATON, GEORGE, *The Apostles' Doctrine of the Atonement* (Banner of Truth, 1991.

SOUTER, ALEXANDER, *A Pocket Lexicon of the Greek New Testament* (OUP, 1956).

SWETE, H. B., *The Ascended Christ* (Macmillan, 1922).

TRAPP, JOHN, *Commentary on the New Testament* (Sovereign Grace Book Club, 1958).

TRENCH, R. C., *Synonyms of the New Testament* (James Clarke, 1961).

VAUGHAN, C. J., *The Epistle to the Hebrews* (Macmillan, 1890).

VENNING, RALPH, *The Plague of Plagues* (Banner of Truth, 1965; reprinted as *The Sinfulness of Sin*, 1993).

VINCENT, MARVIN R., *Word Studies in the New Testament* (MacDonald, n.d.).

WARFIELD, B. B., *The Inspiration and Authority of the Bible* (Marshall, Morgan & Scott, 1959).

—— *Counterfeit Miracles* (Banner of Truth, 1972).

WESTCOTT, B. F., *The Epistle to the Hebrews* (Eerdmans, 1974).

WUEST, KENNETH S., *Hebrews in the Greek New Testament* (Eerdmans, 1947).

Revelation

INTRODUCTION

It is generally acknowledged that the last book in the Bible is the most difficult to understand, and yet its very place in the canon of Scripture underlines the vital importance of grasping the meaning of its message, for Revelation is the capstone in the edifice of divinely revealed truth. In this great unveiling of God's redemptive purpose, victory is assured to the followers of the Lamb even in the midst of their struggle with the powers of darkness, and the heavenly perspective thus granted has enabled believers in every age to stand fast against their persecutors. Hence the purpose of the book is supremely practical: it is a revelation given to promote patient endurance but not to stimulate fanciful speculation.

As to its form, Revelation (*apocalypsis*) is at once an *apocalypse* [1:1], a *prophecy* [1:3] and an *epistle* [1:4, 11; 22:21]. Arising within Judaism after the gift of prophecy had ceased, *apocalyptic* was a type of literature in which despair associated with the present evil age encouraged reflection upon the glories of the age to come. But though Revelation draws heavily upon the symbolic imagery of apocalyptic, the differences between them are more striking than the similarities. Unlike the Jewish apocalyptists, the writer of Revelation claims the inspiration of a prophet [1:3; 22:7] and uses his own name instead of hiding his identity under some great name from the past [1:4]. He does not retell history under the guise of prophecy, but teaches that the hope of future glory is firmly rooted in the historic victory of the cross [7:14]. Finally, in place of the passive despair of the apocalyptists, John's faith in the power of the gospel will not allow him to abandon the present to the forces of evil, which is why he so urgently charges his readers to 'keep the sayings of this book'.

As a *prophetic book,* Revelation is not predictive in the sense that it is history written in advance, but it does clearly show the working out of

God's purpose in history by revealing the eternal issues which were at stake in the crisis that confronted the churches of the Roman province of Asia. John insists that his book is a prophecy [1:3; 22:10, 18, 19] and, as a true forth-teller of God's will, he delivers the word of promise and judgment to the seven churches. Thus the key to a right understanding of the book must be sought in the 'life situation' of those to whom it was first addressed. In other words, he does not predict the future in a vacuum, but relates the present to the future and so communicates what must have been an intelligible message to the men of his own time. It is not surprising that those who lose sight of this fact are inclined to treat Revelation as if it were *Old Moore's Almanac!*

It is evident from the introduction [1:4] and conclusion; [22:21] that Revelation also takes the form of an *epistle* which was intended to be read to the seven churches [chapters 2, 3] as they met for worship [1:3; Col. 4:16]. Since the writer was well known to his brethren in Asia, he introduces himself simply as John. It is as a sharer in their tribulation [1:9] that he exhorts them to remain faithful in the face of persecution, which threatened the church from without, and the heresies which would undermine it from within. Most scholars agree in dating the book towards the end of the reign of Domitian (AD 96), who was the first emperor to persecute Christians for their refusal to join in the worship of the imperial cult. The authority with which the author speaks and the august nature of the revelation vouchsafed to him both suggest that he was the apostle John, whose sojourn in Asia was virtually proved by Isbon Beckwith after a thorough examination of the early tradition. It has been widely claimed in modern times that the differences between Revelation and the fourth Gospel rule out the possibility of common authorship. But at the end of a careful investigation H. B. Swete concluded that the evidence 'creates a strong presumption of affinity between the Fourth Gospel and the Apocalypse, notwithstanding their great diversity both in language and thought'.

There are three further features of Revelation which should be noted:

1. ITS NUMEROUS ALLUSIONS TO THE OLD TESTAMENT. John's thought is so steeped in the Hebrew Scriptures that the whole book is a richly-woven tapestry of Old Testament words, phrases and near quotations.

2. ITS RICH TREASURY OF HYMNS. The book is filled with the songs of heaven which have constantly inspired and guided the worship of the church on earth.

3. ITS FIGURATIVE LANGUAGE AND SYMBOLIC USE OF NUMBERS. John employs strange and sometimes monstrous images to impress upon his readers the reality of the unseen spiritual contest which lies behind the persecuting power of a hostile state. Numbers are freely used to convey ideas rather than mathematical units, and the dominant place which is given to the number seven has convinced some scholars that the book consists of a series of seven parallel sections, each of which depicts the church's conflict throughout the gospel age from a different standpoint. This view was expounded by William Hendriksen in *More than Conquerors* and is also followed here.

A SUMMARY OF THE BOOK OF REVELATION

Section 1: Christ among the Seven Churches (chs. 1–3).

The seven letters speak to the church in every age, because they show that the glorified Christ is always with his people, both in judgment to call them to repentance and in grace to assure them of victory.

Section 2: The Lamb and the Seven Seals (chs. 4–7).

The vision of heaven reveals the victorious Lamb as the only one who is worthy to take the book with seven seals. These he opens one by one, thus securing the judgment of the wicked and the bliss of the redeemed.

Section 3: The Seven Trumpets of Judgment (chs. 8–11).

The first six warning judgments fail to bring the wicked to repentance and, though the witnessing church must suffer persecution, all these wrongs are avenged when the seventh trumpet heralds the final judgment.

Section 4: The Woman and the Dragon (chs. 12–14).

As the woman gives birth to a son, the dragon (Satan) waits to devour him, but the child is caught up to heaven. The dragon now persecutes the woman and is assisted by the beast from the sea and the beast from the earth. The section ends with a vision of Christ's coming in judgment.

Section 5: The Seven Bowls of Wrath (chs. 15–16).

In this vision there is portrayed the outpouring of God's wrath upon the impenitent and the terror of the last judgment.

Section 6: The Fall of Babylon (chs. 17–19).

The fall of the godless city is followed by rejoicing in heaven, and the destruction of the beast and the false prophet is depicted in a further account of Christ's second coming.

Section 7: Christ's Victory over Satan (chs. 20–22).

During the gospel age Satan is bound so that he may no longer deceive the nations, but he is released for the last battle, only to be overthrown at Christ's return, when the present universe is replaced by the new heaven and the new earth.

It will be seen that the above outline identifies the so-called 'millennium' of chapter 20 with the day of salvation, and the binding of Satan during this period demonstrates Christ's *present* lordship over the powers of evil, even as it also assures the church of the success of her witness in what nevertheless remains an *evil* age.

It is hoped that the interpretation offered in this book may encourage a more sober assessment of the Apocalypse, for it is very strange that the same evangelicals who refuse to allow sceptical scholars to turn Genesis into a book of myths are still credulous enough to let Revelation become the playground for the wild fantasies of some popular writers.

1: CHRIST AMONG THE SEVEN CHURCHES
CHAPTER ONE

The revelation given to John is a prophecy which is to be read to the seven churches of Asia [verses 1–8]. On Patmos John sees the Christ, who instructs him to write to these churches. He describes the majestic appearance of Christ and the overwhelming effect of this vision upon him [verses 9–20].

1: The Revelation of Jesus Christ, which God gave him to show unto his servants, even the things which must shortly come to pass: and he sent and signified it by his angel unto his servant John;

'The Revelation of Jesus Christ' means the revelation given by him (NEB). Although John is the *writer*, Jesus Christ is the real *Author* of the book. As the Mediator [5:9], Christ is the unveiler of God's purpose for his people ('his servants'), and he sent his angel [22:8, 16] to convey this transcendent mystery to John through signs and symbols ('signified'). The revelation has for its content the things which '*must* (of divine necessity) shortly come to pass'. The phrase shows that the main burden of the prophecy was intended to meet the need of John's own day by warning believers of the impending crisis of persecution, though, of course, it also speaks of more distant events [verse 18]. Christians may never regard history as a random and meaningless succession of events, because they know that whatever happens must serve to advance the divine plan of salvation [*Rom.* 8: 28, 35–39].

2: who bare witness of the word of God, and of the testimony of Jesus Christ, even of all things that he saw.

In telling all that he saw, John gave witness to the Word of God and the testimony borne by Jesus Christ. John thus describes his book as 'a revelation from God mediated by the testimony of Jesus Christ, and made known to himself in visions' (Beckwith).

3: Blessed is he that readeth, and they that hear the words of the prophecy, and keep the things which are written therein: for the time is at hand.

This is the first of the seven beatitudes recorded in the book [14:13; 16:15; 19:9; 20:6; 22:7, 14]. Here a blessing is pronounced upon the one who reads the prophecy to the congregation and upon those who both hear and obey its message [22:7]. The prophecy is not mere prediction, but a true forth-telling of the will of God for his people, who are urgently summoned to keep the words of the book because the time of their fulfilment is at hand. Thus the admonition and counsel given in the prophecy were intended to prepare the church for the hour when its faith would be tried sorely [note also verse 1].

4, 5a: John to the seven churches that are in Asia: Grace to you and peace, from him who is and who was and who is to come; and from the seven Spirits that are before his throne; and from Jesus Christ, who is the faithful witness, the firstborn of the dead, and the ruler of the kings of the earth.

John to the seven churches that are in Asia: Although there were other churches in Asia (e.g. Colossae, Hierapolis), the fact that John was instructed to write only to seven shows that the number is used in a symbolic sense to indicate completeness. These seven churches were selected as representative of the whole church in every age. This is evident from the repeated formula, 'He that hath an ear, let him hear what the Spirit saith to the churches,' which underlines the universal application of the message addressed to each of the churches [2:7, 11, 17, 29; 3:6, 13, 22].

There is no ground for supposing that the letters to the churches are prophetic and represent successive periods of church history. R. C. Trench justly remarks on the 'arbitrary artificial character of all the attempted adaptations of Church history to these Epistles', and points out that this error results from 'a futile looking into Scripture for that which is not to be found there, from a resolution to draw out from it that which he who draws out must first himself have put in. Men will never in this way make Scripture richer. They will have made it much poorer for themselves, if they nourish themselves out of it with the fancies of men, their own or those of others, instead of with the truths of God.'

Grace to you and peace: This is the distinctive Christian greeting which is found in most of the New Testament epistles. All the benefits of the gospel are summed up in the twin blessings of grace and peace. 'Grace' is the free and unmerited favour of God, and 'peace' is the state of spiritual well-being secured by that favour. The threefold source of these blessings is next set forth.

From him who is and who was and who is to come: In this expansion of the Greek version of *Exod.* 3:14, 'I am he who is', God the Father is described in terms of his eternal self-existence. As the one who eternally is, God's lordship over time embraces both the past and the future, and this truth would minister much needed comfort at a time when the church stood under the threat of persecution. The phrase 'who is to come' is especially significant, because it foreshadows 'the general purpose of the book, which is to exhibit the comings of God in human history' (Swete) [verse 7].

And from the seven Spirits that are before his throne: In another instance of the symbolic use of the number seven, this image represents the

Holy Spirit in the fulness of his manifold operations in the church [3:1] and in the world [4:5; 5:6]. 'The seven Spirits' are seen 'before his throne' to show the readiness of the Holy Spirit to accomplish the will of God. The imagery here is borrowed from *Zech.* 4, where the prophet sees a lampstand with seven lamps ['the eyes of the Lord, which range through the whole earth', verse 10], and the meaning of the vision is 'Not by might, nor by power, but by my Spirit, says the Lord of hosts' [verse 6].

And from Jesus Christ, who is the faithful witness, the first-born of the dead, and the ruler of the kings of the earth: This triple title is clearly in accord with John's pastoral purpose. To encourage the fidelity of his readers, he reminds them that Jesus Christ is

1. *'The faithful witness'*, who bore witness to the truth of God even to the point of death [*John* 18:37; *1 Tim.* 6:13; *Rev.* 2:13 where the same title is given to Antipas, who also sealed his witness with his blood];

2. *'The first-born of the dead'*, whose unique triumph over death has given him the rank of first-born and guaranteed the resurrection of all who are found in him [*Psa.* 89:27; *Col.* 1:18];

3. *'The ruler of the kings of the earth'*, who is already reigning over Caesar, their persecutor, despite all appearances to the contrary [*Eph.* 1:20–22; *Phil.* 2:9–11; *Col.* 1:15–18].

5b, 6: Unto him that loveth us, and loosed us from our sins by his blood; and he made us to be a kingdom, to be priests unto his God and Father; to him be the glory and the dominion for ever and ever. Amen.

In the first of the many doxologies of the book, praise is offered to Jesus Christ for his abiding love and finished work of redemption. As the one who lives, he ever loves those whom he purchased from sin's dreadful bondage at the cost of his own blood. John next states the privileges won by the Redeemer for his people. He collectively constituted them a 'kingdom' in which they individually serve 'his God and Father' [the expression points to a unique relationship, 2:27; 3:5, 21; 14:1] as 'priests'. It is because believers recognize Christ as the Messiah that they are viewed in the New Testament as the true heirs of the promises made to Israel [*Exod.* 19:6; *1 Pet.* 2:9]. First, regal dignity belongs to the members of Christ's kingdom, for they are destined to share in his kingly rule [5: 10]. Secondly, each believer is a priest. This priesthood is not limited to any order of ministry. 'All may offer the sacrifice of praise and thanksgiving: all have direct access to the holiest through the blood of Jesus: all Christians, as priests, are to minister to one another and to plead for one another' (Marvin R. Vincent). It is to Christ as the Author of these blessings that John gratefully ascribes 'the glory and the dominion for ever and ever. Amen'. In a salutary comment, Trench contrasts the prominent place which is given to doxological praise in this book with the very subordinate place it often occupies in our worship.

7: Behold, he cometh with the clouds; and every eye shall see him, and they that pierced him; and all the tribes of the earth shall mourn over him. Even so, Amen.

This announcement of the coming of Christ in glory to judge the world is an adaptation of *Dan.* 7:13 and *Zech.* 12:10. The latter prophecy bears its original favourable sense when applied to the first advent of Christ [*John* 19:37], but here the mourning is not that of repentance but of hopeless remorse, because the second advent will end the age of gospel opportunity and usher in the eternal state [6:16, 17]. Hence all the tribes of the earth will then wail on account of Christ's judgment upon them. The expression 'coming with the clouds' is best understood as symbolizing this approaching judgment [*Isa.* 19:1]. 'Every eye shall see him' clearly means that Christ's glorious advent will be visible to all and hidden from none. The Bible nowhere speaks of a 'secret' second coming. John endorses the awesome truth thus set forth with the solemn double seal: 'Even so, Amen.'

8: I am the Alpha and the Omega, saith the Lord God, who is and who was and who is to come, the Almighty.

In Revelation it is only here and in 21:5–8 that God is introduced as the speaker. The prophecy of the previous verse is guaranteed by the one who is 'the Alpha and the Omega'. These are the first and last letters of the Greek alphabet, and the title means that as God is both the beginning and the end, the A to Z of history, nothing lies outside the scope of his sovereignty [see verse 4 for comment on the second title]. According to F. J. A. Hort, 'the Almighty' means 'not One who can do anything, but One who holds together and controls all things'. The title 'would thus have special force in this book as reminding the fainthearted that in spite of all appearances of a God-forsaken world, the Ruler in the heavens was Lord over all the doings of men and controlling them all in obedience to His supreme purposes'.

9: I John, your brother and partaker with you in the tribulation and kingdom and patience which are in Jesus, was in the isle that is called Patmos, for the word of God and the testimony of Jesus.

To express his oneness with his readers, John omits his official title and introduces himself as their 'brother' in the fellowship of suffering. It is 'in Jesus' that he shares with them 'in the tribulation and the kingdom and the patient endurance' (RSV). The order of the words is significant. As union with Jesus attracts the hostility of the world [*John* 16:33], so the lively assurance of a share in his kingdom enables believers patiently to endure to the end [*Matt.* 24:13]. 'Were it not for the kingdom, which the world opposes, there would be no affliction for the partakers of the kingdom; were it not for the powers of the kingdom, its partakers could not endure' (R. C. H. Lenski). John had been banished to Patmos, a small rocky island in the Aegean Sea lying about thirty-seven miles west-southwest of Miletus, because of his preaching of 'the word of God and the testimony borne by Jesus' [verse 2]. Committal to an island was a device used by provincial governors to rid themselves of men of high rank whose influence upon others was deemed to be harmful.

10: I was in the Spirit on the Lord's day, and I heard behind me a great voice, as of a trumpet

John's extraordinary experience on Patmos must not be confused with the normal condition of the Christian life [*Rom.* 8:9]. 'In the Spirit' here means that John was caught up by the Spirit into a state of rapture in which he lost contact with the things of time and sense and was transported into the invisible world of spiritual realities [*Ezek.* 2:2; *Acts* 10:10; 22:7; *2 Cor.* 12:1–4]. This took place on the day which was known to believers as 'the Lord's day', because Christ made it pre-eminently his own when he rose from the dead and inaugurated the new age of gospel grace [*John* 20:1, 19; *Acts* 20:7; *1 Cor.* 16:2]. John heard behind him a voice of such penetrating power that he could only liken it to that of a trumpet, and on turning he found that it was the voice of Christ [verse 12].

11: saying, What thou seest, write in a book and send it to the seven churches: unto Ephesus, and unto Smyrna, and unto Pergamum, and unto Thyatira, and unto Sardis, and unto Philadelphia, and unto Laodicea.

It is in obedience to Christ's command that John writes this book and sends it to the seven churches [see comment on verse 4]. The seven cities are mentioned in the order in which it would be natural to visit them, travelling north from Ephesus to Smyrna and Pergamum, and then inland to Thyatira, and going south to Sardis, Philadelphia and Laodicea in a rough semi-circle.

12: And I turned to see the voice that spake with me. And having turned I saw seven golden candlesticks;

In John's vision these churches are symbolized by seven golden 'lampstands' (ASV margin, verse 20]. The seven-branched lampstand represents Israel in *Zech.* 4, but here there are seven separate lampstands to emphasize the duty of each local church to reflect the light of Christ in a sin-darkened world [*Matt.* 5:14; *Phil.* 2:15, 16]. It is obvious that the purpose of the lampstand is to provide light, but if it fails to fulfil this function the very reason for its existence disappears [2:5]. The adjective 'golden' is frequently used in Revelation to indicate the preciousness of all that pertains to the true church of God. 'No base metal belongs in the church. In all the world there is nothing so valuable as the churches which hold aloft the shining Word of the gospel' (Lenski).

13: and in the midst of the candlesticks one like unto a son of man, clothed with a garment down to the foot, and girt about at the breasts with a golden girdle.

Although now glorified, Christ is far from being remote and removed from his people, for he is seen walking in the midst of the seven lampstands [2:1]. The expression 'one like unto a son of man' comes from *Dan.* 7:13. The word 'like' not only affirms a similarity with man, but also indicates that he is more than man and thus points to his deity (See E. J. Young's 'Daniel's Vision of the Son of Man' reprinted in *The Law and the Prophets*, p.443.) As befits his divine dignity, he is arrayed in a long robe and a golden girdle [*Dan.* 10:5]. To show that the work of redemption is complete [*John* 19:30], the girdle is not around the waist, as though prepared for action, but is worn high round the breast 'as by one who rests from toil in the repose of sovereignty' (W. Boyd Carpenter).

14: And his head and his hair were white as white wool, white as snow; and his eyes were as a flame of fire;

Here the white hair of 'the Ancient of days' in *Dan.* 7:9 is assigned to Christ to show that he shares the divine attributes of eternity and purity [*Isa.* 1:18]. The description of Christ's eyes has its source in *Dan.* 10:6, and it symbolizes his omniscience [*Heb.* 4:13]. The image not only depicts 'the penetrating insight of the Son of Man; but it also expresses his indignation at the sin which his divine insight detects' (Vincent).

15: and his feet like unto burnished brass, as if it had been refined in a furnace; and his voice as the voice of many waters.

The rare word here rendered 'burnished brass' was probably an alloy for which the metal-workers of Thyatira were famous [2:18]. The appearance of Christ's feet was like this metal 'glowing in a furnace' (NIV), thus signifying the consuming fire of his approaching judgment [*Dan.* 10:6]. His voice is compared to the deafening roar of many waters to indicate his sovereign authority over all the inhabitants of the earth [*Ezek.* 43:2].

16: And he had in his right hand seven stars: and out of his mouth proceeded a sharp two-edged sword: and his countenance was as the sun shineth in his strength.

In his right hand, the symbol of power and protection, Christ held seven stars, which are later identified as 'the angels of the seven churches' [see comment on verse 20]. Out of his mouth came a sharp two-edged sword, and this vigorous image points to the executive power of his Word, which renders any other weapon unnecessary [*Isa.* 11:4; *2 Thess.* 2:8]. For it is with this same sword that Christ purges his church [2:16] and punishes the nations [19:15]. The dazzling splendour of Christ's face was like the brightness of the noonday sun. As Swete points out, this would have reminded John of the transfiguration, 'which anticipated the glory of the ascended Christ' [*Matt.* 17:2].

17,18: And when I saw him, I fell at his feet as one dead. And he laid his right hand upon me, saying, Fear not; I am the first and the last, and the Living one; and I was dead, and behold, I am alive for evermore, and I have the keys of death and of Hades.

John was so overwhelmed by the awesome majesty of Christ that he fell at his feet as though dead, for, like the prophets before him, he felt utterly unfit for the divine presence [*Isa.* 6:5; *Ezek.* 1:28; *Dan.* 8:17; 10: 8, 9]. Christ then laid his right hand upon John in strengthening grace as he spoke the familiar and comforting words of reassurance: 'Fear not' [*Matt.* 17:7].

I am the first and the last: This is an express claim to deity [*Isa.* 44:6], which is well explained by Richard of St Victor (died 1173): 'First, because before me a God was not formed; last, because after me there shall not be another. First, because all things are from me; last, because all things are to me; from me the beginning, to me the end. First, because I am the cause of origin; last, because I am the judge and the end' (cited by Vincent).

I am the Living One; I was dead, and behold I am alive for ever and ever! (NIV): As 'the Living One' Christ possesses life in himself [*John* 5:26], but he is the source of life for us because he once came under the power of death to make our doom his own and is now alive for evermore. 'There are two wonders here: the living One becomes dead, and the dead One is alive for evermore' (Carpenter).

And I have the keys of death and of Hades: Having risen victorious from the grave, Christ has the keys of death and of Hades, for he not only controls the gates of death, but also exercises authority over the abode of departed spirits. As Christ's power thus extends even to the unseen realm of the dead, his people need not fear that the death threatened by their persecutors will be able to separate them from his love [*Rom.* 8:35–39].

19: Write therefore the things which thou sawest, and the things which are, and the things which shall come to pass hereafter.

Having received such an assurance of Christ's power [verses 17,18], John is *therefore* to write to the churches of the things he has seen. In this repetition of the command given in verse 11, the content of the book is further defined ('and', *kai*, here means *that is*) as a revelation of things present ('which are') and of things to come (which shall come to pass hereafter'). But this does not mean that the Apocalypse can be neatly divided into two watertight compartments (e.g. present, chs. 1–3; future, chs. 4–22). Hence this verse does not announce the 'programme' of Revelation, except insofar as it constantly relates the present to the future. For as Beckwith points out, 'A very considerable part of the book has to do with a revelation of things existent, upon which the future is conditioned.'

20: The mystery of the seven stars which thou sawest in my right hand, and the seven golden candlesticks. The seven stars are the angels of the seven churches: and the seven candlesticks are seven churches.

As for the mystery of the seven stars which you saw in my right hand, and the seven golden lampstands, the seven stars are the angels of the seven churches and the seven lampstands are the seven churches (RSV): In revealing the secret meaning of the stars in his right hand [verse 16], Christ identifies them as the angels of the seven churches, and many equate these angels with the pastors of the churches. But it is better to understand the angels as personifying the prevailing spirit of the various churches. In the double symbolism of the stars and the lampstands there seems to be an intended contrast between the inward spiritual life of the churches and their outward earthly embodiment. Yet these are not separate entities, for though each letter is addressed to the *angel* of the church [2:1], the concluding appeal is made directly to the *churches* [2:7]. In other words, the angel and the church are the same under different aspects: 'The one is its spiritual character personified; the other is the congregation of believers who collectively possess this character' (A. Plummer).

CHAPTER TWO

This chapter contains the first four of the letters to the seven churches of Asia. Ephesus is both faithful and discerning but has lost her first love [verses 1– 7]. Smyrna is commended for remaining steadfast amid

Jewish persecutions [verses 8–11]. Pergamum is still loyal despite heathen opposition, but some have fallen into moral laxity and are urged to repent [verses 12–17]. Thyatira is rebuked for permitting immorality to go unchecked, and the faithful are commanded to hold fast to what they have [verses 18–29].

The structure of each letter follows the same general pattern:

1. *A greeting:* 'To the angel of the church in . . .'
2. *A description of Christ*, usually taken from the vision in chapter 1.
3. *A commendation* for faithfulness and good works (absent in the case of Laodicea).
4. *A condemnation* of sin (except in the case of Smyrna and Philadelphia).
5. *A word of warning.*
6. *A call to hear:* 'He that hath an ear . . .'
7. *A promise* to the victor.

1. *THE LETTER TO THE CHURCH IN EPHESUS* [2:1–7]

Situated near the mouth of the Cayster River, Ephesus, which Pliny called 'the Light of Asia', was the largest and most important city in the province (population: 250,000). It was a key commercial centre and was famous for its devotion to the cult of Artemis (Latin, *Diana*), whose temple was one of the seven wonders of the ancient world [*Acts* 19:35]. It was appropriate that the first letter should be sent to the leading church of Asia. The church in Ephesus was founded by the apostle Paul, who, on his departure after three years of ministry there, had warned its elders against false teachers [*Acts* 20:28 –31].

1: To the angel of the church in Ephesus write: These things saith he that holdeth the seven stars in his right hand, he that walketh in the midst of the seven golden candlesticks:

As we have gathered from 1:20, the stars are the heavenly counterparts of the churches, while the lampstands represent their earthly existence [1:13, 16]. The verse thus conveys an assurance and a warning. From a heavenly point of view, Christ firmly holds the seven stars in his right hand to show that he guarantees the salvation of his people [*John* 10: 28]. But from an earthly perspective the churches stand in need of constant correction, and so Christ is also seen walking in the midst of the lampstands to inspect their condition and administer necessary reproofs [3:19].

2,3: I know thy works, and thy toil and patience, and that thou canst not bear evil men, and didst try them that call themselves apostles, and they are not, and didst find them false; and thou hast patience and didst bear for my name's sake, and hast not grown weary.

'I know' indicates Christ's intimate acquaintance with the condition of the church [2:9, 13, 19; 2:1, 8, 15], for this particular word emphasizes 'the absolute clearness of mental vision which photographs all the facts of life as they pass' (Swete). The works for which the Christians in Ephesus are commended are 1. Their intolerance of evil men and their toil in unmasking the pretensions of these self-styled 'apostles' or itinerant 'Missionaries', who are identified as the Nicolaitans in verse 6 [*1 John* 4: 1]; 2. Their steadfast endurance for the sake of Christ's name [verse 3]. 'Tired in loyalty, not of it. The Ephesian church can bear anything except the presence of impostors in her membership' (James Moffatt).

4: But I have this against thee, that thou didst leave thy first love.

Christ's charge against the church in Ephesus reveals a condition which is fraught with danger. Despite their zeal for the truth, their devotion had suffered a serious decline. They had lost the fervour of their first love for Christ and for his people, the latter being the indispensable evidence of the former [*John* 13:35]. Hence they are urged to repent and 'do the first works' by showing their love for Christ in self-giving love of the brethren [verse 5]. Mere orthodoxy is not enough for the Searcher of all hearts, for the greatest works are worthless without love [*1 Cor.* 13:1–3].

5: Remember therefore whence thou art fallen, and repent, and do the first works; or else I come to thee, and will move thy candlestick out of its place, except thou repent.

To correct and restore the church to the love of her espousals [*Jer.* 2:2], Christ uses three striking imperatives: 'Remember . . . repent . . . do.' They are summoned to compare the warmth of their past devotion with the coldness of their present service, and this humbling exercise must lead to a decisive act of repentance resulting in the doing of the first works. It is worth noting that the command is not, 'Feel thy first feelings,' but, 'Do the first works.' 'The way to regain this warmth of affection is neither by working up spasmodic emotion nor by theorizing about it, but by doing its duties' (Moffatt). Otherwise Christ will come in swift judgment and remove its lampstand so that it ceases to be a church.

6: But this thou hast, that thou hatest the works of the Nicolaitans, which I also hate.

But Christ commends the Ephesian church for hating what (not whom) he hates, namely the *works* of the Nicolaitans. 'To share His hatred of evil is to manifest an affinity of character with Him, which is a sign of grace in Churches and in individuals' (Swete). The Nicolaitans were an early Gnostic sect, who evidently advocated sinful licence in the name of Christian liberty, on the ground that spiritual perfection could not be impaired by sensual indulgence. As Lenski points out, their founder Nicolaus is more likely to have been a disciple of Cerinthus (AD 95) than the deacon mentioned in *Acts* 6:5 (AD 31).

7: He that hath an ear, let him hear what the Spirit saith to the churches. To him that overcometh, to him will I give to eat of the tree of life, which is in the Paradise of God.

He that hath an ear: The admonition of the glorified Christ to all the churches echoes the saying he repeated so often during his earthly ministry [*Matt.* 11:15]. His appeal to the individual stresses the need for a 'spiritual' hearing of 'spiritual' truth, for those who harden their hearts become deaf to the voice of truth [*Matt.* 13:15].

Let him hear what the Spirit saith to the churches: The words are indeed spoken by Christ, but his voice is now heard in the churches through the testimony of the Spirit as recorded in Scripture [*John* 16:12–15].

To him that overcometh: This is the first of Christ's promises to the 'overcomer' in the spiritual conflict against sin. To the one who is faithful to the end, Christ will give 'to eat of the tree of life' [22:14]. 'Man's exclusion from the Tree of life [*Gen.* 3:22f.] is repealed by Christ on condition of a personal victory over evil. To eat of the Tree is to enjoy all that the life of the world to come has in store for redeemed humanity' (Swete). 'Paradise', originally a Persian word meaning 'pleasure park', was applied to the Garden of Eden in the Greek Old Testament [*Gen.* 2:8; *Ezek.* 28:13], and finally here denotes heaven itself.

2. *The Letter to the Church in Smyrna* (2: 8–11)

Smyrna, the only one of the seven cities still in existence (modern Izmir), lay some thirty-five miles north of Ephesus. A beautiful city and a prosperous port (population: 200,000), it claimed to be the first in Asia, and as a faithful ally of Rome, was in fact the first in the province to build a temple to the goddess Roma in 195 BC. Its large colony of Jews used their influence with the authorities to persecute Christians, and they later assisted in the martyrdom of the aged Polycarp (AD 156). The faithful church in Smyrna receives the shortest letter and the warmest praise.

8: And to the angel of the church in Smyrna write: These things saith the first and the last, who was dead, and lived again.

In contrast to the city which claimed to be the first of Asia in beauty and loyalty to Rome, Christ here presents himself to his suffering church in Smyrna as both 'the first and the last', and therefore as the supreme controller of all that lies between [1:17]. The second title [1:18], 'who died and came to life' (RSV), emphasizes his conquest of death to assure them that the suffering he ordains must also end in victory [verses 10, 11].

9: I know thy tribulation, and thy poverty (but thou art rich), and the blasphemy of them that say they are Jews, and they are not, but are a synagogue of Satan.

Christ knows that his people in Smyrna are hard pressed and in dire poverty because of their unflinching loyalty to him. In a hostile environment they found it difficult to make a living, and probably pagan mobs had aggravated their plight by plundering their goods [*Heb.* 10:34]. But in contrast to the false self-estimate of the Laodicean church [3:17], Christ pronounces them rich. 'Men saw nothing there save poverty, but He who sees not as man seeth, saw the true riches which this seeming poverty concealed . . . even as He too often sees the real poverty which may lie behind the show of riches; for there are both poor rich-men and rich poor-men in his sight' (Trench). Christ also knows 'the slander' to which they are subjected by those who have forfeited the name of Jew, and are 'a synagogue of Satan' because they follow the father of lies in accusing the brethren [12:10]. It is worth noticing that the three terms, 'a synagogue of Satan' [verse 9], 'Satan's throne' [verse 13] and 'the deep things of Satan' [verse 24], respectively denote Jewish, pagan and heretical antagonism to the church.

10: Fear not the things which thou art about to suffer: behold, the devil is about to cast some of you into prison, that ye may be tried; and ye shall have tribulation ten days. Be thou faithful unto death, and I will give thee the crown of life.

Christ has no word of censure for this church, but warns that worse things are in store than poverty and slander, for the devil is about to cast some of them into prison to await trial and perhaps death. They must not fear the things they are about to suffer, for though the devil's design in motivating their persecutors is destructive, the divine purpose is that, when tried, they may be found faithful. The limited time the devil is allowed for his evil work – 'ten days' indicating a short period of intense testing – shows that the whole process remains under God's control. To the one who is faithful to the end, whether he dies as a martyr or not, Christ promises the festive crown of eternal life [*James* 1:12]. 'The Lord wants only a limited number of martyrs, but he wants all of us to be faithful unto death in whatever measure of tribulation he allots to us in order to try us' (Lenski) [*Matt.* 24:13].

11: He that hath an ear, let him hear what the Spirit saith to the churches. He that overcometh shall not be hurt of the second death.

He that hath an ear . . .: See comment on verse 7.

He that overcometh . . . In a situation where faithfulness to Christ may demand the ultimate sacrifice, the 'overcomer' is assured that he shall in no way be hurt by 'the second death'. This expression is used in Revelation to designate eternal punishment [20:14, 15; 21:8]. 'The essence of punishment is suffering, and suffering is consciousness. In order to be punished, the person must be conscious of a certain pain, must feel that he deserves it, and know that it is inflicted because he does . . . If God by a positive act extinguishes, at death, the remorse of a hardened villain, by extinguishing his self-consciousness, it is a strange use of language to denominate this a punishment' (W. G. T. Shedd, *The Doctrine of Endless Punishment,* p.92).

3. *The Letter to the Church in Pergamum* (2:12–17)

Pergamum, the provincial capital of Asia, was about fifty-five miles north-east of Smyrna. The city was renowned for its great buildings, its library of 200,000 volumes and its many pagan temples. The most famous of these was dedicated to Asclepius, the serpent-god of healing, and the popularity of this cult made Pergamum the 'Lourdes' of the ancient world (R. H. Charles). As the first in Asia to erect a temple to Augustus (29 BC), it was also the stronghold of the imperial cult, and this combination of politics and religion presented the greatest threat to Christians living in Pergamum.

12: And to the angel of the church in Pergamum write: These things saith he that hath the sharp two-edged sword.

It was important that those who were living under the threat of the Roman sword should be reminded that Christ wielded a far more powerful sword [1:16], with which he would visit the unfaithful in summary judgment [verse 16].

13: I know where thou dwellest, even where Satan's throne is; and thou holdest fast my name, and didst not deny my faith, even in the days of Antipas my witness, my faithful one, who was killed among you, where Satan dwelleth.

Christ knows how difficult it is to be a Christian in Pergamum where Satan dwells and has his throne. As the city was the official centre of emperor worship in Asia, any refusal to confess that 'Caesar is Lord' would be regarded as an act of disloyalty to the emperor and punishable by death.

But despite the danger, the church continued to hold fast to Christ's name and had already faced one crisis without denying the faith. It was during this time of persecution that Antipas was killed. We know no more of this early martyr than is said here, but Christ's commendation of his fidelity is indeed noteworthy.

14: But I have a few things against thee, because thou hast there some that hold the teaching of Balaam, who taught Balak to cast a stumbling block before the children of Israel, to eat things sacrificed to idols, and to commit fornication.

In turning from praise to censure, Christ rebukes the church for tolerating within the membership a few ('a few things' = 'some') who held to the teaching of Balaam. This false prophet appears here as the prototype of all who advocate compromise with paganism, because he taught Balak, King of Moab, how to ensnare the children of Israel by enticing them into idolatry and immorality [*Num.* 25:1–3; 31:16]. Thus the church 'which could resist Satan in the form of the Emperor-cult was not equally proof against an insidious heresy within its own ranks' (Swete).

Secure in the knowledge that the heathen gods had no real existence [*1 Cor.* 8: 4], these 'liberated' Christians saw no harm in attending idol-feasts and embracing temple prostitutes in order to obtain pagan approval.

15: So hast thou also some that hold the teaching of the Nicolaitans in like manner.

So hast thou also. . . : The comparison suggests that the two immoral sects at Pergamum were really one and the same, for those who held to the teaching of Balaam are here identified as the Nicolaitans [verse 6]. Christ thus brands the Nicolaitans as Balaamites to show his abhorrence of their vile practices [verse 20].

16: Repent therefore; or else I come to thee quickly, and I will make war against them with the sword of my mouth.

The whole church is urgently summoned to repent, or else Christ will visit it in swift judgment, for, unlike vigilant Ephesus [verse 6], they had allowed this evil to go on unchecked. And just as Balaam perished by the sword [*Num.* 31:8], so Christ threatens to make war against his present-day followers with the sword of his mouth [19:11–15]. As might be expected in a book describing the cosmic conflict with evil, there are more references to war in Revelation than in any other book in the New Testament. 'The glorified Christ is in this book a Warrior, who fights with the sharp sword of the word' (Swete).

17: He that hath an ear, let him hear what the Spirit saith to the churches. To him that overcometh, to him will I give of the hidden manna, and I will give him a white stone, and upon the stone a new name written, which no one knoweth but he that receiveth it.

He that hath an ear . . .: See comment on verse 7.

To him that overcometh . . .: The one who abstains from the forbidden idol-food will be abundantly rewarded by the gift of the hidden manna in the heavenly kingdom, for then what is now hidden will be revealed [*1 John* 3:2]. 'The seeing of Christ as He is, and, through this beatific vision, being made like to Him, is identical with the eating of the hidden manna, which shall, as it were, be then brought forth from the sanctuary, the holy of holies of God's immediate presence, where it was withdrawn from sight so long, that all may partake of it; the glory of Christ, now shrouded and concealed, being then revealed at once to his people and in them [*Col.* 3:4]' (Trench). There are many explanations of what is signified by the 'white stone', but the suggestion that it is the *tessera* or token that gives admission to the heavenly banquet is the one best suited to the context ['hidden manna']. The secret name inscribed on the stone is the victor's new name, which expresses his own distinctive character. The unity of heaven does not entail loss of individuality in a vague universal oneness of being. Glorification does not eliminate the human personality but rather brings it to perfection.

4. *The Letter to the Church in Thyatira* (2:18–29)

Paradoxically the longest letter is sent to the city of least importance. Thyatira lay some forty miles south-east of Pergamum, and was notable only for its industry. Each craft had its own trade guild, and as membership involved participation in licentious pagan feasts, this naturally posed an acute problem for Christians, since it was difficult for a man to make a living without belonging to the guild of his trade (W. M. Ramsay). The daring 'solution' of the problem proposed by the self-styled prophetess 'Jezebel' accounts for the severe tone of the letter [verse 20].

18: And to the angel of the church in Thyatira write: These things saith the Son of God, who hath his eyes like a flame of fire, and his feet are like unto burnished brass.

Christ presents himself to this church as the divine Judge, whose flaming eyes penetrate the deceptions of the prophetess and whose brazen feet are ready to crush the enemies of truth [1:14, 15]. Here the title 'the Son of God' anticipates the later allusion to *Psa.* 2 [verses 26, 27].

19: I know thy works, and thy love and faith and ministry and patience, and that thy last works are more than the first.

Christ knows there is much to praise in the church of Thyatira. He approves the love shown in service, the faith manifested in patient endurance and the progress proved by the growth of good works. This advance in love and faith is in sharp contrast to the sad decline at Ephesus [verse 5]. 'In Ephesus there is much zeal for orthodoxy, but little love; in Thyatira there is much love, but a carelessness about false doctrine' (Plummer).

20: But I have this against thee, that thou sufferest the woman Jezebel, who calleth herself a prophetess; and she teacheth and seduceth my servants to commit fornication, and to eat things sacrificed to idols.

The devotion of the church, though warm, was lacking in discernment and this had led to the toleration in their midst of a woman who claimed prophetic inspiration for her antinomian practices. She is here branded by Christ as 'Jezebel', because the Baal-worship introduced to Israel by that pagan queen fostered idolatry and ritual prostitution [*2 Kings* 9:22].

Trench attributes her success to the possession of genuine spiritual powers, 'only they were such as reached her from beneath, not such as descended on her from above; for as at this time miraculous gifts of grace and power were at work in the Church, so were also their counterfeits' [*1 John* 4: 1]. By her words and shameless example [verse 22], she doubtless taught that immorality and sacrificial meals could not defile those in whom the Spirit dwells, because the gods of the trade guilds were gods in name only [*1 Cor.* 8:4]. This doctrine was the same as that of the Nicolaitans in Pergamum [verses 14, 15]. But despite the evils found in these churches, it is significant that Christ never counsels true believers to leave in order to found a 'pure' church of their own (Harry Buis).

21: And I gave her time that she should repent; and she willeth not to repent of her fornication.

Although Christ had given the false prophetess time to repent, she continued in her determination not to change her wicked ways. 'The fact that punishment does not at once overtake sinners is constantly misunderstood by them as an evidence that it never will overtake them [*Eccles.* 8:11; *Isa.* 26:10; *Psa.* 26:11]; that God does not see, or, seeing, does not care to avenge' (Trench).

22,23a: Behold, I cast her into a bed, and them that commit adultery with her into great tribulation, except they repent of her works. And I will kill her children with death.

'Behold,' arrests attention and marks the suddenness of the judgment. Christ will turn Jezebel's bed of pleasure into a bed of suffering, and her misguided followers will share that suffering in full measure unless they repent of 'her works'.

Although it may seem strange to speak of repenting of another person's works, 'the point is that those who have become partakers in her sins have abandoned their own works for hers; and it is therefore from her works that they are bidden to repent' (Plummer). But her real devotees, in contrast to those she has misled for a time, Christ will kill 'with death', which is a very emphatic way of expressing their final doom.

23b: And all the churches shall know that I am he that searcheth the reins and hearts: and I will give unto each one of you according to your works.

As Jezebel and her followers were probably notorious, this terrible judgment will be a salutary object lesson for all the churches in the province.

'The reins' or kidneys were regarded as the seat of the emotions, while the term *'hearts'* covers the thoughts and motives [*Jer.* 17:10]. 'Both are subject to the scrutiny of him whose eyes are as a flame of fire [verse 18]' (Swete). Works are the sole criteria of judgment because they are the indisputable proof of character. In the Day of Judgment these works shall be seen by all as Christ sees them now, and not according to our present superficial estimates of their value [20:12; 22:12].

24: But to you I say, to the rest that are in Thyatira, as many as have not this teaching, who know not the deep things of Satan, as they are wont to say; I cast upon you none other burden.

Christ now turns to the faithful in Thyatira who do not hold this teaching, and who are willingly ignorant of 'the deep things of Satan' which the 'liberated' Jezebel and her brood claimed the right to plumb. In thus boasting of their freedom to explore Satan's domain, they would taunt timid Christians for refusing to join in the activities of the trade guilds. Presumably they argued that the immunity granted by the Spirit enabled them even to indulge in immorality without contracting defilement. 'I cast upon you none other burden' is a clear echo of *Acts* 15:28, and means 'I put upon you no other burden than abstinence from and protest against these abominations' (Vincent).

25: Nevertheless that which ye have, hold fast till I come.

Instead of imposing any new demands upon the faithful [verse 24], Christ commands them once and for all to take a firm hold upon what they have been taught. 'What they have of sound doctrine, of holy living, this they must hold fast, must so grasp it that none shall wrest it from them, till the day when the Lord shall come, and bring this long and painful struggle for the maintenance of his truth to an end' (Trench).

26,27: And he that overcometh, and he that keepeth my works unto the end, to him will I give authority over the nations: and he shall rule them with a rod of iron, as the vessels of the potter are broken to shivers; as I also have received of my Father.

The overcomer is here identified as the one who keeps Christ's works to the end. 'My works' are in marked contrast to 'her works' [verse 22]. 'The works are those which Christ commands, which He does, and which are the fruits of His Spirit'(Vincent). A free quotation of *Psa.* 2:9 shows that part of the overcomer's reward will consist of a share in Christ's rule over the nations. Having received this authority from his Father as the reward for his obedience [*Phil.* 2:9–11], Christ will rule as a Shepherd in the interests of his flock by smiting their enemies with a staff of iron and smashing them to pieces like pottery. As Lenski explains, the meaning of the promise is to be sought in 3:21 and 20:4.

'One by one, as we reach the end here on earth, we shall pass into heaven and there sit with Christ on his throne and together with him exercise kingly rule and authority over the nations until his Parousia.'

28, 29: and I will give him the morning star. He that hath an ear, let him hear what the Spirit saith to the churches.

Since Christ declares that he is 'the bright, the morning star' [22:16], he here promises to give himself to the overcomer. 'The conqueror is not only to share Christ's activities; he is to possess Christ' (Swete). The general exhortation is placed at the end of the last four letters, whereas in the first three it precedes the promise. See comment on verse 7.

CHAPTER THREE

This chapter contains the last three of the letters to the seven churches of Asia. Sardis is a dead church whose few living members are bidden to awake [verses 1–6]. The faithful church of Philadelphia is promised protection in the coming hour of trial [verses 7–13]. The lukewarm church of Laodicea is summoned to repent and receive Christ who stands at the door and knocks [verses 14–22].

5. *The Letter to the Church in Sardis* (3:1–6)

Sardis, the old capital of Lydia, was about thirty miles southeast of Thyatira. In the first century AD it was still famous for its woollen and dyed goods [verse 4], but its glory was long since past. The city was addicted to a life of ease and this was sadly reflected in the church. The failure to keep watch had twice led to the capture of the city, and now the church was showing the same lack of vigilance [verse 3]. No external opposition or internal heresy disturbed the church, which was as peaceful as the grave.

And to the angel of the church in Sardis write: These things saith he that hath the seven Spirits of God, and the seven stars: I know thy works, that thou hast a name that thou livest, and thou art dead.

As the ascended Christ controls the mission of the Holy Spirit to the seven churches [see comment on 1:4, 16] the Sardians must choose whether to experience his power in quickening grace or in sudden judgment [verse 3]. The phrase 'I know thy works' here introduces Christ's condemnation of the church whose reputation for life was devoid of reality. Beneath the fair facade of bustling activity, Christ saw that the church at Sardis was in fact spiritually dead.

2: Be thou watchful, and establish the things that remain, which were ready to die: for I have found no works of thine perfected before my God.

The admonition was especially appropriate to Sardis because twice in its history the acropolis had been captured through the failure of the defenders to keep watch – first by Cyrus in 549 BC and then by Antiochus the Great in 218 BC [*Matt.* 24:42–44]. Although almost past hope of recovery, a residue of spiritual life remained in the church, but prompt action was essential if the embers of devotion were to be rekindled.

For I have not found any work of yours completed in the eyes of my God (NEB): What would have made their deeds acceptable to God was lacking, for 'works' are 'fulfilled' only when 'they are animated by the Spirit of life' (Swete). As in *John* 20:17, 'my God' expresses Christ's special relationship with the Father, which is here connected with the work of judgment [verse 5].

3: Remember therefore how thou hast received and didst hear; and keep it, and repent. If therefore thou shalt not watch, I will come as a thief, and thou shalt not know what hour I will come upon thee.

To stimulate a desire for recovery, Christ bids the church of Sardis to bear in mind the gospel which was entrusted to their safekeeping ('received') from the moment they came to faith ('didst hear'). They must continue to keep what they had received and, by repenting forthwith, turn from present neglect to recover their lost fervour. If this warning fails to awaken the church, Christ will come as unexpectedly as a thief and his swift judgment will take them completely by surprise [*Luke* 12:39]. There are many preliminary visitations in judgment upon churches and individuals before the final coming in glory [2:5].

4: But thou hast a few names in Sardis that did not defile their garments: and they shall walk with me in white; for they are worthy.

But in spite of the spiritual torpor of the majority, there were a few in Sardis who had not besmirched their garments by worldly compromise. In the pagan religions 'soiled clothes disqualified the worshipper and dishonoured the god. Moral purity qualifies for spiritual communion' (Moffatt). Hence Christ promises that the undefiled minority shall walk with him in the white garments of holiness [19: 8].

For they are worthy: 'To be accounted worthy by the Lord means to be reckoned so by his grace, the grace which gave life, developed it, kept it sound and clean to the end' (Lenski) [*1 Cor.* 15:10].

5: He that overcometh shall thus be arrayed in white garments; and I will in no wise blot his name out of the book of life, and I will confess his name before my Father, and before his angels.

Here the promise of the previous verse is repeated, but it is clear from the passive tense of the verb that the overcomer does not clothe himself, for this is the investiture of grace. The emphatic negative, 'I will in no wise blot out his name', really amounts to the strongest affirmation that the victor's name shall ever remain in the book of life. Thus the perseverance of the saints to glory confirms their foreordination in the heavenly register of the redeemed [13:8; 17:8; 21:27]. Christ further promises to confess the name of the victor before his Father and his angels [*Matt.* 10:32; *Luke* 12:8]. 'We may observe of this Epistle that in great part it is woven together of sayings which the Lord had already uttered in the days during which he pitched his tent among men; he is now setting his seal from heaven upon his words uttered on earth' (Trench).

6: He that hath an ear, let him hear what the Spirit saith to the churches.

See comment on 2:7.

6. *The Letter to the Church in Philadeplphia* (3:7–13)

Like nearby Sardis, Philadelphia was destroyed by the great earthquake of AD 17. But even after it was rebuilt, many citizens were afraid to return and chose to live in the surrounding countryside. Although the city had its share of pagan cults, the letter shows that the main opposition to the church came from the synagogue. Christ has no word of blame for this church, which had remained faithful despite the active hostility of the Jews [cf. verse 9 with 2:9].

7: And to the angel of the church in Philadelphia write: These things saith he that is holy, he that is true, he that hath the key of David, he that openeth and none shall shut, and that shutteth and none openeth:

This needful word of reassurance is addressed to the church which upheld Christ's Messianic claims in the face of Jewish gibes. As the one who is holy and true [6:10], Christ shares the divine attributes and, as the possessor of the key of David [*Isa.* 22:22], he exercises supreme authority in giving or withholding admission to the new Jerusalem. Thus the Jews who claimed the power to exclude from the synagogue would find themselves shut out of the heavenly kingdom. While Christ has committed the keys of the kingdom to his church [*Matt.* 16:19], 'He still retains the highest administration of them in his own hands. If at any time there is error in their binding and loosing, if they make sad the heart which He has not made sad, if they speak peace to the heart to which He has not spoken peace [*Ezek.* 13:19], then his sentence shall stand, and not theirs' (Trench).

8: I know thy works (behold, I have set before thee a door opened, which none can shut), that thou hast a little power, and didst keep my word, and didst not deny my name.

Christ knows the works of the church in Philadelphia, for as a small company of believers they have little power, and yet they have kept his Word and not denied his name [2:13]. The parenthetical promise, 'Behold, I have set before thee a door opened, which none can shut,' is taken by many in the Pauline sense of a door of missionary opportunity [*1 Cor.* 16:9; *2 Cor.* 2:12]. But in the light of the previous verse, it is more likely to be the door of the Messianic kingdom. Although the Jews boasted that the kingdom belonged to ethnic Israel, Christ assures the loyal Philadelphians that he has placed before them an open door to glory, which no one can shut.

9: Behold, I give of the synagogue of Satan, of them that say they are Jews, and they are not, but do lie; behold, I will make them to come and worship before thy feet, and to know that I have loved thee.

The repeated 'behold' marks the unexpected reversal of Jewish hopes. Those who call themselves 'the chosen of God' Christ brands 'the synagogue of Satan', for in rejecting the Messiah and persecuting his people they have shown that they are not true Jews [*Rom.* 2:28, 29]. These bitter opponents of the gospel will find out their mistake when it is too late. In the Day of Judgment Christ will make them pay homage to Gentile believers and they will know that he has loved those whom they despised. This will be the final irony for Jews who expected the Gentiles to acknowledge them [*Isa.* 60:14], but who will then play the role of the heathen in confessing that Christians are the true Israel (Charles).

10: Because thou didst keep the word of my patience, I also will keep thee from the hour of trial, that hour which is to come upon the whole world, to try them that dwell upon the earth.

Because the Philadelphians had kept 'the word of my endurance', Christ will keep them 'from' the hour of trial (i.e. protection from the power of Satan, rather than exemption from suffering, *John* 17:15). 'To embrace and hold fast the gospel of the Crucified was to embrace and hold fast the Gospel of Christ's own endurance, at once as an example and as a power' (Hort). The hour of trial which was about to break upon the whole Roman world was the wave of persecution which followed the enforcement of emperor worship as a test of loyalty. The church's time of trial would test all men by bringing their true character to light, for whenever unbelievers persecute Christ's people they thereby pass judgment upon themselves.

11: I come quickly: hold fast that which thou hast, that no one take thy crown.

It is clear from 2:16 that 'I come quickly' does not refer to Christ's final coming in glory, but to his coming to help the Philadelphians in their hour of need. He comes in every trial to succour his people and judge their persecutors. Like the faithful in Thyatira [2:25], they must hold fast to what they have, 'that no one take thy crown' [2:10]. For if wicked men caused them to be unfaithful, they would forfeit this crown, and so they must always be on their guard [*1 Cor.* 10: 1 2].

12: He that overcometh, I will make him a pillar in the temple of my God, and he shall go out thence no more: and I will write upon him the name of my God, and the name of the city of my God, the new Jerusalem,

which cometh down out of heaven from my God, and mine own new name.

He that overcometh, I will make him a pillar in the sanctuary of my God, and he shall go out thence no more (ASV margin): This promise would have special significance for those who knew the insecurity of living in a city troubled by frequent earthquakes, which caused people to flee from the danger of falling masonry. The language is metaphorical but it conveys a great spiritual truth [21:22]. 'As the pillar cannot be moved out of its place while the house stands, so a lapse from goodness will be impossible for the character which has been fixed by the final victory' (Swete).

And I will write upon him the name of my God: In view of the unsettling effect of Jewish taunts, the victor's place in glory is here trebly assured.

1. *Christ will write on him the divine name* to mark his possession by God. 'The struggling Christian is encouraged by hearing that a time will come when he will without any doubt become God's own, incapable of being removed or claimed by another' (Plummer).

And the name of the city of my God, the new Jerusalem, which cometh down out of heaven from my God:

2. *Christ will write on him the name of the heavenly city* (see comment on 21:2, 10). Even during this present life the Christian's true citizenship is in heaven [*Phil.* 3:20], though it is now hidden; but then 'he is openly avouched, and has a right to enter in by the gates into the city' (Trench).

And mine own new name:

3. *Christ will write on him his own new name* [19:12]. This mark of ownership will initiate the victor into the mystery of Christ's full glory, which is beyond our present understanding [*1 Cor.* 13:12].

13: He that hath an ear, let him hear what the Spirit saith to the churches.

See comment on 2:7.

7. *The Letter to the Church in Laodicea* (3:14–22)

Prosperous Laodicea was famous for its banks, its clothing and carpets made from the local glossy black wool and its medical school, which produced a noted ear ointment and eye salve [verse 18]. But for all their wealth, the Laodiceans had to drink the poor water which was piped to them from hot springs six miles away [verse 16]. Although apparently flourishing, this church receives Christ's sharpest rebuke for having absorbed the complacent spirit of an affluent society. Yet the lukewarm church also receives the most cordial invitation to enjoy the tender favours of Christ's love [verse 20].

14: And to the angel of the church in Laodicea write: These things saith the Amen, the faithful and true witness, the beginning of the creation of God:

Christ presents himself to the church, which is woefully ignorant of its real condition, as 'the Amen, the faithful and true witness' [1:5; *Isa.* 65:16]. Since he is the divine Amen, 'in whom verity is personified' (Beckwith), he is the reliable and true witness, 'whose testimony never falls short of the truth' (Swete). As the pre-existent Son, he is also 'the beginning of the creation of God' [*Col.* 1:15], the uncreated source and sustainer of all things [*John* 1:3; *Col.* 1:18; *Heb.* 1:3]. This familiar title [*Col.* 4:16] would remind the Laodiceans of the supreme authority and power of Christ against whose judgment there was no appeal.

15: I know thy works, that thou art neither cold nor hot: I would thou wert cold or hot.

Christ here shatters the fatal illusion of self-sufficiency by revealing the church's true condition [verse 17]. The works of the Laodiceans show that they are neither cold nor hot, but lukewarm [verse 16]. They had lost their former warmth, and lapsed into a spirit of complacency which was blind to any shortcoming. There is more hope of winning the 'cold' sinner than of reheating the 'lukewarm' Christian!

I would thou wert cold or hot: 'The wish is not that they might grow cold rather than remain in this lukewarm state; it is more a regret that they are among those who are in a condition which is so liable to self-deception' (Carpenter).

16: So because thou art lukewarm, and neither hot nor cold, I will spew thee out of my mouth.

A startling expression of disgust at the lukewarm religion of the Laodiceans, which was as nauseating to Christ as their own water supply was to them. This came from the hot springs at Denizli and was still tepid when it reached them. 'I will spew thee' is better rendered, 'I am about to spew thee'. It is not an irrevocable sentence of doom, but a timely word of warning which is intended to lead to their repentance [verse 18–20].

17,18: Because thou sayest, I am rich, and have gotten riches, and have need of nothing; and knowest not that thou art the wretched one and miserable and poor and blind and naked: I counsel thee to buy of me gold refined by fire, that thou mayest become rich; and white garments, that thou mayest clothe thyself, and that the shame of thy nakedness be not made manifest; and eyesalve to anoint thine eyes, that thou mayest see.

The disease is first diagnosed [verse 17] and then the remedy prescribed [verse 18]. Although rich in pride, the church was poor in grace and ignorant of its destitute condition.

Because thou sayest: Evidently Laodicea's self-sufficiency in *material* things was reflected in the *spiritual* life of the church, which not only claimed to be rich but also boasted that this wealth was self-acquired. Many today cherish the same delusion that they have need of nothing when, in fact, they are spiritual paupers.

And knowest not: But the true state of the church is revealed in the divine indictment: '*Thou* art the wretched one!' They had an unenviable pre-eminence in wretchedness, and this pitiable condition was due to a complete lack of the very things on which they prided themselves. 'Poor and blind and naked' shows that such confidence in their prosperity, discernment and acceptance with God was totally misplaced.

I counsel thee to buy of me: Christ counsels the poverty-stricken Laodiceans to buy of him, and thus have all their needs supplied. This is that 'gospel-buying' which is without money and without price [*Isa.* 55:1]. Discarding the counterfeit coinage of merit, they must trust in the gold of grace refined by Christ in the furnace of affliction, so that they may be truly rich [*2 Cor.* 8:9]. As they could not hide their nakedness with their own black woollens, they must cover their shame with the white garments of salvation, the robe of Christ's righteousness [*Isa.* 61:10; Toplady: 'Naked, come to thee for dress']. Finally, they must recognize that they needed more than the local eye ointment to restore their clouded vision, for only Christ could give them the anointing which would enable them to see clearly both their need and his provision for it.

19: As many as I love, I reprove and chasten: be zealous therefore, and repent.

In an abrupt change of tone, Christ assures the Laodiceans that his rebukes are the proof of his love for them. 'As many as' admits of no exceptions, for chastening is not the mark of rejection but an evidence of adoption [*Prov.* 3:11, 12; *Heb.* 12:5, 6]. 'The Lord is no soft Eli to his children' (Lenski).

Be zealous therefore, and repent: Lukewarmness must be replaced by a life of continuing zeal and this dramatic change in their condition is to be marked by a decisive act of repentance.

20: Behold, I stand at the door and knock: if any man hear my voice and open the door, I will come in to him, and will sup with him, and he with me.

'Behold' is a summons to each individual to heed the promise of Christ, who condescends to stand at the heart's door and seek admittance. He not only knocks but also speaks and by his gracious words he awakens a responding love which enables the sinner to open the door and let him in. The fellowship which at once follows the sinner's reception of Christ is represented by the image of a shared meal, which was to the oriental mind a sign of the most intimate friendship. The present enjoyment of this spiritual communion anticipates the heavenly banquet, but its scope is unduly restricted by those who refer these words to the Lord's Supper.

21: He that overcometh, I will give to him to sit down with me in my throne, as I also overcame, and sat down with my Father in his throne.

This extension of the promise made to the Twelve gives every faithful disciple the same privilege of sharing in Christ's heavenly reign [*Matt.* 19:28]. The overcomer is pictured as enthroned with Christ and his exaltation follows the pattern set by Christ who also overcame before he sat down with his Father on his throne [*2 Tim.* 2:12]. 'My throne' and 'his throne' are the same, for Christ shares the Father's throne [22:1]. 'This crowning promise is made to the most unpleasing of the churches. But it is well that thus the despondency which often succeeds the sudden collapse of self-satisfied imaginations should be met by so bright a prospect' (Carpenter).

22:He that hath an ear, let him hear what the Spirit saith to the churches.

See comment on 2:7.

2: THE LAMB AND THE SEVEN SEALS

CHAPTER FOUR

In this vision the door of heaven is opened to reveal God seated upon his throne [verses 1–3]. He is attended by the twenty-four elders and the four living beings who worship him as the sovereign Creator of all [verses 4–11].

1: After these things I saw, and behold, a door opened in heaven, and the first voice that I heard, a voice as of a trumpet speaking with me, one saying, Come up hither, and I will show thee the things which must come to pass hereafter.

The change of scene from earth to heaven marks a new beginning in the book. A door in heaven is opened so that John may enter and see that God is still on the throne. It is because the destiny of the world is determined by God that his hard-pressed people on earth are assured of final victory over all their foes. The voice John hears is that of Christ [1:10], who summons him to heaven to show him what *must* (in furtherance of the divine plan, 1:1) happen hereafter. For it is only from the vantage-point of heaven that earthly events can be seen in their true perspective [*Rom.* 8:31].

2: Straightway I was in the Spirit: and behold, there was a throne set in heaven, and one sitting upon the throne;

Probably John repeats his earlier statement to show that his rapture to heaven was 'in the Spirit' and not the body [1:10]. His creaturely limitations were temporarily suspended to enable him to see the heavenly realities which are hidden from human gaze. *'Behold'* indicates that the vision is centred upon the throne of God, which is the symbol of his divine authority and power. John does not attempt to describe the form of God, whose glory is manifested in brilliant light [verse 3;

1 Tim. 6:16], but simply says that he saw 'one sitting upon the throne'. The image depicts God as reigning from the throne and points to his continuing activity in accomplishing the divine decrees.

3: and he that sat was to look upon 1ike a jasper stone and a sardius: and there was a rainbow round about the throne, like an emerald to look upon.

According to 21:11, the jasper stone is 'clear as crystal', and it perhaps represents the dazzling brightness of God's holiness, while the blood-red sardius may stand for his avenging judgments. But a much-needed note of comfort is brought to this awesome vision by the rainbow of God's grace which surrounds the throne [*Gen.* 9:13]. For it gives believers an impregnable assurance of their salvation 'even in and with the intimation of God's judgment on the race' (K. Rengstorf, *TDNT*, vol. 3, p. 342).

4: And round about the throne were four and twenty thrones: and upon the thrones I saw four and twenty elders sitting, arrayed in white garments; and on their heads crowns of gold.

Many suppose that the twenty-four elders represent the church in its totality, but in their song of praise to the Lamb they refrain from identifying themselves with the redeemed (according to the true text of 5:9, 10], and in fact it is not until 7:9, 10 that the saints appear and ascribe their salvation to God (N. B. Stonehouse, 'The Elders and Living-Beings in the Apocalypse' in *Paul before the Areopagus*, pp. 88–108.). It is therefore more in keeping with the context to regard the elders as angelic princes (probably belonging to the highest rank of 'thrones', *Col.* 1:16], who exercise priestly functions in worshipping God and presenting the prayers of the saints [5:8] as the heavenly counterparts of the twenty-four priestly orders in *1 Chron.* 24:9–19. Holiness and royal dignity are symbolized by their white garments and golden crowns.

5: And out of the throne proceed lightnings and voices and thunders. And there were seven lamps of fire burning before the throne, which are the seven Spirits of God;

As in the manifestation of God's presence at Sinai [*Exod.* 19:16], the lightnings and the ominous sounds ('voices') of thunder that proceed from the throne proclaim the dreadful power and majesty of God [8:5; 11:19; 16:18]. The seven blazing torches before the throne represent the presence of the Holy Spirit in the plenitude of his power (see comment on 1:4).

6–8: and before the throne, as it were a sea of glass like unto crystal; and in the midst of the throne, and round about the throne, four living creatures full of eyes before and behind. And the first creature was like a lion, and the second creature like a calf, and the third creature had a face as of a man, and the fourth creature was like a flying eagle. And the four living creatures, having each one of them six wings, are full of eyes round about and within: and they have no rest day and night, saying, Holy, holy, holy, is the Lord God, the Almighty, who was and who is and who is to come.

What John likened to 'a sea of glass' is best understood as an image of God's transcendence. 'It suggests the vast distance which, even in the case of one who stood at the door of heaven, intervened between himself and the Throne of God' (Swete).

Four living-beings (Arndt-Gingrich): The resemblance of the four living beings to the cherubim and seraphim [*Isa.* 6:1–3; *Ezek.* 1:1, 5–25; 10:20] suggests that they are the angelic throne attendants who lead the heavenly hosts in the unceasing praise of God. Their strange appearance is not intended to represent the created order before the throne, but rather depicts their characteristic qualities. They are in strength like the lion, in service like the ox, in intelligence like man and in swiftness like the eagle (so Hendriksen). With prompt obedience ('six wings') and ceaseless vigilance ('full of eyes'), they continually praise God as the thrice holy one, whose eternal being guarantees his lordship over all ages and his forthcoming triumph over the powers of evil [1:4].

9–11: And when the living creatures shall give glory and honour and thanks to him that sitteth on the throne, to him that liveth for ever and ever, the four and twenty elders shall fall down before him that sitteth on the throne, and shall worship him that liveth for ever and ever, and shall cast their crowns before the throne, saying, Worthy art thou, our Lord and our God, to receive the glory and the honour and the power: for thou didst create all things, and because of thy will they were, and were created.

In addition to the continuous praise of the previous verse, this appears to point to the spontaneous acclamation which occurs as God manifests his sovereignty in the progressive accomplishment of redemption [5:8, 14; 11:16; 19:4]. 'When' here has frequentative force and means 'as often as'. As often as the living beings give glory and honour and thanks to God, the twenty-four elders prostrate themselves before him and cast down their crowns in acknowledgement that their authority is derived from him. The sovereignty and eternity of God are stressed to show that he will rule for as long as he lives. In verse 8 the living beings praise God for his essential nature as the holy and eternal one, but the twenty-four elders celebrate the manifestation of the glory and power of God in creation.

As the Creator to whom all things owe their existence, God alone is worthy of the glory, honour and power which are often usurped by finite creatures, like the Emperor Domitian, who in his madness claimed the title 'our Lord and our God'. God's will is the originating cause of all things. They existed in the mind of God ('they were') before he gave them actual existence at the appointed time ('and were created'). 'The Divine Will had made the universe a fact in the scheme of things before the Divine Power gave material expression to the fact' (Swete).

CHAPTER FIVE

God is seen holding in his right hand the seven-sealed book of the divine decrees, which only the Lamb is worthy to open, and the vision ends in a paean of praise to the victorious Lamb [verses 1–14].

1: And I saw in the right hand of him that sat on the throne a book written within and on the back, close sealed with seven seals.

John next saw a scroll on the open palm of the one seated on the throne. The scroll was filled with writing on both sides of the papyrus, but it was sealed with seven seals to ensure the secrecy of its contents. Although the future is unknown to us, it clearly contains no surprises for God, who has already determined the destiny of the world. But the vision shows that these decrees can only be fulfilled by Christ, because he alone is the appointed executor of the divine purposes [verses 5, 6]. The scroll is never read, but as each seal is broken the drama of judgment and salvation is set forth in further symbols, which disclose only as much as God intends to reveal.

2: And I saw a strong angel proclaiming with a great voice, Who is worthy to open the book, and to loose the seals thereof?

A strong angel with a mighty voice 'is needed to be the herald of a challenge addressed to the whole creation' (Swete). He cries for someone who is 'worthy' to open the book and break its seals. The call is not for a person of superhuman strength, but for one who has the moral and spiritual fitness to fulfil God's decrees and bring history to its appointed goal.

History is not a random succession of events without meaning, but it remains an enigma to those who fail to realize that Christ holds the key to the world's destiny.

3: And no one in the heaven, or on the earth, or under the earth, was able to open the book, or to look thereon.

Although the angel's challenge embraced the whole creation, no one in heaven, or on earth, or in the place of departed spirits, was able to open the book or to look inside it. This emphasis on the complete inability of any other being to open the book stresses 'the supreme worthiness of the One who is able' (Buis).

4: And I wept much, because no one was found worthy to open the book, or to look thereon:

John's unrestrained grief is not due to disappointment or self-pity; it expresses his distress at the apparent set-back to the divine plan for creation. As one who longs to see the accomplishment of God's purpose, he weeps because he knows that purpose will remain unfulfilled unless the scroll is opened.

5: And one of the elders saith unto me, Weep not; behold, the Lion that is of the tribe of Judah, the Root of David, hath overcome to open the book and the seven seals thereof.

John's weeping is checked by one of the elders (see comment on 4:4). *'Behold'* directs John's attention to the one whose conquest over sin and death gives him the right to open the seven-sealed scroll [verse 9]. He is introduced by two titles which identify him as the long-promised Messiah. 'The Lion that is of the tribe of Judah' points to his royal power. The designation is derived from *Gen.* 49:9, 10 which promises that the sceptre shall not depart from Judah until the advent of the One to whom all sovereignty is given. 'The Root of David' alludes to *Isa.* 11:1, which predicts that a new shoot will restore the rule of the house of David. As the seed of David, he entered history to become the ideal king, whose universal dominion was secured by that triumph which made all history his story.

6: And I saw in the midst of the throne and of the four living creatures, and in the midst of the elders, a Lamb standing, as though it had been slain, having seven horns, and seven eyes, which are the seven Spirits of God, sent forth into all the earth.

But instead of the victorious Lion [verse 5], John saw a Lamb which appeared to have been slain, standing in the centre of the throne, surrounded by the four living beings and the elders [3:21; 7:17]. This striking paradox shows that the Lion of Judah overcame when he offered himself in lamb-like submission as the perfect sacrifice for sin [*Isa.* 53:7].

It is through the abiding merit of his death that the risen Christ now occupies the place of highest honour in heaven [verse 9]. In Revelation there are twenty-eight references to Christ as the Lamb, and this concept so dominates the rest of the book that the word virtually becomes a proper name. The seven horns symbolize the fulness of Christ's power, and the seven eyes the penetrating, creation-wide thoroughness of his vision. These all-seeing eyes are identified with 'the seven Spirits of God' [1:4] to show that the Holy Spirit is sent forth into the world by the ascended Christ [*John* 14:26; 15:26; 16: 7–11].

7: And he came, and he taketh it out of the right hand of him that sat on the throne.

The drama of the scene is vividly conveyed by the tenses of the verbs: 'And he came and has taken possession of the book from the right hand of the one upon the throne.' The Lamb's victory over sin and death proved he was worthy to take the book from the right hand of God. When Christ ascended to heaven he was invested with the authority and power to rule the world and the church in accordance with the divine decrees [*Matt.* 28:18; *Eph.*1:20–23].

8: And when he had taken the book, the four living creatures and the four and twenty elders fell down before the Lamb, having each one a harp, and golden bowls full of incense, which are the prayers of the saints.

As soon as the Lamb had taken the book, it is reasonable to assume that he sat down with God on the throne [3:21; *Heb.* 1:3]. Then the four living beings and the twenty-four elders acknowledged his deity as they fell down before him in worship [22:9]. In accordance with their priestly function, each of the elders had a harp or lyre (a symbol of praise, *Psa.* 33:2], and precious golden bowls full of incense, representing the accumulated prayers of God's people for the fulfilment of the divine purpose in the world [8:3–5]. 'The saints are not to be thought of as present there in the court of heaven, for their prayers would not then be presented by others in their behalf' (Beckwith).

9, 10: And they sing a new song, saying, Worthy art thou to take the book, and to open the seals thereof: for thou wast slain, and didst purchase unto God with thy blood men of every tribe, and tongue, and people, and nation, and madest them to be unto our God a kingdom and priests; and they reign upon the earth.

These celestial attendants around the throne sing a 'new' song in praise of the Lamb, whose death inaugurated the 'new' covenant and accomplished the long-awaited redemption of God's people [*Psa.* 96:1; *Matt.* 26:28]. Christ is worthy to take the book and open its seals because he was slain! He purchased for God with his blood men out of every tribe and tongue and people and nation [*Acts* 20:28]. The universal scope of his sacrifice thus embraces men of every group to form one people. Having been made a kingdom and priests (see comment on 1:6), the redeemed already reign on earth by means of their prayers [verse 8; *Eph.* 2:6; *1 Pet.* 2:9]. As this is a *spiritual* reign, it must not be equated with the exercise of visible authority over their fellow-men.

'The "new song" vindicates for Jesus Christ the unique place which He has taken in the history of the world. By a supreme act of self-sacrifice He has purchased men of all races and nationalities for the service of God, founded a vast spiritual Empire, and converted human life into a priestly service and a royal dignity. He who has done this is worthy to have committed into His hands the keeping of the Book of

Destiny, and to break its seals and unroll its closely packed lengths; to preside over the whole course of events which connects His Ascension with His Return' (Swete).

11, 12: And I saw, and I heard a voice of many angels round about the throne and the living creatures and the elders; and the number of them was ten thousand times ten thousand, and thousands of thousands; saying with a great voice, Worthy is the Lamb that hath been slain to receive the power, and riches, and wisdom, and might, and honour, and glory, and blessing.

Next, John saw and heard an innumerable host of angels responding to this worship and praising the Lamb with a mighty shout of acclamation. Their seven-fold ascription is a complete unit governed by the definite article before the first item ('*the* power'). They acknowledge the worthiness of the Lamb who was slain to receive adoration for the qualities he possesses: his divine *power* [*1 Cor.* 1:24], inexhaustible *riches* [*Eph.* 3:8]; infinite *wisdom* [*Col.* 2:3], executive *might* [*Luke* 11:22], supreme *honour* [*Phil.* 2:11] and eternal *glory* [*John* 1: 14] – all of which call for the *blessing* or praise of his creatures.

13: And every created thing which is in the heaven, and on the earth, and under the earth, and on the sea, and all things that are in them, heard I saying, Unto him that sitteth on the throne, and unto the Lamb, be the blessing, and the honour, and the glory, and the dominion, for ever and ever.

John now hears all creation joining in a great fourfold doxology to God and to the Lamb, whose complete equality is acknowledged in the confession that all blessing, honour, glory and dominion belong to them for ever and ever [1:6]. The adoration of creation is not a song of universal salvation, but the outcome of an assurance that God will renew his fallen world through Christ's reconciling work [*Rom.* 8:20–22; *Col.* 1:20].

This linking of the Lamb with God is found throughout the book. 'Here they are linked in praise; in 6:16 they are linked in wrath; in 7:17 they are linked in ministering consolation; in 19:6, 7 they are linked in triumph. In the final vision of the book the Lord God and the Lamb are the temple [21:22] and the light [21:23], the refreshment [22:1] and sovereignty [22:3] of the celestial city' (Carpenter).

14: And the four living creatures said, Amen. And the elders fell down and worshipped.

Here the exalted spirits nearest to the throne fittingly conclude the praise they began [4:8]. As the four living beings say, 'Amen' (So be it), the twenty-four elders fall down in silent worship. In the key vision of the book [chs. 4, 5], John's readers are shown that the seat of sovereignty is not in Rome but in heaven and that the unfolding of God's decrees has been entrusted to their Redeemer. Persecutors cannot have the last word when God has determined to overrule even the tribulations of his people for their final good [*Rom.* 8:28–39].

CHAPTER SIX

As each of the first four seals is broken, a horse and its rider appear, representing conquest, war, famine and death [verses 1–8]. The opening of the fifth seal brings to view the souls of the martyrs awaiting the day of their vindication [verses 9–11]. The dreadful calamities which follow the breaking of the sixth seal are a manifestation of the Lamb's righteous wrath [verses 12–17].

1, 2: And I saw when the Lamb opened one of the seven seals, and I heard one of the four living creatures saying as with a voice of thunder, Come. And I saw, and behold, a white horse, and he that sat thereon had a bow; and there was given unto him a crown: and he came forth conquering, and to conquer.

As John saw the Lamb open the first seal of the book, he heard one of the four living beings summon the first horseman with a voice of thunder. In Revelation the colours of the four horses symbolize the woes they bring: white for conquest, red for bloodshed, black for famine and pale for death [*Zech.* 1:8–11; 6:1–8]. The rider on the white horse is often identified with Christ or the progress of the gospel in the world, but the Lamb who opens the seal cannot be expected to reappear as the rider thus sent forth. In fact the only similarity between this vision and that of Christ in 19:11–16 is the colour of the horse, for the rider here holds a bow whereas Christ wields the sword of the Word. This horseman at once embarks on his career of conquest, but only because 'there was given unto him a crown' [*Isa*. 10:5–7]. 'Doubtless he thought of his own might as producing the victory. But John is sure of the sovereignty of God. The conqueror has only what God allows him to have' (Leon Morris).

3,4: And when he opened the second seal, I heard the second living creature saying, Come. And another horse came forth, a red horse: and to him that sat thereon it was given to take peace from the earth, and that they should slay one another: and there was given unto him a great sword.

The remaining horsemen reveal the inevitable consequences of conquest: bloodshed, famine and death! 'Victory, white-horsed and crowned, wears another aspect when viewed in the lurid light of the battlefield' (Swete). Thus John is further shown that the rider on the red horse was given the power to take peace from the earth and to cause men to slay one another. For when peace is removed the destructive instincts of men are no longer restrained. The extent of this carnage is indicated by the great sword the rider is given. War is one of the judgments of God upon an apostate race. 'The history of the world is the judgment of the world' (Friedrich von Schiller).

5, 6: And when he opened the third seal, I heard the third living creature saying, Come. And I saw, and behold, a black horse; and he that sat thereon had a balance in his hand. And I heard as it were a voice in the midst of the four living creatures saying, A measure of wheat for a shilling, and three measures of barley for a shilling; and the oil and the wine hurt thou not.

The breaking of the third seal releases a black horse whose rider held in his hand a balance for the careful weighing of food [*Ezek*. 4:16]. This symbol is explained by the voice John heard saying, 'A measure of wheat for a shilling (literally, a *denarius*), and three measures of barley for a shilling.' At these 'famine' prices, which were twelve times the ordinary rate, a man's daily wage would only buy enough wheat to support himself, and if he wished to provide something for his family he would have to buy barley instead. The command not to hurt the oil and the wine limits the extent of the famine. The drought is severe enough to destroy most of the cereal crops, but the deeper-rooted olive and the vine are not seriously affected.

7,8: And when he opened the fourth seal, I heard the voice of the fourth living creature saying, Come. And I saw, and behold, a pale horse: and he that sat upon him, his name was Death; and Hades followed with him. And there was given unto them authority over the fourth part of the earth, to kill with sword, and with famine, and with death, and by the wild beasts of the earth.

When the fourth seal was opened there appeared a pallid horse ridden by Death and followed by Hades, for those slain by death are then delivered to the realm of the dead [1:18; 20:13, 14]. This rider does not personify death in general, but is only the symbol of the deaths inflicted by the 'four sore judgments' mentioned here [*Ezek.* 14:21]. As with the severe but not catastrophic famine [verse 6], these are evidently preliminary judgments of warning, since they affect only 'the fourth part of the earth'.

The meaning of the first four seals is helpfully summarized by Swete: 'The first group of seal-openings, now completed, describes the condition of the Empire as it revealed itself to the mind of the Seer. He saw a vast world-wide power, outwardly victorious and eager for fresh conquests, yet full of the elements of unrest, danger, and misery; war, scarcity, pestilence, mortality in all its forms, abroad or ready to show themselves. This series of pictures repeats itself in history, and the militarism and lust of conquest, which it represents both in their attractive and repellent aspects, are among the forces set loose by the hand of Christ to prepare the way for His coming and the final publication of the secrets of the Sealed Book.'

9, 10: And when he opened the fifth seal, I saw underneath the altar the souls of them that had been slain for the word of God, and for the testimony which they held: and they cried with a great voice, saying, How long, O Master, the holy and true, dost thou not judge and avenge our blood on them that dwell on the earth?

The opening of the fifth seal reveals the souls of the martyrs safely resting under the heavenly altar of incense, from where their impatient cry for vindication ascends to the throne of God [8:3, 4]. Although they had been slain for the Word of God 'and for the witness they had borne' (RSV), John saw that they lived on in heaven, for men had no power to destroy their 'souls' (the seat and centre of that life which transcends the earthly physical existence, 20:4]. The martyrs address God as their 'Sovereign Lord' (NIV), and in further acknowledging him as 'the holy and true', they reinforce their plea for swift vengeance upon the wicked inhabitants of the earth who had shed their blood. They do not thirst for private revenge, but cry for public justice [*Luke* 18:7, 8; *Rom.* 12:19]. For the truth they confessed will not be vindicated until the sentence of condemnation passed upon them is reversed by God's judgment of their persecutors (G. B. Caird).

11: And there was given them to each one a white robe; and it was said unto them, that they should rest yet for a little time, until their fellow-servants also and their brethren, who should be killed even as they were, should have fulfilled their course.

This discloses the present condition of the martyrs: 'Though they have not yet reached their final bliss, they have received the *white robe,* they are free from possibility of defilement, the victory is won, and they have *rest*' (Plummer). God's answer to their cry, 'How long?' [verse 10], is that they should rest 'for a little time' until 'the number of their fellow-servants and brothers who were to be killed as they had been, was completed' (NIV). God knows the exact number of martyrs. They are his shock troops against the powers of evil, for he has ordained that the final victory is to be won through the suffering of his chosen witnesses. The way of the cross is the way to glory [3:21]. 'The vision of the martyrs under the altar shows the security of those who have already suffered, explains why God delays his final judgment, and greatly inspires John's readers to be faithful unto death and join their brethren in the company of victors' (Morris Ashcraft).

12: And I saw when he opened the sixth seal, and there was a great earthquake; and the sun became black as sackcloth of hair, and the whole moon became as blood;

With the opening of the sixth seal John is given his first vision of the end. In the succeeding visions he is 'permitted to see some things more than once, but each time from a different perspective' (Lenski).

Here we have a symbolic description of the physical catastrophes which will herald the end of the age. As man's revolt against his Maker is associated with his belief in the stability of the created order, the final shaking of the universe will convince the proudest rebels of their arrant folly [verse 15].

The effects of this cosmic upheaval could be conveyed only by means of traditional poetic language, but those who dismiss such images as the stock phrases of Jewish apocalyptic do not thereby make the judgment they represent any less certain of fulfilment. The six signs of this day of wrath involve the complete dislocation of the universe [verses 12–14]. Of the first three, John here says that when he saw the sixth seal opened, there was a great earthquake, when the sun became as black as sackcloth and the moon as the colour of blood [*Joel* 2:10, 31].

13, 14: and the stars of the heaven fell unto the earth, as a fig tree casteth her unripe figs when she is shaken of a great wind. And the heaven was removed as a scroll when it is rolled up; and every mountain and island were moved out of their places.

In three further images John shows how the unleashing of God's judgment completely shatters what the ancients regarded as the fixed points of an ordered world: the stars of heaven fell to the earth like unripe figs in a violent wind; the vault of heaven was rolled up like a scroll; and on earth every mountain and island was shaken out of its place [*Isa.* 34:4].

15: And the kings of the earth, and the princes, and the chief captains, and the rich, and the strong, and every bondman and freeman, hid themselves in the caves and in the rocks of the mountains;

This terrifying judgment reduces men of every class to the same condition of abject fear, as they vainly seek refuge in the caves and rocks of the mountains [*Isa.* 2:19]. The sixfold enumeration gives special stress to the utter helplessness of those who once wielded great worldly power and influence. The kings, princes and chief captains are stripped of their authority, the rich of their security and the strong of their courage. 'Every slave and free man' covers the rest of mankind and shows that none can escape the final visitation of divine wrath.

16,17: and they say to the mountains and to the rocks, Fall on us, and hide us from the face of him that sitteth on the throne, and from the wrath of the Lamb: for the great day of their wrath is come; and who is able to stand?

The people plead for the mountains and rocks to fall on them [*Hos.* 10:8], because what 'sinners dread most is not death, but the revealed presence of God' (Swete). Now that the great day of reckoning has come, they shrink in terror from the sight of God, and 'from the wrath of the Lamb'. This paradoxical expression identifies Christ as the agent of divine judgment, for those who spurn his sacrifice must endure his wrath.

As the phrase 'their wrath' indicates, the Lamb's wrath is the manifestation of the wrath of God upon a sinful world. There is nothing impersonal about God's wrath; it is the necessary response of his holiness to persistent wickedness (F. F. Bruce). Since the question, 'Who is able to stand?' assumes that nobody can do so, John next describes the preservation of the righteous 'and their raptured praises, a joyous contrast with the despairing fate of those whose doom has just been narrated' (Plummer).

CHAPTER SEVEN

In contrast to the doom of the wicked, John next sees the sealing of the 144,000, who represent the true Israel of God in all its fulness [verses 1–8]. This pledge of security is followed by the vision of its realization in heaven, where the 144, 000 are seen to be an innumerable host, who have triumphed over tribulation and entered into the state of final blessedness [verses 9–17].

1: After this I saw four angels standing at the four corners of the earth, holding the four winds of the earth, that no wind should blow on the earth, or on the sea, or upon any tree.

'After this' does not indicate chronological sequence, but simply introduces the vision which answers the solemn question of the last chapter: 'Who is able to stand?' As the four winds are another symbol for the four horsemen (see the explicit identification in *Zech.* 6:5), the first scene of this vision shows that the sealing of God's people is effected *before* the judgments of 6:1–8 can take place [verses 1–8]. John saw four angels holding back the winds of judgment which were ready to blow from every quarter, for 'those tempests would not arise or shake a single leaf till the securing of God's servants was accomplished' (Carpenter).

2, 3: And I saw another angel ascend from the sunrising, having the seal of the living God: and he cried with a great voice to the four angels, to whom it was given to hurt the earth and the sea, saying, Hurt not the earth, neither the sea, nor the trees, till we shall have sealed the servants of our God on their foreheads.

The approach of another angel from the east ('sunrising') is appropriate, as God's gracious manifestations were expected from that direction [*Ezek.* 43:2; *Mal.* 4:2]. The angel's task is to impress 'the seal of the living God' upon the foreheads of God's servants as the mark of divine ownership and protection [*Ezek.* 9:1–4; *Eph.* 4:30; *2 Tim.* 2:19], and so his first care is to prevent the angels of the winds from unleashing their judgments until the work of sealing is done. This sealing does not guarantee immunity from suffering [6:9], but though God's servants 'must suffer, many of them even unto death, they will finally be brought in safety out of all the woe into the eternal kingdom' (Beckwith).

4–8: And I heard the number of them that were sealed, a hundred and forty and four thousand, sealed out of every tribe of the children of Israel: of the tribe of Judah were sealed twelve thousand; of the tribe of Reuben twelve thousand; of the tribe of Gad twelve thousand; of the tribe of Asher twelve thousand; of the tribe of Naphtali twelve thousand; of the tribe of Manasseh twelve thousand; of the tribe of Simeon twelve thousand; of the tribe of Levi twelve thousand; of the tribe of Issachar twelve thousand; of the tribe of Zebulun twelve thousand; of the tribe of Joseph twelve thousand; of the tribe of Benjamin were sealed twelve thousand.

John does not witness the sealing, but he hears the number of those sealed – 144,000 consisting of 12,000 from each of the twelve tribes of Israel. This symbolic number represents the church as the true spiritual Israel [2:9; 3:9; 14:1; *Rom.* 2:29; *Gal.* 3:29; 6:16]. According to K. Rengstorf, 'twelve' indicates the divine will to save; 'thousands' stresses the size of the community; the 12,000 from each tribe 'brings out the orderly nature of the divine action and the perfection of the result' and the total number 'attests the absolute unity of those who are sealed' (*TDNT*, vol. 2, p. 324).

That ethnic Israel is not in view is confirmed by the irregular listing of the tribes. Judah is placed first as the Messiah's own tribe, Dan is omitted, Levi is included as an ordinary tribe and Joseph replaces Ephraim. Lenski observes that the two parts of this chapter constitute '*the revelation of the church. Sealed – Glorified!* This is to be our picture and vision of *the church*. It is transcendent.'

9: After these things I saw, and behold, a great multitude, which no man could number, out of every nation, and of all tribes and peoples and tongues, standing before the throne and before the Lamb, arrayed in white robes, and palms in their hands ...

'*After these things*' introduces a fresh aspect of the vision as the scene shifts from earth to heaven. This preview of the final bliss of the redeemed is the logical sequel to the sealing of the 144,000. In John's vision the glorified church is revealed as a cosmopolitan body, for the vast throng which cannot be counted is drawn from every tribe and nation and made one in Christ [5:9]. The saints stand accepted in the place of honour before the throne of God and before the Lamb, clothed in 'white robes' [verse 14] and with 'palms' in their hands [*John* 12:13], symbols which denote the purity and victory that is theirs by grace alone.

10: and they cry with a great voice, saying, Salvation unto our God who sitteth on the throne, and unto the Lamb.

As with one voice, the great multitude of the redeemed ascribe their deliverance to the sovereign will of God and the sacrifice of the Lamb. 'Salvation unto our God' means that 'The praise and honour due for our salvation belongs to God, since he is the Cause of our salvation' (Plummer).

11, 12: And all the angels were standing round about the throne, and about the elders and the four living creatures; and they fell before the throne on their faces, and worshipped God, saying, Amen: Blessing, and glory, and wisdom, and thanksgiving, and honour, and power, and might, be unto our God for ever and ever. Amen.

The view that the elders and the four living beings are angelic powers is supported by the fact that they join in the worship offered by all the angels around the throne (see comment on 4:4 and 4:6). The angels' first 'Amen' confirms the praise of the redeemed [verse 10], before they add their own tribute to God in a sevenfold doxology similar to that addressed to the Lamb in 5:12. God is praised as the fount of all the *blessing, glory* and *wisdom* which are so conspicuously displayed in the salvation of men [*Eph.* 3:10], and is therefore the One to whom all the *thanksgiving* and *honour* belong for the exercise of his *power* and *might* in this great work of grace. 'For ever and ever' puts this adoration 'into the realm of eternal verities' (Morris) and the final 'Amen' sets the seal upon the truth just confessed.

13, 14: And one of the elders answered, saying unto me, These that are arrayed in the white robes, who are they, and whence came they? And I say unto him, My lord, thou knowest. And he said to me, These are they that come out of the great tribulation, and they washed their robes, and made them white in the blood of the Lamb.

One of the elders interprets the vision by anticipating John's unspoken questions concerning the white-robed multitude [5:5]. 'My lord' is the language of reverent regard for a heavenly being, but not that of worship [19:10; 22:8, 9]. 'Thou knowest' is at once a confession of ignorance and a plea for enlightenment.

And he said to me, 'These are they who have come out of the great tribulations' (RSV): This translation is preferable, since the ASV could be taken as implying that those whom John saw were still coming out of tribulation, whereas from the future standpoint of the vision the number of the redeemed is complete. Here 'the great tribulation' does not refer to any particular time of suffering, but includes all the afflictions through which the saints have passed on their way to glory [*Acts* 14:22]. 'This tribulation is now completed and past, and is therefore referred to as "the great tribulations"' (Plummer).

And they washed their robes, and made them white in the blood of the Lamb: This striking language applies to all believers alike, and there is nothing in the context to support the strange notion that it refers only to martyrs. By his sacrifice Christ merited salvation for his people, but the benefits won by that death must be appropriated by faith, and the aorist verbs here look back to the time on earth when they washed and whitened their robes in the blood of the Lamb. 'This blood and nothing else in the universe whitens us so that we may stand before God' (Lenski).

15: Therefore are they before the throne of God; and they serve him day and night in his temple: and he that sitteth on the throne shall spread his tabernacle over them.

Because of this washing ('therefore'), the redeemed are before the throne of God, which is not only a place of safety but also of service. For heaven is the sanctuary in which they all constantly offer to God the priestly service of worship [5:10]. The elder's concluding words depict the final bliss of God's people in a series of beautiful images [verses 15–17]. The promise that God 'shall spread his tabernacle over them' means that he will shelter his people from all harm by the glory ('*Shekinah*') of his abiding presence [21:3; *Ezek.* 37:27].

16: They shall hunger no more, neither thirst any more; neither shall the sun strike upon them, nor any heat.

Blessed relief is promised from the privations suffered by Christ's faithful witnesses on earth. They shall be delivered from the inward pangs of hunger and thirst and from those outward trials which are symbolized by the scorching heat of the sun [*Isa.* 49:10]. But these negatives also imply the satisfaction of all their needs (for food and drink, see *John* 6:35; for divine protection, see previous verse).

17: For the Lamb that is in the midst of the throne shall be their shepherd, and shall guide them unto fountains of waters of life: and God shall wipe away every tear from their eyes.

The Lamb as *Shepherd* may seem to be a surprising reversal of roles, but as the Saviour of his blood-bought flock, he alone has the authority 'to guide them unto fountains of waters of life' [*Psa.* 23:1, 2; *John* 10: 14]. This figure promises the complete satisfaction of every need, even though the heavenly reality it represents is beyond our present understanding [*1 Cor.* 13:12]. The state of glory will also be marked by the absence of all suffering and sorrow. The tender assurance that 'God shall wipe away every tear from their eyes' is taken from *Isa.* 25:8

[cf. 21:4]. Words like these 'must sound as a divine music in the ears of the persecuted. God will comfort as a mother comforts' (J. M. S. Baljon).

3: THE SEVEN TRUMPETS OF JUDGMENT
CHAPTER EIGHT

As the Lamb opens the seventh seal, seven angels prepare to blow the seven trumpets of judgment in response to the prayers of the saints [verses 1–5]. After a description of the destruction wrought by the first four trumpets, a flying eagle warns that three fearful woes are yet to come [verses 6–13].

1, 2: And when he opened the seventh seal, there followed a silence in heaven about the space of half an hour. And I saw the seven angels that stand before God; and there were given unto them seven trumpets.

The opening of the seventh seal cannot follow the sixth in chronological sequence, because the contents of that seal portrayed the final day of wrath [6:12–17]. The seven trumpets rather serve to introduce a series of judgments which are synchronous with those of the seals. Hence the vision covers the same ground again, but from a different point of view. The calamities described are typical judgments which recur throughout this dispensation, and should not be regarded as symbolizing particular events.

When the Lamb opened the seventh seal, there was a dramatic pause for about half an hour as the praise of the heavenly hosts was hushed in dread anticipation of the judgments to follow. John then saw that seven trumpets were given to 'the seven angels' that stand before God. The definite article points to a specific group of angels, who are possibly to be identified with the seven angels of the Presence whose names are given in the apocryphal book *1 Enoch* [20:2–8] as Uriel, Raphael, Raguel, Michael [12:7; *Jude* 9], Sariel, Gabriel [*Luke* 1:19] and Remiel. As the blowing of trumpets signalled the fall of Jericho [*Josh.* 6:13], so those assigned to the angels herald the 'end-time' judgments of God [verses 7–12; 9:1, 12; 11:15].

3, 4: And another angel came and stood over the altar, having a golden censer; and there was given unto him much incense, that he should add it unto the prayers of all the saints upon the golden altar which was before

the throne. And the smoke of the incense, with the prayers of the saints, went up before God out of the angel's hand.

Another angel with a golden censer next appears on the scene, and John saw that 'there was given unto him' much incense to offer with the prayers of all the saints upon the altar of incense before the throne [6:9]. The angel is neither a mediator nor an intercessor. He does not bring his own offering, but is given 'much incense' and this symbol 'represents the intercession of Christ for his church, which adds power and efficacy to the prayers of the church' (Lenski). For it is only as the prayers of the saints are purified by Christ's intercession that they ascend to God as a fragrant offering.

5: And the angel taketh the censer; and he filled it with the fire of the altar, and cast it upon the earth: and there followed thunders, and voices, and lightnings, and an earthquake.

Having emptied the censer of incense, the angel takes it again in order to fulfil another office. It is to be used now, not for the offering of prayers, but for the work of judgment. He fills the censer with fire from the altar, and casts its contents upon the earth [*Ezek.* 10:2]. This is a partial answer to the cry of the martyrs for justice [6:10], and it means that 'the prayers of the saints return to the earth in wrath' (Swete). The awesome portents that follow – thunders, voices of the storm, lightnings and earthquake – underline the power of God which is about to be manifested in his righteous judgments [*Exod.* 19:16 –25].

6: And the seven angels that had the seven trumpets prepared themselves to sound.

The seven angels know that these portents are the signal for them to play their part in the great drama, and they prepare to sound their trumpets to 'usher in the judgments which shall fulfil the prayers of God's people' (Beckwith). For the vindication of the saints calls for retribution on the wicked (see comment on 6:10).

7: And the first sounded, and there followed hail and fire, mingled with blood, and they were cast upon the earth: and the third part of the earth was burnt up, and the third part of the trees was burnt up, and all green grass was burnt up.

The first four trumpets form a group of warning judgments directed against the sources of life which men in their blindness take for granted.

These judgments resemble the Egyptian plagues which were sent to move Pharaoh to repentance, but, as in the case of their prototypes, they only serve to harden the hearts of the wicked [9:20, 21]. Hail and fire recall the fourth plague [*Exod.* 9:23–26], while the phrase 'mingled with blood' adds to the dramatic intensity of the picture [*Ezek.* 38:22]. In the third part of the earth which was affected by this judgment, the fire burnt all the grass and a third of the trees. John's purpose is to show that there are no *natural* disasters in a world which is governed by God. The curse does not come without a cause. The trumpets thus depict God's judgments 'on the world, not the trials of the Church. The Church is the true Israel which exists uninjured by these manifestations of God's wrath in the midst of the world of Egyptian wickedness' (Plummer).

8, 9: And the second angel sounded, and as it were a great mountain burning with fire was cast into the sea: and the third part of the sea became blood; and there died the third part of the creatures which were in the sea, even they that had life; and the third part of the ships was destroyed.

When the second trumpet sounded something that looked like a blazing mountain was cast into the sea, turning a third of it to blood. This brought death to all marine life and destroyed the ships in that part of the sea. Here the turning of the water into blood and the destruction of the fish bring to mind the first Egyptian plague [*Exod.* 7:20, 21]. But to attempt to interpret the blazing mountain in terms of volcanic eruptions, like that of Vesuvius in AD 79, is to misunderstand the nature of such apocalyptic images. The evident meaning of the terrible picture is that the sea can also be used by God to punish and warn mankind. For if the loss of lives and property in all the sea disasters throughout the centuries could be calculated, this vision would not seem at all extravagant.

10, 11: And the third angel sounded, and there fell from heaven a great star, burning as a torch, and it fell upon the third part of the rivers, and upon the fountains of the waters; and the name of the star is called Wormwood: and the third part of the waters became wormwood; and many men died of the waters, because they were made bitter.

At the third trumpet-blast a great fiery star called Wormwood fell upon a third part of the rivers and springs [*Jer.* 9:15]. This made the fresh water as bitter as wormwood, in contrast to the miracles which sweetened bitter waters [*Exod.* 15:25; *2 Kings* 2:21]. It is off the mark to say that wormwood is not actually poisonous. The expression simply means that the waters became charged with sorrow and disaster, so that many died through floods, drought, water pollution, pestilence etc. The star points to 'the awe-striking nature of the punishment, and is indicative of the fact that the judgment is the act of God, and proceeds directly from heaven, and is not to be attributed to merely natural circumstances' (Plummer).

12: And the fourth angel sounded, and the third part of the sun was smitten, and the third part of the moon, and the third part of the stars; that the third part of them should be darkened, and the day should not shine for the third part of it, and the night in like manner.

At the sound of the fourth trumpet the heavenly luminaries are so darkened that they cease to give any light for a third of the day and night. This judgment recalls the ninth Egyptian plague [*Exod.* 10: 21–23]. The first part of the verse seems to mean that the intensity of light was reduced by a third, whereas the second part indicates that there was total darkness for a third of the day and night. However, it should be obvious that John is painting a picture and not writing a treatise on astronomy! The darkness prefigures the doom of the ungodly [*Isa.* 13:10], and is also the prelude to the new exodus of God's people from under the hands of their oppressors [11:8; *Luke* 21:28]. In an age which looks to the stars for guidance, this verse reminds us that God exercises complete control over the solar system. 'God can turn even the benign influences of the sun and planets into means for the destruction of man. In the countless evils which have their origin in the excess or defect of the power of the sun, we may see an illustration of the fulfilment of this judgment' (Plummer).

13: And I saw, and I heard an eagle, flying in mid heaven, saying with a great voice, Woe, woe, woe, for them that dwell on earth, by reason of the other voices of the trumpet of the three angels, who are yet to sound.

The bird of prey John next sees flying in mid-heaven is an omen of worse to come. The eagle proclaims a triple woe 'for them that dwell on earth' (i.e. the wicked, as can be seen from 9:4, 20), because of the three trumpets yet to sound.

CHAPTER NINE

The woes inflicted by the fifth and sixth trumpets attack men directly. The former of these releases a swarm of satanic locusts from the bottomless pit which torment men for five months [verses 1–12]. The latter looses four angels with a vast army of fiendish horsemen to kill a third of mankind. But those unaffected by this judgment still refused to repent of their wickedness [verses 13–21].

1: And the fifth angel sounded, and I saw a star from heaven fallen unto the earth: and there was given to him the key of the pit of the abyss.

At the sounding of the fifth trumpet John saw a star which had fallen from heaven to earth. From what follows [verse 11], it appears that the star is a fallen angel named *Apollyon* (i.e. Destroyer), who is permitted 'to exercise malicious power on earth in furtherance of divine judgment' (Moffatt). There is a vast difference between this fallen angel who 'was given' the key of the abyss, and the angel of 20:1, who descends from heaven with this key in his hand as the willing agent of the divine purpose (Caird). 'The abyss' is the abode of demons before the final judgment [*Luke* 8:31], and the reservoir of evil from which the worst dangers arise [11:7; 17:8].

2: And he opened the pit of the abyss; and there went up a smoke out of the pit, as the smoke of a great furnace; and the sun and the air were darkened by reason of the smoke of the pit.

When the fallen angel unlocked the shaft of the abyss, there rose up a dense cloud of smoke like that from a great furnace, obscuring the sun and befouling the air with its noxious fumes. The verse presents a vivid picture of the pervasive power of evil, 'which clouds men's minds and darkens their understandings' (Plummer).

3: And out of the smoke came forth locusts upon the earth; and power was given them, as the scorpions of the earth have power.

Out of the smoke John saw a swarm of locusts come upon the earth, but they were unlike ordinary locusts which merely devour all the vegetation, as in the Egyptian plague and the prophecies of punishment in Joel [*Exod.* 10:1–20; *Joel* 1:2–2:11]. For these fearsome creatures were given the authority to inflict torment upon the ungodly with their scorpion-like stings [verses 5, 10]. 'The scorpion takes its place with the snake and other creatures hostile to man, and with them symbolizes the forces of spiritual evil which are active in the world' (Swete).

4: And it was said unto them that they should not hurt the grass of the earth, neither any green thing, neither any tree, but only such men as have not the seal of God on their foreheads.

The locusts were not permitted to harm the vegetation of the earth, but only the men who had not the seal of God on their foreheads [7:1–8]. As the Israelites were protected from the plagues which punished the Egyptians [*Exod.* 8:22; 9:4, 26; 10:23; 11:7], so the new Israel is exempted from the torments arising from the abyss. This means that the children of God are strangers to the spiritual torments that plague the wicked [*Luke* 10:19]. 'No real injury can happen to them; pain and death might be encountered, but all things work together for their higher good . . . No plague can hurt those who have the seal of God on their foreheads. A plague from which those whose way is through tribulation are exempt can hardly be a physical one' (Carpenter).

5, 6: And it was given them that they should not kill them, but that they should be tormented five months: and their torment was as the torment of a scorpion, when it striketh a man. And in those days men shall seek death, and shall in no wise find it; and they shall desire to die, and death fleeth from them.

The power of the locusts is limited by the will of God to a period of five months, perhaps corresponding to the natural life-span of these creatures. A torment which lasts for five months is a long time, but is still of limited duration. It is clear from verse 6 that the anguish inflicted by the locusts' scorpion-like stings is restricted to the present life of the ungodly, or they would not desire death to release them from it. 'The withholding of death, instead of being an alleviation, is really a refinement of torture; so infernal is the pain, that the sufferers crave, but crave in vain, for death' (Moffatt).

7–10: And the shapes of the locusts were like unto horses prepared for war; and upon their heads as it were crowns like unto gold, and their faces were as men's faces. And they had hair as the hair of women, and the teeth were as the teeth of lions. And they had breastplates, as it were breastplates of iron; and the sound of their wings was as the sound of chariots, of many horses rushing to war. And they have tails like unto scorpions, and stings; and in their tails is their power to hurt men five months.

John's description of the demonic appearance of these locusts shows that the attempt to compare them with an ordinary swarm of locusts is quite misguided. 'They are locusts, but they have the malice of scorpions; they advance like horse-soldiers to battle; they wear crowns; they bear a resemblance to men; there is something womanlike also in their appearance, and in their voracity they are as lions. The exigencies of the symbolism are quite beyond the features of the ordinary locust: the sacred writer shows us a plague in which devastation, malice, king-like authority, intelligence, seductiveness, fierceness, strength, meet together under one directing spirit, to torment men' (Carpenter).

11: They have over them as king the angel of the abyss: his name in Hebrew is Abaddon, and in the Greek tongue he hath the name Apollyon.

In contrast to ordinary locusts [*Prov.* 30:27], these locusts have the angel of the abyss as their king, for they obey his orders and do his work [verse 1]. John knows the name of this fallen angel: it is in Hebrew *Abaddon* and in Greek *Apollyon*, meaning the Destroyer. He is not Satan but one of his minions; Satan himself does not appear before the vision of the woman and the dragon in chapter 12.

12: The first Woe is past: behold, there come yet two Woes hereafter.

This dramatic announcement marks the end of the first woe and warns that two more are yet to come [8:13; 9:12; 11:14].

13–15: And the sixth angel sounded, and I heard a voice from the horns of the golden altar which is before God, one saying to the sixth angel that had the trumpet, Loose the four angels that are bound at the great river Euphrates. And the four angels were loosed, that had been prepared for the hour and day and month and year, that they should kill the third part of men.

The voice that John heard commanding the sixth angel to release the second woe came from the horns of the golden altar of incense [*Exod.* 30:2], which shows that this judgment is in response to the prayers of the saints [6:9, 10; 8:3–5]. The four evil angels who were kept bound at the Euphrates were not permitted to embark upon their strictly limited mission of destruction ('that they should kill the third part of men', verse 18) until the exact moment determined by God. There is symbolic significance in the direction from which the judgment is launched, because the world powers God used to punish apostate Israel for her idolatry came from beyond the river Euphrates [*Isa.* 7:20]. Thus a corrupt civilization which indulges in the same sin will incur the same judgment. 'The aim of the plague is to exhibit the death-working power of false thoughts, false customs, false beliefs, and to rouse men to forsake the false worships, worldliness, and self-indulgence into which they had fallen [verses 20, 21]' (Carpenter).

16–19: And the number of the armies of the horsemen was twice ten thousand times ten thousand: I heard the number of them. And thus I saw the horses in the vision, and them that sat on them, having breastplates as of fire and of hyacinth and of brimstone: and the heads of the horses are as the heads of lions; and out of their mouths proceedeth fire and smoke and brimstone. By these three plagues was the third part of men killed, by the fire and the smoke and the brimstone, which proceeded out of their mouths. For the power of the horses is in their mouth, and in their tails: for their tails are like unto serpents, and have heads; and with them they hurt.

This is the only place in the book where John specifically states that he is describing what he saw in a vision, because only thus could he perceive the vast forces which were armed with supernatural powers to torment and kill a third of mankind. He saw an immense host of two hundred million horsemen, the colour of whose breastplates matched the three plagues of fire, smoke ('hyacinth' = dark blue) and sulphur that proceeded from the lion-like mouths of their fiendish mounts. These diabolical animals also had tails like serpents, with which to torment their victims. The whole judgment 'portrays the spiritual evils which afflict the ungodly in this life . . . The number of such inflictions is, indeed, great enough to be described as "two myriads of myriads" [verse 16]; they destroy a part, but not the greater part [verse 15, "the third part"] of men; and yet how largely they fail to bring men to repentance! Such punishment is a foretaste of hell, as seems to be foreshadowed in the "fire and smoke and brimstone" of verses 17, 18' (Plummer).

20, 21: And the rest of mankind, who were not killed with these plagues, repented not of the works of their hands, that they should not worship demons, and the idols of gold, and of silver, and of brass, and of stone, and of wood; which can neither see, nor hear, nor walk: and they repented not of their murders, nor of their sorceries, nor of their fornication, nor of their thefts.

The majority who escaped this terrible judgment might have been expected to take warning from the fate of their fellows, and to become servants of God and of Christ. But they were so far from doing this that they did not even repent of their idolatry. Such repentance would have led them 'to abandon the worship of unclean spirits and of the idols that represented them' (Swete) [*Deut.* 32:17; *1 Cor.* 10:20.] These idols are scornfully described as 'the works of their hands', because the gods they make from existing materials like gold and silver 'can neither see, nor hear, nor walk' [*Psa.* 115:5–7; *Dan.* 5:23]. The further charge of verse 21 shows that they were no more willing to repent of their evil deeds than of their idolatry, for false worship leads to every kind of wickedness [*Rom.* 1:18–32]. John later reveals that the lake of fire awaits all who persist in idolatry and the sins that accompany it [21: 8].

CHAPTER TEN

John sees a mighty angel descend from heaven with a little book in his hand and hears him announce that the mystery of God will shortly be fulfilled. The angel gives John the book to eat. First it tastes sweet, but then turns bitter because of the woes it contains.

1: And I saw another strong angel coming down out of heaven, arrayed with a cloud; and the rainbow was upon his head, and his face was as the sun, and his feet as pillars of fire;

Apparently John is now back on earth, for he sees a mighty angel coming down from heaven. The description of this angel has led some to identify him with Christ, but John could never introduce Christ as 'another angel' [8:3], The angel's appearance points to his celestial dignity. He is clad in a cloud, 'the vehicle in which heavenly beings descend and ascend' (Swete); the rainbow upon his head gives the church further assurance of God's covenant faithfulness (see note on 4:3); while his face shone like the sun, and his feet were like pillars of fire. 'The last two clauses express the same idea, viz. the bright and glorious appearance of the angel. God's glory is reflected in his messenger, as formerly it was in Moses [*Exod.* 34:29, 30]' (Plummer).

2: and he had in his hand a little book open: and he set his right foot upon the sea, and his left upon the earth;

The angel had a little book which lay open in his hand, thus showing that its contents were to be made known to men. No great stress should be placed on the diminutive. The 'little' book contained prophecies of world-wide significance [verses 6, 11], yet it was small enough for John to eat [*Ezek.* 2:8-3:3]. In this vision the angel appears as a colossal figure, who bestrides sea and land, 'and cries with a loud voice, because his message is addressed to the whole world' (Beckwith).

3, 4: and he cried with a great voice, as a lion roareth: and when he cried, the seven thunders uttered their voices. And when the seven thunders uttered their voices, I was about to write: and I heard a voice from heaven saying, Seal up the things which the seven thunders uttered, and write them not.

The shout of the angel was like the roar of a lion [*Hos.* 11: 10; *Amos* 3:8]; 'and when he shouted, the seven thunders spoke' (NEB). John evidently understood the meaning of this utterance, and was just about to write it down when a voice from heaven (presumably the voice of God or Christ) forbids him to reveal what he has heard [*Dan.* 12:4]. 'The Seer's enforced reticence witnesses to the fragmentary character of even apocalyptic disclosures. The Seer himself received more than he was at liberty to communicate' (Swete) [*2 Cor.* 12:4]. It is thus pointless to speculate on the nature of what is purposely concealed from us [*Deut.* 29:29].

5, 6: And the angel that I saw standing upon the sea and upon the earth lifted up his right hand to heaven, and sware by him that liveth for ever

and ever, who created the heaven and the things that are therein, and the earth and the things that are therein, and the sea and the things that are therein, that there shall be delay no longer:

The angel then lifted up his right hand to heaven [*Deut.* 32:40; *Dan.* 12:7], and solemnly swore by the eternal God, who is the Creator of all things, that there should be no more delay in the fulfilment of the divine purpose [verse 7].

1. Because God is *eternal*, he is certain to fulfil what he has planned. The 'problem' of evil cannot baffle or outwit the one who is a stranger to improvisation and frustration [*Prov.* 21:30].

2: Because God is *the Creator*, he is sure to accomplish the purpose he had in creating the world [4:11]. The sovereignty of God over the whole creation means that all things must contribute to his glory and work together for the final good of his people [*Rom.* 8:28].

7: but in the days of the voice of the seventh angel, when he is about to sound, then is finished the mystery of God, according to the good tidings which he declared to his servants the prophets.

The angel proclaims that there shall be no further delay [verse 6], but within the period to be introduced by the sounding of the seventh trumpet the mystery of God will be accomplished [11:15–18]. 'The mystery of God' is the eternal purpose of God, which was once kept secret but is now revealed [*Rom.* 16:25, 26]. The consummation of this mystery includes the final judgment of the wicked, and 'the full salvation of the saints in the perfected kingdom' (Beckwith). This will be no 'surprise' ending, but the fulfilment of the good tidings that God gave 'to his servants the prophets' [*Amos* 3:7]. The promise given here is good news indeed for the fainting Christian, for it tells of the end of his trials and the overthrow of his enemies' (Plummer).

8: And the voice which I heard from heaven, I heard it again speaking with me, and saying, Go, take the book which is open in the hand of the angel that standeth upon the sea and upon the earth.

This is the same heavenly voice that forbade John to write down what the seven thunders uttered [verse 4]. He now hears another command requiring the same prompt obedience. He is to approach the angel and take the book that lies open in his hand.

9, 10: And I went unto the angel, saying unto him that he should give me the little book. And he saith unto me, Take it, and eat it up; and it shall make thy belly bitter, but in thy mouth it shall be sweet as honey. And I took the little book out of the angel's hand, and ate it up; and it was in my mouth sweet as honey: and when I had eaten it, my belly was made bitter.

The angel instructs John to take the little book and eat it up, but warns him that it will be bitter to digest, even though it will taste as sweet as honey [*Psa.* 19: 10]. John's experience proved to be similar to that of Ezekiel, who found that God's Word tasted sweet [*Ezek.* 3:3], but because the scroll was filled with woe his mood was soon changed to one of bitterness [*Ezek.* 2:10; 3:14]. Hence the physical bitterness John felt matched the terrible nature of the judgment he had to announce [verse 11]. 'The true preacher of God's Word will faithfully proclaim the denunciations of the wicked it contains. But he does not do this with fierce glee. The more his heart is filled with the love of God, the more certain it is that the telling forth of "woes" will be a bitter experience' [Morris].

11: And they say unto me, Thou must prophesy again over many peoples and nations and tongues and kings.

'They say' is rather strange, but is probably the equivalent of the passive 'it was said' (RSV: 'I was told').

'Thou must prophesy again concerning many peoples and nations and tongues and kings' (ASV margin). The fourfold enumeration shows that the prophecy embraces the whole of mankind. The burden of woe that concerns so many is laid upon John by the 'must' of divine necessity. It is to be done 'again', because he has already 'to some extent set forth God's will in the earlier part of the book; and he is now required to proceed with the delivery of his message' (Plummer).

CHAPTER ELEVEN

John is told to measure the temple and count the worshippers [verses 1, 2]. After God's two witnesses have prophesied for 1260 days, they are killed by the beast from the abyss, but rise again and ascend to heaven [verses 3–13]. At the seventh trumpet blast, the proclamation of Christ's victory in heaven is followed by the outpouring of God's wrath upon the world [verses 14–19].

1: And there was given me a reed like unto a rod: and one said, Rise, and measure the temple of God, and the altar, and them that worship therein.

John is given a reed like a measuring rod, and is instructed to measure the inner sanctuary of God, the altar of incense [8:3] and those who worship therein [*Ezek.* 40]. The last clause is significant, for only the priests were allowed to enter the Holy of Holies in the temple at Jerusalem, but now all believers enjoy immediate access to God. Hence this is a picture of God's new temple, the church [*1 Cor.* 3:16; *Eph.* 2:19–22]. The church is measured to show that it will be protected and preserved from spiritual danger, though not from physical suffering, and the assurance thus conveyed corresponds to the sealing of the 144,000 [7:1–8].

2: And the court which is without the temple leave without, and measure it not; for it hath been given unto the nations: and the holy city shall they tread under foot forty and two months.

From the aspect of its eternal security the church is preserved inviolate [verse 1], but in regard to its earthly existence it is subject to persecution by 'the heathen' (i.e. 'the nations' or 'the Gentiles'). So John is forbidden to measure the outer court of the temple, because God has given the heathen the power to trample on 'the holy city' (i.e. the church viewed as the new Jerusalem) for 'forty and two months'. The time limit which is set for this trial is derived from *Dan.* 7:25, and refers to the three and a half years of terror under Antiochus Epiphanes when the temple at Jerusalem was desecrated (June 168 to December 165 BC). In this book, forty-two months [13:5], 1260 days [verse 3; 12:6] and 'a time, and times, and half a time' [12:14] are equivalent designations for the same period. 'By comparing these passages with the present context we get the equation: the duration of the triumph of the Gentiles = the duration of the prophesying of the Two Witnesses = the duration of the Woman's sojourn in the wilderness. The time-limit serves of course no further purpose than to synchronize the several periods, and to compare them with the greatest crisis through which the Jewish people passed between the Exile and the Fall of Jerusalem' (Swete).

3: And I will give unto my two witnesses, and they shall prophesy a thousand two hundred and threescore days, clothed in sackcloth.

The two witnesses are appointed by God to prophesy for 1260 days, and are clothed in sackcloth because their message is a call to repentance [*Matt.* 11:21]. These witnesses are not actual men like Moses and Elijah, even though they exercise similar powers [verses 5, 6]. They are rather a collective symbol of the church, for two witnesses were necessary to give competent legal testimony [*Deut.* 17:6; 19:15]. The purpose of the vision is to promote obedience: it is a summons to the church to bear witness to the truth before a hostile world [2:10].

4: These are the two olive trees and the two candlesticks, standing before the Lord of the earth.

The two witnesses are now identified as the two olive trees and two lampstands that stand before the Lord of the earth [*Zech.* 4:2–14]. It is because the church is constantly supplied with the oil of the Spirit that the lamp of witness is not quenched by the opposition of evil men.

In Zechariah the two olive trees represent Zerubbabel the prince and Joshua the priest, who thus symbolize the royal and priestly prerogatives of the church [1:6; 5:10; 20:6]. But instead of Zechariah's single lampstand, there are two lampstands here to match the two witnesses. These lampstands depict the whole church, and not just a minority of martyrs. For all believers are called to be faithful witnesses, not fearing what man can do, as befits those who are privileged to stand 'before the Lord of the earth'.

5: And if any man desireth to hurt them, fire proceedeth out of their mouth and devoureth their enemies; and if any man shall desire to hurt them, in this manner must he be killed.

John next proceeds to show that those who oppose God's witnesses only succeed in bringing destruction upon themselves [verses 5, 6]. There is an allusion to Elijah, who called down fire from heaven on the soldiers sent to arrest him [*2 Kings* 1:10–12], but here the fire comes out of the mouths of the witnesses. This means that their enemies are inevitably killed by the power of God's Word [*Jer.* 5:14]. 'The Word in the mouth of the Lord's prophet-witnesses may be scorned but it is not an empty sound. Its judgments are fire that devours its enemies' (Lenski).

6: These have the power to shut the heaven, that it rain not during the days of their prophecy: and they have power over the waters to turn them into blood, and to smite the earth with every plague, as often as they shall desire.

These witnesses also have the same power as Elijah to shut the heavens to prevent rain during the time of their prophecy [*1 Kings* 17:1]. And like Moses they can also turn water into blood and inflict whatever plague they wish [*Exod.* 7:20–25]. John's purpose here may be to express 'the truth that God's servants in the new dispensation have just as great resources as did Moses and Elijah in the old' [Morris].

7: And when they shall have finished their testimony, the beast that cometh up out of the abyss shall make war with them, and overcome them, and kill them.

The witnesses are immortal until they have completed their testimony, but at the end of the period determined by God they are killed by the beast that 'comes up' from the abyss [13:1; 17:8]. The present tense of the verb points to a permanent attribute of the beast, for the abyss is the place of its origin and the source of its power [9:1]. The beast appears to represent those antichristian powers in the world which seek to silence the church's witness. However, the fact that the beast finally prevails over the two witnesses does not mean that the whole church will be martyred. John's intention is to show that the church will experience increasing opposition from the power of Satan, which will result 'in the apparent triumph of the forces of evil. But the triumph will be brief; it will but usher in the end and the final subjugation of the devil' (Plummer).

8: And their dead bodies lie in the street of the great city, which spiritually is called Sodom and Egypt, where also their Lord was crucified.

In a display of the utmost contempt, the dead bodies of the witnesses are left unburied in the street of the great city, which is stained with the blood of all the prophets [*Matt.* 23:35; *Luke* 13:33]. Thus Jerusalem, 'where also their Lord was crucified', is that secular city which has the character of Sodom and Egypt: it is a place of uncleanness and the oppressor of the true people of God [*Isa.* 1: 9, 10; *Jer.* 23:14]. As such, it is the ignoble prototype of the great city of Babylon (which in John's day was Rome), wherein was found 'the blood of prophets and of saints, and of all that have been slain upon the earth' [18: 24].

9: And from among the peoples and tribes and tongues and nations do men look upon their dead bodies three days and a half, and suffer not their dead bodies to be laid in a tomb.

The unburied bodies of the witnesses are viewed by men of every race and nation. But the three and a half days of their humiliation are a short period compared with the three and a half years of their ministry [verse 3]. So the triumph of the ungodly is in fact very brief, though 'long enough to bear the semblance of being complete and final' (Swete).

10: And they that dwell on the earth rejoice over them, and make merry; and they shall send gifts one to another; because these two prophets tormented them that dwell on the earth.

The men of the world are jubilant at the death of the two prophets whose fearless testimony had tormented their consciences for so long [verses 4, 5; *1 Kings* 18:17]. In typical oriental fashion, they celebrate the festive occasion by sending gifts to one another [*Esther* 9:19, 22]. 'Such a sense of relief is not seldom felt by bad men when a preacher of righteousness or a signal example of goodness is removed, though good breeding may prevent outward manifestation of joy' (Swete).

11: And after the three days and a half the breath of life from God entered into them, and they stood upon their feet; and great fear fell upon them that beheld them.

But the rejoicing of the wicked was short-lived, for after the three and a half days God sent the breath of life into the dead bodies of the witnesses, and they stood upon their feet [*Ezek.* 37:10]. The spectators of their return to life were panic-stricken at the power of God thus displayed. The world has often celebrated the death of the church, only to see it rise again from the verge of extinction. 'Each such resurrection strikes consternation into the hearts of her oppressors' [Morris].

12: And they heard a great voice from heaven saying unto them, Come up hither. And they went up into heaven in the cloud; and their enemies beheld them.

A great voice then called the two witnesses to heaven, and they went up in full view of their enemies. The event John describes is clearly no secret rapture; God's vindication of his persecuted people will be visible to all. But this final triumph of the church 'has been partly anticipated in the sight of the world by the tribute paid to the victims of a persecution, sometimes within a few years after their dishonour and death . . . paganism saw the men it had hated and killed called up to heaven before its eyes' (Swete).

13: And in that hour there was a great earthquake, and the tenth part of the city fell; and there were killed in the earthquake seven thousand persons: and the rest were affrighted, and gave glory to the God of heaven.

The hour of victory for the church is the hour of judgment for the world. But here John describes only the first shock of the final catastrophe, because he is concerned to stress the terrified reaction of the rest of humanity [cf. the parallel scene in 6:15–17]. The revelation of God's irresistible might fills them with terror, and they are forced to acknowledge his sovereignty. Men will give glory to God when it is too late for them to repent. Indeed such repentance is impossible without the witness of the Word. Hence the rapture of the church is the end of all hope for the world.

14: The second Woe is past: behold, the third Woe cometh quickly.

It is surprising that the announcement of the third woe is not followed by a description of the final judgment. But the seventh trumpet 'does something greater, it pictures a scene in heaven *after* the judgment and lets us hear what the judgment signifies for God and his Christ, for the obdurate world, and for Christ's prophets and saints' (Lenski).

15: And the seventh angel sounded; and there followed great voices in heaven, and they said, The kingdom of the world is become the kingdom of our Lord, and of his Christ: and he shall reign for ever and ever.

When the seventh trumpet sounded, John heard the voices of the angelic hosts in heaven proclaiming the final triumph of the kingdom of God. They rejoice that the kingdom of the world has become the kingdom of their Lord (i.e. God) and of his Christ (i.e. 'his anointed', *Psa.* 2:2). This means that the world, which was once under the usurped dominion of Satan, has now at last passed into the hands of its true owner and king (Swete).

And he shall reign for ever and ever: Although the subject of the verb is God, the joint sovereignty of Christ is implied in the preceding phrase 'and of his Christ' (Beckwith).

16: And the four and twenty elders, who sit before God on their thrones, fell upon their faces and worshipped God,

As already noted (see comment on 4:4), the twenty-four elders are a superior order of angelic beings, and are not to be identified with the redeemed. N. B. Stonehouse observes that they refer to 'the saints' and 'them that destroy the earth' with equal detachment [verses 17, 18], and asks how one can account for this attitude, 'if we are meant to understand that the redeemed people of God, represented by the elders, are glorifying God for their own salvation?' (*Paul before the Areopagus and Other New Testament Studies*, p. 102).

17,18: saying, We give thee thanks, O Lord God, the Almighty, who art and who wast; because thou hast taken thy great power, and didst reign. And the nations were wroth, and thy wrath came, and the time of the dead to be judged, and the time to give their reward to thy servants the prophets, and to the saints, and to them that fear thy name, the small and the great; and to destroy them that destroy the earth.

The song of the elders celebrates the final victory of God, who has demonstrated his great power and entered upon his triumphant reign (NIV, RSV). It is significant that God is not here praised as the one 'who is to come' [1:8], because he has now come and decisively defeated the powers of evil. For the last fierce assault of the nations against the church has called down the wrath of God and ushered in the Day of Judgment. This is the day of *reward* for all God's people, both the small and the great, of whom the prophets are singled out for special mention. It is also the day of *retribution* for God's enemies. Those now bent on destroying the earth shall then justly be consigned to everlasting destruction. This clearly 'contradicts those who try to divide the judgment day into completely separate events' [Buis].

19: And there was opened the temple of God that is in heaven; and there was seen in his temple the ark of his covenant; and there followed lightnings, and voices, and thunders, and earthquake, and great hail.

The divine response to this praise is seen in the opening of the heavenly sanctuary to disclose the ark of the covenant, which is the visible sign that God's covenant with his people has been fulfilled. The manifestation of God's grace is followed by the awesome tokens of his majesty and power, 'the solemn salvos, so to speak, of the artillery of Heaven' (Alford).

4: THE WOMAN AND THE DRAGON
CHAPTER TWELVE

The woman with child is threatened by the dragon, but the child is taken up to God [verses 1–6]. Michael and his angels war against the dragon and victory is proclaimed in heaven [verses 7–12]. But the dragon continues to persecute the woman on earth [verses 13–17].

1: And a great sign was seen in heaven: a woman arrayed with the sun, and the moon under her feet, and upon her head a crown of twelve stars;

In this chapter we are shown the purpose which lies behind Satan's attacks upon the people of God. The great wonder John sees displayed in the sky is a woman whose appearance is dazzling. She is clothed with the sun, crowned with twelve stars and stands upon the moon. The description simply emphasizes the dignity of her position. The woman should be regarded as an ideal symbol of God's people in both dispensations. Many have noted the glaring contrast between the heavenly glory of the woman and the earthly glitter of the great harlot [17:4].

2: and she was with child; and she crieth out, travailing in birth, and in pain to be delivered.

The woman is pictured as pregnant, and she cries in anguish as she labours to give birth to her child. This cry of travail fills the Old Testament as the chosen community longs for the advent of 'the seed of the woman' [*Gen.* 3:15; *Isa.* 26:17; *Mic.* 4:9, 10; 5:2, 3]. In Scripture no sharp dividing line is drawn between the true Israel and the new

Israel, because the people of the promise are one people, whether they lived before or after the coming of Christ [*Matt.* 8:11; *Rom.* 4:16; *Gal.* 3:9].

3: And there was seen another sign in heaven: and behold, a great red dragon, having seven heads and ten horns, and upon his heads seven diadems.

The second sign John sees in the sky is a great red dragon with seven heads, which he later identifies as 'the old serpent, he that is called the Devil and Satan' [verse 9]. The red colour of the dragon symbolizes his murderous character [*John* 8:44]. On his seven heads are seven diadems, which are the symbols of his usurped dominion, while the ten horns indicate the completeness of his power over the kingdoms of the world [*Dan.* 7:7].

4: And his tail draweth the third part of the stars of heaven, and did cast them to the earth: and the dragon standeth before the woman that is about to be delivered, that when she is delivered he may devour her child.

The power of the dragon was such that the sweep of his tail was able to drag away a third of the stars of heaven and cast them to the earth [*Dan.* 8:10]. This dramatic figure has the introductory function of illustrating the destructive power of the dragon, but the main purpose of the verse is to show that this power is directed against God's Messiah. Thus the dragon stands before the woman waiting to devour her child as soon as he is born. 'The pregnant woman is the church which is pregnant with the promise of the Messiah beginning with Genesis 3:15. Satan's one aim was "to devour" or destroy this Messiah' (Lenski).

5: And she was delivered of a son, a man child, who is to rule all the nations with a rod of iron: and her child was caught up unto God, and unto his throne.

The woman gives birth to a male child, who is clearly the Lord's anointed, for he is destined to rule the nations with a rod of iron [*Psa.* 2:9; *Rev.* 19:15]. Without referring to the earthly life, John passes straight from Christ's birth to the ascension, because he wishes to stress the fact that the dragon's plan was foiled by an act of divine power. The child was caught up to God, 'and unto his throne'. These words 'are added to emphasize the completeness of Satan's failure; the

Messiah, so far from being destroyed, is caught up to a share in God's throne' (Beckwith).

6: And the woman fled into the wilderness, where she hath a place prepared of God, that there they may nourish her a thousand two hundred and threescore days.

Since the woman is now the object of the dragon's fury [verse 13], she flees to a refuge prepared by God in the wilderness, where she will be nourished for 1260 days (see comment on 11:2). The church is thus assured that she will be divinely protected and sustained throughout the short period of her testing on earth, just as the Israelites who fled from the Egyptian dragon [*Ezek.* 29:3] found safety and food in the wilderness.

7, 8: And there was war in heaven: Michael and his angels going forth to war with the dragon; and the dragon warred and his angels; and they prevailed not, neither was their place found any more in heaven.

The next scene in the drama reveals the effect of Christ's victory in heaven. Michael, as the guardian angel of God's people [*Dan.* 10:13, 21; 12:1], leads an attack upon the dragon and his angels, which results in their defeat and expulsion from heaven [*Luke* 10:18]. 'The reference here is to a definitive fall of Satan from heaven, so that he no longer has any access to God as accuser, 12:10' (W. Foerster, *TDNT*, vol. 3, p. 157). In former times Satan could enter heaven as the accuser of God's people [*Job.* 1:6–12; *Zech.* 3:1, 2], but now that the price of their redemption has been paid he can do so no longer [verse 11; *Rom.* 8:34]. But if the victory is really Christ's, why is Michael represented as the victor of the war in heaven? The answer is that Michael was only able to conquer in heaven in virtue of Christ's decisive conquest on earth [*Col.* 2:15]. G. B. Caird helpfully likens Michael to the staff officer who is able to remove Satan's flag from the heavenly map because the officer in the field has won the real victory on Calvary.

9: And the great dragon was cast down, the old serpent, he that is called the Devil and Satan, the deceiver of the whole world; he was cast down to the earth, and his angels were cast down with him.

The identity of the dragon is here put beyond all doubt. He is called:

1. *'The old serpent'*, whose first act of deceit was to beguile Eve in the garden [*Gen.* 3:1–7];
2. *'The Devil'*, [which means *'slanderer'*] because he is the calumniator of God's servants, verse 10;
3. *'Satan'* [which means *'adversary'*], because he is the great enemy of mankind;
4. *'The deceiver of the whole world'*, which is blinded by his lies [*2 Cor.* 4:4].

The ejection of Satan from heaven means that his fury is now directed against the church on earth [verse 13], but he is a defeated foe whose days are numbered and whose doom is sealed [20:10].

10: And I heard a great voice in heaven, saying, Now is come the salvation, and the power, and the kingdom of our God, and the authority of his Christ: for the accuser of our brethren is cast down, who accuseth them before our God day and night.

The great voice in heaven John hears is probably that of an angel, despite the reference to 'our brethren', for the angels are united with the redeemed in the kinship of mutual service [19:10]. The voice announces the triumph of God's salvation, power and kingdom, in which Christ has assumed his right to rule, following his enthronement in heaven [verse 5]. Nothing can now hinder the salvation of God's people, for the adversary who constantly accused them before God has been 'cast down', i.e. stripped of his power to condemn by Christ's satisfaction of the claims of divine justice on their behalf [*Rom.* 8:33, 34].

11: And they overcame him because of the blood of the Lamb, and because of the word of their testimony; and they loved not their life even unto death.

The victory of Christ's faithful witnesses is so certain that it is spoken of here as though it were already an accomplished fact. They overcame Satan by 'the blood of the Lamb', an evocative phrase which points to the redemptive power of Christ's sacrifice [1:5; 5:9; 7:14]. The power of Christ's love for them was also the source of their own fidelity to him, enabling them to remain true to 'the word of their testimony' without regard to the consequences. For they chose to die rather than deny the Lord who bought them with his blood [6:9; 11:7].

12: Therefore rejoice, O heavens, and ye that dwell in them. Woe for the earth and for the sea: because the devil is gone down unto you, having great wrath, knowing that he hath but a short time.

The angel bids the inhabitants of heaven to rejoice in the downfall of the accuser [verse 10], but warns of woe for the earth and sea because the devil has descended in great wrath. He is spurred on by the knowledge that he has only a short time in which to do his evil work [verses 6, 13, 14]. 'The troubles of the persecuted righteous arise not because Satan is too strong, but because he is beaten. He is doing all the harm he can while he can. But he will not be able to do this for much longer' [Morris].

13: And when the dragon saw that he was cast down to the earth, he persecuted the woman that brought forth the man child.

Having been cast down from heaven [verse 9], it is hardly surprising that the dragon now pursues (in order to persecute, *Exod.* 14:8; *Acts* 26:11) the woman whose Son had conquered him. 'If he cannot directly attack the Woman's Son, he can hurt the Son through the Mother [*Matt.* 25:45; *Acts* 9:4]' (Swete).

14: And there were given to the woman the two wings of the great eagle, that she might fly into the wilderness unto her place, where she is nourished for a time, and times, and half a time, from the face of the serpent.

This explains how the woman escaped from the dragon [verse 6], who is here called 'the serpent' because of the flood of lies that pours from his mouth [verses 9, 15]. As God delivered his people from the Egyptians, so the woman was borne on eagle's wings to the safety of the wilderness and nourished with food from heaven [*Exod.* 19:4; *Deut.* 32: 10, 11]. She is thus divinely preserved throughout the period of her trial, which extends from the time of Christ's enthronement [verse 5] until the judgment (so Lenski: see also comment on 11:2).

15, 16: And the serpent cast out of his mouth after the woman water as a river, that he might cause her to be carried away by the stream. And the earth helped the woman, and the earth opened her mouth and swallowed up the river which the dragon cast out of his mouth.

Although the serpent is unable to follow the woman in her flight, he sends forth a great flood of water to sweep her away, but she is rescued by the earth which swallows up the torrent. The proverbial deceit of the serpent is manifested in a stream of deadly delusions which would engulf the church if they were not providentially diverted. This river of lies is the satanic parody of the river of life which flows from the heavenly throne [21:1].

17–13:1: And the dragon waxed wroth with the woman, and went away to make war with the rest of her seed, that keep the commandments of God, and hold the testimony of Jesus: and he stood upon the sand of the sea.

The dragon was enraged at the escape of the woman, and went off to make war against the rest of her seed, who are characterized as those 'that keep the commandments of God, and maintain the testimony that Jesus bore' [1:2; *1 Tim.* 6:13]. 'If he can neither unseat the Throned Christ nor destroy the Church, yet individual Christians may enjoy no such immunity' (Swete). So the dragon stood by the seashore to summon the beast from the sea to assist him in his fierce campaign of persecution [chapter 13].

CHAPTER THIRTEEN

The beast with seven heads and ten horns which rises from the sea is given power by the dragon, and becomes the object of an idolatrous worship [verses 1–6]. He persecutes the saints, and is assisted by the beast that emerges from the earth, which kills all who will not receive the mark of the first beast [verses 7–18].

1b: And I saw a beast coming up out of the sea, having ten horns and seven heads, and on his horns ten diadems, and upon his heads names of blasphemy.

At the behest of the dragon [verse la], there appeared a terrible beast rising up from the sea, whose chaotic depths are the abode of demonic powers [11:7; *Dan.* 7:2–8]. The dragon's deputy is like the dragon, for it also has ten horns and seven heads [12:3]. It represents the persecuting power of human government, first as manifested in the Roman Empire, and later to be realized in full in the reign of Antichrist. The ten horns with ten diadems symbolize the ten kings who will be the allies of Antichrist in the final conflict [17:12–14]. The titles of blasphemy written on the seven heads clearly point to the divine honours assumed by the Roman emperors, which culminated in Domitian's demand that he be addressed as 'our Lord and God'.

2: And the beast which I saw was like unto a leopard, and his feet were as the feet of a bear, and his mouth as the mouth of a lion: and the dragon gave him his power, and his throne, and great authority.

This beast combined the characteristics of the first three beasts of *Dan.* 7:4–6 together with the horns of the fourth beast [*Dan.* 7:7, 8] and was thus the summation of the evil powers manifested in successive world empires. But it was the dragon which gave the beast such power. 'The Dragon works through the Beast as his agent; the war is of Satan's making, but the Empire is his tool for waging it' (Swete).

3: And I saw one of his heads as though it had been smitten unto death; and his death-stroke was healed: and the whole earth wondered after the beast;

In a parody of the death and resurrection of the Lamb [5:6], the mortal wound received by the beast in one of its heads was healed. This probably refers to Nero, whose notoriety as the arch-persecutor of God's people made him the fit symbol of Antichrist, the last incarnation of evil (see the further comments on 17:8–13). Nero's suicide in AD 68 seemed to be the death of the beast as a persecuting power. But the fact that this wound was healed shows that the beast's capacity 'to make war with the saints' [verse 7] was soon renewed. Nero's death had been followed by a series of political upheavals which threatened to destroy the empire, but when it was rescued from ruin by Vespasian (AD 69–79), the whole world wondered at the recuperative power of the beast. 'The vitality of the pagan empire, shown in this power of righting itself after the revolution, only added to its prestige. The infatuation of loyalty, expressing itself in the worship of the emperor as the personal embodiment of the empire, grew worse and worse' (Moffatt).

4: and they worshipped the dragon, because he gave his authority unto the beast; and they worshipped the beast, saying, Who is like unto the beast? and who is able to war with him?

As the authority of the beast came from the dragon, those who worshipped the beast also worshipped the evil power which was behind it. John thus equates the imperial cult with the worship of Satan. The praise given to the beast is a parody of the true worship of God [*Exod.* 15:11]. The second question reflects the crisis facing the churches of Asia Minor when John wrote this book, for Domitian (AD 81–96) was the first emperor to demand that his subjects should worship him as 'Lord and God'.

5: And there was given to him a mouth speaking great things and blasphemies; and there was given to him authority to continue forty and two months.

The blasphemous pretensions of the Roman emperors are only the first stage in the beast's career, which is to continue for 'forty and two months', i.e. throughout the period of the church's witness [*Dan.* 7:8, 25; see also comment on 11: 2]. It was the dragon who gave the beast power and authority [verses 2, 4], but the repeated passive ('was given') indicates that the beast always remains under the control of God [verses 5, 7]. The saints are thus assured that the power of evil is not absolute. For not only has God set a limit upon it, but he will even make it contribute to the final good of his people [*Rom.* 8:28].

6: And he opened his mouth for blasphemies against God, to blaspheme his name, and his tabernacle, even them that dwell in the heaven.

The beast opens his mouth to blaspheme against God's name and his tabernacle, which is identified with those 'that dwell in heaven'. This either denotes 'the heavenly host', or the church viewed ideally as seated in heaven [*Eph.* 2:6]. If 'tabernacle' is understood in the light of 21:3, 'The tabernacle of God is with men, and he shall dwell with them', then the phrase will refer to God's faithful people on earth, whose 'citizenship is in heaven' [*Phil.* 3:20]. This means that God regards the persecution of those who bear his name as a blasphemy which is directed against him.

7: And it was given unto him to make war with the saints, and to overcome them: and there was given to him authority over every tribe and people and tongue and nation.

The beast was also allowed to make war with the saints and overcome them [*Dan.* 7:21]. He was given the power to persecute and kill the saints, but not to overcome their faith. Thus the beast enjoys only an apparent success; the real victory belongs to the saints who remain faithful unto death [12:11]. The fourfold enumeration in the second part of the verse emphasizes the universal authority granted to the beast. 'Wherever the Gospel was carried, Rome was there beforehand; the Beast's authority extended over all the nations and races which surrounded the Mediterranean' (Swete).

8: And all that dwell on the earth shall worship him, every one whose name hath not been written from the foundation of the world in the book of life of the Lamb that hath been slain.

Every one whose name hath not been written in the book of life of the Lamb that hath been slain from the foundation of the world [ASV margin]: All the (unbelieving) inhabitants of the earth will join in the worship of the beast, because their names have not been written in the Lamb's book of life [21:27]. The plain inference is that those who are enrolled in that heavenly register will refuse to bow to the beast. Although 17:8 supports the ASV text, it is more natural here to connect 'from the foundation of the world' with 'slain' rather than with 'written', as in the ASV margin cited above. In the eternal purpose of God, Christ is the Lamb who has been slain from the foundation of the world [*1 Pet.* 1:20]. Those whose names are written in the Lamb's book of life are those for whom he died. Thus election to eternal life also includes the means of redemption.

9, 10: If any man hath an ear, let him hear. If any man is for captivity, into captivity he goeth: if any man shall kill with the sword, with the sword must he be killed. Here is the patience and the faith of the saints.

The repetition of the formula that occurs at the end of each of the letters to the seven churches here introduces a solemn charge to the readers [2:7, etc.]. The first couplet points to the inevitability of the forthcoming test of their fidelity. If any man is destined for captivity, then he must be willing to accept it in a spirit of humble submission [*Jer.* 15:2]. The second couplet warns them against the folly of resorting to force, and recalls the saying of Jesus: 'All that take the sword shall perish with the sword' [*Matt.* 26:52]. To meet the persecution inflicted by the beast in this spirit demonstrates the steadfast endurance and unwavering faith of the saints.

11: And I saw another beast coming up out of the earth; and he had two horns like unto a lamb, and he spake as a dragon.

John next saw arising from the earth another beast, whose harmless appearance was betrayed by its roaring voice [*Matt.* 7:15]. For though it looked like a lamb, it spoke like a dragon. This beast, which is later called 'the false prophet' [16:13; 19:20; 20:10], represents false religion as the servant of the secular power. In John's day the beast operated through the priests who acted as the propagandists of the Caesar-cult by aping a spiritual power which they did not possess in the interests of a persecuting state.

12: And he exerciseth all the authority of the first beast in his sight. And he maketh the earth and them that dwell therein to worship the first beast, whose death-stroke was healed.

The second beast has all the authority of the first beast and exercises it with his approval ('in his sight'). This is because the sole aim of the second beast is to make all men worship the first beast, 'whose death-stroke was healed' (see comment on verse 3). 'The true prophet lives in the presence of God, taking his orders from Him and doing His pleasure; the False Prophet stands before the Beast, whose interpreter and servant he is' (Swete).

13: And he doeth great signs, that he should even make fire to come down out of heaven upon the earth in the sight of men.

The false prophet authenticates his mission of deceit by means of pseudo-miracles, and in a parody of true spiritual power even makes fire come down from heaven for the admiration of his dupes [*Deut.* 13:1; *1 Kings* 18:38; *Matt.* 24:24; *Rev.* 11:5]. Such trickery was practised by all the religious charlatans of the day, and the apparent miracle of producing fire from heaven was evidently used by the priests of the imperial cult to persuade men to worship the emperor's image [verses 14, 15].

14, 15: And he deceiveth them that dwell on the earth by reason of the signs which it was given him to do in the sight of the beast; saying to

them that dwell on the earth, that they should make an image to the beast who hath the stroke of the sword and lived. And it was given unto him to give breath to it, even to the image of the beast, that the image of the beast should both speak, and cause that as many as should not worship the image of the beast should be killed.

The second beast was given the power to deceive 'them that dwell on the earth', i.e. the unbelieving world [6:10]. He instructs the people to make an image of the beast that recovered from the stroke of the sword [verse 3]. And he was given the power to animate the idol, which not only spoke, but also demanded the death of all who refused to worship it. In the ancient world statues were regarded as the natural means by which gods could have intercourse with their worshippers and were accredited with the power of working miracles (Charles). There is good reason to believe that the trick of making the statue of the emperor speak was well within the power of the imperial priesthood, for similar ventriloquism was practised by the priests of the oriental cults. ' "Might is right" is the motto of worldliness; "Right is might" is the motto of faith, and those who hold it cannot worship the beast, even though the stroke of his death-wound is healed. Men have appealed to lying miracles on behalf of a death-wounded creed: the cleverness of self-interested partisanship is seldom barren of imposing expedients' (Carpenter).

16,17: And he causeth all, the small and the great, and the rich and the poor, and the free and the bond, that there be given them a mark on their right hand, or upon their forehead; and that no man should be able to buy or to sell, save he that hath the mark, even the name of the beast or the number of his name.

In a parody of the sealing of the redeemed [7:3], the second beast demands that universal allegiance be given to the first beast and forces all to receive the mark of the monster. Although this was a visible mark in the vision, there is no need to imagine that the emperor's worshippers were literally stamped with the number of his name [verse 18]. To receive the mark is to partake of the character of the beast, but as believers are identified with a very different image, they would easily be distinguished from the beast's followers. It would seem that the Christians in Smyrna were already subject to economic sanctions because of their faith [2:9]. Here the purpose of the boycott is to bring them to the notice of the imperial authorities so that none should escape (Charles).

18: Here is wisdom. He that hath understanding, let him count the number of the beast; for it is the number of a man: and his number is Six hundred and sixty six.

The announcement, 'Here is wisdom', is followed by the call to the man of understanding to calculate the number of the beast: it is the number of a man and his number is 666. In Hebrew and Greek the letters of the alphabet were used as numerical symbols, so that a name could be equated with the number which consisted of the sum of its letters, e.g. Jesus = 888. It has been shown that when Nero Caesar is rendered into Hebrew it yields the required number 666, and this strongly suggests that the identification first arose among believers who spoke Hebrew or Aramaic [cf. 'Maranatha', *1 Cor.* 16:22]. John's readers were probably acquainted with this tradition, and the use of such a code would have protected them from further charges of subversion against the state. There is additional significance in the number itself, for each digit of 666 falls short of the perfect number 7. Moreover, the contrast between 666 and 888 shows the gulf which separates the Devil's 'Christ' from God's Christ (see G. R. Beasley-Murray's excellent exposition).

CHAPTER FOURTEEN

John sees the Lamb with the 144, 000 who have been sealed and hears the song of the redeemed [verses 1–5]. Three angels announce the nearness of the end, the fall of Babylon and the doom of the beast's worshippers [verses 6–11]. The faithful who die in the Lord are promised blessing and rest [verses 12, 13]. Two visions depict the harvest of the earth and the winepress of God's wrath [verses 14–20].

1: And I saw, and behold, the Lamb standing on the mount Zion, and with him a hundred and forty and four thousand, having his name, and the name of his Father, written on their foreheads.

The grim scenes of the previous chapter are now followed by a vision of glorious hope. John saw the victorious Lamb standing on the heavenly Mount Zion with 144,000, a figure which signifies the whole company of the redeemed (see comment on 7:4). This means that all the sealed were saved; not one of the elect was lost. The seal on the foreheads of the chosen is here shown to consist of the name of the Lamb and that of his Father [7:3]. 'These two names are the seal because no man comes to the Father save by the Son' [*John* 14:6]' (Lenski).

2: And I heard a voice from heaven, as the voice of many waters, and as the voice of a great thunder: and the voice which I heard was as the voice of harpers harping with their harps:

The voice [or sound] which John heard from heaven made such an impression upon him that he uses three similes to describe it. It was like the roar of many waters; it was as loud as a peal of thunder, and its entrancing melody resembled the music made by many harpists. This is the song of redemption which can only be sung by those who have experienced its joys [verse 3].

3: and they sing as it were a new song before the throne, and before the four living creatures and the elders: and no man could learn the song save the hundred and forty and four thousand, even they that had been purchased out of the earth.

As it were a new song: 'Not actually new, It is the old, old song of redemption which is their theme. But their circumstances are so changed that it is sung with new joy, and through endless ages it will be ever new. Only those can learn this song who are redeemed from the earth. It befits only the Church of God; and not only is their position clearly defined, but their character is definitely given [verse 4]' (Clemance).

4: These are they that were not defiled with women; for they are virgins. These are they that follow the Lamb whithersoever he goeth. These were purchased from among men, to be the first-fruits unto God and unto the Lamb.

The virginity of the 144,000 must be understood symbolically of their complete separation from the pollution of idolatry. They kept their spiritual chastity by resisting the seductions of the great harlot [17:2; *2 Cor.* 11: 2]. They are free of impurity because they did not worship the beast and his image [13:15]. Such a capitulation to the powers of evil was ruled out by their commitment to Christ. It was their habit on earth to render implicit obedience to the Lamb, for, as the purchase of his passion, they knew themselves to be wholly consecrated to God and to their Saviour. Since the 144,000 are the totality of the redeemed, 'firstfruits' cannot here mean that there are more to follow, but carries the more usual sense of an offering to God (see Charles, vol. 2, p. 6).

5: And in their mouth was found no lie: they are without blemish.

More is meant than simple honesty, for unlike the pagan world 'which exchanged the truth of God for a lie' [*Rom.* 1:25], the 144,000 had rejected the deceit of the beast and cast Satan's lie behind them [21:27; 22:15; *John* 8:44; *1 John* 2:21, 22]. The last thing that John says about the condition of the redeemed in glory is that they are without blemish and without fault. 'Their being without fault is but the completion of a work which was going on here; it is a receiving the last finishing touch and impress of the Spirit's seal. That last impress stamped out the marks of the last sin' (Clemance).

6, 7: And I saw another angel flying in mid heaven, having eternal good tidings to proclaim unto them that dwell on the earth, and unto every nation and tribe and tongue and people; and he saith with a great voice, Fear God, and give him glory; for the hour of his judgment is come: and worship him that made the heaven and the earth and sea and fountains of waters.

After this anticipation of the bliss of the redeemed [verses 1–5], three angels appear to warn of the approaching judgment [verses 6–11]. It is important to realize that John saw a series of visions which were intended to convey an intelligible message that was permanently valid. Hence it is a mistake to become preoccupied with the bizarre details of the visions to the detriment of the clear declarations they contain. There is no need for any angel to fly in mid-heaven at some future date, for the warning thus conveyed to the world through John holds good to the end of the age. In contrast to the beast's empty claim to universal dominion, the everlasting sovereignty of the Creator of the world is indeed 'eternal good tidings' to those with reverent and submissive hearts. The angelic summons is not a preaching of *the* gospel [the Greek lacks the article], but is a call to the earth's inhabitants to awake to the reality of God's rule before it is too late [*Acts* 14:15].

8: And another, a second angel, followed, saying, Fallen, fallen, is Babylon the great, that hath made all the nations to drink of the wine of the wrath of her fornication.

The second angel announces the fall of Babylon [*Jer.* 51:7]. The image is a fit symbol of human society organized against God, and to the early Christians new Rome was but old Babylon writ large [*1 Pet.* 5:13]. Here the prophetic past tense points to the certainty of the judgment which is vividly portrayed in chapter 18. Two ideas are combined in the phrase, 'the wine of the wrath of her fornication'. Babylon is represented as the great harlot who intoxicates the nations with the wine of her fornication [17:2, 4, 6], but God will punish these infidelities by making her drain the cup of his wrath [verse 10; 16:19; *Jer.* 25:15].

9, 10: And another angel, a third, followed them, saying with a great voice, If any man worshippeth the beast and his image, and receiveth a mark on his forehead, or upon his hand, he also shall drink of the wine of the wrath of God, which is prepared unmixed in the cup of his anger; and he shall be tormented with fire and brimstone in the presence of the holy angels, and in the presence of the Lamb:

The third angel warns of the terrible punishment which will befall any man who worships the beast and receives his mark. He shall drink of the wine of God's wrath, which is 'mingled unmixed' [ASV margin] in the cup of his anger. The first word of this paradoxical phrase refers to the ancient practice of mixing wine with spices to make it more powerful; the second word means that its strength is not diluted by the addition of water. To drink the cup of God's wrath involves being tormented with fire and brimstone in the presence of the holy angels and of the Lamb [19:20; 20:10; 21:8]. This suggests that the most poignant factor in the pain of the wicked will be to see 'the triumph of the Lamb, against whom as worshippers of the Beast they had made war' (Beckwith).

11: and the smoke of their torment goeth up for ever and ever; and they have no rest day and night, they that worship the beast and his image, and whoso receiveth the mark of his name.

The phrase 'for ever and ever' is predicated of God in 4:9, and this means that the torment of the beast's followers is as endless as God himself (Anthony Hoekema). Had John wished to convey the impression that the punishment of the wicked was only of limited duration, he could hardly have chosen a more misleading phrase to describe it! However, their punishment is endless because their guilt is endless. 'The demand that penal suffering shall stop when it has once begun, is as irrational as the demand that guilt shall stop when it has once begun. The *continuous* nature of guilt necessitates the endlessness of retribution' (Shedd, *Dogmatic Theology*, vol. 2, p. 722).

12: Here is the patience of the saints, they that keep the commandments of God, and the faith of Jesus.

Since such a judgment will overtake the worshippers of the beast, John issues a call to the saints to exhibit that patient endurance which consists in keeping the commandments of God and trusting in Jesus. Those with a living faith in Jesus would rather die than be disloyal to their Lord. 'The Caesar-cult supplied the saints with a test of loyalty which strengthened and matured those who were worthy of the name' (Swete).

13: And I heard a voice from heaven saying, Write, Blessed are the dead who die in the Lord from henceforth: yea, saith the Spirit, that they may rest from their labours; for their works follow with them.

John then heard a voice from heaven instructing him to write down an important message which promises blessedness to all who die in the Lord 'from henceforth'. This final phrase does not deny the same blessedness to saints who died previously, but is added to bring special comfort to those who would soon be required to seal their testimony with their blood. But though the message is here applied to the particular crisis that faced the church of John's day, the assurance thus given belongs to believers in every age. This promise is confirmed and further explained by an emphatic utterance of the Spirit. For the blessedness of those who die in union with the Lord consists not only in rest from their exhausting toil, but also in the enjoyment of their works of faith which follow them to heaven [2:2]. No labour for the Lord is ever lost [*1 Cor.* 15:5 8].

14: And I saw, and behold, a white cloud; and on the cloud I saw one sitting like unto a son of man, having on his head a golden crown, and in his hand a sharp sickle.

John next saw the advent in judgment of one 'like unto a son of man', sitting on a white cloud and wearing a golden crown [*Dan.* 7:13]. This description could apply to no one but Christ. He is holding a sharp sickle in readiness to reap the harvest of the earth [verse 15]. As the harvest is the end of the world, that which is reaped should not be restricted to the righteous only. 'The figure is comprehensive, including in a word the whole process of the winding up of the ages, and the recompense of both the good and the bad' (Beckwith).

15, 16: And another angel came out from the temple, crying with a great voice to him that sat on the cloud, Send forth thy sickle, and reap: for the hour to reap is come; for the harvest of the earth is ripe. And he that sat on the cloud cast his sickle upon the earth; and the earth was reaped.

Some have felt it inappropriate that an angel should convey a command to Christ, but this objection overlooks the fact that the angel is sent from the temple by God. 'The angel acts as the messenger of the will of God to Christ in his capacity as Son of man, because the command is one concerning the times and seasons which the Father hath kept in his own power' (Plummer). It is remarkable that mere men should still presume to predict the time of the end when even Christ cannot reap the harvest of the earth until the moment determined by God [*Mark* 13:32; *Acts* 1: 7].

17: And another angel came out from the temple which is in heaven, he also having a sharp sickle.

The general picture of the last judgment given in the previous vision is now followed by a gruesome close-up of the effect of God's vengeance upon the wicked [verses 17–20]. The appearance of another angel from the heavenly temple is significant, for it shows that he is the agent of God's judgment. He also wields a sharp sickle for his task of reaping the vintage of the earth [*Joel* 3:13].

18: And another angel came out from the altar, he that hath power over fire; and he called with a great voice to him that had the sharp sickle,

saying, Send forth thy sharp sickle, and gather the clusters of the vine of the earth; for her grapes are fully ripe.

There now appears on the scene yet another angel. This one comes from the altar and has power over fire, which presumably means the fire of judgment. 'He comes from the altar, upon which was offered the incense accompanying the prayers of the saints for judgment' (Beckwith). It is in response to those prayers that he instructs the angel with the sharp sickle to cut down the clusters from the vine of the earth, for its grapes are at last fully ripe for judgment [6:9; 8: 3].

19: And the angel cast his sickle into the earth, and gathered the vintage of the earth, and cast it into the winepress, the great winepress, of the wrath of God.

The angel at once obeyed and gathered the vintage of the earth, and cast it into the great winepress of God's wrath. Here the primitive method of treading the grapes to extract their juice becomes a graphic symbol of the fierceness of the divine anger [19:1 5; *Isa.* 63:3].

20: And the winepress was trodden without the city, and there came out blood from the winepress, even unto the bridles of the horses, as far as a thousand and six hundred furlongs.

The judgment is depicted as taking place 'without the city', which probably refers to the exclusion of the wicked from the society of the redeemed [20:9]. The universality of the judgment is indicated by a ghastly image. The red juice of the grape pours from an ordinary winepress, but a sea of blood flows from this winepress, and reaches as high as the bridles of horses and extends as far as 1600 stadia. The number is again symbolic, and is derived from the square of 4 (the number of the earth, 7:1) multiplied by the square of 10 (the number of completeness). It thus signifies 'completeness as regards the created world, and the inability of anyone to escape God's judgment' (Plummer).

5: THE SEVEN BOWLS OF WRATH

CHAPTER FIFTEEN

After a vision of seven angels holding the last seven plagues, John saw those who had overcome the beast singing the song of Moses and of the Lamb [verses 1–4]. The seven angels then came forth from the heavenly temple with the seven bowls of God's wrath [verses 5 –8].

1: And I saw another sign in heaven, great and marvellous, seven angels having seven plagues, which are the last, for in them is finished the wrath of God.

As the previous chapter closed with another account of the end, it is evident that the events portrayed in these visions are not presented in chronological order. Hence it seems best to regard the cycles of judgment represented by the seals, the trumpets and the bowls as covering the same period in history from three different viewpoints. This verse stands as the frontispiece to what follows, for John introduces the seven angels as if they were all present at one moment, when in fact he sees their actions in succession. The entire vision [chs. 15, 16] is a great and marvellous portent because the wrath of God reaches its goal in the end-time judgments which are symbolized by these last seven plagues.

2: And I saw as it were a sea of glass mingled with fire; and them that come off victorious from the beast, and from his image, and from the number of his name, standing by the sea of glass, having harps of God.

John first saw what looked like 'a sea of glass' in 4:6, where it represents God's transcendence, but here it is 'mingled with fire', to show that God's wrath is about to fall upon the persecutors of his saints [8:5]. The conquerors of the beast are those who have not worshipped his image nor received as a mark the number of his name [13:14–18]. Having safely emerged from their time of trial, they now stand on the crystal pavement of heaven, holding harps to accompany their hymn of grateful praise to God [verses 3, 4].

3,4: And they sing the song of Moses the servant of God, and the song of the Lamb, saying, Great and marvellous are thy works, O Lord God, the Almighty; righteous and true are thy ways, thou King of the ages. Who shall not fear, O Lord, and glorify thy name? For thou only art holy; for all the nations shall come and worship before thee; for thy righteous acts have been made manifest.

Although they sing one song of praise to God, it is called the song of Moses and the song of the Lamb, because the deliverance God wrought through his servant Moses foreshadowed that which he wrought through the Lamb. The continuity of God's saving purpose in both dispensations means that the Old Testament phrases which make up the hymn can be applied to the greater exodus which he accomplished through Christ [*Exod.* 15:1–18]. Verse 3 celebrates the great and marvellous works of Almighty God; all his ways are righteous and true, as befits the King whose sovereignty spans the ages [*Psa.* 139:14; *Amos* 4:13; *Deut.* 32:4; *Jer.* 10: 10]. The challenge of verse 4, 'Who shall not fear, O Lord, and glorify thy name?' [*Jer.* 10:7], is followed by three clauses giving the reasons for paying this tribute of praise to God.

1. *God is the Holy One*, who is unapproachably great [*Psa.* 99:3].
2. *His universal dominion* must lead to universal homage [*Psa.* 86:9].
3. *The righteousness of his judicial sentences* is now manifest to all [*Psa.* 98:2]. 'The teaching of Scripture is that in the end the whole universe shall acknowledge the righteousness of all God's acts and verdicts' (Lenski).

5, 6: And after these things I saw, and the temple of the tabernacle of the testimony in heaven was opened: and there came out from the temple the seven angels that had the seven plagues, arrayed with precious stone, pure and bright, and girt about their breasts with golden girdles.

After hearing this song [verses 3, 4], John saw the heavenly temple opened and there came out the seven angels with the seven plagues. Here the temple is called 'the tabernacle of the testimony' [*Exod.* 38:21], because that tent 'contained the ark with the law of God which testifies against sin' [Vincent]. As nothing but sin calls forth God's wrath, his punitive judgments must be recognized as the just recompense of man's sinfulness. The celestial purity of these angels is indicated by their dress. They were clothed in 'pure bright linen, and their breasts girded with golden girdles' (RSV). The ASV follows the harder reading advocated by Westcott and Hort, but 'stone' makes no sense here and must be rejected as a transcriptional error [see Metzger, *A Textual Commentary on the Greek New Testament*, p. 756].

7: And one of the four living creatures gave unto the seven angels seven golden bowls full of the wrath of God, who liveth for ever and ever.

One of the angelic throne-attendants (see comment on 4:6) acts as an intermediary in giving the avenging angels the seven bowls which were full of the wrath of God (Robert Mounce). The fact that God 'liveth for ever and ever' means that his promised judgments are no idle threats, but a dreadful reality which the wicked will soon experience in full measure.

8: And the temple was filled with smoke from the glory of God, and from his power; and none was able to enter into the temple, till the seven plagues of the seven angels should be finished.

The smoke that filled the temple was the symbol of the glory and power of God [*Exod.* 40:34; *Isa.* 6:4]. It was also the sign of the imminence of his judgments. 'Smouldering fires of indignation are now on the point of bursting into punishment from the arsenal of anger. Hence, till the plagues are over, God's presence is unendurable' [Moffatt].

CHAPTER SIXTEEN

The seven angels are commanded to empty the bowls of God's wrath upon the earth, and the plagues which follow reach their climax in the destruction of Babylon [verses 1–21].

1: And I heard a great voice out of the temple, saying to the seven angels, Go ye, and pour out the seven bowls of the wrath of God into the earth.

As no one could enter the temple until the seven plagues were finished [15:8], it would seem that the great voice John heard from the temple was that of God himself. Although the angels have received the seven bowls of wrath [15:7], they must await the command of God before they can pour them out. The contents of the bowls are very similar to the woes announced by the trumpets. The plagues in both series recall those that fell upon Egypt before the exodus, and cover the same period in history terminating with the last judgment day.

2: And the first went, and poured out his bowl into the earth; and it became a noisome and grievous sore upon the men that had the mark of the beast, and that worshipped his image.

The first plague of foul and malignant sores is like the Egyptian plague of boils [*Exod.* 9:9–11], and is a fitting punishment for those who had received the mark of the beast. 'The victims of the scourge are declared to be the worshippers of the Beast; that this is true of the other plagues is clear, though not expressly stated' (Beckwith).

3,4: And the second poured out his bowl into the sea; and it became blood as of a dead man; and every living soul died, even the things that were in the sea. And the third poured out his bowl into the rivers and the fountains of the waters; and it became blood.

The second plague turns the sea into blood and destroys all marine life, while the third also turns the sources of fresh water into blood [*Exod.* 7:17–21]. The judgment of the second and third bowls is total, whereas that of the second and third trumpets was only partial [8:8–11].

5,6: And I heard the angel of the waters saying, Righteous art thou, who art and who wast, thou Holy One, because thou didst thus judge: for they poured out the blood of saints and prophets, and blood hast thou given them to drink: they are worthy.

John next heard the angel in charge of the waters acknowledge the righteousness of God's judgment in turning them into blood. 'The spirit of the waters is so far from resenting the plague that he bears witness to the justice which inflicts it' (Swete). It is because God is righteous, eternal and holy that he has made the punishment fit the crime (on the omission of 'who is to come', see comment on 11:17). As the worshippers of the beast poured out the blood of saints and prophets, so God has given them blood to drink. 'They are worthy' means 'They have their deserts!' (NEB).

7: And I heard the altar saying, Yea, O Lord God, the Almighty, true and righteous are thy judgments.

The altar is here said to speak because it is associated with the martyrs' plea for vindication in 6:9. 'The altar beneath which the souls of the martyrs cried, and on which the prayers of saints were offered, is represented as confirming the testimony to the just dealings of God' (Carpenter).

8, 9: And the fourth poured out his bowl upon the sun; and it was given unto it to scorch men with fire. And men were scorched with great heat:

and they blasphemed the name of God who hath the power over these plagues; and they repented not to give him glory.

Whereas the fourth trumpet had reduced the power of the sun by a third [8:12], the fourth bowl so increased its intensity that men were scorched with the excessive heat. But though they clearly saw the hand of God in this and the other plagues, they not only refused to repent but were further hardened and blasphemed the name of God. 'The members of the kingdom of evil are characterized by willing, wilful, and intense hatred of God and holiness, and by an impenitent and blaspheming spirit' (Shedd).

10, 11: And the fifth poured out his bowl upon the throne of the beast; and his kingdom was darkened; and they gnawed their tongues for pain, and they blasphemed the God of heaven because of their pains and their sores; and they repented not their works.

As the fifth plague is poured out upon the throne of the beast, his kingdom is plunged into darkness and his subjects gnaw their tongues in pain [*Exod.* 10:21–23]. They have preferred darkness to light, and now that dreadful choice is confirmed as the darkness of God's anger overwhelms them with anguish. But far from confessing their guilt, they cursed the God of heaven for the spiritual and physical torments, and would not repent of their works. Now where there is no acknowledgement of God's justice, there can be no experience of his mercy. 'Accordingly, in all the Biblical descriptions of the lost, the absence of sorrow for sin as related to justice, and the hatred of justice itself, are invariable elements. Satan and his angels, together with condemned men, are utterly and malignantly impenitent' (Shedd).

12: And the sixth poured out his bowl upon the great river, the river Euphrates; and the water thereof was dried up, that the way might be made ready for the kings that come from the sunrising.

The sixth bowl prepares the way for the final conflict by drying up the river Euphrates to allow the kings from the east (literally, 'from the sunrising') to advance on Rome (Babylon). This apparently alludes to the contemporary belief that a revived Nero would return from the east with the dreaded Parthian hordes to ravage the empire. What follows shows that Nero will indeed return – not literally, but in the shape of that persecuting ruler who will be the last opponent of the people of God (see comments on 17:8–11). Here the kings from the east represent the Parthian provincial governors, who are probably to be identified with the ten kings of 17:12, 13.

13,14: And I saw coming out of the mouth of the dragon, and out of the mouth of the beast, and out of the mouth of the false prophet, three unclean spirits, as it were frogs: for they are spirits of demons, working signs; which go forth unto the kings of the whole world, to gather them together unto the war of the great day of God, the Almighty.

John sees three unclean spirits that look like frogs coming out of the *mouths* of the dragon (Satan, 12:3), the beast (world power, 13:1) and the false prophet (false religion, 13:11). The fact that these demonic spirits proceed from the mouths of this unholy trinity indicates the nature of their task. As the lying spirit enticed Ahab into battle [*1 Kings* 22:21–23], so they are sent forth with deceitful words and signs to persuade the kings of the world to join in the great final battle [19:11–21]. But though the unclean spirits thus gather the world rulers against the Lord and his anointed [*Psa.* 2:2], they fail to understand that their preparations only pave the way for 'the great day of God, the Almighty'.

15: (Behold, I come as a thief. Blessed is he that watcheth, and keepeth his garments, lest he walk naked, and they see his shame.)

It is entirely appropriate that Christ should interject a warning at this point concerning the unexpectedness of his coming [3:3; *Matt.* 24:43; *2 Pet.* 3:10]. 'Blessed are they who are ready, watching. But vigilance is not enough: the garments must be kept. The powers of evil are abroad. Sloth and pleasure may counsel ease, and tempt the watcher to lay aside his garments and take rest and sleep. The earnest watcher desires, like Paul, to be found in Christ, clad in the true righteousness of faith [*Phil.* 3:9]' (Carpenter) [3:18].

16: And they gathered them together into the place which is called in Hebrew Har-Magedon.

The unclean spirits fulfilled their mission by gathering the kings together at Har-Magedon. The fact that no translation of the Hebrew word is supplied should alert us to its symbolic significance. The word means 'Mountain of Megiddo', and this presents a serious difficulty as there is no mountain on the plain of Megiddo. Beckwith suggests that 'mountain' may have been drawn from *Ezek.* 38:8–21; 39:2, 4, 17, where the last battle takes place on 'the mountains of Israel', and then 'Megiddo' was added because of its fame as the place where Jehovah's enemies perished [*Judg.* 5:19, 31]. Hence the name represents an event rather than a recognizable geographical location. Har-Magedon is then 'an imaginary name for designating the scene of the great battle between Antichrist and the Messiah' (Beckwith) [19:11–21].

17: And the seventh poured out his bowl upon the air; and there came forth a great voice out of the temple, from the throne, saying, It is done :

The pouring out of the seventh bowl upon the air is followed by a storm and an earthquake of unexampled severity [verse 18]. The voice of God is again heard coming from the throne of the temple, saying, 'It is done' [see verse 1]. The declaration marks the end of God's judgments and the accomplishment of his purpose.

18: and there were lightnings, and voices, and thunders; and there was a great earthquake, such as was not since there were men upon the earth, so great an earthquake, so mighty.

The appalling portents of God's wrath in the sky are accompanied by the most devastating earthquake the world has ever known. 'Writing in a century remarkable for the number and severity of its earthquakes, and to men whose country was specially subject to them, St John is careful to distinguish this final shock from even the greatest hitherto known' (Swete).

19: And the great city was divided into three parts, and the cities of the nations fell: and Babylon the great was remembered in the sight of God, to give unto her the cup of the wine of the fierceness of his wrath.

The earthquake brought about the complete disintegration of the great city ('split into three'), and it also destroyed the cities of the nations, thus bringing antichristian civilization to an end. It is because the great city of Babylon (Rome) made the whole earth drunk with 'the wine of her fornication' [17:2] that she is now made to drink 'the wine of the fierceness of his wrath'. God appeared to have forgotten the great city during the time that she filled up the cup of her iniquities, but when judgment strikes at last, it becomes clear that God has not forgotten her offences.

20: And every island fled away, and the mountains were not found.

The completeness of the destruction is indicated by the disappearance of every island and mountain. 'No city, even on the most remote island, no fortress of the antichristian empire on a single mountain height escaped the destructive final wrath' (Lenski).

21: And great hail, every stone about the weight of a talent, cometh down out of heaven upon men: and men blasphemed God because of the plague of the hail; for the plague thereof is exceeding great.

The dreadful effusion of God's wrath reaches its climax in a plague of hailstones so huge that they weighed about a hundred pounds each. Yet even this terrible visitation fails to move the wicked to repentance. 'Even Pharaoh had shown signs of repentance under the hail [*Exod.* 9:27], though he relapsed into impenitence as soon as it had ceased; but the age of the last plague blasphemed while it suffered' (Swete).

6: THE FALL OF BABYLON

CHAPTER SEVENTEEN

John is first shown the harlot, Babylon the great, who is drunk with the blood of the saints [verses 1–6]. The angel then explains that the woman represents Rome, and that the beast and his allies will act as the instrument of God in destroying the wicked city [verses 7–18].

1: And there came one of the seven angels that had the seven bowls, and spake with me, saying, Come hither, I will show thee the judgment of the great harlot that sitteth upon many waters;

One of the seven angels calls John to see the judgment of the great harlot. She is clearly a parody of the bride whom the same angel will later show to John [21:9]. As the apotheosis of worldly influence, she is aptly called Babylon the Great, but she represents Rome because the mantle of Babylon's iniquities has now fallen upon that city. Since she is the harlot and not the spouse, her sin is not described as adultery but as fornication. This means that she turns people away from God and lures them into idolatry and immorality [verses 4, 5]. She is depicted as sitting upon many waters, for Babylon was irrigated by an elaborate system of canals [*Jer.* 5 1:13]. But as applied to Rome, these waters represent the many peoples who are subject to her evil influence [verse 15].

2: with whom the kings of the earth committed fornication, and they that dwell in the earth were made drunken with the wine of her fornication.

Rome is the great harlot 'with whom the kings of the earth committed fornication'. The fornication 'of which these kings were guilty consisted in purchasing the favour of Rome by accepting her suzerainty and with it her vices and idolatries' (Swete). Thus Rome was the metropolis of corruption, who had made the inhabitants of the earth drunk with the wine of her fornication [14:8].

3: And he carried me away in the Spirit into a wilderness: and I saw a woman sitting upon a scarlet-coloured beast, full of names of blasphemy, having seven heads and ten horns.

The angel then carried John away in the Spirit [1:10] into a wilderness, where he saw a woman sitting on a fearsome beast, for her powers of seduction rest upon the might of the Roman empire [13:1]. The beast is richly draped in scarlet, to indicate the ostentatious magnificence of that empire, and it is covered with the blasphemous claims to deity made by its emperors. The meaning of its seven heads and ten horns is later explained by the angel [verses 9–14, 16, 17].

4: And the woman was arrayed in purple and scarlet, and decked with gold and precious stone and pearls, having in her hand a golden cup full of abominations, even the unclean things of her fornication,

The woman is arrayed in costly garments and adorned with gold and precious jewels, but the golden cup she holds is full of the abominations of her fornication [21:27; *Jer.* 51:7]. Although she appears to offer a satisfying drink, the golden cup is filled with the 'abominations' of idolatry, which she promotes by her spiritual 'fornication' [*Mark* 13:14]. 'Rome is pronounced luxurious, licentious, and loathsome' (Moffatt).

5: and upon her forehead a name written, MYSTERY, BABYLON THE GREAT, THE MOTHER OF THE HARLOTS AND OF THE ABOMINATIONS OF THE EARTH.

And written on her forehead was a name with a secret meaning: 'Babylon the great, the mother of whores and of every obscenity on earth' (NEB): It was the custom for Roman prostitutes to wear a headband which displayed their names. The word 'mystery' is not part of the name, but warns the reader that the name must be interpreted spiritually [11: 8]. John calls the woman Babylon, but the initiated will realize that he is in fact referring to Rome. The mother city is here 'viewed as the source and furtherer of all the abominations of the earth' (Beckwith).

6: And I saw the woman drunken with the blood of the saints, and with the blood of the martyrs of Jesus. And when I saw her, I wondered with a great wonder.

With the blood of the saints, and with the blood of the witnesses of Jesus [ASV margin]: The capital charge against this woman is that she is a murderess. She kills those who refuse to participate in her abominable idolatries. Her victims are doubly defined as 'the saints' and 'the witnesses of Jesus' – they belong to God, and had borne testimony to Jesus. Probably the primary reference is to those who were martyred at Rome by Nero. Thus the woman not only makes others drunk with the wine of her fornication [verse 2], but she is herself drunk with the blood of God's people (Caird). Having expected to see the judgment of the great harlot [verse 1], John is astonished to be shown a vision in which she glories and triumphs in her sin.

7: And the angel said unto me, Wherefore didst thou wonder? I will tell thee the mystery of the woman, and of the beast that carrieth her, which hath the seven heads and the ten horns.

John's amazement at the harlot's apparent success is rebuked by the angel, who proceeds to interpret the mystery of the woman and of the beast which carries her.

8: The beast that thou sawest was, and is not: and is about to come up

out of the abyss, and to go into perdition. And they that dwell on the earth shall wonder, they whose name hath not been written in the book of life from the foundation of the world, when they behold the beast, how that he was, and is not, and shall come.

The angel first reveals the fate of the beast and thus exposes the emptiness of its divine pretensions. In contrast to the One 'who *is* and who was and who is to come' [1: 4], the beast John saw 'was, and *is not*, and is about to come up', which is but a feeble parody of the divine title. The career of the beast also parodies that of the Lamb. For the Lamb descends from heaven and returns to heaven, whereas the beast ascends from the abyss only to sink back into perdition [19:20].

It is clear from what follows that the beast is to be identified with Nero, who symbolizes the future Antichrist (see also comments on 13:1, 3). Nero committed suicide in AD 68, but for twenty years after his death many believed that he had gone to the east and would return at the head of a Parthian army. When this expectation was no longer credible, it was replaced by the still stranger myth that Nero would return from the dead to regain his lost power. At the time of John's vision the Neronic persecution was in the past ('was'), and it would seem from 2:13 that Antipas was the only contemporary martyr ('and is not'), but a revival of the beast's power is now imminent in the renewal of emperor worship by Domitian ('and is about to come up out of the abyss'). But the primary application of the vision to the church of John's day does not rule out its secondary fulfilment in the last days before Christ's return. The beast's supernatural powers will excite the wonder and worship of the unbelieving world. 'True, he *goes to perdition* eventually, but not before all except the elect have succumbed to the fascination of his second advent' [Moffatt].

9–11: Here is the mind that hath wisdom. The seven heads are seven mountains, on which the woman sitteth: and they are seven kings; the five are fallen, the one is, the other is not yet come; and when he cometh, he must continue a little while. And the beast that was, and is not, is himself also an eighth, and is of the seven; and he goeth into perdition.

This difficult passage is prefaced by the warning that spiritual discernment is required in order to understand the mystery of the beast [13:18]. A double interpretation is given of the beast's seven heads.

They are first said to be the seven mountains on which the woman sits, an unmistakable reference to Rome which no one could fail to recognize, and they are also seven kings representing the full series of Roman emperors. The point of interest lies not in the imperial line which has nearly run its course, but in the coming of an eighth who is also one of the seven. 'The Roman empire must fill out its destined place in history, it must have its complete tale of kings denoted by the typical number seven; then Antichrist comes, who succeeds the Roman power which he destroys; he forms an eighth ruler added to the seventh . . . but at the same time he is "of the seven", inasmuch as he is one of the seven [Nero] reincarnate' (Beckwith).

12,13: And the ten horns that thou sawest are ten kings, who have received no kingdom as yet; but they receive authority as kings, with the beast, for one hour. These have one mind, and they give their power and authority unto the beast.

The angel further explains that the ten horns John saw are ten kings who have received no kingdom as yet, but they will receive their kingly authority with the beast and will reign with him 'for one hour', i.e. a very short time. They are united in consenting to give their power and authority to the beast, because God put it into their hearts to do this until his words were accomplished [verse 17]. These willing allies of the beast are probably the kings from the east mentioned in the previous section (see comment on 16:12).

14: These shall war against the Lamb, and the Lamb shall overcome them, for he is Lord of lords, and King of kings; and they also shall overcome that are with him, called and chosen and faithful.

This brief preview of the last battle shows that the allies of the beast shall war against the Lamb [19:11–21]. Initially this means they will attack the Lamb's followers, but their martyrdom amounts to a victory [13:7], because they have refused to deny their Lord even in the midst of this final onslaught by the powers of evil [12:11]. But when the Lamb suddenly appears from heaven he will overcome all his enemies, for he is Lord of lords and King of kings [19:16]. The saints with the Lamb will share in his victory as they are 'called and chosen and faithful'. They were effectually called by grace because they were first chosen, and so they have remained faithful [2:10, 13].

15: And he saith unto me, The waters which thou sawest, where the harlot sitteth, are peoples, and multitudes, and nations, and tongues.

The angel next identifies the waters upon which the harlot sits as the multitudes who are subjected to her corrupting influence [verse 1]. Rome was the centre of a civilization which had become drunk 'with the wine of her fornication' [verse 2]. Yet Rome's 'greatest danger lay in the multitudes which were under her sway, and out of which would arise the "ten kings" who were to bring about her downfall'(Swete).

16: And the ten horns which thou sawest, and the beast, these shall hate the harlot, and shall make her desolate and naked, and shall eat her flesh, and shall burn her utterly with fire.

Here the angel reveals the fate of Rome in language that recalls the judgment of the harlot city of Jerusalem [*Ezek.* 23:25 –30]. It is because evil contains the seeds of its own destruction that the beast and the ten kings will turn in hatred upon the harlot and completely destroy her. 'Wicked men are not just one happy band of brothers. Being wicked, they give way to jealousy and hatred. At the climax their mutual hatreds will result in mutual destruction' (Morris).

17: For God did put in their hearts to do his mind, and to come to one mind, and to give their kingdom unto the beast, until the words of God should be accomplished.

Since this is such a surprising development, the angel explains that the unanimity of the ten kings was no accident, for God moved them to put their power at the disposal of the beast until all God's words were fulfilled. A sovereign God leaves no room for any form of dualism. 'A divine overruling controls all political movements [11:2; 13:5, 7] . . . The irony of the situation is that the tools of providence are destroyed, after they have unconsciously served their purpose (as in *Isa.* 10:12f.)' (Moffatt).

18: And the woman whom thou sawest is the great city, which reigneth over the kings of the earth.

This puts the identity of the woman beyond all doubt. The great harlot is Rome, which rules over the kings of the earth. But Babylon the great represents more than first-century Rome; it also stands for the final Babylon which is yet to be overthrown [so Mounce].

CHAPTER EIGHTEEN

A glorious angel proclaims the fall of Babylon [verses 1–3]. God's people are called out before the judgment falls upon her [verses 4–8]. There is great lamentation on earth and rejoicing in heaven [verses 9–20]. Her total destruction is signified by the casting of a great millstone into the sea [verses 21 –24].

1: After these things I saw another angel coming down out of heaven, having great authority; and the earth was lightened with his glory.

After the interpreting angel had done his work, John saw another angel coming down from heaven with the divine authority to announce the doom of Babylon. 'So recently has he come from the Presence that in passing he flings a broad belt of light across the dark earth' (Swete) [*Ezek.* 43:2.]

2: And he cried with a mighty voice, saying, Fallen, fallen is Babylon the great, and is become a habitation of demons, and a hold of every unclean spirit, and a hold of every unclean and hateful bird.

The dramatic declaration, 'Fallen, fallen is Babylon the great,' transfers to the past what is still future, to denote the certainty of the event [*Isa.* 21:9]. The once proud city is viewed as having already become 'a dwelling for demons, a haunt for every unclean spirit, for every vile and loathsome bird' (NEB). This prophetic picture presents a scene of utter desolation and degradation. Deserted of human inhabitants, Babylon is now the dwelling-place of demons, and the haunt of every unclean spirit and bird [*Isa.* 13:19–22; 34:11; *Jer.* 50:39].

3: For by the wine of the wrath of her fornication all the nations are fallen; and the kings of the earth committed fornication with her, and the merchants of the earth waxed rich by the power of her wantonness.

For all nations have drunk deep of the fierce wine of her fornication (NEB): Babylon is so judged because she has intoxicated the nations with the wine of her fornication [*Jer.* 51:7]. The kings of the earth have shared in her idolatries and its merchants have grown rich from the power of her wanton luxury. 'The history of human civilization is to a great extent the history of human luxury; and the history of human luxury is the history of bodily appetites growing more and more inordinate, and growing by what they feed upon' (W. G. T. Shedd, 'Christian Moderation' in *Sermons to the Spiritual Man*, p. 25) [3:17].

4,5: And I heard another voice from heaven, saying, Come forth, my people, out of her, that ye have no fellowship with her sins, and that ye receive not of her plagues: for her sins have reached even unto heaven, and God hath remembered her iniquities.

The voice John heard from heaven must be that of an angel who speaks on God's behalf, for the placing of God in the third person in verse 5 clearly shows that God is not the speaker. The call to God's people to come out from Babylon does not require local removal from the place itself [*1 Cor.* 5:10], but is rather a demand to the churches for complete moral separation from her iniquities so that they do not participate in her plagues [*Isa.* 51 :11; *Jer.* 51:45; *2 Cor.* 6:17]. 'The constant danger confronting God's people is to be taken in by the antichristian seduction which seeks to entice and entangle them' (Lenski). The angel further declares that Babylon's sins have been heaped up to heaven like a latter-day tower of Babel, thus forcibly reminding God that the time for judgment has come [*Gen.* 11: 4; *Jer.* 51:9].

6: Render unto her even as she rendered, and double unto her the double according to her works: in the cup which she mingled, mingle unto her double.

This command is not addressed to believers, but to the angelic ministers of the divine vengeance [*Rom.* 12:19]. They are instructed to give back the double punishment Babylon deserves for her double sin [*Jer.* 16:18; 17:18]. 'The "double" must not be taken to mean double her sins; her sins are themselves called double, and her judgment is according to her sins. She is double-stained in wickedness, and "the law of retribution fiercely works" in her. The cup of her luxuriousness becomes the cup of vengeance' (Carpenter).

7,8: How much soever she glorified herself, and waxed wanton, so much give her of torment and mourning: for she saith in her heart, I sit a queen, and am no widow, and shall in no wise see mourning. Therefore in one day shall her plagues come, death, and mourning, and famine; and she

shall be utterly burned with fire; for strong is the Lord God who judged her.

The punishment of Babylon will be in direct proportion to her self-glorification and sinful extravagance [*Isa.* 47:7–9]. As she thought no disaster could ever interrupt her reign of pleasure, her plagues will come in a single day, for the strong city [verse 10] is no match for the strong God who judges her [John Sweet]. 'The "plagues" of Babylon, when they come, will make a dire antithesis to her present condition; death, mourning, dearth will reign where life at its gayest and fullest has long prevailed. Fire will complete the work of destruction' (Swete).

9, 10: And the kings of the earth, who committed fornication and lived wantonly with her, shall weep and wail over her, when they look upon the smoke of her burning, standing afar off for the fear of her torment, saying, Woe, woe, the great city, Babylon, the strong city! For in one hour is thy judgment come.

What Moffatt calls 'this magnificent doom song' is modelled on the prophetic dirge over the city of Tyre [*Ezek.* 27]. Kings [verses 9, 10], merchants [verses 11–17] and mariners [verses 17–19] all mourn over the fall of Babylon. All cry, 'Woe', at the beginning of their lament and end with the words, 'in one hour' [verses 10, 17, 19], thus marking the suddenness of the judgment 'with the monotony of a passing bell heard at intervals amid the strains of sad music' (Carpenter). Here the client kings of Rome wail over the fall of their seducer and protector ('the strong city'), because it has brought their own power and influence to a swift end.

11: And the merchants of the earth weep and mourn over her, for no man buyeth their merchandise any more;

The mourning of the merchants was also prompted by self-interest [*Ezek.* 27:28–36]. Their prosperity had been founded upon Rome's insatiable appetite for the most expensive merchandise, and the sudden loss of this luxury market meant economic ruin for them.

12, 13: merchandise of gold, and silver, and precious stone, and pearls, and fine linen, and purple, and silk, and scarlet: and all thyine wood, and every vessel of ivory, and every vessel made of most precious wood, and

of brass, and iron, and marble; and cinnamon, and spice, and incense, and ointment, and frankincense, and wine, and oil, and fine flour, and wheat, and cattle, and sheep; and merchandise of horses and chariots and slaves; and souls of men.

This catalogue falls into six groups:

1. *Treasure:* gold, silver, precious stones and pearls;

2. *Expensive fabrics*: fine linen, purple, silk and scarlet;

3. *Materials used in furnishing:* citron wood, ivory, costly wood, bronze, iron and marble;

4. *Aromatic articles:* cinnamon, spice, incense, ointment and frankincense;

5. *Foods:* wine, oil, fine flour and wheat;

6. *Live stock:* cattle, sheep, horses, chariots and 'slaves, that is, human souls' (RSV).

The harlot's profligacy is demonstrated by the fact that the list thus concludes with the least valuable 'article'. 'The world of St John's day ministered in a thousand ways to the follies and vices of its Babylon, but the climax was reached in the sacrifice of human life which recruited the huge *familiae* of the rich, filled the *lupanaria* [brothels], and ministered to the brutal pleasures of the amphitheatre' (Swete).

14: And the fruits which thy soul lusted after are gone from thee, and all things that were dainty and sumptuous are perished from thee, and men shall find them no more at all.

In this verse Babylon herself is directly addressed. 'It is in harmony with the fervour of the whole chapter that the descriptive tone should for a moment give place to this apostrophe' (Carpenter). The fruits she lusted after are now gone for ever and the dainty luxuries and extravagant splendours have all disappeared,

15–17a: The merchants of these things, who were made rich by her, shall stand afar off for the fear of her torment, weeping and mourning; saying, Woe, woe, the great city, she that was arrayed in fine linen and purple and scarlet, and decked with gold and precious stone and pearl! For in one hour so great riches is made desolate.

The merchants, like the kings, stand at a safe distance from the city to bemoan their loss. Each group sees the fall of the city in terms of its own interests. The kings lamented the fall of Rome's power, whereas the merchants grieve over the sudden destruction of her wealth.

17b–19: And every shipmaster, and every one that saileth any whither, and mariners, and as many as gain their living by sea, stood afar off, and cried out as they looked upon the smoke of her burning, saying, What city is like the great city? And they cast dust on their heads, and cried, weeping and mourning, saying, Woe, woe, the great city, wherein all that had their ships in the sea were made rich by reason of her costliness! For in one hour is she made desolate.

The third group who mourn the fall of the great city are the sea-captains, passengers, sailors and those who earn their living from the sea. They also view the disaster from a distance, but they give more vivid expression to their sorrow by casting dust upon their heads [*Ezek.* 27:30]. However, their lament chiefly concerns their own commercial loss, for they had profited from the expensive goods in which Rome had so freely indulged.

20: Rejoice over her, thou heaven, and ye saints, and ye apostles, and ye prophets; for God hath judged your judgment on her.

This further apostrophe [verse 14] is a call to the glorified church in heaven to rejoice over the judgment of Babylon. It is not an expression of vindictive delight in the suffering of the unrighteous, but 'a summons to all who have fought on the side of their Lord to rejoice at the removal of one of the great obstacles to the manifestation of God's kingdom' (Carpenter; see also comments on 6:9, 10).

For God hath judged your judgment on her: Caird argues that this should be understood in the light of the law of malicious witness which required that the one who brought a false accusation should be repaid with the evil he intended for his brother [*Deut.* 19:16–19]. Thus Babylon had brought malicious charges against Christians which resulted in their death, but she has been found guilty of perjury and now God has exacted the same penalty from her.

21–23a: And a strong angel took up a stone as it were a great millstone and cast it into the sea, saying, Thus with a mighty fall shall Babylon, the great city, be cast down, and shall be found no more at all. And the

voice of harpers and minstrels and flute players and trumpeters shall be heard no more at all in thee; and no craftsman, of whatsoever craft, shall be found any more at all in thee; and the voice of a mill shall be heard no more at all in thee; and the light of a lamp shall shine no more at all in thee; and the voice of the bridegroom and of the bride shall be heard no more at all in thee;

In a symbolic act of judgment, a strong angel then took up a stone like a great millstone and hurled it into the sea, declaring that thus shall Babylon fall to rise no more [*Jer.* 51:63]. The impressive repetition of the phrase 'no more at all' here rings out like a funeral knell over the dead city. No sound shall break the silence of the desolate place which was once throbbing with life. The strains of music are no longer heard in her; no craftsman pursues his trade; no grain is ground for bread; no lamp relieves her darkness and no marriages are celebrated in that house of death [*Jer.* 25: 10].

23b, 24: for thy merchants were the princes of the earth; for with thy sorcery were all the nations deceived. And in her was found the blood of prophets and of saints, and of all that have been slain upon the earth.

The angel's proclamation concludes with three reasons for the judgment of Babylon.

1. Her merchant princes had acted as missionaries in corrupting the world with her false standards.

2. She had also duped the nations with the sorcery of her idolatries [*Nahum* 3:4; *Rev.* 17:2];

3. In her was found the blood of all the saints [17:6].

The last charge reveals the heinous nature of Babylon's guilt, for, not content with rejecting the way of godliness herself, she killed those who were faithfully following that path [*Matt.* 23:35–39].

CHAPTER NINETEEN

The hymn of praise to God for judging the great harlot and avenging his martyred saints is followed by the marriage hymn of the Lamb [verses 1–9]. John is forbidden to worship the angel who showed him these things [verse 10]. The Word of God appears at the head of his armies to destroy his enemies, and the beast and the false prophet are cast into the lake of fire [verses 11–21].

1, 2: After these things I heard as it were a great voice of a great multitude in heaven, saying, Hallelujah; Salvation, and glory, and power, belong to our God: for true and righteous are his judgments; for he hath judged the great harlot, her that corrupted the earth with her fornication, and he hath avenged the blood of her servants at her hand.

In this vision John hears a vast throng in heaven praising God for judging the great harlot and avenging the blood of his servants. The word 'Hallelujah' [= 'Praise ye Jehovah'] introduces a number of Psalms [*Psa.* 111:1; 112:1; 113:1; 146:1], but this is the only passage in the New Testament where it occurs [verses 1, 3, 4, 6]. Those familiar with Handel's *Messiah* cannot read this passage without being reminded of the great 'Hallelujah chorus', which consists of words taken from *Rev.* 19:6; 11:15; 19:16. The heavenly choir praises God as the author of that salvation which is effected by his glory and power. For by vindicating his servants and judging the harlot, he has again demonstrated that his judgments are true and righteous [15:3; 16:7]. They are not capricious and arbitrary, but absolutely in accordance with the truth and justice of the case. She who had defiled the earth with her fornication and shed the blood of God's servants clearly deserved nothing but destruction!

3: And a second time they say, Hallelujah. And her smoke goeth up for ever and ever.

The image of Babylon's doom recalls the oracle against Edom [*Isa.* 34:10]. 'The words are those of the Seer, who points to the unquenchable smoke rising as the accompaniment to the song and the proof of its truth' (Beckwith).

4: And the four and twenty elders and the four living creatures fell down and worshipped God that sitteth on the throne, saying, Amen; Hallelujah.

In their last appearance in the book of Revelation, the twenty-four elders and the four living beings confirm the praise of God's righteous judgments with this 'Amen' and add their own 'Hallelujah' (see comments on 4:4, 6; *Psa.* 106:48).

5: And a voice came forth from the throne, saying, Give praise to our God, all ye his servants, ye that fear him, the small and the great.

'Our God' shows that the voice cannot be that of God or Christ; it must be that of one of the elders or living beings. The voice calls the whole church to join in the praise of God. [*Psa.* 113:1; 115:13]. 'The small and the great' embraces all the redeemed, from the most insignificant saint to the greatest apostle [11:18].

6–8: And I heard as it were the voice of a great multitude, and as the voice of many waters, and as the voice of mighty thunders, saying, Hallelujah: for the Lord our God, the Almighty, reigneth. Let us rejoice and be exceeding glad, and let us give the glory unto him: for the marriage of the Lamb is come, and his wife hath made herself ready. And it was given unto her that she should array herself in fine linen, bright and pure: for the fine linen is the righteous acts of the saints.

In response to this summons [verse 5], John heard the voice of a great multitude which was like the roar of many waters and great peals of thunder. The voice is not identified, but if the choir of verse 1 was angelic, then presumably this praise is offered by the innumerable company of the redeemed [7:9].

The last hymn in the book strikes a new note of praise, for what the church celebrates is not the doom of Babylon, but its sequel in the setting up of the kingdom of God [NEB: God . . . 'has entered on his reign!']. There is also rejoicing because the day of the Lamb's marriage has arrived.

'The marriage day of Christ and his church is the day of his second advent' [Moffatt]. The most intimate of all relationships is a fit symbol of the union between Christ and his people, which will be perfected at his return [*2 Cor.* 11:2; *Eph.* 5:23–33].

But though the marriage is here announced, the actual event is nowhere described, because even this metaphor cannot do justice to the reality it represents [*1 John* 3:2]. The Lamb's wife has made herself ready by donning the divinely provided garment of fine linen. Her bridal dress is bright and pure, in marked contrast to the purple and scarlet garments of the great harlot [17:4]. John explains that the fine linen stands for 'the righteous acts of the saints' [*Eph.* 2:10]. This is 'the sum of the saintly acts of the members of Christ, wrought in them by His Spirit . . . so corporately the whole Church is seen to be attired in the dazzling whiteness of their collective purity' (Swete).

9: And he saith unto me, Write, Blessed are they that are bidden to the marriage supper of the Lamb. And he saith unto me, These are true words of God.

The unnamed speaker is probably the interpreting angel of 17:1. He commands John to write down the fourth beatitude in the book, which concerns the blessedness of those who are called to the marriage supper of the Lamb. This beatitude makes apparent the fluidity of biblical metaphors, for the saints are not only the bride, but are also the guests at the wedding! As the Spirit endorses the beatitude spoken by a voice from heaven [14:13], so the angel here confirms the truthfulness of these words of God [Martin Rist].

10: And I fell down before his feet to worship him. And he saith unto me, See thou do it not: I am a fellow-servant with thee and with thy brethren that hold the testimony of Jesus: worship God: for the testimony of Jesus is the spirit of prophecy.

John was so overwhelmed by this message that he fell at the feet of the angel. But the angel rebuked him for offering to a fellow-servant the worship that belongs to God, the giver of revelation [verse 9; comment on 1:2]. According to the parallel passage [22:9], it would appear that the brethren who hold the testimony borne by Jesus are not simply believers but Christian prophets. This helps to clarify the angel's explanation: 'For the testimony of Jesus is the spirit of prophecy,' i.e. the testimony given by Jesus is the word that the Spirit puts into the mouths of the prophets. This is the special obligation resting upon them. 'They have it, not as a secure possession, but as a task, i.e., in order that they may pass it on, as John himself attests the witness of Jesus. This is why they are prophets' [H. Strathmann, *TDNT*, vol. 4, p. 501].

11: And I saw the heaven opened; and behold, a white horse, and he that sat thereon, called Faithful and True; and in righteousness he doth judge and make war.

This section of the book reaches its climax in the vision of the conquering Messiah's return [verses 11–21]. As John sees heaven open, there appears a white horse of victory, whose rider is called Faithful and True. The title distinguishes Christ from the deceivers of mankind [verses 19–21] and guarantees the reliability and truthfulness of his promises (comment on 3:14). It is to fulfil those promises that he comes forth in righteousness to judge and make war on the beast and all his followers [*Isa.* 11:4; *Psa.* 96:13]. 'The Christ who comes is both Judge and Warrior, and He judges first, for in the Divine order judgment precedes victory' (Swete).

12: And his eyes are a flame of fire, and upon his head are many diadems; and he hath a name written, which no one knoweth but he himself.

Nothing is hidden from the penetrating gaze of this Judge, whose eyes are like a flame of fire [1:14; 2:18]. 'These *flame-like eyes* have been fixed upon the moving scenes of human life, and have been reading the hearts of men, and the true meaning of all events and actions' (Carpenter). Upon his head are many crowns of royalty which proclaim his universal kingship [verse 16; 12:3; 13:1]. In addition to the many titles which may be understood, he bears a name which is known to no one but himself, for 'only the Son of God can understand the mystery of His own Being' (Swete) [*Matt.* 11: 27].

13: And he is arrayed in a garment sprinkled with blood: and his name is called The Word of God.

As the symbol of his mission of vengeance [*Isa.* 63:1–6], the Rider wears a robe 'dipped in blood' [ASV margin]. Christ's victory is so certain that he is here depicted as the Warrior whose garment is stained with the blood of his enemies before the battle is joined. He is fittingly called the Word of God because the punishment he inflicts upon them is the work of this all-powerful Word [verse 15].

14: And the armies which are in heaven followed him upon white horses, clothed in fine linen, white and pure.

Mounted on white horses, the armies of heaven follow the conquering Messiah and share in his victory, while the purity of their dress shows that this is the triumph of righteousness. These are not the angels, but the overcomers of 17:14, the redeemed who follow the Lamb wherever he goes [14:4].

15: And out of his mouth proceedeth a sharp sword, that with it he should smite the nations: and he shall rule them with a rod of iron: and he

treadeth the winepress of the fierceness of the wrath of God, the Almighty.

The only weapon which is used by Christ to judge the nations is the sharp sword which issues from his mouth [1:16]. 'The sword is now wielded for but one work – the *word* that Christ spoke will judge men at the last day [*John* 12:48]' (Carpenter). The dreadful finality of this judgment is emphasized in three Old Testament figures: he smites the nations [*Isa.* 11:3, 4]; he rules them with a rod of iron [*Psa.* 2:9]; he treads the winepress of God's furious wrath [*Isa.* 63:1–6]. Christ is the sole executor of that wrath. The armies who accompany him play no part in the judgment, but are simply witnesses of it.

16: And he hath on his garment and on his thigh a name written, King of Kings, and Lord of Lords.

'And on his thigh' explains where the name was written on his garment. It was emblazoned on that part of the garment which falls over the Rider's thigh, and was thus plainly visible to all. So when Christ returns to judge the wicked, his absolute sovereignty will at last be acknowledged by all.

17, 18: And I saw an angel standing in the sun; and he cried with a loud voice, saying to all the birds that fly in mid-heaven, Come and be gathered together unto the great supper of God; that ye may eat the flesh of kings, and the flesh of captains, and the flesh of mighty men, and the flesh of horses and of them that sit thereon, and the flesh of all men, both free and bond, and small and great.

In anticipation of Christ's triumph, an angel stands in the sun and calls the birds of prey in mid-air to come to the great supper that God has provided for them [*Ezek.* 39:17–20]. This supper presents a grim contrast to the marriage supper of the Lamb [verse 9], for the feast consists of the flesh of God's enemies! The birds are invited to gorge themselves, not only on the flesh of kings and captains, but on that of men from every class.

'All classes – the great and small, the master and slave – are mentioned. Those who follow the world-power, and array themselves in hostility to the true King, belong not to one class, but may be found among all. The war is not between class and class, but between righteousness and unrighteousness, truth and falsehood, Christ and Belial' (Carpenter).

19: And I saw the beast, and the kings of the earth, and their armies, gathered together to make war against him that sat upon the horse, and against his army.

John sees the beast and his allies gathered together against the Lord's Anointed and his army [*Psa.* 2:2]. The forces of evil willingly gather for the final conflict [16:14], but their plans are overruled by God and made to serve his ends. 'Those who take note of the tendencies of modern civilization will not find it impossible to conceive that a time may come when throughout Christendom the spirit of Antichrist will, with the support of the State, make a final stand against a Christianity which is loyal to the Person and teaching of Christ' (Swete).

20,21: And the beast was taken, and with him the false prophet that wrought the signs in his sight, wherewith he deceived them that had received the mark of the beast and them that worshipped his image: they two were cast alive into the lake of fire that burneth with brimstone: and the rest were killed with the sword of him that sat upon the horse, even the sword which came forth out of his mouth: and all the birds were filled with their flesh.

John gives no description of the battle, perhaps because the mightiest army can do nothing against an omnipotent adversary. Hence he simply records the outcome of the confrontation. The beast and the false prophet were taken and cast into the lake of fire [20:10]; the rest were slain by the word of Christ [verse 15] and their bodies devoured by the birds. 'Spiritual death is inflicted upon those who have proved themselves hostile to God. The last sentence emphasizes the nature of the punishment by the reference to the indignity offered to their bodies after death' (Plummer).

7: CHRIST'S VICTORY OVER SATAN
CHAPTER TWENTY

Satan is bound for a thousand years and the glorified saints reign with Christ for the same period [verses 1–6]. Satan is then released to gather the nations for the last battle. But the wicked are devoured by fire from heaven, and the devil is cast into the lake of fire [verses 7–10]. This is followed by the general resurrection and the last judgment [verses 11–15].

1: And I saw an angel coming down out of heaven, having the key of the abyss and a great chain in his hand.

John sees an angel descend from heaven with the key of the abyss and a great chain in his hand. The angel does not act on his own initiative, but, like Michael, is authorized to put into effect the victory of Christ (see comment on 12:7). As the conqueror of Satan, Christ has the power to confine him to the abyss. But if this passage is regarded as a continuation of the previous chapter, then Christ refuses to exercise that power until the end of the age, a conclusion which is clearly at variance with the teaching of the entire New Testament!

2, 3: And he laid hold on the dragon, the old serpent, which is the Devil and Satan, and bound him for a thousand years, and cast him into the abyss, and shut it, and sealed it over him, that he should deceive the nations no more, until the thousand years should be finished: after this he must be loosed for a little time.

John leaves us in no doubt of the identity of the one whom the angel binds and casts into the abyss (see comment on 12:9). Satan is thus bound for a thousand years so that he can no longer deceive the nations. If this follows the desolating judgment of chapter 19 in chronological sequence, it is rather surprising to find that there is anyone left to deceive! But the problem disappears when the thousand years are seen to be coextensive with the gospel age. This binding of Satan means that he cannot prevent the heralding of the gospel to all the nations (Lenski). It is Christ's victory over Satan that restrains him from deceiving the nations during the long day of grace [*Matt.* 12:26–29; 28:18–20; *Luke* 10:17–19; *John* 12:31, 32]. But at the end of this period, Satan must be loosed for a little while to gather together the enemies of Christ for the last attack on his church [verses 8, 9].

4: And I saw thrones, and they sat upon them, and judgment was given unto them: and I saw the souls of them that had been beheaded for the testimony of Jesus, and for the word of God, and such as worshipped not the beast, neither his image, and received not the mark upon their

forehead and upon their hand; and they lived, and reigned with Christ a thousand years.

The scene now shifts from earth to heaven. 'Here we are told of men *from* earth – not of men *on* it. That the expression 'the souls' refers to men in what is called the disembodied state, scarcely admits of question . . . The text indicates not that Christ came down to earth to live with them, but that they had soared upward to live and reign with Christ' (Clemance). John sees the believers who have died seated on thrones and sharing in the judgments of Christ [3:21]. He then singles out for special mention the martyrs who, having refused to worship had suffered for the testimony of Jesus [13:15].

These 'souls' lived and reigned with Christ 'a thousand years', i.e. throughout the gospel age [verses 1–3]. 'Those true to Christ during the comparatively brief period of persecution will reign with him for a long time. Again the very practical lesson is that it is worth dying to remain true to Christ' (Buis).

5: The rest of the dead lived not until the thousand years should be finished. This is the first resurrection.

What is true of the 'souls' in the previous verse does not pertain to 'the rest of the dead'. They do not 'live' in this period, as they are both physically and spiritually dead (though this does not mean that they cease to exist). And because they have not participated in the first resurrection, they are destined to suffer the second death [verse 6]. 'The first resurrection is the rising of the saint at death to a higher life in Christ, which will be consummated at the general resurrection when the thousand years have expired' (Clemance).

6: Blessed and holy is he that hath part in the first resurrection: over these the second death hath no power; but they shall be priests of God and of Christ, and shall reign with him a thousand years.

This is the fifth beatitude in the book. Those who share in the first resurrection are pronounced blessed and holy. Not only does the second death have no power over them [verse 14], but they shall be priests of God and Christ, and they shall reign with him a thousand years [verse 4; 1:6; 5:10]. 'They who are the Lord's rise twice, and die but once. They who are not the Lord's rise but once, and die twice' (Clemance).

7, 8: And when the thousand years are finished, Satan shall be loosed out of his prison, and shall come forth to deceive the nations which are in the four corners of the earth, Gog and Magog, to gather them together to the war: the number of whom is as the sand of the sea.

At the end of the gospel age, Satan will be released from his imprisonment and will go out to deceive the nations and gather them together for the final assault on God's people [verse 9]. The passage emphasizes the crucial role of Satan at the end of the age, for his gathering of the nations for the last conflict leads to the denouement of divine judgment. This is no new battle which unaccountably occurs at the end of an earthly millennium, but is in fact the same battle of Har-Magedon which has already been depicted three times in previous visions [16:12–16; 17:14–18; 19:11–21]. The nations from the four corners of the earth are further identified as 'Gog and Magog' [*Ezek*. 38:2]. As used by John, the term has no geographical significance, and has become the symbol of pagan opposition against God. This is in line with rabbinic thought, which equated Gog and Magog with the rebellious nations of *Psa*. 2. The final phrase points to an immense multitude.

9: And they went up over the breadth of the earth, and compassed the camp of the saints about, and the beloved city: and fire came down out of heaven, and devoured them.

The vast armies gathered by Satan advanced over the broad plain of the earth and encircled 'the camp of the saints' and 'the beloved city'. The people of God are here described under the double symbolism of a camp and a city. The first image recalls the encampments of Israel in the wilderness [*Exod*. 14:19, 20; *Num*. 2], and the second distinguishes the community that willingly lives under the rule of God from the rebellious secular city. It is again made clear that no battle takes place, for fire descends from heaven and consumes this apparently invincible host [*Ezek*. 38: 22; *2 Thess*. 1: 7].

10: And the devil that deceived them was cast into the lake of fire and brimstone, where are also the beast and the false prophet; and they shall be tormented day and night for ever and ever.

The devil shares the same fate as the beast and the false prophet. This does not mean that they were cast into hell before Satan, but only that their punishment has already been described [19:20]. 'They all go down together, Satan, the beast and the false prophet . . . In this lake of fire and brimstone all three are tormented for ever and ever, [*Matt.* 25:46]' (Hendriksen).

11: And I saw a great white throne, and him that sat upon it, from whose face the earth and the heaven fled away; and there was found no place for them.

The one whom John sees seated upon the great white throne is presumably God himself [5:1, 7, 13], but this should not be taken as excluding Christ from the judgment, since he also shares the throne with God [3:21; 22:1, 3]. The majesty of the Judge was so awesome that even earth and heaven fled away, and no place was left for them. As Ladd rightly insists, the poetic imagery here conveys the profound theological truth that God's judgment must fall upon the creation, which was marred by man's sin [*Rom.* 8:19–22]. Yet this judgment is not merely destructive, for the removal of the old order makes way for the new creation [*2 Pet.* 3:13].

12: And I saw the dead, the great and the small, standing before the throne; and books were opened: and another book was opened, which is the book of life: and the dead were judged out of the things which were written in the books, according to their works.

All the dead, both great and small, stand before the great white throne, and the books containing the record of their deeds are opened [*Dan.* 7:10]. The judgments of the last assize are not arbitrary, but are in perfect accord with the evidence thus presented [2:23; 22:12; *Rom.* 2:6]. Then another book is opened to reveal the names of those elected to eternal life [3:5; 13:8; 17:8; 21:27]. The principle of judgment according to works cannot disclose any disagreement between the testimony of the books and the book of life. 'Judgment according to works does not contravene salvation by grace. Salvation is by grace through faith. But the faith that is saving bears fruit in good works, and faith without works is dead. Good works are therefore the index to a state of salvation' (John Murray, *Collected Writings*, vol. 2, p. 416).

13: And the sea gave up the dead that were in it; and death and Hades gave up the dead that were in them: and they were judged every man according to their works.

The sea is specially mentioned to show that 'the accidents of death will not prevent any of the dead from appearing before the Judge' (Swete). In the ancient world death by drowning was considered to be a desolate fate, as it meant that the body could not be buried properly, and some Jews believed that this made resurrection impossible (Bruce). The universal extent of the resurrection is emphasized by the statement that death and Hades gave up the dead that were in them [1:18]. Not only are all the dead included in the judgment, but it is again affirmed that all are judged according to their works [verse 12].

14, 15: And death and Hades were cast into the lake of fire. This is the second death, even the lake of fire. And if any was not found written in the book of life, he was cast into the lake of fire.

This bold personification signifies the end of the intermediate state. As the realm of the dead, Hades receives souls after death, and then delivers them up again at the resurrection. The resurrection marks its end, and it is replaced by hell as the final place of punishment (J. Jeremias, *TDNT*, vol. 1, p. 148). Anyone whose name was not found written in the book of life was cast into the lake of fire, which is the second death [21:8]. As in *Matt.* 25:40–46, the qualification for the second death is a negative one, because the 'negation of eternal life is eternal death' (Swete).

CHAPTER TWENTY-ONE

In a vision of a new heaven and earth, John sees the new Jerusalem coming down from heaven [verses 1, 2]. The blessedness of God's people is described and the judgment of the wicked confirmed [verses 3–8]. The chapter concludes with a glowing account of the splendours of the new Jerusalem [verses 9 –27].

1: And I saw a new heaven and a new earth: for the first heaven and the first earth are passed away; and the sea is no more.

The judgment which removed the old order makes way for a new heaven and a new earth [20:11; *Isa.* 65:17]. Here 'new' [*kainos*] does not mean new in time, but new in quality. The new order does not evolve from the historical process, but is entirely due to the creative interposition of God. There is no room in the new earth for the sea, as it is the symbol of separation, wickedness and restless rebellion [13:1; *Psa.* 65: 7; 93:3; *Isa.* 57:20]. The sea has disappeared, because 'it is associated with ideas which are at variance with the character of the New Creation' (Swete).

2: And I saw the holy city, new Jerusalem, coming down out of heaven from God, made ready as a bride adorned for her husband.

John depicts the bliss of the perfected community under the dual image of a city and a bride. He sees the holy city, new Jerusalem [verse 1], coming down out of heaven from God, prepared as a bride adorned for her husband [19:7]. The continuity of God's redemptive purpose is indicated by the name of the city, new *Jerusalem*, which stands for the whole church of God, including the saints of both dispensations. The city descends *from* heaven because the church is God's creation; it descends *to* earth for that is where the glorified saints will enjoy uninterrupted fellowship with God throughout eternity [verse 3].

3: And I heard a great voice out of the throne saying, Behold, the tabernacle of God is with men, and he shall dwell with them, and they shall be his peoples, and God himself shall be with them, and be their God:

John then heard a great voice from the throne announcing the ultimate fulfilment of the Old Testament promise [*Lev.* 26:11, 12; *Ezek.* 37: 27; *Zech.* 8: 8]. 'Behold' arrests the attention and marks the wonder of the permanent tabernacling of God with men. The original promise to Israel is here expanded to include men of all nations who now constitute 'his peoples' [7:9]. The assurance that God will be with them and be their God is an obvious echo of the Immanuel prophecy [*Isa.* 7:14].

4: and he shall wipe away every tear from their eyes; and death shall be no more; neither shall there be mourning, nor crying, nor pain, any more: the first things are passed away.

The blessedness of eternal fellowship with God means that the first things which belonged to the old order have passed away. Gone for ever is that grim harvest of sin: sorrow, suffering and death. God will graciously console his people by wiping away every tear from their eyes

[*Isa*. 25: 8]. 'So many descriptions of eternal blessedness are either figurative or couched in negation because the realities are inconceivable to us in our present state' (Lenski).

5: And he that sitteth on the throne said, Behold, I make all things new. And he saith, Write: for these words are faithful and true.

Apart from 1: 8, this paragraph is the only place in Revelation where God is definitely represented as the speaker [verses 5–8; 16:1, 17]. It is from the throne that the sovereign God declares that he is making all things new. There is nothing that can frustrate the fulfilment of his creative purpose and therefore the regeneration which is rooted in Christ's redemptive achievement shall be consummated in the cosmic renewal of all things [*2 Cor.* 5:17]. God commands John to write down this message to the churches, because the revelation is trustworthy and true [19:9; 22:6].

6: And he said unto me, They are come to pass. I am the Alpha and the Omega, the beginning and the end. I will give unto him that is athirst of the fountain of the water of life freely.

God here proclaims that these things have come to pass, because the future blessedness of the saints is so secure that it can be regarded as already accomplished. For he who is the Alpha and Omega determines both the beginning and the end according to the counsel of his own will [1: 8; *Eph.* 1: 11]. To the one who thirsts for him, God offers to give of the fountain of the water of life freely [22:17; *Psa.* 42:1, 2; 63:1; *Isa.* 55:1, 2; *Matt.* 5:6].

7: He that overcometh shall inherit these things; and I will be his God, and he shall be my son.

As in the letters to the seven churches, it is the victor in the present spiritual conflict who shall inherit all the blessings of the new creation [2:7, 11, 17, 26; 3:5, 12, 21]. 'I will be his God, and he shall be my son' further defines the promise of the previous verse; 'the thirst for God will be satisfied in the relation of perfect sonship with God' (Beckwith). It is significant that the Messianic prophecy of *2 Sam.* 7:14 could only be applied to the Christian when the word 'father' was replaced by 'God', for God is uniquely the Father of Christ and believers are God's sons only by the adoption of grace.

8: But for the fearful, and unbelieving, and abominable, and murderers, and fornicators, and sorcerers, and idolaters, and all liars, their part shall be in the lake that burneth with fire and brimstone; which is the second death.

In contrast to the assurance given to the overcomer, God warns that the lot of the wicked shall be in the lake of fire, which is the second death [20:14, 15]. Those who exclude themselves from the holy city are characterized by eight epithets [22:15]. Perhaps only the first two relate to apostates, and the rest apply to pagans in general. 'The cowardly' and 'the faithless' are those who have denied the faith under the pressure of persecution. 'Abominable' describes those who shared in the impurities of the harlot [17:4, 5]. In this context 'murderers' possibly refers to the persecutors who killed the martyrs [13:15]. 'Fornicators', 'sorcerers' and 'idolaters' are common descriptions of the heathen, while 'liars' includes all the lovers and inventors of falsehoods [2:2; 3:9; 14:5; 21:27; 22:15]. These all have their place in the lake of fire, because their 'moral affinities are with evil . . . Character determines environment, and character is destiny' [R. A. Finlayson, *God's Light on Man's Destiny*, p.66].

9: And there came one of the seven angels who had the seven bowls, who were laden with the seven last plagues; and he spake with me, saying, Come hither, I will show thee the bride, the wife of the Lamb.

One of the angels with the seven bowls, presumably the angel who had shown John the great harlot [17:1], now comes to show him the bride, the wife of the Lamb [verse 2]. The use of the same angel to introduce both visions thus presents a striking contrast between the doom of the harlot city and the glory of the holy city.

10: And he carried me away in the Spirit to a mountain great and high, and showed me the holy city Jerusalem, coming down out of heaven from God,

The angel carried John away in the Spirit to a high mountain, and there showed him 'the holy city' Jerusalem descending from God out of heaven [*Ezek.* 40:2]. What is stressed here is not the newness of Jerusalem [verse 2], but her distinctive character as the holy city. This shows that the purpose of the vision is not so much predictive as pastoral, for the holiness of the glorified church provides a great incentive for holy living in the present age.

11: having the glory of God: her light was like unto a stone most precious, as it were a jasper stone, clear as crystal:

The most important feature of the holy city is mentioned first. John saw that it shone with the glory of God, 'and its brilliance was like that of a very precious jewel, like a jasper, clear as crystal' [NIV, 4:3]. And because the city thus rejoiced in the light of God's own presence, it needed no other source of illumination [21:23].

12,13: having a wall great and high; having twelve gates, and at the gates twelve angels; and names written thereon, which are the names of the twelve tribes of the children of Israel: on the east were three gates; and on the north three gates; and on the south three gates; and on the west three gates.

The city is square, and is surrounded by a great wall with three gates on each side, on which are inscribed the names of the twelve tribes of Israel [*Ezek.* 48:30–34]. In the new Jerusalem each tribe of the whole Israel of God (see comment on 7:4) 'is assured of its right of equal approach into the place of God's presence' (Beckwith). To allow easy access for the elect the gates of the city are never shut [verse 25], but to protect its purity each gate has its guardian angel [*Isa.* 62:6; *Rev.* 22:15].

14: And the wall of the city had twelve foundations, and on them twelve names of the twelve apostles of the Lamb.

The wall of the city rests on twelve foundations, upon which are inscribed the names of the twelve apostles of the Lamb. The thought is similar to that of *Eph.* 2:20. The church is founded upon the apostolic testimony to Christ. Since the apostolate as a whole is in view, there can be 'no question as to individual names of apostles, e.g. whether St Matthias or St Paul is the twelfth' (Plummer).

15: And he that spake with me had for a measure a golden reed to measure the city, and the gates thereof, and the wall thereof.

The angel had a golden reed to measure the city, so that John might realize its vast size and admire its perfect symmetry [*Ezek.* 40:3].

16, 17: And the city lieth foursquare, and the length thereof is as great as the breadth: and he measured the city with the reed, twelve thousand furlongs: the length and the breadth and the height thereof are equal. And he measured the wall thereof, a hundred and forty and four cubits, according to the measure of a man, that is, of an angel.

The city is in the shape of a perfect cube, and thus corresponds to the Holy of Holies in the temple [*1 Kings* 6:20]. The high priest could only enter the holy place once a year, but free access to God is the constant privilege of all the inhabitants of this city. Although John tells us that the angel was using the human system of measurements, the enormous dimensions of the city are clearly symbolic, and the attempts to reduce them to a mathematical statement are quite futile (Vincent). No light is thrown on the passage by observing that the city extends for 1500 miles in each direction and that its walls are 216 feet thick! The numbers are again in multiples of twelve, and simply indicate that there will be plenty of room in the city for all the people of God.

18: And the building of the wall thereof was jasper: and the city was pure gold, like unto pure glass.

The wall of the city was built of jasper, which shows that even its boundaries were suffused with the glory of God [verse 11]. The city itself was built of gold so pure that it was like clear glass. This image perhaps points to the purity of the glorified church [*Eph.* 5:27].

19,20: The foundations of the wall of the city were adorned with all manner of precious stones. The first foundation was jasper; the second, sapphire; the third, chalcedony; the fourth, emerald; the fifth, sardonyx; the sixth, sardius; the seventh, chrysolite; the eighth, beryl; the ninth, topaz; the tenth, chrysoprase; the eleventh, jacinth; the twelfth, amethyst.

The glory of the city is further enhanced by the precious stones which adorn the foundations of the wall [*Isa.* 54:11, 12]. These gems recall the jewelled breastplate of the high priest, on which were engraved the names of the twelve tribes of Israel [*Exod.* 28:15–21]. Most of the stones are the same in both lists, and 'their function here is to express the priestly character of Christ and his church as the foundation of the renewed world' [John Sweet].

21: And the twelve gates were twelve pearls; each one of the several gates was of one pearl: and the street of the city was pure gold, as it were transparent glass.

Each of the twelve gates of the city consisted of a single pearl. Although we cannot imagine pearls of such a size, the image suggests the transcendent worth of the kingdom, and brings to mind the parable of the merchant who sold all to gain the pearl of greatest price [*Matt.* 13:45, 46]. The main street of the city was made of pure gold which looked like transparent glass. The royal dignity of walking upon gold belongs to those who are joint-heirs with Christ.

22: And I saw no temple therein: for the Lord God the Almighty, and the Lamb, are the temple thereof.

In sharp contrast to Ezekiel's vision of the restored temple [*Ezek.* 40–46], John sees that there is no temple in the new Jerusalem, for the city itself is now the Holy of Holies (see comment on verse 16). 'No temple building is needed, for the presence of God and the Lamb makes every place where they are a sanctuary, and the whole new Jerusalem is filled with their presence' (Beckwith).

23: And the city hath no need of the sun, neither of the moon, to shine upon it: for the glory of God did lighten it, and the lamp thereof is the Lamb.

As the divine presence removes the need for any material temple in the city [verse 22], so it needs no created light, since the same Presence illuminates it unceasingly [*Isa.* 60:19, 20]. Another indirect proof of the deity of Christ is provided by this further linking together of God and the Lamb [22:3].

24: And the nations shall walk amidst the light thereof: and the kings of the earth bring their glory into it.

Here the universal diffusion of the knowledge of God in the eternal order is expressed in the language of Old Testament prophecy. Isaiah spoke of the day when the brightness of God's presence in Jerusalem would attract the homage of Gentile nations and kings [*Isa.* 60:1–3]. It is appropriate for John to apply this prophecy to the eternal state, because the redeemed are drawn from all the nations of the earth [7:9].

As it appears that these peoples will retain their national identity, the saints of each nation will have a distinctive contribution to make to the glory of God [verse 26].

25: And the gates thereof shall in no wise be shut by day (for there shall be no night there):

This is taken from *Isa.* 60:11, but because Isaiah says the gates 'shall not be shut day *nor night'*, John adds his parenthetical remark to explain this omission. 'In peace by day, the city gates will be open; nor can there be night when God the Almighty is the Sun' (Carpenter).

26: and they shall bring the glory and the honour of the nations into it:

This further allusion to *Isa.* 60:11 reaffirms the thought of verse 24 (see comment there).

27: and there shall in no wise enter into it anything unclean, or he that maketh an abomination and a lie: but only they that are written in the Lamb's book of life.

The unclean shall not enter the holy city, but only those whose names are written in the Lamb's book of life [20:15]. John warns his readers that no one who now indulges in the impurities of Babylon shall gain access to the new Jerusalem [22:15]. For the freedom of that city belongs to those who have made their calling and election sure by the obedience of faith [22:14]. 'The Bible does not teach universalism. Here is great blessedness for God's people, but those who remain in their sin are excluded' [Buis].

CHAPTER TWENTY-TWO

After the vision of the river and tree of life, the blessedness of God's servants is described [verses 1–7]. John is forbidden by the angel to worship him and is commanded to seal up the prophecy [verses 8–11]. The promise of Christ's coming is followed by the response of the Spirit and the church [verses 12–17]. John adds a solemn warning against tampering with the teaching of the book and concludes with the benediction [verses 18–21].

1, 2a: And he showed me a river of water of life, bright as crystal,

proceeding out of the throne of God and of the Lamb, in the midst of the street thereof.

The first five verses of this chapter conclude John's vision of the new Jerusalem and provide a brief but glorious description of what life is like in the city. Eternal life in all its fulness is symbolized by the river of the water of life, which flows out from the throne through the midst of the city [*Psa.* 46:4]. The image recalls the river of Eden [*Gen.* 2:10] and the river that flowed from the temple in Ezekiel's vision [*Ezek.* 47:1–12]. But as there is no temple in the holy city, the source of this river is the throne of God and of the Lamb, who are thus regarded as the joint source of the blessing.

2b: And on this side of the river and on that was the tree of life, bearing twelve manner of fruits, yielding its fruit every month: and the leaves of the tree were for the healing of the nations.

Here the singular 'tree' is used collectively, for each side of the river was lined with these trees. They produced twelve kinds of fruit every month, and their leaves 'were for the healing of the nations' [*Ezek.* 47:12].

This does not mean that there is any disease which needs healing in the new Jerusalem. The expression simply contrasts the suffering of the present life with the complete absence of all ills in the next. Hence 'the tree of life' is another symbol of eternal life [2:7; 22:14]. It brings to mind the tree in Eden from which man was barred after he had sinned [*Gen.* 2:9; 3:22]. 'The consummation of God's dealings with creation and man thus takes up and transcends what was given in Paradise' [K. Rengstorf, *TDNT*, vol. 6, p. 604].

3: And there shall be no curse any more: and the throne of God and of the Lamb shall be therein: and his servants shall serve him;

In contrast to the present evil age, there shall be no more curse in the new Jerusalem, because the rule of God and the Lamb banishes all sin [*Gen.* 3:17; *Zech.* 14:11]. Their unity is such that they share the same throne and the same glory, and their servants are said to 'serve *him*' [*John* 10:30]. 'To the final revelation of God there corresponds a perfected service; where the Throne is always in sight the service must be perpetual' (Swete) [7:15].

4: and they shall see his face; and his name shall be on their foreheads.

What was denied to Moses will be the ultimate privilege of all God's people [*Exod.* 33:20]. 'To see God is the reward of purity, and conversely the sight of God in Christ will perfect the process of purification [*Matt.* 5:8; *1 John* 3:2]' (Swete). As a mark of ownership, they will bear on their foreheads the name of God [3:12]. Since each epoch of God's self-revelation to man was associated with some new name of God, it is not surprising that the future age will be marked by a further disclosure of the divine glory (T. F. Glasson).

5: And there shall be night no more; and they need no light of lamp, neither light of sun; for the Lord God shall give them light: and they shall reign for ever and ever.

Darkness is utterly banished from the holy city, where there is no night and no need of lamp or sun, for its inhabitants will rejoice in the radiance of the Lord God [21:23]. And they shall reign for ever and ever [3:21]. With this final promise of the unending bliss of the redeemed the visions of the Apocalypse reach a fitting conclusion.

6: And he said unto me, These words are faithful and true: and the Lord, the God of the spirits of the prophets, sent his angel to show unto his servants the things which must shortly come to pass.

The epilogue to the whole book begins with the angel's guarantee of its veracity. He tells John that these words are trustworthy and true [21:5] for they come from the Lord, who sent his angel to show his servants the things that must shortly come to pass (see comment on 1:1). The remarkable expression, 'the God of the spirits of the prophets', is clarified by 19:10. It means that God illuminates the spirits of the prophets by the inspiration of the Holy Spirit; 'they are the natural faculties of the Prophets, raised and quickened by the Holy Spirit' (Swete).

7: And behold, I come quickly. Blessed is he that keepeth the words of the prophecy of this book.

The angel here quotes the words of Christ and does so again in verse 12. As the nearness of the Lord's advent should promote watchfulness, this announcement is appropriately followed by the sixth beatitude in the book, which pronounces a blessing upon the obedient. 'It is not in reading, or wondering, or talking, but in keeping, that the blessing comes. He that loves Christ will keep His commandments [*John* 14:15], even as Christ loved His Father and kept His commandments [*John* 15:10]' (Carpenter).

8, 9: And I John am he that heard and saw these things. And when I heard and saw, I fell down to worship before the feet of the angel that showed me these things. And he saith unto me, See thou do it not: I am a fellow-servant with thee and with thy brethren the prophets, and with them that keep the words of this book: worship God.

John now vouches for the authenticity of the revelation he has received, and confesses that he was so overcome by the divine authority of the message that he fell at the feet of the angel through whom it was mediated [19:10]. But the angel forbids the homage and directs him to worship God, because he is only a fellow-servant with John and his brethren the prophets, and with all the faithful who keep the words of the book.

10: And he saith unto me, Seal not up the words of the prophecy of this book; for the time is at hand.

Daniel was told to seal up the words of the book [*Dan.* 12:4, 9], but John must publish the prophecy for the encouragement of the churches. In Daniel's case the end was far off, but now the time is at hand. Such is the difference between the prophecy of the old and the new dispensation. The first belonged to the preliminary state; the other to the final fulfilment. So however 'long the gospel age may have lasted, or may yet continue, *it is the last time* [*1 John* 2:18]' (Carpenter).

11: He that is unrighteous, let him do unrighteousness still: and he that is filthy, let him be made filthy still: and he that is righteous, let him do righteousness still: and he that is holy, let him be made holy still.

The apparent determinism of the verse in fact conceals a solemn warning and an implicit appeal to the readers [*Dan.* 12:10]. There is obvious irony in commanding the wicked to continue in their evil ways. But the intention is surely to show that as character determines destiny, so the time will soon come when change is no longer possible. Although the exhortation to the righteous presents no problem, it is equally relevant since only those who endure to the end shall be saved [*Matt.* 10: 22].

12, 13: Behold, I come quickly; and my reward is with me, to render to each man according as his work is. I am the Alpha and the Omega, the first and the last, the beginning and the end.

Once more the angel quotes the words of Christ [verse 7]. He will come quickly to reward the righteous and the wicked by rendering 'to each man according as his work is' (see comment on 20:12). The total life of each man will be 'his work': 'the public evidence of what is in his heart, either faith or unbelief' (Lenski). The titles claimed by God [1:8; 21:6] also belong to Christ [1:17; 2:8], and they here give solemn assurance that he has the divine authority to judge all men. It is because God and the Lamb share the same throne [verse 1] that the judgment-seat of Christ is also the judgment-seat of God [*Rom.* 14:10; *2 Cor.* 5: 10].

14: Blessed are they that wash their robes, that they may have the right to come to the tree of life, and may enter in by the gates into the city.

The evangelical tone of the last beatitude in the book is unmistakable. The blessing is pronounced upon those who wash their robes, for only they have the right to the tree of life, and may enter in triumph through the gates of the city (see comment on verse 2b). This washing of their robes in the blood of the Lamb must continue throughout their earthly pilgrimage, whereas the washing is regarded as past when the glorified saints are in view [7:14]. The right to eternal life rests entirely upon washing in the blood of Christ the garments soiled by sin.

Dear dying Lamb, Thy precious blood
Shall never lose its power,
Till all the ransomed church of God
Be saved to sin no more.

William Cowper

15: Without are the dogs, and the sorcerers, and the fornicators, and the murderers, and the idolaters, and every one that loveth and maketh a lie.

This verse does not mean that the wicked are just outside the holy city, but rather emphasizes their eternal exclusion from it. Five of the six types of evildoers mentioned also appear in 21:8, but the term 'dogs' significantly heads the list. The wild scavenging dogs which roamed about eastern cities were a fit symbol of the unclean and the impure. 'All liars' [21:8] is here expanded to 'every one that loveth and maketh a lie'. 'He who loves falsehood is in his nature akin to it, and has through his love of it proved his affinity to Satan, who is *the father of it* [*John* 8:44]' (Swete).

16: I Jesus have sent mine angel to testify unto you these things for the churches. I am the root and the offspring of David, the bright, the morning star.

The emphatic 'I Jesus' shows that this is the direct utterance of Christ. He has sent his angel 'to testify unto you these things for the churches'. As 'you' is plural, it would seem that the seven churches are addressed. If so 'the churches' would then refer to the churches outside Asia. Jesus presents himself as 'the root and offspring of David' because he is the fulfilment of the Messianic promise [*Isa*. 11:1; *Rev*. 5:5]. He is also 'the bright, the morning star' who heralds the dawn of everlasting day [*Num*. 24:17; *2 Pet*. 1: 19].

17: And the Spirit and the bride say, Come. And he that heareth, let him say, Come. And he that is athirst, let him come: he that will, let him take the water of life freely.

'Come' is the ardent response of the Holy Spirit and the church to the words of the Lord, and every man who listens to the reading of the book is bidden to join in this prayer for the Lord's return. Finally, any outsider who is thirsty is urged to come and take the water of life freely [21:6]. Although the supply is gratuitous, 'take' suggests that 'the responsibility of accepting and using it rests with the individual' (Swete).

18, 19: I testify unto every man that heareth the words of the prophecy of this book, If any man shall add unto them, God shall add unto him the plagues which are written in this book: and if any man shall take away from the words of the book of this prophecy, God shall take away his part from the tree of life, and out of the holy city, which are written in this book.

John issues a severe warning against tampering with the message of the book [*Deut.* 4:2; 12:32]. If any man adds words of his own God shall add to him the plagues threatened in it, and if any man takes away any words God shall take away his part from the tree of life and the holy city. By this wilful distortion of God's Word he would forfeit 'his share' of eternal life, i.e. he would lose what he seemed to have by profession, though as such an act would prove, not by possession!

20: He who testifieth these things saith, Yea: I come quickly. Amen: come, Lord Jesus.

The book concludes with Christ's promise to come quickly, and the response of the church is expressed by John: 'Come, Lord Jesus'. This expression is the equivalent of the Aramaic saying, *Maranatha* [*1 Cor.* 16:22]. 'It is the cry of the waiting and longing community for His coming again in glory – a cry which is made to the Lord of the community with particular force and fervour at the Lord's Supper ["Lord, come"]' [K. G. Kuhn, *TDNT*, vol. 4, p. 472].

21: The grace of the Lord Jesus be with the saints. Amen.

Since the opening of the book has the form of an epistle [1:4], it ends appropriately with a benediction. John prays that the grace of the Lord Jesus may be with the saints of Asia who have heard the prophecy read to them in church.

SOLI DEO GLORIA

BIBLIOGRAPHY

ARNDT, W. F., AND GINGRICH, F. W., *A Greek-English Lexicon of the New Testament* [University of Chicago Press, 1957].

ASHCRAFT, MORRIS, *Revelation* [Broadman Bible Commentary, 1972].

BANKS, ROBERT [ed.], *Reconciliation and Hope* [Eerdmans, 1974].

BEASLEY-MURRAY, G. R., *The Book of Revelation* [Oliphants, 1974].

BECKWITH, ISBON T., *The Apocalypse of John* [Baker, 1967].

BERKHOF, L., *Systematic Theology* [Banner of Truth, 1959].

BOWMAN, JOHN WICK, 'The Revelation of John: Its Dramatic Structure and Message' [in *Interpretation*, October 1955].

BRUCE, F. F., *Revelation – A Bible Commentary for Today* [Pickering & Inglis, 1979].

BUIS, HARRY, *The Book of Revelation – A Simplified Commentary* [Presbyterian & Reformed, 1974].

BUIS, HARRY, *The Doctrine of Eternal Punishment* [Presbyterian & Reformed, 1957].

CAIRD, G. B., *The Revelation of St John the Divine* [A. & C. Black, 1966].

CARPENTER, W. BOYD, *The Revelation of St John – Bible Commentary for English Readers*, ed. C. J. Ellicott, vol. 8] [Cassell].

CHARLES, R. H., *The Revelation of St John* [*ICC*], [T. & T. Clark, 1975].

FINLAYSON, R. A., *God's Light on Man's Destiny* [Knox Press, n.d.].

GLASSON, T. F., *The Revelation of John* [*CBC*], [CUP, 1965].

GRIER, W. J., *The Momentous Event* [Banner of Truth, 1970].

GUTHRIE, DONALD, *New Testament Introduction* [Tyndale, 1970].

HARRISON, EVERETT F., [ed.] *Baker's Dictionary of Theology* [Baker, 1960].

HENDRIKSEN, WILLIAM, *More than Conquerors* [Tyndale, 1962].

HOEKEMA, ANTHONY A., *The Bible and the Future* [Eerdmans, 1979].

HORT, F. J. A., *Expository and Exegetical Studies* [Klock & Klock, 1980].

HUGHES, P. E., *Interpreting Prophecy* [Eerdmans, 1976].

JOHNSON, ALAN F., *Revelation* [*EBC*], [Zondervan, 1981].

JONES, R. BRADLEY, *What, Where, and When is the Millennium?* [Baker, 1975].

KIDDLE, MARTIN, *The Revelation of St John* [*MNTC*], [Hodder & Stoughton, 1940].

KITTEL, G., [ed.] *Theological Dictionary of the New Testament* [Eerdmans, 1964 –76].

LADD, GEORGE ELDON, *A Commentary on the Revelation of John* [Eerdmans, 1972].

LENSKI, R. C. H., *The Interpretation of St John's Revelation* [Augsburg, 1943].

MCKELVEY, R. J., *The New Temple* [OUP, 1969].

METZGER, BRUCE M., *A Textual Commentary on the Greek New Testament* [UBS, 1971].

MOFFATT, JAMES, *Revelation* [*EGT*], [Eerdmans, 1974].
MORRIS, LEON, *Apocalyptic* [IVP, 1972].
—— *Revelation* [*TNTC*], [Tyndale, 1969].
MOUNCE, ROBERT H., *The Book of Revelation* [*NICNT*], [Eerdmans, 1977].
MURRAY, GEORGE L., *Millennial Studies* [Baker, 1977].
MURRAY, JOHN, *Collected Writings*, vol. 2 [Banner of Truth, 1977].
PLUMMER, A., AND CLEMANCE, C., *Revelation* [*Pulpit Commentary*], [Kegan Paul, 1890].
PRESTON, R. H., AND HANSON, A. T., *Revelation of Saint John the Divine* [*TBC*], [SCM, 1968].
RAMSAY, W. M., *The Letters to the Seven Churches of Asia* [James, 1978].
ROBERTSON, A. T., *Word Pictures in the New Testament*, vol. 6 [Broadman Press, 1931].
ROBBINS, RAY FRANK, *The Revelation of Jesus Christ* [Broadman Press, 1975].
RIST, MARTIN, *The Revelation of St John the Divine* [*IB*], [Abingdon, 1957].
SHEDD, W. G. T., *The Doctrine of Endless Punishment* [1885; reprinted Banner of Truth, 1986].
—— *Dogmatic Theology* [Klock & Klock, 1979].
—— *Sermons to the Spiritual Man* [Banner of Truth, 1972].
SKILTON, JOHN H., [ed.] *The Law and the Prophets* [Presbyterian & Reformed, 1974].
STONEHOUSE, N. B., *Paul before the Areopagus and Other New Testament Studies* [Tyndale, 1957].
SWEET, JOHN, *Revelation* [SCM, 1979].
SWETE, H. B., *The Apocalypse of St John* [Macmillan, 1909].
TRENCH, R. C., *The Epistles to the Seven Churches in Asia* [Macmillan, 1867].
VINCENT, MARVIN R., *Word Studies in the New Testament* [MacDonald, n.d.].
VOS, GEERHARDUS, *Redemptive History and Biblical Interpretation* [Presbyterian & Reformed, 1980].
WARFIELD, B. B., *Works*, vol. 2 [Baker, 1981].

—— *Selected Shorter Writings*, vol. 2, [Presbyterian & Reformed, 1973].

YAMAUCHI, EDWIN, *The Archaeology of New Testament Cities in Western Asia Minor* [Pickering & Inglis, 1980].

ZORN, RAYMOND O., *Church and Kingdom* [Presbyterian & Reformed, 1962]; reprinted as *Christ Triumphant* [Banner of Truth, 1999].